ZAGAT®

Los Angeles
So. California
Restaurants
2011

LA EDITORS
Todd Cohen, Elizabeth Hurchalla,
Grace Jidoun and Helen Sillett

ORANGE COUNTY EDITORS
Cynthia Furey and Gretchen Kurz

SENIOR CONSULTING EDITOR
Merrill Shindler

STAFF EDITORS
Michelle Golden and Cynthia Kilian

Published and distributed by
Zagat Survey, LLC
4 Columbus Circle
New York, NY 10019
T: 212.977.6000
E: losangeles@zagat.com
www.zagat.com

ACKNOWLEDGMENTS

We thank Kathy Aaronson, Jon Baer, Kent Hayward, Lea Healy, Jean Hurchalla, Eva Ingvarson, Thomas Mohler, Maggie Nemser, Bernard Onken, Becky Ruthenburg and Mona Shah, as well as the following members of our staff: Caitlin Eichelberger (associate editor), Danielle Borovoy (editorial assistant), Brian Albert, Sean Beachell, Maryanne Bertollo, Jane Chang, Sandy Cheng, Reni Chin, Larry Cohn, John Deiner, Carol Diuguid, Alison Flick, Jeff Freier, Matthew Hamm, Justin Hartung, Garth Johnston, Natalie Lebert, Mike Liao, Jacqueline Wasilczyk, Art Yaghci, Sharon Yates, Anna Zappia and Kyle Zolner.

The reviews in this guide are based on public opinion surveys. The ratings reflect the average scores given by the survey participants who voted on each establishment. The text is based on quotes from, or paraphrasings of, the surveyors' comments. Phone numbers, addresses and other factual data were correct to the best of our knowledge when published in this guide.

Maps © Antenna Audio

© 2010 Zagat Survey, LLC
ISBN-13: 978-1-60478-304-9
ISBN-10: 1-60478-304-4
Printed in the
United States of America

Contents

Ratings & Symbols	4	Sleepers	318
About This Survey	5	Special Occasions	319
What's New	6	Stargazing	319
Most Popular	7	Tasting Menus	320
		Teen Appeal	321
LOS ANGELES		Transporting Experiences	321
Key Newcomers	9	Trendy	321
Top Ratings:		Views	322
Food	10	Visitors on Expense Acct.	323
Decor	15	Wine Bars	324
Service	16	Winning Wine Lists	325
Best Buys	17	Worth a Trip	326

LA Directory

Names, Locations, Contact
Info, Ratings & Reviews 20

ORANGE COUNTY

Top Ratings	328
Directory	329

LA Indexes

Cuisines	250
Locations	269
Location Maps	291

PALM SPRINGS

Top Ratings	342
Directory	342

SANTA BARBARA

Top Ratings	354
Directory	354

Special Features:

Beachside/Waterside	295
Breakfast	295
Brunch	296
Buffet	296
Business Dining	296
Celebrity Chefs	297
Cheese Trays	298
Chef's Table	299
Child-Friendly	299
Cool Loos	301
Dancing	301
Dessert Specialists	301
Dining Alone	301
Entertainment	302
Family-Style	303
Fireplaces	303
Food Trucks	304
Green/Local/Organic	305
Historic Places	305
Holiday Meals	307
Hotel Dining	307
Late Dining	308
Microbreweries	310
Newcomers	310
Outdoor Dining	311
Parties/Private Rooms	312
People-Watching	313
Power Scenes	314
Quiet Conversation	315
Raw Bars	316
Romantic Places	316
Singles Scenes	317

**Orange County, Palm Springs,
Santa Barbara Indexes**

Cuisines	364
Locations	368
Special Features	372
Wine Chart	380

Ratings & Symbols

Zagat Top Spot	Name	Symbols		Cuisine	Zagat Ratings			
					FOOD	DECOR	SERVICE	COST
					▽ 23	9	13	$15

Area, Address & Contact

Z Tim & Nina's ◗ *Asian*

Hollywood | 346 Sunset Blvd. (1st St.) | 213-555-2570 | www.zagat.com

Review, surveyor comments in quotes

"Trend"-spotters hail this "high-concept" production on Sunset offering "fantastic" Asian-deli fare that includes "tantalizing tongue sushi" slathered in "to-die-for hijiki coleslaw"; decor that "hasn't changed since Cecil B. DeMille" was a regular and "reeeal New Yawk–style" service don't seem to deter "agents", "stars" and "working gals" hooked on the "delicious sake-celery soda-tinis."

Ratings

Food, Decor and **Service** are rated on the Zagat 0 to 30 scale.

0	– 9	poor to fair
10	– 15	fair to good
16	– 19	good to very good
20	– 25	very good to excellent
26	– 30	extraordinary to perfection
	▽	low response | less reliable

Cost

Our surveyors' estimated price of a dinner with one drink and tip. Lunch is usually 25 to 30% less. For unrated **newcomers** or **write-ins,** the price range is shown as follows:

I	$25 and below	E	$41 to $65
M	$26 to $40	VE	$66 or above

Symbols

Z	highest ratings, popularity and importance
◗	serves after 11 PM
Ⓢ	closed on Sunday
Ⓜ	closed on Monday
⌀	no credit cards accepted

Maps

Index maps show restaurants with the highest Food ratings in those areas.

Menus, photos, voting and more – free at ZAGAT.com

About This Survey

Here are the results of our **2011 Los Angeles/ So. California Restaurants Survey,** covering 2,016 eateries in the greater Los Angeles area as well as Orange County, Palm Springs and Santa Barbara. Like all our guides, this one is based on input from avid local consumers – 10,852 all told. Our editors have synopsized this feedback and highlighted representative comments (in quotation marks within each review).

OUR PHILOSOPHY: Three simple premises underlie our ratings and reviews. First, we've long believed that the collective opinions of large numbers of consumers are more accurate than the opinions of a single critic. (Consider that, as a group, our surveyors bring some 1.9 million annual meals' worth of experience to this Survey. They also visit restaurants year-round, anonymously – and on their own dime.) Second, food quality is only part of the equation when choosing a restaurant, thus we ask surveyors to separately rate food, decor and service and report on cost. Third, since people need reliable information in a fast, easy-to-digest format, we strive to be concise and to offer our content on every platform.

ABOUT ZAGAT: In 1979, we started asking friends to rate and review restaurants purely for fun. The term "user-generated content" had not yet been coined. That hobby grew into Zagat Survey; 31 years later, we have over 375,000 surveyors and cover everything from airlines to shopping in over 100 countries. Along the way, we evolved from being a print publisher to a digital content provider, e.g. **ZAGAT.com, ZAGAT.mobi** (for web-enabled mobile devices), **ZAGAT TO GO** (for smartphones) and **nru** (for Android phones). We also produce customized gifts and marketing tools for a wide range of corporate clients. And you can find us on Twitter (twitter.com/zagatbuzz), Facebook and other social media networks.

THANKS: We're grateful to our local editors, Merrill Shindler, an ABC radio commentator and columnist, food writer, critic and a Zagat editor for 25 years; Gretchen Kurz, a Zagat editor for 15 years, who covers OC dining for publications including *Orange Coast* magazine; Todd Cohen, a freelance food writer; Cynthia Furey, a food writer for *The Orange County Register* and *Orange Coast* magazine; Elizabeth Hurchalla, a writer for publications including Yahoo! Food, Blackboard Eats and *InStyle*; Grace Jidoun, a food writer and cookbook editor; and Helen Sillett, who edits and writes for numerous travel publications. Thank you, guys. We also sincerely thank the thousands of surveyors who participated – this guide is really "theirs."

JOIN IN: To improve our guides, we solicit your comments; it's vital that we hear your opinions. Just contact us at **nina-tim@zagat.com.** We also invite you to join our surveys at **ZAGAT.com.** Do so and you'll receive a choice of rewards in exchange.

New York, NY
September 22, 2010

Nina and Tim Zagat

What's New

The recession continues to affect LA restaurant-goers – 44% of surveyors say they're more attentive to prices when ordering and 41% are choosing less-expensive places – but the City of Angels is still blessed with an adventurous dining scene that encompasses everything from trucks to pop-ups to the high-end places that top our Food ratings list.

IT'S ONLY MONEY: Despite the economy, splurging hasn't entirely gone out of style. Testifying to the enduring lure of pristine Japanese raw fish, five of the Top 10 Food restaurants are pricey sushi specialists, with the omakase-only **Sushi Zo** the new No. 1 for Food. Yet thanks to its many affordable eateries, including arrivals like **Chego!** (from the **Kogi** truck team) and **Slaw Dogs**, LA remains overall a surprisingly reasonable town in which to eat, with an average per-meal cost of $34.85 (vs. $38.78 in San Francisco and $41.81 in New York).

CATCH 'EM IF YOU CAN: Angelenos gladly eat and run at the many transient restaurants roving the city: 28% of surveyors frequent gourmet food trucks, and 58% have sampled a pop-up. Indeed, chef Ludo Lefebvre's **LudoBites** pop-up has become one of the town's hottest tables. Other moveable feasts include the taco-wielding **Border Grill**, Asian **Flying Pig** and Vietnamese **Phamish** trucks. The latest wrinkle in the food truck trend: convoys convening at festivals such as First Friday on Abbot Kinney in Venice.

GO WEST, TASTY CRITTERS: London's nose-to-tail craze first landed in LA a few years ago via **Animal,** with its pig- and foie-heavy offerings, and now other PETA-unfriendly eateries are following suit. Downtown newcomer **Lazy Ox Canteen** turns out pig's-ear chicharrons and lamb-neck hash; Culver City's **Waterloo & City** pairs libations with smoked tongue and trotters; and Fairfax's **Bistro LQ** whips up veal sweetbreads and rabbit tart. Likewise, droves of restaurants are making their own charcuterie, sausages and terrines.

TOQUE SHOW: The 39% of surveyors who say they're more likely to dine at a restaurant from a celebrity chef have fresh options with openings including Thomas Keller's **Bouchon** and **Bar Bouchon**, **Red O** (Rick Bayless), the **Tar Pit** (**Campanile**'s Mark Peel) and **WP24** (Wolfgang Puck). *Top Chef* fans can head for **The Gorbals** and **Stefan's at L.A. Farm** from winner Ilan Hall and finalist Stefan Richter, respectively.

NEW RESTAURANT ROWS: Downtown is now a bona fide dining destination thanks to the success of **Church & State, Ciudad, Drago Centro** and **Rivera** paving the way for newcomers like **Bottega Louie** and **Starry Kitchen,** plus the slew of midrange arrivals (**Rock'n Fish, Wolfgang Puck B&G**) at LA Live. Meanwhile, the unveiling of Santa Monica Place and its attendant six restaurants – including Richard Sandoval's **La Sandia** and Chris Yeo's **Xino** – should get some buzz going at the beach.

Los Angeles, CA
September 22, 2010

Merrill Shindler

Menus, photos, voting and more – free at ZAGAT.com

Most Popular

A full list is plotted on the map at the back of this book.

LOS ANGELES

1. Pizzeria Mozza | *Pizza*
2. Bazaar/José Andrés | *Spanish*
3. Spago | *Californian*
4. Osteria Mozza | *Italian*
5. Angelini Osteria | *Italian*
6. Café Bizou | *Californian/French*
7. Mélisse | *American/French*
8. A.O.C. | *Californian/French*
9. Mastro's | *Steak*
10. Bouchon | *French*
11. Providence | *American/Seafood*
12. Campanile | *Cal./Med.*
13. Brent's Deli | *Deli*
14. Lucques | *Cal./Med.*
15. Joe's | *Californian/French*
16. Cheesecake Factory | *American*
17. CUT | *Steak*
18. In-N-Out | *Burgers*
19. Chinois on Main | *Asian/French*
20. Gjelina | *American*
21. Lawry's Prime Rib | *Steak*
22. Matsuhisa | *Japanese*
23. JiRaffe | *American/French*
24. Bottega Louie | *Italian*
25. Fraîche | *French/Italian*
26. Water Grill | *Seafood*
27. Apple Pan | *American*
28. Din Tai Fung | *Chinese*
29. Ruth's Chris | *Steak*
30. Church & State | *French*
31. Valentino | *Italian*
32. Crustacean | *Asian/Vietnamese*
33. Fleming's | *Steak*
34. Boa | *Steak*
35. Katsuya | *Japanese*
36. Father's Office | *Amer./Burgers*
37. Houston's | *American*
38. Katsu-ya | *Japanese*
39. Palm | *Steak*
40. Roy's | *Hawaiian*

Many of the above restaurants are among the Los Angeles area's most expensive, but if popularity were calibrated to price, a number of other restaurants would surely join their ranks. To illustrate this, we have added two pages of Best Buys on pages 17 and 18.

ORANGE COUNTY

1. Marché Moderne | *French*
2. Napa Rose | *Californian*
3. In-N-Out | *Burgers*
4. Charlie Palmer | *American*
5. Five Crowns | *Continental*
6. Roy's | *Hawaiian*
7. Park Ave | *American*
8. 230 Forest Ave. | *Californian*
9. Mr. Stox | *American*
10. Tabu Grill | *Seafood/Steak*

PALM SPRINGS

1. Le Vallauris | *French/Med.*
2. Jillian's | *Continental*
3. Cuistot | *Californian/French*
4. Johannes | *Eclectic*
5. LG's Prime | *Steak*

SANTA BARBARA

1. La Super-Rica | *Mexican*
2. Downey's | *Californian/French*
3. Ca' Dario | *Italian*
4. Hitching Post | *BBQ*
5. Brophy Bros. | *Seafood*

Regional Map (Greater Los Angeles Area)

2 · 134 · Glendale · 60 · Downey · Compton · 710 · Long Beach

Burbank · 2 · Los Angeles · Inglewood · 110 · 405 · Torrance · Rancho Palos Verdes

Santa Clarita · San Fernando · 210 · 5 · 101 · 10 · El Segundo · Manhattan Beach · Redondo Beach

14 · 5 · 405 · DETAIL AT LEFT · 1

118 · Thousand Oaks · 101 · Santa Monica

Simi Valley · Val Verde Park · Piru · Malibu · Café Habana

Moorpark · Somis · Camarillo · Westlake Village

Fillmore · 126 · 23 · 23 · 118 · 101 · 1

PACIFIC OCEAN

Detail Map

Altadena · *Slaw Dogs* ★ · *Noir* ★ ★ · *DISH* ★ ★ · *Café 140 South* · S. Pasadena · *Cheval Blanc* ★ ★

Alhambra · 10 · Monterey Park · 710 · 5 · E. Los Angeles · 710

134 · York Blvd. · Huntington Dr. · 60 · Whittier Blvd. · Washington Blvd. · 710

2 · Rd. · 2 · *Lazy Ox* ★ · 101 · *Gorbals* ★ · 5 · Soto St. · 10

Glendale · San Fernando Rd. · SILVER LAKE · *WP24* ★ · *First & Hope* ★ · MID-WILSHIRE · DOWNTOWN · Alameda St. · 10

Burbank · 5 · 134 · Los Feliz Blvd. · 110 · Vermont · 110 · Ave.

101 · HOLLYWOOD · Western · W. Olympic Blvd. · W. Pico Blvd. · Ave. · Vernon · Slauson

NORTH HOLLYWOOD · 170 · *Delphine &* · *Drai's* ★ · Santa Monica Blvd. · 2 · Melrose Ave. · *Tar Pit* ★ · W. 3rd St. · Arlington · Ave.

STUDIO CITY · 101 · *Olive* ★ · *Hudson* ★ · *Red O* ★ · Beverly Blvd. · *Eva* ★ · Wilshire · Crenshaw Blvd. · 10 · View Park

Burbank Blvd. · Magnolia Blvd. · WEST HOLLYWOOD · *Bouchon* ★ · BEVERLY HILLS · *Culina* ★ · La Cienega Blvd. · Jefferson · Windsor Hills

SHERMAN OAKS · 405 · BEL AIR · *Momed* ★ · *Oliverio* ★ · CENTURY CITY · 2 · *Chego!* ★ · Culver City · 405 · 90

Ventura Blvd. · 101 · *Stefan's at L.A. Farm* ★ · *Waterloo & City* ★ · Venice Blvd.

Los Angeles · San Vicente Blvd. · Santa Monica Blvd. · Wilshire Blvd. · *BP Oysterette* ★ · 10 · Lincoln Blvd. · VENICE

Santa Monica · 1 · Santa Monica Bay

LA Key Newcomers

Our editors' take on the year's top arrivals. See page 310 for a full list.

Bouchon | *French* | Thomas Keller's long-awaited Beverly Hills bistro

BP Oysterette | *Seafood* | New England clam shack in Santa Monica

Café Habana | *Cuban* | Eco-friendly NYC import in the Malibu Lumber Yard

Café 140 South | *Cal.* | Casual Pasadenan from the Smith Brothers

Chego! | *Korean/Mexican* | Kogi rice bowls lose the wheels in Palms

Cheval Blanc | *French* | Smith Brothers' cozy, cool bistro in Pasadena

Culina | *Italian* | The Four Seasons Beverly Hills plus pizza and crudo

Delphine | *French/Med.* | The South of France, W Hollywood–style

DISH Bistro | *Cal./Med.* | Creative plates in Old Town Pasadena

Drai's | *Continental* | Elegant eatery-cum-nightclub at the W Hollywood

Eva | *Cal.* | Minimal digs and seasonal dishes on Beverly Boulevard

First & Hope | *Amer.* | Handsome retro Downtowner with a Southern accent

Gorbals | *Eclectic* | Scottish-Jewish fusion Downtown from Ilan Hall

Hudson | *Amer.* | Comfort food plus cocktails, tap beer and wine in WeHo

Lazy Ox | *Eclectic* | Seasonal cuisine and of-the-moment offal in Little Tokyo

Momed | *Med.* | Beverly Hills spot with a menu that roams the Middle East

Noir | *Eclectic* | Small plates and wines in Pasadena from Claud Beltran

Olive | *Cal./Italian* | Casual dining in the Grafton Hotel on the Sunset Strip

Oliverio | *Italian* | Poolside scene in Beverly Hill's Avalon Hotel

Red O | *Mexican* | Instant hit on Melrose with a menu by Rick Bayless

Slaw Dogs | *Hot Dogs* | Gourmet fast food in Pasadena

Stefan's/L.A. Farm | *Eclectic* | Top Cheffer debut in Santa Monica

Tar Pit | *Eclectic* | Supper club on Melrose from Mark Peel

Waterloo & City | *British* | A modern gastropub in Culver City

WP24 | *Chinese* | Wolfgang Puck's latest in Downtown's Ritz-Carlton

---

As we go to press, hot on the horizon is Suzanne Tracht's long-awaited Beverly Boulevard Pan-Asian, **Suzpree.** Meanwhile, Bryant Ng, chef de cuisine at **Pizzeria Mozza**, is prepping **The Spice Table**, a Pan-Asian in Little Tokyo. The Mediterranean **Mezze** is set to take over the space that was last home to the much-revered **Sona** in West Hollywood, chef Paul Shoemaker is readying **Savory**, a locally sourced New American in Malibu and NYC's Scott Conant is bringing his Italian **Scarpetta** to Beverly Hills. Next year, look for **Grace** to be resurrected in a former rectory on Second Street Downtown. Finally, two Thomas Keller vets are following their former boss into town, with Jordan Kahn opening a modern Vietnamese in Beverly Hills called **Red Medicine,** and Jeffrey Cerciello debuting **FARMshop Market & Restaurant** in the Brentwood Country Mart.

Top Food

29 Sushi Zo | *Japanese*

28 Matsuhisa | *Japanese*
Mélisse | *American/French*
Brandywine | *Continental*
Shiro | *French/Japanese*
Providence | *Amer./Seafood*
Angelini Osteria | *Italian*
Sushi Nozawa | *Japanese*

27 Asanebo | *Japanese*
Wa | *Japanese*
Saam/The Bazaar | *Eclectic*
Hatfield's | *American*
Leila's | *Californian*
Babita | *Mexican*
Sushi Sasabune | *Japanese*
Saddle Peak | *American*
Lucques | *Cal./Med.*
Water Grill | *Seafood*
Mori Sushi | *Japanese*
Spago | *Californian*
Urasawa | *Japanese*
Orris | *French/Japanese*
Pizzeria Mozza | *Pizza*
Sushi Masu | *Japanese*
Osteria Mozza | *Italian*

Hamasaku | *Japanese*
Bastide | *French*
Bashan | *American*
A.O.C. | *Californian/French*
CUT | *Steak*
Café 14 | *Cal./Continental*
Langer's Deli | *Deli*

26 Nobu Malibu | *Japanese*
Bistro 45 | *Californian*
Mako | *Asian*
Derek's | *Californian/French*
Piccolo | *Italian*
Bazaar/José Andrés | *Spanish*
Valentino | *Italian*
Jitlada | *Thai*
Patina | *American/Californian*
JiRaffe | *American/French*
Katsu-ya | *Japanese*
Mastro's | *Steak*
Vincenti | *Italian*
Chinois on Main | *Asian/French*
Nobu LA | *Japanese*
Il Grano | *Italian*
Sam's by the Beach | *Cal./Med.*
Amarone | *Italian*

BY CUISINE

AMERICAN (NEW)
28 Mélisse
Providence
27 Hatfield's
Saddle Peak
Bashan

AMERICAN (TRAD.)
25 Grill on Alley
24 Lasher's
Martha's 22nd St. Grill
Clementine
23 Laurel Tavern

ASIAN/ASIAN FUSION
26 Mako
Chinois on Main
24 Gina Lee's
Crustacean
Chaya Downtown

BAKERIES
26 Susina
24 Clementine

Sweet Lady Jane
Porto's
23 Jin Patisserie

BARBECUE
25 Phillips BBQ
23 Johnny Rebs'
22 JR's BBQ
Lucille's BBQ
Dr. Hogly Wogly's

BURGERS
24 In-N-Out
23 Tommy's
Apple Pan
22 Golden State
Father's Office

CALIFORNIAN
27 Leila's
Lucques
Spago
A.O.C.
Café 14

Excludes places with low votes, unless otherwise indicated

CARIBBEAN/CUBAN

24 Porto's
   Asia de Cuba
21 Versailles
   Bamboo
20 Cha Cha Chicken

CHINESE

26 Yujean Kang's
25 Din Tai Fung
   Sea Harbour
24 Elite
23 Bamboo Cuisine

COFFEE SHOP/DINER

23 Cora's Coffee
22 Original Pancake
   Uncle Bill's
   Nickel Diner
   Pie 'N Burger

CONTINENTAL

28 Brandywine
27 Café 14
25 Dal Rae
23 Polo Lounge
21 Bistro Garden/Coldwater

DELI

27 Langer's Deli
26 Brent's Deli
22 Barney Greengrass
20 Art's Deli
   Nate 'n Al

DIM SUM

25 Sea Harbour
21 NBC Seafood
   Ocean Star
   Empress Harbor
   Ocean Seafood

ECLECTIC

27 Saam/The Bazaar
25 Lou
   Noir
   Chez Mélange
24 Lazy Ox

FRENCH

28 Mélisse
   Shiro
27 Orris
   Bastide
   A.O.C.

FRENCH (BISTRO)

26 Julienne
   Mistral
25 Frenchy's Bistro
24 Bouchon
   Pinot Bistro

GREEK

24 Papa Cristo's
23 Petros
22 George's Greek
21 Taverna Tony
   Le Petit Greek

INDIAN

24 Addi's Tandoor
23 Nawab of India
22 Bombay Café
   Electric Lotus
   Akbar

ITALIAN

28 Angelini Osteria
27 Osteria Mozza
26 Piccolo
   Valentino
   Il Grano

JAPANESE

29 Sushi Zo
28 Matsuhisa
   Shiro
   Sushi Nozawa
27 Asanebo

KOREAN

24 Park's BBQ
23 Tofu-Ya
   ChoSun Galbee
   Soot Bull Jeep
   Kogi

MEDITERRANEAN

27 Lucques
26 Sam's by the Beach
   Campanile
25 Christine
   Lou*

MEXICAN

27 Babita
25 Alegria/Sunset
   La Cabanita
   El Tepeyac
24 Lotería!

---

* Indicates a tie with restaurant above

MIDDLE EASTERN

24 Carousel
   Carnival
23 Azeen's
   Sunnin*
22 Open Sesame

PIZZA

27 Pizzeria Mozza
25 Village Pizzeria
23 Mulberry St. Pizzeria
   Casa Bianca
   Joe's Pizza

SEAFOOD

28 Providence
27 Water Grill
24 Hungry Cat
23 Lobster
   Malibu Seafood

SMALL PLATES

27 Orris
   A.O.C.
26 Mako
   Izaka-Ya
   Gjelina

SOUL FOOD/ SOUTHERN

25 Les Sisters
24 Lasher's
23 Johnny Rebs'
21 Roscoe's
   Big Mama's

SOUTH AMERICAN

24 Carlitos Gardel
23 Fogo de Chão
   1810 Restaurant
   Galletto B&G
22 Mario's Peruvian

STEAKHOUSES

27 CUT
26 Mastro's
   Lawry's Prime Rib
25 Jar
   555 East

THAI

26 Jitlada
23 Chadaka
   Cholada
   Saladang
22 Talésai

VEGETARIAN

23 Veggie Grill
   Native Foods
22 M Café de Chaya
   Real Food Daily
20 A Votre Sante

VIETNAMESE

24 Crustacean
   Pho 79
23 Blossom
   Golden Deli
22 Gingergrass

BY SPECIAL FEATURE

ALL YOU CAN EAT

23 Fogo de Chão
   Nawab of India
21 Bombay Palace
   Picanha
19 Green Field

BREAKFAST

24 Lotería!
   Martha's 22nd St.
   Clementine
23 Griddle Cafe
22 Huckleberry Café

BRUNCH

27 Saddle Peak
26 Campanile
   Joe's
   Gjelina
25 Belvedere

BUSINESS DINING

28 Mélisse
   Providence
27 Hatfield's
   Water Grill
   Spago

GARDEN DINING

27 Bastide
25 Belvedere
   Michael's
   Raymond
24 Koi

HOTEL DINING

27 Saam/The Bazaar (SLS)
   CUT (Beverly Wilshire)
26 Bazaar/José Andrés (SLS)
25 Belvedere (Peninsula Hotel)
   RH (Andaz)

LATE DINING

27	Pizzeria Mozza
26	Gjelina
25	Lou
	Iroha
24	Lazy Ox

LUNCH

29	Sushi Zo
28	Matsuhisa
	Brandywine
	Providence
	Angelini

NEWCOMERS (RATED)

25	Noir
	Eva
24	Lazy Ox
	Bouchon
23	Stefan's/L.A. Farm

PEOPLE-WATCHING

27	Spago
23	XIV
21	Ivy
20	Cecconi's
19	Chateau Marmont

POWER SCENES

28	Matsuhisa
	Providence
	Angelini
27	Water Grill
25	Grill on Alley

TRENDY

27	Pizzeria Mozza
26	Bazaar/José Andrés
	Gjelina
25	Rivera
23	Tavern

WINNING WINE LISTS

28	Mélisse
27	Lucques
	Water Grill
	Bastide
26	Valentino

WORTH A TRIP

27	Leila's (Oak Park)
	Babita (San Gabriel)
	Saddle Peak (Calabasas)
26	Tuscany (Westlake Village)
25	Din Tai Fung (Arcadia)

BY LOCATION

BEVERLY BOULEVARD

28	Angelini Osteria
26	Hirozen
25	Jar
	Eva
23	Lemonade Cafe

BEVERLY HILLS

28	Matsuhisa
27	Saam/The Bazaar
	Spago
	Urasawa
	CUT

BRENTWOOD

26	Vincenti
	Takao
24	Osteria Latini
	Divino
	Palmeri

CHINATOWN

22	Yang Chow
	Philippe the Original
	Sam Woo
21	Ocean Seafood
20	Empress Pavilion

DOWNTOWN

27	Water Grill
	Langer's Deli
26	Patina
	Drago Centro
25	Rivera

FAIRFAX

26	Animal
24	Lotería!
	Bistro LQ
23	Nyala
22	Golden State

HOLLYWOOD

28	Providence
27	Pizzeria Mozza
25	Lou
	Village Pizzeria
24	Hungry Cat

LA BREA

26	Campanile
	Susina
25	Cube
22	Ca'Brea
20	Pink's Chili Dogs

LONG BEACH

26 Michael's/Naples
25 555 East
Frenchy's Bistro
24 Lasher's
23 La Creperie Cafe

LOS FELIZ/SILVER LAKE

25 Alegria/Sunset
24 Farfalla
Blair's
23 Yuca's
Aroma

MALIBU

26 Nobu Malibu
23 Malibu Seafood
Cholada
22 Terra
Tra Di Noi

MELROSE

27 Hatfield's
25 Angeli Caffe
Osteria Mozza
24 Sweet Lady Jane
Carlitos Gardel

PASADENA/ SOUTH PASADENA

28 Shiro
26 Bistro 45
Derek's
Parkway Grill
Maison Akira

SAN FERNANDO VALLEY

28 Brandywine
Sushi Nozawa
27 Asanebo
Saddle Peak
Bashan

SAN GABRIEL VALLEY

27 Babita
25 Sea Harbour

Dal Rae
24 Elite
Pho 79

SANTA MONICA

28 Mélisse
26 Valentino
JiRaffe
Chinois on Main
Sam's by the Beach

SOUTH BAY

26 Izaka-Ya
25 Christine
Phillips BBQ
Chez Mélange
Musha

THIRD STREET

27 A.O.C.
26 Izaka-Ya
25 Locanda Veneta
Ortolan
23 Joan's on Third

VENICE

26 Piccolo
Joe's
Gjelina
25 Ado
24 Axe

WEST HOLLYWOOD

27 Wa
Lucques
Bastide
26 Nobu LA
Amarone

WEST LA

29 Sushi Zo
27 Sushi Sasabune
Mori Sushi
Orris
Sushi Masu

Top Decor

28 Cicada
Edison*
Belvedere

27 Bazaar/José Andrés
Bistro Garden/Coldwater
Saddle Peak
Polo Lounge
mar'sel
Gonpachi
Tar Pit
Drago Centro

26 Inn/Seventh Ray
Sur
Dar Maghreb
RockSugar
Mélisse
Saam/The Bazaar
Penthouse
Yamashiro
Michael's

Geoffrey's
Il Cielo
Crustacean
Patina
Bouchon
Asia de Cuba
One Pico

25 Vibrato
Bastide
Providence
Cliff's Edge
Chateau Marmont
Tavern
Craft
Catch
Larsen's Steak*
Parkway Grill
Water Grill
Spago
La Boheme

OUTDOORS

26 Michael's
Geoffrey's
Il Cielo
25 Chateau Marmont
23 Katana

22 Ca' del Sole
Beechwood
21 Cafe des Artistes
19 Firefly Bistro
18 Beacon

ROMANCE

27 Bazaar/José Andrés
Saddle Peak
26 Mélisse
Il Cielo
25 Getty Center

Rivera
24 Hatfield's
Lucques
23 Capo
19 Brentwood

STARGAZING

25 Chateau Marmont
Tavern
Spago
CUT
Cecconi's

24 Koi
22 Ivy
21 Mr. Chow
19 Brentwood
18 Il Sole

VIEWS

27 Saddle Peak
26 Penthouse
Yamashiro
Geoffrey's
One Pico

24 Cafe Del Rey
23 Lobster
22 Parker's Lighthouse
Moonshadows
20 Beachcomber Café

Top Service

27	Mélisse
	Belvedere
	Providence
	Sam's by the Beach
	Brandywine
	Bastide

26	Shiro
	Urasawa
	Saddle Peak
	Bistro 45
	Polo Lounge
	Grill on Alley
	Il Tiramisù
	Valentino
	Water Grill
	CUT
	Hatfield's
	Lawry's Prime Rib
	Spago

| 25 | Patina |

Vincenti
Derek's
Tuscany
Lucques
Japon Bistro
Sur*
Brunello
Mistral
La Vecchia
Bashan
Michael's
Saam/The Bazaar
JiRaffe
Josie
Maison Akira
Carlitos Gardel
Arroyo
Bouchon
Parkway Grill
Noir

BEST BUYS: BANG FOR THE BUCK

In order of Bang for the Buck rating.

1. In-N-Out
2. Best Fish Taco
3. Let's Be Frank
4. Tommy's
5. Yuca's
6. Carney's Express
7. Caffe Luxxe
8. Lamonica's
9. Astro Burger
10. Portillo's
11. Kogi
12. Chipotle
13. Five Guys
14. Border Grill Truck
15. Porto's
16. Poquito Más
17. Apple Pan
18. Sharky's
19. Spitz
20. Joe's Pizza
21. Philippe the Original
22. Bay Cities Deli
23. Susina
24. Veggie Grill
25. Pink's Chili Dogs
26. Baja Fresh
27. Jody Maroni's
28. El Tepeyac
29. Uncle Bill's
30. Martha's 22nd St.
31. Blossom
32. Asahi Ramen
33. Village Pizzeria
34. 101 Noodle
35. California Chicken
36. Stand
37. Original Pancake
38. Abbot's Pizza
39. Bamboodles
40. Cafe 50's

GOOD VALUE NEWCOMERS

Burger Kitchen
CaCao
Chego!
Cuvee
8½ Taverna
K-Town BBQ
Libra
Mac & Cheeza
Market Café
Phamish
Starry Kitchen
Villains Tavern

OTHER GOOD VALUES

Alejo's
Angelique Café
Antonio's
Auntie Em's Kitchen
Baby Blues BBQ
BCD Tofu
Benley Vietnamese
BLD
Blue Hen
Breadbar
Brent's Deli
California Pizza
Casa Bianca
Chili John's
Clifton's Cafeteria
Falafel King
Griddle Cafe
Gumbo Pot
Hole in the Wall
Jinky's
Jin Patisserie
Jitlada
Johnnie's Pastrami
Johnny Reb's
John O'Groats
JR's BBQ
Lemonade Cafe
Lemon Moon
Local Place
Mandarin Deli
Nickel Diner
Papa Cristo's
Pei Wei
Pho 79
Rae's
Ragin' Cajun
Shack
Slaw Dogs
Sunnin
Yang Chow

BEST BUYS

For prix fixe menus, call ahead for availability.

BYO

23	Malibu Seafood
22	Doughboys
21	Bloom Cafe
	Cobras & Matadors
	Angelique
20	Cha Cha Chicken
	Gaby's
19	Aroma Café

CHEAP DATE

24	Farfalla
	Girasole
23	Il Capriccio
	Café Bizou
	Nyala
22	Tlapazola Grill
	Corkbar
21	Palms Thai
20	Figaro Bistrot
19	Cha Cha Cha

CHILD-FRIENDLY

27	Pizzeria Mozza
26	Brent's Deli
25	Angeli
24	Lotería!
23	Apple Pan
22	Uncle Bill's
	bld
21	Border Grill
	Alejo's

EARLY-BIRD

24	Pinot Bistro
	2117
22	vermont
21	Fritto Misto
	Asakuma
20	Emle's
19	Chart House
18	Marmalade Café
17	Taix
	Castaway

HOLE-IN-THE-WALL

25	Alegria/Sunset
	Les Sisters
23	Tofu-Ya
	Ruen Pair∇
22	Mario's Peruvian

	Chung King∇
21	Versailles
	Poquito Mas
	Flore∇
20	Le Saigon

NOODLE SHOPS

24	Pho 79
23	Blossom
	Mandarin
22	101 Noodle
21	Viet Noodle Bar∇
	Chabuya
20	Asahi Ramen
	Bamboodles
19	Pho Café∇
	9021Pho

PRIX FIXE LUNCH

26	Echigo ($14)
24	Carousel ($20)
	Carlitos Gardel ($24)
	Craft ($25)
	2117 ($18)
	Roy's ($25)
23	1810 Restaurant ($13)
	Café Provencal ($16)
22	Beacon ($13)
	Comme Ça ($20)

PRIX FIXE DINNER

27	Bashan ($40)
26	Il Grano ($44)
	Sam's by the Beach ($38)
24	Carousel ($39)
	Piccolo Paradiso ($37)
	2117 ($38)
	Fleming's ($40)
	Roy's ($35)
23	Café Pierre ($35)
	1810 Restaurant ($23)

VEGAN/VEGETARIAN

28	Madeleine
27	Elf Café
25	Fatty's & Co.
23	Vegan Glory∇
	Veggie Grill
	Native Foods
	Tiara
21	Flore

Menus, photos, voting and more – free at ZAGAT.com

LOS ANGELES
RESTAURANT
DIRECTORY

	FOOD	DECOR	SERVICE	COST

Abbey, The ◐ *American* | 16 | 21 | 17 | $29 |

West Hollywood | 692 N. Robertson Blvd. (Santa Monica Blvd.) | 310-289-8410 | www.abbeyfoodandbar.com

A "lovely patio by day" and "nonstop gay dance party" by night, this "mostly outdoor" SBE-owned "see-and-be-scene" WeHo American is known for its "pricey cocktails" and "chic" "ultramodern" digs with fireplaces and cabanas; "average" fare (mac 'n' cheese is a standout) is "more than made up for in eye candy" – and that includes the "slow"-moving but "cute" waiters; P.S. open till 2 AM.

Abbot's Pizza *Pizza* | 22 | 7 | 15 | $13 |

Santa Monica | 1811 Pico Blvd. (18th St.) | 310-314-2777
Venice | 1407 Abbot Kinney Blvd. (California Ave.) | 310-396-7334
www.abbotspizzaco.com

It's all about the "bagel crust" and "unique", "high-quality toppings" (the "salad pizza rocks") at this "bohemian Venice hang" and its Santa Monica sibling "cranking out awesome" pies for very little dough; there's "absolutely no frills, no comfort", little seating and "curt service", but for such "creative, delicious" 'za, stalwarts say that's "no problem."

ABC Seafood *Chinese/Seafood* | 20 | 11 | 15 | $25 |

Chinatown | 205 Ord St. (New High St.) | 213-680-2887

"Loud, rushed and a bit frumpy", Chinatown's stalwart seafooder still serves up "inspiring" dim sum and "traditional" "family-style" fin fare plucked "fresh" from the tank, all at "bargain-basement" prices; though some say it's getting "eclipsed by Monterey Park" competition, it's "still a winner", with a "hospitable staff" to boot.

Absolutely Phobulous *Vietnamese* | 18 | 10 | 14 | $16 |

West Hollywood | 350 N. La Cienega Blvd. (Beverly Blvd.) | 310-360-3930
Encino | 15928 Ventura Blvd. (bet. Gaivota & Gloria Aves.) | 818-788-3560 Ⓢ
www.abpho.com

"For noodles and soup" fast, this Vietnamese duo "with the cutesy name" in West Hollywood and Encino does the trick with "large bowls" of "simple" pho and other "solid" "everyday" eats that are "easy on the wallet"; the "bare-bones decor" and "indifferent" service aren't so troubling, considering the cuisine is "rare to find" in these parts.

Adagio Ⓜ *Italian* | 22 | 17 | 23 | $39 |

Woodland Hills | 22841 Ventura Blvd. (Fallbrook Ave.) | 818-222-0533

Owner Claudio Gontier "is always there" "making sure everyone feels at home" at this "old favorite" in Woodland Hills proffering "reliable" Northern Italian meat dishes and "delicious Caesar salads made tableside" at "reasonable prices"; maybe the "dark", "cozy" setting could use "a boost", but for the "locals who keep coming back", it's a "gem."

❷ Addi's Tandoor *Indian* | 24 | 17 | 21 | $31 |

Redondo Beach | 800 Torrance Blvd. (bet. PCH & Prospect Ave.) | 310-540-1616 | www.addistandoor.com

"Flavorful" Goan fare will "take you on a trip" to India assure acolytes of this "authentic" Redondo Beach strip-mall "treasure" that's LA's No. 1 Indian; also known for its "polite, helpful" staff led by host-owner Addi Decosta, it's deemed "one of the best in the South Bay" for the genre, so its "tiny", "tastefully appointed" dining room is naturally "always crowded", often with a "line out the door."

Admiral Risty *Seafood*
20 | 18 | 22 | $42

Rancho Palos Verdes | Golden Cove Shopping Ctr. | 31250 Palos Verdes Dr. W. (Hawthorne Blvd.) | 310-377-0050 | www.admiral-risty.com

Longtime fans "delight in sunsets over the ocean" at this "expensive" Rancho Palos Verdes seafooder known for "fresh fish" served in a variety of ways by "polite" servers who "let you take your time"; though a few carp about the "old-school" nautical-inspired decor, the bar offering "live tunes" Wednesday–Sunday lures in loyalists too.

Ado *Californian/Italian*
25 | 20 | 21 | $51

Venice | 796 Main St. (Abbot Kinney Blvd.) | 310-399-9010 | www.adovenice.com

Expect "effusive greetings" from owner Paolo Cesaro as you enter this "charming, creaky beach house" in Venice that's gaining followers with "celestial homemade pastas" and other "creative" pricey Italian fare delivered by servers "who know their way around a wine list"; sure, the "noise is deafening" in the "crowded", candlelit dining room, but most agree "it's much Ado about something."

Adobe Cantina *Mexican*
17 | 16 | 17 | $24

Agoura Hills | 29100 Agoura Rd. (Cornell Rd.) | 818-991-3474

"Fantastic" patio seating and "gargantuan margaritas" stoke "the relaxed feel of summer all year long" for Agoura Hills regulars of this "mellow" Mexican, where "the drinks keep coming" and the "extensive" menu of cheap, "hearty" south-of-the-border standards includes "tasty Southwest BBQ"; "friendly" servers further factor in for "lazy" lingering.

Ago *Italian*
21 | 20 | 20 | $55

West Hollywood | 8478 Melrose Ave. (La Cienega Blvd.) | 323-655-6333 | www.agorestaurant.com

"You may suffer whiplash from all the head-turning you'll do" at this "pricey" "showbiz" "hot spot" in West Hollywood backed by Robert De Niro and touted for its "solid" Tuscan fare and some 600 wines delivered by "charming" servers; it's "high-energy" and "always packed", making for a "fantastically loud" experience, but conversations are "secondary" to the "glam" people-watching "scene" here.

Agra Cafe *Indian*
∇ 22 | 11 | 19 | $23

Silver Lake | 4325 Sunset Blvd. (Fountain Ave.) | 323-665-7818 | www.agracafela.com

Masala mavens beat a path to this Silver Lake Indian approximating "mother's home cooking" with affordable dishes "unmodified for American tastes" and as "fiery hot" as you can handle; "courteous" servers are a plus, but most choose to "carry out" considering the strip-mall setting and "small", no-frills burgundy-hued room.

Ahi Sushi *Japanese*
21 | 17 | 20 | $36

Studio City | 12915 Ventura Blvd. (Coldwater Canyon Ave.) | 818-981-0277 | www.ahisushi.com

Generally considered a "solid" "standby" on Studio City's Sushi Row, this "casually elegant", midpriced Japanese turns out "complex" rolls that "tantalize the taste buds" alongside "unusual house specials", all delivered by a "friendly staff"; the less-"inventive" traditional setting features mirrors and Japanese paintings, with a bamboo-shielded patio providing extra seating.

Akasha *American*   20 | 21 | 20 | $39

Culver City | 9543 Culver Blvd. (Washington Blvd.) | 310-845-1700 | www.akasharestaurant.com

Chef-owner Akasha Richmond's "upscale" Culver City New American gets props for its "local, sustainable" approach, with a "spare, modern" room setting the stage for a market-driven menu and goods from an on-site organic bakery, plus "out-of-this-world, seasonal" cocktails and biodynamic wines; add in "conscientious" servers and you can't help but "feel good about eating here", except perhaps for the somewhat "pricey" bill.

Akbar Cuisine of India *Indian*   22 | 16 | 19 | $29

Marina del Rey | 3115 Washington Blvd. (Yale Ave.) | 310-574-0666
Santa Monica | 2627 Wilshire Blvd. (bet. Princeton & 26th Sts.) | 310-586-7469
Hermosa Beach | 1101 Aviation Blvd. (Prospect Ave.) | 310-937-3800
Pasadena | 44 N. Fair Oaks Ave. (Union St.) | 626-577-9916
www.akbarcuisineofindia.com

The spice is "right" at this "reliable", midpriced Indian chain known for "authentic", "vibrant" curries and kebabs, "tongue-tingling" specials and "thoughtful" "wine pairings" suggested by a "knowledgeable" staff; Santa Monica gets a shout-out for its recent dining room "makeover", though the decor "could use an update" at the other locations.

Alcove *American*   20 | 20 | 16 | $19

Los Feliz | 1929 Hillhurst Ave. (Franklin Ave.) | 323-644-0100 | www.alcovecafe.com

"Actors trying to be inconspicuous", "wannabe models" and "hip" Los Feliz locals fill the "pretty", "people-watching" courtyard of this inexpensive American bakery/cafe in a "cozy" converted bungalow that proffers "luscious desserts", "freshly made sandwiches" and "breakfast all day"; given the "intense crowds", the staff can sometimes seem "grumpy", but it's the "stand-in-line", "order-at-the-counter" setup that regulars rate a "hassle."

Alegria *Nuevo Latino*   21 | 20 | 21 | $29

Long Beach | 115 Pine Ave. (bet. B'way & 1st St.) | 562-436-3388 | www.alegriacocinalatina.com

"Mouthwatering" Nuevo Latino tapas "served with flair" and "sangria that will have you seeing double" are just part of the attraction at this "lively" late-night Long Beacher where "flamenco"-lovers stomp to the bar for weekend performances; factor in a colorful fiestalike atmosphere with murals and mosaics and live music including salsa and jazz Tuesday–Sunday, and it's no wonder "everyone" leaves "happy."

☑ Alegria on Sunset ⓧ⇄ *Mexican*   25 | 14 | 21 | $20

Silver Lake | Sunset Plaza | 3510 W. Sunset Blvd. (Golden Gate Ave.) | 323-913-1422 | www.alegriaonsunset.com

South-of-the-border standards with "fresh", "unexpected twists" lure local "hipsters" to this "funky, friendly" "mini-mall Mexican" in Silver

	FOOD	DECOR	SERVICE	COST

Lake that offers a hefty "bang for the buck"; surveyors suggest it's best to ignore the "crowded" pocketsize location and just focus on the "flavorful" feast.

Alejo's *Italian* | 21 | 9 | 18 | $20 |

Marina del Rey | 4002 Lincoln Blvd. (Washington Blvd.) | 310-822-0095
Westchester | 8343 Lincoln Blvd. (84th St.) | 310-670-6677 | www.alejosrestaurant.com

"Garlic lovers" breathe heavily over the "enormous portions" of "rustic, homey" spaghetti and meatballs and other fare that could "rid the world of vampires" at these separately owned, "affordable" Italians; devotees don't expect "fancy", just a "friendly vibe" with a "neighborhood feel"; there's BYO only at Marina del Rey, while Westchester offers wine and beer.

Alessio Ristorante Italiano *Italian* | 21 | 18 | 20 | $30 |

Northridge | 9725 Reseda Blvd. (Superior St.) | 818-709-8393
West Hills | Platt Vill. | 6428 Platt Ave. (Victory Blvd.) | 818-710-0270

Delivering "well-prepared" Italian meals to the North Valley for years, this "reliable" duo remains a "classy" refuge from Los Angeles prices, with an "eager-to-please staff" and "fairly sophisticated" modern decor; though some say it's "noisy" (especially with "live music" weekends at West Hills), most concede it's "convenient" for an "authentic" taste of Italy.

All India Cafe *Indian* | 21 | 14 | 19 | $25 |

West LA | Santa Monica Plaza | 12113 Santa Monica Blvd. (Bundy Dr.) | 310-442-5250
Pasadena | 39 S. Fair Oaks Ave. (bet. Colorado Blvd. & Green St.) | 626-440-0309
www.allindiacafe.com

Not "your run-of-the-mill" chainlet, these "authentic", "reasonably priced" Indians in Pasadena, West LA and Santa Barbara blend a "variety of flavors" from the North and South regions in "fresh, vibrant" cuisine that's ferried by a "helpful, prompt" staff; despite the name, you "can't fit all of India" into the "small" quarters, but most "go for the food, not the feel" anyway.

Allora Cucina Italiana *Italian* | - | - | - | M |

Third Street | 8432 W. Third St. (La Cienega Blvd.) | 323-782-9576

"Personal service" is the hallmark of this "great little spot" on Third Street run by native Italians who turn out "solid" midpriced dishes of veal, pasta, pizza and such with a "home-cooked feel"; it's "totally unpretentious" right down to the spare trattoria setup, and considered a local "gem", especially now that it has a beer and wine license.

Amalfi *Italian* | 19 | 20 | 20 | $35 |

La Brea | 143 N. La Brea Ave. (bet. Beverly Blvd. & 1st St.) | 323-938-2504 | www.amalfiristorante.com

While live music in the upstairs lounge may recall its jazz-club days (it's where Nat 'King' Cole's trio was born), this "tried-and-true Italian eatery" on La Brea co-owned by comic Adam Carolla is decidedly modern with "cozy fireplaces", high ceilings and a "something-for-everyone" menu of "reliable" dishes such as risotto and pumpkin ravi-oli; add in "reserved, professional" service for what fans find an overall "pleasant dining experience."

Amarone Kitchen & Wine ⊠ *Italian*   26 | 18 | 24 | $55

West Hollywood | 8868 W. Sunset Blvd. (San Vicente Blvd.) | 310-652-2233 | www.amarone-la.com

Surveyors "feel like *famiglia*" at this "dimly lit" West Hollywood Italian where the "perfectly al dente" "homemade pastas" and other Bologna-inspired fare is just as "authentic" as the "accented waiters"; in spite of its "tiny" dimensions and Sunset Strip locale, fans find it "charming" and "well worth" the "pricey" tab.

American Girl Place Cafe *American*   11 | 23 | 22 | $32

Fairfax | The Grove | 189 The Grove Dr. (bet. Beverly Blvd. & 3rd St.) | 877-247-5223 | www.americangirlplace.com

"An enchanting experience for young girls" is offered at this pink-and-black cafe in The Grove on Fairfax, where "cheery servers" "make a fuss" over the little ones while dolls "sit in mini high-chairs" with "their own place setting at the table"; "it's corny" and the midpriced American fare is "average at best", but for a "special afternoon", it's a mother-daughter "must."

Amici *Italian*   21 | 19 | 20 | $41

Beverly Hills | Beverly Terrace Hotel | 469 N. Doheny Dr. (Santa Monica Blvd.) | 310-858-0271 | www.tamici.com
Brentwood | 2538 San Vicente Blvd. (26th St.) | 310-260-4900 | www.amicibrentwood.com

"Cute little date places", these "casual", separately owned Italians of-fer spaghetti with lobster and other "upscale", "authentic" delights set down by an "attentive", "considerate" staff; the more casual spot in the Beverly Terrace Hotel boasts a "lovely patio" while Brentwood has high ceilings, "exposed brick and sleek wood", but both offer "big bang for reasonable bucks."

Ammo *Californian*   23 | 20 | 22 | $37

Hollywood | 1155 N. Highland Ave. (bet. Fountain Ave. & Santa Monica Blvd.) | 323-871-2666 | www.ammocafe.com

Aiming for "farm-fresh", "organic" ingredients whenever possible, this "super-cool" midpriced Californian in Hollywood hits the mark with "simple" yet "irresistible" seasonal dishes and a "top-notch" cocktail menu; a "helpful" staff and "chic, minimalist design" with warm wood paneling cements its status as a power-lunch "favorite", especially among a "high-energy entertainment crowd" including more than a few "celebs."

Angeli Caffe Ⓜ *Italian*   25 | 16 | 23 | $34

Melrose | 7274 Melrose Ave. (bet. Alta Vista Ave. & Poinsettia Pl.) | 323-936-9086 | www.angelicaffe.com

Acolytes attest it just "gets better and better" at Evan Kleiman's "long-time" Melrose Italian, where "small, tight" quarters are a backdrop for "transcendent", "Slow Food"–inspired dishes, including "fabulous" "homemade breads" and pizzas from the wood-burning oven; add in "sweet, attentive" servers for a "warm, hospitable" atmosphere to "know why it's been around" – and "loved" – "all these years."

⚡ Angelini Osteria Ⓜ *Itali[...]*
Beverly Boulevard | 7313 Bever[...]
323-297-0070 | www.angelini[...]
"Dazzling" dishes from che[...]
crusted branzino" "to die[...]
experience" – are accompa[...]
Beverly Boulevard trattoria[...]
surveyors say "solicitous[...]
to ensure such an "overa[...]
much "cares" about the "sardine[...]
a bit "pricey."

Angelique Café Ⓜ *French*   `21` `15` `17` `[...]`
Downtown | 840 S. Spring St. (bet. 8th & 9th Sts.) | 213-623-8698
A French "oasis" in the "heart of Downtown", this "absolutely cute"
cafe is a Garment District "lunch meet-up" known for dishing out
"reasonably priced" "light fare" including "divine" charcuterie and
pâté and delivering it with "unpretentious" service; as for the "unusual" location "squished into a triangular" intersection on Spring,
regulars usually retreat to the "pleasant" "roof deck" for a view of
the "traffic" below.

Angel's Ⓜ *Californian*   `-` `-` `-` `M`
Santa Monica | 2460 Wilshire Blvd. (25th St.) | 310-828-2115 |
www.angelssantamonica.com
Old-school with a 21st-century edge, this Santa Monican inspired by
supper clubs of the '30s and '40s complete with jazz piano, late hours
and retro decor makes naughty night owls "want to do the Charleston";
the seasonal Californian cuisine isn't quite "as dialed-in yet", but a
"staff that tries hard to please" and moderate prices compensate;
P.S. the piano bar is open till 2 AM.

Animal *American*   `26` `16` `22` `$50`
Fairfax | 435 N. Fairfax Ave. (bet. Oakwood & Rosewood Aves.) |
323-782-9225 | www.animalrestaurant.com
"Not for vegetarians" or "the faint-of-heart", this "friendly" Fairfax
"meatfest" "from rock 'n' roll chef-team" Jon Shook and Vinny Dotolo
"will blow your mind" with an "innovative", "well-executed" New
American menu that's "an ode to all things pork" and beef; carnivores
call it "worth a splurge", so forget the "spartan decor" (and your "cho-
lesterol level" for that matter) – it's futile to resist when "there's even
bacon in dessert."

⚡ Anisette Brasserie *French*   `21` `24` `19` `$47`
Santa Monica | 225 Santa Monica Blvd. (bet. 2nd St. & 3rd St. Promenade) |
310-395-3200 | www.anisettebrasserie.com
"Classy" quarters with "tile floors, high ceilings" and a zinc bar give
this Santa Monica French from Alain Giraud "all the charm and au-
thenticity of a real Parisian brasserie", which extends to the "well-
executed" fare ("superb oysters" are a "highlight") and "disaffected
waiters"; though it's "overpriced and overpacked" with a "noise level
off the charts", it's "one of the most beautiful restaurants" around and
"worth a visit for a special occasion"; P.S. "scrumptious" brunch at
"more reasonable" prices appeals to wallet-watchers.

	FOOD	DECOR	SERVICE	COST
	21	15	19	$26

...*izza*

...la Marina Mktpl. | 13455 Maxella Ave. (Glencoe Ave.) |
...www.anticapizzeria.net

...e of the "most authentic Neapolitan pizza in LA", this
...Marina del Rey "gem" features a wood-burning oven baking
...elievable crusts" topped with "mozzarella made on-site" and
..."authentic" ingredients; the "odd" mall location and "nothing-
...cial" decor is forgotten once you're seated on the "breezy" "bal-
...ony" biting into a "real Italian" slice.

Antonio's Ⓜ *Mexican*
	22	18	22	$26

Melrose | 7470 Melrose Ave. (bet. Fairfax & La Brea Aves.) | 323-658-9060 |
www.antoniosonmelrose.com

It's "been around forever for a reason" say fans of this "venerable"
Melrose Mexican purveying "solid" moles and other midpriced delights while pouring "tasty" margaritas and 150 different tequilas in a
setting decorated with bright murals and autographed photos of "Old
Hollywood"; mariachi music on the weekends fits the "warm, friendly"
vibe established by owner Antonio, who "greets guests at the door."

🅩 A.O.C. *Californian/French*
	27	23	24	$54

Third Street | 8022 W. Third St. (bet. Crescent Heights Blvd. & Fairfax Ave.) |
323-653-6359 | www.aocwinebar.com

"A rare treat for the senses", this food-lovers' "mainstay" on Third
Street from Suzanne Goin (Lucques, Tavern) offers a "remarkable
roster of wines by the glass" coupled with "brilliant", "farm-driven"
Cal-French small plates, including "tremendous" charcuterie and
cheese; "professional, savvy" servers add to the overall "delight", so
even if tables in the "elegant, simple" space are a bit "close" and it's all
too "easy to rack up a substantial bill", "there's no other place quite
like it in LA"; P.S. if you're feeling "lucky", try for a spot at the wine
bar – no reservations required.

🅩 Apple Pan ●Ⓜ⇗ *American*
	23	11	20	$14

West LA | 10801 W. Pico Blvd. (bet. Glendon Ave. & Westwood Blvd.) |
310-475-3585

"LA wouldn't be LA" without this family-owned, cash-only "culinary
landmark", a circa 1947 "throwback to post-war diners" that makes
"lip-smackin'" American favorites like "hickory burgers", "phenomenal pies" and "a mean tuna sandwich"; the "quick-and-to-the-point",
"counter-only" service and "no-frills" Westside setting where patrons
"hover over your chair waiting to pounce" also "hark back to" another
era, but that's "part of the charm."

Armstrong's Fish Market & Seafood Restaurant *Seafood*
	-	-	-	M

Catalina Island | 306 Crescent Ave. (Whitney Ave.) | Avalon |
310-510-0113 | www.armstrongseafood.com

Overlooking Avalon Bay with a "relaxing view" of boats bobbing up
and down, this venerable midpriced family-owned seafooder on Catalina
Island turns out fresh, seasonal fin fare – from jumbo fried shrimp to
sashimi – that can be washed down with fruity and classic cocktails;
the wood-paneled, nautical setting is "nothing fancy", just a fine
"place to watch the world go by."

	FOOD	DECOR	SERVICE	COST

Aroma *Italian*
| 23 | 16 | 22 | $30 |

Silver Lake | 2903 W. Sunset Blvd. (bet. Reno St. & Silver Lake Blvd.) | 323-644-2833 | www.aromaatsunset.com

Surveyors head to a "nondescript strip mall" in Silver Lake for this "cozy, charming" midpriced Italian with a "long list" of "superb" "daily specials" and "tasty pastas" delivered by "prompt", "personable servers"; white tablecloths, original artwork and a "lovely patio with plenty of seating" give a boost to the otherwise "noisy", "run-of-the-mill storefront" digs.

Aroma Café *E European/Mediterranean*
| 19 | 13 | 15 | $22 |

West LA | Rancho Park Plaza | 2530 Overland Ave. (bet. Ayres & Cushdon Aves.) | 310-836-2919 | www.aromacafe-la.com

For a taste of Eastern European–Med "home cooking" Bosnian-style, devotees seek out this "affordable" spot in a West LA strip mall offering "big portions" of "simple, well-prepared" "comfort food" and "energetic service"; despite a "plain setting", it's a favored "hang" for expats and curious converts, with a "mini-grocery store" that's a sure thing for a Balkan fix.

☒ Arroyo Chop House *Steak*
| 25 | 24 | 25 | $58 |

Pasadena | 536 S. Arroyo Pkwy. (California Blvd.) | 626-577-7463 | www.arroyochophouse.com

This "classic" Pasadena steakhouse is a "clubby", "masculine", "martinis and red meat" kind of place, where locals exercise their "expense accounts" on "impressive" "cuts of steer" and an "extensive" list of fine California wine; "top-notch service", nightly "live piano" and a "beautiful" mahogany bar seal the deal.

Arsenal, The ●☒ *American*
| 16 | 16 | 17 | $24 |

West LA | 12012 W. Pico Blvd. (bet. Bundy Dr. & Westgate Ave.) | 310-575-5511 | www.arsenalbar.com

In a circa-1874 building that was formerly a Spanish arsenal, an Old West saloon and a speakeasy, this "dark" "neighborhood bar" in West LA has retained its "old-school" charm with jukeboxes, lemon drop cocktails and a "surprisingly good" American menu featuring "lotsa meat and potatoes" delivered by a "hip", "friendly" staff; but it's really the "strong drinks" and "fantastic happy hour" that make it such a "great scene" (it closes at 2 AM).

Artisan Cheese Gallery *Cheese/Sandwiches*
| 24 | 14 | 17 | $18 |

Studio City | 12023 Ventura Blvd. (Laurel Canyon Blvd.) | 818-505-0207 | www.artisancheesegallery.com

"Cheese fanatics love this gem" in Studio City for its "impressive selection of rare-to-find *fromages* (some 300 kinds) as well as its "crave"-worthy salads and "fresh, interesting sandwiches"; a "knowledgeable staff" can verge on "pretentious" but "encourages sampling", which helps to compensate for "pricey tabs" and "long waits" for a "coveted table" in a mostly retail setting; P.S. closes at 7 PM most nights.

Art's Deli *Deli*
| 20 | 12 | 19 | $21 |

Studio City | 12224 Ventura Blvd. (bet. Laurelgrove & Vantage Aves.) | 818-762-1221 | www.artsdeli.com

"Fantastically delicious" pastrami and "corned beef piled high on fragrant rye" has made this family-owned Studio City deli a "Valley institution" for over 50 years – and the close proximity to film studios means the "people-watching is outta-sight"; service is "quick" and the "comfortable", "old-fashioned setting fits" the fare, though grumblers gripe it's "expensive for what it is", despite "plenty of leftovers to take home."

Asahi Ramen ⊅ *Japanese*   20 | 8 | 16 | $13
West LA | 2027 Sawtelle Blvd. (bet. La Grange & Mississippi Aves.) | 310-479-2231 | www.asahiramen.com

"Slurping" surveyors say the "best cold-day restaurant in town" is this "amazingly consistent" Japanese in West LA, where the "big bowls of steaming ramen" are "cheap" and "satisfying"; there's "no decor" to speak of, and "service is so quick your cash is gone before your soup is"; still, expect "long waits" and "get there early" to avoid the "crowds."

Asaka *Japanese*   ▽ 16 | 14 | 15 | $34
Rancho Palos Verdes | Golden Cove Shopping Ctr. | 31208 Palos Verdes Dr. W. (Hawthorne Blvd.) | 310-377-5999 | www.asakausa.com

"An ocean view and outside seating make dining a treat" ("especially at sunset") at this "casual", midpriced Rancho Palos Verdes Japanese offering "fresh" sushi and teriyaki that appeals to kids as much as adults; less "memorable" is an inside that's "a bit like a sports bar" – "crowded and uncomfortable" – with service that's sometimes "overtaxed."

Asakuma *Japanese*   21 | 15 | 19 | $34
Beverly Hills | 141 S. Robertson Blvd. (bet. Charleville & Wilshire Blvds.) | 310-659-1092
Venice | Hoyt Plaza | 2805 Abbot Kinney Blvd. (Washington Blvd.) | 310-577-7999
West LA | Brentwood Shopping Ctr. | 11701 Wilshire Blvd. (Barrington Ave.) | 310-826-0013
West LA | 11769 Santa Monica Blvd. (bet. Granville & Stoner Aves.) | 310-473-8990
www.asakuma.com

"Quick" delivery of "fresh sushi to your door" is the deal at most outposts of this "dependable" midpriced Japanese foursome in Beverly Hills, Venice, and West LA, where most laud the "exceptional quality and service for takeout"; eating in gets mixed reactions, given the "erratic service", "miserable parking" and "strip-mall ambiance", though the separately owned Wilshire location has a sizable dining room.

⚡ Asanebo Ⓜ *Japanese*   27 | 16 | 23 | $69
Studio City | 11941 Ventura Blvd. (bet. Carpenter & Radford Aves.) | 818-760-3348

It might be a "hole-in-the-wall" on Studio City's "Sushi Row", but "genius" chef-owner Tetsuya Nakao's "top-notch" Japanese presents sushi and sashimi that's "sublime", along with "perfectly flavored cooked fish dishes", for an omakase experience that is "one incredible course after another"; though it could almost be "less expensive to actually fly to Japan", fans say "it never fails to amaze" and is "worth the cost."

⚡ Asia de Cuba *Asian/Cuban*   24 | 26 | 21 | $61
West Hollywood | Mondrian Hotel | 8440 Sunset Blvd. (bet. La Cienega Blvd. & Olive Dr.) | 323-848-6000 | www.chinagrillmanagement.com

A "spectacular view of the city" combined with "white minimalist decor" (by Philippe Starck) makes this "sexy" Asian fusioner in West

	FOOD	DECOR	SERVICE	COST

Hollywood's Mondrian Hotel a "romantic destination" and a "first pick to impress out-of-state visitors" with a "sophisticated" seasonal menu of Cuban-influenced fare; it gets bonus points for being a "people-watching paradise", though "waiters with attitude" and "pricey" tabs come with the territory.

Astro Burger ⊄ *Burgers* | 20 | 11 | 17 | $11 |

Hollywood | 5601 Melrose Ave. (Gower St.) | 323-469-1924 | www.astroburger.com ●
West Hollywood | 7475 Santa Monica Blvd. (bet. Fairfax & La Brea Aves.) | 323-874-8041 ●
Montebello | 3421 W. Beverly Blvd. (Bradshawe St.) | 323-724-3995
Fans "never leave without" indulging in the "tip-top onion rings" at this "late-night" threesome dishing up a slice of "burger heaven" and "lots of vegetarian selections" (including Greek food at the Hollywood location) in retro "diner" digs sporting "oldies in the jukebox" and a "cool" drive-thru; sure, it's a "greasy spoon", but "beloved by many" as a "fast, inexpensive joint to hit before a show" or after a "night out."

Asuka *Japanese* | 19 | 14 | 19 | $32 |

Westwood | 1266 Westwood Blvd. (Wilshire Blvd.) | 310-474-7412
"One of the first sushi restaurants in LA", this Westwood Japanese is "still going strong", drawing in a "neighborhood" clientele with "basic" but "fresh" fish and "friendly service"; the light-wood "decor is quite dated", but it's "convenient" "before a movie" or with kids in tow, and "you can't beat the price for the quality."

Auld Dubliner, The *Pub Food* | 16 | 18 | 18 | $24 |

Long Beach | Pike at Rainbow Harbor | 71 S. Pine Ave. (Ocean Blvd.) | 562-437-8300 | www.aulddubliner.com
"They pour a perfect pint" at this "authentic Irish pub" in Long Beach serving "filling" Celtic fare in appropriately dark-wood environs (the furniture came from Ireland); ok, it's "a bit loud at night" with the live music and "booty-shaking" "crowds" having "alcohol-induced fun", but you can always count on a "friendly", "awesome atmosphere."

Auntie Em's Kitchen *American* | 21 | 13 | 18 | $17 |

Eagle Rock | 4616 Eagle Rock Blvd. (Corliss St.) | 323-255-0800 | www.auntieemskitchen.com
"My favorite aunt" is what fans call this "quirky", "casual" Eagle Rock spot, where a "friendly" staff plates up inexpensive "home-cooked" American eats including "killer cupcakes", "terrific" breakfasts and "fresh" salads and sandwiches, all "with just enough flair to be distinctive"; "colorful oil tablecloths" and mismatched furniture assure that "cutesy kitsch abounds", which is just fine by the "college kids" and local "hipsters" who "hang out" here; there are also "artisan cheeses" at the small attached shop.

Aunt Kizzy's Back Porch *Southern* | 19 | 13 | 17 | $23 |

Marina del Rey | Marina Connection | 523 Washington Blvd., 2nd fl. (Via Marina) | 310-578-1005 | www.auntkizzys.com
"Down-home cookin'" is "hard to find" in LA, and this wallet-loving Marina del Rey Southern spot has been filling the void for some 25 years with "soul food" "classics" like "good ol' fried chicken" and mac 'n' cheese that are "worth the caloric splurge"; "family-run" and "friendly",

it gets the "hospitality" thing right for the most part, though mini-mall digs are dissed for lack of "charm."

Austen's at the Pierpont Inn *Californian*   − | − | − | M
Ventura | Pierpont Inn | 550 Sanjon Rd. (Harbor Blvd.) | 805-643-6144 | www.pierpontinn.com

For "leisurely meals with family and friends", Ventura locals hit this "old mainstay" (circa 1910) in the Craftsman-style Pierpont Inn, where expertly served Sunday brunch is a highlight of the Californian menu; a "beautiful" "view of the coastline" from the candlelit dining room "adds to the enjoyment", as do "reasonable" prices.

A Votre Sante *Vegetarian*   20 | 15 | 20 | $24
Brentwood | 13016 San Vicente Blvd. (26th St.) | 310-451-1813 | www.avotresantela.com

French for *to your health,* this aptly named, stalwart Brentwood vegetarian "revamps" burgers and breakfasts "with a nutritious twist", appealing to vegans, carnivores "in a rabbit type of mood" (though turkey and chicken are also on the menu) and more than a few "celebrities"; sure, it's "trendier these days", but the "smiley" staff and "earthy ambiance" with local artwork on the walls still channel a "wholesome goodness" that makes "you feel healthy just walking in."

Azeen's Afghani Restaurant *Afghan*   23 | 17 | 22 | $27
Pasadena | 110 E. Union St. (Arroyo Pkwy.) | 626-683-3310 | www.azeensafghanirestaurant.com

"Who knew Afghani food" was so "delicious" exclaim newcomers to the "tender, juicy kebabs", "excellent dumplings" and other "authentic", "wallet-friendly" fare at this "wonderful little" "storefront" in Old Town Pasadena that's "adorned with tapestries" and artwork; its staff is "extraordinarily friendly", and it's a local "favorite" for "out-of-town guests."

Babalu *Californian*   20 | 15 | 18 | $26
Santa Monica | 1002 Montana Ave. (10th St.) | 310-395-2500 | www.babalu.info

"Incredible" "gooey homemade desserts" including banana brownie cream pie are the stars at this longtime Santa Monica "favorite" known for its "delightful Island twist" on Californian fare in a "cool Caribbean atmosphere" with bamboo ceilings; "spotty service" and "noisy", "tightly packed" quarters mean "it's not a place to linger", unless you "can score an outdoor table" for prime "people-watching."

Z Babita Mexicuisine M *Mexican*   27 | 16 | 24 | $41
San Gabriel | 1823 S. San Gabriel Blvd. (Norwood Pl.) | 626-288-7265

Don't let the "dive" exterior "fool you", this San Gabriel Mexican rated "best in class" is "adored" for its "exceptional" "haute cuisine" as well as its "gracious" chef-owner Roberto Berrelleza, who ensures a "friendly, warm" experience; it's "small" and "not cheap", but for fans "there's nothing comparable" and it's "well worth the trip getting here."

Baby Blues BBQ *BBQ*   21 | 12 | 18 | $24
West Hollywood | 7953 Santa Monica Blvd. (Hayworth Ave.) | 323-656-1277 | www.babyblueswh.com

(continued)

Baby Blues BBQ

Venice | 444 Lincoln Blvd. (Rose Ave.) | 310-396-7675 |
www.babybluesvenice.com

"Smoky, hot deliciousness – and that's just the waitresses" cheer fans of this "reasonable" BBQ duo in Venice and West Hollywood that has gained a reputation for "lick-your-plate-clean", "falling-off-the-bone" ribs, "quality fixin's" and "unbelievable banana pudding"; "junkyard-chic" digs with local artwork and "graffiti-ed walls" are "appropriately casual", but "getting there early" to "avoid long lines" is essential.

Back Home in Lahaina *Hawaiian*

| 17 | 16 | 18 | $18 |

Carson | 519 E. Carson St. (Grace Ave.) | 310-835-4014
Manhattan Beach | 916 N. Sepulveda Blvd. (bet. 9th & 10th Sts.) |
310-374-0111
www.backhomeinlahaina.com

"Onolicious!" exclaim followers of these inexpensive Hawaiian eateries in Carson and Manhattan Beach where "huge portions" of "tasty fried chicken" and other "homestyle" fare provide a "quick" "fix" for those "jonesin'" for tropical tastes; with a staff that captures "the spirit" of the islands and a "genuine laid-back atmosphere", "the only thing missing is the ocean breeze."

Baja Fresh Mexican Grill *Mexican*

| 17 | 10 | 15 | $11 |

Third Street | Beverly Connection | 8495 W. Third St. (La Cienega Blvd.) |
310-659-9500
Beverly Hills | 475 N. Beverly Dr. (Santa Monica Blvd.) | 310-858-6690
Brentwood | 11690 San Vicente Blvd. (bet. Barrington & Darlington Aves.) |
310-826-9166
Marina del Rey | Villa Marina Mktpl. | 13424 Maxella Ave. (Glencoe Ave.) |
310-578-2252
Santa Monica | 720 Wilshire Blvd. (Lincoln Blvd.) | 310-393-9313
Westwood | Westwood Vill. | 10916 Lindbrook Dr. (bet. Gayley Ave. &
Westwood Blvd.) | 310-208-3317
Long Beach | Los Altos Shopping Ctr. | 2092 Bellflower Blvd. (Britton Dr.) |
562-596-9080
Burbank | 877 N. San Fernando Blvd. (Burbank Blvd.) | 818-841-4649
Studio City | Bistro Ctr. | 12930 Ventura Blvd. (Coldwater Canyon Ave.) |
818-995-4242
Woodland Hills | Winnetka Sq. | 19960 Ventura Blvd. (Winnetka Ave.) |
818-888-3976
Oxnard | Tower Plaza | 2350 Vineyard Ave. (St. Marys Dr.) | 805-988-7878
Ventura | Telephone Plaza | 4726-2 Telephone Rd. (bet. Market St. &
Ventura Frwy.) | 805-650-3535
www.bajafresh.com
Additional locations throughout Southern California

Fans find "everything fast food usually is not" at this "always fresh" SoCal Mexican chain where the "fish tacos are a highlight" and the "salsa bar is a hit"; though critics find it "under-spiced" with "hit-or-miss" service, most consider it "worthwhile" for a "cheap" meal "on the run."

Baleen Los Angeles *American*

| 19 | 22 | 18 | $46 |

Redondo Beach | Portofino Hotel & Yacht Club | 260 Portofino Way
(Harbor Dr.) | 310-372-1202 | www.hotelportofino.com

"Not your typical beach fare", the "upscale" seasonal seafood has special allure in the candlelit dining room and "pretty" patio setting of this

	FOOD	DECOR	SERVICE	COST

New American at the Portofino Hotel & Yacht Club in Redondo Beach which affords "wonderful views of boats in the harbor"; diners grousing over "slow" service and "expensive" tabs are buoyed by live music in the lounge on Fridays.

Bamboo *Caribbean*
	21	14	20	$26

Culver City | 10835 Venice Blvd. (bet. Overland Ave. & Sepulveda Blvd.) 310-287-0668 | www.bamboorestaurant.net

"Culver City's answer to the Caribbean" is this spot with an eclectic menu of "basic" but "delightful" "chicken, shrimp, vegetable" and other dishes that are all "wonderfully washed down" with signature mojitos served by a "fast and friendly" staff; while the "simple" setting with "traffic zooming past" the patio won't exactly "sweep you away" to the islands, the prices are so "reasonable" that no one seems to mind.

Bamboo Cuisine *Chinese*
	23	17	21	$25

Sherman Oaks | 14010 Ventura Blvd. (bet. Costello & Murietta Aves.) | 818-788-0202 | www.bamboocuisine.com

For "upscale Chinese" in the Valley, a "devoted following" frequent this Sherman Oaks veteran dishing out "generous portions" of "dependable", "well-prepared" fare served "promptly" by an "attentive staff"; "noisy, crowded" digs with "big, round tables and lazy Susans" make it a popular pick for "families and large parties", so "don't even think of coming on the weekend without a reservation."

Bamboodles *Chinese*
	20	10	15	$13

San Gabriel | 535 W. Valley Blvd. (New Ave.) | 626-281-1226 | www.bamboodlesrestaurant.com

"Supple" yet "al dente" "handcrafted noodles are masterfully created" daily at this inexpensive San Gabriel Chinese say samplers who get a kick out of watching the staff in the "glass-enclosed prep room" "hopping on a giant bamboo stick to knead dough"; the "menu is limited" and the "room is basic", so as not to distract from the "teeter-tottering" show.

Bandera *American/Southwestern*
	22	21	21	$37

West LA | 11700 Wilshire Blvd. (Barrington Ave.) | 310-477-3524 | www.hillstone.com

Brace for a "raging bar scene" at this "always packed" "part of the Houston's chain" that "beckons" with "spot-on" midprice Southwestern-American "comfort food" including "perfectly grilled artichokes" and "ribs that melt off the bone", plus live jazz and "dark" setting with "comfortable booths"; a "good-looking, cheerful staff" keeps the good "vibes" flowing, though it's the "huge martinis", "generous pours of wine" and no-corkage that are the real catalysts for fun.

Banzai Sushi *Japanese*
	▽ 20	14	19	$31

Calabasas | 23508 Calabasas Rd. (Valley Circle Blvd.) | 818-222-5800 www.banzaisushi.com

"All types" of "creative" specialty rolls and moderate tabs make this "must for sushi lovers" "in the heart of Calabasas"; it's known for "accommodating service" and short wait times, and despite a "small" setting a "friendly atmosphere" keeps it on locals' short list.

	FOOD	DECOR	SERVICE	COST

Bar*Food ● Ⓜ Eclectic
▽ 15 | 15 | 15 | $22

West LA | 12217 Wilshire Blvd. (Amherst Ave.) | 310-820-3274 |
www.bar-food.us

"Gourmet burgers" and other "simple food" is on the "surprisingly inexpensive" "small menu" at this Eclectic West LA gastropub from "focused, enthusiastic" owner (and Irish actor) Jason Killalee, whose "friendly staff" delivers an "extensive selection of specialty beers on tap"; for a "neighborhood bar", the "ambiance is cool", with marble floors and exposed wooden beams.

Barbara's at the Brewery Ⓢ Eclectic
▽ 15 | 10 | 12 | $19

Downtown | Brewery Art Complex | 620 Moulton Ave. (Main St.) |
323-221-9204 | www.bwestcatering.com

This inexpensive Downtown "local hangout for the art crowd" tucked inside the Brewery Art Complex remains a "good place for a beer or three" to wash down "decent" burgers, tacos and other Eclectic eats; its industrial space with rotating art is a lure when you want to "experience a different side of LA."

NEW Bar Bouchon ● French
23 | 25 | 22 | $52

Beverly Hills | 235 N. Cañon Dr. (Dayton Way) | 310-271-9910 |
www.bouchonbistro.com

Nestled below "star"-chef Thomas Keller's "elegant" Bouchon is this "lively", "stylish bistro", a relatively "informal" French "oasis in the heart of Beverly Hills" where locals can nibble on "superb", pricey seasonal small plates and sip wine at the nickel-plated bar; with a "charming" garden view and "wonderful" service, no wonder it's "packed."

Barbrix Italian/Mediterranean
23 | 20 | 22 | $40

Silver Lake | 2442 Hyperion Ave. (Tracy St.) | 323-662-2442 |
www.barbrix.com

A "breath of fresh air" for Silver Lake, this "vibrant" late-night Italian-Mediterranean from chef Don Dickman is "hopping with a very chic crowd" that "loves" the "exciting, contemporary small plates" and "adventurous", "reasonably priced" wine list; "attentive" staffers and "dimly lit" environs in a "comfortable" "converted house" brand it a "neighborhood" "find", despite "jet engine" acoustics.

Bar Celona Spanish
17 | 19 | 18 | $31

Pasadena | 46 E. Colorado Blvd. (bet. Fair Oaks & Raymond Aves.) |
626-405-1000 | www.barcelonapasadena.com

Go for "happy hour and enjoy the tapas" counsel fans of this crimson-hued Spaniard in Old Town Pasadena where a "happening" scene at the "outstanding bar" is the focus; despite a midpriced menu that's "a bit of a snooze" (but includes paella), nightly flamenco dancers and DJs add spice, plus there's a "cheery staff", all making it a "great place to meet friends" for "after-work drinks."

Barefoot Bar & Grill Ⓜ Californian/Eclectic
17 | 18 | 18 | $35

Third Street | 8722 W. Third St. (bet. George Burns Rd. & Robertson Blvd.) |
310-276-6223 | www.barefootrestaurant.com

Apart from its "beautiful" vine-covered patio, this "reasonably priced" Third Street Cal-Eclectic near Cedars-Sinai has a "relaxing" feel with a "broad enough menu to satisfy anyone's needs" and "one of the most consistent happy hours around"; foes fault "mixed" service and "average" fare, though even they concede the private "garden room upstairs" is among the "best party places" in the city.

Bar Hayama 🅂 *Japanese* 22 | 22 | 22 | $44
West LA | 1803 Sawtelle Blvd. (Nebraska Ave.) | 310-235-2000 |
www.bar-hayama.com
A "cool setting" with a "giant fire pit" on the patio provides a "romantic" backdrop for the "innovative, imaginative Japanese" dishes of chef-owner Toshi Sugiura, whose seasonal plates come "with a fusion twist" at this West LA "gem"; somewhat "pricey" tabs are softened by "terrific service" and an "outstanding selection of sakes."

Bariloche Restaurant *S American* ∇ 22 | 16 | 21 | $26
Ventura | 500 E. Main St. (California St.) | 805-641-2007 |
www.mybariloche.com
Surveyors "feel miles from the mainstream of Main Street Ventura" at this "small" South American named after an Argentinean city, thanks to the "unique", "fresh" fare including "must-try" desserts and some of the "best empanadas" around; maybe the decor is nothing to write home about, but "friendly servers", "large portions" and nightly live music make it "worth a try" for "something different."

Barney Greengrass *Deli* 22 | 17 | 18 | $33
Beverly Hills | Barneys New York | 9570 Wilshire Blvd., 5th fl. (bet. Camden & Peck Drs.) | 310-777-5877 | www.barneygreengrass.com
For "ex-Gothamites craving lox and real bagels" it's hard to beat this "upscale" NYC-import "power-lunch spot" "on top of Barneys department store", where "you'll likely trip over an agent, producer or studio exec" chowing down on "generous portions" of "fine" deli fare; service is hit-and-miss, but regulars tout a "lovely outdoor patio" with a "super view of the Hollywood Hills" and the "beautiful people", adding "yes, it's overpriced, but it's the scene, baby."

Barney's Beanery ● *Eclectic* 15 | 15 | 15 | $20
West Hollywood | 8447 Santa Monica Blvd. (bet. Holloway & Olive Drs.) | 323-654-2287 | www.barneysbeanery.com
Once a hangout for the likes of Janis Joplin and Jim Morrison, this "classic Route 66" WeHo "favorite" still packs them in on "game" night with an "astounding" selection of beers and an Eclectic menu that "includes everything but the kitchen sink" – complete with the "greasyspoon chili you'd expect" from a "funky" roadhouse; sure, it's hard to "hustle up" a table and the "alcohol-scented" setting is "jammed full" of "knickknacks", but as far as cheap "bar fare goes, it delivers."

Barney's Gourmet Hamburgers *Burgers* 20 | 11 | 16 | $16
Brentwood | 11660 San Vicente Blvd. (Darlington Ave.) | 310-447-6000
Santa Monica | Brentwood Country Mart | 225 26th St. (San Vicente Blvd.) | 310-899-0133
Sherman Oaks | Westfield Fashion Sq. | 14006 Riverside Dr. (Woodman Ave.) | 818-808-0680
www.barneyshamburgers.com
The "huge variety" of "thick, juicy burgers cooked to perfection" "could convert a vegetarian" say satisfied samplers of this "reasonable" family-friendly chain from San Francisco that also offers lots of

meatless patties and "amazing" "fresh-cut fries"; "service with a smile" can be "painfully slow", and don't expect "much in the way of atmosphere" except at the Brentwood Country Mart, which sports a "cozy courtyard" with a "fire pit" and the "occasional" "movie star."

Bar Pintxo *Spanish*

| 21 | 17 | 20 | $34 |

Santa Monica | 109 Santa Monica Blvd. (Ocean Ave.) | 310-458-2012 | www.barpintxo.com

A "convivial, unpretentious" atmosphere recalls a "charming bodega" in "Barcelona" as the "after-work" Santa Monica crowd "perches" on "high stools" and "elbows their neighbors" while nibbling "tasty" seasonal tapas and sipping "interesting" wines at this late-night Spaniard from chef-owner Joe Miller (Joe's); even the "casually indifferent service" adds a certain "authentic" flair, but be careful, as "those little plates can add up"; P.S. Spanish products are also available at the attached gourmet shop.

NEW bar210 🖼Ⓜ *Eclectic*

| - | - | - | M |

Beverly Hills | Beverly Hilton | 9876 Wilshire Blvd. (Santa Monica Blvd.) | 310-887-6060

In the former Beverly Hills branch of Trader Vic's, this Las Vegas–style Eclectic features decor by Tom Ford (yes, that Tom Ford!), who went rather over-the-top filling the intensely purple and ochre rooms; expect fluffy chandeliers, low couches out of the last days of Rome and soft goat-hair pillows – in other words, a setting equally hospitable for cocktails, orgies and food by *Top Chef* finalist Marcel Vigneron (formerly of The Bazaar by José Andrés).

☑ Bashan Ⓜ *American*

| 27 | 20 | 25 | $54 |

Montrose | 3459 N. Verdugo Rd. (bet. Oceanview & Sunview Blvds.) | 818-541-1532 | www.bashanrestaurant.com

This "culinary delight" in suburban Montrose from husband-and-wife team Nadav and Romy Bashan is "splendid" for "simple, classy and inspired" New American fare made with "quality" farmer's market ingredients; add in "knowledgeable servers", "interesting offbeat wines" and a "cozy", modern setting conducive to "conversation", and there's no doubt it's "worth the trek" for "serious foodies."

Basix Cafe *Californian/Italian*

| 19 | 15 | 18 | $25 |

West Hollywood | 8333 Santa Monica Blvd. (Flores St.) | 323-848-2460 | www.basixcafe.com

"Just as the name implies", this "WeHo standard" and sibling of Marix is "nothing fancy" with "simple" Cal-Italian "comfort food" set down by a "friendly" staff in a "comfortable, uncrowded" setting; it's the budget-friendly prices – including a "tempting array of happy-hour specials" – that set it apart, as does the "sidewalk" seating where "locals" and their "furry friends" like to watch the "neighborhood" go by.

☑ Bastide 🖼Ⓜ *French*

| 27 | 25 | 27 | $86 |

West Hollywood | 8475 Melrose Pl. (La Cienega Blvd.) | 323-651-5950 | www.bastidela.com

This "refined" New French in West Hollywood is "always changing" and "reinventing itself", and its latest "incarnation" boasts a "substantially simpler" menu featuring "creative" global twists and "more pocket-friendly prices" than before; "polite service" and an

FOOD | DECOR | SERVICE | COST

"exquisite" environment incorporating an Assouline bookstore get kudos, though the "lovely" walled-in "garden is still the place" for "extended romantic evenings."

⚡ Bay Cities Deli Ⓜ *Italian* 25 | 9 | 15 | $13

Santa Monica | 1517 Lincoln Blvd. (B'way) | 310-395-8279 | www.bcdeli.com

A "perennial favorite" of deli devotees, this circa-1925 Italian "institution" in Santa Monica "satisfies" with "huge sandwiches of delicious, top-quality meats", especially the Godmother, a "quintessential sub" that's a taste of "spicy heaven"; "there are hardly any tables", it's "always crazy-busy" and counter "service is brusque", "but oh, those meatballs!" – so it's all "worth it"; P.S. "pre-order your lunch via fax" or e-mail "for quicker service."

⚡ Bazaar by José Andrés, The *Spanish* 26 | 27 | 24 | $77

Beverly Hills | SLS at Beverly Hills | 465 S. La Cienega Blvd. (Clifton Way) | 310-247-0400 | www.thebazaar.com

Prepare to be "blown away" by chef José Andrés' "crazy-brilliant molecular gastronomy" – "cotton candy foie gras", "liquid olives" – that's "balanced" by more traditional yet no less "magical" tapas at this Beverly Hills Spaniard in the SLS hotel; Philippe Starck's "deliciously outrageous" "high-concept decor" provides a variety of backdrops including a *blanco* room ("quiet"), *rojo* room ("noisier"), pink patisserie and a "chic" bar; surveyors are split on service ("attentive" vs. "casual"), but the majority agrees "it's worth every penny" for such a "memorable", "over-the-top" experience; afterwards, pick up a "unique souvenir" from the Moss retail store also on-site.

BCD Tofu House *Korean* 20 | 10 | 13 | $17

Koreatown | 3575 Wilshire Blvd. (bet. Ardmore & Kingsley Aves.) | 213-382-6677 ☽
Koreatown | 869 S. Western Ave. (bet. 8th & 9th Sts.) | 213-380-3807 ☽
Cerritos | 11818 South St. (Pioneer Blvd.) | 562-809-8098
Torrance | 1607 Sepulveda Blvd. (Western Ave.) | 310-534-3480
Reseda | 18044 Saticoy St. (Lindley Ave.) | 818-342-3535 ☽
Rowland Heights | Yes Plaza | 1731 Fullerton Rd. (Colima Rd.) | 626-964-7073
www.bcdtofu.com

"Boiling cauldrons" of "spicy tofu soup" are the thing at this "casual" Korean chain, which curbs the "craving for something warm and hearty" on "cold winter nights" (late hours make it "perfect for post-club grub"); despite "convenient tabletop buzzers", service is practically "nonexistent" in the "frenetic, noisy" space, but when it's this "cheap" and "tasty", who cares?; P.S. Koreatown locations are open 24/7.

Beachcomber Café *Californian* 18 | 20 | 18 | $36

Malibu | 23000 PCH (Malibu Pier) | 310-456-9800 | www.thebeachcombercafe.com

"Perched over the Pacific" in a "wonderful location on the Malibu Pier", this "lovely" spot with surfer decor conjuring the "interior of a beautiful ship" also offers "hearty" Californian fare; the service (when you can "get someone") is "family-friendly", but at least "they don't charge a mint" and anyway, "you came for the view", no?

	FOOD	DECOR	SERVICE	COST

Beacon *Asian*
22 | **18** | **21** | **$37**

Culver City | Helms Bldg. | 3280 Helms Ave. (Washington Blvd.) |
310-838-7500 | www.beacon-la.com

Having helped "put Culver City on the map" when it opened in 2004,
this "unpretentious" Pan-Asian from chef/co-owners Kazuto Matsusaka
and Vicki Fan remains a "beacon" for "foodies" thanks to its "simple"
yet "inventive" fare including – "believe it or not – one of the best burgers in town"; a few mutter about "poor acoustics", but "expert" service
and "reasonable prices" quell complaints.

Beau Rivage Ⓜ *Mediterranean*
19 | **21** | **21** | **$49**

Malibu | 26025 PCH (Corral Canyon Rd.) | 310-456-5733 |
www.beaurivagerestaurant.com

Perhaps Malibu's "most romantic location", this "casually elegant"
Mediterranean "overlooking the Pacific" evokes a "back-in-time"
"Tuscan villa" ambiance with "unhurried" service, rustic wooden
beams and a leafy upstairs terrace that can be reserved for private
parties; though some wish the fare lived up to the "lovely setting", it's
still an "old favorite" for "date night", just don't "forget your checkbook."

Beckham Grill *American*
19 | **19** | **21** | **$34**

Pasadena | 77 W. Walnut St. (Fair Oaks Ave.) | 626-796-3399 |
www.beckhamgrill.com

For better or worse, "time seems to grind to a halt" at this "quaint"
Pasadena tavern, a piece of "jolly old England" complete with a red
phone booth, British taxi and "warm, cozy" tables by the fireplace;
though the "predictable" steakhouse fare is thoroughly American (tip:
"get the prime rib"), "friendly" service and reasonable tabs have kept
it a "welcoming" "hangout" for 30-plus years.

Beechwood Ⓩ Ⓜ *American*
19 | **22** | **18** | **$35**

Marina del Rey | 822 Washington Blvd. (Abbot Kinney Blvd.) |
310-448-8884 | www.beechwoodrestaurant.com

The outdoor lounge with fire pit "rules" at this "chic, modern" American
in Marina del Rey known for a "lively" bar scene fueled by "creative
drinks"; so even if the seasonal menu of midpriced steak and ribs is
"solid" and the staff "talented", it's all "eclipsed" by the "beautiful setting", which, naturally, is "perfect for a first date."

Bel-Air Bar & Grill *Californian*
20 | **20** | **21** | **$44**

Bel-Air | 662 N. Sepulveda Blvd. (bet. Moraga Dr. & Ovada Pl.) |
310-440-5544 | www.belairbarandgrill.com

You'll find "lots of *Mad Men* downing martinis" at this "reliable
standby" in Bel-Air "between the city and the valley" serving an "extensive menu" of "solid" Californian fare in "cozy" environs (think brick
fireplaces, a "pretty patio" and a mirrored bar); while it's a bit too "old
school" for some, "terrific service" and a "low-key" vibe assuage most.

Bella Roma SPQR Ⓜ *Italian*
∇ **24** | **14** | **20** | **$32**

Pico-Robertson | 1513 S. Robertson Blvd. (bet. Cashio & Horner Sts.) |
310-277-7662 | www.bellaromaspqr.com

Die-hard fans of "charming" chef-owner Roberto Amico's "unassuming
little Italian" in Pico-Robertson "hope it's never found by the rest of the
Westside", the better to keep its "fresh, light" Roman fare (including
handmade pastas) to themselves; besides, there's already "elbow-

to-elbow" seating, due in part to the "bang-for-your-buck" tabs; P.S. "nominal corkage" is a "plus."

Bellavino Wine Bar ⬕ *Eclectic*   ▽ 19 | 18 | 18 | $39

Westlake Village | Paseo Market Pl. | 3709 E. Thousand Oaks Blvd. (Marmon Ave.) | 805-557-0202 | www.bellavinowinebar.com

A "wine list that never ends" – including 1,200 bottles and 50 by the glass – attracts oenophiles to this trendy Westlake Village bistro presenting "flavorful" risotto, Kobe burgers and other seasonal Eclectic eats in an art-filled setting; a few flag service issues and tabs that run "a bit pricey", but "if nothing else, go for the great live sounds" (jazz Thursday–Saturday).

NEW Bellini Osteria Bar & Lounge *Italian*   - | - | - | M

Westlake Village | 951 S. Westlake Blvd. (Hampshire Rd.) | 805-497-8482 | www.belliniosteria.com

Westlake Villagers are all aglow about this Italian newcomer, where everything is "*bellissimo*", from the "hot waiters" and "good-looking patrons" to the "modern", "tastefully done" setting and "quiet patio"; "well-prepared" pastas and veal chops "draw big appreciative crowds", even if a few unimpressed sorts deem service simply "fair" and the plates "overpriced."

Belmont, The *American*   16 | 15 | 16 | $31

West Hollywood | 747 N. La Cienega Blvd. (Sherwood Dr.) | 310-659-8871 | www.thebelmontcafe.com

"Watch sports, hang out with friends" and dig into "mac 'n' cheese, steak skewers" and other American comfort favorites at this "inviting" late-night lounge in West Hollywood; though the chow gets decidedly mixed marks, reasonable prices and a full bar make it a "happy-hour staple"; P.S. dress code enforced after 7 PM.

Belmont Brewing Co. *American*   18 | 20 | 19 | $28

Long Beach | 25 39th Pl. (1 block south of Ocean Blvd.) | 562-433-3891 | www.belmontbrewing.com

When the "sun is shining" in Long Beach, the patio "is the place to be" say fans of this Belmont Pier brewpub boasting "fabulous ocean views" and "ample portions at small prices"; sure, the seafood-centric American chow is "tasty" enough, but remember "you're here for the beer, not the food", so "knock back a pitcher" of the "excellent" housemade suds delivered by servers as "laid-back" as the scene.

⦿ Belvedere, The *American*   25 | 28 | 27 | $74

Beverly Hills | Peninsula Hotel of Beverly Hills | 9882 S. Santa Monica Blvd. (Wilshire Blvd.) | 310-788-2306 | www.peninsula.com

"An oasis of refinement", this "see-and-be-seen" Beverly Hills "classic" at the Peninsula Hotel stars chef James Overbaugh's "top-flight" American cuisine, delivered by "gracious" servers to the city's "rich and famous" amid "elegant yet unpretentious" English-inspired surroundings; regulars who deem it "perfect for that special night" (and for a "one-of-a-kind" Sunday jazz brunch) admit, yes, "you pay for it", but "if you want to feel coddled, this is the place."

Benihana *Japanese*   19 | 18 | 21 | $36

Beverly Hills | 38 N. La Cienega Blvd. (Wilshire Blvd.) | 323-655-7311

(continued)

Benihana

Santa Monica | 1447 Fourth St. (bet. Broadway St. & Santa Monica Blvd.) | 310-260-1423
Torrance | 21327 Hawthorne Blvd. (Village Ln.) | 310-316-7777
Ontario | 3760 E. Inland Empire Blvd. (Haven Ave.) | 909-483-0937
Encino | 16226 Ventura Blvd. (bet. Libbit & Woodley Aves.) | 818-788-7121
City of Industry | Plaza at Puente Hills | 17877 Gale Ave. (Fullerton Rd.) | 626-912-8784
www.benihana.com

"Bring on the onion volcano" clamor customers who count on an "entertaining" "show" for "all ages" (even "jaded teenagers") at this Japanese steakhouse chain where tableside teppanyaki chefs perform feats while delivering "reliable" eats, including sushi and other "updated" items; critics call it "tired", "tacky" and "overpriced", but it works as a place to "take the kids and still have an edible meal."

Benley Vietnamese Kitchen 🔡 *Vietnamese*   ▽ 24 | 13 | 20 | $26

Long Beach | 8191 E. Wardlow Rd. (Norwalk Blvd.) | 562-596-8130

"You'll be floored" by the "clean, assertive flavors" and "exotic" aromas at this inexpensive Long Beach Vietnamese, where the "skilled kitchen" puts a "modern", French-accented spin on the cuisine and servers are "friendly and knowledgeable"; it's "tucked in the back of a strip mall" and features a "sparse interior", but devotees decree it's a "definite winner" nonetheless.

Berri's Pizza Cafe *Pizza*   15 | 13 | 16 | $26

Third Street | 8412 W. Third St. (bet. Croft & Orlando Aves.) | 323-852-0642 ◑
Playa del Rey | 8415 Pershing Dr. (Manchester Ave.) | 310-823-6658
www.berrispizzacafe.net

It's "not the cheapest" pizza-pasta purveyor around and critics deem it "decent" at best, but since this "resilient" Third Streeter is "open till 4 AM", club-hoppers looking for a "late-night" nosh cheer it (the "pleasant" service and BYO help); the Marina del Rey offshoot closes earlier but sports a liquor license, prompting some to proclaim it "better for cocktails than dining."

Beso 🔡 *Pan-Latin*   21 | 24 | 20 | $51

Hollywood | 6350 Hollywood Blvd. (Ivar Ave.) | 323-467-7991 | www.besohollywood.com

Actress Eva Longoria Parker's "glamorous" – and "expensive" – Hollywooder "hits the mark" with "creative", "surprisingly good" takes on Pan-Latin cuisine from "celeb chef"/co-owner Todd English; still, while the "cavernous space" awash in leather and chandeliers is filled with a "sea of beautiful people" (servers "couldn't be nicer" to mere mortals too), the unimpressed just "don't get the hype" – and good luck "people-watching" in a dining room so "dark" you can "hardly see what you're eating."

🖪 Best Fish Taco in Ensenada 🏴 *Mexican*   21 | 6 | 17 | $8

Los Feliz | 1650 Hillhurst Ave. (Prospect Ave.) | 323-466-5552 | www.bestfishtacoinensenada.com

"The name says it all (except for the Ensenada part)" at this "no-frills" Mexican "shack" in Los Feliz whose "amazingly cheap" fish and shrimp tacos are enhanced by a "plethora" of "unusual" salsas; add in a "super-friendly owner" and "welcoming staff", and most wish there could "be one on every street corner."

Big Mama's Rib Shack ☒ *BBQ/Soul Food*   21 | 12 | 18 | $23
Pasadena | 1453 N. Lake Ave. (Rio Grande St.) | 626-797-1792 | www.bigmamas-ribshack.com

The BBQ "meat is so tender it almost melts" at this "friendly" soul-fooder in Pasadena where most everything is "down-home delicious", especially the "falling-off-the-bone ribs"; true, it's not much to look at and service can be "slow", but it pleases most looking for a well-priced, "Southern-style" sojourn, only "without the humidity and air travel."

Billingsley's *Steak*   15 | 11 | 19 | $27
West LA | 11326 W. Pico Blvd. (Sawtelle Blvd.) | 310-477-1426 | www.billingsleysrestaurant.com

Go for the "early-bird special and a strong cocktail" at this "old-style" West LA steakhouse opened by Barbara Billingsley's husband in 1946 that offers "lots of food for the money" along with a side of "nostalgia"; the service is "crusty", the decor (red leather booths, wood paneling) is "older than the hills" and you "expect Dean Martin" to pop "out from behind a plant" at any moment, but "loads of loyalists" endorse this "blast from the past."

BiMi ☒ *Japanese*   23 | 17 | 21 | $36
West LA | 11917 Wilshire Blvd. (Westgate Ave.) | 310-479-2464 | www.bimirestaurant.com

It's "more than just sushi" at this West LA Japanese that goes beyond its "creative", "gorgeous" rolls to offer an "eclectic" mix of small plates from "reasonably priced sashimi" to traditional meat skewers; the casual setting plus "gracious, attentive service", an "invigorating" happy hour and "reasonable prices" make it feel like a true "Tokyo izakaya."

Bistro de la Gare ☒ *French*   19 | 19 | 19 | $36
South Pasadena | 921 Meridian Ave. (bet. El Centro & Mission Sts.) | 626-799-8828 | www.bistrodelagare.com

South Pasadenans "craving a taste of France" look no further than this "comfortable neighborhood" wine bar "conveniently" located next to a Gold Line metro stop, that captures a certain "je ne sais quois"; "well-executed" bistro fare, "charming", "accented" waiters and "softly lit, deep-red walls" add up to an "intimate date spot" that won't bust your budget; P.S. closed Monday and Tuesday.

☒ Bistro 45 ☒ *Californian*   26 | 23 | 26 | $57
Pasadena | 45 S. Mentor Ave. (bet. Colorado Blvd. & Green St.) | 626-795-2478 | www.bistro45.com

A "continued standout" in Pasadena, this "upscale but friendly" Californian mixes a "stunningly beautiful setting" in an art deco building (including an enclosed twinkle-lit terrace) with "imaginative" seasonal cuisine and a "carefully constructed" 800-bottle wine list; "wonderful" host Robert Simon leads a staff that "treats you like an old friend" from "the first time you go", but expensive tabs mean you'll only get there on "special occasions."

	FOOD	DECOR	SERVICE	COST

🗹 Bistro Garden at Coldwater *Continental* | 21 | 27 | 23 | $52

Studio City | 12950 Ventura Blvd. (Coldwater Canyon Ave.) | 818-501-0202 | www.bistrogarden.com

"One of the most elegant restaurants in the Valley", this "oldie but goodie" "splurge" in Studio City draws "ladies who lunch" and "special-occasion" diners to its "gorgeous" "indoor-garden" setting; cheers over the "delightful" nightly jazz piano, "efficient service" and "divine" "signature chocolate soufflé" drown out drones who dis the "rather boring" Continental menu.

Bistro LQ 🗒📵 *French* | 24 | 20 | 22 | $64

Fairfax | 8009 Beverly Blvd. (bet. Edinburgh & Laurel Aves.) | 323-951-1088 | www.bistrolq.com

"Adventurous palates" needn't search far for "audacious" cooking: chef "Laurent Quenioux is back" at this "fabulous" Fairfax bistro where the "expensive" menu of "innovative" globally inspired French dishes (many available in half-portions) includes one of the "best cheese carts" in the city; the "simple", sleek, art-filled setting is made invitingly "friendly" by an "informed", "enthusiastic" staff.

Bistro Provence 🗒 *French* | 23 | 18 | 22 | $40

Burbank | Lakeside Ctr. | 345 N. Pass Ave. (Rte. 134) | 818-840-9050 | www.bistroprovenceburbank.com

With "elegant fare", a "warm, helpful" staff and a "bargain" prix fixe dinner, the only reason this "gem" of a French bistro remains "Burbank's hidden secret" may be its "nondescript""mini-mall" location; luckily, the "inviting" interior doesn't match the facade.

Bistro 31 🗒📵 *Californian* | - | - | - | M

Santa Monica | Art Institute of LA | 2900 31st St. (Ocean Park Blvd.) | 310-314-6057 | www.artinstitutes.edu

Prepare for an "interesting experience" at this midpriced, BYO student-run Californian at Santa Monica's Art Institute of LA, where aspiring chefs "learning their craft" create and serve weekly changing lunch menus in a minimalist space; fans say even when service lags and the dishes are a miss, it's "hard to find fault" with a staff that "tries its hardest" to please; it's open Tuesday–Thursday, but hours are seasonal.

BJ's *Pub Food* | 17 | 16 | 17 | $21

Cerritos | 11101 183rd St. (I-605) | 562-467-0850
Westwood | 939 Broxton Ave. (bet. Le Conte & Weyburn Aves.) | 310-209-7475 ☾
Long Beach | 5258 E. Second St. (bet. Covina & Laverne Aves.) | 562-439-8181
Moreno Valley | 22920 Centerpoint Dr. (Frederick St.) | 951-571-9370
Arcadia | 400 E. Huntington Dr. (bet. 5th & 2nd Aves.) | 626-462-1494 ☾
Burbank | 107 S. First St. (bet. Angeleno & Olive Aves.) | 818-557-0881
Woodland Hills | 6424 Canoga Ave. (bet. Erwin St. & Victory Blvd.) | 818-340-1748
West Covina | Eastland Shopping Ctr. | 2917 E. Eastland Center Dr. (Baranca Ave.) | 626-858-0054
Oxnard | Esplanade Plaza | 461 W. Esplanade Dr. (bet. Oxnard Blvd. & Vineyard Rd.) | 805-485-1124
Westlake Village | 3955 E. Thousand Oaks Blvd. (Westlake Blvd.) | 805-497-9393

(continued)

(continued)

BJ's

Valencia | Valencia Town Ctr. | 24320 Town Center Dr. (McBean Pkwy.) |
661-288-1299
www.bjsbrewhouse.com
Additional locations throughout Southern California

"Deep-dish" pies, a "rockin' pizookie" ("cookie in a pizza pan") and
"darn good beers on tap" elevate this "decently priced", "friendly",
"packed" SoCal franchise "above the average chain"; expect the usual
American "sports bar trappings", like "plenty of TVs" and a "rowdy"
crowd on game nights, along with a fair share of families.

Blair's *American*   24 | 19 | 21 | $41

Silver Lake | 2903 Rowena Ave. (bet. Glendale Blvd. & Hyperion Ave.) |
323-660-1882 | www.blairsrestaurant.com
This "warm" and "cozy neighborhood" "hang" "does Silver Lake proud",
and has "maintained its quality" throughout the years with "dependable" New American seasonal fare (try the "amazing" short ribs), a
"lovely" wine list and a "welcoming staff"; even if a handful pleads for
"something new" on the "pricey" menu, it remains a "favorite" for
"dinner with friends."

bld *American*   22 | 20 | 20 | $33

Beverly Boulevard | 7450 Beverly Blvd. (Vista St.) | 323-930-9744 |
www.bldrestaurant.com
"A favorite" "for B and L" – as well as dinner – this "popular" New
American diner on Beverly Boulevard courtesy of chef Neal Fraser
(Grace) offers "new takes on traditional fare" in "light-filled" "contemporary" surroundings; a "young, hip crowd" and "eager" "service to
match" keep the place "bumping", especially on weekends, so for the
quickest "in and out", "snag a seat at the bar."

Bloom Cafe *American/Californian*   21 | 15 | 15 | $22

Mid-City | 5544 W. Pico Blvd. (Sierra Bonita Ave.) | 323-934-6900 |
www.bloomcafe.com
Organic cuisine fans "tingle over" the "interesting menu" at this
"bright", art-filled Mid-City BYO eatery that serves "simple" salads
and other "ultrafresh" Californian–New American fare that's so "delicious" you hardly know it's "healthy"; though service can be "forget-
ful" and it's "a bit overpriced" for its type, loyal locals come "once or
twice a week", saying "we need more" places like this.

Blossom 🗷 *Vietnamese*   23 | 13 | 18 | $15

Downtown | 426 S. Main St. (Winston St.) | 213-623-1973 |
www.blossomrestaurant.com
Always a "pho-vorite" for "quick", "cheap" Vietnamese noodle and
rice dishes, coupled with a "great selection" of Asian beers, this
"solid" Downtowner keeps patrons "coming back"; just don't expect
much from the "unremarkable setting" with sage-toned decor.

BLT Steak *Steak*   24 | 22 | 22 | $73

West Hollywood | Sunset Plaza | 8720 Sunset Blvd. (Sherbourne Dr.) |
310-360-1950 | www.bltsteak.com
"A bit of Manhattan at the Sunset Plaza", Laurent Tourondel's "expertly executed" West Hollywood outpost of the BLT brand boasts

"excellent" steaks à la carte, "rich and buttery sides" and "heavenly popovers" delivered by an "agreeable" staff; sure, the "noisy", "celeb-heavy" "scene" and "pricey" tabs aren't for everyone, but the majority calls it "a winner" "all around."

NEW Blue Dog Beer Tavern *American*   21 | 20 | 20 | $19
Sherman Oaks | 4524 Saugus Ave. (Greenleaf St.) | 818-990-2583 | www.bluedogbeertavern.com
Valley-dwellers deem this Sherman Oaks pub a "neighborhood find" thanks to its "tasty" burgers and other "uncomplicated" American fare, "fantastic" draft beers and a "comfy", "industrial" setting with walls made from the room's original 1940s-era floors and posted with "photos of patrons' dogs"; with a staff that "knows your name" and does "everything short of throwing a Frisbee to make you happy", boosters bark it "feels like it's been here for years."

Blue Hen *Vietnamese*   17 | 15 | 19 | $18
Eagle Rock | 1743 Colorado Blvd. (Argus Dr.) | 323-982-9900 | www.eatatbluehen.com
Locally sourced organic chicken and produce is the hallmark of this modern, "casual" Vietnamese kitchen in Eagle Rock where the "fresh" pho, banh mi and other "reasonably priced" dishes on the "limited menu" are delivered by a "lovely" staff; you "feel healthy just walking in", though peckish patrons shouldn't expect much space in the "tiny", "cramped" digs.

Blue Velvet ⓩ Ⓜ *American*   20 | 23 | 20 | $46
Downtown | The Flat | 750 S. Garland Ave. (bet. 7th & 8th Sts.) | 213-239-0061
"Hipsters love the view" of the Downtown skyline as well as the "sultry, laid-back atmosphere" of this "gorgeous", pricey New American that incorporates produce from its rooftop garden into "innovative" seasonal cuisine; considering the "so LA" bar that wraps "around a pool" and the weekend DJ (not to mention the "cool" "coed bathroom"), the fare and "snooty" service are clearly "secondary to the scene."

Bluewater Grill *Seafood*   20 | 20 | 19 | $36
Redondo Beach | King Harbor Marina | 665 N. Harbor Dr. (Beryl St.) | 310-318-3474 | www.bluewatergrill.com
"Fine, moderately priced seafood" comes "with views of where the stuff came from" at this Redondo Beach fin fare specialist with a "water-front location" and a menu that offers up to 20 varieties of fresh fish daily along with "wonderful, warm" sourdough bread; "service is ser-viceable" and "friendly enough" and the weekday "happy hour" has its fans too, all adding up to a "relaxing way to finish a sun-kissed day."

Blu LA Café *American*   - | - | - | I
Downtown | Pacific Electric Lofts | 126 E. Sixth St. (bet. Los Angeles & Main Sts.) | 213-488-2088 | www.blu.la
"Deliciously meaty, cheesy burgers", "outstanding pastries" and other American comfort fare satisfies diners from morning until late night at this Downtowner set in the landmark Pacific Electric Lofts; though the decor is highlighted by shades of blue, the "friendly" staff and afford-able pricing leave patrons anything but the namesake color.

Blvd, The *Californian*
23 | 24 | 24 | $54

Beverly Hills | Beverly Wilshire | 9500 Wilshire Blvd. (Rodeo Dr.) |
310-385-3901 | www.fourseasons.com

An "interesting crowd" of "well-heeled" locals "enjoys the good life" at
this "classic" art deco Californian with a "perfect location" in the "posh"
Beverly Wilshire; the "outdoor seating" "opposite Rodeo Drive" is "great
for people-watching" and the "unobtrusive service" works for "showbiz
dealmakers", but the seasonal menu, including dry-aged rib-eye, "terrific brunches" and "late afternoon tea", is "pricey" for mere mortals.

Blvd 16 *American*
21 | 23 | 21 | $45

Westwood | Hotel Palomar | 10740 Wilshire Blvd. (Selby Ave.) |
310-474-7765 | www.blvd16.com

A "hideaway" for the Westwood crowd, this "modern" New American
with "semi-reasonable prices" in the Hotel Palomar is just "waiting for
its moment of fame" say fans; the "awesome", sleek decor has a certain
"futuristic elegance", the "inspired", farm-to-table seasonal menu
embraces "fresh" finds "from local markets" and the "savvy staff"
pulls it all together; P.S. early-risers favor the "delicious" breakfasts.

◪ Boa *Steak*
22 | 24 | 21 | $63

West Hollywood | 9200 Sunset Blvd. (Doheny Dr.) | 310-278-2050
Santa Monica | 101 Santa Monica Blvd. (Ocean Ave.) | 310-899-4466
www.boasteak.com

Dry-aged chops and other "prime meats" are delivered by a "professional" staff at these "flashy", seriously priced steakhouses in West
Hollywood and Santa Monica that put a "modern" spin on the
genre with "sexy, stylish" digs (think leather walls); the "celebrity"-
studded clientele mirrors the "ultratrendy" surroundings, though traditionalists who detect "too much 'tude" tend to say "it's more of a
nightspot with steak."

Boccaccio's *Continental*
20 | 22 | 22 | $38

Westlake Village | 32123 Lindero Canyon Rd. (Lakeview Canyon Rd.) |
818-889-8300 | www.boccacciosonthelake.com

The "enchanting lake view" and "relaxed", "romantic" ambiance are
the "best parts" of this "beautiful", midpriced Continental in Westlake
Village, where the fare and service "can sometimes fall short" of the
"pretty" indoor and outdoor scenery; still, it's "worth" the time "for
drinks" or "Sunday brunch on the [waterside] patio."

Boccali's ♥ *Italian*
▽ 19 | 14 | 17 | $22

Ojai | 3277 Ojai-Santa Paula Rd. (Reeves Rd.) | 805-646-6116 |
www.boccalis.com

"Lush lawn" seating in an idyllic Ojai location may be "the star" at this
family-owned Italian, but the pasta and "chewy, gooey pizza" featuring "fresh" homegrown vegetables isn't far behind; fans of the casual,
cash-only spot "relax and enjoy" it all, including microbrews and local
wines from the family's own vineyard.

BoHo *Eclectic*
17 | 20 | 18 | $29

Hollywood | The Arclight | 6372 W. Sunset Blvd. (Vine St.) | 323-465-8500 |
www.bohorestaurant.com

"Movies at the ArcLight get better" when paired with this "on-site
hang" from André Guerrero (The Oinkster) serving moderately priced

	FOOD	DECOR	SERVICE	COST

Eclectic "comfort food" ranging from "ordinary"(pizza, burgers) to "sophisticated" (braised short ribs, Chinese duck confit), plus "craft brews" and plenty of wines by the glass; though service is so-so, the "dark", "kitschy" Hollywood setting, with deer heads and lanterns, evokes a cool "1970s basement lair."

Boiling Crab, The Cajun

| 23 | 13 | 15 | $26 |

Alhambra | 33 W. Main St. (bet. 1st St. & Garfield Ave.) | 626-300-5898 ⓈⓂ
Alhambra | 742 W. Valley Blvd. (bet. 7th & 8th Sts.) | 626-576-9368
www.theboilingcrab.com

Prepare to "get down and dirty" at this Cajun duo in Alhambra that "satisfies crustacean cravings" for "messy" piles of "spicy" shrimp, crabs and crawfish laid out on butcher paper and "eaten with your hands"; though "service is nothing to rave about" and neither is the "boat-themed decor", there's a reason why people "wait for hours" to get in – it's just so "darn good."

NEW Boiling Shrimp, The Cajun/Vietnamese

| – | – | – | M |

Hollywood | 5112 Hollywood Blvd. (bet. Normandie Ave. & Winona Blvd.) | 323-668-9113

A Vietnamese-Cajun wave sweeps into Thai Town with this functionally decorated room that's packed with locals hungry for crab, shrimp, mussels, corn on the cob and spicy fries dumped unceremoniously on the table, where plastic bib-sporting diners attack the food with wooden mallets; the process is sloppy, the fare tasty, the hours late – a great new destination after a night in Hollywood.

Bokado Spanish

| ∇ 19 | 17 | 22 | $35 |

Studio City | 12345 Ventura Blvd. (Whitsett Ave.) | 818-752-9222 | www.bokadorestaurant.com

Locals are "happy to have" this Studio City restaurant and gourmet market from chef Frank Leon (La Loggia) offering "creative" Spanish small plates and "exceptional fish specials" in a red-and-black-accented space; even if a few frown over limited, "hit-or-miss" choices, the "unhurried" service and "enjoyable" outdoor seating are pluses.

Bollywood Cafe Indian

| 17 | 12 | 17 | $23 |

Studio City | 11101 Ventura Blvd. (Vineland Ave.) | 818-508-8400 | www.bollywoodcafela.com
Studio City | 3737 Cahuenga Blvd. (Lankershim Blvd.) | 818-508-5533 | www.bollywoodcafe2.com Ⓢ

Despite the name, don't expect anything flashy or even "spicy" at these Studio City Indians known for "dependable", if "predictable", masala and tandoor specialties at "fabulous prices"; service varies from "curt" to "kindly", decor veers toward "hole-in-the-wall" and they're usually "jammed at lunch", so some opt for takeout instead.

Bombay Bite Indian

| ∇ 19 | 15 | 16 | $24 |

Westwood | 1051 Gayley Ave. (Kinross Ave.) | 310-824-1046 | www.bombaybite.com

"The spice is right" and so is the price at this Indian "bargain for Westwood", a "quiet haven" in the surrounding hubbub, where "flavorful, if not innovative, curries" and other "tasty" specialties gain favor; it might not be exciting, but the "small", "inviting" space and "happy" staff make for a "pleasant" meal.

Bombay Cafe *Indian*

22 | 15 | 19 | $31

West LA | 12021 W. Pico Blvd. (Bundy Dr.) | 310-473-3388 |
www.bombaycafe-la.com

Fan say the "interesting" menu including "street-style specialties" and
"curry of the day" will "blow you away" at this "long-standing" West
LA Indian where the "chutney trio should not be missed" and the
"knowledgeable" staff "knows its way around" a "ginger margarita";
considering the "informal" setting and "difficult parking", however,
wallet-watchers deem it on the "pricey" side.

Bombay Palace *Indian*

21 | 21 | 22 | $38

Beverly Hills | 8690 Wilshire Blvd. (bet. Hamel & Willaman Drs.) |
310-659-9944 | www.bombaypalace.com

Living up to its name, this "elegant", "pricey" Beverly Hills Indian delivers "delicious" subcontinental classics in a "gorgeous" dining room
filled with lighted niches holding "glittering" statues; with perhaps the
"classiest lunch buffet" in town and "friendly" service, no wonder it
has "outlasted" a lot of its competitors.

BonChon Chicken *Korean*

∇ 19 | 10 | 11 | $17

Koreatown | 3407 W. Sixth St. (Catalina St.) | 213-487-7878

The "fantastic" fried chicken at this K-town branch of a South Korean
fast-food chain is "much better than expected" insist fans who find
both the soy-garlic and spicy versions "delicious"; the decor, however,
elicits more yawns than yums, and the "so-o-o slow" service means
you have to call ahead to avoid "long waits."

Bond Street Beverly Hills *Japanese*

20 | 22 | 18 | $59

Beverly Hills | Thompson Beverly Hills Hotel | 9360 Wilshire Blvd.
(Crescent Dr.) | 310-273-1400 | www.thompsonbeverlyhills.com

A "sleek, sophisticated" setting with a terrace and a "cool" brown-
leather lounge designed by Dodd Mitchell and attended by an "attractive staff" makes this "swanky" Japanese in the Thompson Beverly
Hills Hotel an easy choice for "after-work" sake and sushi; but a handful who believe they're "paying for atmosphere" over substance dis the
"tiny portions", "pretentious" service and "trendy 90210" vibe.

Boneyard Bistro *BBQ/Eclectic*

21 | 15 | 19 | $32

Sherman Oaks | 13539 Ventura Blvd. (Woodman Ave.) | 818-906-7427 |
www.boneyardbistro.com

"High-end BBQ" "may be an oxymoron", but it sure is "tasty" claim those
who dig the Eclectic menu at this Sherman Oaks mash-up that features
both "wonderful smoked and barbecued meats" and "unexpectedly
fine" seasonal bistro fare, coupled with an "extensive beer list"; if you
find the "concept" confusing, let the "capable staff" "lead you down"
a "lip-smacking" path, just remember it's "not for the faint" of palate
or wallet; N.B. a recent expansion may not be reflected in Decor score.

NEW Bonnie B's Smokin' Barbeque Heaven Ⓜ *BBQ*

- | - | - | I

Pasadena | 1280 N. Lake Ave. (Washington Blvd.) | 626-794-0132 |
www.bonniebssmokin.com

This down-home Southerner, with roots in San Diego, is flavoring the
air north of the 210 Freeway with the aroma of BBQ ribs and chicken
smoked long and slow; the storefront setting features peace signs on

the walls, a mural of Gold Rush miners cooking 'cue and framed photos of African-American icons like MLK, MJ and Muhammad Ali.

Bono's *Californian*
21 | 20 | 20 | $43

Long Beach | 4901 E. Second St. (St. Joseph Ave.) | 562-434-9501 | www.bonoslongbeach.com

Even if the majority enjoys the "delightful" Californian fare and "stiff drinks" at this "pricey", open-air Long Beach bistro courtesy of Christy Bono (daughter of the late Sonny), it's all about the "bustling scene" and "terrific outdoor seating" for "prime people-watching" on Second Street; the "beautiful" interior includes a waterwall and amber-lit bar and service is "friendly", if "uneven", but it's "loud" "when it's busy, which is most of the time."

Border Grill *Mexican*
21 | 18 | 19 | $35

Santa Monica | 1445 Fourth St. (bet. B'way & Santa Monica Blvd.) | 310-451-1655 | www.bordergrill.com

Surveyors agree the "Too Hot Tamales" (celeb owners Susan Feniger and Mary Sue Milliken) are "still innovative" "after all these years", offering "zesty", "imaginative" midpriced Mexican fare and "potent margaritas" at this "legendary" Santa Monica cantina; "quirky, colorful wall paintings", a "friendly" staff and a "lively" crowd make it feel like "there's always a party going on", so be prepared to shout over all the "noise."

Border Grill Truck ⊅ *Mexican*
20 | 8 | 19 | $12

Location varies; see website | 213-542-1102 | www.bordergrill.com

"The best parts of Border Grill come to you" via this roving taco truck that turns out the same "unique twist on Mexican" as the restaurant, but in "small" handheld portions (think "ceviche cones" and "churro bites"); even if a few warn of "slow" lines and high prices "for what you get", most advise "if you can find it, eat it"; P.S. it's open from 11 AM-2:30 PM, check website for locations.

NEW Borracho Cantina ● *Mexican*
- | - | - | I

West Hollywood | 8570 W. Sunset Blvd. (Alta Loma Rd.) | 310-289-8809 | www.borrachocantina.com

This West Hollywood Mexican serves a budget-friendly menu of many tacos, platters and even a lunchtime 'bento box' – accompanied by a drink list whose signature option is called 'The Horny Margarita' – in a modern setting decorated with oversized beer labels and boasting a heated front patio with a fine view of the Strip; P.S. there are two happy hours daily – from 3-6 PM and 10 PM-1 AM.

Bossa Nova *Brazilian*
20 | 14 | 17 | $22

Hollywood | 7181 W. Sunset Blvd. (Formosa Ave.) | 323-436-7999 ●
Pico-Robertson | 10982 W. Pico Blvd. (bet. Greenfield & Veteran Aves.) | 310-441-0404 ●
West Hollywood | 685 N. Robertson Blvd. (bet. Melrose Ave. & Santa Monica Blvd.) | 310-657-5070 ●
Beverly Hills | 212 S. Beverly Dr. (Charleville Blvd.) | 310-550-7900
www.bossafood.com

Surveyors "eat their hearts out" at this Brazilian chainlet with a "sprawling menu" of "cheap", "consistently satisfying" choices ranging "from

pastas to plantains to pizza" ("would you like starch with that?");
"friendly waiters are more than happy to point you in the right di-
rection", though many diners opt for "late-night delivery" since the
"tropical-themed" decor falls "flat" (the Hollywood branch is open
until 4 AM nightly).

Boss Sushi *Japanese*   25 | 15 | 19 | $41
Beverly Hills | 270A S. La Cienega Blvd. (Gregory Way) | 310-659-5612 |
www.bosssushi.com
Sushi "boss" Tom Sagara "continues to rule" at his pricey Beverly Hills
Japanese where the "enormous" rolls are always "inventive" and "if
you're a regular you may get one named after you"; "decor is random
at best", service varies and "parking can be a drag", but the "top-
notch" fish in "amazing presentations" "makes up for it."

Z Bottega Louie *Italian*   22 | 23 | 21 | $33
Downtown | 700 S. Grand Ave. (7th St.) | 213-802-1470 |
www.bottegalouie.com
Channeling a "raucous" "New York vibe" with "marble" tables, an
open kitchen, "soaring ceilings and lots of clang and clatter", this
"sparkling" Downtown Italian with a "to-go" market "in a converted
bank building" also generates "definite buzz" with its "innovative" pizzas, pastas and other "modern" trattoria fare; even with the "excruci-
ating waits" (there's a "no-reservations" policy), all that "urban
charm" coupled with a "hot" staff makes loyalists "love it."

Bottle Inn *Italian*   - | - | - | M
Hermosa Beach | 26 22nd St. (Hermosa Ave.) | 310-376-9595 |
www.thebottleinn.com
This old-school Hermosa Beach Italian has been a South Bay destination for pasta, veal, chicken and seafood for more than three decades,
serving moderately priced fare in a kitschy room that could have been
lifted straight out of Naples; an outdoor patio is washed by ocean
breezes, and (as the name suggests) there's an extensive wine list.

BottleRock *European*   16 | 16 | 18 | $30
Downtown | Met Lofts | 1050 S. Flower St. (11th St.) |
213-747-1100
Culver City | 3847 Main St. (bet. Culver & Venice Blvds.) |
310-836-9463
www.bottlerock.net
"The tasting experience is the draw" at this "unpretentious" Culver City
wine bar and store where a wide "variety" of wines, shelved throughout
the room, are available by the glass with a "limited menu" of European
nibbles ("homemade charcuterie", "wonderful cheese"); a handful of
oenophiles, however, are left "cold" by the "modern" look and service
that ranges from "knowledgeable" to "ditzy", while some patrons of
the Downtown sib say its more substantial menu misses "the mark."

Z NEW Bouchon *French*   24 | 26 | 25 | $68
Beverly Hills | 235 N. Cañon Dr., 2nd fl. (Dayton Way) | 310-271-9910 |
www.bouchonbistro.com
"Commando chef" "Thomas Keller has done it again" with this "long-
awaited" Beverly Hills bistro ("sister" to the Yountville original) that
"lives up to its reputation" with "perfectly prepared", "quintessential"

	FOOD	DECOR	SERVICE	COST

French classics like "exquisite roast chicken", "impressive *fruits de mer*" and "divine desserts"; service is "meticulous" and "well trained", though the "spacious, airy" decor gets mixed reviews ("transporting" and "beautiful" vs. "faux Paris" à la "Vegas"), and naturally such a "glam scene" does not come "cheap", but most say "it's worth every cent."

Bouzy Gastropub at Chez Mélange *American* | 22 | 19 | 22 | $29 |

Redondo Beach | 1611 S. Catalina Ave. (bet. Aves. H & I) | 310-540-1222 | www.chezmelange.com

"Innovative" twists (e.g. fish 'n' chips curry tartar) inflect the American "comfort" fare at this "cozy" Redondo Beach gastropub in the front room of Chez Mélange – and the "bouze isn't bad either" quip tipplers who declare it a "relaxed place to hang"; don't let the "informal", dimly lit setting fool you, though – it offers the same kind of "dedicated service" and "extensive" wine list as its "more upscale" neighbor.

Bowery ◐ *American/French* | 20 | 17 | 18 | $29 |

Hollywood | 6268 Sunset Blvd. (bet. Argyle Ave. & Vine St.) | 323-465-3400 | www.theboweryhollywood.com

"Great for pre- or post-"ArcLight bites, this "darling" Hollywood "hole-in-the-wall" serving "high-quality burgers" and other "tasty" American-French fare "feels just like NYC" with its subway tiles and tin ceilings, but has "half the attitude" thanks to a "friendly staff"; "strong drinks" and an "impressive selection" of brews lead to a "convivial atmosphere" after 11 PM, when it becomes more bar than "boîte."

NEW Boxwood Café *Californian/Continental* | ▽ 22 | 24 | 20 | $44 |

West Hollywood | London West Hollywood | 1020 N. San Vicente Blvd. (Sunset Blvd.) | 310-358-7788 | www.thelondonwesthollywood.com

Gordon Ramsay gets "cute" with this "hidden jewel"-box tucked away in the London West Hollywood, serving a "lovely", "granny"-approved afternoon tea, brunch on weekends and "upscale" Californian-Continental fare for "half the price" of his adjacent fine-dining restaurant; contrary to the chef's TV persona, it's voted "pleasant" all-around, mixing a "shiny", "bright" bistro setting with a "kind" staff.

NEW BP Oysterette *Seafood* | 22 | 17 | 21 | $36 |

Santa Monica | 1355 Ocean Ave. (Santa Monica Blvd.) | 310-576-3474 | www.blueplatesantamonica.com

Santa Monicans take a "trip to New England" at this "upscale clam shack" (whose initials stand for Blue Plate) offering an "array" of oysters and other seafood so "fresh" "you could have picked it out of the ocean yourself"; "helpful" servers and a "cozy" space featuring a "great raw bar" give it a "been-here-forever feel", all leading most to agree it's "worth shelling out for."

☑ Brandywine ⧄ *Continental* | 28 | 20 | 27 | $64 |

Woodland Hills | 22757 Ventura Blvd. (Fallbrook Ave.) | 818-225-9114

"Elegant" Continental cuisine "priced for perfection" is the forte of this "romantic" Woodland Hills "gem" overseen by a "husband-and-wife team" who "bend over backwards" to please patrons; though the "cozy" French country-inn decor strikes some as too "'70s"-style, loyalists still consider it "one of the best places in the Valley for that special date", adding "they just don't make 'em like this anymore."

	FOOD	DECOR	SERVICE	COST

Bravo Cucina *Italian/Pizza* — 19 | 13 | 20 | $23

Santa Monica | 1319 Third St. Promenade (bet. Arizona Ave. & Santa Monica Blvd.) | 310-394-0374

Bravo Pizzeria *Italian/Pizza*

Santa Monica | 2400D Main St. (bet. Hollister Ave. & Ocean Park Blvd.) | 310-392-7466

www.bravosantamonica.com

For "deliciously predictable" pizzas, pastas and "people-watching" on Santa Monica's Third Street Promenade, check out this "reasonably priced" Italian, a "great place to grab a bite", sit outside and take in the "casual" scene; if its Main Street sibling lacks the same ambiance, it compensates with "huge slices" of "creative" pies and "late-night" hours.

Breadbar *American/Bakery* — 18 | 14 | 14 | $22

West Hollywood | 8718 W. Third St. (Robertson Blvd.) | 310-205-0124
Century City | Westfield Century City Shopping Ctr. | 10250 Santa Monica Blvd. (bet. Ave. of the Stars & Century Park W.) | 310-277-3770

www.breadbar.net

It's all about the "bread, glorious bread" at these "slightly pricey" bakeries in Century City and West Hollywood where patrons "carb out" on a "plethora" of "fresh"-baked loaves, pastries and other "guilty pleasures"; "tasty" seasonal sandwiches and soups also find favor, but the same can't be said of the "cold atmosphere" and "lackadaisical" servers "who are more interested in updating their Facebook pages than getting you your food."

Breeze *Californian/Seafood* — 18 | 20 | 18 | $44

Century City | Hyatt Regency Century Plaza Hotel | 2025 Ave. of the Stars (Constellation Ave.) | 310-551-3334 | www.centuryplaza.hyatt.com

"Filled with Hollywood agents and lawyers", this "modern" Californian in the Hyatt Regency Century Plaza "has the lock on the lunch crowd" as big deals go down along with the "fresh" sushi and other "solid" seafood; the plant-filled patio is "super when weather permits", though service is "spotty" and even expense-account types carp about pricing.

Ⓩ Brent's Deli *Deli* — 26 | 15 | 21 | $21

Northridge | 19565 Parthenia St. (bet. Corbin & Shirley Aves.) | 818-886-5679
Westlake Village | 2799 Townsgate Rd. (Westlake Blvd.) | 805-557-1882

www.brentsdeli.com

Whether or not "it's the best deli west of NYC", it's safe to say "your Jewish grandmother would feel at home" thanks to "pastrami like butta", double-baked rye "to die for" and other "classic" noshes served "with a smile" by "savvy waitresses" at this affordable Westlake Village and Northridge duo; "always crowded and noisy", it's a bit "like eating in Grand Central" but still "so worthwhile."

Brentwood, The ◑ *American* — 22 | 19 | 20 | $49

Brentwood | 148 S. Barrington Ave. (Sunset Blvd.) | 310-476-3511 | www.brentwoodrestaurant.com

"Seductive" quarters trimmed in mahogany and black leather give this "pricey" Brentwood "retreat" an "old-school" ambiance that befits its "classic, varied" menu of New American fare, including "great steaks" partnered with "killer martinis"; even loyalists lament "it's so dark you can go in wearing anything and look good", but "friendly" staffers and "late-night hours" keep it "packed" nonetheless.

Briganti *Italian*
21 | 18 | 22 | $36

South Pasadena | 1423 Mission St. (bet. Fair Oaks & Fremont Aves.) | 626-441-4663 | www.brigantisouthpas.com

"You feel like part of the family" at this South Pasadena "storefront" Italian that "delights" diners with "beautifully presented", "high-quality" fare ferried by "friendly servers"; a "lovely courtyard" contributes to a "nice little slice of Italy" at a moderate price, making it a fallback for families and many a mature "local."

Brighton Coffee Shop *Diner*
18 | 9 | 20 | $16

Beverly Hills | 9600 Brighton Way (Camden Dr.) | 310-276-7732

"An escape from chichi Beverly Hills", this "classic coffee shop" "that's been here forever" refreshes weary "shoppers" with "no-frills" "feel-good" diner fare (try the "wonderful meatloaf sandwich") at un-"fancy prices"; "charming, efficient" service and "cozy", "honest-to-good-ness" old-time decor complete with original '30s posters are more reasons why it's been a perennial favorite for "grabbing lunch and gab-bing with the gals."

Broadway Deli *Deli*
15 | 13 | 14 | $24

Santa Monica | 1457 Third St. Promenade (B'way) | 310-451-0616 | www.broadwaydeli.com

"More coffee shop than deli", this "Santa Monica staple" on the Promenade offers "plenty of choices" whether your "comfort food" of choice is "modern or old-fashioned", dishing out everything from "high-quality smoked fish" to pizzas from a wood-burning oven; ser-vice is "slow" and prices somewhat "inflated", but "late-night" hours and a "gargantuan" setting mean you can "most always get a table."

Brooks ⊠ *American*
25 | 21 | 24 | $51

Ventura | 545 E. Thompson Blvd. (California St.) | 805-652-7070 | www.restaurantbrooks.com

"Fine but unpretentious", this New American in Ventura proffers "in-ventive", "well-prepared" cuisine and local, boutique wines along with the "personal attention" of husband-and-wife team Andy and Jayme Brooks, who are "always there" to ensure a "dining adventure" that "measures up to the best of LA"; the "pleasant" decor is contemporary in blue-grays and browns, completing an "experience" most agree is "worth every pricey penny."

⊠ Brophy Bros. Clam Bar & Restaurant *Seafood*
21 | 17 | 18 | $29

Ventura | 1559 Spinnaker Dr. (Harbor Blvd.) | 805-639-0865 | www.brophybros.com

See review in Santa Barbara Directory.

⊠ Brunello Trattoria *Italian*
23 | 15 | 25 | $29

Culver City | 6001 Washington Blvd. (La Cienega Blvd.) | 310-280-3856

Culver City's "hidden treasure", this "family-run trattoria" is "like vis-iting Italy" with "solid home cooking" that's just as "authentic" as the "hospitable owner"; white tablecloths and an open kitchen add pizzazz to the "comfortable", traditional space, but it's the "fair prices" that prompt regulars to "recommend" it as a "once-a-week place."

Buca di Beppo *Italian*   15 | 17 | 17 | $24

Santa Monica | 1442 Second St. (bet. Broadway St. & Santa Monica Blvd.) | 310-587-2782

Redondo Beach | 1670 S. PCH (Palos Verdes Blvd.) | 310-540-3246

Pasadena | 80 W. Green St. (De Lacey Ave.) | 626-792-7272

Encino | 17500 Ventura Blvd. (Encino Ave.) | 818-995-3288

Universal City | Universal CityWalk | 1000 Universal Studios Blvd. (off Rte. 101) | 818-509-9463

Claremont | 505 W. Foothill Blvd. (Indian Hill Blvd.) | 909-399-3287

Thousand Oaks | Janss Mall | 205 N. Moorpark Rd. (Hillcrest Dr.) | 805-449-3688

Valencia | 26940 Theater Dr. (McBean Pkwy.) | 661-253-1900

www.bucadibeppo.com

"Loads of red-sauced pastas" fuel the "merry" "gluttony" at this family-style Italian chain that's always "loud" and "crowded with groups" indulging in "monster portions" amid "kitschy", "over-the-top" decor (including "wacky photos"); despite "average" fare, the "ridiculously perky" crew, relatively "cheap" tabs and "Dean Martin songs" make it a staple for big "get-togethers" in a "Mamma Leone's" vein.

Buddha's Belly *Asian*   19 | 15 | 19 | $26

Beverly Boulevard | 7475 Beverly Blvd. (Gardner St.) | 323-931-8588

Santa Monica | 205 Broadway (2nd St.) | 310-458-2500

www.bbfood.com

Serving an "eclectic mix" of "reliable" Pan-Asian fare (though a bit too "Americanized" for some), this "lively" Beverly Boulevard and Santa Monica duo works just as well for a "girls' night out" as it does for "fun, flirty dates"; "service varies" and the "casual" settings can get "noisy and crowded", but prices that "aren't too frightening" keep them bustling.

Buffalo Club ⊠ *American*   19 | 21 | 19 | $54

Santa Monica | 1520 Olympic Blvd. (bet. 14th & 16th Sts.) | 310-450-8600 | www.thebuffaloclub.com

An "early 20th-century speakeasy" atmosphere appointed in wood and leather is the backdrop for this "discretely located" American in Santa Monica that attracts a "party scene" on weekends with "music and dancing" on the "gorgeous patio"; while the "private club" vibe and "personable" service can be a "treat", merely "decent" "comfort food" "leaves you wanting more" and the bill "wishing you had more."

Buffalo Fire Department ⊠ *American*   19 | 19 | 20 | $24

Torrance | 1261 Cabrillo Ave. (Torrance Blvd.) | 310-320-2332 | www.buffalofiredepartment.com

"Upscale" wings, "burgers and brews" in a "clever", "funky" "fire-house setting" draw "families" and the "after-work" crowd to this "terrific" Torrance American from Buffalo, NY, native Michael Shafer (The Depot); a "lovely staff" and affordable tabs add to the appeal.

Buggy Whip *Seafood/Steak*   18 | 17 | 20 | $40

Westchester | 7420 La Tijera Blvd. (74th St.) | 310-645-7131 | www.thebuggywhip.com

Beloved for its "classic" "clubby" atmosphere with "tall red-leather booths" and "piano entertainment", this "oldie" but "goodie" in

	FOOD	DECOR	SERVICE	COST

Westchester is also known for "huge portions" of chops, seafood and "scrumptious Green Goddess dressing" just like they served "50 years ago"; even critics calling for an "upgrade" appreciate getting "lots for your money" and a staff that "always remembers you."

Bull Pen *Seafood/Steak*

∇ 15	10	16	$34

Redondo Beach | 314 Ave. I (bet. Elena Ave. & PCH) | 310-375-7797
It's a "time warp" at this "dark", '50s-era surf 'n' turfer in Redondo Beach, where an "older crowd" sidles up to the "saloon" and slips into "red booths" for "standard meat-and-potatoes" fare; though some say service is "erratic", prices are "moderate" and it's counted as one of the "best" "old-school" "dives" in the South Bay, with "live music" several nights a week.

Buona Sera *Italian*

∇ 18	17	20	$44

Redondo Beach | 247 Avenida del Norte (Catalina Ave.) | 310-543-2277
"*Bella*" is how surveyors describe "relaxed" meals of handmade pastas, lasagna and pizza from a wood-burning oven at this Redondo Beach Italian just one block from the shore; though the service is "hit-and-miss", "decent" if a bit "pricey" fare cements its status as a "neighborhood spot."

Burger Continental *Mideastern*

18	11	16	$19

Pasadena | 535 S. Lake Ave. (California Blvd.) | 626-792-6634 | www.burgercontinentalpasadena.com
"Don't let the burger name fool you" (though they have those too), "variety" is the operative word at this "Pasadena institution", a longtime "Cal-Tech hangout" that "shocks" newcomers with its "extensive" array of Mideastern specialties at "starving-student" prices ("you won't be hungry for a week") plus a bottomless Sunday brunch; sure, the "funky" setting, mostly a tented patio, could use a "makeover", but a "jovial" staff and live entertainment including "weekend belly dancers" supplement the "wow" factor.

NEW Burger Kitchen *Burgers*

-	-	-	I

Mid-City | 8048 W. Third St. (Crescent Heights Blvd.) | 323-944-0503
There are more than 20 burgers to choose from at this Mid-City arrival, ranging from a Texas chili burger to a lobster burger to a Thai burger, along with an eggs Benedict burger for breakfast and a chocolate one for dessert; with green walls, a marble counter and wooden shelves, the handsome space offers a nice spot for refueling during Third Street shopping adventures.

Cabbage Patch, The 🗷 *Californian/Mediterranean*

∇ 23	12	20	$17

Beverly Hills | 214 S. Beverly Dr. (bet. Charleville Blvd. & Gregory Way) | 310-550-8655
West LA | 12531 Beatrice St. (bet. Grosvenor Blvd. & Westlawn Ave.) | 310-305-1547
www.cabbagepatchbh.com
For "quick lunches" of organic and sustainable fare in Beverly Hills, this casual cafe with a West LA sibling fills the bill offering a "limited menu" of inexpensive burgers, tofu bowls and other "creative, fresh"

Cal-Med morsels; a "friendly, helpful staff" adds to the reasons locals say anyone "would be lucky to have this in their neighborhood."

Ca'Brea *Italian*

22 | 20 | 21 | $46

La Brea | 346 S. La Brea Ave. (bet. 3rd & 4th Sts.) | 323-938-2863 | www.cabrearestaurant.com

Italian cuisine that's a "little more genuine than most" draws surveyors to this "charming" La Brea "classic" that's "a little pricey but worth it" for "dependable" Tuscan fare and "fabulous" wines transported by a "professional" staff; "full of dark woods and beautiful flowers", the multilevel space captures a "cozy, quiet" vibe conducive to "romantic evenings", "business lunches" and even "group dinners", thanks to three upstairs private rooms.

NEW CaCao Mexicatessen Ⓜ *Mexican*

▽ 25 | 18 | 19 | $17

Eagle Rock | 1576 Colorado Blvd. (Townsend Ave.) | 323-478-2791 | www.cacaodeli.com

An "off-the-charts surprise", this "casual", colorfully decorated Mexican in Eagle Rock supplies an "authentic" experience via its "scrumptious", "out-of-the-ordinary tacos", "serious" coffee and *cacao* (hot chocolate), and overall "interesting take" on south-of-the-border "classics" at wallet-friendly prices; locals "love" it so much, even the "sometimes spacey service" is chalked up to its "newfound popularity."

Ca' del Sole *Italian*

21 | 22 | 22 | $41

North Hollywood | 4100 Cahuenga Blvd. (Lankershim Blvd.) | 818-985-4669 | www.cadelsole.com

"Industry" types "meet for lunch in the Studio Zone" and enjoy "comforting" Northern Italian cuisine and "gracious, relaxed service" at this "solid" North Hollywood "establishment" with a "villa-like atmosphere"; a "delightful garden patio" and "quiet surroundings" for "conversation" also help make it a "value for the price."

Café Beaujolais Ⓜ *French*

20 | 16 | 21 | $33

Eagle Rock | 1712 Colorado Blvd. (bet. La Roda Ave. & Mt. Royal Dr.) | 323-255-5111

Feeling "like a neighborhood cafe in Southern France", this "warm, congenial" French bistro in Eagle Rock purveys "authentic" fish and meat dishes at moderate prices; though the menu is the main "draw", "charming waiters don't hurt", making it a "nice break from the typical trendy LA scene."

Z Café Bizou Ⓜ *Californian/French*

23 | 19 | 22 | $32

Pasadena | 91 N. Raymond Ave. (Holly St.) | 626-792-9923
Sherman Oaks | 14016 Ventura Blvd. (bet. Costello & Murietta Aves.) | 818-788-3536

Z Bizou Grill Ⓢ *Californian/French*

Santa Monica | Water Gdn. | 2450 Colorado Ave. (26th St.) | 310-453-8500
www.cafebizou.com

"High-quality" "gourmet food at a reasonable price" is the raison d'être of these "charming", wildly popular Cal-French bistros dishing up "solid" pastas and other "comfort" classics that "never fail to satisfy"; with $2 corkage and "gracious service", it's a "terrific" pick for "date night", but downsides include a "noisy" setting with tables "so close" you can practically "kiss" your neighbors.

	FOOD	DECOR	SERVICE	COST

Café Brasil *Brazilian*

| 19 | 13 | 15 | $19 |

Palms | 10831 Venice Blvd. (Westwood Blvd.) | 310-837-8957
West LA | 11736 W. Washington Blvd. (McLaughlin Ave.) |
310-391-1216
www.cafe-brasil.com

"Just like in Rio", these "charming" Brazilian "shacks" in Palms and West LA dish up "authentic", "hearty plates" of rice, beans and "seasoned meats" with a heaping side of "colorful, tropical kitsch"; "unpretentious" "mostly outdoor" settings with "mismatched furniture" are just as "low-key" as the "friendly folks" who work here, and inexpensive prices are even better.

Café Chez Marie ⊠ *French*

| - | - | - | I |

Century City | 10681 Santa Monica Blvd. (Manning Ave.) | 310-475-2949 |
www.cafechezmarie.com

Housed in an "adorable" Normandy-style cottage, this "hard-to-find" French brasserie is a "tranquil haven" tucked amid Century City office complexes, offering weekday warriors "informal" breakfasts and lunches in its "small but adequate" interior and out on the "beautiful patio"; the "delightful" eponymous owner is usually "on-site" overseeing the "simple meals" of salads, sandwiches, soups and such; P.S. closed weekends.

Cafe Del Rey *Californian/Mediterranean*

| 22 | 24 | 21 | $48 |

Marina del Rey | 4451 Admiralty Way (bet. Bali Way & Via Marina) |
310-823-6395 | www.cafedelreymarina.com

Get into a "divine" "marina state of mind" at this Marina del Rey "classic on the water", where "unbeatable" views of "boats and seabirds" reel in locals and tourists alike for "delicious", "imaginative" Cal-Med cuisine; the standout Sunday jazz brunch, "VIP" service and "lovely piano bar" are more reasons it's an "all-time favorite" for a "romantic" repast or to "blow away out-of-town guests" – "especially when they pick up the tab."

Cafe des Artistes ● *French*

| 20 | 21 | 20 | $45 |

Hollywood | 1534 N. McCadden Pl. (Sunset Blvd.) | 323-469-7300 |
www.cafedesartistes.info

Given its "cozy" fireplace, "delightful garden" and "relaxed", "1960s-bohemian" vibe, it's easy to mistake this "funky" French "retreat" in the heart of Hollywood for a "small inn somewhere in France"; a "charming" staff delivers the "fine" bistro fare at prices deemed "reasonable" for the overall "wonderful" experience, which makes this "romantic" "date spot" and "hipster hangout" ideal for "good friends and a glass of wine."

Cafe 50's *Diner*

| 16 | 17 | 18 | $15 |

Venice | 838 Lincoln Blvd. (Lake St.) | 310-399-1955 ⊟
West LA | 11623 Santa Monica Blvd. (bet. Barry & Federal Aves.) |
310-479-1955 ●
Sherman Oaks | 4609 Van Nuys Blvd. (Hortense St.) |
818-906-1955
www.socafe50s.com

For "milkshakes, burgers and board games", these "throwback" diners are "super swell", dishing up all the favorite "comfort foods" of the '50s at "reasonable prices"; with a "funky" atmosphere, "friendly servers" and "old-time music" playing from "jukeboxes" at every table, "it's fabulous for the kids without torturing the adults", and if "some of the decor is showing its age", regulars can't help but remark, isn't that "the point"?

Cafe FIORE *Italian*

22 | 21 | 21 | $34

Ventura | 66 S. California St. (bet. Main & Santa Clara Sts.) | 805-653-1266 | www.fiorerestaurant.net

"Delicious", affordable Southern Italian classics, courteous service and a "comfortable" atmosphere make this trattoria a "favorite" in the "center of Old Town" Ventura; regulars seeking a "hopping" "scene" head straight for the "crazy-busy martini bar" offering "live music" Tuesday–Saturday, while those looking for quiet conversation gravitate to the "delightful patio."

Cafe Firenze M *Italian*

19 | 22 | 19 | $41

Moorpark | Mission Bell Plaza | 563 W. Los Angeles Ave. (bet. Park Ln. & Shasta Ave.) | 805-532-0048 | www.cafefirenze.net

Though it's located "smack dab in an unremarkable strip mall" in Moorpark, this upscale Northern Italian boasts an interior that's "surprisingly cozy" and "trendy"; while it generally wins favor with its "classic", "authentic" pastas and such dished up in "portions so large it's ludicrous", there are gripes about "hit-or-miss" service ("varies with the phases of the moon").

Z Café 14 M *Californian/Continental*

27 | 20 | 24 | $46

Agoura Hills | Reyes Adobe Plaza | 30315 Canwood St. (Reyes Adobe Rd.) | 818-991-9560 | www.cafe-14.com

"Exciting", "elegant" fare served in a "romantic" ambiance with oak floors, mirrors and an "intimate patio" makes this "tiny", "memorable" Californian-Continental a true "gem" in underserved Agoura Hills, with "excellent service", fans say "go once and you'll be hooked", if you can find it, that is – "tucked in a nondescript strip mall", "you couldn't hide it any better."

NEW Café Habana *Cuban*

- | - | - | M

Malibu | Malibu Lumber Yard | 3939 Cross Creek Rd. (PCH) | 310-317-0300 | www.cafehabana.com

One of the anchors of the newly repurposed Malibu Lumber Yard, the first West Coast branch of this well-regarded New York spot is so eco-friendly, the cooking oil used for its midpriced menu of Cuban fare is recycled to power owner Sean Meenan's car; the celeb-heavy green scene continues with salvaged wood (including some from Coney Island), solar power, a human-powered bike blender for smoothies, and utensils, plates and cups made from organic materials.

Cafe Med *Italian*

19 | 17 | 17 | $36

West Hollywood | Sunset Plaza | 8615 Sunset Blvd. (Sunset Plaza Dr.) | 310-652-0445 | www.cafemedsunset.com

"Celebs are a fixture" at this West Hollywood Italian that's a "dependable local hangout" and "place to fall into for lunch"; yes, it's appreciated for its "wonderfully authentic" pastas and pizzas delivered by a "friendly" staff, but to most "it's all about sitting on the patio" and taking in the Sunset Strip "scene" – including a steady stream of the "latest sports vehicles" passing by.

	FOOD	DECOR	SERVICE	COST

Cafe Montana *Californian*

18 | 16 | 18 | $33

Santa Monica | 1534 Montana Ave. (16th St.) | 310-829-3990 |
www.cafemontana.info

"Shop and stop for a bite" at this "treasure" on Santa Monica's boutique-chic Montana Avenue, where "see-and-be-seen" types "power lunch" (or brunch) on "solid" Californian fare plus "desserts to die for"; though all-glass walls and "close tables" make some feel as if they're "eating in a crowded fishbowl" ("pedestrians can read your lips!"), its "reasonable prices", "attentive" service and "convenient" location ensure it's "popular" as ever even "after all these years."

Café Nouveau *Californian*

∇ 21 | 18 | 19 | $25

Ventura | 1497 E. Thompson Blvd. (San Jon St.) | 805-648-1422

Locals "love the patio on a sunny afternoon" and commend the "helpful staff" and "prices low enough" for a spur-of-the-moment meal "when you just feel like going out" at this "casual" Californian cafe on a "residential Ventura street"; though it's a breakfast and brunch "favorite", lunch and dinner are also "tasty."

NEW Café 140 South *Californian*

∇ 19 | 19 | 21 | $27

Pasadena | 140 S. Lake Ave. (bet. Cordova & Green Sts.) | 626-449-9900 |
www.cafe140south.com

A "great redo" of the old Crocodile Cafe in Pasadena, this Californian from the Smith Brothers ("little brother to Smitty's next door") is a "real treat", offering a "varied" menu of pizza and burgers that's "kid-friendly" and delivered with "hospitable service"; the "casual, elegant setting" with a patio and open kitchen is much the same as before and happily it all still comes "without sticker shock."

Café Pacific *Mediterranean*

∇ 22 | 26 | 25 | $56

Rancho Palos Verdes | Trump Nat'l Golf Course | 1 Ocean Trails Dr.
(Palos Verdes Dr.) | 310-303-3260 | www.trumpgolf.com

"Hard to beat" as a "place to watch the sun set over the ocean" is this "grand" Med dining room at the Trump National Golf Course, perched above the cliffs in Rancho Palos Verdes; the few surveyors who've weighed in call it a "treat" for "special occasions", even if some say the "high-priced" fare is outshined by the "terrific" view, plush gilt-and-velvet setting and "super-attentive" service.

Café Piccolo *Italian*

22 | 21 | 23 | $37

Long Beach | 3222 E. Broadway (bet. Coronado & Obispo Aves.) |
562-438-1316 | www.cafepiccolo.com

At this "inviting" Italian "treasure" in a run-down corner of Downtown Long Beach, "gracious and entertaining host" Moe Shabani greets customers as if he were "welcoming them into his home"; candlelit "romance" reigns here, especially on "warm, starry nights" in the big "lovely garden" equipped with fire pits and a gurgling fountain, with "delicious" fare sealing its status as a "wonderful date place."

Café Pierre *French*

23 | 19 | 22 | $48

Manhattan Beach | 317 Manhattan Beach Blvd. (bet. Highland Ave. &
Morningside Dr.) | 310-545-5252 | www.cafepierre.com

Guy Gabriele's "long-standing" "high-end" French bistro along Manhattan Beach's main drag remains a "local favorite" thanks to its "consistent" "golden touch" with fare that's "simple" and "true to

French flavors", matched with "wonderful" wines and delivered by a "knowledgeable" staff; sure, the quarters are "cramped" and get "crowded on weekends", but the generally "relaxed ambiance" has most calling it a "lovely hangout by the beach" all the same.

Cafe Pinot   *Californian/French* | 23 | 24 | 22 | $51 |

Downtown | 700 W. Fifth St. (Flower St.) | 213-239-6500 | www.patinagroup.com

"OMG, I love this place!" exclaim patrons of this pricey, "wonderful patio"–equipped Patina Group "oasis amid skyscrapers" that provides "meals to remember" under the "stars and twinkly lights" of Downtown's theater and Central Library district; the "carefully prepared", "artistically plated" Cal-French cuisine and "impressive wines" are deemed "sophisticated but not snooty", likewise the "gracious staff" that treats all customers like their "rich relatives."

Café Provencal   *French* | 23 | 16 | 23 | $38 |

Thousand Oaks | 2310 E. Thousand Oaks Blvd. (Conejo School Rd.) | 805-496-7121 | www.cafeprovencal.biz

"Fan-flippin-tabulous" is the word on the prix fixe deals at this "little French gem hidden" in a Thousand Oaks strip mall, where suburbanites are transported to "the back roads of France" via "gracious" service and "delectable" classics at recession-friendly rates; the "intimate" interior is "romantic" to some, "super-tacky" ("disco ball and all") to others – but all seem to agree the overall vibe's "endearing."

Cafe Rodeo   *Californian*   ∇ | 15 | 15 | 14 | $37 |

Beverly Hills | Luxe Hotel Rodeo Dr. | 360 N. Rodeo Dr. (bet. Santa Monica & Wilshire Blvds.) | 310-273-0300 | www.luxehotelrodeodrive.com

"Not as stuffy as the location might warrant", this relatively "relaxed" cafe inside the Luxe Hotel on Rodeo Drive is made for shopping breaks given its moderately priced, three-meal-a-day Californian menu served in "friendly" environs; those in-the-know ask for the "lovely outdoor seating" and watch the passing parade – hey, "you just might find a star or two out for a nosh."

Café Santorini   *Mediterranean* | 22 | 21 | 20 | $33 |

Pasadena | 64 W. Union St. (bet. De Lacey & Fair Oaks Aves.) | 626-564-4200 | www.cafesantorini.com

Be "whisked away to the Greek Isles" at this Pasadena Mediterranean mainstay, where "must-try white-wine sangria" goes down well with the "contemporary", moderately priced Med fare; try for a table on the balcony with "views of the San Gabriel Mountains" – on a "warm summer night" it's the perfect perch for "romance", or to "bring your frost-bitten friends from the East Coast."

Cafe Sevilla Long Beach   *Spanish*   ∇ | 21 | 23 | 21 | $36 |

Long Beach | 140 Pine Ave. (B'way) | 562-495-1111 | www.cafesevilla.com

"*Mas* sangria!" is the rallying cry at this "fun", festive Long Beach Spaniard where bossa nova, flamenco guitar and other live music take center stage most nights, harmonizing with a "wonderful array" of tapas and "delightful libations"; prices are moderate, but given all the "great things to try", some say it's easy to "leave poor and stuffed" – though you can always dance it off at the nightclub upstairs.

Cafe Stella *French*

21 | 21 | 17 | $40

Silver Lake | 3932 W. Sunset Blvd. (bet. Hyperion & Sanborn Aves.) | 323-666-0265 | www.cafestella.com

"No longer a well-kept secret", this "lovely" Silver Lake "neighborhood Frenchie" draws local "hipsters" for "palate-pleasing" Gallic classics served "without the attitude"; given "kinda steep prices", it's more of a "date-night" place than an anyday standby, but the "beautiful off-street patio" and overall "romantic", "like-in-Paris" vibe have most gushing "*c'est magnifique*" all the same.

Cafe Surfas *American*

20 | 10 | 15 | $16

Culver City | 8777 W. Washington Blvd. (National Blvd.) | 310-558-1458 | www.cafesurfas.com

"Recover after an orgy of utensil-buying" at this "beloved" Culver City cafe adjoining Surfas restaurant supply and gourmet store offering "tasty, creative takes" on American "gourmet deli treats" (sandwiches, soups, salads); given the skimpy seating, however, many recommend devouring its low-cost "quick bites" "on the go"; P.S. breakfast and lunch only.

Cafe Sushi ● *Japanese*

▽ 21 | 13 | 19 | $41

Beverly Boulevard | 8459 Beverly Blvd. (La Cienega Blvd.) | 323-651-4020

"Leave behind the glitz and glam of other area sushi joints – as well as the huge price tag" at this nearly 30-year-old Beverly Boulevard Japanese standby that's a "reliable" source for "fresh, delicious" fish, sliced into the late hours; it's nothing fancy, to say the least, and some report "parking" headaches, but loyal locals "highly recommend" it all the same.

Café Was ● *French*

17 | 25 | 22 | $42

Hollywood | 1521 N. Vine St. (Sunset Blvd.) | 323-466-5400 | www.cafewas.com

Like "an old cabaret of eras gone by", this whimsical Hollywood brainchild of nightlife trendsetter Ivan Kane showcases nightly live piano music and Friday burlesque in a "swanky" "New Orleans"–esque setting that's one part "kitschy brothel", one part "adventure in wonderland"; opinions on the French bistro fare vary ("mediocre" vs. "mouthwatering"), but "strong drinks", "friendly service" and that "bottomless-beverage brunch" keep "hip" types "coming back"; P.S. the kitchen's open till 2 AM.

Caffè Delfini *Italian*

23 | 19 | 23 | $48

Santa Monica | 147 W. Channel Rd. (PCH) | 310-459-8823 | www.caffedelfini.com

Just steps from the "hustle and bustle of the PCH" is this "beachside" Italian "getaway", which has been satisfying Santa Monicans for more than two decades with "delicious" pastas and other "authentic" dishes ferried by a "warm", "attentive" crew; it's a bit pricey and its "dimly lit" ("ask for a flashlight") quarters are a "tight" "squeeze", but never mind because to most this "darling" place is "one of the most romantic" going.

Caffe Luxxe *Coffeehouse*

20 | 15 | 19 | $12

Brentwood | 11975 San Vicente Blvd. (Montana Ave.) | 310-394-2222

(continued)

(continued)

Caffe Luxxe

Santa Monica | Brentwood Country Mart | 225 26th St. (bet. Brentwood Terr. & San Vicente Blvd.) | 310-394-2222 🅂🅜
Santa Monica | 925 Montana Ave. (bet. 9th & 10th Sts.) | 310-394-2222
www.caffeluxxe.com

"Coffee snobs" get their fixes at these "very European" Santa Monica–Brentwood coffeehouses, where "personable" baristas treat "coffee as art", elevating luscious lattes and cappuccinos to "frothy heaven"; though kinda "expensive" pricing and "limited seating" can be buzz-kills, "melt-in-your-mouth" pastries and "bend-over-backwards" service are two more reasons they're "the place to start the day" nonetheless.

Caffe Pinguini 🅜 *Italian*   22 | 19 | 21 | $43

Playa del Rey | 6935 Pacific Ave. (Culver Blvd.) | 310-306-0117 | www.caffepinguini.com

One of "Playa del Rey's well-kept secrets", this "off-the-beaten-path" "hangout" is a "locals'" choice for "rich-with-flavor" seafood, pastas and other "authentic" Italian dishes "after a stroll on the beach"; "romantic" alfresco dining in an enclosed patio and "friendly Italiano service" are two other reasons this "old-school" standby is declared *"molto bene."*

Caffe Primo ❶ *Italian*   ▽ 18 | 19 | 18 | $23

West Hollywood | Sunset Millennium Plaza | 8590 Sunset Blvd. (La Cienega Blvd.) | 310-289-8895 | www.iloveprimo.com

Most could linger "for hours" at this West Hollywood Italian "hang" whose "European vibe" is boosted by the "pretty" clientele that congregates on its "comfortable" patio for modestly priced Italian snacks like panini, pizzettes, salads and such; sweet tooths suggest surrendering to the "smiling staff" and ordering some "delicious" artisanal gelati or sorbetto to enjoy while you "people-watch."

Caffe Roma ❶ *Italian*   18 | 19 | 18 | $39

Beverly Hills | 350 N. Cañon Dr. (bet. Brighton & Dayton Ways) | 310-274-7834 | www.cafferomabeverlyhills.com

Owned by Agostino Sciandri of Ago fame, this "always-interesting" Beverly Hills "standby" serves up midpriced Italiana rated "solid", if "not spectacular"; it was "retooled" a couple of years back and sports a "fresher", contemporary look plus a DJ on weekends, but still the bread and butter of this "hangout" is its "old-school crowd" that power-lunches on the "pleasant" patio, "watching the pretty girls (and boys) walk by."

Caioti Pizza Cafe *Pizza*   21 | 12 | 17 | $20

Studio City | 4346 Tujunga Ave. (Moorpark St.) | 818-761-3588 | www.caiotipizzacafe.com

The late Ed LaDou's "legacy lives on" at this "other California kitchen" in Studio City, where "old-world" ingredients and new-world "interesting combos" collide in a "creative" explosion of "soul pizzas" and reasonably priced "build-your-owns"; maybe the space "needs some updating", but that doesn't bother "grateful" locals and others who know to sit outside for "doggy social hour"; P.S. it's known as "the originator" of the BBQ chicken 'za.

	FOOD	DECOR	SERVICE	COST

Cajun Kitchen *Cajun* — 20 | 12 | 19 | $18

Ventura | 301 E. Main St. (Palm St.) | 805-643-7701 |
www.cajunkitchensb.com
See review in Santa Barbara Directory.

California Chicken Cafe *American* — 21 | 10 | 16 | $13

Hollywood | 6805 Melrose Ave. (Mansfield Ave.) |
323-935-5877 🛃
Santa Monica | 2401 Wilshire Blvd. (24th St.) | 310-453-0477 🛃
Venice | 424 Lincoln Blvd. (bet. Flowers & Sunset Aves.) |
310-392-3500
West LA | 2005 Westwood Blvd. (La Grange Ave.) |
310-446-1933 🛃
Encino | 15601 Ventura Blvd. (bet. Firmament & Haskell Aves.) |
818-789-8056 🛃
Northridge | University Plaza | 18445 Nordhoff St. (Reseda Blvd.) |
818-700-9977 🛃
Woodland Hills | 22333 Ventura Blvd. (Shoup Ave.) |
818-716-6170 🛃
www.californiachickencafe.com
There must be "Prozac in the chicken" at this "healthy" "fast-food alternative" chain, because its "quick", "satisfying", "fresh-off-the-spit" rotisserie birds – plus "standout" wraps and "generously portioned" salads – have surveyors seriously "happy"; factor in "really affordable prices", and no wonder its "cafeteria"-like setups are "jammed" and "noisy" at lunchtime, with "blue and white collars" dining "elbow to elbow"; P.S. closed on Sunday, except for the Venice location.

California Pizza Kitchen *Pizza* — 18 | 14 | 17 | $22

Downtown | Wells Fargo Ctr. | 330 S. Hope St. (bet. 3rd & 4th Sts.) |
213-626-2616
Hollywood | Hollywood & Highland Ctr. | 6801 Hollywood Blvd.
(Highland Ave.) | 323-460-2080
Beverly Hills | Beverly Ctr. | 121 N. La Cienega Blvd. (bet. Beverly Blvd. &
3rd St.) | 310-854-6555
Beverly Hills | 207 S. Beverly Dr. (Charleville Blvd.) | 310-275-1101
Santa Monica | 210 Wilshire Blvd. (bet. 2nd & 3rd Sts.) |
310-393-9335
Westwood | Westwood Vill. | 1001 Broxton Ave. (Weyburn Ave.) |
310-209-9197
Manhattan Beach | Manhattan Vill. | 3280 N. Sepulveda Blvd. (33rd St.) |
310-796-1233
Pasadena | Plaza Las Fuentes | 99 N. Los Robles Ave. (Union St.) |
626-585-9020
Burbank | 601 N. San Fernando Blvd. (Cypress Ave.) |
818-972-2589
Studio City | 12265 Ventura Blvd. (Laurel Grove Ave.) |
818-505-6437
www.cpk.com
Additional locations throughout Southern California
"Clever", "unusual" pizzas (such as Thai) and "creative" salads are the "stars" at this Beverly Hills–bred "gourmet" pie chain providing "something for everyone's taste"; it's "inexpensive", "prompt" and "consistent", though some complain the "wannabe eclectic offerings" have grown "tired" and the "overlit" surroundings just "don't have any charm."

	FOOD	DECOR	SERVICE	COST

California Wok *Chinese*   16 | 8 | 15 | $18
Third Street | Cienega Plaza | 8520 W. Third St. (La Cienega Blvd.) |
310-360-9218
Brentwood | 12004 Wilshire Blvd. (Bundy Dr.) | 310-479-0552
Encino | Encino Vill. | 16656 Ventura Blvd. (bet. La Maida St. & Petit Ave.) |
818-386-0561

California Wok Express *Chinese*
Marina del Rey | 4006 Lincoln Blvd. (Washington Blvd.) | 310-305-8801
Though this "order-at-the-counter" mini-chain doesn't exactly "wok
the boat", its separately owned locations have earned a loyal fan base for
"real-deal" Chinese fare that's surprisingly "consistent" and "healthy",
with lots of veggie options; wallet-friendly "deals" make it a "fast-bite"
fixture, but "nonexistent" decor has most opting for "takeout."

Camilo's ⓜ *Californian*   21 | 20 | 22 | $28
Eagle Rock | 2128 W. Colorado Blvd. (Caspar Ave.) | 323-478-2644
An "outstanding" Sunday brunch is just one of the reasons locals flock
to this "anchor in the Eagle Rock dining scene", where a "creative chef"
puts "new twists" on Californian "classics", offering "something for
every appetite and disposition"; "gracious" service and a "cozy" atmosphere "blend together very well", making this reasonably priced approach to "casual fine dining" "worth the visit."

🄲 Campanile *Californian/Mediterranean*   26 | 24 | 24 | $57
La Brea | 624 S. La Brea Ave. (bet. 6th St. & Wilshire Blvd.) |
323-938-1447 | www.campanilerestaurant.com
"After all these years" ("20-plus"), Mark Peel's "quintessential LA experience" remains a La Brea "star" seducing "foodies" with "exceedingly well-prepared" Cal-Med cuisine that amounts to a "splendid"
"assault" of "flavor" and "imagination"; it's best "to bring a big wallet",
then "relax" as the "unassuming" pro staff unveils varying menus and
popular weekly specials (such as Thursday's "grown-up" Grilled
Cheese night) in a cinematic 1929 space boasting a tile fountain and
"unforgettable" high ceilings; P.S. Peel has opened the Tar Pit and also
now owns sandwich shop The Point in Culver City.

Canal Club *Californian/Eclectic*   18 | 18 | 18 | $32
Venice | 2025 Pacific Ave. (Venice Blvd.) | 310-823-3878 |
www.canalclubvenice.com
"Funky vibes" wash ashore at this Venice "diamond in the rough" where,
yes, Mexican and sushi lead the "interesting" cast of Cal-Eclectic dishes;
"Polynesian fantasy" decor and "killer margaritas" ensure it's a "fun"
place to "meet friends", with a "welcoming" staff keeping spirits high -
especially during the "well-priced" happy hour, which "is indeed happy."

Candela Taco Bar & Lounge ⓓ *Mexican*   - | - | - | I
Mid-City | 831 S. La Brea Ave. (bet. 8th & 9th Sts.) | 323-936-0533 |
www.candelatacobar.com
Run by members of the family that owns and operates a nightclub next
door, this Mid-City Mexican cafe "lures" locals with a plethora of
"great-tasting" takes on tacos, sopas and other classics; a few warn
that "close seating" and "loud" acoustics are a part of the "small"
package, but nonetheless prices that "can't be beat" and "super-
strong" margaritas keep many lingering "longer than planned."

	FOOD	DECOR	SERVICE	COST

C & O Cucina *Italian*
19 | 17 | 20 | $26

Marina del Rey | 3016 Washington Blvd. (Thatcher Ave.) | 310-301-7278 | www.cocucina.com

C & O Trattoria *Italian*

Marina del Rey | 31 Washington Blvd. (Pacific Ave.) | 310-823-9491 | www.cotrattoria.com

"You won't leave hungry" from this Italian trattoria in Marina del Rey where the "heavenly" "garlic knots" are "unlimited", "wine flows from never-empty carafes" and Italian waiters lead nightly "sing-alongs" to "That's Amore"; though the Cucina is more modern, both offer "cheap food in large quantities" and are considered tops for "tourists, college students" and "families" seeking "friendly", "festive" feasts.

Canelé Ⓜ *Mediterranean*
23 | 17 | 20 | $40

Atwater Village | 3219 Glendale Blvd. (bet. Brunswick & Edenhurst Aves.) | 323-666-7133 | www.canele-la.com

It's "the definition of a neighborhood gem", and this "hideaway" in "sleepy little Atwater Village" makes its mark with "adventurous", "rustic" Mediterranean cooking, varied seasonally by chef-owner Corina Weibel (who cut her teeth at Campanile and Lucques); maybe it's "a little pricey" and the quarters "a bit close", but with an "open kitchen" and a communal table where it's easy to "make new friends", overall the mood is "jubilant" – plus, "who can turn down a free canele" at meal's end?; P.S. no reservations.

Canter's ◗ *Deli*
19 | 11 | 16 | $21

Fairfax | 419 N. Fairfax Ave. (bet. Oakwood & Rosewood Aves.) | 323-651-2030 | www.cantersdeli.com

"Any time of the day" works for noshers at this "quintessential", circa-1924 Fairfax deli and bakery whose "old-school" Jewish delights served 24/7 include "curative" matzo-ball soup, "sandwiches so big you'll plotz" and "pickles to satisfy any pregnant woman's craving"; however, aficionados agree the real "charm" of this "landmark" is in its "beyond-retro" interior, "cranky" "waitresses who've been there since the Roman Empire" and "entertaining" clientele providing some of the "best people-watching in town."

🆕 Capital Grille, The *Steak*
- | - | - | M

West Hollywood | Beverly Ctr. | 8614 Beverly Blvd. (San Vicente Blvd.) | 310-358-0650 | www.thecapitalgrille.com

The most sophisticated of the Darden restaurants (a brand best known for Red Lobster and Olive Garden), this American steakhouse sits on the northwest edge of the Beverly Center, offering a selection of upscale steaks like the porcini-rubbed Delmonico with 12-year-aged balsamic and the bone-in, Kona-crusted dry-aged sirloin with caramelized shallot butter; the sprawling former Hard Rock Cafe space is now dominated by red carpets, banquettes and ornate hanging lamps – with nary a photo of Eric Clapton in sight.

Capo 🅱Ⓜ *Italian*
25 | 23 | 23 | $80

Santa Monica | 1810 Ocean Ave. (Vicente Terr.) | 310-394-5550 | www.caporestaurant.com

"Tuscan farm house"-like though Bruce Marder's "upscale" Santa Monica Italian may be, the waves of "beautiful people" and "Bentleys" it attracts remind diners that in fact they're at one of Ocean Avenue's "continuing hot spots", where "see-and-be-seen" types wrestle over reservations; what makes it a "true destination" is its "inspired" pastas, steaks and seafood, exhaustive wine list and "romantic", fireplace-enhanced interior – just be sure to "bring someone else's wallet" to settle the "outta-sight" tab.

NEW Capriotti's *Sandwiches*
▽ 23 | 9 | 21 | $13

Encino | Encino Place | 16101 Ventura Blvd. (Woodley Ave.) | 818-986-2838
Beverly Hills | 9683 Wilshire Blvd. (Bedford Dr.) | 310-858-8381
www.capriottis.com

"More like Crackpriotti's", this "gourmet sub" chain based out of Delaware has Beverly Hills habitués "hooked" with its "divine" sandwiches made from "quality ingredients" (like the Bobbie, which fans dub "Thanksgiving at its best on a bun"); factor in solid service, and those who've discovered it are saying it's a "wonderful addition to the city's fast-food options"; N.B. the Encino branch opened post-Survey.

☑ Carlitos Gardel *Argentinean/Steak*
24 | 19 | 25 | $49

Melrose | 7963 Melrose Ave. (bet. Edinburgh & Hayworth Aves.) | 323-655-0891 | www.carlitosgardel.com

It's a trip back to "old Buenos Aires" at this "family-run Argentine steakhouse" on Melrose where "hefty", "savory", midpriced cuts tango with a "vast" South American wine list, not to mention the "absolute must" appetizer of "garlic fries" and the "perfect finishing note" of housemade desserts; most have "no problemo recommending" this "memorable" "diversion from the ordinary", where the "impeccable" service ensures "you and yours feel welcome."

Carney's Express *Hot Dogs*
20 | 14 | 16 | $11

West Hollywood | 8351 W. Sunset Blvd. (bet. Kings Rd. & Sweetzer Ave.) | 323-654-8300 ●
Studio City | 12601 Ventura Blvd. (bet. Coldwater Canyon & Whitsett Aves.) | 818-761-8300
www.carneytrain.com

"You can diet tomorrow" might as well be the mantra of these Studio City–Sunset Strip "landmarks" where "locals", "visitors" and "families with screaming kids" make "quick" pit stops for "habit-forming" hot dogs, burgers and fries – and "cover everything" in its chili considered "the best this side of the Mississippi"; fans who feel "you can't go wrong" here muse "why is eating so much more fun in a train car?"

☑ Carnival *Lebanese*
24 | 10 | 16 | $21

Sherman Oaks | 4356 Woodman Ave. (bet. Moorpark St. & Ventura Blvd.) | 818-784-3469 | www.carnivalrest.com

With fare so "wonderfully fresh", this "bustling", 25-year-old Sherman Oaks Lebanese offers its "off-the-hook kebabs", hummus and other "to-die-for" classics in "value"-size portions that please even the most "budgetarily challenged"; however, sometimes-"cranky" service and a "crowded" "strip-mall" setup has many suggesting "takeout."

☑ Carousel Ⓜ *Mideastern*
24 | 16 | 21 | $28

East Hollywood | High Plaza | 5112 Hollywood Blvd. (bet. Normandie Ave. & Winona Blvd.) | 323-660-8060

(continued)

Carousel

Glendale | 304 N. Brand Blvd. (California Ave.) | 818-246-7775
www.carouselrestaurant.com

"The only problem is figuring out what to order" because "everything is so good" at this well-priced Mideastern duo where the "pass-and-share" plates of "knockout" meze, kebabs and such are delivered by an "accommodating" crew; aesthetes say the East Hollywood branch "lacks the handsome, exotic decor of its Glendale sibling", which also offers a full bar and "live band and belly dancing" on weekends.

Casa ⑤ *Mexican*   19 | 19 | 19 | $24

Downtown | 350 S. Grand Ave. (bet. 3rd & 4th Sts.) | 213-621-2249 |
www.casadowntown.com

Located amid Downtown's "granite canyons", this "upscale", "mod"-looking Mexican dispenses "tasty" takes on tacos and small plates that draw the corporate "lunch crowd" by day and a mix of "high-rise denizens", concert hall patrons and others come evening; the less-impressed shrug "all style, no substance", but few find fault with its solid "happy-hour specials" and "cool adobe patio."

Casa Bianca ●⑤Ⓜ⇱ *Pizza*   23 | 11 | 17 | $19

Eagle Rock | 1650 Colorado Blvd. (bet. Mt. Royal Dr. & Vincent Ave.) |
323-256-9617 | www.casabiancapizza.com

"Awesomely addictive pizza" is the thing at this Eagle Rock "mom-and-pop shop" whose "classic" "thin-crust" pies ("get the sausage and eggplant") have made it a beloved "local" "institution" for 50-plus years; parking is a "pain", the red-checkered-tablecloth decor is "worn around the edges" and a contingent "disappointed" by the fare "wonder why people rave about it", but nonetheless the "crowds" keep coming – so expect "excruciatingly long waits" (even "for takeout").

Casablanca *Mexican*   20 | 18 | 20 | $26

Venice | 220 Lincoln Blvd. (Rose Ave.) | 310-392-5751 |
www.casablancacatering.com

"Kitschy" decor "straight out of the movie" is part of the charm of this Venice "neighborhood" Mexican, though the true star here is the "little lady making tortillas in the middle of the room"; its "reasonably" priced, "dependable" "standard" dishes are that much more "delicious" when paired with a "fantastic margarita" mixed by a "tableside bartender."

Casablanca Mediterranean *Mediterranean*   ▽ 23 | 19 | 17 | $32

Claremont | The Packing House | 500 W. First St. (Oberlin Ave.) |
909-626-5200 | www.casablancabarandgrill.com

A converted lemon-packing plant from the 1920s "doesn't necessarily scream 'Mediterranean'", but that's the setting for the "authentic" meze, kebabs and more at this standout in a "chic" corner of Claremont; "inconsistent" service can irk, but its large patio and "asset-shaking belly dancers" (Friday nights) have the majority "definitely going back."

Casa Vega ● *Mexican*   17 | 16 | 18 | $26

Sherman Oaks | 13301 Ventura Blvd. (bet. Fulton & Nagle Aves.) |
818-788-4868 | www.casavega.com

"There's a reason it's been around for half a century" say the "sentimental" of this "old-style" Sherman Oaks Mexican whose "campy" dining room and "hoppin' bar" are perpetually "slam-packed" with a "new Hollywood–meets-Valley" crowd; "cranked-up decibels" and "very dark" digs ("vampires and rock stars love this place") provide good cover for "lethal" margaritas and "gooey, cheesy" midpriced "standards" that "stay with you for a while", whether you like it or not.

Cassell's ☒ *Burgers*   21 | 4 | 14 | $13
Koreatown | 3266 W. Sixth St. (bet. Berendo St. & New Hampshire Ave.) | 213-480-5000
"Sloppy good" grub has been "going strong" at this Koreatown "joint" since 1948, making it a "high-calorie, high-carb institution" for those seeking "big burgers", fries and "lumpy" "horseradish" potato salad that's "much better than it sounds"; though the "old" "strip-mall" setup is "shabby at best", just consider it an inexpensive "trip back" in time.

Castaway *Californian*   17 | 22 | 19 | $37
Burbank | 1250 E. Harvard Rd. (Sunset Canyon Dr.) | 818-848-6691 | www.castawayrestaurant.com
"Wow out-of-town guests" with the "wonderful views" from the "fireplace"-equipped "outdoor patios" of these Burbank–San Bernardino Californian "banquet and wedding reception standbys" that have been going strong for half a century; "friendly" service and a brunch buffet boasting "tremendous variety" are pluses, though the eats are deemed merely "standard", especially for the price.

Catalina Ⓜ *American*   ▽ 22 | 19 | 19 | $42
Redondo Beach | 320 S. Catalina Ave. (Torrance Blvd.) | 310-374-6929 | www.320catalina.com
Providing a little "sophistication near the sea" is this uncrowded New American in Redondo Beach whose modern setting is deemed "simple but inviting"; "accommodating" service and "excellent" fare heavy on seafood help take the sting out of somewhat "high prices."

Catalina Country Club ☒Ⓜ *American*   - | - | - | M
Catalina Island | Catalina Country Club | 1 Country Club Dr. (Las Lomas Dr.) | Avalon | 310-510-7404
Situated in "historic Avalon" on "romantic" Catalina Island, this "quiet" American housed in a 1928 building is an oasis of "civilization" for dining; the "lovely" setting features a patio, courtyard and dining room with a fireplace and views of the bay and canyon; P.S it's open Thursday-Monday during the summer and Friday–Monday the rest of the year.

Cat & Fiddle ❶ *Pub Food*   15 | 19 | 16 | $24
Hollywood | 6530 W. Sunset Blvd. (bet. Highland & Wilcox Aves.) | 323-468-3800 | www.thecatandfiddle.com
"Throw back a few and play some darts" at this "affordable" "supersize English pub" housed in a "historic" old building "in the middle of Hollywood"; maybe the classic "bar fare" is "just ok" and the service so-so, but those who "pop in for a pint" on the crowded but "charming" patio call it the "cat's meow."

Ⓩ Catch *Californian/Seafood*   22 | 25 | 23 | $57
Santa Monica | Hotel Casa del Mar | 1910 Ocean Way (Pico Blvd.) | 310-581-7714 | www.hotelcasadelmar.com
"Gorgeous ocean views" through floor-to-ceiling windows and a "stunning" fireplace-enhanced setting have surveyors "in heaven" at this

	FOOD	DECOR	SERVICE	COST

seaside Californian in Santa Monica's Hotel Casa del Mar; the "solid" sushi and other dishes, "warm yet formal" service and all-around "elegant" experience come at a price, but for a "special occasion", it's hard to beat.

CBS Seafood *Seafood*
Chinatown | 700 N. Spring St. (Ord St.) | 213-617-2323

`20` `8` `12` `$20`

"Yum yum dim sum" is the refrain at this inexpensive Chinatown seafooder featuring "Hong Kong–style" cart-borne tidbits, plus a lengthy menu of other "quality" fare, including plenty plucked from the "big fish tanks"; those preferring to avoid the inevitable "crowds", slapdash service and nonexistent decor hit the "busy" take-out counter instead.

Cecconi's ● *Italian*
West Hollywood | 8764 Melrose Ave. (Robertson Blvd.) | 310-432-2000 | www.cecconiswesthollywood.com

`20` `25` `20` `$57`

The "comfortable, glam" setting complete with "seductive patio" is a perfect foil for the "celebs", "British expats" and other "'in'-crowd" types who dine on "fine" Italian fare "attentively" served at this "lively" WeHo offshoot of a London hot spot; it gets "oppressively crowded" and can take a toll on the wallet, but nonetheless it remains "one of the hardest reservations in town."

Celestino *Italian*
Pasadena | 141 S. Lake Ave. (bet. Cordova & Green Sts.) | 626-795-4006 | www.celestinopasadena.com

`25` `20` `23` `$44`

"Still awesome after all these years", this Drago brothers "classic" in Pasadena is beloved for its "fabulous" "gourmet Italian" fare, "excellent wine list" and "responsive", "knowledgeable" staff; no wonder it's "always crowded" and "noisy", despite slightly "pricey" tabs and claims from some that the Venetian-inspired digs are "starting to look a little tired."

🆕 Centanni Deli & Trattoria *Italian*
Venice | 1700 Lincoln Blvd. (Palms Blvd.) | 310-314-7275 | www.centannivenice.com

∇ `19` `16` `21` `$24`

This "casual", "friendly" Venice spot dubs itself the 'Original Old Italian Deli', and in a city with a shallow tradition of Italian groceries, it's a much appreciated addition; the "unpretentious" space is half market and half "small trattoria", with affordable menus for lunch and dinner, and more than a dozen "quality" panini options; P.S. it's BYO.

Central Park *American/Californian*
Pasadena | 219 S. Fair Oaks Ave. (bet. Orange Pl. & Valley St.) | 626-449-4499 | www.centralparkrestaurant.net

`19` `18` `21` `$26`

At this Pasadena grill, "friendly" staffers serve up "satisfying", "good-value" American-Californian sandwiches, salads, soups and such three meals a day in "pleasant", "retro" environs; though its location "near Old Town" may require a "search", the reward is "better parking."

Cézanne *Californian/French*
Santa Monica | Le Merigot Hotel | 1740 Ocean Ave. (bet. Colorado Ave. & Pico Blvd.) | 310-899-6122 | www.lemerigothotel.com

∇ `22` `24` `25` `$53`

With "incredible service", "consistently well-prepared" Cal-French fare, "ocean views" and an "upscale" setting whose "cushy" booths and "quiet" acoustics allow for "relaxing talk", this Santa Monica "hidden gem" in the Le Merigot Hotel is a "rarity" in the area; however, the "wonderful" dining experiences here are best when on an "expense account."

Chaba ⓜ *Thai*
▽ 22 | 20 | 21 | $30

Redondo Beach | 525 S. PCH (bet. Ruby & Sapphire Sts.) | 310-540-8441 | www.chabarestaurant.com

Redondo Beach residents relish this Thai's cuisine, including some "healthy, nontraditional" dishes, all served by an "efficient" crew in relatively "upscale" quarters with a South Pacific feel; its prices are already "value"-oriented, but they get even better during daily happy hour.

Chabuya Tokyo Noodle Bar *Japanese*
21 | 15 | 19 | $18

West LA | 2002 Sawtelle Blvd. (La Grange Ave.) | 310-473-9834

Addicts who "constantly crave" ramen that "squeaks slightly as you chew" find their fixes at this West LA Japanese slurp shop, where those in-the-know "sit at the bar" and "watch the big wads of steaming noodles" being made before their eyes; "casual", "reliably fast" and reasonably priced, it's an ideal choice for "dinner with the family."

Cha Cha Cha *Caribbean*
19 | 17 | 19 | $27

Silver Lake | 656 N. Virgil Ave. (bet. Clinton St. & Melrose Ave.) | 323-664-7723 | www.theoriginalchachacha.com

"Never dull", this "funky" Silver Lake Caribbean standby offers a "vibrant", "mismatched", tiki-inspired setting and "friendly, attentive" service that add up to an overall "casual", "fun" vibe; if a few find the "modestly priced" cuisine "a bit uninspired", the majority declares it "delicious", giving particular praise to its brunch ("can you say chilaquiles?") and "easy-to-drink sangria."

Cha Cha Chicken *Caribbean*
20 | 11 | 14 | $15

Santa Monica | 1906 Ocean Ave. (Pico Blvd.) | 310-581-1684 | www.chachachicken.com

"Grab a bite before or after hitting the sand" at this "little" Caribbean counter in Santa Monica dishing up "spicy jerk chicken" and other "tasty" edibles "with a serious island vibe"; an unpretentious, almost "all-outdoor" setting featuring "tropical plants in colorfully painted oil drums" and a "no-corkage-BYO" policy keep the vibe "laid-back" and the tabs minimal.

⛚ Chadaka *Thai*
23 | 20 | 21 | $30

Burbank | 310 N. San Fernando Blvd. (bet. Magnolia Blvd. & Palm Ave.) | 818-848-8520 | www.chadaka.com

"Fantastic Thai cuisine" in a setting "surprisingly lovely for Burbank's main drag" keeps 'em coming to this "modern", "mirrored" "retreat" from the nearby "chains"; efficient service and "value pricing", especially at lunchtime, are two more reasons it's considered a Valley standout.

Chalet Edelweiss *German*
▽ 17 | 12 | 20 | $28

Westchester | 8740 Sepulveda Blvd. (bet. La Tijera Blvd. & Manchester Ave.) | 310-645-8740 | www.chaletedelweiss.us

For "gooey, bubbly cheese fondue" and other Swiss-German staples, plus "thin-crust pizzas" from a wood-burning oven, locals head to this "hard-to-find" Westchster spot just north of LAX offering solid "on-tap drafts" and a beer garden in which to enjoy them; its "strip-mall"

FOOD | DECOR | SERVICE | COST

etup is "nothing fancy", but "friendly" service overseen by a "delight-
ul" owner shores up the overall "pleasant" vibe.

Chan Dara *Thai*   21 | 17 | 19 | $28

West LA | 11940 W. Pico Blvd. (Bundy Dr.) | 310-479-4461 |
www.chandararestaurant.com

Chan Darae *Thai*

Hollywood | 1511 N. Cahuenga Blvd. (Sunset Blvd.) | 323-464-8585 |
www.chan-darae.com

House of Chan Dara *Thai*

Hancock Park | 310 N. Larchmont Blvd. (Beverly Blvd.) | 323-467-1052 |
www.chandararestaurant.com

Regulars warn "don't bring a date" or you'll risk "wandering eyes"
thanks to the "knockout waitresses" at this "casual", "bustling" threesome; it's "been around for decades" and the "dated" decor looks it,
but "Americanized", Thai flavors "delight your tongue", and the prices
are "reasonable" too; N.B. the Hollywood branch is separately owned.

NEW Charcoal Grill 🅾 *Mexican*   - | - | - | I

Downtown | Higgins Bldg. | 108 W. Second St (Main St.) | 213-687-8040 |
www.thecharcoalgrill.com

There have been lines since day one at this Downtown newcomer, a
counter-serve Traditional Mexican that allows diners to design their
own burritos, or choose from budget-friendly, cheese-intensive house
specials like a Monster Quesadilla and molletes (Mexican bread
topped with refried beans and melted cheese); the utilitarian-looking
space inside a red-brick warehouse includes a few tables.

Chart House *Seafood/Steak*   19 | 21 | 19 | $42

Malibu | 18412 PCH (Topanga Canyon Blvd.) | 310-454-9321
Marina del Rey | 13950 Panay Way (Via Marina) | 310-822-4144
Redondo Beach | 231 Yacht Club Way (Harbor Dr.) | 310-372-3464
www.chart-house.com

"Beautiful" water views enhance the "well-prepared" surf 'n' turf selections at this upscale chain seafooder that's "known more for its
scenery" than its "consistent" cuisine; "attentive" service helps keep
it a "safe" bet, though critics who contend a "pretty space can't mask
the lackluster chow" call it "average for the price."

⬛ Chateau Marmont ● *Californian/French*   19 | 25 | 19 | $51

West Hollywood | Chateau Marmont | 8221 W. Sunset Blvd.
(bet. Havenhurst Dr. & Marmont Ln.) | 323-656-1010 |
www.chateaumarmont.com

Hang on the "beautiful" "hideaway patio" and "watch the stars stroll in"
at this "legendary" WeHo hotel "hot spot" that's known as the ultimate place to "see and be seen on the Sunset Strip"; the "forgettable"
Cal-French cuisine is "good" but certainly "not the draw", ditto the
service – and be prepared to pay for all that "celeb"-gazing when the
check comes; P.S. shutterbugs beware: there's a "no-photo policy."

Chaya Brasserie *Asian/French*   24 | 23 | 22 | $52

West Hollywood | 8741 Alden Dr. (Robertson Blvd.) | 310-859-8833 |
www.thechaya.com

"Lovely presentations" of "imaginative" Asian-French "fusion" dishes
and a "buzzy", "distinctive" atmosphere – including a bamboo garden

in the middle of the room and glass doors opening onto the patio – en
sure that this "pricey" WeHo "old-time favorite" is "still cool"; the ic
ing on the cake is "polished" "but not annoying" service.

Chaya Downtown *Asian/French*

24 | 24 | 22 | $51

Downtown | City Nat'l Plaza | 525 S. Flower St. (bet. 5th & 6th Sts.) |
213-236-9577 | www.thechaya.com

A "chandelier made of colorful plastic" "trinkets" lights up the "con
temporary", "fashionable" dining room at this "sophisticated
Downtown "standout" featuring "fresh, inventive" Asian-French cui
sine and "fab" service – which extends to a complimentary "shuttle t
the Music Center"; yes, prices are geared to the "power-lunch" set
but bargain-hunters know to "head to happy hour" for "cheap" eat
and drinks on the patio.

Chaya Venice *Japanese/French*

23 | 22 | 21 | $45

Venice | 110 Navy St. (Main St.) | 310-396-1179 |
www.thechaya.com

Still "hopping after all these years", this "hip" Venice "institution
boasts a "comfortable but chic dining room" and a happy-hour "ba
scene" that's "louder" and just "slightly less crowded than the Nev
York subway"; if you're "not sure what you're craving", the "friendly
staffers will guide you through the "broad", "expensive" Japanese
French menu, though regulars suggest "sticking with the seafood."

Checkers Downtown *Californian*

21 | 22 | 23 | $54

Downtown | Hilton Checkers | 535 S. Grand Ave. (bet. 5th & 6th Sts.) |
213-891-0519 | www.checkersdowntown.com

"Elegance lives" at this Hilton Checkers Downtown dining room with
"sedate atmosphere conducive to conversation" and "lovely" deco
featuring photos of the building through the years; though it's a "ta
expensive", attentive service, a convenient "pre-theater" location an
"unadventurous but well-prepared" Californian cuisine have most de
claring it "does not thrill, but it never disappoints."

Cheebo *Italian*

20 | 15 | 18 | $27

Hollywood | 7533 W. Sunset Blvd. (bet. Gardner St. & Sierra Bonita Ave.) |
323-850-7070 | www.cheebo.com

"Über-hip" Hollywood types "squish" into this "narrow" Sunse
Boulevard "neighborhood" "joint", where the roster of "reliable" Italia
eats offers "something for everyone"; locals say you can get a "tasty
meal "for the money" so long as "you can get past" the "off-the-wal
"orange" decor and "hit-or-miss service" heavy on the "attitude."

☑ Cheesecake Factory *American*

19 | 18 | 19 | $27

Fairfax | The Grove | 189 The Grove Dr. (bet. Beverly Blvd. & 3rd St.) |
323-634-0511
Beverly Hills | 364 N. Beverly Dr. (bet. Brighton & Dayton Ways) |
310-278-7270
Brentwood | 11647 San Vicente Blvd. (bet. Barrington & Darlington Aves.) |
310-826-7111
Marina del Rey | 4142 Via Marina (Admiralty Way) | 310-306-3344
Redondo Beach | 605 N. Harbor Dr. (bet. Beryl & Herondo Sts.) |
310-376-0466
Arcadia | 400 S. Baldwin Ave. (Huntington Dr.) | 626-447-2800
Pasadena | 2 W. Colorado Blvd. (Fair Oaks Ave.) | 626-584-6000

	FOOD	DECOR	SERVICE	COST

(continued)

Cheesecake Factory

Sherman Oaks | Sherman Oaks Galleria | 15301 Ventura Blvd. (Sepulveda Blvd.) | 818-906-0700
Woodland Hills | Warner Ctr. | 6324 Canoga Ave. (bet. Erwin St. & Victory Blvd.) | 818-883-9900
Thousand Oaks | Thousand Oaks Mall | 442 W. Hillcrest Dr. (bet. Lynn & Moorpark Rds.) | 805-371-9705
www.thecheesecakefactory.com
Additional locations throughout Southern California

"Humongous portions and humongous lines" characterize this American chain where the "textbook"-size menu offers "lots of choices" and a "broad price spectrum" to keep families "stuffed and happy"; the "herd 'em in, herd 'em out" feel isn't for everyone and critics knock "mass-produced" fare and "overdone" decor, but overall it's a "crowd-pleaser", especially when it comes to the "amazing" namesake dessert – even if you need to "take it home for much later."

Chef Melba's Bistro ⓜ *Californian* ▽ 27 | 15 | 21 | $44

Hermosa Beach | 1501 Hermosa Ave. (15th St.) | 310-376-2084 | www.chefmelbasbistro.com

Chef Melba's admirers call her a "delight" "who really cares about quality" and cooks up "glorious", "imaginative" Californian fare in her open kitchen at this Hermosa Beach "hidden gem"; though some say the "cozy dining area" could use "some sound dampening" and others claim it "needs a designer", a "friendly staff" helps stoke the "cool vibe."

NEW Chego! 🄢ⓜ *Korean/Mexican* - | - | - | I

Palms | 3300 Overland Ave. (Rose Ave.) | 310-287-0331 | www.eatchego.com

The mini-mall sibling of Kogi provides a permanent Palms home for the food truck chef's Korean-Mexican rice bowls, plus other affordable items including fried meatballs, charred asparagus with blueberry jalapeño salsa and a glazed pork belly bowl (but no tacos); the wildly busy, counter-serve setting includes wood tables with red chairs and walls decorated with giant letters that spell out the name.

NEW Cheval Blanc Bistro *French* 22 | 22 | 22 | $40

Pasadena | 41 S. De Lacey Ave. (Colorado Blvd.) | 626-577-4141 | www.chevalblancbistro.com

"Lovely" "traditional" French bistro favorites are delivered by a "welcoming staff" at this "winning" "addition to the Pasadena scene" from the Smith brothers (Arroyo Chop House, Parkway Grill, Smitty's Grill); a few purists find the feel "formulaic", but to most it's "cozy" and "cool", with a "beautiful" 100-year-old bar and fair prices boosting the appeal.

Chez Jay *Steak* 16 | 14 | 17 | $31

Santa Monica | 1657 Ocean Ave. (Colorado Ave.) | 310-395-1741 | www.chezjays.com

"Jay may be gone, but his spirit lives on" in this "dark", circa-1959 Santa Monica "dive of the finest pedigree", where sawdust and "peanut shells on the floor", red-checked tablecloths and a jukebox complete the "time-warp" scene; the surf 'n' turf fare is "mediocre" and the "crusty" staff "challenging", but it's such an "institution", most maintain "you've gotta go at least once."

Chez Mélange *Eclectic*
25 | 20 | 24 | $45

Redondo Beach | 1611 S. Catalina Ave. (Ave. I) | 310-540-1222 |
www.chezmelange.com

This Redondo Beach "classic" "sets the standard" for "fine dining" in
the South Bay, given its "fresh", "creative" Eclectic cooking, "excellent"
wines and "exceptional" service led by "warm" owners; a "quiet atmosphere with well-spaced tables" and "reasonable prices" round out
the endorsement – "what's not to like?"

Chichen Itza *Mexican*
∇ 24 | 11 | 19 | $15

Downtown | Mercado La Paloma | 3655 S. Grand Ave. (bet. 35th &
37th Sts.) | 213-741-1075 | www.chichenitzarestaurant.com

A "little piece of the Yucatán in LA, true to the cuisine and culture", this
Downtown "treasure" run by a "warm, wonderful owner" offers "excellent" Mexican dishes, "especially for the price", via either counter
or table service; its food-court location is "out of the way" and a little
on the "depressing" side, but loyalists keep coming all the same; P.S. the
Sixth Street branch has closed.

Chi Dynasty *Chinese*
21 | 15 | 20 | $25

Los Feliz | Los Feliz Plaza | 1813 Hillhurst Ave. (bet. Melbourne &
Russell Aves.) | 323-667-3388 | www.chidynasty.com

"Welcoming" staffers "remember you" at this Los Feliz "neighborhood
Chinese" where the "delicious" dishes may be "slightly more expensive" than typical Sino fare, but to most it's well "worth it"; the interior's a little "nicer" than the "strip-mall exterior" suggests, but it's
"small" and gets "loud when busy."

Chili John's 🚫 *American*
18 | 9 | 17 | $13

Burbank | 2018 W. Burbank Blvd. (Keystone St.) | 818-846-3611

At this "tiny" Burbank "old-school mom-and-pop joint from the '40s",
the "folksy", "cantankerous waitresses" behind a horseshoe-shaped
counter dish out "damn hot" beef, chicken and vegetarian chili so
"greasy" they "supply bibs"; the look is strictly "hokey" "coffee shop",
but the tabs are cheap; it's closed July–August.

China Grill *Californian/Chinese*
19 | 17 | 18 | $33

Manhattan Beach | Manhattan Vill. | 3282 N. Sepulveda Blvd.
(bet. Ardmore Ave. & 30th St.) | 310-546-7284 | www.chinagrillbistro.com

"Flavorful", "creative" Cal-Cantonese offerings at a "not-bad price"
make this "casual" Manhattan Beach "neighborhood" standby just a
"nice little place" for a "quick bite"; it fills a niche in "an area without
a lot of Chinese food", but to bypass the "plain" decor, "get a spot
on the patio."

Chin Chin *Chinese*
17 | 15 | 17 | $25

West Hollywood | Sunset Plaza | 8618 W. Sunset Blvd. (Sunset Plaza Dr.) |
310-652-1818
Beverly Hills | 206 S. Beverly Dr. (Charleville Blvd.) | 310-248-5252
Brentwood | San Vincente Plaza | 11740 San Vicente Blvd. (bet. Barrington &
Montana Aves.) | 310-826-2525
Studio City | 12215 Ventura Blvd. (Laurel Canyon Blvd.) | 818-985-9090
www.chinchin.com

Though everybody "loves the Chinese chicken salad" that "made it famous", this chain otherwise serves mostly "predictable" "American-

ized" Sino dishes that aficionados deem strictly "for those who don't know better"; "tacky" settings make it "seem like a fast-food place without the fast-food prices" – so it's "better to call ahead for takeout."

☑ Chinois on Main Asian/French   26 | 20 | 23 | $63

Santa Monica | 2709 Main St. (Hill St.) | 310-392-9025 |
www.wolfgangpuck.com

"Phenomenal" Asian-French flavors ferried by "fabulous" servers are the hallmark of this "Puck empire" "winner" in Santa Monica that's "still going strong" after more than 25 years; you may "need earplugs" and a shoehorn to handle its "jammed", "dated" (think *Miami Vice*) dining room, but nonetheless it remains a "memorable experience" – "if you've got the dough."

Chipotle Mexican   19 | 11 | 15 | $11

Fairfax | Farmers Mkt. | 110 S. Fairfax Ave. (bet. Beverly Blvd. & 3rd St.) |
323-857-0608

Hawthorne | 5330 Rosecrans Ave. (bet. Hindry & Isis Aves.) | 310-297-0850

Lakewood | 5310 Lakewood Blvd. (Candlewood St.) | 562-790-8786

Beverly Hills | Beverly Ctr. | 121 N. La Cienega Blvd. (bet. Beverly Blvd. & 3rd St.) | 310-855-0371

Beverly Hills | 244 S. Beverly Dr. (bet. Charles Blvd. & Gregory Way) |
310-273-8265

Marina del Rey | 4718 Admiralty Way (Mindanao Way) | 310-821-0059

El Segundo | 307 N. Sepulveda Blvd. (Grand Ave.) | 310-426-1437

Torrance | Torrance Crossroads | 24631 Crenshaw Blvd. (Skypark Dr.) |
310-530-0690

Pasadena | Hastings Ranch Shopping Ctr. | 3409 E. Foothill Blvd.
(Halstead St.) | 626-351-6017

Burbank | 135 E. Palm Ave. (1st St.) | 818-842-0622
www.chipotle.com
Additional locations throughout Southern California

"Tasty", "gut-busting" burritos "custom-made for you" are the draw at this "fresh-Mex" chain, which earns extra "respect" for its "commitment to organic ingredients" and "well-sourced" meats; the "line moves quickly" and prices are "fair", so even if the "sparse" setting is "not too comfortable", it works for "lunch or takeout."

Cholada Thai   23 | 9 | 18 | $23

Malibu | 18763 PCH (Topanga Canyon Blvd.) | 310-317-0025

NEW Thousand Oaks | 1724 Thousand Oaks Blvd. (Erbes Rd.) |
805-557-0899
www.choladathaicuisine.com

"It doesn't get any better" than chowing down on "fresh, spicy", "outstanding" Thai eats "right across the street from the surfers" at this "funky", "dilapidated" Malibu "favorite" (with a new Thousand Oaks offshoot); service is "prompt" and "friendly" and prices "low", but as it's usually a "crowded", "loud" "circus on weekends", sit outdoors if it's warm – it's just the place to "watch the sun set over the Pacific."

ChoSun Galbee Korean   23 | 18 | 18 | $38

Koreatown | 3330 W. Olympic Blvd. (Manhattan Pl.) | 323-734-3330 |
www.chosungalbee.com

A "go-to" for "delicious", "upscale" Korean barbecue, this "hip" K-town "cook-it-yourself" place is manned by an "efficient", "no-nonsense" staff that's "almost too quick"; its sleek interior is "pleasant", but most recommend the "nice patio", where "letting all the smoke go up to the sky" means "you don't leave smelling like a BBQ pit."

Choza Mama *Peruvian* ∇ 19 | 12 | 15 | $19
NEW **Pasadena** | 96 E. Colorado Blvd. (Raymond Ave.) | 626-432-4692
Burbank | 3121 Olive Ave. (Alameda Ave.) | 818-566-9888
www.chozamama.com

Be "transported to Peru" via this arrival in a former Hooters space in the middle of Old Pasadena, a combination restaurant/bakery whose "tasty, exotic" fare replaces wings and beer with ceviche and Inka Cola (plus there's live music Friday–Sunday); the takeout-oriented Burbank original features a big sign in front promoting its specialty, rotisserie chicken.

Christine *Mediterranean/Pacific Rim* 25 | 19 | 24 | $43
Torrance | Hillside Vill. | 24530 Hawthorne Blvd. (Via Valmonte) | 310-373-1952 | www.restaurantchristine.com

Chef-owner Christine Brown "continues to delight South Bay diners" "year after year" with her "fresh", "sophisticated", "well-crafted" Med–Pacific Rim dishes at this "delightful", "reasonably priced" Torrance "treat"; the "inviting", "intimate" quarters may be "cramped", but the "attentive", "friendly" staff ensures you're "comfortable."

Chung King *Chinese* ∇ 22 | 7 | 14 | $19
Monterey Park | 206 S. Garfield Ave. (bet. Garvey & Newmark Aves.) | 626-280-7430

So "spicy" they "will blow your socks off", the Sichuan specialties at this Monterey Park Chinese "hole-in-the-wall" are both "excellent" and reasonably priced; however, even admirers concede the atmosphere's "not much", ditto the service.

Z Church & State *French* 25 | 21 | 21 | $49
Downtown | 1850 Industrial St. (Mateo St.) | 213-405-1434 | www.churchandstatebistro.com

"Go for" the "crunchy pig ears", "succulent marrow bone" and other "rich", "fabulous" French delicacies at this former biscuit factory-turned–"trendy" bistro "reminiscent of a bustling Paris cafe" hidden in an "out-of-the-way" "gritty neighborhood" Downtown; considering the "hip factor" and "chic", airy setting, prices are relatively "reasonable", though some give demerits for staff "attitude"; N.B. the Food score may not reflect a recent chef change.

Z Cicada **M** *Californian/Italian* 23 | 28 | 24 | $56
Downtown | 617 S. Olive St. (bet. 6th & 7th Sts.) | 213-488-9488 | www.cicadarestaurant.com

The "stunning" art deco setting inside a "historic" "former haberdashery" makes everything "taste even better" at this "fantastic" Downtown "destination" tied for LA's No. 1 Decor, whose "amazing" Cal-Italian cuisine makes for "fine dining" that's "expensive" but "so worth the price"; factor in "impeccable" service and a live big band with dancing on Sundays and it "can't be beat."

Circa 55 *American/Californian* ∇ 19 | 20 | 19 | $57
Beverly Hills | Beverly Hilton | 9876 Wilshire Blvd. (Santa Monica Blvd.) | 310-887-6055 | www.circa55beverlyhills.com

"Sitting out on the patio" by the pool is "a must" at this pricey Beverly Hilton eatery featuring "well-prepared", if not remarkable, New

	FOOD	DECOR	SERVICE	COST

American–Cal dishes, delivered by a competent crew; insiders tout the "lavish" Sunday brunch buffet with "unlimited" champagne.

Citizen Smith ⬤ *American* | 17 | 20 | 17 | $37 |

Hollywood | 1600 N. Cahuenga Blvd. (bet. Hollywood & Sunset Blvds.) | 323-461-5001 | www.citizensmithhollywood.com

"Young", "hip" types dig the "rock-star vibe" and "mammoth booths" at this "loud, covered-in-cowhide" Hollywood restaurant/late-night lounge, where "taken-with-themselves" staffers serve up "down-home" American "comfort" grub ("jalapeño mac 'n' cheese"); those who're "over it" say it's "overpriced" for just-"fair" edibles; P.S. open till 4 AM.

Ciudad *Nuevo Latino* | 22 | 19 | 20 | $41 |

Downtown | Union Bank Plaza | 445 S. Figueroa St. (bet. 4th & 5th Sts.) | 213-486-5171 | www.ciudad-la.com

"Imaginative", "flavorful" Nuevo Latino fare combines with "fabulous" "signature drinks" at this Downtown '60s retro-look mainstay from the Too Hot Tamales – Mary Sue Milliken and Susan Feniger of Border Grill; the "lively bar" and "happy-hour deals" stoke a "festive" vibe that can get "deafening" and make for "uneven service", so for some the quieter "delightful patio" is "preferable."

Clafoutis *French/Italian* | 19 | 19 | 18 | $34 |

West Hollywood | Sunset Plaza | 8630 W. Sunset Blvd. (Sunset Plaza Dr.) | 310-659-5233

The "international tourist crowd" is among the "people-watchers" at this WeHo French-Italian where patrons sit at the "sunny" "little sidewalk cafe" on Sunset Boulevard to "see the fancy cars pull up"; "harried waiters" mean "long waits" for fare that's just "ok", but on the upside, prices are reasonable and there's "copious free parking."

Claim Jumper *American* | 18 | 17 | 19 | $26 |

Long Beach | Marketplace Shopping Ctr. | 6501 E. PCH (2nd St.) | 562-431-1321
Torrance | Torrance Crossroads | 24301 Crenshaw Blvd. (Lomita Blvd.) | 310-517-1874
Monrovia | 820 W. Huntington Dr. (Foothill Fwy.) | 626-359-0463
Northridge | Northridge Fashion Ctr. | 9429 Tampa Ave. (Plummer St.) | 818-718-2882
City of Industry | 18061 Gale Ave. (Fullerton Rd.) | 626-964-1157
Thousand Oaks | The Lakes at Thousand Oaks |
2150 E. Thousand Oaks Blvd. (Conejo School Rd.) | 805-494-9656
Valencia | 25740 The Old Rd. (bet. McBean Pkwy. & Pico Canyon Rd.) | 661-254-2628
www.claimjumper.com

Surveyors "expect Paul Bunyan to walk in any second" at this "family-friendly" chain with a "miner forty-niner decor" and "hectic, loud", "zoo"-like atmosphere; though servers sometimes "drop the ball when they get busy" and "formerly" "pig-out" "portions have shrunk" a bit, most agree "if you gotta feed a soccer team, this is the place", even if the "big-value" American eats strike uppity sorts as "mostly fool's gold."

Clay Pit *Indian* | 21 | 15 | 21 | $28 |

Brentwood | 145 S. Barrington Ave. (Sunset Blvd.) | 310-476-4700

A "quick" staff "anticipates your every need" at this Brentwood "neighborhood Indian place" serving "reliably tasty" dishes in a "quiet atmosphere"; though the "decor is practically nonexistent" and some find the portions "small" and "a bit pricey" for the genre, the "lunch buffet is a bargain."

Clearman's Galley *American*   19 | 18 | 17 | $20

San Gabriel | 7215 N. Rosemead Blvd. (Huntington Dr.) | 626-286-1484 | www.clearmansrestaurants.com

Known to locals as "the boat", this San Gabriel American offers an "inexpensive", "relaxed meal" in a setting with "peanut shells on the floor" and plenty of "TVs for watching sports"; the fare may be "predictable" "burgers, hot dogs, fries and chili", but fans fawn "it's just so good, especially with an ice-cold beer" – and "best of all, cafeteria service means you get it fast."

☒ Clementine ☒ *American/Bakery*   24 | 12 | 16 | $19

Century City | 1751 Ensley Ave. (Santa Monica Blvd.) | 310-552-1080 | www.clementineonline.com

Chef Annie Miler's "mouthwatering pastries" and "fresh", "seasonal" American eats – including "creative salads" and "fantastic sandwiches" – "delight" fans of this "casual, low-key" Century City "hit"; just "allow plenty of time" for "problematic parking" and "long lines" at the counter as you "hope to snag a table" – or else opt for takeout.

☒ Cliff's Edge *Californian/Italian*   19 | 25 | 17 | $39

Silver Lake | 3626 Sunset Blvd. (Edgecliffe Dr.) | 323-666-6116 | www.cliffsedgecafe.com

Regulars "sit outside on a starry night" at this "romantic" Silver Lake "hideaway" where the bi-level garden patio "makes you feel like you're eating in a tree house"; though the service and Cal-Italian fare are "nothing special", moderate prices and the "lovely setting" assure there's "always a good crowd."

Clifton's Cafeteria *American*   13 | 18 | 14 | $14

Downtown | 648 S. Broadway (bet. 6th & 7th Sts.) | 213-627-1673 | www.cliftonscafeteria.com

"Long live Clifton's!" shout fans of this Downtown "old-time cafeteria" and 1930s-era "blast from the past" where "you can get Thanksgiving dinner every day of the year"; the "quick, cheap" American eats may be "mediocre", but loyalists contend the "kitschy" waterfall and "national forest"–theme decor "should be declared a historic landmark."

Coast *Californian/Seafood*   21 | 24 | 21 | $45

Santa Monica | Shutters on the Beach | 1 Pico Blvd. (Ocean Ave.) | 310-458-0030 | www.coastsantamonica.com

"Ocean breezes" and views of the Pacific make this Californian getaway in Santa Monica's Shutters hotel (with a spin-off in Santa Barbara's Canary Hotel) feel "like a holiday"; a "delectable raw bar" and other "light, fresh" items from the seafood-based menu come at a rather "high price", but most don't mind given the "caring service" while "sitting outside looking at the sunset."

Cobras & Matadors *Spanish*   21 | 15 | 18 | $34

Beverly Boulevard | 7615 Beverly Blvd. (bet. Curson & Stanley Aves.) | 323-932-6178

"Little bites" promise "big satisfaction" at Steven Arroyo's "loud, funky" and "hip" Beverly Boulevard Spanish standby "packed" with a "young" crowd; wallet-watchers applaud the BYO no-corkage policy and affordable tapas, but warn that tabs can still "add up fast"; P.S. sibling sandwich shop Potato Chips is next door.

Cole's *American*
17 | 18 | 17 | $18

Downtown | 118 E. Sixth St. (Main St.) | 213-622-4090 |
www.colesfrenchdip.com

A "slice of LA history", this Downtown "trip down memory lane" features red banquettes and the 1908 building's original fixtures as its "old-school" setting for the signature "crusty" French-dip sandwich fans call a "simple delight"; service is "friendly", but those less-impressed with the affordable American grub head straight for the "superb from-scratch drinks" and the "interesting scene" at The Varnish, the "secret speakeasy" "hidden in the back."

NEW Collection, The Ⓜ *Eclectic*
- | - | - | M

Malibu | Malibu Country Inn | 6506 Westward Beach Rd. (PCH) | 310-457-2602 | www.thecollectionmalibu.com

Situated in a rustic inn overlooking Zuma Beach, with a view of the Pacific that goes on forever, this Eclectic offers breakfast, lunch and dinner to hotel guests and those who journey north from LA in need of the soothing breezes (and celebs) of Malibu; while nothing on the midpriced menu surprises – think reliable coastal fare like crab cakes, shrimp scampi and a burger of considerable heft – that may not matter after a day at the beach.

NEW Colony, The Ⓞ🅾Ⓜ *Californian*
- | - | - | M

Hollywood | 1743 N. Cahuenga Blvd. (Hollywood Blvd.) | 323-525-2450

It's an 18-mile drive from the Pacific to the heart of Hollywood, but you wouldn't know it at this SBE Group (The Bazaar by José Andrés, XIV) Californian with a weathered wood setting designed to look as if it's lived through many a storm, chairs resembling boats and a makeshift beach out front; dishes on the midpriced menu are designed to go well with the sort of drinks favored by Young Hollywood – paging Ms. Hilton!

Colony Café *American*
▽ 18 | 16 | 15 | $19

West LA | 10939 W. Pico Blvd. (bet. Veteran Ave. & Westwood Blvd.) | 310-470-8909 | www.thecolonycafe.com

Despite its urban West LA location, this "cute little" American cafe popular with families is decorated in a blue-and-white "beachfront theme"; "if you want to eat quickly but avoid fast food", colonists concur the "fresh salads" and other "decent" "cheap" eats at this counter-service spot fit the bill.

Comme Ça *French*
22 | 20 | 20 | $48

West Hollywood | 8479 Melrose Ave. (La Cienega Blvd.) | 323-782-1104 | www.commecarestaurant.com

"As close to Saint-Germain as you'll get in LA", this WeHo brasserie from David Myers (the shuttered Sona) delivers "well-executed French classics", a "standout burger" and "superb" "speakeasy"-inspired cocktails to the "trendy", "handsome crowd" filling its "chic black-and-white room"; service may be "spotty" and prices "dear", but conversationalists note that "recent renovations have brought the deafening crowd noise down to a dull roar"; P.S. a Costa Mesa outpost is in the works.

Cook's Tortas *Mexican* ▽ 25 | 11 | 17 | $12

Monterey Park | 1944 S. Atlantic Blvd. (bet. Brightwood St. & Floral Dr.) | 323-278-3536 | www.cookstortas.com

"Cheap and cheerful", this Monterey Park torta spot offers "unique" "Mexican sub" sandwiches (including a "slow-cooked pork" version) on housemade bread along with "fresh fruit drinks"; patrons order at the deli counter from "selections written on a huge chalkboard" that "change daily."

Copa d'Oro ●⛨ *American* ▽ 17 | 20 | 19 | $21

Santa Monica | 217 Broadway (2nd St.) | 310-576-3030 | www.copadoro.com

A "youngish crowd" gravitates to this "dark, clublike" Santa Monica "oasis" where a "mixologist" whips up an "extensive" albeit "pricey" selection of "killer cocktails" from "farmer's market fruits"; though it's really "more a drinks place", the American "bar food" including panini is quite "serviceable" and delivered by a "knowledgeable staff."

Coral Tree Café *Californian/Italian* 17 | 14 | 14 | $18

Brentwood | 11645 San Vicente Blvd. (Darlington Ave.) | 310-979-8733
Encino | 17499 Ventura Blvd. (Encino Ave.) | 818-789-8733

Coral Tree Express *Californian/Italian*

Century City | Westfield Century City Shopping Ctr. |
10250 Santa Monica Blvd. (bet. Ave. of the Stars & Century Park W.) |
310-553-8733
www.coraltreecafe.com

For a "fast-and-easy" "casual bite", these "convenient" chain links offer "fresh" Cal-Italian fare, including baked goods and a variety of "healthy" options; while a few find them "overpriced" "for the quality" and call counter service "inconsistent", backers mention that they "don't rush you", making the patios at the Brentwood and Encino locations a draw for those "studying" or "reading the paper"; N.B. the Century City location is in a food court.

⛨ Cora's Coffee Shoppe *Diner* 23 | 16 | 19 | $23

Santa Monica | 1802 Ocean Ave. (bet. Colorado Ave. & Pico Blvd.) | 310-451-9562 | www.corascoffee.com

Surveyors "don't mind the noise" from "one of the busiest streets in Santa Monica" when dining at this "hidden secret" from Bruce Marder (Capo, The Brentwood) that "charms" with its "outstanding" diner fare and "lovely" patio "shaded with vines"; some balk at "breakfast for the price of dinner" and "spotty service", but on the upside, "if you have to wait", you can just "take a walk on the beach"; P.S. closes at 3 PM.

Corkbar *Eclectic* 22 | 21 | 23 | $33

Downtown | 403 W. 12th St. (Grand Ave.) | 213-746-0050 |
www.corkbar.com

Grape nuts seek out this "well-priced" "little" Downtown "secret" for "innovative, delicious", "seasonal" Eclectic "nibbles" accompanied by a "wide choice of excellent California wines"; the "cleverly designed space" features shelves of vino and the staff "makes you feel right at home", making it also a "great date place."

Counter, The *Burgers* 20 | 13 | 17 | $18

NEW West Hollywood | 7919 Sunset Blvd. (bet. Fairfax & Hayworth Aves.) | 323-436-3844

	FOOD	DECOR	SERVICE	COST

(continued)

Counter, The

Marina del Rey | 4786 Admiralty Way (Fiji Way) | 310-827-8600
Santa Monica | 2901 Ocean Park Blvd. (bet. 29th & 30th Sts.) | 310-399-8383
El Segundo | Plaza El Segundo | 700 Allied Way (bet. Hughes Way & Rosecrans Ave.) | 310-524-9967
NEW Torrance | 21209B Hawthorne Blvd. (Torrance Blvd.) | 310-406-3300
NEW Pasadena | 140 Shoppers Ln. (Mentor Ave.) | 626-440-1008
Studio City | 12117 Ventura Blvd. (Laurel Canyon Blvd.) | 818-980-0004
Westlake Village | 30990 Russell Ranch Rd. (Lindero Canyon Rd.) | 818-889-0080
www.thecounterburger.com

"Creative" types "have it their way" at this "affordable" chain offering an "awesome" "customizable" "gourmet burger" (including what many call "the best veggie" patty in town) "built to their specifications from the bun up" and crowned with an "expansive choice of toppings" from "dried cranberries" to spicy sour cream; "standout" shakes (plus beer and wine) wash it down and the "modern" setting is "cheerful" and "family-friendly", though those who want to "save their hearing" or avoid the "long lines" "recommend takeout."

Coupa Café *Eclectic*

▽ 19 | 19 | 20 | $23

Beverly Hills | 419 N. Cañon Dr. (bet. Brighton Way & Santa Monica Blvd.) | 310-385-0420 | www.coupacafe.com

Fans say the joe "alone is worth the trip" to this Beverly Hills Eclectic hangout "specializing in coffee" and Venezuelan dishes delivered "fast" and at "great value"; there's occasional live music and regulars recommend sitting among the "lush" greenery on the patio in front to "people-watch."

Cowboys & Turbans *Indian*

- | - | - | I

NEW Echo Park | 2815 Sunset Blvd. (Silver Lake Blvd.) | 213-483-7778
Mid-Wilshire | 5515 Wilshire Blvd. (Dunsmuir Ave.) | 323-936-7070 🅰🍴
www.cowboysandturbans.com

Street food–inspired "bites" including a "spicy naanwich" and "masala fries" meet "cooling homemade limeade" on the "limited" but "decent" Indian menu at this casual duo; the small tabs and proximity to the El Rey make the Wilshire branch a convenient stop before a show.

Coyote Cantina *Southwestern*

21 | 18 | 21 | $29

Redondo Beach | King Harbor Marina | 531 N. PCH (Beryl St.) | 310-376-1066 | www.coyotecantina.net

"Modern", "upscale gourmet" south-of-the-border dishes such as sweet-corn ravioli and Mexican lasagna get washed down with some 110 types of tequila at this well-priced "small neighborhood haunt" in Redondo Beach; a "whimsical" setting and "friendly atmosphere" keep it popular with "locals."

☒ Craft *American*

24 | 25 | 24 | $71

Century City | 10100 Constellation Blvd. (bet. Ave. of the Stars & Century Park E.) | 310-279-4180 | www.craftrestaurant.com

Celebrity chef Tom Colicchio's Century City "entertainment industry" haven (aka the "CAA" commissary) "delivers the goods" via "superb" American dishes "shared family-style", which emphasize "seasonal ingredients" and are served by a "well-informed" staff that "showers you with TLC" and "surprise bites from the kitchen"; for those who might "experience bill shock", the lower-priced craftbar menu is available on the patio or in the bar.

Crazy Fish *Japanese* | 18 | 8 | 13 | $30 |

Beverly Hills | 9105 W. Olympic Blvd. (Doheny Dr.) | 310-550-8547
Sushi rolls in "crazy-big portions" for "crazy-low prices" ("at least for LA") are the draw at this "low-key" Beverly Hills "favorite" serving "reliably" "tasty" Japanese fare; the "decor is nonexistent" and "you have to fight to get the attention of the "overworked servers", but "there's always a throng of people waiting to get in", so they're obviously "doing something right."

☑ Crustacean *Asian/Vietnamese* | 24 | 26 | 22 | $62 |

Beverly Hills | 9646 Little Santa Monica Blvd. (Bedford Dr.) |
310-205-8990 | www.houseofan.com
An "aquarium walkway" featuring fish swimming "beneath your feet" is the highlight of the "sumptuous decor" at this Beverly Hills spot known for its "addictive crab, garlic noodles" and other "fantastic" Vietnamese and Asian fusion plates; surveyors are split on service, with some calling it "accommodating" and others "challenging", but most agree the big tabs can "sting."

Cuban Bistro Ⓜ *Cuban* | ▽ 20 | 17 | 18 | $28 |

Alhambra | 28 W. Main St. (Garfield Ave.) | 626-308-3350 |
www.cubanbistro.com
"Wonderful fresh-baked bread" and what devotees dub the "best mojitos bar none" set the tone at this casual Alhambra stop dishing out "melt-in-your-mouth lechon asado" (roast pork) and other Cuban favorites at "value" prices; a granite-and-stone bar and "nice service" complete the package.

Cube Ⓢ *Italian* | 25 | 17 | 23 | $37 |

La Brea | 615 N. La Brea Ave. (Clinton St.) | 323-939-1148 |
www.cubemarketplace.com
A "dizzying cheese selection", salumi and "top-quality" "seasonal" Italian dishes meet wine pairings suggested by "knowledgeable" servers at this "reasonably priced" La Brea "gourmet food store" and eatery; there are "just a handful of tables", so patrons warn that trying to score a seat "on a busy night" without a reservation "may end in heartbreak."

NEW Cucina Rustica Ⓢ *Italian* | - | - | - | M |

Downtown | 888 Wilshire Blvd. (Figueroa Ave.) | 213-988-8880 |
www.cucinarustica.com
This centrally located Italian in LA's Financial District has become an immediate destination for traders and brokers hungry for some 'rustica'-style pasta, antipasti and classic entrees; dominated by an overhead skylight, the casually elegant, pleasantly noisy room sports polished wood, tablecloth-free tables and tall windows looking out on the street.

NEW Culina Modern Italian *Italian* | - | - | - | E |

Beverly Hills | Four Seasons Beverly Hills | 300 S. Doheny Dr. (Burton Way) |
310-860-4000 | www.culinarestaurant.com
Follow a garden path to this Italian located in the celeb-heavy Four Seasons Beverly Hills, where options on the upscale menu range from

brick-oven pizza to selections from a crudo bar; the casually elegant setting features a huge glass-bubble chandelier, outdoor seating, a large wine room with a communal table made from a 200-year-old magnolia tree and a mini-shop selling artisanal foods.

Z CUT ☒ *Steak* | 27 | 25 | 26 | $94 |

Beverly Hills | Beverly Wilshire | 9500 Wilshire Blvd. (Rodeo Dr.) | 310-276-8500 | www.wolfgangpuck.com

Meat mavens "feast on" "exceptional", "decadent" steaks and "wonderful sides" delivered by "spot-on servers" at Wolfgang Puck's "glorious paean to the cow" in the Beverly Wilshire hotel; the "dramatic" dining room features "huge pictures" of stars (including "Clooney, Blanchett and Pitt"), and naturally, it's "crazy expensive", but at least the "celebrity sightings are free."

NEW Cuvee *Californian* | - | - | - | I |

West Hollywood | 145 N. Robertson Blvd. (Burton Way) | 310-271-4333 | www.mycuvee.com

After closing for an extensive remodel, what used to be a serviceable WeHo take-out shop has grown into a popular neighborhood casual Californian with a sizable selection of sandwiches, salads and light entrees (along with early-morning breakfast for those heading for the towers of nearby Cedars-Sinai); the slickly modern setting mixes marble and steel, with large windows to let in the abundant light.

Daily Grill *American* | 19 | 17 | 20 | $30 |

Downtown | Pegasus Apartments | 612 S. Flower St. (6th St.) | 213-622-4500

Brentwood | Brentwood Gdns. | 11677 San Vicente Blvd. (Barrington Ave.) | 310-442-0044

Santa Monica | Yahoo! Ctr. | 2501 Colorado Ave. (bet. Cloverfield Blvd. & 26th St.) | 310-309-2170 ☒

LAX | LA Int'l Airport, Tom Bradley Terminal | 380 World Way (Sepulveda Blvd.) | 310-215-5180

Burbank | Burbank Marriott | 2500 Hollywood Way (bet. Empire & Thornton Aves.) | 818-840-6464

Studio City | Laurel Promenade | 12050 Ventura Blvd. (Laurel Canyon Blvd.) | 818-769-6336

www.dailygrill.com

"Solid", "traditional American dishes" like chicken pot pie fill a "gigantic menu", making this midpriced chain a "sure thing" that "suits all tastes" "without breaking the bank"; though the "lively, comfortable setting" featuring lots of wood is "attractive" and service is "pleasant", detractors sniff it's all rather "formulaic" and "more a compromise than a destination."

Dal Rae *Continental* | 25 | 21 | 24 | $50 |

Pico Rivera | 9023 E. Washington Blvd. (Rosemead Blvd.) | 562-949-2444 | www.dalrae.com

"Outstanding" waiters who "look like they've been around forever" "aim to please" with "heavenly" Caesar salad and steak Diane "prepared tableside" plus other "excellent" if "high-priced" Continental "classics" at this Pico Rivera "blast from the past"; "dim lighting, large rounded booths and dark wood" add to the "'50s feel", and fans say they "wouldn't change a thing"; there's live piano music too, Tuesday–Saturday.

Damon's Steakhouse *Steak*

19 | 17 | 20 | $29

Glendale | 317 N. Brand Blvd. (bet. California Ave. & Lexington Dr.) | 818-507-1510 | www.damonsglendale.com

Decidedly "cheaper than a trip to Hawaii", this "old-school tacky tiki steakhouse" in Glendale boasts "funky Polynesian decor", tropical cocktails and a "friendly" staff; the "bargain" eats, though "not for the gourmet", are "straightforward" and "surprisingly good."

D'Amore's Famous Pizza *Pizza*

20 | 7 | 16 | $16

Malibu | 22601 PCH (Cross Creek Rd.) | 310-317-4500
Westwood | 1136 Westwood Blvd. (bet. Kinross Ave. & Lindbrook Dr.) | 310-209-1212
Canoga Park | 7137 Winnetka Ave. (Sherman Way) | 818-348-5900
Tarzana | 18663 Ventura Blvd. (Yolanda Ave.) | 818-905-3377
Thousand Oaks | Skyline Shopping Ctr. | 2869 Thousand Oaks Blvd. (Skyline Dr.) | 805-496-0030

D'Amore's of Camarillo *Pizza*

Camarillo | 300 N. Lantana St. (Daily Dr.) | 805-445-6534
www.damoresfamouspizza.com

"Water shipped from Boston could be the secret to the delicious dough" at this "dependable", reasonably priced "family-owned" chain serving "tasty" pizza; the "hole-in-the-wall setting" contains only a "handful of tables", but "most of the business is takeout" anyway.

NEW Daniels Bistro + Bar *American*

– | – | – | I

LAX | Tom Bradley International Terminal | 380 World Way (Sepulveda Blvd.) | 310-215-4215

Situated on the arrivals level of the Bradley International Terminal at LAX, this Traditional American gives those waiting for friends and family an affordable place to eat, drink and linger; there's a cafe with seating on one side, and, on the other, a bar with big screens serving numerous mixed drinks, which should come in handy if any luggage has vanished in transit.

Dan Tana's ● *Italian*

23 | 18 | 22 | $56

West Hollywood | 9071 Santa Monica Blvd. (Doheny Dr.) | 310-275-9444 | www.dantanasrestaurant.com

"Step back to the Rat Pack years" at this West Hollywood "landmark" where "crusty but engaging" waiters who have "been there forever" deliver "satisfying" "old-world" Italian fare and "strong drinks" to the "showbiz types" occupying "red booths"; it's "crowded and noisy" with "regulars" and "celebrities" alike, so "expect waits even with a reservation" plus a "hefty price tag", and prepare for a "fun adventure."

Da Pasquale 🗷 *Italian*

23 | 16 | 23 | $33

Beverly Hills | 9749 Little Santa Monica Blvd. (bet. Linden & Roxbury Drs.) | 310-859-3884 | www.dapasqualecaffe.com

"No one cooks homestyle Italian like" "mama" (head chef and wife of the eponymous Pasquale) at this "family-run" "neighborhood" trattoria in Beverly Hills serving up "simple, flavorful" dishes, including "superb pizza" and "perfectly cooked fresh pasta" for "value" prices; "warm, welcoming service" along with "pretty alfresco seating on the sidewalk" and a "cozy" (if "tight") interior add to the appeal.

	FOOD	DECOR	SERVICE	COST

☑ Dar Maghreb *Moroccan* — 23 | 26 | 23 | $47

Hollywood | 7651 Sunset Blvd. (Stanley Ave.) | 323-876-7651 | www.darmaghrebrestaurant.com

"You feel like you're in a movie" sitting at "low tables" "while belly dancers glide through" the "lush, exotic" room at this "over-the-top" Hollywood Moroccan "feast for the eyes, ears and palate"; despite prices some deem too dear, "personal service" and "interesting", "flavorful" dishes help make this an "unforgettable" place to "take out-of-towners."

Darren's *American/Californian* — 24 | 21 | 24 | $57

Manhattan Beach | 1141 Manhattan Ave. (Manhattan Beach Blvd.) | 310-802-1973 | www.darrensrestaurant.com

"Inventive" chef-owner Darren Weiss whips up "spectacular" Californian–New American dishes and "makes the rounds" at this "upscale" Manhattan Beach spot with a "cozy", "relaxed atmosphere" sans "attitude"; "prices are high but worth it", making this many locals' "go-to for special occasions and expense-report dinners" alike.

NEW Da Vinci ☑ *Mediterranean* — - | - | - | E

Beverly Hills | 9737 S. Santa Monica Blvd. (Wilshire Blvd.) | 310-888-0090

After closing for a year and a half, this old-school Beverly Hills watering hole has reopened with new owners and moved the menu from classic Italian to modern Mediterranean (fried artichokes, grilled asparagus with eggplant purée, house-cured bacon); the space has been redone too, boasting a massive marble bar and an illustration of Leonardo Da Vinci gazing benevolently at diners.

D'Caché ⓜ *Pan-Latin* — ▽ 23 | 24 | 22 | $46

Toluca Lake | 10717 Riverside Dr. (bet. Cahuenga & Lankershim Blvds.) | 818-506-9600 | www.dcacherestaurant.com

"Enter through a lovely hidden garden" to step into the "dark", "sexy" interior of this "hidden gem" located in a 1920s Toluca Lake house, where a capable staff serves Pan-Latin cuisine; though it's "a little pricey", there's also "terrific" nightly entertainment including live Spanish guitar and a band.

Delancey Hollywood *Italian* — ▽ 20 | 18 | 23 | $29

Hollywood | 5936 W. Sunset Blvd. (Tamarind Ave.) | 323-469-2100 | www.delanceyhollywood.com

Italian eats including "thin-crust" "gourmet pizzas" with "fresh", "unique toppings" are ferried by "knowledgeable" servers at this Hollywood "neighborhood hang"; the "affordable" tabs and "chill vibe" make it a "great spot for drinks and dinner" "with friends", though the "tin ceiling" means it "can get loud."

Delmonico's Lobster House *Seafood* — 22 | 19 | 22 | $46

Encino | 16358 Ventura Blvd. (Noeline Ave.) | 818-986-0777 | www.delmonicossteakandlobsterhouse.com

An "extensive menu" of the "freshest seafood" makes this Encino surf 'n' turf "institution" popular with "families and large groups"; patrons say "ask for one of the semi-secluded booths" for a "special occasion" but prepare for tabs that can be "pricey" "for what you get", and "go early" to indulge in the all-you-can-eat Sunday champagne brunch buffet.

	FOOD	DECOR	SERVICE	COST

Delphi Greek ● *Greek* — 16 | 12 | 16 | $23

Westwood | 1383 Westwood Blvd. (bet. Rochester & Wilkins Aves.) |
310-478-2900 | www.delphirestaurant.com

"Basic" dishes "much like you might get on the back streets of Athens"
are on the menu at this small Westwood Greek that's simply decorated in blue and white; while some call the fare "uninspired", the service is mostly "solicitous", and best of all, the "price is right."

NEW Delphine *French/Mediterranean* — 20 | 23 | 22 | $43

Hollywood | W Hollywood Hotel | 6250 Hollywood Blvd. (Vine St.) |
323-798-1355 | www.restaurantdelphine.com

A "young" crowd "dressed in black" flocks to this upscale "hot spot" in
the W Hollywood Hotel where a "well-trained staff" delivers "seriously
good" French-Mediterranean dishes in a "beautiful interior" conjuring
the South of France; the location is "convenient for the Pantages", and
there's also a "comfortable adjacent lounge" for a "post-dinner drink."

Depot, The ⊠ *Eclectic* — 24 | 21 | 23 | $43

Torrance | 1250 Cabrillo Ave. (Torrance Blvd.) | 310-787-7501 |
www.depotrestaurant.com

"Who would have thought such a gem would be in Old Torrance" remark admirers of the "inviting experience" coming via chef-owner
Michael Shafer's "excellent", "original" Eclectic cuisine delivered with
"personable service"; the "warm, intimate atmosphere" in a "historic"
"former railroad depot" further helps make tabs that run "a bit
expensive" seem "reasonable."

Derby, The *Steak* — 20 | 22 | 22 | $41

Arcadia | 233 E. Huntington Dr. (bet. Gateway Dr. & 2nd Ave.) |
626-447-2430 | www.thederbyarcadia.com

"After a day at the Santa Anita track" this "old-fashioned" Arcadia
steakhouse is a "treat" "worth the expense", from the "first-rate" beef
to the "warm service"; "big" "red booths" and a wealth of horse-
racing" "memorabilia" – thanks to the original owner and Seabiscuit
jockey George Woolf – make the environs extra "inviting", as does live
jazz Fridays and Saturdays.

⊠ Derek's ⊠Ⓜ *Californian/French* — 26 | 23 | 25 | $62

Pasadena | 181 E. Glenarm St. (Marengo Ave.) | 626-799-5252 |
www.dereks.com

"Tantalizing" fare is served by a "helpful", "professional" staff at this
"special-occasion" Cal-French "surprise" "tucked in a nondescript strip
mall in Pasadena"; whether on the "patio" or "by the fireplace" (for an
"extra romantic touch"), the "relaxing" setting and "above-par wine
list" encourage "unhurried" "conversation"; N.B. the Food and Service
ratings do not reflect recent changes in the owner and chef.

Desert Rose *Californian/Mediterranean* — ▽ 19 | 20 | 20 | $34

Los Feliz | 1700 N. Hillhurst Ave. (Prospect Ave.) | 323-666-1166 |
www.desertroserestaurant.com

For a "beautiful night under the stars", it's tough to beat the "romantic" patio featuring two fountains and over 100 rosebushes at this Los
Feliz Cal-Med "sleeper"; service is "friendly" and the "tasty", "varied
menu" includes vegan options, making for an "interesting" selection
at moderate prices.

Devon, Restaurant Ⓜ *Californian/French* ▽ 24 | 21 | 22 | $53

Monrovia | 109 E. Lemon Ave. (Myrtle Ave.) | 626-305-0013
A "vast selection of game" (such as black-bear ravioli and quail with
lamb mousse) is the highlight of the "excellent" Cal-French menu at
this Monrovia find in a modern, elegant setting that's "so quiet you
can hear a pin drop"; add in an "outstanding wine list", "unique" desserts and fine service for a "quality" meal at matching prices.

NEW Dillon's Irish Pub & Grill ◑ *Pub Food* – | – | – | I

Hollywood | 6263 Hollywood Blvd. (Vine St.) | 323-465-1680 |
www.dillonsirishpub.com
"You can't afford not to go" to this Hollywood sports bar with over 30
"beers on tap" and prices that are "so cheap" ($3 a pint) rave the "real
dudes" who hang out in its "wonderful" wood-filled rooms; sure, the
Traditional American "food is an afterthought", but "if the best-looking
waitresses in short skirts are your thing", you're in luck.

Dining Room at
The Shangri-La Hotel *American* ▽ 22 | 25 | 23 | $48

Santa Monica | The Shangri-La Hotel | 1301 Ocean Ave. (Arizona Ave.) |
310-451-0717 | www.shangrila-hotel.com
"Creative" New American dishes "in an amazing room with amazing
views" overlooking the Pacific "marks a return to civilized dining" at
this "undiscovered gem" in Santa Monica's Shangri-La Hotel; though
tabs aren't cheap, service is a class act and the "lovingly restored" "art
deco room" "looks like Fred and Ginger might dance in at any moment."

☒ Din Tai Fung *Chinese* 25 | 15 | 16 | $21

Arcadia | 1088 S. Baldwin Ave. (Arcadia Ave.) | 626-446-8588
Arcadia | 1108 S. Baldwin Ave. (bet. Arcadia Ave. & Duarte Rd.) |
626-574-7068
www.dintaifungusa.com
Despite "brusque" (if "efficient") service, "basic decor" and "pricey
for the area" tabs, "massive crowds" gather every weekend to experience the "holy grail" of "juicy pork dumplings" at these neighboring
Arcadia links in a Taipei-based chain; though there are other "fresh"
Chinese dishes on the menu, their trademark "mouthwatering" "morsels from heaven" are the real stars here.

Dish *American* 18 | 16 | 17 | $24

La Cañada Flintridge | 734 Foothill Blvd. (bet. Commonwealth &
Oakwood Aves.) | 818-790-5355 | www.dishbreakfastlunchanddinner.com
It feels like the "heartland" at this La Cañada Flintridge "local institution" with a "cozy fireplace" and "toasters on the tables" (before
noon) and where the "down-home" Traditional American cooking
comes at "reasonable prices"; if "lunch and dinner are less inspired"
and the "service is unpredictable", it's "definitely" the "go-to destination for weekend family breakfasts."

NEW DISH Bistro
& Bar Ⓜ *Californian/Mediterranean* – | – | – | M

Pasadena | 53 E. Union St. (Raymond Ave.) | 626-795-5546 |
www.dishbistroandbar.com
"Unique" Cal-Med small and large plates put this "pleasant" Old
Pasadena newcomer on the map; despite prices some find "costly" for

the "small portions", "attentive service" and a "warm", "convivial" atmosphere elevate the experience.

NEW District Ⓜ Eclectic
— | — | — | M

Hollywood | 6600 Sunset Blvd. (Seward St.) | 323-962-8200
Hollywood restaurateur George Abou-Daoud (Mercantile, Delancey) teams with local-favorite chef Kris Morningstar (ex A.O.C., Grace, Patina) for this Eclectic bistro with a midpriced menu that wanders across the culinary landscape; the environs bring to mind a pub as designed by a movie studio, with a carved wooden bar, old-style hanging lights and bartenders in vests with their sleeves rolled.

Divino Italian
24 | 19 | 24 | $43

Brentwood | 11714 Barrington Ct. (Sunset Blvd.) | 310-472-0886
"Gracious owner" Goran Milic "makes you feel like he's been waiting" just for you to "walk through the door" at this "little" "neighborhood" "treasure" in Brentwood with a "terrific" staff serving up "incredible pasta", "excellent seafood" and other "high-quality" Italian dishes; "interesting wines" add to the "value" in a two-level setting that feels "quaint" and "relaxed."

Dolce Isola Ⓩ Bakery/Sandwiches
— | — | — | I

Pico-Robertson | 2869 S. Robertson Blvd. (bet. Cattaraugus Ave. & Hargis St.) | 310-776-7070
"Under the same ownership as the Ivy and boy, can you taste it", this "outstanding bakery" in the Pico-Robertson neighborhood feels "like a trip to Italy"; despite few tables and long "lines" suggesting lapses in the service department, the fairly priced "never-fail pastries" and "amazing sandwiches and breads" bring in breakfast and lunch crowds all the same.

Dominick's ❶ Italian
21 | 22 | 20 | $35

Beverly Boulevard | 8715 Beverly Blvd. (bet. Robertson & San Vicente Blvds.) | West Hollywood | 310-652-2335 | www.dominicksrestaurant.com
Expect to see the "hip, young crowd" "drinking wine" on the "buzzing", "beautiful patio" or eating "tasty" Italian plates indoors near the fireplace at this Beverly Boulevard standby where diners "feel like family"; adding to the "good value", "rollicking" $15 three-course Sunday night dinners with $10 bottles of vino are a "steal."

Doña Rosa ❶ Bakery/Mexican
17 | 13 | 13 | $15

Pasadena | 577 S. Arroyo Pkwy. (California Blvd.) | 626-449-2999 | www.dona-rosa.com
When you want to "grab" a meal without resorting to a drive-thru, this Mexican bakery and taqueria in Pasadena (an El Cholo spin-off) is a "nice alternative" with a rustic, "fast-food atmosphere" and "casual service"; penny-pinchers proclaim the $1.25 tacos and $1.50 margaritas on Tuesdays perfect when "your belly and your wallet are fairly empty", though some proclaim the everyday fare a bit "pricey."

Doughboys ❶ Bakery
22 | 15 | 18 | $20

Third Street | 8136 W. Third St. (Crescent Heights Blvd.) | 323-852-1020 | www.doughboyscafe.com
"It's back!" "rejoice" fans of this recently "reincarnated" Third Street favorite (shuttered in 2007 over zoning issues) that's once again dis-

pensing "baked goods galore" – including the "reigning king of red velvet cake" – plus "comfort food" like pancakes and "beefy mac 'n' cheese"; some find the simple, woody new environs "more comfortable", while others find them "tight", but most agree the service is "personable" and the prices affordable.

Drago *Italian*   23 | 20 | 22 | $56
Santa Monica | 2628 Wilshire Blvd. (26th St.) | 310-828-1585 | www.celestinodrago.com
At this "mature" Santa Monica "classic" from chef-owner Celestino Drago, "attentive", "warm" waiters deliver "divine" "old-world" Italian dishes, including "melt-in-your-mouth pumpkin tortellini"; add an "extensive list" of over 1,000 wines and a "lovely", "formal" room, and it's clear why most maintain the experience is "worth every penny."

Z Drago Centro *Italian*   26 | 27 | 25 | $58
Downtown | City Nat'l Plaza | 525 S. Flower St. (bet. 5th & 6th Sts.) | 213-228-8998 | www.dragocentro.com
Celestino Drago's "Downtown oasis of excellence" "has it all", offering a menu of "tremendous pastas" and other "scrumptious" Italian fare served by an "attentive" staff that "makes you feel special" amid a "spectacular", "sleek" space (some "can't believe it used to be a bank"); that said, it's "expensive", so "let's hope the boss is picking up the tab."

NEW Drai's Hollywood *Continental*   - | - | - | E
Hollywood | W Hollywood Hotel | 6250 Hollywood Blvd., 12th fl. (Vine St.) | 323-962-1111 | www.draishollywood.com
More than a decade after leaving LA to find fame and fortune in Las Vegas, restaurateur (and *Weekend at Bernie's* producer) Victor Drai returns with this restaurant-cum-nightclub on the 12th floor of the W Hollywood, where former Ma Maison chef Claude Segal oversees the pricey Continental menu; the elegant setting comes complete with a dazzling view, a VIP lounge and a massive rooftop deck with a swimming pool, around which guests can assemble for cocktails and nibbles.

Dr. Hogly Wogly's BBQ *BBQ*   22 | 8 | 18 | $20
Van Nuys | 8136 Sepulveda Blvd. (bet. Lanark St. & Roscoe Blvd.) | 818-780-6701 | www.hoglywogly.com
Believers think they've "died and gone to Texas" thanks to the "towering mountains" of "classic BBQ", including "juicy ribs", "awesome hot links" and what fans call the "best brisket in Southern California" at this "little shack" in Van Nuys; "sassy waitresses" and "reasonable prices" help compensate for the "retro dive" decor.

Duke's *Pacific Rim*   17 | 20 | 18 | $34
Malibu | 21150 PCH (Las Flores Canyon Rd.) | 310-317-0777 | www.hulapie.com
"Come for the view, stay for the view" say surveyors about this "little taste of Maui in Malibu" where "fantastic" surfside seating makes "you forget about" "just ok" Pacific Rim fare; considering the "beachy" (i.e. variable) service and tabs that are "pricey" "for what you get", some advise "skipping the dining room" and heading to the Barefoot Bar for "delicious tropical drinks" instead.

	FOOD	DECOR	SERVICE	COST

Dukes West Hollywood ● *Diner*

| 18 | 11 | 16 | $17 |

West Hollywood | 8909 Sunset Blvd. (San Vicente Blvd.) | 310-652-3100 | www.dukeswesthollywood.com

"Rock on!" cheer champions of this West Hollywood "greasy spoon" "right next to Whisky a Go Go"; with new ownership, the formerly "skuzzy" coffee-shop interior has been "cleaned up and feels a lot lighter and cleaner" than it used to, though longtime fans grumble that the "magic is gone", leaving mostly the "rude" service and "cheap", "basic" diner fare (though with more vegetarian and vegan options).

Du-par's ● *Diner*

| 16 | 11 | 16 | $18 |

Fairfax | Farmers Mkt. | 6333 W. Third St. (Fairfax Ave.) | 323-933-8446 | www.dupars.com
Studio City | Studio City Plaza | 12036 Ventura Blvd. (Laurel Canyon Blvd.) | 818-766-4437 | www.dupars.com
Oxnard | 2420 E. Vineyard Ave. (bet. Hwy. 101 & Oxnard Blvd.) | 805-983-2232 | www.du-pars.com

"With precious few 24-hour options in the city", this chainlet "stands out" for its late hours and "retro vibe", including "waitresses who seem to have been there for 50 years" and "good old-fashioned" (if "unremarkable") diner eats from pancakes to pies; indeed, "the only thing that's changed" is the "modern-day prices."

Dusty's *American/French*

| 21 | 20 | 21 | $32 |

Silver Lake | 3200 W. Sunset Blvd. (Descanso Dr.) | 323-906-1018 | www.dustysbistro.com

"Hipsters" "love" the "simple, delicious" brunch dishes and other affordable American-French fare at this "funky" Silver Lake "neighborhood spot"; just don't go in a rush, since service (though improved) "tends to be relaxed", as is the "warm and cozy" setting.

NEW East *Eclectic*

| ∇ 25 | 27 | 22 | $47 |

Hollywood | 6611 Hollywood Blvd. (bet. Cherokee & Whitley Aves.) | 323-462-3278 | www.east-hollywood.com

Scene-makers "ask for" one of the "intimate" carved wood "private booths" at this "trendy" Hollywood "date destination" with an Eclectic menu and a "gorgeous", modern interior featuring a soaring skylight and a 10-ft.-wide glass fireplace; though "expensive", the "thoughtfully prepared" "small plates meant to be shared" are "exceptional" and are delivered by a "helpful, knowledgeable staff."

NEW Eatalian ⑤ *Italian*

| - | - | - | I |

Gardena | 15500 S. Broadway (Redondo Beach Blvd.) | 310-532-8880
This Gardena arrival set in a high-ceilinged former textile factory offers an affordable Italian menu dominated by ultra-thin-crust pizzas and numerous pastas; the space features a gelato bar off to one side, and stools along the open kitchen allow you to watch the chefs at work – a free cooking lesson with every meal.

Eat Well Cafe *American*

| 17 | 10 | 18 | $18 |

West Hollywood | 8252 Santa Monica Blvd. (Harper Ave.) | 323-656-1383
Glendale | 1013 S. Brand Blvd. (Chevy Chase Blvd.) | 818-243-5928
Known for "breakfast", this twinset dishes up inexpensive "home-style American" "comfort food" served by a "laid-back" staff in a "minimal" "diner" setting; "great people-watching" and "man candy" are

	FOOD	DECOR	SERVICE	COST

attractions at the "colorful" WeHo branch, while the Glendale location, which closes at 3 PM, is more popular with families.

E. Baldi ⊠🅜 *Italian*

| 23 | 18 | 19 | $57 |

Beverly Hills | 375 N. Cañon Dr. (bet. Brighton & Dayton Ways) | 310-248-2633 | www.ebaldi.com

"Ladies who lunch" and "power" players go "to see and be seen" at this Beverly Hills spot with "divine pasta" and other "fantastic" fare from Giorgio Baldi's son Edoardo; naysayers lament "ridiculous prices", "indifferent" service and "tight quarters", but keep returning anyway for a convenient Northern "Italian fix" that "can't be beat."

Echigo ⊠ *Japanese*

| 26 | 9 | 19 | $51 |

West LA | 12217 Santa Monica Blvd. (Amherst Ave.) | 310-820-9787

"Sushi snobs are amply rewarded" at this "secret spot" that serves "amazingly fresh", "exquisite" "warm-rice sushi" (and "no California rolls"), including an "excellent" "bang-for-the-buck omakase"; despite its clientele of "regulars", there's rarely a "wait for tables" in its "hole-in-the-wall" setting on the top floor of a West LA "strip mall."

Edendale Grill 🅜 *American*

| 18 | 23 | 19 | $35 |

Silver Lake | 2838 Rowena Ave. (bet. Glendale Blvd. & Hyperion Ave.) | 323-666-2000 | www.edendalegrill.com

"Lovely patios" in "both the front and back" increase the allure of this "converted" 1924 Craftsman-style "firehouse" in Silver Lake with a "fun bar" and "friendly staff"; "homey" American eats are "alright", though surveyors suggest they be "kicked up a notch" to match the midpriced tabs and "great space."

🆉 Edison, The ⊠🅜 *American*

| 15 | 28 | 16 | $31 |

Downtown | Higgins Bldg. | 108 W. Second St. (Main St.) | 213-613-0000 | www.edisondowntown.com

Nightcrawlers slip into an alley and "into another world" at this "meticulously restored" power plant and "1920s speakeasy"-style lounge Downtown – tied for LA's No. 1 Decor – where a "sophisticated crowd" sneaks off to "nooks" amid a massive multiroomed space filled with "old generators"; the "pricey" American "bites" "could use improvement", but "specialty" drinks are the "highlight", and it's all a "spectacular" "reason to get dressed up" (there's a dress code); P.S. open Wednesday–Saturday only.

NEW 8½ Taverna �'*Italian*

| - | - | - | I |

Studio City | 11334 Moorpark St. (Tujunga Ave.) | 818-308-1100

The gastropub craze reaches Studio City at this Italian-themed artisanal beer and wine hot spot, with a blackboard menu of small dishes and pizzas both traditional and exotic – a white pizza topped with bechamel sauce, corn and potatoes, anyone?; as a bonus, the dark wood-decorated space is open till midnight every night – and the Gelato Bar by Gail Silverton (Nancy's sister) is right around the corner.

1810 Restaurant *Argentinean/Steak*

| 23 | 19 | 22 | $28 |

Pasadena | 121 W. Colorado Blvd. (bet. De Lacey & Pasadena Aves.) | 626-795-5658 | www.1810restaurant.com

When "Argentinean cravings" hit, surveyors seek out this midpriced Old Town Pasadena steakhouse that puts "Pampas" on the plate with

FOOD | DECOR | SERVICE | COST

its "quality" cuts, "amazing" empanadas and other "fresh" fare "with flair"; a "pleasant brick-walled room" "takes you back to the old country", and service satisfies too.

8 oz. ● *Burgers*   22 | 16 | 18 | $23

Melrose | 7661 Melrose Ave. (bet. Spaulding & Stanley Aves.) | 323-852-0008 | www.8ozburgerbar.com

At the forefront of LA's "gourmet-burger craze", this "crowded" Melrose meatery from celeb chef Govind Armstrong turns out a "variety" of "exceptional-quality" patties and equally "hefty" cocktails such as the "addictive" bacon-infused Bloody Mary; a "friendly staff, late hours" and "reasonable prices" make it a "good bet all-around", if you can get past a setting that falls somewhere between a "sports bar" and a "frat-house basement."

El Carmen ● *Mexican*   ∇ 15 | 20 | 17 | $23

Third Street | 8138 W. Third St. (bet. Crescent Heights Blvd. & La Jolla Ave.) | 323-852-1552

It's "all about the scene" at this Third Street "late-night hangout" with "funky" "south-of-the-border decor" featuring posters of masked wrestlers and 400 varieties of tequila; sure, you can order "decent inexpensive Mexican bar food" like taquitos and enchiladas, but most "come here for the booze and ambiance."

El Cholo Cafe *Mexican*   18 | 18 | 19 | $25

Mid-City | 1121 S. Western Ave. (11th St.) | 323-734-2773 | www.elcholo.com
Santa Monica | 1025 Wilshire Blvd. (bet. 10th & 11th Sts.) | 310-899-1106 | www.elcholo.com
Pasadena | 958 S. Fair Oaks Ave. (Glenarm St.) | 626-441-4353 | www.elcholopasadena.com

El Cholo Cantina *Mexican*

LAX | LA Int'l Airport, Terminal 5 | 209 World Way (Sepulveda Blvd.) | 310-417-1910

"Killer margaritas", "excellent enchiladas" and seasonal "green-corn tamales" will "seduce even the snobbiest critic" with "Americanized" but nonetheless "tasty" Mexican fare at this "reasonably" priced "old-school" LA chain; add "friendly" waitresses in traditional "costumes" and a "colorful", "kitschy" setting to complete the "experience."

NEW El Cholo Downtown *Mexican*   - | - | - | I

Downtown | 1037 S. Flower St. (10th St.) | 213-746-7750 | www.elcholo.com
More than 75 years after the original El Cholo opened Downtown, owner Ron Salisbury returns to the old neighborhood (just a block away from LA Live and Staples) to open this souped-up newest location with a large outdoor patio; it offers the classic Mexican cooking of the rest of the chain, and also serves a limited selection of dishes from the now-defunct Sonora Cafe.

El Coyote Cafe *Mexican*   15 | 15 | 18 | $21

Beverly Boulevard | 7312 Beverly Blvd. (bet. Fuller Ave. & Poinsetta Pl.) | 323-939-2255 | www.elcoyotecafe.com

Popular with a colorful crowd, including the occasional "starlet" and "washed-up rocker", this "superbly tacky" Mexican "icon" on Beverly Boulevard "isn't "fine dining, but it is fine-feeling", thanks to its "ebullient atmosphere" and "potent margaritas"; "fast, friendly service" and "incredibly low prices" help compensate for the "forgettable", 'saucy, oozy-cheesy" eats.

Electric Lotus ● *Indian*   22 | 19 | 20 | $25

Los Feliz | 1870 N. Vermont Ave. (Franklin Ave.) | 323-953-0040 | www.electriclotus.com

The "young crowd" takes to the "loud", "rockin' music" and "booths with curtains" at this "dark", "happening" Indian in Los Feliz; "surprisingly good" (if "slightly overpriced") fare and "always decent service" make it "worth the wait" for a table in the room with golden saris on the walls.

NEW Elements Kitchen Ⓜ *American/Eclectic*   ∇ 23 | 18 | 20 | $34

Pasadena | Pasadena Playhouse | 37 S. El Molino Ave. (bet. Green St. & Colorado Blvd.) | 626-440-0044 | www.elementskitchen.com

"Playful" New American–Eclectic dishes based on seasonal ingredients come from the "open kitchen" at this midpriced "superior newcomer in the Pasadena Playhouse"; even with a few "outdoor tables" overlooking the "street", the "limited seating" in the "tiny" space means "it's best to book ahead."

Elf Café Ⓜ⇌ *Mediterranean/Vegetarian*   ∇ 27 | 13 | 20 | $27

Echo Park | 2135 W. Sunset Blvd. (Alvarado St.) | 213-484-6829

"Locals" promise "you'll never miss the meat" at this "cute", "hidden" Echo Park vegetarian serving "outstanding", "good-value" Med dishes at dinner only Wednesday–Sunday; they don't offer liquor, but diners can BYO for a $5 corkage fee.

Elite Restaurant *Chinese*   24 | 15 | 16 | $23

Monterey Park | 700 S. Atlantic Blvd. (El Portal Pl.) | 626-282-9998 | www.elitechineserestaurant.com

Order what devotees dub the "best dim sum in LA" from "off the menu instead of from rolling carts" at this Monterey Park Chinese that also offers "exotic dinner" options; service is "quick once you're seated", and though prices are higher than most places in the area, so is the "quality."

El Pollo Inka *Peruvian*   20 | 12 | 18 | $18

Lawndale | Lawndale Plaza | 15400 Hawthorne Blvd. (154th St.) | 310-676-6665
Gardena | Gateway Plaza | 1425 W. Artesia Blvd. (Normandie Ave.) | 310-516-7378
Hermosa Beach | 1100 PCH (Aviation Blvd.) | 310-372-1433
Torrance | 23705 Hawthorne Blvd. (bet. Skypark Dr. & 238th St.) | 310-373-0062
www.elpolloinka.com

A "loyal following" lauds the "signature rotisserie chicken", lomo saltado ("beef sautéed with onions and tomatoes then tossed with fries") and other "interesting dishes" at this Peruvian chain with varying decor; "friendly", "efficient service", "value" pricing and live "music and dancing" on weekends at the Torrance and Hermosa Beach branches are added enticements.

El Tepeyac *Mexican*   25 | 10 | 19 | $15

East LA | 812 N. Evergreen Ave. (Winter St.) | 323-267-8668

"If you want more authentic Mexican food, go to Mexico" assert admirers of this East LA "institution" that dishes out "humongous burritos" and other "cheap" "homestyle" eats courtesy of owner Manuel Rojas, a "charming" "character" with a "big personality"; the digs are "one step above a fast-food joint", but there's "always a wait in line, and for good reason."

El Torito *Mexican*   15 | 15 | 17 | $21

Hawthorne | 11855 Hawthorne Blvd. (bet. 118th & 119th Sts.) | 310-679-0233
Marina del Rey | 13715 Fiji Way (Lincoln Blvd.) | 310-823-8941
Long Beach | 6605 PCH (bet. 2nd St. & Westminster Ave.) | 562-594-6917
Redondo Beach | Fisherman's Wharf | 100G Fisherman's Wharf (Catalina Ave.) | 310-376-0547
Pasadena | 3333 E. Foothill Blvd. (Sierra Madre Villa Ave.) | 626-351-8995
NEW Burbank | 3113 W. Olive Ave. (Alameda Ave.) | 818-841-4433
Northridge | 8855 Tampa Ave. (bet. Nordhoff & Parthenia Sts.) | 818-349-1607
Sherman Oaks | 14433½ Ventura Blvd. (Van Nuys Blvd.) | 818-990-5860
Woodland Hills | Warner Ctr. | 6040 Canoga Ave. (Oxnard St.) | 818-348-1767
Thousand Oaks | 449 N. Moorpark Rd. (Brazil St.) | 805-497-3952
www.eltorito.com
Additional locations throughout Southern California

A "Disney kind of south-of-the-border experience", this "kid-friendly" chain "will do in a pinch", but the "plain Jane" Mexican fare is "nothing special"; if "well-intentioned but stressed servers" and interiors that "look a bit worn around the edges" come up short at some locations (the Burbank outpost is new), at least it's "reasonably priced."

El Torito Grill *Mexican*   19 | 18 | 19 | $25

Beverly Hills | 9595 Wilshire Blvd. (Camden Dr.) | 310-550-1599
Torrance | 21321 Hawthorne Blvd. (Torrance Blvd.) | 310-543-1896
Sherman Oaks | Sherman Oaks Galleria | 15301 Ventura Blvd. (Sepulveda Blvd.) | 818-907-7172
www.etgrill.com

It's "a little classier" than "its sister El Torito" at this Mexican chain that "surprises from the get-go with warm, fresh tortillas in lieu of chips" and "tableside guacamole" "made to your specifications"; considering the "upscale" fare, it provides good "value", making it worth enduring the sometimes "noisy" environs.

Emle's *Californian/Mediterranean*   20 | 13 | 21 | $21

Northridge | 9250 Reseda Blvd. (Prairie St.) | 818-772-2203 | www.emlesrestaurant.com

In the "middle of chain mediocrity", this Northridge "mom-and-pop oasis" in a strip-mall "nook" "surprises with an extensive menu" of "wonderful" Cal-Med eats for "breakfast, lunch and dinner"; the "welcoming" owner and his family aim to "please" with "reliable satisfaction at reasonable prices."

Empress Harbor Seafood Restaurant *Chinese* 21 | 15 | 14 | $22

Monterey Park | Atlantic Plaza | 111 N. Atlantic Blvd. (Garvey Ave.) | 626-300-8833 | www.empressharbor.com

"Cart-pushing" servers wheel around "lots of small plates" of "irresistible dim sum" at this Chinese standby in Monterey Park that's also "excellent for dinner"; though the decor is less than dazzling, the price is right, so "get there early to avoid a long wait" on weekends.

	FOOD	DECOR	SERVICE	COST

Empress Pavilion *Chinese*   20 | 13 | 15 | $23

Chinatown | Bamboo Plaza | 988 N. Hill St. (Bamboo Ln.) | 213-617-9898 | www.empresspavilion.com

"Massive crowds" head to this "cavernous" "granddaddy of dim sum" palaces" in Chinatown for a "wide selection" of "small-plate delicacies" ferried by a "hectic" staff "racing" steam carts "around the tables" like it's "Grand Central"; fans attest the Chinese dinners are also well prepared", and the "price can't be beat."

Encounter *Eclectic*   ▽ 16 | 26 | 18 | $31

LAX | LA Int'l Airport, Theme Bldg. | 209 World Way (Sepulveda Blvd.) | 310-215-5151 | www.encounterlax.com

"Austin Powers would feel right at home" at this "wacky outer-space-themed" eatery perched at the top of LAX's famed Theme Building; though the Eclectic eats are strictly so-so, solid service and a 360-degree view of the airport" elevate it beyond just an overpriced "tourist trap."

Engine Co. No. 28 Ⓩ *American*   21 | 22 | 21 | $39

Downtown | 644 S. Figueroa St. (bet. 7th St. & Wilshire Blvd.) | 213-624-6996 | www.engineco.com

"Set in an old firehouse complete with a pole", this Downtown grill with "serious cocktails" and "old-school service" is "convenient" "before a sporting event" or "show"; "all-American" "gourmet comfort food" is "solid" and "well prepared" but not "knock-your-socks-off", and though some say "prices are high for what you get", it's "handy for concertgoers" with a free shuttle to selected events at the Music and Staples Centers.

Enoteca Drago *Italian*   22 | 20 | 22 | $44

Beverly Hills | 410 N. Cañon Dr. (bet. Brighton Way & Santa Monica Blvd.) | 310-786-8236 | www.celestinodrago.com

Like "a trip to Italian wine country without the plane fare", Celestino Drago's "reasonably priced" Beverly Hills enoteca offers an "incredible list" of bottles and "irresistible", "simple" small plates served by a "friendly" staff; the "happening bar" "beckons with soccer on TV" while the "few outside tables" offer a respite from the "noisy" interior.

Enoteca Toscana   ▽ 25 | 21 | 25 | $37
Wine Bistro Ⓜ *Italian/Spanish*

Camarillo | 2088 E. Ventura Blvd. (Fir St.) | 805-445-1433 | www.enotecatoscanawinebistro.com

"limited but well-thought-out" menu of "delicious", "moderately priced" Spanish and Italian "tapas" "pleases just about any palate" at his "cute" wine bar in Old Town Camarillo; the "owners know" their ino and offer a sizable selection by the glass, and live jazz Saturday ights sweetens the deal.

Enterprise Fish Co. *Seafood*   19 | 17 | 18 | $35

Santa Monica | 174 Kinney St. (Main St.) | 310-392-8366

For a "reminder you live in a beach town", look no further than these casual", "dependable" Santa Monica and Santa Barbara twins where friendly servers" ferry "fresh", "simply" prepared seafood that doesn't "break the bank", including an "amazing" "$29.95 lobster meal" Monday–Thursday and half-off happy hours; the "noisy", "pub-like" nautically themed setting is "nothing fancy", but it's a "good place to bring a kid" or "meet friends."

	FOOD	DECOR	SERVICE	COST

Enzo & Angela *Italian* — 21 | 16 | 22 | $39

West LA | 11701 Wilshire Blvd. (Barrington Ave.) | 310-477-3880 | www.enzoandangela.com

This "well-priced", "unassuming" "mom-and-pop" "sleeper" in West LA "gets it right" with "authentic", "wonderful" Italian dishes that are a "step above the upstairs strip-mall setting"; the "welcoming staff" "remembers regulars", which helps make the experience feel even more "like eating in Florence."

NEW Eva Ⓜ *Californian* — 25 | 18 | 24 | $49

Beverly Boulevard | 7458 Beverly Blvd. (bet. Gardner & Vista Sts.) | 323-634-0700 | www.evarestaurantla.com

"Minimalist atmosphere and menu, maximalist satisfaction and service" is how surveyors sum up this Beverly Boulevard newcomer where "enthusiastic chef"-owner Mark Gold "chats with everyone" and "guides" diners through his "exquisite" seasonal Californian menu; some find the "tiny" former Hatfield's space "cozy" and "homey", while even those calling it "cramped" admit the "experience" is "habit-forming", particularly given the "reasonable prices" and the Sunday night family-style dinner "party" ($35 including wine is a "real bargain."

Fab Hot Dogs *Hot Dogs* — - | - | - | I

Reseda | Loehmann's Plaza | 19417½ Victory Blvd. (Tampa Ave.) | 818-344-4336 | www.fabhotdogs.com

Wiener wizard Joe Fabrocini's down-home Reseda doggery is fabled for its eccentric selection of red hots, including the charred deep-fried Ripper, Bald Eagle (a Ripper with housemade mustard relish) and Carolina Slaw Dog; double dogs are available for those with a bigger appetite, and the only downside is that it closes at 10 PM on weekends – and fare like this seems to cry out to be consumed après midnight.

Fabiolus Café, The *Italian* — 18 | 14 | 19 | $30

Hollywood | 6270 W. Sunset Blvd. (Vine St.) | 323-467-2882 | www.fabiolus.org

"If you're going to the Pantages" or ArcLight, this Hollywood Northern Italian trattoria is "conveniently located" and the gracious "but not overbearing" "staff is good at getting you out on time"; though some find the "cramped" interior disappointing, the "patio is comfy" and the "value-priced" fare is "satisfying."

Factor's Famous Deli Ⓓ *Deli* — 18 | 11 | 19 | $23

Pico-Robertson | 9420 W. Pico Blvd. (Beverly Dr.) | 310-278-9175 | www.factorsdeli.com

A "never-ending menu" including "humongous sandwiches", "matzo ball soup" and other "old-fashioned", "satisfying" "Jewish deli" eats means there's "something for everyone" at this "family-owned" Pico-Robertson "local" "favorite"; though the interior "could use a face-lift" and tabs are "pricey", "rushing waitresses" fetch your order and "valet parking makes it easy to get in and out."

Falafel King *Mideastern* — 19 | 5 | 12 | $12

Santa Monica | The Promenade | 1315 Third St. Promenade (bet. Arizona Ave. & Santa Monica Blvd.) | 310-587-2551

continued/

alafel King
Westwood | 1010 Broxton Ave. (bet. Kinro
10-208-4444

Go for the "fast, fresh and filling" Middle Easter
icious falafel" and what seems to some like "a n
"don't expect much else" from this Santa Monica and
the decor "could use some improvement" and the "staf
ferent", but prices are "unbeatable."

| 24 | 17 | 20 |

Farfalla Trattoria *Italian*
Los Feliz | 1978 Hillhurst Ave. (Finley Ave.) | 323-661-7365 |
www.farfallatrattoria.com

"Delectable" pasta, "wood-fired pizzas" and other Italian dishes draw
a "neighborhood" crowd" to this "affordable" Los Feliz "find"; "brick
walls" and a "friendly staff" contribute to the "warm atmosphere",
though there's "often a wait" since they don't take "reservations" (except for large parties).

| 18 | 16 | 18 | $30 |

Farm of Beverly Hills *American*
Downtown | LA Live | 800 W. Olympic Blvd. (Figueroa St.) | 213-747-4555
Fairfax | The Grove | 189 The Grove Dr. (bet. Beverly Blvd. & 3rd St.) |
323-525-1699
Beverly Hills | 439 N. Beverly Dr. (bet. Brighton Way & Santa Monica Blvd.) |
310-273-5578
www.thefarmofbeverlyhills.com

"Convenient" for a show at LA Live or shopping in Beverly Hills or at
The Grove, this trio of "casual", "crowded" eateries is "reliable" "for a
quick bite" of "wholesome", "upscale" American "comfort food" and
"irresistible" desserts; if some find the offerings "overpriced and un-
derwhelming", they come with service that's generally "easygoing."

| 22 | 17 | 21 | $28 |

Farm Stand *Eclectic*
El Segundo | 422 Main St. (Holly Ave.) | 310-640-3276 | www.farmstand.us
An "attentive" staff aims to "please" at this "winner" offering a "nice
change of pace for El Segundo" and "good value" in its "unusual",
"well-prepared" Eclectic dishes "made with fresh ingredients"; considering the "small", "noisy" interior, it's "best to sit on the covered patio."

| 23 | 19 | 21 | $39 |

Far Niente *Italian*
Glendale | 204½ N. Brand Blvd. (Wilson Ave.) | 818-242-3835 |
www.farnienteristorante.net

Regulars say "don't miss" this "long-standing" Glendale "favorite" with a
"varied menu" of "exceptional" Italian fare served amid a "dark",
"quiet", "warm" setting; the "amenable", "knowledgeable" staff extends
the experience, making slightly pricey meals "worth every penny", and
it's also convenient for "performances at the Alex Theatre" nearby.

| 19 | 17 | 20 | $35 |

Fat Fish *Asian/Japanese*
Koreatown | 3300 W. Sixth St. (Berendo St.) | 213-384-1304
West Hollywood | 616 N. Robertson Blvd. (bet. Melrose Ave. &
Santa Monica Blvd.) | 310-659-3882
"Rolls are the strong point" at this Japanese–Asian fusion pair where
the service is "friendly" and prices are "cheap" for the genre; the "casual" Koreatown location, which lacks a liquor license, delivers sushi

...h is "trendier", of-
...r dining space."

2	15	13	$24

...enice &

...ts.) | 310-736-2224

...titutions" (or even
..."n", found at these
...n "outstanding list
...st-served seating,
...lver City location,
...king to one", since
...still, most say the

...rience is "worth it", P.S. you must be 21 to enter.

Fatty's & Co. Ⓜ Vegetarian

▽			
25	21	21	$31

Eagle Rock | 1627 Colorado Blvd. (Vincent Ave.) | 323-254-8804 |
www.fattyscafe.com

"Every plate looks and tastes like a work of art" at this affordable, still largely "undiscovered gem" in Eagle Rock where "mouthwatering" dishes, "impressive cocktails" and an "exceptional wine list" mean "you don't feel you're denying yourself" by eating vegetarian; capable servers and a "converted garage" setting with vaulted ceilings and garden seating complete the package.

Feast from the East Ⓢ Asian

21	7	14	$14

West LA | 1949 Westwood Blvd. (bet. La Grange & Missouri Aves.) |
310-475-0400 | www.ffte.com

A "good place to stop for a quick lunch", this "cheap, fast" West LA Pan-Asian is "famous" for its "addictive Chinese chicken salad", though the sesame wings are so "haunting" some are "tempted to steal them from the next table"; the "decor leaves much to be desired", but you can always get your meal "to go" – and whether eating in or out, just "don't forget to pick up" a bottle of "their salad dressing."

FIG American/French

22	21	21	$49

Santa Monica | Fairmont Miramar Hotel & Bungalows | 101 Wilshire Blvd.
(Ocean Ave.) | 310-319-3111 | www.figsantamonica.com

"Locavores" love this French-New American in Santa Monica's Fairmont Miramar Hotel for its "fresh, organic", "seasonal" menu and "cre-...on the ...ishes at "all three meals"; "sit overlooking the ...terior and enjoy the "polite" serv...lax in the "fancy yet comfortable" in-...which of course all comes at a price.

Figaro Bistrot French

20	21	18	$31

Los Feliz | 1802 N. Vermont Ave. (Melbourne Ave.) | 323-662-1587 |
www.figarobistrot.com

The "funky clientele" adores "sitting at a sidewalk table on a date" and "people-watching" at this "cute" "neighborhood" French bistro especially "popular" for brunch; it "feels like a little slice of Paris in Los Feliz" (right down to the service with "attitude"), and those who call the prices "très cher" "for what it is" are outvoted by those calling it all they "could want."

	FOOD	DECOR	SERVICE	COST

Figtree's Café & Grill *Eclectic* | − | − | − | I |

Venice | 429 Ocean Front Walk (Paloma Ave.) | 310-392-4937 |
www.figtreescafe.com

A Venice Beach favorite since 1978, this affordable mostly outdoor cafe offers a prime view of the side show on the boardwalk – bicyclers, skateboarders, slackers, in-line skaters and lots of guys with big muscles and gals in thongy things – a modern-day circus playing out before diners eating an Eclectic assortment of omelets, salads, sandwiches and such.

ins *Continental/Seafood* | 21 | 19 | 20 | $41 |

Calabasas | 23504 Calabasas Rd. (Mulholland Dr.) | 818-223-3467
Westlake Village | Westlake Plaza | 982 S. Westlake Blvd. (bet. Agoura & Townsgate Rds.) | 805-494-6494
www.finsinc.com

"If it swims, you'll find it on the menu" at these finny Continental twins where the seafood "consistently delivers" and so does the "attentive" service; while the "relaxed" settings at both boast comfy booths and patios (and live music on weekends), the creekside Calabasas branch is so close to the water, "you can hear the bullfrogs."

irefly ◐ *American* | 20 | 23 | 18 | $43 |

Studio City | 11720 Ventura Blvd. (Colfax Ave.) | 818-762-1833

Hipsters have a "drink" in the "comfortable" "library"-themed lounge, then flit to the "large", "trendy", "heated patio" to dine at this "charming Valley oasis" in Studio City; the "well-prepared" New American fare pleases most, though service can be "erratic", but the "atmosphere is cool enough to make up for" any flaws.

irefly Bistro Ⓜ *American* | 20 | 19 | 22 | $31 |

South Pasadena | 1009 El Centro St. (Meridian Ave.) | 626-441-2443 |
www.eatatfirefly.com

At this "welcoming", midpriced South Pasadenan, a tented setting surrounded by foliage makes for a "relaxed atmosphere"; though "not everything works", the "eclectic" New American "twists on old favorites" are "mostly hits" and there's live music Thursdays and Sundays.

🆕 Firenze Osteria *Italian* | 20 | 18 | 19 | $40 |

North Hollywood | 4212 Lankershim Blvd. (Valley Spring Ln.) |
818-760-7081 | www.firenzeosteria.com

Fans of *Top Chef* vet Fabio Viviani find the Italian fare more "predictable" than "expected" at this North Hollywood "neighborhood joint", where the "homey" vibe is bolstered with sunny art-hung walls; "knowledgeable service" and "fair prices" add to the appeal, not to mention a menu of "unique martinis" (including one made with balsamic vinegar) that cocktail mavens "dream about."

🆕 First & Hope *American* | − | − | − | M |

Downtown | 710 W. First St. (Hope St.) | 213-617-8555 |
www.firstandhope.com

Just a short stroll from the Walt Disney Concert Hall, this Downtown arrival offers a fine alternative for pre- or post-show dinner and drinks, with a moderately priced menu of Southern-inflected Traditional American cuisine; the handsomely retro, white-tableclothed space boasts glowing walls, modernist chandeliers and a wine lounge with a pour-it-yourself Enomatic machine.

	FOOD	DECOR	SERVICE	COST

Fish Grill *Seafood* | 19 | 9 | 15 | $18

Beverly Boulevard | 7226 Beverly Blvd. (bet. Alta Vista Blvd. &
Formosa Ave.) | 323-937-7162
Pico-Robertson | 9618 W. Pico Blvd. (Beverwil Dr.) | 310-860-1182
Brentwood | 12013 Wilshire Blvd. (bet. Bundy Dr. & Saltair Ave.) |
310-479-1800
Malibu | 22935 PCH (Malibu Pier) | 310-456-8585
www.fishgrill.com
For "fresh fish fast", fin fans favor this kosher chainlet offering "simple
grilled" seafood for "bargain" prices; the "surroundings aren't much to
look at", so many opt for "takeout", "but hey, a deal's a deal"; just
know that there's no alcohol or shellfish, and they're closed Friday
nights and Saturdays.

555 East *Steak* | 25 | 22 | 24 | $55

Long Beach | 555 E. Ocean Blvd. (bet. Atlantic & Linden Aves.) |
562-437-0626 | www.555east.com
From the "New York feel" with "stamped-metal ceilings" and "rich,
dark wood" to the "soft jazz pianist", there's no mistaking that this
Long Beacher is a "classic chophouse" that's "serious" about "tender", "cooked-to-perfection steaks" and "fantastic" wines; the "upscale" approach will cost you, but it's "perfect for business" or
impressing a "special someone", complete with "impeccable" service
and "no attitude."

Five Guys *Burgers* | 20 | 10 | 15 | $11

Carson | South Bay Pavilion | 20700 Avalon Blvd. (Del Amo Blvd.) |
310-515-7700
Cerritos | Cerritos Promenade | 11461 South Street | 562-809-0055
www.fiveguys.com
"Juicy, greasy, tasty" burgers "with all the trimmings" "blow away" the
competition according to fans of this "presidential favorite" with Carson
and Cerritos branches that's also prized for its "farm-to-fryer" fries
and "free peanuts while you wait"; so even if doubters "don't get the
hype", these "bare-bones" but "cheery" East Coast–based franchises
are "taking the world by storm."

Five Sixty-One 🗷 *Californian/French* | ▽ 23 | 18 | 18 | $36

Pasadena | Le Cordon Bleu College of Culinary Arts | 561 E. Green St.
(Madison Ave.) | 626-405-1561 | www.561restaurant.com
"Try out haute cuisine from aspiring chefs" at this Monday–Friday Cal-
French "training restaurant" at Pasadena's Le Cordon Bleu College of
Culinary Arts, where brick walls and big windows are the backdrop for
the "relaxed setting"; those who ask for a seat near the open kitchen
can watch the "earnest" cooks turning out "adventurous" dishes that
range from "eh to excellent" – and remember that "everyone is still
learning", so forgive the "uneven service."

Flavor of India *Indian* | 21 | 15 | 19 | $28

West Hollywood | 9045 Santa Monica Blvd. (Nemo St.) | 310-274-1715 |
www.theflavorofindia.com
Burbank | 161 E. Orange Grove Ave. (bet. 1st St. & San Fernando Blvd.) |
818-558-1199 | www.flavorofindia.com
"Well-prepared" Indian food comes at "great prices" at this Burbank
and West Hollywood pair that also offers a lunch buffet; service is

personable", and if the setting is nothing special, the WeHo branch feels "comfortable and cozy", thanks to a heated patio twinkling with "Christmas lights."

Fleming's Prime Steakhouse & Wine Bar *Steak*

24 | 23 | 24 | $58

Downtown | LA Live | 800 W. Olympic Blvd. (Figueroa St.) | 213-745-9911
El Segundo | 2301 Rosecrans Ave. (Douglas St.) | 310-643-6911
Woodland Hills | 6373 Topanga Canyon Blvd. (Victory Blvd.) | 818-346-1005
www.flemingssteakhouse.com

Beef eaters savor the "delicious" steaks, "unique" wines by the glass and "subdued" ambiance at this "chain-chic" chophouse that offers a "high level of service", showing impressive "attention to detail" all round; while the tabs are "prime" too, "seasonal prix fixe menus" are a "recession-budget treat", and the "affordable happy hour" makes it a "perfect after-office wind-down spot."

Flore Vegan Cuisine *Vegan*

▽ 21 | 11 | 17 | $18

Silver Lake | 3818 W. Sunset Blvd. (Hyperion Ave.) | 323-953-0611 | www.florevegan.com

Meet Market *Vegetarian*
(fka Flore Cafe)

Echo Park | 3206 W. Sunset Blvd. (Descanso Dr.) | 323-667-0116
"Even meat eaters" "come out believers" at these "tiny", affordable vegetarian "finds" where "fresh, organic", "vegan" "soups, salads, desserts" and more are a "pleasant surprise"; though takeout is available from the deli counter at Silver Lake, there's also table service for eating on the sidewalk and in the "hole-in-the-wall" interior, while the Echo Park location is more of a cafe/market than a sit-down restaurant.

NEW Flying Pig Truck 🗷🖘 *Asian/Pacific Rim*

- | - | - | I

Location varies; see website | 714-234-5107 | www.flyingpigtruck.com
"Flavorful" sliders and braised pork belly on a steamed bun join more "unusual" items such as duck tacos among the offerings at this BBQ food truck with Asian–Pacific Rim leanings; though "each bite bursts with flavor", roving regulars squeal that portions are "small", so tabs can add up.

Fogo de Chão *Brazilian/Steak*

23 | 21 | 24 | $61

Beverly Hills | 133 N. La Cienega Blvd. (bet. Clifton Way & Wilshire Blvd.) | 310-289-7755 | www.fogodechao.com
"A blast" if you're in a "red-meat frenzy", this Brazilian steakhouse chain proffers skewers laden with "glorious" "hand-carved" cuts that "keep on coming", courtesy of a "fantastic staff" in gaucho get-ups; the "extraordinary" salad bar and "terrific" digs are pluses, but just remember it's an "expensive" all-you-can-eat feast, "so you'd better be hungry" – and "you won't want to see a cow for a year" afterward.

Fonz's *Seafood/Steak*

21 | 19 | 20 | $45

Manhattan Beach | 1017 Manhattan Ave. (bet. 10th Pl. & 11th St.) | 310-376-1536 | www.fonzs.com
The "likable staff" welcomes "locals" to this "happening", "cozy hang" in Manhattan Beach with a patio and casual setting as well as a traditional dining room a block from the sand; though a few say the surf 'n'

turf selections could use a "refresh", most appreciate the "reliable" "wonderful" fare and are "willing to pay for it."

FOOD *American*   21 | 13 | 19 | $20

Rancho Park | 10571 W. Pico Blvd. (Prosser Ave.) | 310-441-7770 | www.food-la.com

For "exceptional baked goods" in the morning or an "honest, healthful lunch", "locals" flock to this Rancho Park "cafe and market" where "homey" American eats are high-"quality" and relatively "high priced"; never mind the "austere" setting, the "wonderful people" "behind the counter" seem so "genuinely interested that you're happy with your meal", it "feels like you're in your mom's kitchen."

Food + Lab *Austrian/Californian*   ▽ 20 | 13 | 15 | $17

West Hollywood | 7253 Santa Monica Blvd. (bet. Formosa Ave. & Poinsettia Dr.) | 323-851-7120 | www.foodlabcatering.com

"Hipsters", "studio folk and WeHo regulars" "pack into" this "small but mighty" cafe and market (an offshoot of a catering company "tucked away in a nondescript little building" in Rancho Park; "delicious, innovative" Austrian-Cal salads and other items are good to-go or eat on-site amid the "humble" yet "cute" surroundings.

NEW Forage 🈺Ⓜ *Californian*   ▽ 25 | 17 | 24 | $21

Silver Lake | 3823 W. Sunset Blvd. (bet. Hyperion & Lucille Aves.) | 323-663-6885 | www.foragela.com

"Beautiful" displays of "fresh", "imaginative" Californian fare let you "see exactly what you're getting" at this "fantastic" Silver Lake "order at-the-counter" spot; "reasonable prices" "for the quality" "impress" but "be prepared", it's a "very small space", so sidewalk seating or takeout may be your best bet.

Ford's Filling Station *American*   20 | 18 | 19 | $38

Culver City | 9531 Culver Blvd. (bet. Cardiff & Watseka Aves.) | 310-202-1470 | www.fordsfillingstation.net

"Aptly named", this "casual" Culver City "anchor" from Harrison's son Ben dishes out an ever-changing "daily menu" of "sophisticated but approachable" New American small plates, "fantastic charcuterie and cheese", "impressive burgers" and "specialty drinks"; though the tabs are "not cheap", service is "polite" and the two patios are the "place to be" for "people-watching."

Formosa Cafe *Asian*   13 | 17 | 17 | $27

West Hollywood | 7156 Santa Monica Blvd. (Formosa Ave.) | 323-850-9050

"Imagine you're Humphrey Bogart or Edward G. Robinson" at this circa-1939 West Hollywood "landmark", where "nostalgia" is on tap nightly at the "legendary bar with a long history" and the headshots of "past patrons on the wall" to prove it; as for the subpar Asian fusion fare, "forget" it – focus instead on the view-riffic "roof deck" and "dingy" but "fun" interior at this "place you should try" at least "once."

Foundry on Melrose *American*   22 | 19 | 21 | $55

Melrose | 7465 Melrose Ave. (bet. Gardner & Vista Sts.) | 323-651-0915 | www.thefoundryonmelrose.com

Chef-owner Eric Greenspan's "bonhomie" is evident in this "classy" yet "unpretentious" Melrose American, where he "merges

| | FOOD | DECOR | SERVICE | COST |

"reativity and comfort food" with "magic" (if "pricey") results; an nimpressed few cite "uneven" experiences, but they are outvoted / those who say its "trendy" milieu complete with "top-notch" bar, omantic" outdoor courtyard and live music (jazz, blues and singer-ngwriters) "never disappoints."

ountain Coffee Room *Diner*
▽ 25 | 20 | 25 | $27

everly Hills | Beverly Hills Hotel | 9641 Sunset Blvd. (Crescent Dr.) | 10-276-2251 | www.thebeverlyhillshotel.com

hough the Beverly Hills Hotel has been a beacon of celebs and hopefuls nce 1912, its circa-1949 "fun, pink" coffee shop remains one of its nsung stars, offering up "delicious", affordable diner staples from an't-be-beat" breakfasts to "thick shakes", floats and other soda foun-in treats; its 20-stool curving counter is "the place to be" for "Sunday orning" "stargazing" – "even if you don't intend to be discovered."

10 Boyd *Californian*
20 | 17 | 19 | $27

owntown | 410 Boyd St. (San Pedro St.) | 213-617-2491 | ww.410boyd.com

"urprisingly sophisticated" Californian cuisine makes this "cool little oot" "hidden" away Downtown a no-brainer for "casual" "pre-eater" dinners or "snappy lunches" say the "artists and City Hall ower brokers" who "hang out" here; wallet-friendly tabs, "friendly, ompt" service and "uncrowded" environs with rotating "local art on e walls" keep the "regulars" coming back.

Fraîche *French/Italian*
23 | 20 | 20 | $49

ulver City | 9411 Culver Blvd. (Bagley Ave.) | 310-839-6800 | ww.fraicherestaurantla.com

EW Santa Monica | 312 Wilshire Blvd. (3rd St. Promenade) | 10-451-7482 | www.fraicherestaurantsm.com

nese "trendy", "very popular" "destinations" seem to have "survived e hype", "continuing to excite" with "inventive culinary flourishes" in e "seasonal, market-driven menu" of French-Italian "epicurean de-ghts"; service can be of the "hoity-toity" variety, and though both lo-ations strut "sleek", "stylish" decor, the "high-energy" Culver City iginal can be "crowded" and "cacophonous" ("food vibrates on the ate") while the Santa Monica "incarnation" is "open", "airy" and has new lounge with its own menu.

rascati *Italian*
23 | 18 | 22 | $42

olling Hills Estates | Promenade on the Peninsula | 550 Deep Valley Dr. Crossfield Dr.) | Rolling Hills | 310-541-8800 | www.frascatirestaurant.com

his "high-end Italian" in Rolling Hills Estates "doesn't disappoint", offering "tempting" pizzas, pastas and small plates that "can make whole dinner"; an extensive wine list and "value"-oriented pricing e other reasons its "relatively small" space can "fill up early" with a yal local crowd.

red 62 ● *Diner*
17 | 15 | 14 | $20

os Feliz | 1850 N. Vermont Ave. (bet. Franklin & Prospect Aves.) | 23-667-0062 | www.fred62.com

er the "late-night hipster hangout", this 'round-the-clock "retro" diner Los Feliz is "definitely not your mother's coffee shop", spinning wisted interpretations" of "comfort" classics; maybe the staff

"needs a serious attitude check", but "trendy", "diverse locals" kee[p]
crowding into its "groovy vinyl booths" all the same.

French Crêpe Co. *French*
21 | 11 | 15 | $14

Fairfax | Farmers Mkt. | 6333 W. Third St. (Fairfax Ave.) |
323-934-3113
Hollywood | Hollywood & Highland Ctr. | 6801 Hollywood Blvd.
(Highland Ave.) | 323-960-0933
www.frenchcrepe.com

"Refuel during your shopping trip" at the Farmers Market o[r]
Hollywood & Highland via this French "quick-bite" duo whose "larg[e]
variety" of "made-to-order" crêpes come in versions both "savory an[d]
sweet"; some consider it "overpriced" considering the basic, "sit-o[n]
a-stool" decor and "so-so" service, but all the same "don't expect you[r]
dining partner to share."

Frenchy's Bistro Ⓜ *French*
25 | 17 | 23 | $48

Long Beach | 4137 E. Anaheim St. (bet. Belmont & Roswell Aves.) |
562-494-8787 | www.frenchysbistro.com

"Chef-owner Andre Angles' personal touch continues to be golden" a[t]
this "off-the-beaten-track" French "treasure" in Long Beach whe[re]
"oh-so-Provençal" "country cooking" and an "extensive" wine list (["a]
"labor of love") have many saying "it's as close to France" as SoC[al]
gets; don't let the "iffy neighborhood" and "unassuming" "storefro[nt]
setting" "fool you" as the "simple yet enchanting" bistro decor an[d]
"friendly" family service make this midpriced spot a true "diamo[nd]
in the rough."

Frida *Mexican*
20 | 18 | 18 | $32

Beverly Hills | 236 S. Beverly Dr. (bet. Charleville Blvd. & Gregory Way)[|]
310-278-7666
Santa Monica | Brentwood Country Mart | 225 26th St. (San Vicente Blvd.)[|]
310-395-9666
Glendale | Americana at Brand | 750 Americana Way (Central Ave.)[|]
818-551-1666
www.fridarestaurant.com

"*Muy bueno*" say fans of these spots specializing in "upscale" "Mexica[n]
with a twist", where a "modern" menu makes "even the standards fe[el]
new"; though naysayers sniff it's "overpriced", most agree the atm[o]
sphere is "fun" and "informal" and the staff is "attentive" (and oft[en]
"more authentic than the dishes"); P.S. The Brentwood Country Ma[rt]
outpost is more of a quick-bite taqueria.

Fritto Misto *Italian*
21 | 12 | 19 | $23

Santa Monica | 601 Colorado Ave. (6th St.) | 310-458-2829
Hermosa Beach | 316 Pier Ave. (Monterey Blvd.) | 310-318-6098

"Nothing extravagant, just solid cooking" sums up this "lovely litt[le]
neighborhood" Italian duo in Hermosa Beach and Santa Monica whe[re]
"families, dates" and "students" "carbo-load" on "generous portion[s]
of "customizable pasta dishes" that "aren't exactly authentic" but a[re]
a "great bang for the buck"; while "long waits confirm the quality" [of]
the fare, the "friendly" staff keeps things "comfy" and "homey", ensu[r]
ing it's "always a hit."

Fromin's Deli *Deli*
15 | 10 | 17 | $19

Santa Monica | 1832 Wilshire Blvd. (bet. 18th & 19th Sts.) | 310-829-544[4]

continued)

romin's Deli

ncino | 17615 Ventura Blvd. (bet. Encino & White Oak Aves.) | 18-990-6346

Old-fashioned" but "serviceable", these separately owned Santa Monica and Encino delis have a "patient" staff placating a mostly Older" crowd; though the "value"-minded fare is "not worth going out f the way for", it's "satisfying", and the "chicken soup" has its fans.

rysmith ☒ *American* | - | - | - | I |

ocation varies; see website | 818-371-6814 | www.eatfrysmith.com

Fries on wheels" make this roaming truck (that runs on recycled vegtable oil) an affordable favorite for "unexpected but delicious combiations" of "golden" hand-cut spuds topped with "creative ingredients" ke kimchi and pork belly or free-range chicken and a tomatillo-tamarind auce; most fans agree "they do one thing and they do it well" and adly remind all "new friends" that "sharing is caring."

🆕 Fuego at the Maya *Mexican/Pan-Latin* | ▽ 19 | 25 | 20 | $41 |

ong Beach | Hotel Maya | 700 Queensway Dr. (Harbor Scenic Dr.) | 62-481-3910 | www.fuegolongbeach.com

urveyors seek out this "beautiful" waterside Mexican–Pan-Latin at he Hotel Maya for its "wonderful views" of the "Long Beach skyline" and he Queen Mary from a "pleasant", "happy hour"–friendly patio; prices ight be a tad high considering the fare looks "more interesting on the ienu than on the plate", but a "friendly" staff and "über-modern" decor ake this relatively "hard-to-get-to" "hangout" "worth the journey."

u-Shing *Chinese* | 19 | 12 | 19 | $22 |

asadena | 2960 E. Colorado Blvd. (El Nido Ave.) | 626-792-8898 | ww.fu-shing.com

A "smiling" staff "welcomes" "families" and "large groups" to this 30-ear-old Pasadena "go-to" where the multigenerational Chang family elivers "consistently" "tasty" Chinese at a "terrific value"; though the ecor is nothing special, to most the Sichuan-based menu is "better han expected" (which explains why it's "always crowded").

iaby's Mediterranean *Mediterranean* | 20 | 9 | 15 | $19 |

Marina del Rey | 20 Washington Blvd. (bet. Pacific Ave & Speedway) | 10-821-9721 ◑

Vest LA | 10445 Venice Blvd. (Motor Ave.) | 310-559-1808

iaby's Express *Mediterranean*

Marina del Rey | 3216 Washington Blvd. (Lincoln Blvd.) | 310-823-7299 ww.gabysexpress.com

Vestsiders agree these "informal" Meds "hit the spot" with "big" porons of meats and other "fresh" fare that "won't break a budget"; nough the "decor may be lacking" (the West LA locale is "tented") and ervice can be "spotty" ("don't be in a hurry, they won't be"), the patios f the two full-service stops continue to be "jammed on summer nights."

iale's ☒ *Italian* | 24 | 19 | 24 | $35 |

asadena | 452 S. Fair Oaks Ave. (bet. California & Del Mar Blvds.) | 26-432-6705 | www.galesrestaurant.com

his "secret" Northern Italian in Pasadena "knows how to please" with feel-good" favorites of "melt-in-your-mouth" pastas, "superb" salads

| | FOOD | DECOR | SERVICE | COST |

and a "wine list for everyone's wallet"; sure, the brick-walled room is often "noisy", but "locals" insist it's "cozy" and doesn't detract from the "knowledgeable" staff and "welcoming", "neighborhood feel" just ask the "crowd" "waiting" for a table.

Galletto Bar & Grill ● Brazilian/Italian   23 | 17 | 18 | $34
Westlake Village | Westlake Plaza | 982 S. Westlake Blvd. (bet. Agoura & Townsgate Rds.) | 805-449-4300 | www.gallettobarandgrill.com
"Outstanding Brazilian specialties" join Italian dishes at this Westlake Village "gem", where "crowds" congregate for a "change from the usual" via the "unique", moderately priced menu featuring "more choices than can be imagined"; with the "loud" interior often shaking to the beat of "live music", many opt for the "festive" patio boasting "lots of greenery."

Galley, The Seafood/Steak   17 | 17 | 20 | $38
Santa Monica | 2442 Main St. (bet. Hollister Ave. & Ocean Park Blvd.) 310-452-1934 | www.thegalleyrestaurant.net
Since 1934, this Santa Monica "surf 'n' turf on the surf" has been "satisfying" "locals" with service that "makes you feel at home" and "generous portions" of midpriced fare in a "funky" "maritime" setting starring props from *Mutiny on the Bounty* (including the steering wheel used in the movie) and other nautically themed "kitsch"; despite detractors who claim "it's past its prime", many fans stand by the "old school" "experience", saying "it is what it is and we like it that way."

Gaucho Grill Argentinean/Steak   18 | 14 | 17 | $27
Brentwood | 11754 San Vicente Blvd. (Gorham Ave.) | 310-447-7898 | www.gauchobrentwood.com
Woodland Hills | 6435 Canoga Ave. (Victory Blvd.) | 818-992-6416 www.gauchogrillwh.com
Carnivores unite at these "value"-friendly Argentineans for "consistently" "solid" steaks, "garlicky chicken" and kebabs that fans suggest "dousing" with "housemade chimichurri"; for those seeking truly "memorable" cuts, they're "not worth a special trip", but "moderately cheerful" decor (modern in Brentwood, traditional in Woodland Hills) and "reliable" service assure there are "never rude surprises."

Geisha House ● Japanese   18 | 21 | 16 | $44
Hollywood | 6633 Hollywood Blvd. (Cherokee Ave.) | 323-460-6300 www.dolcegroup.com
This "über-trendy sushi joint" is a "rollicking good time" for young "scene"-makers and "tourists" who prefer to "laugh and dine" amid Hollywood's "beautiful people" in a setting that resembles a sexy, futuristic Tokyo club; think "expense account", but you can expect "speedy" service "even when it's crazy busy."

Genghis Cohen Chinese   21 | 14 | 18 | $29
Fairfax | 740 N. Fairfax Ave. (Melrose Ave.) | 323-653-0640 | www.genghiscohen.com
"Catch a show and get some chow" at this reasonably priced Chinese on Fairfax where "homesick East Coasters" "whet their appetites with" "genuine New York egg rolls" and a "dependable" Sichuan menu served with a Jewish slant (i.e. "pickles and coleslaw"); the "weird combo" doesn't stop there however, as the "slick" dining room shares

| | FOOD | DECOR | SERVICE | COST |

a wall with an adjacent "mini-theater" where "local artists on the rise" perform nightly.

Gennaro's Ristorante 🗷 *Italian* — ▽ 22 | 22 | 22 | $45

Glendale | 1109 N. Brand Blvd. (Dryden St.) | 818-243-6231 | www.gennarosristorante.com

A "genuinely quiet" environment sets the stage for "expensive" "fine dining" delivered via a "helpful staff" at this "very pleasant" Northern Italian in Glendale; persnickety types insist it's stuck "in a time warp" with "'80s"-decor matching a "tired menu", but appreciative patrons call it "a throwback to when things were slower."

☑ Geoffrey's *Californian* — 20 | 26 | 21 | $61

Malibu | 27400 PCH (4 mi. north of Malibu Canyon Rd.) | 310-457-1519 | www.geoffreysmalibu.com

"Breathtaking ocean views" "wow" diners at this "upscale" Malibu "oasis" where the "romantic" patio dining area is a "picture-perfect" setting for "dates" to turn into "proposals" and eventually "anniversaries"; while it's generally agreed the "pricey" Californian cuisine isn't quite "as wonderful as the ambiance", "celebs" and "out-of-towners" gladly "splurge" for the popular brunch where a "cheerful" staff delivers "mimosas on a beautiful day."

George's Greek Café *Greek* — 22 | 15 | 20 | $24

Downtown | Seventh Street Market Pl. | 735 S. Figueroa St. (7th St.) | 213-624-6542 🗷
NEW Lakewood | 5252 Faculty Ave. (Candlewood St.) | 562-529-5800
Long Beach | 135 Pine Ave. (bet. B'way & 1st St.) | 562-437-1184
Long Beach | 5316 E. Second St. (Pomona Ave.) | 562-433-1755
www.georgesgreekcafe.com

"*Opa!*" shout backers of this "modestly priced" Greek chainlet that takes a "traditional" approach to "hearty", "homey" gyros, hummus, lamb chops, salads and more; "lunch"-friendly patios and occasional "live music" (at the Long Beach spots) make for a "casual" atmosphere, but it's the "attentive service" sometimes topped by "a kiss on the cheek" from George himself that is the real "icing on the baklava."

Getty Center, Restaurant at the 🅼 *Californian* — 22 | 25 | 22 | $45

Brentwood | The Getty Ctr. | 1200 Getty Center Dr. (Sepulveda Blvd.) | 310-440-6810 | www.getty.edu

"One of the best works of art at the Getty" Center is how admirers describe the museum's "surprisingly" "sumptuous" Californian offering "million-dollar views" of "mountaintops", "sunsets" and "architectural treats" as a "serene respite" for a "civilized meal"; service is "knowledgeable" in the modern dining space with white decor and "floor-to-ceiling windows", and the "creative", seasonally "changing menu" of "meticulously prepared" dishes are "worth the splurge"; P.S. dinner is served only on Saturdays.

Gina Lee's Bistro 🅼 *Asian/Californian* — 24 | 14 | 24 | $42

Redondo Beach | Riviera Plaza | 211 Palos Verdes Blvd. (bet. Catalina Ave. & PCH) | 310-375-4462

Owners Gina and Scott Lee "continue to please" at their "affordable" "neighborhood gem", serving "reliable" yet "inventive" Cal-Asian cuisine out of an "obscure" "strip-mall" storefront in Redondo Beach; a "louder-

than-normal setting" can make it "hard to have a conversation", still
host Gina makes "everyone feel like an old friend" by taking a "per
sonal interest" in every plate that comes out of chef Scott's kitchen.

Gingergrass *Vietnamese* 22 | 16 | 19 | $25

Silver Lake | 2396 Glendale Blvd. (Silver Lake Blvd.) | 323-644-1600 |
www.gingergrass.com

"A far cry from the typical bland pho joint", this "sleek, polished"
Vietnamese in Silver Lake serves a "fantastic array" of "imaginative"
"decently priced" fare that's "not tremendously authentic" "bu
tasty"; though service can be "unpredictable", the "lively" atmosphere
and "hip" industrial setting continues to attract "arty, young" "crowds"
making for "long waits" that can border on "unbearable" at times.

Giorgio Baldi Ⓜ *Italian* 26 | 16 | 18 | $72

Santa Monica | 114 W. Channel Rd. (PCH) | 310-573-1660 |
www.giorgiobaldi.us

Italian fare "worthy of one's last meal" is served at this "old favorite"
in Santa Monica that "squeezes" in the "haute class" of the "Pacifi
Palisades and Malibu" for "consistently superb" dishes including "to-
die-for" pastas in a "romantic", "bustling" setting that's predictably a
"stargazer's paradise"; just keep in mind that servers can be "snooty"
"unless you're a regular or celebrity" and you may have to "apply for a
loan before checking out."

Girasole Cucina Italiana Ⓜ *Italian* 24 | 16 | 22 | $32

Hancock Park | 225½ N. Larchmont Blvd. (Beverly Blvd.) | 323-464-6978 |
www.girasolecucina.com

"Real Italian" fare from the Veneto region of Northern Italy pleases patrons of this "well-kept secret" in Hancock Park that serves "homemade" pastas, soups "to die for" and osso buco that "melts in your
mouth"; though no alcohol is served in the "tiny", "tight" space, a "relaxed" vibe, "truly likable" service and "very reasonable prices" have
crowd-fearing regulars pleading "don't tell too many people about it."

⚡ Gjelina ◗ *American* 26 | 22 | 20 | $45

Venice | 1429 Abbot Kinney Blvd. (Milwood Ave.) | 310-450-1429 |
www.gjelina.com

Chef/co-owner Travis Lett's much-"hyped" Venice New American
takes "crowds" on a "true culinary journey" with an "eclectic", "seasonal" menu featuring small plates and "thin-crust pizzas" in a "hip yet
homey" space that's "not for the claustrophobic"; an occasionally
"aloof" staff means "all bets are off servicewise when it gets hopping",
but a "relaxing patio" and "amazing" butterscotch pot de crème keep
"well-heeled creative types" returning; P.S. requests for modifications
to dishes are declined.

Gladstone's *Seafood* 13 | 18 | 15 | $40

LAX | LA Int'l Airport, Terminal 3 | 201 World Way (Sepulveda Blvd.) |
310-646-8056

Gladstone's Malibu *Seafood*

Pacific Palisades | 17300 PCH (Sunset Blvd.) | 310-573-0212
www.gladstones.com

"Seagull alerts" come with the territory at this Malibu "hangout" with
a "beachside patio" where "tourists" and "bikini-clad surfers" dig into

FOOD | DECOR | SERVICE | COST

seafood and a "few brews" while "watching the sun sink into the Pacific"; some say "mediocre service is just fine with a view like this", but "mammoth portions" cannot make up for "overpriced", "uninspired" fare ("fish giving their lives for nothing!") and "parking can be a zoo"; P.S. the airport location is separately owned.

NEW Glendon Bar & Kitchen, The ● Californian `- | - | - | M`

West LA | 1071 Glendon Ave. (Kinross Ave.) | 310-208-2023 | www.theglendonla.com

This stylish Californian (in the old Moustache Café space) is dominated by the most impressive bar in Westwood, a grand carved and polished wood-and-glass construct, lined with a phalanx of tall, well-padded chairs perfect for sipping the cocktail-of-the-moment; there are also spacious banquettes for digging into the student-friendly menu of upscale pizzas, sliders and mac 'n' cheese, plus an overhead loft for parties and get-togethers.

NEW Goal ● American `- | - | - | I`

Fairfax | 8334 W. Third St. (Flores St.) | 323-655-5955

Slick and high-tech, this bar and grill near the Beverly Center feels a bit like a spaceship for sports aficionados, offering a dozen flat-screens broadcasting every game that's on at the moment; burgundy leatherette booths provide cozy spots for watching fave teams in action while nibbling on affordable Traditional American fare like mini corn dogs with three dipping sauces.

NEW Gold Class Cinema *Eclectic* `▽ 18 | 20 | 20 | $35`

Pasadena | One Colorado | 42 Miller Alley (Colorado Blvd.) | 626-639-2260 | www.goldclasscinemas.com

Hungry cinephiles check out "the latest Hollywood releases" "in style" at this "pampering" Pasadena "experience" complete with "plush recliners, pillows and blankets" plus midpriced Eclectic eats; sure it's "a bit challenging to watch a film and enjoy a meal at the same time", and the "setting is more noteworthy than the fare", but with a "discreet staff" summoned at the push of a "call button", it's one "fancy schmancy" movie setup.

Golden Deli *Vietnamese* `23 | 5 | 12 | $14`

San Gabriel | Las Tunas Plaza | 815 W. Las Tunas Dr. (Mission Dr.) | 626-308-0803 | www.goldendelirestaurant.com

"For a quick Vietnamese fix" of "better-than-most" pho and "addicting" egg rolls, this storefront in a San Gabriel strip mall delivers "crave"-worthy cuisine that is "so authentic" and "very affordable"; though service is less than stellar, the simple setting is "crowded" with admirers who reluctantly spread the word as "lines are too long already."

Golden State Ⓜ *Californian* `22 | 11 | 17 | $18`

Fairfax | 426 N. Fairfax Ave. (bet. Oakwood & Rosewood Aves.) | 323-782-8331 | www.thegoldenstatecafe.com

Fans say this "simple" "storefront" on Fairfax "scores" with "juicy" "gourmet" "burgers for grown-ups", a "crazy assortment of California brews" and a "surprisingly good selection" of gelato flavors (e.g. caramel-bacon); the "super-friendly owners" and "on-staff beer nerds will help you understand" the "reasonably priced" fare, but "don't go when it' busy", lest the limited seating leave you "hovering like a vulture" whil "waiting" for a table.

☑ Gonpachi *Japanese*
21 | 27 | 20 | $50

Beverly Hills | 134 N. La Cienega Blvd. (bet. San Vincente & Wilshire Blvds.)
310-659-8887 | www.globaldiningca.com

Surveyors feel "transported" to a "traditional home" in "old Kyoto" a this Beverly Hills Japanese with a "multimillion-dollar" setting of vari ous "grand" rooms and a "beautiful koi pond" garden; though some sigh "if only the dining matched the decor", service is "caring" and most "enjoy" the "expensive" variety of sushi, robata and small plates starring "homemade soba noodles to die for."

⬛ᴺᴱᵂ Gorbals, The ●☒ *Eclectic*
21 | 13 | 19 | $35

Downtown | Alexandria Hotel | 501 S. Spring St. (5th St.) | 213-488-3408 |
www.thegorbalsla.com

"Interesting" is how surveyors describe *Top Chef* Ilan Hall's "quirky" "inventive" Eclectic in Downtown's renovated "historic Alexandria Hotel", where "gourmet" "Scottish-Jewish fusion" is the "oddly win ning combination" behind seasonal "small bites" such as the "highly touted bacon-wrapped matzo balls"; though some find the relatively "easy-on-the-wallet" menu and service "uneven", the "friendly hipster crowd" filling the communal tables amid "bare-bones industrial-type decor" agrees it's "an experience."

Gordon Biersch *Pub Food*
16 | 16 | 17 | $25

Burbank | 145 S. San Fernando Blvd. (bet. Angeleno & Olive Aves.) |
818-569-5240 | www.gordonbiersch.com

"If you can't find a true local microbrewery", this affordable chain link in Burbank is a "fine substitute", serving up "delicious" "craft beers" that "beat" the "decent" American pub grub (though all "hail" the "amazing" garlic fries); an "enjoyable happy-hour kinda place", it's not particularly "exciting", but the "relaxed" atmosphere is well suited to "kicking back with friends."

Gordon Ramsay ⓜ *French*
23 | 24 | 23 | $78

West Hollywood | The London West Hollywood |
1020 N. San Vicente Blvd. (Sunset Blvd.) | 310-358-7788 |
www.thelondonwesthollywood.com

"Prepare to be wowed" at this WeHo hot spot in the London hotel that "lives up to the buzz" by delivering "thought-provoking" French fare with Asian accents in a "classy space" that "sparkles" with "fabulous views" of the city; though the service might be "a touch pretentious" and some feel "it's lost its edge" since the "celebrity chef" sold his share (he remains as a consultant), most "discriminating palates" agree it's "worth the steep price."

Gram & Papas *American*
- | - | - | I

Downtown | 227 E. Ninth St. (Los Angeles St.) | 213-624-7272 |
www.gramandpapas.com

Serving weekday breakfast and lunch only, this wallet-friendly spot is the occasional home to chef Ludo Lefebvre's LudoBites, one of the hot test tickets in town; when Ludo's not in the kitchen, other chefs (with experience that includes stints with Rick Bayless, Todd English and

	FOOD	DECOR	SERVICE	COST

Tim Goodell) churn out burgers and braised short ribs, making this American one more reason to head Downtown.

Grand Lux Cafe *Eclectic*

19 | 19 | 19 | $30

Beverly Hills | Beverly Ctr. | 121 N. La Cienega Blvd. (bet. Beverly Blvd. & 3rd St.) | 310-855-1122 | www.grandluxcafe.com

Offering "pages and pages of options", this Beverly Center "classier counterpart" to the Cheesecake Factory serves "nicely done" Eclectic dishes in a "loud", somewhat "over-the-top" "high-ceilinged" setting inspired by European grand cafes; portions are as "ridiculously large" as the original's (but a bit "more expensive"), so there's still "no room" for the "decadent" desserts.

Great Greek *Greek*

20 | 15 | 20 | $30

Sherman Oaks | 13362 Ventura Blvd. (bet. Dixie Canyon & Nagle Aves.) | 818-905-5250 | www.greatgreek.com

It's a "rollicking good" time at this reasonably priced Sherman Oaks Greek where an "upbeat" staff dishes out "ginormous portions" of "authentic grub" in an environment known for "loud" live music and "customers dancing around" "like Zorba"; while perhaps not so "great" for those who "like to hear their dinner partner", for those "in the mood", it delivers "all-day grins."

Greenblatt's Deli & Fine Wines ● *Deli*

19 | 10 | 17 | $23

Hollywood | 8017 Sunset Blvd. (Laurel Ave.) | 323-656-0606 | www.greenblattsdeli.com

Deli mavens "chow down" at this Hollywood "favorite" that dishes out "old standards" including "skyscraper" sandwiches and "matzo-ball soup that would make a grandmother jealous"; sure, the decor has grown "tired" over the "decades", but "hustling", "friendly service" and cheap corkage (with bottles from the attached wine store) make it "heaven" for those seeking a "value" or some "late-night" Jewish soul-food "staples" (it's open till 2 AM).

Green Field Churrascaria *Brazilian*

19 | 16 | 22 | $35

Long Beach | 5305 E. PCH (Anaheim St.) | 562-597-0906
West Covina | 381 N. Azusa Ave. (bet. Rowland & Workman Aves.) | 626-966-2300
www.greenfieldchurrascaria.com

"Stuff yourself silly" at this "carnivore's delight" duo in Long Beach and West Covina where "handsome gauchos" slice a "big selection" (e.g. beef, pork, chicken, lamb, rabbit) of "all-you-can-eat" Brazilian grilled meats directly at the table, making for a "lazy glutton's paradise"; though it's "not the most luxurious" setting, the cuts are "juicy and tender" and the "fixed price" is right, plus there's a "salad bar too, but who cares."

Green Street Restaurant *American*

22 | 17 | 20 | $25

Pasadena | 146 Shoppers Ln. (Cordova St.) | 626-577-7170 | www.greenstreetrestaurant.com

This "casual" "Pasadena fixture" is a neighborhood "favorite" for "light, fresh" American "comfort food" for breakfast, lunch or dinner – such as a "salad Dianne worthy of its fame" and zucchini bread that's "better than dessert"; tack on a sunny patio and "reasonable" prices and it's naturally "perfect for families" and "ladies who lunch."

Green Street Tavern *Californian/European* | 24 | 20 | 22 | $39

Pasadena | 69 W. Green St. (bet. De Lacey & Fair Oaks Aves.) | 626-229-9961 | www.greenstreettavern.net

Located "off the beaten path in Old Town Pasadena", this "small", "cozy" Californian "aims to please" with a "creative" menu of locally sourced fare with European touches delivered by "friendly" servers specializing in "personal attention"; mix in a "noisy" ambiance and "intimate" setting with earthy colors and warm woods for a "pleasantly surprising" package that comes at "reasonable prices."

Griddle Cafe, The *American* | 23 | 12 | 16 | $18

Hollywood | 7916 Sunset Blvd. (bet. Fairfax & Hayworth Aves.) | 323-874-0377 | www.thegriddlecafe.com

Pancakes "twice the size of your head" and "rich" "French-press coffee" lead a "first-class" lineup of "decadent" breakfasts and lunches at this "easy-on-the-wallet" Hollywood "hole-in-the-wall", where "hearty" American fare attracts "lines a block long on weekends"; though the space is "noisy", "you don't come for the ambiance or service", but the "funky" spot filled with "hipsters", "celebs in their pj's" and "out-of-towners" makes for "good people-watching."

Grilled Cheese Truck *American* | - | - | - | I

Location varies; see website | www.grilledcheesetruck.com

Along with Kogi, one of the most popular of the endless wave of food trucks is this free-wheeler serving gooey creations including a "grilled sammy with Southern mac 'n' cheese, house-smoked BBQ pork and caramelized onions" and a version made with "Brie, brown-butter apples and fresh herbs"; those who hunger for even more trick up their sandwiches with bacon, crust them with Parmesan and order sides of tomato soup, bread and butter pickles and Tater Tots.

Grill on Hollywood, The *American* | 22 | 19 | 23 | $47

Hollywood | Hollywood & Highland Ctr. | 6801 Hollywood Blvd. (Highland Ave.) | 323-856-5530

Grill on the Alley Westlake, The *American*

Thousand Oaks | Promenade at Westlake | 120 E. Promenade Way (bet. Lakeview Canyon Rd. & Westlake Blvd.) | 805-418-1760 | www.thegrill.com

Hollywood & Highland habitués hit this "old-school" American near the Kodak theater (with a Westlake Village sibling) for "nourishing, satisfying" fare of "quality and quantity" in a menu of pricey but "reliable grill offerings"; the atmosphere is "less frenzied" than at the "movie-crowd" original Grill on the Alley, and most "hardly remember they are in a mall" as the "servers do it like it should be done."

Z Grill on the Alley, The ● *American* | 25 | 22 | 26 | $58

Beverly Hills | 9560 Dayton Way (bet. Camden & Rodeo Drs.) | 310-276-0615 | www.thegrill.com

A "true classic" that sparked a national chain, this Beverly Hills "institution" earns kudos as a "first-rate", "old-fashioned" American where "it's a win no matter what you choose" including "mouthwatering" cuts of steak and "fresh seafood", all delivered by "polished servers" (many "have been there for years"); the "East Coast-retro" decor is "clubby", if also "testosterone"-laden, luring in

	FOOD	DECOR	SERVICE	COST

"agents, lawyers and execs" bearing "big wallets" to "power lunch" with their celebrity clients.

Grub *American*

| 22 | 16 | 21 | $23 |

Hollywood | 911 N. Seward St. (bet. Romaine St. & Willoughby Ave.) | 323-461-3663 | www.grub-la.com

"Bounteous" portions of "standout" American "favorites" that taste "like mom's cooking" and don't cost a bundle make this "cute", "funky" bungalow a Hollywood go-to all day long from brunch and "working lunches" through dinner; with "friendly owners and servers" giving a "warm, informal welcome" and the outdoor patio adorned with "lots of plants", the whole package is so "quaint" and "unpretentious" it "feels like it doesn't belong in LA."

Guelaguetza *Mexican*

| 21 | 13 | 19 | $20 |

Huntington Park | 2560 E. Gage Ave. (bet. Pacific Blvd. & Rugby Ave.) | 323-277-9899
Koreatown | 3014 W. Olympic Blvd. (Normandie Ave.) | 213-427-0608
Koreatown | 3337½ W. Eighth St. (Irolo St.) | 213-427-0601
Lynwood | 11215 Long Beach Blvd. (Beechwood Ave.) | 310-884-9234
www.guelaguetzarestaurante.com

"Viva Mexico!" cheer champions of this clutch of "reasonably priced" eateries where "authentic" black mole that "can't be beat" headlines a "massive, traditional" Oaxacan menu; "cavernous" digs can "feel like a mall" and service is "sometimes slow", but at some locations live music serenading "lots of families and groups" amps up the "charm."

Guido's *Italian*

| 20 | 19 | 23 | $41 |

Malibu | 3874 Cross Creek Rd. (PCH) | 310-456-1979 | www.guidosmalibu.com
West LA | 11980 Santa Monica Blvd. (Bundy Dr.) | 310-820-6649 | www.guidosla.com

"They've been doing it right for years" at these "standby" Italian siblings where staffers "treat you like honored family" as they ferry "classic", definitely "not *nuovo*" dishes; the West LA room is "dark" and "clubby" with "waiters in tuxedos" and "spacious red booths", while the light-filled Malibu locale feels more like "a scene from *Miami Vice*."

Gulfstream *American/Seafood*

| 21 | 20 | 21 | $40 |

Century City | Westfield Century City Shopping Ctr. | 10250 Santa Monica Blvd. (bet. Ave. of the Stars & Century Park W.) | 310-553-3636 | www.hillstone.com

"Virtually always crowded", this "reliable" "Houston's cousin" in Century City caters to a "mostly corporate" clientele with "fresh", "straightforward" American seafood dishes and "cheery" service set off by "classy", "modern" decor; it can be "noisy", but "frosty martinis" and other "killer cocktails" add another boost, making it an "all-around winner."

Gumbo Pot *Cajun*

| 20 | 6 | 14 | $15 |

Fairfax | Farmers Mkt. | 6333 W. Third St. (Fairfax Ave.) | 323-933-0358 | www.thegumbopotla.com

It "sure ain't fancy", but Southern supporters say the "thoroughly enjoyable gumbo", "addictive" shrimp po' boys and beignets at this "friendly" "food stall" in the Fairfax Farmers Market are the "real

Cajun thing"; while spice-lovers lobby for more "punch", "pricewise you can't beat it", so most agree it's a "must" for a "N'Awlins"-style "feast."

Gus's BBQ *BBQ*
20 | 18 | 20 | $26

South Pasadena | 808 Fair Oaks Ave. (bet. Hope & Mission Sts.) | 626-799-3251 | www.gussbbq.com

"Melt-in-your-mouth BBQ" and "sinful" sides make for a "hearty" "finger-lickin'" meal at this affordable South Pasadena classic in business since 1946 and "brought back in fine style" recently after a "cool" nostalgic "makeover"; detractors say it's "not the same" as it used to be, but service is "attentive" and in this "sleepy" neighborhood the "lively crowds" speak for themselves.

Gyenari Korean BBQ & Lounge *Korean*
20 | 23 | 20 | $38

Culver City | 9540 Washington Blvd. (Culver Blvd.) | 310-838-3131 | www.gyenari.com

"Korean BBQ with style" lures grill-it-yourself fans to this "upscale", "modern" midpriced spot in Culver City where "high-quality" meats in "tasty" marinades plus "plentiful" sides are refilled by "engaging" servers; critics claim it's "not the most authentic", but defenders say the "loungey" atmosphere and "awesome drinks" make it a "most enjoyable" experience.

Gyu-Kaku *Japanese*
20 | 17 | 18 | $34

Beverly Hills | 163 N. La Cienega Blvd. (Clifton Way) | 310-659-5760
West LA | 10925 W. Pico Blvd. (bet. Veteran Ave. & Westwood Blvd.) | 310-234-8641
Torrance | Cross Road Plaza | 24631 Crenshaw Blvd. (Skypark Dr.) | 310-325-1437
Pasadena | 70 W. Green St. (De Lacey Ave.) | 626-405-4842
Canoga Park | Westfield Topanga Ctr. | 6600 Topanga Canyon Blvd. (Victory Blvd.) | 818-888-4030
Sherman Oaks | 14457 Ventura Blvd. (Van Nuys Blvd.) | 818-501-5400
www.gyu-kaku.com

"Do-it-yourself grilling" "at your table" is a "novel", "festive" experience – especially for "groups" and "families with young kids" – at this yakiniku chain; prices are basically moderate but "bills can creep up" and some say "portions are pee-wee", so savvy surveyors suggest hitting "happy hour" for better value.

Hall, The Ⓜ *French*
▽ 21 | 23 | 18 | $52

West Hollywood | Palihouse | 8465 Holloway Dr. (bet. Hacienda Pl. & La Cienega Blvd.) | 323-656-4020 | www.thehallbrasserie.com

Exuding "European cool", this French brasserie inside WeHo's Palihouse hotel appeals to a "chill LA" crowd with its "hip lounge" and "beautiful interior courtyard" that's "perfect on warm nights" or for "Sunday brunch"; the plates are somewhat pricey, but service is generally "attentive", leading most to agree it's a "lovely place to meet up with friends"; P.S. a post-Survey chef change is not reflected in the Food score.

Hal's Bar & Grill *American*
21 | 20 | 20 | $37

Venice | 1349 Abbot Kinney Blvd. (California Ave.) | 310-396-3105 | www.halsbarandgrill.com

This "good old" "favorite" remains the "quintessential Venice" scene "after all these years", playing host to a "boho" crowd of "local artists and their art dealers" who gather as much for "hanging out at the bar" as for the "reliable" American fare (including the "famous turkey burger"); given the frequent "live music" downstairs, the more "insulated" "upstairs room" works better for "conversation", but despite "loud" acoustics it's "packed every night" with loyalists who agree things "wouldn't be the same without it."

–	–	–	M

Hamakaze *Japanese*

Marina del Rey | 13327 W. Washington Blvd. (Glencoe Ave.) | 310-822-9900
Chef Nick Nishi (ex Chez Mélange, Michi) "practices his art" at this Japanese boîte in Marina del Rey, turning out "creatively prepared" yet basically "authentic" fin fare and izakaya items; though "modest", the velvet-upholstered, red-chandeliered setting is more plush than the typical sushi specialist, and "early-bird bento boxes are a deal", so converts claim "this is definitely the place" for "traditional" Nipponese.

27	17	22	$64

Z Hamasaku Ⓢ *Japanese*

West LA | 11043 Santa Monica Blvd. (Sepulveda Blvd.) | 310-479-7636 | www.hamasakula.com
"No words can describe the ecstasy" say afishionados of this "*très* hip" West LA Japanese that may "not be for sushi purists" but is prized nonetheless for "ceaselessly inventive", "fantastic rolls" that are "named after celebrities"; though inhabiting somewhat "plain" digs, it's "ridiculously expensive", but "fabulous" co-owner Toshi is often on hand to "make everyone" (including lots of "stars") "feel welcome", so "it's worth every dollar."

22	14	18	$43

Hama Sushi *Japanese*

Venice | 213 Windward Ave. (Main St.) | 310-396-8783 | www.hamasushi.com
"Locals" "line" up to feast on "straight-ahead sushi", rolls and a menu of cooked Japanese standards in this somewhat "sparse" ocean-adjacent Venice locale with a "kitschy" "surfer vibe" and an outdoor patio that's a favorite "on summer nights"; detractors say prices are "steep" but "happy-hour deals" (twice daily) add value, so even if it's "nothing fancy" it remains a "solid" standby.

18	16	18	$24

Hamburger Hamlet *American*

West Hollywood | 9201 Sunset Blvd. (Doheny Dr.) | 310-278-4924
Pasadena | 214 S. Lake Ave. (bet. Cordova St. & Del Mar Blvds.) | 626-449-8520
Sherman Oaks | 4419 Van Nuys Blvd. (Ventura Blvd.) | 818-784-1183
www.hamletrestaurants.com
Combining "familiar, comforting" "coffee-shop" fare (burgers, salads, "famous" lobster bisque) with "warm, welcoming" service, this "dependable" chain of "old standbys" still satisfies longtime loyalists; critics counter that they're a "bit shopworn", but prices are "modest" and the atmosphere is "easy and comfortable", so despite menu tweaks and multiple name changes, most are glad they just "keep going and going."

14	13	16	$22

Hamburger Mary's ◑ *Diner*

West Hollywood | 8288 Santa Monica Blvd. (Sweetzer Ave.) | 323-654-3800 | www.hamburgermarysweho.com
It's "crazy (in a good way)" say steadfast supporters of this "funky" WeHo staple where the affordable menu "is not the main attraction" as "cute waiters" sling "large drinks" and "your basic crowd-pleasing

American standards" to a "young, gay-friendly" clientele; if all the "people-watching" isn't enough, frequent events like karaoke night and "drag-queen bingo" provide plenty of "festive entertainment."

Hampton's ☒ *Californian* ▽ 21 | 24 | 22 | $58

Westlake Village | Four Seasons Westlake Vill. | 2 Dole Dr. (bet. Via Colinas & Via Rocas) | 818-575-3000 | www.fourseasons.com

With a "bewitching view" over the gardens and waterfalls, "gushing service" and an "elegant" Californian menu, allies attest this Westlake Villager at the Four Seasons proves a "wonderful" option for "celebratory occasions"; the seafood buffet on Friday evenings is "nirvana" and Sunday brunch is "fit for a king", so naturally, it's "expensive."

Hard Rock Cafe *American* 13 | 20 | 15 | $27

Universal City | Universal CityWalk | 1000 Universal Studios Blvd. (off Rte. 101) | 818-622-7625 | www.hardrock.com

"Rock memorabilia" is the claim to fame of this "noisy", "nostalgic", music-driven American chain link in Universal CityWalk, and if the food doesn't exactly rock, it's fine for "enjoying a burger and a beer"; but those who deem the concept "so yesterday" feel it may be best left to "headbangers", "tourists" and youngsters who "love" those T-shirts.

Harold & Belle's *Creole* 24 | 16 | 22 | $35

Mid-City | 2920 W. Jefferson Blvd. (bet. 9th & 10th Aves.) | 323-735-3376 | www.haroldandbellesrestaurant.com

Partisans praise "down-home cooking" that's "the next-best thing" to New Orleans at this warm, homey Mid-City Creole "institution" that's one of the "nicer places in the area"; "huge portions" are "more than one person can (or should) eat", so "take home a doggy bag and forget the doggy", but "plan ahead", or you'll "stand and wait for a table" on weekends when it's "crowded."

Hash & High *American* - | - | - | M

Venice | Hotel Erwin | 1697 Pacific Ave. (17th Ave.) | 310-452-1111 | www.jdvhotels.com/hotels/erwin

Two separate venues inside Venice's ultramodern Hotel Erwin, Hash is a "ground-floor" cafe/bistro where Gordon Ramsay alum Micah Fields oversees an American menu, while High is a "cool" rooftop bar with ocean views; the few reviewers who've been say it's a "wonderful concept" but it's still working on the "execution."

☑ Hatfield's *American* 27 | 24 | 26 | $66

Melrose | 6703 Melrose Ave. (Citrus Ave.) | 323-935-2977 | www.hatfieldsrestaurant.com

"Better than ever" swoon supporters of this "jewel in the crown" of LA eateries, where husband-and-wife team Quinn and Karen Hatfield are "outdoing themselves" with "meticulous", "pricey" American cuisine (including a "fabulous" chef's tasting menu) in a new, "expansive" and "prettier" setting on Melrose (formerly Michel Richard's Citrus); factor in "impeccable" service and most "can't wait to go back."

Havana Mania *Cuban* - | - | - | M

Redondo Beach | 3615 Inglewood Ave. (Manhattan Beach Blvd.) | 310-725-9075 | www.havanamania.com

Just off the Inglewood exit of the 405, this Redondo Beach mini-mall Cuban offers a full bar that specializes in mojitos and Cuba libres to

	FOOD	DECOR	SERVICE	COST

wash down a full menu of Havana favorites; the setting's both relaxed and upscale, and there's live music Friday–Sunday nights.

Hayakawa M *Japanese*
∇ 28 | 17 | 25 | $52

Covina | 750 Terrado Plaza (bet. Citrus & Workman Aves.) | 626-332-8288
With "outstanding sashimi" and an omakase that acolytes swear "comes close to Nobu's" (chef Kazuhiko Hayakawa worked at Matsuhisa) at a "much more reasonable cost", this Covina Japanese is a "hidden jewel"; servers are "warm and friendly" without a hint of "attitude", so it all adds up to "an incredible find" surveyers deem "worthy of support."

Henry's Hat *American*
∇ 18 | 16 | 20 | $24

Universal City | 3413 Cahuenga Blvd. W. (Universal Studios Blvd.) | 323-512-2500 | www.henrys-hat.com
"Tasty" American "comfort food" gives a "gourmet" edge to "game nights" at this Universal City hang (by the team behind Luna Park), where multiple flat-screens and "excellent drinks" ("bottomless" mimosas with weekend brunch) foster an "upscale sports bar" vibe; a wide selection of board games, Wii and homey furnishings inspire settling in and "enjoying the company" of friends.

Heroes and Legends *Pub Food*
17 | 16 | 17 | $21

Claremont | 131 N. Yale Ave. (bet. 1st & 2nd Sts.) | 909-621-6712
"Burgers and such" in "abundant" portions at the right price lure "lively" crowds to this "college-town pub" in Claremont; the casual atmosphere – "toss your peanut shells on the floor" – is fueled by "dozens of brews" on tap, so even if "waits can be ridiculous", most "enjoy" the Southland's "answer to Boston's *Cheers*."

Hideout at the
Hollywood Heights Hotel *American*
- | - | - | M

Hollywood | Hollywood Heights Hotel | 2005 N. Highland Ave. (Franklin Ave.) | 323-876-8600 | www.hollywoodheightshotel.com
A "retro-cool" setting inside the mod-"chic" Hollywood Heights Hotel forms just the right backdrop for "delicious", moderately priced American comfort-food classics like mac 'n' cheese and roasted chicken; amid the stylized surroundings, "unpretentious, amiable" bartenders and servers create an "easy, uncontrived" mood, so that the few surveyors who've weighed in say it's just what "LA needed."

Hide Sushi M⊖ *Japanese*
24 | 10 | 17 | $29

West LA | 2040 Sawtelle Blvd. (bet. La Grange & Mississippi Aves.) | 310-477-7242
"Best bang for your sushi buck" assess value-hounds, who swear by the "substantial" servings and "bargain" prices at this "cash-only" "perennially" "popular" Japanese in West LA; cuts are "authentic" but "basic", so "don't expect paper-thin hamachi with jalapeño slices" or "fancy rolls", but even after "long waits" for "cramped seating" and "zero decor", it might "make you wonder why you go to the more expensive places."

Hirosuke *Japanese*
19 | 12 | 19 | $33

Encino | Plaza de Oro | 17237 Ventura Blvd. (Louise Ave.) | 818-788-7548
"Friendly and reliable", this "pleasant" midpriced Encino Japanese sates "neighborhood" cravings for "fresh fish" and "creative" "specialty rolls"; though the basic decor could use "an update", and "dis-

	FOOD	DECOR	SERVICE	COST

appointed" surveyors sigh it "used to be better", defenders deem it still a "favorite."

Hirozen ⊠ *Japanese*   26 | 13 | 21 | $40

Beverly Boulevard | 8385 Beverly Blvd. (bet. Kings Rd. & Orlando Ave.) | West Hollywood | 323-653-0470 | www.hirozen.com

An "unsung gem", this Beverly Boulevard Japanese is far "less trendy" than more fashionable hot spots, while it "stuns" afishionados with "sublime" sushi, "extraordinary specials" and a "reasonably priced omakase"; the decor may be "minimal", but since prices "won't burn a hole in your wallet" and there's "no attitude", the consensus is it "will not let you down."

Holdren's Steaks & Seafood *Steak*   20 | 19 | 20 | $52

Thousand Oaks | 1714 Newbury Rd. (bet. Hillcrest Dr. & Ventu Park Rds.) | 805-498-1314 | www.holdrens.com

This duo of "club-style" steakhouses in Thousand Oaks and Santa Barbara pleases partisans with "terrific" cuts of meat – including the "amazing cowboy rib-eye"– and a "cozy bar atmosphere"; though prices are "reasonable", dissenters say they're "underperforming" and "don't live up to their reputation."

Hole in the Wall Burger Joint ⊠⊅ *Burgers* 21 | 8 | 17 | $15

West LA | 11058 Santa Monica Blvd. (Bentley Ave.) | 310-312-7013 | www.holeinthewallburgerjoint.com

"Buns down", "full-flavored" burgers at this "well-hidden" West LA locale (behind Winchell's Donuts) stand out as "some of the juiciest" around; the surroundings are basic, "parking can be a big pain" and wallet-watchers warn that it's "a bit overpriced for what's basically a hamburger stand", but given the variety of "housemade sauces" and "add-ons" to doctor things up, most enthusiastically agree that it's a "find."

Holy Cow Indian Express *Indian*   ▽ 22 | 5 | 17 | $15

Third Street | 8474 W. Third St. (La Cienega Blvd.) | 323-852-8900 | www.holycowindianexpress.com

"Quick Indian fixes" take a "healthy" turn at this reasonably priced "neighborhood" spot on Third Street where "fresh, bright flavors" are ghee-free and vegan-friendly; perhaps the "spartan decor needs aesthetic help", but it fills the bill for "fast" meals or "takeout."

Honda-Ya ● *Japanese*   22 | 16 | 17 | $31

Little Tokyo | Mitsuwa Shopping Ctr. | 333 S. Alameda St. (3rd St.) | 213-625-1184

You've "gotta appreciate the late-night hours" making it easy to sample from an assortment of "authentic" little plates including yakitori, sushi and other "Japanese pub" grub at this hip "hangout" in Little Tokyo; cost-conscious critics warn that the tab "can add up" but "lines out front are a telling sign" of their appeal.

Hop Li *Chinese*   19 | 11 | 16 | $22

Chinatown | 526 Alpine St. (Hill St.) | 213-680-3939
Pico-Robertson | 10974 W. Pico Blvd. (Veteran Ave.) | 310-441-3708
West LA | 11901 Santa Monica Blvd. (Armacost Ave.) | 310-268-2463

(continued)

Hop Li

Arcadia | 855 S. Baldwin Ave. (bet. Fairview Ave. & Huntington Dr.) | 626-445-3188
www.hoplirestaurant.com

"Not hip, never trendy", this "classic Chinese" quartet instead offers "lots of value" in its "abundant portions" of "traditional" fare ideal "for sharing" with the "family" or "big groups"; "you don't go for the decor" (though a "recent remodel" left the Chinatown digs "much improved"), and even if somewhat "brisk" service impedes "leisurely" dining, it's "always noisy and crowded."

Hop Woo *Chinese*

19 | 8 | 14 | $22

Chinatown | 845 N. Broadway (bet. Alpine & College Sts.) | 213-617-3038 ◐
West LA | 11110 W. Olympic Blvd. (Sepulveda Blvd.) | 310-575-3668
Alhambra | 1 W. Main St. (Garfield Ave.) | 626-289-7938 ◐
www.hopwoo.com

This separately owned Chinese trio is "treasured" for its "large menu" of "close-to-authentic" "traditional Cantonese" dishes with a seafood emphasis; basic digs that lead some to wonder "who came up with the decor" and service that's a middling "fine" lead some to "prefer take-out", but "huge portions" help compensate.

NEW House Café *Eclectic*

21 | 16 | 19 | $38

Beverly Boulevard | 8114 Beverly Blvd. (Crescent Heights Blvd.) | 323-655-5553 | www.housecafe.com

As a "new local hangout", this "casual" Beverly Boulevard bistro owned by Bruce Marder (Capo, Cora's) proves a "pleasant" "addition to the neighborhood" with a "solid" menu of "high-quality", "reasonably priced" Eclectic dishes (pasta, tacos, lamb couscous) served under a wood-beamed ceiling; service "can't be faulted" and the list of wines by the glass is "impressive", so the majority "wants to go back."

House of Blues Ⓜ *Southern*

16 | 20 | 16 | $34

West Hollywood | 8430 Sunset Blvd. (Olive Dr.) | 323-848-5100 | www.houseofblues.com

Sunday's "gospel brunch is the way to go" at this "rustic" "Southern-style" Sunset Strip chain link with a "bluesy, jazzy" feel and frequent "fabulous" music by big touring acts; the moderately priced soul food plays "second fiddle", so "keep it basic" when you order, or just "stick with the booze and bands."

Ⓩ Houston's *American*

22 | 20 | 22 | $37

Century City | Westfield Century City Shopping Ctr. | 10250 Santa Monica Blvd. (bet. Ave. of the Stars & Century Park W.) | 310-557-1285
Santa Monica | 202 Wilshire Blvd. (2nd St.) | 310-576-7558
Manhattan Beach | 1550-A Rosecrans Ave. (bet. Aviation & Sepulveda Blvds.) | 310-643-7211
Pasadena | 320 S. Arroyo Pkwy. (Del Mar Blvd.) | 626-577-6001
www.hillstone.com

The "crème de la crème" of "grill chains", this "stylish, adult" place delivers "properly done", midpriced American eats in a "fern bar" setting with a "happening" after-work scene; "well-informed, efficient" servers add to the "welcoming" vibe, but "long" weekend waits are a drawback.

	FOOD	DECOR	SERVICE	COST

Huckleberry Café & Bakery Ⓜ American   22 | 14 | 15 | $21

Santa Monica | 1014 Wilshire Blvd. (bet. 10th & 11th Sts.) | 310-451-2311 | www.huckleberrycafe.com

"How sweet (and savory) it is" swoon Santa Monicans smitten with chef-owner Zoe Nathan's "masterpiece" pastries and "beautiful" American cafe creations – all oozing "sustainable organic-ness"; critics complain it's "a tad pricey" and the "cafeteria-style" ordering system followed by a frantic table-hunt is a major "headache", especially during "madhouse brunch" hours, but "Huckleberry friends" agree that it's an "absolute must-go."

NEW Hudson, The American   - | - | - | I

West Hollywood | 1114 N. Crescent Heights Blvd. (Santa Monica Blvd.) | 323-654-6686 | www.thehudsonla.com

It's "always crowded" at this WeHo spot that's equal parts eatery and watering hole, matching up American comfort food with specialty cocktails, beers on tap and a California-strong wine list; moody lighting, deep booths and plenty of fresh air via a large patio – not to mention a 50-ft. tree in the dining room – all inspire lingering even when it's "packed."

Hudson House ❶ Pub Food   ▽ 23 | 18 | 18 | $24

Redondo Beach | 514 N. PCH (Beryl St.) | 310-798-9183 | www.hudsonhousebar.com

"Excellent gastropub" fare combines "quality and creativity" at this affordable Redondo Beach "hangout" where "locals" soak up the "relaxed-but-hip vibe"; the drinks menu tempts with "so many choices for beer and cocktails" and "they serve food late into the night", so backers insist "you'll want to return again and again."

Hugo's Californian   20 | 13 | 18 | $24

West Hollywood | 8401 Santa Monica Blvd. (bet. Kings Rd. & Orlando Ave.) | 323-654-3993

Studio City | 12851 Riverside Dr. (Coldwater Canyon Ave.) | 818-761-8985 | www.hugosrestaurant.com

"Vegetarians, vegans and omnivores" meet at these WeHo and Studio City cafe twins, where the "something-for-everyone" menu of Cal-New American fare is "on the healthy tip", including smoothies, "flavorful" salads that "win over even the most greens-resistant" types and an "astounding variety of teas"; the "unpretentious" vibe is "hippie-ish coffee shop", and the crowd is dotted with "celebs" and other "beautiful boys and girls" who "filter in post-clubbing" for their recovery brunch.

Hungry Cat, The Seafood   24 | 17 | 20 | $47

Hollywood | 1535 N. Vine St. (bet. Selma Ave. & Sunset Blvd.) | 323-462-2155 | www.thehungrycat.com

Patrons "purr" over the "raw-bar delights" and "maybe the best burger in town" (at a seafood place – "who'da thunk") "pleasantly" served at this "pricey" duo from chef-owner David Lentz (Suzanne Goin's husband); the Hollywood outpost has a "hip" "industrial" look while Santa Barbara sports pictures of cats, and at both cocktail "wizardry" with "niche liquors" and "California fruits" provides an additional boost, so it's "still hard to get in."

| | FOOD | DECOR | SERVICE | COST |

Hurry Curry of Tokyo *Japanese*
| | 18 | 12 | 15 | $18 |

West LA | 2131 Sawtelle Blvd. (bet. Mississippi Ave. & Olympic Blvd.) | 310-473-1640 | www.hurrycurryoftokyo.com

"Weekly fixes" keep "withdrawals" at bay for spice-hounds "addicted" to the "traditional Japanese" "comfort food" at this "unassuming" West LA curry house held dear by "UCLA students" and workers looking for a "quick biz lunch"; the decor is on the plain side, but tabs are "reasonable" and the service has gotten even "speedier."

Hu's Szechwan *Chinese*
| | 22 | 7 | 19 | $19 |

Palms | 10450 National Blvd. (bet. Motor & Overland Aves.) | 310-837-0252 | www.husrestaurant.com

After more than 30 years, Palms diners still turn to this "mainstay" for "heaping portions" of Sichuan-style Chinese classics "for cheap"; it's "not much to look at" and "parking can be a problem", but "attentive service" adds to the reasons why it's "always crowded" with locals who consider it a "go-to."

i Cugini *Italian/Seafood*
| | 21 | 21 | 21 | $43 |

Santa Monica | 1501 Ocean Ave. (B'way) | 310-451-4595 | www.icugini.com

"Fine seafood" selections top a "rock-solid" "fairly priced" menu at this "upscale" oceanside Santa Monica Italian resembling a grand cafe with an "outstanding patio" for taking in "sunset views over the beach"; waiters pour on the "charm", and the Sunday jazz brunch buffet is a "nice tradition", so even if some find it "ho-hum", most agree it "satisfies."

Il Buco *Italian*
| | 22 | 16 | 23 | $38 |

Beverly Hills | 107 N. Robertson Blvd. (Wilshire Blvd.) | 310-657-1345 | www.giacominodrago.com

The "quiet cousin in the Drago" family, this "likable", "fairly priced" Italian in Beverly Hills keeps "locals" loyal with the likes of "delicious" thin-crust pizza and "done-just-right" pasta proffered by an "accommodating", "gracious" staff; the "informal" "neighborhood" setting is conversation-friendly, and it all adds up to an "eminently enjoyable" experience.

Il Capriccio di Carlo
Wood Fire Pizzeria *Italian*
| | 23 | 16 | 22 | $27 |

Los Feliz | 4518 Hollywood Blvd. (Hillhurst Ave.) | 323-644-9760 | www.carlopizzeria.com

Il Capriccio on Vermont *Italian*
Los Feliz | 1757 N. Vermont Ave. (bet. Kingswell & Melbourne Aves.) | 323-662-5900 | www.ilcapriccioonvermont.com

There's "homestyle flavor in everything they serve" at this Los Feliz "joint" "crowded" with "neighborhood" types jonesing for "perfect pastas" and "tasty" sauces'; "friendly" servers complete the "unpretentious" vibe and tabs are "affordable" to boot, making it a "favorite" choice for a "simple evening out"; the Hollywood Boulevard pizzeria has a wood-burning brick oven and is separately owned.

Il Chianti *Italian*
| | ∇ 21 | 15 | 16 | $36 |

Lomita | 24503 Narbonne Ave. (Lomita Blvd.) | 310-325-5000 | www.il-chianti.com

"Japanese flair and nuances" provide a "fresh, unique" twist to "delicious", "never-heavy" Italian cuisine at this unexpected Lomita offshoot of a Nipponese chain; the white-walled surroundings have modern appeal, so South Bay supporters say "it's definitely a keeper."

☑ Il Cielo *Italian*

22 | 26 | 24 | $55

Beverly Hills | 9018 Burton Way (bet. Almont & Wetherly Drs.) | 310-276-9990 | www.ilcielo.com

So "astonishingly beautiful" "you'll think you've stepped onto a movie set", this Beverly Hills Italian is relished by "romantics" for its "delightful outdoor space", which may be the "best" locale in the city for saying "I love you or I'm sorry", especially "at night when it's all lit up" with twinkle lights; "accommodating" staff and owners "nurture a warm atmosphere", and the cuisine, while "not cheap", is "consistent", making it a "special place for a special evening."

Il Fornaio *Italian*

21 | 20 | 20 | $36

Beverly Hills | 301 N. Beverly Dr. (Dayton Way) | 310-550-8330
Santa Monica | 1551 Ocean Ave. (Colorado Ave.) | 310-451-7800
Manhattan Beach | Manhattan Gateway Shopping Ctr. |
1800 Rosecrans Ave. (Aviation Blvd.) | 310-725-9555
Pasadena | One Colorado | 1 W. Colorado Blvd. (Fair Oaks Ave.) |
626-683-9797
www.ilfornaio.com

Loyalists "love the bread" and "creative" pastas at this "simple" but "civilized" Italian chain that "tries and often succeeds in serving authentic fare with monthly regional specials"; though some say service is "not consistent" and find the food "unremarkable", the "attractive" environs help support its "almost-gourmet prices."

Il Forno *Italian*

21 | 17 | 21 | $35

Santa Monica | 2901 Ocean Park Blvd. (bet. 29th & 30th Sts.) | 310-450-1241 | www.ilfornocaffe.com

This "neighborhood standby" in Santa Monica owes its "strong following" to "quality" Italian cooking and a "welcoming", "comfortable" atmosphere that's pleasing to "couples, kids and older folks"; with generally "decent" tabs to boot, it's a "dependable" "gem."

Il Forno Caldo ☑ *Italian*

21 | 20 | 22 | $34

Beverly Hills | 9705 Santa Monica Blvd. (Roxbury Dr.) | 310-777-0040 | www.ilfornocaldo.com

Proof that "good things" come in "small" packages, this "shoebox-sized" Italian in Beverly Hills draws a "repeat" crowd with "hearty" midpriced fare including "lunch sandwiches" that "make the whole workday worthwhile"; wine bottles displayed in racks complete the "quaint", "no-pretensions" setting, leading "local" loyalists to turn to it as a regular "hangout."

Il Grano ☑ *Italian*

26 | 20 | 23 | $57

West LA | 11359 Santa Monica Blvd. (Purdue Ave.) | 310-477-7886 | www.ilgrano.com

"Talented" young chef-owner Salvatore Marino demonstrates his "genius" with "dynamite" Italian "delicacies" – especially "innovative crudo and fish entrees" – at this "elegant", modern West LA dining room where "charming" service and "fabulous wines" complete the "first-rate" experience; "you do pay more" for this kind of "excellence", but even so, defenders declare that it's always "high on their list."

	FOOD	DECOR	SERVICE	COST

Il Moro *Italian* — 22 | 21 | 22 | $46

West LA | 11400 W. Olympic Blvd. (Purdue Ave.) | 310-575-3530 | www.ilmoro.com

"Genuine" pastas and grilled fare appeals to "business-lunchers" at this "expansive" "upscale" Northern Italian whose "hide-and-seek" location "in the bottom of an office tower" in West LA is offset by a "lovely" "landscaped patio" that will "make you forget" the "high-rise"; a "spread" of "gourmet apps" "free for the price of a drink" make for "outstanding" weekday happy hours, so most maintain that it's "terrific."

Il Pastaio *Italian* — 26 | 17 | 21 | $45

Beverly Hills | 400 N. Cañon Dr. (Brighton Way) | 310-205-5444 | www.giacominodrago.com

It's "always crowded" from "power lunches" through "nights to remember" at this "lively" Beverly Hills "hangout" – and "justifiably" so, given "exquisite pastas" and other "heavenly Italian food at down-to-earth prices" from chef-owner Giacomino Drago; "tightly packed tables" feel a bit like the "last row of coach", but staffers are "friendly" and "outdoor tables" offer a perfect perch for 90210 "people-watching", so it's "worth" contending with the "mob scene."

Il Piccolino 🗷 *Italian* — 22 | 16 | 20 | $56

West Hollywood | 350 N. Robertson Blvd. (Rosewood Ave.) | 310-659-2220 | www.ilpiccolinorestaurant.com

"Traditional" Italian cuisine has regulars going "back again and again" to this "inviting" WeHo ristorante where the owners "make everyone" – including "Hollywood movers and shakers" and "Los Angeles dignitaries" – "feel special"; prices are not for those "on a budget", but "beautiful" English-garden flora add to the "relaxing" environs.

Il Sole *Italian* — 23 | 18 | 21 | $62

West Hollywood | 8741 Sunset Blvd. (Sherbourne Dr.) | 310-657-1182

"Glimpses of Leo" and other "lurking celebrities" may be "the main draw" of this "trendy" WeHo trattoria, but "perfect pastas" and other "solid" offerings win plenty of praise from partisans; opinions split on staff attitudes ("warm" to "snooty") and it's "expensive", but for many, "rubbing elbows with the industry" is "worth it every time."

🗷 Il Tiramisù Ristorante & Bar Ⓜ *Italian* — 24 | 19 | 26 | $36

Sherman Oaks | 13705 Ventura Blvd. (Woodman Ave.) | 818-986-2640 | www.il-tiramisu.com

"Warm and welcoming" father-son owners "bend over backwards" to "treat guests with care" at this midpriced Sherman Oaks kitchen crafting "excellent" Northern Italian meals from "quality ingredients"; the white-tableclothed setting is "pleasant", leaving locals feeling awfully "lucky" to have it in the 'hood.

Il Tramezzino *Italian* — 19 | 11 | 17 | $19

Beverly Hills | 454 N. Cañon Dr. (Santa Monica Blvd.) | 310-273-0501
Studio City | 13031 Ventura Blvd. (bet. Coldwater Canyon Ave. & Valley Vista Blvd.) | 818-784-2244
Tarzana | 18636 Ventura Blvd. (Yolanda Ave.) | 818-996-8726
www.iltram.com

Fans say all "panini should aspire to be" like the "well-executed" sandwiches created at this affordable trio of "casual" cafes, which also do "fresh, tasty" salads; "lots of patio space" make them appealing places to "enjoy the day" or a "balmy evening."

India's Clay Oven *Indian*   ▽ 21 | 14 | 19 | $23

Beverly Boulevard | 7233 Beverly Blvd. (bet. Alta Vista Blvd. & Formosa Ave.) | 323-936-1000 | www.indiasoven.com

The Indian eats are "as good as it gets outside of Artesia" believe boosters of this Beverly Boulevard spot; despite some authentic subcontinental decorations, the surroundings come off as "mediocre", but "family-friendly prices" compensate.

India's Oven at Wilshire *Indian*   ▽ 21 | 12 | 18 | $25

West LA | West Wilshire Medical Bldg. | 11645 Wilshire Blvd., 2nd fl. (Barry Ave.) | 310-207-5522 | www.indiasovenwilshire.com

"One of the best Indians on the Westside" swear supporters of this stalwart, which has new decor and a new chef – both of which may explain why it's "getting more crowded"; buffet-hounds needn't fear, however: the "reasonably priced lunch" spread is still available.

India's Tandoori *Indian*   21 | 13 | 20 | $20

Mid-Wilshire | 5468 Wilshire Blvd. (bet. Cochran & Dunsmuir Aves.) | 323-936-2050 | www.indiastandoori.net
Hawthorne | 4850 W. Rosecrans Ave. (bet. Inglewood & Shoup Aves.) | 310-675-5533 | www.indiastandoorilax.net
West LA | 11819 Wilshire Blvd. (Granville Ave.) | 310-268-9100 | www.indias-tandoori.com
Tarzana | Windsor Ctr. | 19006 Ventura Blvd. (Donna Ave.) | 818-342-9100
Spice-hounds turn to this string of "simple-looking" spots for "well-executed, traditional Indian dishes"; the settings may "lack character", but "attentive service more than makes up" for it, and "reasonable" checks allow it to be a "regular" "en-route stop."

Indo Cafe *Indonesian*   ▽ 20 | 15 | 20 | $24

Palms | 10430 National Blvd. (bet. Mentone & Motor Aves.) | 310-815-1290
"From satay to rendang", the "spicy Indonesian" dishes are "the real thing" at this small, affordable Palms "delight" with an accommodating staff; renovated after a 2009 fire, the space now strikes some as suitable for "a nice, quiet date."

Indochine Vien *Vietnamese*   ▽ 16 | 15 | 19 | $25

Atwater Village | 3110 Glendale Blvd. (Glenhurst Ave.) | 323-667-9591 | www.indochinevien.com

"Big bowls of pho" are "standouts" at this Atwater Village Vietnamese that keeps things "sweet and simple" by sticking to a "small menu" of items "but preparing them well"; with a mod paint scheme and bamboo-lined walls, it exudes more style than the typical noodle house; P.S. "BYO beer and wine."

∅ Inn of the Seventh Ray *Californian*   21 | 26 | 21 | $44

Topanga | 128 Old Topanga Canyon Rd. (8 mi. south of Hwy. 101) | 310-455-1311 | www.innoftheseventhray.com

"A magical masterpiece of fairy-garden fantasy" "tucked into a canyon", this 1975 standard-bearer of Topanga counter-culture encourages "hippies turned industry bigwigs" ("wear a suit with a tie-dyed shirt under it" to blend in) to "chill out" over "expensive" Californian fare that appeals to everyone from vegans to carnivores; grumblers grouse about "inconsistent" cooking and a "staff that has a hard time coming down to earth", but most maintain this "romantic with a capital R" spot "is so worth the drive."

ⓩ In-N-Out Burger ◑ *Burgers*   24 | 11 | 20 | $9

Hollywood | 7009 Sunset Blvd. (Orange Dr.)
Culver City | 13425 Washington Blvd. (bet. Glencoe & Walnut Aves.)
West LA | 9245 W. Venice Blvd. (Canfield Ave.)
Westwood | 922 Gayley Ave. (Levering Ave.)
Westchester | 9149 S. Sepulveda Blvd. (bet. 92nd St. & Westchester Pkwy.)
North Hollywood | 5864 Lankershim Blvd. (bet. Califa & Emelita Sts.)
Sherman Oaks | 4444 Van Nuys Blvd. (Moorpark St.)
Studio City | 3640 Cahuenga Blvd. (Fredonia Dr.)
Van Nuys | 7930 Van Nuys Blvd. (bet. Blythe & Michaels Sts.)
Woodland Hills | 19920 Ventura Blvd. (bet. Oakdale & Penfield Aves.)
800-786-1000 | www.in-n-out.com
Additional locations throughout Southern California
Rated the Survey's No. 1 Bang for the Buck, this "legendary" West Coast hamburger chain inspires a widespread "cult following", with converts to the "church of In-N-Out" swearing that the "cooked-to-order" "never-frozen" patties, "freshly cut french fries" ("order them crispy") and "off-menu" "customizing" options are so "phenomenal" they must have been "created on the eighth day"; yes, they're always "mobbed" and drive-thru "lines are interminable", but "if you don't know why it's the food of the gods, leave LA."

Iroha ◑ *Japanese*   25 | 17 | 22 | $39

Studio City | 12953 Ventura Blvd. (bet. Coldwater Canyon & Ethel Aves.) | 818-990-9559

"You'd never find it" if you weren't really looking and it doesn't "get the attention" that some of the glitzier Japanese do, but this midpriced Studio City "hideaway" holds its own against – and possibly even "edges out" – the bigger guns with "fine fish" (both "sushi and cooked dishes") prepared by chefs aka "artists"; "cozy, intimate" environs and staffers who are "happy to answer questions" encourage you to "sit and linger."

Islands *American*   17 | 16 | 18 | $18

Beverly Hills | 350 S. Beverly Dr. (Olympic Blvd.) | 310-556-1624
Marina del Rey | 404 Washington Blvd. (Via Dolce) | 310-822-3939
West LA | 10948 W. Pico Blvd. (Veteran Ave.) | 310-474-1144
Manhattan Beach | 3200 N. Sepulveda Blvd. (bet. 30th & 33rd Sts.) | 310-546-4456
Torrance | 2647 PCH (Crenshaw Blvd.) | 310-530-5383
Pasadena | 3533 E. Foothill Blvd. (Rosemead Blvd.) | 626-351-6543
Burbank | 101 E. Orange Grove Ave. (1st St.) | 818-566-7744
Encino | 15927 Ventura Blvd. (bet. Gaviota & Gloria Aves.) | 818-385-1200
Glendale | 117 W. Broadway (bet. Brand Blvd. & Orange St.) | 818-545-3555
Woodland Hills | 23397 Mulholland Dr. (Calabasas Rd.) | 818-225-9839
www.islandsrestaurants.com
Additional locations throughout Southern California
"Always a good plan" when "kids are in tow", this "kitschy" "tropical surf-themed" chain dishes out burgers, soft tacos and "addictive" fries that make for a "decent" "quick bite without breaking the bank"; salads and beachy cocktails help "keep the parents happy", so even if wise-acres crack "what islands are they referring to", it "will do in a pinch."

	FOOD	DECOR	SERVICE	COST

Itacho ☒ *Japanese*   21 | 14 | 20 | $39

Beverly Boulevard | 7311 Beverly Blvd. (bet. Fuller Ave. & Poinsettia Pl.) | 323-938-9009 | www.itachorestaurant.com

It's "been around a long time" (over 10 years), but loyalists still turn to this Beverly Boulevard izakaya for "a mixture of hot and cold [small] dishes" that's "perfect when your crowd is half-sushi, half-cooked-food eaters"; "warm" staffers heat up the somewhat "cavernous", industrial environs with high ceilings.

NEW Itzik Hagadol *Israeli*   21 | 14 | 19 | $28

Encino | 17201 Ventura Blvd. (Louise Ave.) | 818-784-4080 | www.itzikhagadol.com

Wear your "stretchy pants" to best accommodate an "onslaught of Middle Eastern appetizers" and "varied" salads (which "keep coming as long as you have room"), plus "the juiciest kebabs", at this "authentic", affordable Encino entry, an offshoot of an Israeli skewer shop; the "bustling" servers win props for their "good attitude", creating a "busy, crazy, delicious experience."

Ivy, The *Californian*   21 | 22 | 20 | $62

West Hollywood | 113 N. Robertson Blvd. (bet. Beverly Blvd. & 3rd St.) | 310-274-8303

"The action can overtake the meal" at this WeHo bungalow where even the "*Flintstones*-sized" Californian eats have trouble competing with the "gawk"-fest that results from the appearances of "minor celebrities" and accompanying paparazzi; the "volume of coin you're handing over" is "outrageous", and some feel the staff "invented the word attitude", but the "grandma's home"–like "French country" digs ("floral, floral everywhere") and "white picket fenced" patio are "beautiful", so most love this "iconic LA" experience anyway.

Ivy at the Shore *Californian/Italian*   22 | 22 | 21 | $61

Santa Monica | 1535 Ocean Ave. (bet. B'way & Colorado Ave.) | 310-393-3113

Striking some as the "shy wallflower cousin of the Robertson Boulevard" original, this Santa Monica outpost "overlooking the ocean" is nonetheless valued for "people-watching" and "star-spotting"; while the Cal-Italian fare comes in "absurdly large portions", equally big prices have some muttering about "the emperor's new clothes" cuisinewise, still, a staff that seems to have "less attitude" than their WeHo counterparts and "beautiful" "views from the patio" do much to mollify.

NEW Ixtapa *Mexican*   - | - | - | I

Pasadena | 119 E. Colorado Blvd. (Arroyo Pkwy.) | 626-304-1000 | www.cantinaixtapa.com

As the name suggests, this Old Pasadena newcomer from the restaurant group behind Bar Celona and Villa Sorriso serves a budget-friendly menu of Mexican beach cuisine – all the basics, along with lots of seafood; the 7,000-sq.-ft. space, designed by Akar Studios features plenty of dark wood, tall windows and tables on several levels; there's also a lounge, weekend DJs and occasional bands.

Izaka-Ya by Katsu-Ya *Japanese*   26 | 15 | 18 | $41

Third Street | 8420 W. Third St. (bet. La Cienega Blvd. & Orlando Ave.) | 323-782-9536

(continued)

Izaka-Ya by Katsu-Ya

NEW **Manhattan Beach** | 1133 Highland Ave. (Center Pl.) | 310-796-1888
www.katsu-yagroup.com

"The secret's out" about at this "bustling" Third Streeter (with a new Manhattan Beach sibling) vending "less-expensive versions" of chef Katsuya Uechi's "delectable" modern Japanese dishes – minus the "sceney-ness of his Katsuya" chain; popularity has its price – "it's impossible to get a seat", the servers tend to "rush you" and "the noise level" is high – but acolytes attest it's "worth it" for the master's creations.

NEW Izakaya Fu-Ga 🅂 *Japanese*   – | – | – | I

Little Tokyo | Kajima Bldg. | 111 S. San Pedro St. (1st St.) | 213-625-1722

This Japanese small-dish pub in Little Tokyo's Kajima Building has quickly become the go-to spot for visitors from Tokyo, who take over tables for hours, drinking sake and eating budget-friendly izakaya fare until last call at 2 AM; the sub-street-level space is windowless, with indirect lighting that makes the walls – and the bar in particular – seem to glow.

Izayoi *Japanese*   ▽ 25 | 13 | 19 | $35

Little Tokyo | 132 S. Central Ave. (bet. 1st & 2nd Sts.) | 213-613-9554

Surveyors say the sushi and sashimi are "extremely fresh" at this diminutive Little Tokyo izakaya, "but the real gems are the small dishes", including "fluffy homemade tofu"; ample soju and "sake selections" complement the "tapas-style" approach, leading supporters to insist they like everything and "anything" on the menu.

Jack n' Jill's *American*   18 | 14 | 18 | $21

Beverly Hills | 342 N. Beverly Dr. (bet. Brighton & Dayton Ways) | 310-247-4500
Santa Monica | 510 Santa Monica Blvd. (5th St.) | 310-656-1501
www.eatatjacknjills.com

"Uncomplicated" "breakfast or lunch" options from "sweet to savory", coupled with "awesome baked goods", "fetch a following" for this duo of "homey" American cafes in Beverly Hills and Santa Monica; though often beset by "screaming kids, baby strollers and long waits", they remain "happy" spots for "unhurried" types to "laze the afternoon away."

Jack n' Jill's Too *Creole*   ▽ 21 | 15 | 20 | $23
(fka Creperie by Jack n' Jill's)

Third Street | 8738 W. Third St. (bet. Arnaz Dr. & Robertson Blvd.) | 310-858-4900 | www.jacknjillstoo.com

Creole dishes join a "not fancy, but fine" assortment of sweet and savory crêpes at this affordable Third Street "concept" and full-menu branch of a SoCal chainlet that also serves up "interesting" breakfast creations and heartier fare such as salads, wraps, Louisiana-spiced rotisserie chicken and BBQ; the inside is decked out in mirrors and modern decor, and it also has a "nice outdoor dining area."

James' Beach *American*   19 | 19 | 21 | $42

Venice | 60 N. Venice Blvd. (Pacific Ave.) | 310-823-5396 | www.jamesbeach.com

Venice "locals unwind" at this "cool hang by the beach" that offers a "laid-back" yet "lively" vibe, "solid" American fare and "friendly" service; those who "stick to the drinking" in the old Craftsman-style house have multiple "terrific" bars from which to choose, where "singles" and "varied crowds" collide "late-night" for something of an "indoor-outdoor disco" with a "neighborhood feel."

Jan's ● Diner   16 | 9 | 18 | $17
West Hollywood | 8424 Beverly Blvd. (Croft Ave.) | 323-651-2866 | www.jansrestaurant.com

Surveyors "step back in time" at this "long-standing" "neighborhood coffee shop in West Hollywood, where "old-fashioned diner food" a an "excellent price" is served from dawn till late into the night (1 AM) "it's been around forever", but a "friendly" staff "makes up for the non decor" and a "late-night burger and beer" still "hits the spot."

☒ Japon Bistro Ⓜ Japanese   25 | 19 | 25 | $42
Pasadena | 927 E. Colorado Blvd. (bet. Lake & Mentor Aves.) | 626-744-1751 | www.japonbistro-pasadena.com

"Creative" sushi pleases patrons of this Pasadena "neighborhoo gem" where the "accommodating chefs" and "helpful servers" offe multiple "fresh" omakase options in addition to the regular menu the "long, narrow space feels like Tokyo", and seeing as it's hom to the Sake Institute of America, the "variety" of "tastings ar educational and delicious."

☒ Jar American/Steak   25 | 22 | 24 | $61
Beverly Boulevard | 8225 Beverly Blvd. (Harper Ave.) | West Hollywood 323-655-6566 | www.thejar.com

"No gimmicks, just solid cooking" sums up Suzanne Tracht's Beverl Boulevard chophouse where "steaks that cut like butter" and "sinful good" pot roast mingle amid American "comfort food" with a season touch in "handsome, dark-wood" digs reminiscent of "the '50s, whe movie stars dressed to the nines"; yes, it's a "total splurge" and "scene", but "engaging service" and "incredible adult beverages" eas a "cool crowd" into "good vibes", making this "retro" "gourmet "always a winner."

Javan Persian   20 | 17 | 19 | $26
West LA | 11500 Santa Monica Blvd. (Butler Ave.) | 310-207-5555 | www.javanrestaurant.com

"Soul-warming stews" and "delicious" kebabs lead this "traditiona Persian's menu of "simple, yet extremely flavorful" fare that's "gene ously" portioned for "hungry" Westsiders; "efficient service" an prices that "won't break the wallet" have many listing it as their "c sual" Iranian "go-to", and the "big, open room" is "pleasant."

Jer-ne American/Steak   ▽ 23 | 24 | 23 | $59
Marina del Rey | Ritz-Carlton, Marina Del Rey | 4375 Admiralty Way (off Lincoln Blvd.) | 310-574-4333 | www.ritzcarlton.com

Dreamers "hanker for the private yachts" viewed from the "abso lutely inspiring" patio at this "lovely" New American steakhouse the Marina Del Rey Ritz-Carlton; overall it's "what you expect fro the Ritz", offering "pricey" plates, a "decent wine list" and cosseti service that's "great for special occasions", and though nitpicke fault the menu's "attempt to be innovative", the majority agrees it an "exquisite" "find."

	FOOD	DECOR	SERVICE	COST

ian Korean BBQ Korean ▽ 23 | 23 | 22 | $41

everly Boulevard | 8256 Beverly Blvd. (Sweetzer Ave.) | 323-655-6556 |
ww.jianbbq.com

urveyors are "pleasantly surprised" at this "nearly authentic" Beverly
oulevard Korean BBQ where "cooking your own meats" and "experi-
nenting with sauces" attract do-it-yourselfers seeking an "easy ac-
ess" alternative to K-town; though it's "a little pricey", there are also
ocktails (honey-ginger mojito, anyone?) and sleek decor that's a
feast for the eyes."

inky's Southwestern 19 | 11 | 17 | $17

Vest Hollywood | 8539 W. Sunset Blvd. (Alta Loma Rd.) |
10-659-9670
anta Monica | 1447 Second St. (bet. B'way & Santa Monica Blvd.) |
10-917-3311
herman Oaks | 14120 Ventura Blvd. (Stansbury Ave.) |
18-981-2250
www.jinkys.com

Breakfast is the big draw" at this "casual" Southwestern-American
aytime trio that "consistently" cranks out "inventive" morning meals
nd "chilies galore" from a reasonably priced menu that's so "exten-
ve", regulars reckon "if you can't find something to eat here, you
hould stay home"; there's "always a wait on weekends", when service
an run "spotty", but most agree it's "worth the trouble"; P.S. the
herman Oaks branch also serves dinner.

in Patisserie Ⓜ Bakery/French 23 | 19 | 20 | $21

enice | 1202 Abbot Kinney Blvd. (Aragon Ct.) | 310-399-8801 |
www.jinpatisserie.com

Poetry in chocolate" and "pretty pastries" inspire sweet-talkers to
ompare this "discreet" Venice cafe and dessert shop to a "charming"
ideaway" "worthy of Paris"; though the French fare may be "a little
n the pricey side" for lunches that look "cuter than they taste", the
erene" garden makes for a "lovingly quiet" setting to savor an "out-
anding tea selection" and steep in an "unhurried" vibe.

JiRaffe American/French 26 | 22 | 25 | $57

anta Monica | 502 Santa Monica Blvd. (5th St.) | 310-917-6671 |
ww.jirafferestaurant.com

anta Monicans swear there's a dash of "magic" added to the "locally
rown materials" chef Raphael Lunetta uses to create "original" French-
ew American fare that "rivals the best LA has to offer"; prices are
easonable for the quality" (though "it ain't cheap"), and while it can
et "noisy when busy", "knowledgeable" service complements the "el-
gant" yet "unpretentious" setting, culminating in an "experience"
at exudes "luxurious relaxation."

Jitlada Thai 26 | 11 | 17 | $27

ast Hollywood | 5233½ W. Sunset Blvd. (bet. Harvard Blvd. &
ngsley Dr.) | 323-667-9809 | www.jitladala.com

Not for the faint of heart", this "amazing Southern Thai" experience
East Hollywood "goes far beyond the standards", forging a "stagger-
g variety" of "authentic" and "eye-wateringly hot" fare that blazes
ith "blow-you-away goodness"; "charming" proprietress Jazz offers
ackground on the food and culture", and though it's not uncommon

to "wait and wait" at the "strip-mall digs", the prices "won't break th
bank", making it "worth a detour or 10."

Joan's on Third *American/Bakery*   23 | 17 | 17 | $24

Third Street | 8350 W. Third St. (bet. Fairfax Ave. & La Cienega Blvd.)
West Hollywood | 323-655-2285 | www.joansonthird.com

"The best takeout this side of Dean and Deluca", this "upscale" ma
ketplace and cafe "encourages grazing" amid a "mouthwatering" de
case, "educational" cheese station and "dazzling" desserts with "A
cupcakes"; make no mistake, it's a "scene", "packed with beautif
people and celebrities", and though "scarce" seating inside and o
makes it more "gourmet-to-go", habitués agree it "always has som
thing new and interesting."

Jody Maroni's Sausage Kingdom *Hot Dogs*   19 | 7 | 14 | $11

Venice | 2011 Ocean Front Walk (20th Pl.) | 310-822-5639
Glendale | The Americana | 668 Americana Way (bet. Central Ave.
Orange St.) | 818-545-9025
Universal City | Universal CityWalk | 1000 Universal Studios Blvd.
(off Rte. 101) | 818-622-5639
www.jodymaroni.com

They "aren't going to slim you down", but just "sink your teeth into o
of these juicy babies" anyway urge dogged devotees of this "cheap
fast-food chainlet slinging a "spectrum" of "tasty", "unusual" sa
sages and "yummy-to-the-tummy" fries; "there's no decor", so ju
"dig in and enjoy" the grub, especially at the Venice Beach original whe
"waves, sun and sand" accompany a "circus" of "boardwalk crazies.

☒ Joe's ⓜ *Californian/French*   26 | 21 | 24 | $54

Venice | 1023 Abbot Kinney Blvd. (B'way) | 310-399-5811 |
www.joesrestaurant.com

"Still the king of Abbot Kinney", chef-owner Joe Miller continues
"wow" Venice diners with "imaginative uses of local, in-season ingr
dients" in a "civilized" yet "savory" Cal-French menu that's "one of t
best near the beach"; "attentive", "unpretentious" servers drift am
the covered patio and "laid-back" rooms, and though expensive, it's
deal for fine dining" – especially at lunch with the prix fixe "steal."

Joe's Pizza ⓞ *Pizza*   22 | 5 | 13 | $11

NEW **West Hollywood** | 8539 Sunset Blvd. (Alta Loma Rd.) |
310-358-0900
Santa Monica | 111 Broadway (Ocean Ave.) | 310-395-9222 ⭐
www.joespizza.com

"NYC-style pizza" fans "have a place to call home" at these San
Monica and West Hollywood offshoots of the Gotham "origina
that remain "true to their roots" with "thin-crust" pies and slic
with a "taste, texture and smell" that's "legit"; they're "open late
and despite "absolutely no ambiance" and "only a handful of tabl
inside and out", purists insist the wallet-friendly goods are "be
eaten on-site."

Johnnie's New York Pizzeria *Pizza*   17 | 9 | 16 | $17

Downtown | California Plaza | 350 S. Grand Ave. (bet. 3rd & 4th Sts.
213-613-9972 🅢
Downtown | City Nat'l Plaza | 505 S. Flower St. (bet. 5th & 6th Sts.)
213-488-0299 🅢

(continued)

Johnnie's New York Pizzeria

Mid-Wilshire | Museum Park Sq. | 5757 Wilshire Blvd. (bet. Curson & Masselin Aves.) | 323-904-4880

Century City | Fox Apts. | 10251 Santa Monica Blvd. (bet. Ave. of the Stars & Century Park W.) | 310-553-1188

Palms | 10401 W. Venice Blvd. (bet. Mentone & Motor Aves.) | 310-845-9470

Santa Monica | 1444 Third St. Promenade (B'way) | 310-395-9062

Venice | Hoyt Plaza | 2805 Abbot Kinney Blvd. (Washington Blvd.) | 310-821-1224

West LA | 11676 Olympic Blvd. (Barrington Ave.) | 310-477-2111

West LA | 3183 Wilshire Blvd. (Vermont Ave.) | 213-385-3100

Long Beach | 7539 Carson Blvd. (Pioneer Blvd.) | 562-425-4600

www.johnniesnypizza.com

Additional locations throughout Southern California

For a carbfest at a good price", this pizza chain delivers "fast-and-easy" pies with "plenty of different toppings" alongside garlic rolls, pastas, calzones, salads and other fare that "serves a purpose"; "lunch specials" keep some outposts "busy", and though fans say "it's pretty close to NYC realistic", others simply call it "not Cali"–style.

Johnnie's Pastrami ●👑 *Diner* 20 | 9 | 18 | $15

Culver City | 4017 Sepulveda Blvd. (bet. Washington Blvd. & Washington Pl.) | 310-397-6654

"Nothing's changed in 50 years (except the prices)" at this "hole-in-the-wall" in Culver City that's a "guilty pleasure" for "meat lovers" seeking "salty, succulent" "pastrami on a bun" and other "belly-filling" fare; sure, "you can actually hear your arteries hardening", but "old-school waitresses" ("fast, loud, scattered") and a retro diner setting including "barstools", "tableside quarter jukeboxes" and a "patio from the '50s" make it "one of those must-go places."

Johnny Rebs' *BBQ* 23 | 18 | 21 | $24

Bellflower | 16639 Bellflower Blvd. (Flower St.) | 562-866-6455

Long Beach | 4663 Long Beach Blvd. (bet. 46th & 47th Sts.) | 562-423-7327

www.johnnyrebs.com

"Finger-lickin' good" 'cue including "just plain ol' awesome" pulled pork and St. Louis–style ribs joins fried chicken, catfish and diet-defying breakfast "biscuits and gravy" at these chain links in Bellflower and Long Beach where the affordable grub is dished out in "large portions"; the "roadhouse" setting is complete with "peanuts on the table and shells on the floor", and service enhances the "come-back-soon-y'all feeling."

Johnny Rockets *Burgers* 16 | 15 | 16 | $14

Fairfax | Farmers Mkt. | 6333 W. Third St. (Fairfax Ave.) | 323-937-2093

Hollywood | Hollywood & Highland Ctr. | 6801 Hollywood Blvd. (Highland Ave.) | 323-465-4456

Melrose | 7507 Melrose Ave. (Gardner St.) | 323-651-3361

Long Beach | Pine Ct. | 245 Pine Ave. (bet. B'way & 3rd St.) | 562-983-1332

Manhattan Beach | Manhattan Mktpl. | 1550 Rosecrans Ave. (Market Pl.) | 310-536-9464

Westchester | Howard Hughes Ctr. | 6081 Center Dr. (bet. Howard Hughes Pkwy. & Sepulvda Blvd.) | 310-670-7555

(continued)

(continued)

Johnny Rockets

Arcadia | Santa Anita Fashion Park Shopping Ctr. | 400 S. Baldwin Ave. (Huntington Dr.) | 626-462-1800

Burbank | Media City Ctr. | 201 E. Magnolia Blvd. (bet. 1st & 3rd Sts.) | 818-845-7055

Encino | 16901 Ventura Blvd. (Balboa Blvd.) | 818-981-5900

www.johnnyrockets.com

Additional locations throughout Southern California

"Classic burgers", "malted milkshakes" and a "big helping of nostalgia" are the bait at these "'50s-style" diners where "singing waiters and waitresses" dole out "good old American food" to "children and the young at heart"; while "jukebox tunes are a bonus", critics call the offerings "so-so" and the prices "positively 21st-century."

John O'Groats *American*   20 | 12 | 19 | $19

Rancho Park | 10516 W. Pico Blvd. (½ block west of Beverly Glen Blvd.) | 310-204-0692

NEW Encino | 16120 Ventura Blvd. (bet. Libbit Ave. & Woodley Park Ln.) | 818-501-2366

www.ogroatsrestaurant.com

Many a "breakfast pilgrimage" has culminated at this American in Rancho Park (with an Encino branch that also serves dinner), where "hearty, stick-to-your-ribs" grub comes in portions so "plentiful", "it's a wonder the tables don't collapse under the sheer weight"; digs are "comfortable and cozy", with service that "makes you feel at home", and though there are "incredible crowds on the weekend", "complimentary coffee" and the "anticipation of fresh, hot biscuits" help ease the "wait."

Jonathan's at Peirano's Ⓜ *Californian/Mediterranean*   ▽ 23 | 23 | 23 | $42

Ventura | Peirano | 204 E. Main St. (bet. Figueroa & Palm Sts.) | 805-648-4853 | www.jonathansatpeiranos.com

The Cal-Med plates by chef/co-owner Jason Collis are "big on flavor and creativity" at this "charmer" that inhabits a "tastefully decorated" "historic building" "directly across from the San Buenaventura Mission"; "it can be noisy", due to the frequent live entertainment, but the staff is "personable", making this an all-around "wonderful" choice; for something lighter, the adjoining J's Tapas dishes up drinks and small bites.

Jones Hollywood ❶ *American/Italian*   18 | 19 | 18 | $29

West Hollywood | 7205 Santa Monica Blvd. (Formosa Ave.) | 323-850-1726

"Known more for its large, loud bar scene", this "Old Hollywood hangout" in WeHo speaks to the "'in' crowd" with a "cool vibe" in a "dark leather-booth–adorned space" that's open "late" for dining on American-Italian fare; adding to the attraction, staffers "aren't exactly hard on the eyes" as they deliver dishes such as "ahi tuna done right", "surprisingly tasty pizzas" or a "steak and a stiff drink", all at moderate prices.

☒ Josie *American*   26 | 23 | 25 | $64

Santa Monica | 2424 Pico Blvd. (25th St.) | 310-581-9888 | www.josierestaurant.com

Chef Josie Le Balch turns out "stunner after stunner" at this Santa Monica "jewel" where devotees who are "game for game" and other "beautifully prepared" New American fare feast on "seasonal, high quality ingredients"; "gracious" service complements the "elegant" yet "comfortable", "quiet" setting, making for an "expensive" but "civilized" experience that's "showing a lovely patina as it ages."

R's BBQ 🗷 *BBQ* — 22 | 9 | 22 | $21

Culver City | 3055 S. La Cienega Blvd. (Blackwelder St.) | 310-837-6838

"Carnivorous cravings" are "satisfied" at this "little" "joint" "on an industrial corner" of Culver City that cranks out "authentic" Memphis BBQ complete with "telltale pink" brisket, "tender ribs" and "slow-cooked tasty pork"; the ever-"friendly" owner is usually on hand and more than happy to talk 'cue, ultimately creating a "down-home pleasant" environment that is "family-friendly."

🗷 Julienne 🗷 *French* — 26 | 22 | 23 | $26

San Marino | 2651 Mission St. (bet. El Molino & Los Robles Aves.) | 626-441-2299 | www.juliennetogo.com

"Truly a delight" for early mornings or afternoons, this "oasis of calm and sophistication" in San Marino serves "decadent", "amazingly prepared" French bistro fare that satiates "ladies who lunch" on the "lovely patio"; it's very "popular", with "long lines on weekends" to prove it, but an attached "marketplace" provides a "wonderful take-home" alternative; P.S. it closes at 3:30 PM.

Junior's *Deli* — 16 | 11 | 17 | $22

West LA | 2379 Westwood Blvd. (Pico Blvd.) | 310-475-5771 | www.jrsdeli.com

"Sit, schmooze and nosh" at this "middle-of-the-road deli" in West LA that proffers "Jewish soul food" and "old standbys" like "traditional sandwiches piled high" and "steaming bowls" of "must-try matzo-ball soup"; sure, some say it's "overpriced" and "past its prime", but seeing as it opened in 1959, it's no wonder that "everything is dated", including the "competent, salty" staff.

Kabuki *Japanese* — 18 | 16 | 17 | $26

Hollywood | 1545 N. Vine St. (bet. Selma Ave. & Sunset Blvd.) | 323-464-6003
Westchester | Howard Hughes Ctr. | 6081 Center Dr. (bet. Howard Hughes Pkwy. & Sepulvda Blvd.) | 310-641-5524
Pasadena | 3539 E. Foothill Blvd. (bet. Halstead St. & Rosemead Blvd.) | 626-351-8963
Pasadena | 88 W. Colorado Blvd. (De Lacey Ave.) | 626-568-9310
Burbank | 201 N. San Fernando Blvd. (Orange Grove Ave.) | 818-843-7999
Woodland Hills | 20940 Ventura Blvd. (De Soto Ave.) | 818-704-8700
www.kabukirestaurants.com

This "affordable" chain delivers "fresh", "artistically" plated sushi that's been "Westernized" for American palates, making it a "safe choice" to "take unadventurous eaters" in the mood for Japanese fare ("not cuisine"); despite sometimes "slow service" and decor that's "nothing special", it's still a "solid" choice made more enjoyable with "happy-hour deals" and "exotic drinks."

Katana ● *Japanese* — 23 | 23 | 20 | $55

West Hollywood | 8439 W. Sunset Blvd. (bet. La Cienega Blvd. & Sweetzer Ave.) | 323-650-8585 | www.katanarobata.com

"See and be seen" at this West Hollywood "scene" that "delivers" with a "variety of sushi" and robata that's "consistently" "high-quality" (though

"sticklers of authentic" Japanese cuisine might say a bit "gimmicky")
the service is "attentive" as the "beautiful people" "buzz" amid the
"trendy" digs indoors and on the patio, and it all comes with a "big bill."

Kate Mantilini American
18 | 18 | 19 | $35

Beverly Hills | 9101 Wilshire Blvd. (Doheny Dr.) | 310-278-3699
Woodland Hills | 5921 Owensmouth Ave. (bet. Califa & Oxnard Sts.)
818-348-1095
www.katemantilini.biz

For fanciers of "gastronomique Americana", this duo is "the place"
with "something for everyone" on its "extensive menu" of "grown-up
diner" "classics", including "reliable" "late-night" chow; though service varies "depending on your actor" and the fare might be "a tad
overpriced", the "gussied-up coffee-shop" setting at the Beverly Hills
flagship attracts "industry" types who wheel and deal in the "big
booths" or "watch the action in the kitchen" from the bar, while the
Woodland Hills offshoot offers a guacamole station.

⊠ Katsu-ya Japanese
26 | 13 | 19 | $44

Encino | 16542 Ventura Blvd. (Hayvenhurst Ave.) | 818-788-2396
Studio City | 11680 Ventura Blvd. (Colfax Ave.) | 818-985-6976
www.katsu-yagroup.com

"Still packing 'em in", these Studio City and Encino "originators" take
"classic and modern approaches" to "high-quality" Japanese fare,
earning "faithful hearts and palates" with specialties including baked
crab hand rolls that are "heaven on earth"; the staff is "knowledgeable", and despite "agonizingly long waits" and "no-frills decor", it's
"go-to" for "celebs" and "locals" who insist the "pricey" tabs are "always worth it"; P.S. "go with the board for ordering."

⊠ Katsuya Japanese
23 | 23 | 19 | $56

Downtown | LA Live | 800 W. Olympic Blvd. (Figueroa St.) | 213-747-9797
Hollywood | 6300 Hollywood Blvd. (Vine St.) | 323-871-8777 ☾
Brentwood | 11777 San Vicente Blvd. (Montana Ave.) | 310-207-8744
Glendale | Americana at Brand | 702 Americana Way (bet. Brand Blvd. &
Central Ave.) | 818-244-5900
www.sbe.com

"Bring your bankroll" to these "flashy" Japanese "glamour-pusses"
showcasing the "freshest" "sushi creations" and "innovative" signature dishes from chef Katsuya Uechi in "swanky", "modern" settings
designed by Philippe Starck; some note it's more "scene" than "substance", with "beautiful" yet "snooty" servers fanning "pretentious"
vibes, but that hasn't deterred "celebs" and a "young, hip crowd" from
returning for an "energetic" experience that "doesn't disappoint."

Kay 'n Dave's Mexican
16 | 15 | 18 | $22

Culver City | 9341 Culver Blvd. (bet. Bagley & Canfield Aves.) | 310-558-8100
Pacific Palisades | 15246 W. Sunset Blvd. (bet. Monument St. &
Swarthmore Ave.) | 310-459-8118
Santa Monica | 262 26th St. (bet. Georgina Ave. & San Vicente Blvd.)
310-260-1355
www.kayndaves.com

Though "health-conscious Mexican" might seem like "an inherent
oxymoron", these "wholesome" chain links have found a way to offer a
"lighter" menu of "interesting" and "traditional" fare that isn't "larded
down" with the guilt of "going to the gym to work off the fat"; though

t's more "gringo" than "authentic" and "service is hit-or-miss", it
works for "families" who tote their "munchkins" to the "cheerful" atmosphere for a "value."

Kendall's Brasserie French
| 19 | 21 | 20 | $47 |

Downtown | Dorothy Chandler Pavilion | 135 N. Grand Ave. (bet. 1st &
Temple Sts.) | 213-972-7322 | www.patinagroup.com

Capitalizing on a "captive audience for the music center and Disney
Hall", this French brasserie Downtown prides itself on a "professional", "prompt" staff intent on getting "theatergoers" "out before
curtain time, every time"; though the "limited menu" lacks this same
"consistency", garnering mixed reviews, the setting stuffed with mirrors
and antique furniture still gets "packed" with "well-dressed crowds"
who don't mind "paying for convenience."

Ketchup ● American
| 15 | 18 | 17 | $38 |

West Hollywood | 8590 W. Sunset Blvd. (Alta Loma Rd.) | 310-289-8590 |
www.dolcegroup.com

"Scene"-makers and "wannabes" descend upon this "trendy" WeHo
concept by the Dolce Group – made famous by *The Hills* – that dishes
upscale takes on American "childhood favorites" such as a "trio of fries"
and ice-cream sandwiches; though naysayers slam "overpriced" fare for
"immature palates", the "clever" decor continues to be "funky fun" for
fans who "take in the Boulevard scene through the big glass windows."

Kincaid's Seafood/Steak
| 20 | 24 | 20 | $41 |

Redondo Beach | Redondo Beach Pier | 500 Fisherman's Wharf
(Torrance Blvd.) | 310-318-6080 | www.kincaids.com

With "ahh"-inducing "sunsets" within eyeshot, this "sophisticated"
chain link in Redondo Beach draws "tourists", "dates" and "groups"
who dig into a "variety" of "well-prepared" surf 'n' turf options while
"watching the waves" roll past the pier; though "somewhat expensive"
fares irks some, "friendly service", a "comfortable" atmosphere and
"wonderful cocktails" from the "large bar area" convince nitpickers to
"just sit back and enjoy the views."

King's Fish House Seafood
| 20 | 18 | 19 | $34 |

Long Beach | 100 W. Broadway Ave. (bet. Pacific & Pine Aves.) |
562-432-7463

Calabasas | The Commons | 4798 Commons Way (Calabasas Rd.) |
818-225-1979

www.kingsfishhouse.com

The "huge menu of fresh fish, beer and such" lures "crowds" to this
"big, rousing fish house" in Long Beach and Calabasas that's "upscale"
enough for "reliable" seafood yet "casual" enough for those who "don't
want to change clothes to go out"; "iffy service" is a part of the catch, and
though "nothing is terribly innovative" here, it's "popular" with "families" who appreciate the "generous portions" at "moderate prices."

King's Hawaiian
Bakery & Restaurant Hawaiian
| 20 | 16 | 19 | $18 |

Torrance | 2808 Sepulveda Blvd. (bet. Crenshaw & Hawthorne Blvds.) |
310-530-0050 | www.kingshawaiianrestaurants.com

"A wonderful aloha spirit" permeates this "reasonably priced"
Hawaiian "coffee shop" and bakery in Torrance that warms bellies

FOOD   DECOR   SERVICE   COST

with "old-school" fare so "authentic" it rivals "the Big Island itself"; th
"specialties" can be "adventurous" for some, and the "noisy" tropic
environment is "fun for kids", but the big kahuna here is the "mouth
watering" baked goods, starring a "Paradise Cake that's a legend i
its own time."

Kings Road Cafe *American*   16 | 12 | 17 | $21

Beverly Boulevard | 8361 Beverly Blvd. (Kings Rd.) | West Hollywood
323-655-9044 | www.kingsroadcafe.com

"Quite the scene", this "reasonably priced" Beverly Boulevard America
is "always crowded at breakfast", drawing locals and "incognit
celebs" for "solid" chow and noteworthy "house-roasted" coffee tha
"has a lovely smokiness"; service is hit-or-miss ("prefer my latte with
out attitude"), but that doesn't stop "lines out the door", with mos
opting for the "outside tables" as the dining room, while "pleasant
can have "deafening noise levels."

Kitchen, The ● *American*   ▽ 20 | 12 | 20 | $24

Silver Lake | 4348 Fountain Ave. (Sunset Blvd.) | 323-664-3663 |
www.thekitchen-silverlake.com

"Flying under the radar", this tiny Silver Lake "hole-in-the-wall" warm
up to diners with "comfort food at comfortable prices", offering
"hearty" yet "limited" menu of American fare via a "friendly staff" wit
"no attitude"; it's "open late" and always casual, securing its reputa
tion as a "reliable neighborhood" spot that some "hope no one els
finds out about."

Kitchen 24 ● *American*   20 | 19 | 17 | $21

Hollywood | 1608 N. Cahuenga Blvd. (Selma Ave.) | 323-465-2424 |
www.kitchen24.info

Hollywood's "sceney" answer to "Denny's" is this "modern diner
slinging "better-than-expected" affordable American grub 24/7 in
"bright", "unique" space "replete with funky music and a full bar
sure, the "friendly model-cum-waiter staff" is slow, but that doesn
stop "hipsters" and the "gorgeous" from swinging by "late-night" afte
hitting "club heaven on Cahuenga."

Kiwami *Japanese*   26 | 21 | 24 | $49

Studio City | 11920 Ventura Blvd. (Carpenter Ave.) | 818-763-3910
www.kiwami.us

"Trend"-seekers go for the "upscale" Japanese "experience" at th
Studio City link in the chain of Katsuya Uechi, who's "raised the bar
by slicing "fresher-than-fresh" fish into "creative" (to some, "over
creative") sushi that speaks to "serious foodies" and the "sashimi cog
noscenti"; service is "attentive", and the "soothing" space is "Zen
like", offering "alfresco" dining as well as a "special bar" where a
omakase menu of "delectable gastronomic treats" is occasionally pre
sented by the esteemed chef himself.

Kogi Korean BBQ-to-Go ⊟ *Korean/Mexican*   23 | 5 | 15 | $10

Location varies; see website | www.kogibbq.com

Roaming raters call it nothing less than a "revelation", "sitting on
street curb" to sample the wares of this "trailblazing food truck" serv
ing cheap Korean-Mexican "tacos and kimchi quesadillas" to a "cu
following" that "chases" its location via Twitter and the Interne

FOOD | DECOR | SERVICE | COST

crazy hype" has resulted in "interminable" lines, leaving some grum-ling "overrated", but the "young clientele" insists it's "worth the vait" for a "quintessential LA experience"; P.S. the fare's also avail-ble at Culver City's Alibi Room 12236 Washington Boulevard.

Koi *Japanese*   24 | 24 | 19 | $65

West Hollywood | 730 N. La Cienega Blvd. (bet. Melrose Pl. & Waring Ave.) | 310-659-9449 | www.koirestaurant.com

Feel like part of the 'in' crowd at this "deliciously high-profile" "hot pot" in West Hollywood where "movie stars galore" and "young, thin irls with guys twice their age" "break the bank" to experience "fresh", creative sushi" and other "eclectic" fare served by "waiters that look ke models"; though naysayers note it's "more about the scene" than he cuisine, the "sexy" setting is sure to "impress a date", marrying Zen gardens with "sleek modernity."

Kokomo Cafe *Southern*   ▽ 19 | 14 | 14 | $20

Beverly Boulevard | 7385 Beverly Blvd. (Martel Ave.) | 323-933-0773 | www.kokomo.com

Prepare to not eat for three days" after gorging on "huge breakfasts" nd "generous" lunches at this Beverly Boulevard Southerner, known or "eclectic" "comfort food" including "catfish and eggs" and "chicken nd waffles"; "don't be in a hurry", as the service is "not always on the all", but the large space with sidewalk seating is "perfect for bringing he kids" and "convenient" as a "weekend go-to."

Koutoubia Ⓜ *Moroccan*   ▽ 25 | 22 | 22 | $46

West LA | 2116 Westwood Blvd. (bet. Mississippi Ave. & Olympic Blvd.) | 310-475-0729 | www.koutoubiarestaurant.com .

Authentic Moroccan home cooking" is the centerpiece of this West LA "experience", where "high-quality ingredients" are "delicately pre-ared" to craft "incredible b'steeya" and "tagine with couscous"; per-haps there's "too much belly dancing" for some, but with decor that feels like a living room" in Marrakesh and an owner who's "informa-ive" and "attentive", most find it most "comfortable."

NEW K-Town BBQ *Korean*   - | - | - | I

Downtown | 738 E. Third St. (Alameda St.) | 213-680-3008

From the restaurateur behind Zip Fusion and e3rd Steakhouse comes this Downtown Korean serving a budget-friendly menu that includes 95¢ skewers, barbecued rock cod and an all-you-can-eat option; with an exterior that looks like it was assembled from old wood crates and ow, loungey tables, this 'cue house is far from the 'seoulful' formality of K-town – both geographically and aesthetically.

K-Zo *Japanese*   24 | 18 | 20 | $46

Culver City | 9240 Culver Blvd. (Washington Blvd.) | 310-202-8890 | www.k-zo.com

This "Culver City jewel" "rivals the big names in sushi", "beauti-fully presenting" "consistent" cuts of "fresh" fish from the hands of 'gifted' chef-owner Keizo Ishiba, who crafts a variety of "modern fu-sion" Japanese small plates as well; the chef's wife, Yuki, "runs the front of the house", overseeing "quality" service within the "hip", con-temporary space that's a "place to splurge" when you "want more than just" the basics.

Lab, The *American*

▽ 17 | 17 | 15 | $22

Downtown | 3500 S. Figueroa St. (Jefferson Blvd.) | 213-743-1843
"Finally, a place to eat near USC" report revelers at this Downtown American, which cooks up "cheap eats" in "fun" digs decked out like a science lab with industrial lighting and slate-topped communal tables; maybe service is "not so great", but after a few "beakers of beer" the "college" crowd'll cheer anyway: "go Trojans!"

La Bistecca *Italian/Steak*

- | - | - | E

Downtown | Millennium Biltmore Hotel | 506 S. Grand Ave. (5th St.) | 213-624-1011 | www.thebiltmore.com
Set in the historic Rendezvous Court of Downtown's "unbelievably beautiful" Biltmore Hotel, this pricey steakhouse uses organic vegetables and hormone-and-antibiotic–free Brandt Farms beef for a seasonal menu rooted in the traditions of Southern Italy and Sicily; the grand space boasts arched ceilings, massive chandeliers and a fountain, creating a "fancy" environment that breathes opulence.

La Boheme *Californian*

21 | 25 | 22 | $43

West Hollywood | 8400 Santa Monica Blvd. (Orlando Ave.) | 323-848-2360 | boheme.globaldiningca.com
Looking like the "stage of an opera" set in "Dracula's castle", this "dramatic" West Hollywood Californian is "all about the ambiance", boasting a "beautiful terrace", "oversized fireplaces" and chandeliers inside a cavernous, imposing space where "everything is red" and oozes "romance"; though the "creative" cuisine is overshadowed by the "dreamy" digs, it's "always a good bet" for a bite, especially during happy hour when the "upscale" prices are slashed.

La Botte *Italian*

24 | 20 | 22 | $56

Santa Monica | 620 Santa Monica Blvd. (7th St.) | 310-576-3072 | www.labottesantamonica.com
With "accented waiters" who treat diners "like family", this Santa Monica Italian is "as authentic as it gets", plating "divine, original" cuisine in a "romantic" "wine-cellar backdrop" that features walls and floors constructed from the wooden planks of barrels; it may be "a bit on the pricey side", but that hasn't deterred "locals" who sum it up in one word: "*magnifico.*"

La Bottega Marino *Italian*

21 | 14 | 21 | $23

Hancock Park | Larchmont Vill. | 203 N. Larchmont Blvd. (bet. Beverly Blvd. & 1st St.) | 323-962-1325
NEW **Beverly Hills** | 9669 Santa Monica Blvd. (Bedford Dr.) | 310-271-7274
West LA | 11363 Santa Monica Blvd. (Purdue Ave.) | 310-477-7777
www.labottegausa.com
"Living up to the Salvatore Marino standards", these "warm neighborhood spots" by the chef-owner of Il Grano serve "simple", "homemade" Italian fare "featuring farmer's market ingredients" and also offer "shelves" of imported products and "authentic" deli "side dishes to take away and enjoy at home"; the rustic setting is "quick and casual" for "fast family getaways", and the "waiters have personality without being too in-your-face", making for an all-in-all "cozy" experience.

	FOOD	DECOR	SERVICE	COST

LOS ANGELES

La Bruschetta Ristorante *Italian* | 23 | 18 | 24 | $42 |

Westwood | 1621 Westwood Blvd. (bet. Massachusetts & Ohio Aves.) | 310-477-1052 | www.lbwestwood.com
"Bellissimo" dishes "with a lot of heart" lure loyalists to this Westwood Italian "well-kept neighborhood secret", where chef-owner Angelo Peloni ("congeniality personified") makes "locals and UCLA employees" alike feel like "they're stepping into his home"; price-conscious pastafarians differ on whether the "reliable, tasty selections" skew "reasonable" or "expensive", but not on the "quiet", "homey" atmosphere that makes "leisurely meals" a "delight."

La Cabanita *Mexican* | 25 | 17 | 21 | $21 |

Montrose | 3447 N. Verdugo Rd. (Ocean View Blvd.) | 818-957-2711
A "genuine" "gem", this Montrose Mexican plates an "expansive" array of "delicious", "authentic" regional dishes "not dumbed-down for the gringo palate"; with "inexpensive" prices, "friendly service" and "homey, if slightly dated" digs done up in traditional style, it's no wonder it's an area "favorite."

La Cachette Bistro *French* | 21 | 21 | 21 | $54 |

Santa Monica | 1733 Ocean Ave. (bet. Colorado Ave. & Pico Blvd.) | 310-434-9509 | www.lacachettebistro.com
This "less-formal" reinvention of Jean Francois Meteigner's much-heralded "fine-dining" restaurant La Cachette focuses on "innovative" takes on bistro classics served "without attitude" in a "big, bright", "modern" venue just blocks from the beach in Santa Monica; yet while admirers "applaud" the "fabulous" fare that would "make Escoffier proud", some fear it's "lost a step" since the move, citing "uneven" execution and tabs that still feel "pricey for what you get."

NEW La Campagna *Italian* | - | - | - | I |

Hermosa Beach | 934 Hermosa Ave. (9th St.) | 310-374-3747
Family- and budget-friendly, this down-home Italian pasta and pizza house sits in a space that's just a short walk from the ocean in Hermosa Beach – you can hear the calls of the pelagic birds while you dine; the room is plain but pleasant, with a view of rollerbladers and skateboarders heading down Hermosa Avenue.

La Creperie Cafe *French* | 23 | 21 | 19 | $25 |

Long Beach | 4911 E. Second St. (bet. Argonne & St. Joseph Aves.) | 562-434-8499 | www.lacreperiecafe.net
Francophiles fawn over this "jewel box of a cafe" in Long Beach turning out *"très bon"* "savory and sweet" crêpes along with other Frenchie fare in a "kitschy" Moulin Rouge-esque setting with a patio; it's "always packed" and "waits can verge on insane", but at least prices remain reasonable enough to "roll in" and "roll out without getting rolled"; P.S. a second location in Downtown Long Beach is in the works for fall.

La Dijonaise Café et Boulangerie *French* | 17 | 14 | 16 | $24 |

Culver City | Helms Bldg. | 8703 Washington Blvd. (Helms Ave.) | 310-287-2770 | www.ladijonaise.com
"Surprisingly inexpensive", this Culver City bistro offers "well-prepared" Gallic "classics" and "divine" pastries in a "modern" "Euro-cafe atmosphere" that's enhanced by the "actual French" staffers; with a "pleas-

ant", newly expanded outdoor patio, it's something of a "neighborhood hangout", especially at brunch.

La Dolce Vita ⊠ *Italian*   22 | 21 | 24 | $60

Beverly Hills | 9785 Santa Monica Blvd. (Wilshire Blvd.) | 310-278-1845 | www.ladolcevitabeverlyhills.com

For an "old-school Italian" experience, seek out this expensive, brick walled Beverly Hills joint where "classic" pastas and dishes like steak Sinatra are washed down with "excellent cocktails" in "romantic" candlelit environs; it remains a taste of the sweet life for its crowd of "regulars" who appreciate being "treated well" by the "wonderful staff."

LA Food Show *American*   17 | 17 | 18 | $28

Beverly Hills | 252 N. Beverly Dr. (bet. Dayton Way & Wilshire Blvd.) | 310-550-9758

Manhattan Beach | Manhattan Vill. | 3212 N. Sepulveda Blvd. (bet. Marine & Rosecrans Aves.) | 310-546-5575 www.lafoodshow.com

There's "something for everyone, even the most finicky" at these Beverly Hills–Manhattan Beach American "comfort-food emporiums" offering a "melting pot" of LA specialties, from chicken and waffles to grilled fish, delivered by a "fast, polite" staff; though some say they're just "so-so", "ample" portions and "spacious" digs have most calling these CPK spin-offs "reliable" "standbys."

La Frite *French*   19 | 15 | 19 | $28

Sherman Oaks | 15013 Ventura Blvd. (bet. Lemona Ave. & Sepulveda Blvd.) | 818-990-1791

Woodland Hills | 22616 Ventura Blvd. (bet. Fallbrook & Sale Aves.) | 818-225-1331 www.lafritecafe.com

Valley dwellers "keep coming back" to these "*très* French" Woodland Hills–Sherman Oaks *frères* for "consistent" bistro standards, "friendly" service and "the magic of romance in the air"; though the "'70s"-era setups may be "starting to show their age", prices are low, so happy patrons keep this "warm and cozy" twosome "crowded" all the same.

La Grande Orange *American*   20 | 19 | 18 | $30

Santa Monica | 2000 Main St. (Bicknell Ave.) | 310-396-9145 | www.lagrandeorangesm.com

La Grande Orange Café *American*

Pasadena | 260 S. Raymond Ave. (Del Mar Blvd.) | 626-356-4444 | www.lgohospitality.com

"All aboard" for "smart versions" of Cal "comfort food" at this "lively", midpriced Pasadena American and its Santa Monica follow-up, "a hit" for their "delish" eats, "snappy service" and "airy" environs, especially the original's "beautifully renovated" locale in the "converted" Del Mar train depot; when it gets "noisy inside", regulars repair to the patios for "refreshing" white sangria on "warm summer nights."

La Huasteca *Mexican*   – | – | – | I

Lynwood | Plaza Mexico | 3150 E. Imperial Hwy. (bet. Long Beach Blvd. & State St.) | 310-537-8800 | www.lahuasteca.com

"Authentic" Mexican cuisine is alive and well in Lynwood at this "relaxing" cantina whose wallet-friendly menu is inspired by the La Huasteca region of Southern Mexico; south-of-the-border artifacts and brightly

	FOOD	DECOR	SERVICE	COST

olored murals enhance the overall experience, as do the exotic mararitas and nightly mariachi music.

al Mirch *Indian*   ▽ 17 | 11 | 19 | $29
tudio City | 11138 Ventura Blvd. (bet. Arch & Fruitland Drs.) | 18-980-2273 | www.lmdining.com
Nothing exceptional" but "not bad", this Studio City Indian is "worth rying" for cost-effective standards served in a nondescript setting redeemed by the "nicest staff" around; though finicky foes sniff it's slipping downhill", the $9.95 weekday lunch buffet remains a "good value."

a Loggia *Italian*   21 | 18 | 19 | $43
studio City | 11814 Ventura Blvd. (bet. Colfax Ave. & Laurel Canyon Blvd.) | 318-985-9222
Ciao bella!" enthuse admirers of this "tried-and-true" Studio City Italian, a "neighborhood favorite" thanks to its "elegantly prepared" seasonal are and servers who "always greet you with a smile"; the networking egulars can get so "loud" "earplugs are needed", but a "lovely covered patio" offers some relief, as does the adjacent "tapas bar."

NEW L.A. Market *American/Californian*   ▽ 19 | 21 | 22 | $41
Downtown | J.W. Marriott at LA Live | 900 W. Olympic Blvd. (Figueroa St.) | 213-765-8600 | www.lalivemarriott.com
Chef Kerry Simon's newest adventure comes in the form of this moderately priced New American–Californian in Downtown's J.W. Marriott at LA Live, offering "tasty", "unique" takes on "creative" comfort food such as a bacon-topped meatloaf and a junk food platter of gourmet Sno Balls, Rice Krispies treats and cotton candy; surveyors stop in "before or after the Staples Center", as the wood-paneled walls and a communal table make for a casual atmosphere.

LAMILL Coffee Boutique *Californian*   21 | 20 | 19 | $24
Silver Lake | 1636 Silver Lake Blvd. (Effie St.) | 323-663-4441 | www.lamillcoffee.com
Get a "glimpse into the culture of java worshipers" at this "chic", "spendy" Silver Lake coffeehouse, a showcase for "sensational cups" and "ridiculously complicated" "brewing techniques" (e.g. "the elaborate dance" of the $11,000 Clover machine); the "inventive" Cal menu courtesy of Michael Cimarusti (Providence) is "surprisingly good", though some "hip" habitués lament "small portions" and staffers who seem "full of themselves."

Lamonica's NY Pizza ●⊄ *Pizza*   22 | 10 | 15 | $11
Westwood | 1066 Gayley Ave. (Kinross Ave.) | 310-208-8671
They "make a mean New York slice" at this no-frills "Westwood tradition", for three decades plus a counter-service "quick" stop for "classic thin-crust" pizza featuring dough imported from Gotham; however, the "blinding", subway-themed decor has even its student-heavy clientele considering "takeout."

Z Langer's Deli Z *Deli*   27 | 11 | 19 | $19
Downtown | 704 S. Alvarado St. (7th St.) | 213-483-8050 | www.langersdeli.com
The "legendary" "hand-sliced" pastrami and "fantastic double-baked rye" really get 'em "drooling" at this 1947-vintage Downtowner, a "clas-

FOOD | DECOR | SERVICE | COST

sic" "old-time deli" (tops in its category) staffed by "wiseacre" "waitresses who aren't afraid to call you 'honey'"; despite the "dicey" 'hood it's "worth the schlep" for a "fix", though regulars know to "call ahead" for curbside pickup; P.S. closes at 4 PM daily, closed Sundays.

La Paella ☒ Spanish   21 | 18 | 20 | $40
Beverly Hills | 476 S. San Vicente Blvd. (bet. La Cienega & Wilshire Blvds.) | 323-951-0745 | www.usalapaella.com

Aficionados of the "marvelous" namesake dish and "tasty" tapas also tout this "petite" Beverly Hills Spaniard for its "knowledgeable" staff and "warm", whitewashed surroundings that conjure up the Iberian "countryside"; it's all so "comfortingly traditional" "you'll swear you're in Spain", especially if you down enough of the "terrific sangria."

La Parolaccia Osteria Italiana Italian   21 | 15 | 21 | $30
Long Beach | 2945 E. Broadway (Orizaba Ave.) | 562-438-1235
Claremont | 201 N. Indian Hill (2nd St.) | 909-624-1516
www.laparolacciausa.com

"Authentic recipes" "straight from the old country" distinguish this "lively" Long Beach "neighborhood osteria" and its Claremont offshoot, where the "fresh pastas", "wood-fired" "Naples-style pizza" and other standards are made with lotsa "Italian lovin'"; affordable and "always welcoming", it's no surprise they're also "popular."

La Pergola Italian   23 | 19 | 23 | $41
Sherman Oaks | 15005 Ventura Blvd. (bet. Lemona & Noble Aves.) | 818-905-8402 | www.lapergolaristorante.net

"Homegrown ingredients" from the chef-owner's neighboring garden are "a major plus" at this Sherman Oaks "find", a longtime "local" "favorite" for the "freshness and flavor" of its "simple" Italian fare; "friendly" staffers add to the "relaxed" feel, and an interior adorned with ceramic "tchotchkes" and "flowers all over" is "loverly" if a little "dated."

La Piazza Italian   ▽ 18 | 22 | 20 | $37
Fairfax | The Grove | 189 The Grove Dr. (bet. Beverly Blvd. & 3rd St.) | 323-933-5050

"Grab a table outside" and "rest your feet after shopping at The Grove" at this Fairfax Italian, which sports two "people-watching" patios and a pizza- and pasta-centric menu that's "better than it needs to be"; it's a "welcoming" stop, but be prepared to "pay for the view."

NEW Larchmont Bungalow American   19 | 19 | 17 | $20
Mid-Wilshire | 107 N. Larchmont Blvd. (Beverly Blvd.) | 323-461-1528 | www.larchmontbungalow.com

"Rest and refuel after shopping" on Larchmont Boulevard at this "convenient" Mid-Wilshire stop, a "casual" "neighborhood" American restaurant known for red-velvet pancakes (breakfast is served all day) and other "enjoyable", "inexpensive" cooking; though it's a "quick in-and-out", it's also "easy" to linger on the patio scoping "all the street life."

Larchmont Grill American   22 | 21 | 24 | $41
Hollywood | 5750 Melrose Ave. (Lucerne Blvd.) | 323-464-4277 | www.larchmontgrill.com

With "a charming converted Craftsman" as the backdrop, this "comfortable" Hollywood New American "feels like home" as one of "the friendliest staffs" in town serves "wonderful" seasonal fare at "reason-

| | FOOD | DECOR | SERVICE | COST |

...ble prices" abetted by daily specials; regulars also commend the "re-
...ent makeover" and a location near Paramount's "main gate" that lets
...double as a "business canteen."

ares ◑ *Mexican* | 20 | 16 | 21 | $23 |

...anta Monica | 2909 Pico Blvd. (29th St.) | 310-829-4559 |
...ww.lares-restaurant.com

"Solid" "without the hype", this long-standing Santa Monica Mexican
...s "a step up from" the average "local" cantina with its "authentic", af-
...ordable chow and "terrific" service; despite a "festive" scene fueled
...y "terrific margaritas", a "mariachi" duo most nights and "lively" bar-
...oers, *novios* note it can be rather "romantic."

.a Rive Gauche *French* | 20 | 19 | 22 | $46 |

Palos Verdes Estates | 320 Tejon Pl. (Via Corta) | 310-378-0267

An "old favorite" in Palos Verdes Estates, this '70s-era French matches
...a "limited but very good" lineup of traditional fare with a lengthy wine
...ist and "warm" atmospherics; its mature clientele clamors it's "time
...o update" the "worn" "country-house" decor, but at least it's "never
...crowded" and there's "a wonderful patio."

.arkin's Ⓜ⇄ *Southern* | ▽ 18 | 18 | 18 | $24 |

Eagle Rock | 1496 Colorado Blvd. (Loleta Ave.) | 323-254-0934 |
www.larkinsjoint.com

"Creativity meets Southern comfort" at Larkin Mackey's cash-only "converted" bungalow in Eagle Rock, where the inventive "down-home
cookin'" is the "American Heart Association's worst nightmare" but devotees are "loving every bite"; "quaint", "arty" decor lends to the "hospitality", though "service can vary" and purists insist "soul food it ain't."

❷ **Larsen's Steakhouse** *Steak* | 23 | 25 | 23 | $62 |

Encino | Encino Pl. | 16101 Ventura Blvd. (Woodley Ave.) | 818-386-9500 |
www.larsensteakhouse.com

Encino's meat eaters maintain this "standout steakhouse" sets itself
apart with "ridiculously huge" slabs of "excellent" beef, "clever" back-
lit menus, "fantastic service" and a "sophisticated" "piano bar vibe"
defined by "rich woods"; it's very "adult", but also "very expensive", so
don't "have a cardiac when you get the check."

ᴺᴱᵂ **La Sandia Mexican**
Kitchen & Tequila Bar *Mexican* | - | - | - | M |

Santa Monica | Dining Deck, Santa Monica Pl. | 395 Santa Monica Pl.
(3rd. St. Promenade) | 310-393-3300 | www.richardsandoval.com

With more than a dozen restaurants worldwide, Richard Sandoval
(and his business partner, Placido Domingo) finally lands in SoCal, in this
dramatic Santa Monica Place space designed by AvroKO to look like an
old-style Mexican hacienda, balancing white stucco with terra-cotta,
reclaimed oak and lots of tiles surrounding a prominent bar specializing
in tequila; the menu offers moderately priced takes on classics such as
chicken mole poblano, achiote salmon and beef barbacoa enchiladas.

La Scala ⓢ *Italian* | 21 | 17 | 21 | $38 |

Beverly Hills | 434 N. Cañon Dr. (bet. Brighton Way & Santa Monica Blvd.) |
310-275-0579

(continued)

FOOD | DECOR | SERVICE | COST

(continued)

La Scala Presto 🖪 *Italian*

Brentwood | 11740 San Vicente Blvd. (bet. Barrington & Montana Aves.) |
310-826-6100
www.lascalabeverlyhills.com

"Dah-ling", the "ladies who lunch" know "it's all about" the "signature" Jean Leon chopped salad that leads the lineup at this "old fashioned" Beverly Hills Italian restaurant, a "comfy", booth-lined "nostalgia" trip tended by a "professional staff"; meanwhile the "smaller" Brentwood spin-off is more contempo-styled, and it's "not as pricey" either.

La Serenata de Garibaldi *Mexican/Seafood*   22 | 15 | 19 | $31

Boyle Heights | 1842 E. First St. (bet. Boyle Ave. & State St.) |
323-265-2887
Santa Monica | 1416 Fourth St. (bet. B'way & Santa Monica Blvd.) |
310-656-7017 Ⓜ

La Serenata Gourmet *Mexican/Seafood*

West LA | 10924 W. Pico Blvd. (bet. Veteran Ave. & Westwood Blvd.) |
310-441-9667
www.laserenataonline.com

"*Muy delicioso*" is the verdict on these "innovative but authentic" Mexican "mainstays", specializing in "mouthwatering" seafood and "unparalleled" sauces that make for a "rewarding" "change of pace"; expect service "with aplomb" and "reasonable prices" at all three, though insiders confide the haciendalike Boyle Heights original offers "more ambiance."

🖪 Lasher's Ⓜ *American*   24 | 23 | 24 | $44

Long Beach | 3441 E. Broadway (bet. Newport & Redondo Aves.) |
562-433-0153 | www.lashersrestaurant.com

Owners Lynn and Ray Lasher put "lots of heart" into this Long Beach "winner", a "quaint" "Craftsman house" "made over" into a "warm and inviting" setting for "top-rate" American cuisine that draws inspiration from New England and the South; with "personal" service and several "delightful" rooms, it "couldn't be more charming" for "a special occasion."

La Sosta Enoteca Ⓜ *Italian*   - | - | - | E

Hermosa Beach | 2700 Manhattan Ave. (27th St.) | 310-318-1556

"Authentic" "cutting-board" specialties like cheese and charcuterie (sliced by the owner himself), "wonderful" bistro bites and fine Italian vinos meet in romantically snug quarters at this "hidden" Hermosa Beach enoteca; some paupers protest it's "way overpriced", but admirers encourage a splurge: "let them pick the wines and have fun."

La Strada *Italian*   ▽ 21 | 17 | 22 | $26
(fka Caffe La Strada)

Long Beach | 4716 E. Second St. (bet. Park & Roycroft Aves.) |
562-433-8100 | www.lastradaon2nd.com

"Hearty" food "like your mama made" is served up with "no pretenses" at this Long Beach Italian on Belmont Shore's collegiate strip; it's a simple "little" storefront "joint", but for "tasty" pizza and pasta "at an affordable price", "it does the trick."

	FOOD	DECOR	SERVICE	COST

Laurel Tavern *American* — 23 | 18 | 16 | $25

Studio City | 11938 Ventura Blvd. (bet. Carpenter Ave. & Laurel Canyon Blvd.) | 818-506-0777 | www.laureltavern.net

Perpetually "hopping", this "friendly" Studio City gastropub is where the "over 30s" turn up for Cali craft beers and "outstanding" "bar food" (notably the "delicious burgers" and "pork-fat french fries") in an exposed-brick "neighborhood" setting; but while the eating "surpasses expectations", it can be a "loud" "zoo" with "atrocious waits" "in prime time."

☑ La Vecchia Cucina *Italian* — 25 | 19 | 25 | $40

Santa Monica | 2654 Main St. (bet. Hill St. & Ocean Park Blvd.) | 310-399-7979 | www.lavecchiacucina.com

"Come hungry, leave happy" at this "unexpected gem" among the many options on Santa Monica's Main Street, a "consistent" local "staple" for "satisfying" Italian cuisine including antipasti, pastas, "mouthwatering osso buco" and "addictive" bread paired with garlic dip; the "cheerful", art-filled surroundings are "busy most nights", but insiders insist the servers will "make you feel welcome" amid the multitudes.

NEW La Vida — - | - | - | E

Restaurant & Lounge Ⓢ Ⓜ *Californian/Spanish*

Hollywood | 1448 N. Gower St. (Sunset Blvd.) | 323-962-0800 | www.lavidahollywood.com

Full of *vida* from day one, this hip, bustling Hollywood destination is the new home of chef Joseph Panarello (ex Rivera) and his upmarket, Spanish-accented Californian cuisine; the former Pinot Hollywood space displays an arresting mash-up of modern Iberian and Moroccan influences – hand-blown lanterns, archways and a wavy aqua bar – but tables in the fire pit–equipped courtyard are the most coveted.

NEW Lawrence of India *Indian* — - | - | - | I

Culver City | 10032 Venice Blvd. (Clarrington Ave.) | 310-841-6559 | www.lawrenceofindia.com

The Lawrence of this Culver City Indian's name is actually chef Lourence Monteiro, who made his name several decades ago at legendary upscale tandoori and curry house Paul Bhalla's Cuisine of India; he returns to the stove at this plain-Jane mini-mall arrival, where he's offering an inexpensive menu that mixes recipes from Southern India, Goa and Delhi.

Lawry's Carvery *American* — 20 | 12 | 16 | $25

Downtown | LA Live | 1011 S. Figueroa St. (Olympic Blvd.) | 213-222-2212

Century City | Westfield Century City Shopping Ctr. | 10250 Santa Monica Blvd. (bet. Ave. of the Stars & Century Park W.) | 310-432-0101

www.lawrysonline.com

Combining "quick with quality", these links in the "Lawry's light minichain" are "easy" "counter-service" stops for "carved-to-order" "sandwich versions" of the "amazing prime rib" found at the "mother ship restaurant in Beverly Hills"; still, many maintain they're "kind of expensive" for "food-court" fare.

LOS ANGELES

Z Lawry's The Prime Rib *Steak* — 26 | 23 | 26 | $53

Beverly Hills | 100 N. La Cienega Blvd. (bet. Beverly Blvd. & 3rd St.) | 310-652-2827 | www.lawrysonline.com

"Tradition tops innovation" at this "time-honored" steakhouse chain and LA "landmark" in Beverly Hills luring guests since 1938 with "superb", "buttery" beef – carved tableside off "elegant" silver carts – and "heavenly" sides; the "retro" digs and somewhat "formal" service are "a hoot", so despite a "touristy" vibe and clientele that "puts the old in old-school", many find it worth the "splurge" for a "special" meal.

Lazy Dog Cafe, The *Eclectic* — 17 | 18 | 18 | $23

Torrance | Del Amo Fashion Ctr. | 3525 W. Carson St. (bet. Hawthorne Blvd. & Madrona Ave.) | 310-921-6080 | www.lazydogcafe.com

"Take the kids" to these "busy" chain outlets, where a "variety" of "substantial" Eclectic SoCal fare is priced for "value" in surroundings featuring "fun" pooch theming and a patio; it works for a "quick bite" "before a movie", though foes growl the noise level's "just a few decibels short of a Who concert."

NEW Lazy Ox Canteen ● *Eclectic* — 24 | 18 | 22 | $45

Little Tokyo | 241 S. San Pedro St. (bet. 2nd & 3rd Sts.) | 213-626-5299 | www.lazyoxcanteen.com

Culinary "wizard" Josef Centeno "effortlessly incorporates" international influences into his "wildly innovative" Eclectic menu at this Little Tokyo canteen, "an instant favorite" for its "impressive" meat-centric small plates, "gracious staff" and "reasonable prices"; the "cool but casual setting" with bare bulbs swinging from the ceiling stays "welcoming" into the late hours (doors usually close at midnight).

Le Chêne *French* — ▽ 25 | 22 | 23 | $39

Saugus | 12625 Sierra Hwy. (bet. Sierra Vallejo Rd. & Steele Ave.) | 661-251-4315 | www.lechene.com

Oui, it's in the "middle of nowhere", but this longtime Saugus "jewel" is a "neat surprise" that "amazes" with "real" traditional French (game and seafood included) served in rustic quarters with a stone facade reminiscent of a rural castle; the "extensive wine list" and leafy patio provide extra incentive to head for "the boondocks."

Z Leila's M *Californian* — 27 | 20 | 24 | $47

Oak Park | Oak Park Plaza | 706 Lindero Canyon Rd. (Kanan Rd.) | 818-707-6939 | www.leilasrestaurant.com

"Gourmet fare in a suburban strip mall" attracts "well-deserved" "attention" to this Oak Park Californian, hailed as the "crown jewel of the Conejo Valley" for its "fabulous" menu (now focused on "imaginative" small plates) and "incredibly diverse" wine list, all "superbly served" at relatively "reasonable prices"; "tucked" into a "cute", newly renovated space, it's a "destination" that "can compete with the best."

Lemonade Cafe *Californian* — 23 | 15 | 18 | $17

West Hollywood | 9001 Beverly Blvd. (Almont Dr.) | West Hollywood | 310-247-2500
NEW Downtown | MOCA | 250 S. Grand Ave. (bet. 2nd & 3rd Sts.) | 213-628-0200
Downtown | 505 S. Flower St. (bet. 5th & 6th Sts.) | 213-488-0299 ⊠

(continued)

Lemonade Cafe
NEW **Venice** | 1661 Abbot Kinney Blvd. (Venice Blvd.) |
310-452-6200
www.lemonadela.com
Named for its "spectacular" flavored lemonades, this burgeoning area
chainlet offers "lots of choice" with a "fresh and original" variety of
Californian fare ("fantastic salads") served "cafeteria-style" in
"bright" venues; "helpful" staffers and nice prices make it a "favorite"
for "healthy" lunching, even if some are sour on the "stark" decor.

Lemon Moon ☒ *Californian/Mediterranean*   20 | 14 | 16 | $19
West LA | Westside Media Ctr. | 12200 W. Olympic Blvd. (Bundy Dr.) |
310-442-9191 | www.lemonmoon.com
Wholesome breakfast fare and an "interesting assortment" of "fresh"
salads and sandwiches draw a "business crowd" at this informal West
LA Cal-Med from Josiah Citrin and Raphael Lunetta, an economical
fave for morning munches and "working lunches"; a few moon the industrial interior is "not very inviting", but there's a patio and it's "efficient" for takeout; P.S. open weekdays till 3 PM.

Le Pain Quotidien *Bakery/Belgian*   20 | 16 | 17 | $21
West Hollywood | 8607 Melrose Ave. (Westbourne Dr.) |
310-854-3700
Beverly Hills | 320 S. Robertson Blvd. (bet. Burton Way & 3rd St.) |
310-858-7270
Beverly Hills | 9630 Little Santa Monica Blvd. (bet. Bedford & Camden Drs.) |
310-859-1100
Brentwood | Barrington Ct. | 11702 Barrington Ct. (Barrington Ave.) |
310-476-0969
Brentwood | 13050 San Vicente Blvd. (26th St.) | 310-393-8909
Santa Monica | 316 Santa Monica Blvd. (bet. 3rd & 4th Sts.) |
310-393-6800
Westwood | 1055 Broxton Ave. (bet. Kinross & Weyburn Aves.) |
310-824-7900
Manhattan Beach | Metlox Plaza | 451 Manhattan Beach Blvd.
(bet. Morningside & Valley Drs.) | 310-546-6411
Pasadena | 88 W. Colorado Blvd. (De Lacey Ave.) | 626-396-0956
Studio City | 13045 Ventura Blvd. (bet. Coldwater Canyon Ave. &
Valley Vista Blvd.) | 818-986-1929
www.lepainquotidien.com
Additional locations throughout Southern California
This "charming chain" of Belgian bakery/cafes satisfies "more than
quotidian" needs with its "awesome coffee", "delightful pastries"
and "fabulous" "organic breads" – not to mention "fresh", "flavorful" soups, salads and tartines – served up "quick" in "accessible",
"communal-dining" settings; some are pained by "European prices"
and "indifferent" staffers, but they're ever "dependable", especially
for "breezy lunches."

Le Petit Bistro *French*   20 | 19 | 20 | $39
West Hollywood | 631 N. La Cienega Blvd. (Melrose Ave.) | 310-289-9797 |
www.lepetitbistro.us
"You'll swear you're on the Left Bank" at this "intimate" West
Hollywood bistro, which boasts "genuine" Gallic grub and a "faux
Parisian setting" that's often "crowded" and "a bit loud"; "service can

be slow", but Francophiles are in for "a "satisfying experience" at a "reasonable price."

Le Petit Cafe ⊠ *French*

21	15	21	$39

Santa Monica | 2842 Colorado Ave. (bet. Stewart & Yale Sts.) | 310-829-6792 | www.lepetitcafebonjour.com

"French food without the attitude" is "easy to love" according to admirers of this "quaint" "local bistro" in Santa Monica, which matches "quality" cooking and *"joie de cuisine"* with "personal service"; installed in "relaxed" digs decorated "with a provincial touch", it's a "keeper" that's "worth searching out."

Le Petit Four *French*

20	19	19	$35

West Hollywood | Sunset Plaza | 8654 W. Sunset Blvd. (Sunset Plaza Dr.) | 310-652-3863 | www.lepetitfour.net

West Hollywood's "sunglasses-wearing" "beautiful people" tout this midpriced French cafe for its "Euro" atmosphere and "sidewalk seating" in Sunset Plaza, an "ideal" site for eyeballing "the Sunset Strip scene"; for most, the "extensive menu" of "generously portioned", globally inflected dishes is "better than average" but "secondary" to the scene.

Le Petit Greek *Greek*

21	16	22	$33

Hancock Park | 127 N. Larchmont Blvd. (bet. Beverly Blvd. & 1st St.) | 323-464-5160 | www.lepetitgreek.com

"Recipes straight from Athens" lure Hancock Park locals to this "dependable neighborhood" Greek for "classic choices" like "falling-off-the-bone" lamb shank and a "cacophony" of "fab" meze; "gracious service" and fair prices help make it "popular" for alfresco meals while "watching life go by" on Larchmont Boulevard.

Le Petit Restaurant *French*

23	19	22	$38

Sherman Oaks | 13360 Ventura Blvd. (Dixie Canyon Ave.) | 818-501-7999 | www.lepetitrestaurant.net

You won't "need your passport" for a "Parisian fix" in Sherman Oaks thanks to this "homey" "neighborhood French bistro", which offers a "classic menu" of "excellent" food and wine "at a modest cost"; the "close" but "comfortable" surroundings are brightened by "wonderful service", and regulars "love their Monday and Tuesday lobster special."

Le Saigon Ⓜ⇥ *Vietnamese*

20	10	21	$16

West LA | 11611 Santa Monica Blvd. (bet. Barry & Federal Aves.) | 310-312-2929 | www.lesaigoncuisine.com

"Get your pho fix" at this "reliable" West LA "hole-in-the-wall", a "low-cost" spot for "comforting" "Vietnamese favorites" served up "fast" in "completely unassuming" surroundings; given the "very friendly" feel, fans can cope with the cash-only and no-alcohol policies.

Le Saint Amour *French*

20	19	20	$40

Culver City | 9725 Culver Blvd. (bet. Duquesne Ave. & Lafayette Pl.) | 310-842-8155 | www.lesaintamour.com

"Paris has landed" in Culver City at this "by-the-book" brasserie from "lovely" husband-and-wife team Bruno and Florence Herve-Commereuc (ex Angelique Café), serving "totally authentic" French "standards" like charcuterie and "housemade terrines" "at moderate prices"; if the

"Francophone" *garçons* don't "sweep you away", the "lively" setting with crimson banquettes, mirrors and a "pleasant" patio will.

Le Sanglier French Restaurant Ⓜ *French*   25 | 23 | 23 | $56

Tarzana | 5522 Crebs Ave. (Ventura Blvd.) | 818-345-0470 | www.lesanglierrestaurant.com

A "little-known gem" in Tarzana, this French vet "skillfully prepares" "hearty" "old-style" fare including the namesake wild boar in "quiet", candlelit environs; it's a trifle "pricey", but the "classy" service and "beautifully decorated" space keep things "warm" and "cozy" for "a special occasion" or "romantic" rendezvous.

🛂 Les Sisters Southern Kitchen Ⓜ *Southern*   25 | 11 | 23 | $20

Chatsworth | 21818 Devonshire St. (Jordan Ave.) | 818-998-0755 | www.lessisters.com

It's only a "family-run hole-in-the-wall", but they "can really cook" those "down-home" Southern staples at this "true" taste of "New Orleans" in Chatsworth; "decor is nonexistent" aside from Mardi Gras beads, but it's "very friendly" and you "can't beat the prices", so "what's not to love?"; P.S. no alcohol or BYO.

🛂 Let's Be Frank Ⓜ⌿ *Hot Dogs*   21 | 9 | 19 | $10

Culver City | Helms Ave. (bet. Venice & Washington Blvds.) | 888-233-7265 | www.letsbefrankdogs.com

"Sustainable", "grass-fed beef" franks with a "satisfying snap" illicit "OMGs" at this "incredible" food truck, a roving hot dog stand parked Wednesday–Sunday outside Culver City's Helms Bakery Complex; brats, turkey dogs and "high-quality" garnishes round out the "addictive" lineup, though a few are frankly "overwhelmed by the price"; P.S. check Twitter for other locations.

NEW Libra *Brazilian*   - | - | - | I

Culver City | 3833 Main St. (Culver Blvd.) | 310-202-1300 | www.bythelibra.com

Wash your hands at the designer sink found at the entrance of this ultramodern Culver City Brazilian before selecting various salads, marinated vegetables and barbecued churrascaria from the buffet line; the reasonable prices are paid by the pound, which, for better or worse, helps you keep track of the damage you're doing to your diet.

Library Alehouse *Eclectic*   19 | 16 | 19 | $23

Santa Monica | 2911 Main St. (bet. Ashland Ave. & Marine St.) | 310-314-4855 | www.libraryalehouse.com

Global "twists" "elevate" this Santa Monica haunt's Eclectic fare "above run-of-the-mill bar food", and an "insanely great" selection of specialty beers (including West Coast microbrews on tap) keeps the mood "relaxed"; set in casual, Craftsman-style quarters with a "lively" back patio, "it gets busy" "for a good reason."

Library Bar *American*   ∇ 17 | 18 | 19 | $25

Downtown | Library Court Bldg. | 630 W. Sixth St. (Hope St.) | 213-614-0053 | www.librarybarla.com

Bibliophiles are "so happy" to have this gastropub near the Downtown Central Library, where walls of books and loungey sofas provide a highbrow backdrop for American "bar food" featuring "some of the best burgers" around; add an international beer selection and those craving a little Chaucer with their chow wonder "what's not to like?"

Lido di Manhattan *Italian/Mediterranean* ▽ 18 | 15 | 18 | $32
Manhattan Beach | 1550 Rosecrans Ave. (bet. Aviation & Sepulveda Blvds.) | 310-536-0730 | www.lidodimanhattan.com

"Recently redone" by TV chef Gordon Ramsay, this affordable Manhattan Beach bistro earns an "A for effort" with its light contempo look, "decent" Italian-Med cooking and new vino-centric leanings (with half-price bottles on Monday); nonfans of the "ordinary" food fear it's "lost a step", but for "neighborhood" loyalists it's still a "mainstay."

Lilly's French Cafe & Wine Bar *French* 19 | 19 | 17 | $38
Venice | 1031 Abbot Kinney Blvd. (bet. Brooks & Westminster Aves.) | 310-314-0004 | www.lillysfrenchcafe.com

Moules frites "are a must" at this "unpretentious" "local" bistro in Venice, providing "well-prepared" "French classics" and 120 wines by the glass in a newly spruced-up setting sporting a "pretty patio"; with a "competent staff" and "fair prices" (especially the prix fixe lunch/brunch "deal"), it's "something a bit special."

Literati Cafe *Californian/Eclectic* 17 | 15 | 17 | $28
West LA | 12081 Wilshire Blvd. (Bundy Dr.) | 310-231-7484 | www.literaticafe.com
Literati Cafe West *Californian/Eclectic*
West LA | 12081 Wilshire Blvd. (Bundy Dr.) | 310-479-3400 | www.literati2.com

Westsiders wanting a "place to relax" over "simple" Cal-Eclectic fare frequent this "literary"-themed coffeehouse and its full-service "satellite" next door, which ply separate menus of "very decent" bites; while "a little pricey", they're "convenient" "neighborhood hangouts" for "laptop tappers" and "UCLA students."

Little Dom's *Italian* 21 | 20 | 20 | $33
Los Feliz | 2128 Hillhurst Ave. (Avocado St.) | 323-661-0055
Deli at Little Dom's *Italian*
Los Feliz | 2128 Hillhurst Ave. (Avocado St.) | 323-661-0088 www.littledoms.com

"Delectable paper thin-crusted pizzas" (including breakfast pies that "can't be beat") and other "enjoyable" Italian dishes satisfy at this "cozy Los Feliz hang" and sib of Dominick's boasting "big", cushy booths and a patio overlooking Hillhurst; although it's a "hipster" favorite, it has a "low-key" vibe and relatively modest prices, especially on Mondays, when it features a $15 supper; P.S. the adjacent Deli at Little Dom's vends salads and sandwiches from its antique deli case.

Little Door, The *Mediterranean* 23 | 25 | 21 | $52
Third Street | 8164 W. Third St. (bet. Kilkea Dr. & La Jolla Ave.) | 323-951-1210 | www.thelittledoor.com

Amorous types are all over this "romantic" Third Street "hideaway" where "wonderful" seasonal Med fare comes served on a lush garden patio lit by "twinkling lights"; yes, it's "spendy", but service is "attentive" and most find it "worth every penny" for a "magical" evening.

	FOOD	DECOR	SERVICE	COST

NEW Living Room/
Station Hollywood ● *Mediterranean*

	-	-	-	M

Hollywood | W Hollywood Hotel | 6250 Hollywood Blvd. (Vine St.) | 323-798-1300 | www.whotels.com

The W Hollywood Hotel is home to this new arrival from Innovative Dining Group (Boa, Katana, Sushi Roku), which plays to a cool clientele with Station, a chic patio lounge named for the adjacent MTA stop, and the Living Room, an airy bar/eatery flaunting updated Tinsel Town swank; the Med small plates come courtesy of chef Sascha Lyon (ex Daniel in New York) at prices the hipoisie can easily live with.

Lobster, The *Seafood*

	23	23	21	$54

Santa Monica | 1602 Ocean Ave. (Colorado Ave.) | 310-458-9294 | www.thelobster.com

"Fabulous" "fresh seafood" showcasing "perfectly cooked lobster" and "jaw-dropping ocean views" provide plenty of claws to celebrate at this green-certified fish house at the "mouth of the Santa Monica Pier"; admittedly it's "loud" and "touristy", but service is "top-notch" and if you're with a "significant other" or an "out-of-town guest", it's one of the "best splurges" around ("especially at sunset").

Lobster Trap *Seafood*

	-	-	-	M

Catalina Island | 128 Catalina Ave. (3rd St.) | Avalon | 310-510-8585 | www.catalinalobstertrap.com

Just a shell's toss from the water, this casual Catalina Island seafooder features fresh fin fare prepared your way and assorted nautical decor, including a boat's stern that doubles as a stage for live bands on weekends; the pool table and tap beers draw a youthful bar crowd, but frequent specials lure in all ages.

Local *American*

	▽ 22	13	19	$21

Silver Lake | 2943 W. Sunset Blvd. (bet. Parkman Ave. & Reno St.) | 323-662-4740 | www.silverlakelocal.com

"Mostly organic, all delicious", this Silver Lake BYO enchants the eco-conscious with seasonal American eats made with "fresh", locally sourced ingredients, spanning a salad bar to "outstanding" carnivorous choices; recycled furniture and mostly open-air seating drive home the theme, and "reasonable prices" conserve the other kind of green.

Local Place, The *Hawaiian*

	17	12	16	$13

Torrance | 18605 S. Western Ave. (186th St.) | 310-523-3233 | www.kingshawaiianrestaurants.com

"Reconnect with your aloha" at this Torrance "quick-fix" Hawaiian, where the "simple" specialties and "excellent" King's Hawaiian baked goods deliver a dose of island "home cooking" "at a great price"; it's "fast-food style" with everything "served on plastic", but "tables inside and out" mean "there's always a place to sit."

NEW Locals Sports Bar & Grill *Pub Food*

	-	-	-	I

Mid-City | 5047 W. Pico Blvd. (La Brea Ave.) | 323-930-1400 | www.localssportsbar.com

Local jocks root for this roomy Mid-City joint, a newcomer to the underserved area around Pico and La Brea that sports spare decor, a 40-ft. bar and "lots of TV screens" beaming the games; though fairly priced, the "snacks and bar food" (think burgers and wings) are not necessarily the main event.

Locanda del Lago *Italian* 22 | 21 | 22 | $39

Santa Monica | 231 Arizona Ave. (2nd St.) | 310-451-3525 | www.lagosantamonica.com

This "warm" Northern Italian is a Santa Monica "staple" for "delicious" cooking from the Lake Como region made "even tastier" by "charming servers" and rusticated quarters with a patio that's "super" for "observing the action" on the Promenade; for those who find price a sticking point, the "upbeat" "happy hour is a real bargain."

NEW Locanda Positano 🖪 *Italian* - | - | - | M

Marina del Rey | 4059 Lincoln Blvd. (Washington Blvd.) | 310-526-3887 | www.locandapositano.com

Looking a bit like a country inn, with cream-colored walls, wood beams and exotically ornate hanging lamps, this Marina-adjacent white-tablecloth Italian offers a small menu with a decided leaning toward fin fare; expect the likes of seafood salad with cannellini beans and shallots and grilled salmon crusted with almonds and pistachios – not surprising, considering you can smell the ocean just down the street.

Locanda Veneta *Italian* 25 | 19 | 22 | $54

Third Street | 8638 W. Third St. (Willaman Dr.) | 310-274-1893 | www.locandaveneta.net

Made for "date nights", this pocket-sized Italian "classic" on Third Street supplies "superb" "homemade" trattoria fare with a Venetian twist and "attentive service" "without the attitude" in a setting that's distinctly "intimate" (if "a bit close"); admittedly, it's "not cheap", but admirers agree the "top-caliber" experience is "worth every penny."

Loft, The *Hawaiian* 19 | 12 | 19 | $17

Cerritos | 20157 Pioneer Blvd. (Del Amo Blvd.) | 562-402-3538
Torrance | 23305 Hawthorne Blvd. (Lomita Blvd.) | 310-375-4051
www.thelofthawaii.com

"Close to the real deal", these family-owned mini-chain outlets in Torrance and Cerritos furnish "plentiful" plates of "satisfying" "Hawaiian home cooking" at "low prices"; service is "friendly and efficient", but be ready for "casual", island-esque settings that pay "little attention to ambiance."

Lomo Arigato *Japanese/Peruvian* - | - | - | I

Location varies; see website | www.lomoarigato.com

Fusion goes mobile as this converted FedEx truck fires up Japanese-Peruvian cheap eats – featuring three takes on its trademark lomo saltado – at stops around the city; the itinerary usually includes Gardena (owner Eric Nakata's home turf), but check Twitter for all of the day's locations.

L'Opera *Italian* 23 | 23 | 24 | $48

Long Beach | 101 Pine Ave. (bet. Broadway & Ocean Blvd.) | 562-491-0066 | www.lopera.com

Let them "pamper you" at this Long Beach Northern Italian, where a landmark "renovated bank" building provides the "elegant" backdrop for "sophisticated" cuisine, "stellar wines" and "truly professional service"; with "live opera arias" filling the spacious interior on weekends, it's "rather expensive" but "memorable" "when only the best will do."

NEW Los Arroyos *Mexican* | 23 | 17 | 20 | $23 |

Camarillo | The Promenade at Camarillo Premium Outlets |
630 Ventura Blvd. (Las Posas Rd.) | 805-987-4000 |
www.losarroyos.net

"The Arroyo family has nailed it" with this low-cost threesome around LA and Santa Barbara, acclaimed as "a cut above" for "authentic", "high-quality" Mexican chow; they're "not haute", but the informal style means it's "possible to get in and out" "fast" or linger and enjoy the "relaxed vibe."

Los Balcones del Peru M *Peruvian* | – | – | – | I |

Hollywood | 1360 N. Vine St. (De Longpre Ave.) | 323-871-9600

"Don't let the humble" digs in a strip center "fool you" advise locals who "absolutely love" the ceviche, lomo saltado and other "first-class" fare at this Hollywood Peruvian; portions are ample, and for penny-pinchers "the price is right"; P.S. a renovation and kitchen expansion were underway at press time.

Lotería! Grill *Mexican* | 24 | 15 | 18 | $23 |

Fairfax | Farmers Mkt. | 6333 W. Third St. (Fairfax Ave.) | 323-930-2211
Hollywood | 6627 Hollywood Blvd. (bet. Cherokee & Whitley Aves.) |
323-465-2500 ◑
NEW Studio City | 12050 Ventura Blvd. (Laurel Canyon Blvd.) |
818-508-5300
www.loteriagrill.com

"Never bland or boring", chef-owner Jimmy Shaw's "crowded" "Farmers Market stall" on Fairfax "is the bomb" for "regional Mexican", notably "thrilling" fillings piled on "handmade" corn tortillas; the "well-priced" Hollywood and Studio City sites add "delicious margaritas" to the mix as the "staff moves fast and furious" in "bright", sometimes "deafening" dining rooms; P.S. Hollywood closes at 2 AM Thursday–Saturday.

Z Lou ◑Z *Eclectic/Mediterranean* | 25 | 16 | 21 | $38 |

Hollywood | 724 Vine St. (Melrose Ave.) | 323-962-6369 |
www.louonvine.com

Run "with passion" by owner and wine guru Lou Amdur, this pint-sized Hollywood "hideaway" offers an ever-changing menu "chock-a-block" with "fantastic" Med-Eclectic dishes ("get the pig candy") along with "inspired", "under-the-radar" vinos; sure, the "strip-mall" venue's "quirky", but once you're busy "expanding your palate" "you'll never notice"; P.S. Mondays feature a $55 prix fixe pairing dinner.

Louise's Trattoria *Californian/Italian* | 17 | 15 | 19 | $26 |

Hancock Park | 232 N. Larchmont Blvd. (Beverly Blvd.) |
323-962-9510
Los Feliz | 4500 Los Feliz Blvd. (Hillhurst Ave.) | 323-667-0777
Santa Monica | 1008 Montana Ave. (10th St.) | 310-394-8888
Santa Monica | 264 26th St. (bet. Georgina Ave. & San Vicente Blvd.) |
310-451-5001
West LA | 10645 W. Pico Blvd. (bet. Manning & Pelham Aves.) |
310-475-6084
Pasadena | 2-8 E. Colorado Blvd. (Fair Oaks Ave.) | 626-568-3030
(continued)

(continued)

Louise's Trattoria

Studio City | 12050 Ventura Blvd. (Laurel Canyon Blvd.) | 818-762-2662 |
www.louises.com

For "big eaters on a small budget", this Cal-Italian chain is "dependable" for "basic" fare set down with "no pretensions"; foes find the "formula" all too "predictable", but they're an "easy" "go-to" for a "family meal."

Lucille's Smokehouse Bar-B-Que BBQ   22 | 18 | 19 | $28

Cerritos | 11338 E. South St. (Gridley Rd.) | 562-916-7427
Long Beach | 4828 E. Second St. (bet. Park & St. Joseph Aves.) | 562-434-7427
Long Beach | Long Beach Towne Ctr. | 7411 Carson St. (Nectar Ave.) | 562-938-7427
Torrance | Del Amo Fashion Ctr. | 21420 Hawthorne Blvd. (Del Amo Circle Blvd.) | 310-370-7427
www.lucillesbbq.com

"Humongous portions" of "meaty ribs" and other "mouthwatering, artery-clogging" BBQ will "make you feel like a caveman" at this "reasonably priced" Southern chain; done up as ersatz roadhouses, the "loud", "kid-friendly" venues are "perpetually busy" with "hungry" "crowds", so expect "slow" going and "the usual wait."

Lucky Devils American   ▽ 21 | 14 | 18 | $22

Hollywood | 6613 Hollywood Blvd. (Whitley Ave.) | 323-465-8259 |
www.luckydevils-la.com

Hollywood denizens are "thrilled with" the "awesome burgers", "exotic" shakes and "craft beers aplenty" at this "relaxed" American "joint" from chef-owner and erstwhile *All My Children* hunk Lucky Vanous; it's "a find" if you're "wandering on" the Boulevard, but expect nondescript digs and "gawking" street folk if you sit outside.

☒ Lucques Californian/Mediterranean   27 | 24 | 25 | $62

West Hollywood | 8474 Melrose Ave. (La Cienega Blvd.) | 323-655-6277 |
www.lucques.com

"Sensational" chef Suzanne Goin is "still the queen of the hill" at this WeHo Cal-Med "standard-bearer", a "charming" carriage house where a "sublime", oft-"changing menu" featuring "the freshest ingredients" is paired with a "thoughtful" wine list curated by co-owner Caroline Styne; "impeccable" service and a "lovely courtyard" add to an "essential" experience, and the prix fixe Sunday suppers are an "amazing" "bargain."

LudoBites Asian/Mediterranean   - | - | - | E

Location varies; see website | www.ludobites.com

One of LA's hottest tickets, this guerilla pop-up phenomenon is the brainchild of chef Ludo Lefebvre, who sets up temporary shop in various eateries (Breadbar, Royal/T and Gram & Papas thus far) and turns out pricey feasts featuring edgy Med-Asian bites; there are no firm plans for the next iteration, but you can sign up on the website for notification – just be quick, as these rezzies go fast.

Lula Mexican   21 | 19 | 21 | $28

Santa Monica | 2720 Main St. (bet. Ashland Ave. & Hill St.) | 310-392-5711 |
www.lulacocinamexicana.com

"Authentic" cooking and 400-plus tequilas make this Santa Monican a "favorite" for "delicious" "regional" Mexican and "killer margarias"; sporting "festive decor" with "larger-than-life" murals and a "bougainvillea-covered patio", it's "lots of fun" for "out-of-towners" and kids, who are treated to magic shows on Saturdays.

Lunada Bayhouse ▣ *Seafood/Steak*

| - | - | - | M |

Palos Verdes Estates | 2325 Palos Verdes Dr. W. (Yarmouth Rd.) | 310-544-1704 | www.lunadabayhouse.com

A "welcome" option in an underserved area, this yearling provides "above-average" surf 'n' turf fare from modestly adorned quarters sited in a Palos Verdes strip center; tabs run "a little high for what you get", but it's staffed by an "attentive and friendly" crew and "they're trying."

Luna Park *American*

| 19 | 19 | 20 | $29 |

La Brea | 672 S. La Brea Ave. (Wilshire Blvd.) | 323-934-2110 | www.lunaparkla.com

"Younger, hip" types frequent this "cool" La Brea eatery where the "tasty" spins on American fare ("save room for s'mores") and "creative" drinks are "priced right"; "professional" service and "private" booths help balance a "vibrant bar scene" that gets "loud during peak times."

Lunasia *Chinese*
(fka Triumphal Palace)

| ▽ 22 | 17 | 15 | $27 |

Alhambra | 500 W. Main St. (5th St.) | 626-308-3222 | www.lunasiachinesecuisine.com

"These folks know how to do dim sum!" enthuse fans of this polished Alhambra Chinese, where servers sans carts deliver "fabulous" morsels that weigh in at "twice the size" of most other joints'; there's also "real" Cantonese seafood, but word is out so "prepare to wait" on weekends.

NEW Lunch ▣ *American*

| - | - | - | I |

Culver City | 3829 Main St. (Culver Blvd.) | 310-837-6200 | www.eatatlunch.com

Not your average grab 'n' go, this relatively new Culver City lunch counter supplies "terrific" salads and sandwiches two ways: choose from their menu of specialties or "build your own" from a lengthy list of fresh ingredients; the streamlined space includes a beer-and-wine bar, and it's also open (with table service) for dinner.

NEW Mac & Cheeza *American*

| - | - | - | I |

Downtown | 223 W. Eighth St. (Main St.) | 213-622-3782 | www.macandcheeza.com

It's mix-and-match time at this storefront Downtown comfort-fooder opened by Larkin's in Eagle Rock, where the budget-friendly menu lets you choose between four sizes (Baby Mac, Momma Mac, Daddy Mac, Mac Daddy) of the titular item; to beef up the already-filling dish, there are add-ons running the gamut from collard greens to BBQ chicken.

Madame Matisse *American*

| - | - | - | I |

Silver Lake | 3536 W. Sunset Blvd. (bet. Golden Gate & Maltman Aves.) | 323-662-4862

"The tiniest kitchen on the planet" turns out "wonderful", "fresh" breakfast and lunch "staples" at this Silver Lake American cafe, which "accommodates" followers with "down-to-earth" service and gentle prices; the limited seating's "mostly outdoors" on a "noisy" stretch of Sunset, but at least it's "good for people-watching."

Madeleine Bistro ⓜ *French/Vegan*
▽ 28 | 20 | 25 | $37

Tarzana | 18621 Ventura Blvd. (bet. Amigo & Yolanda Aves.) | 818-758-6971 | www.madeleinebistro.com

"A must-visit for vegans", this "elegant" Tarzana "find" may "even please the most devoted meat eaters" as chef-owner David Anderson orchestrates French "fine dining" with a "creative and surprisingly delicious" vegetarian twist; factor in "friendly service" and manageable tabs, and it's "like discovering heaven" for the organic set.

Madeo *Italian*
25 | 20 | 23 | $67

West Hollywood | 8897 Beverly Blvd. (Swall Dr.) | 310-859-4903

For "old-school Northern Italian" "classics" "done right", WeHo's "trendy" types and "paparazzi"-dodging "celebs" still pack this "family run" "hot spot" set in a "dark", "underground" space that's like "being transported" to "a different world"; the downsides are "diet-sized portions" and "astronomical prices", and though service can be "superb" "if you're not an Oscar winner" or a "known client", fuhgeddaboudit.

Madison, The ●𝕊 *Seafood/Steak*
▽ 22 | 27 | 20 | $57

Long Beach | 102 Pine Ave. (1st St.) | 562-628-8866 | www.themadisonrestaurant.com

"Soaring ceilings and spectacular chandeliers" lend this capaciously "elegant" Long Beacher in a "former bank building" "tons of character" to admire as you "savor" costly but "wonderful" steaks and seafood jazz piano enhances the mood on weekends, but views still vary on whether the service is "top notch" or "stuck up."

Maggiano's Little Italy *Italian*
19 | 19 | 19 | $31

Fairfax | The Grove | 189 The Grove Dr. (bet. Beverly Blvd. & 3rd St.) | 323-965-9665

Woodland Hills | Westfield Promenade | 6100 Topanga Canyon Blvd. (bet. Erwin & Oxnard Sts.) | 818-887-3777
www.maggianos.com

"Bring a crowd and eat family-style for the best experience" at this "steady-Eddie" Italian chain delivering "gargantuan portions" of "comforting" fare for "reasonable" tabs; its "Little Italy" style and "raucous" environs are a hit with fans, who argue that even if the "assembly-line" food is "nothing special, the total experience is great."

Magnolia *American*
18 | 20 | 19 | $36

Downtown | 825 W. Ninth St. (bet. Cottage Pl. & Figueroa St.) | 213-362-0880 𝕊

Hollywood | 6266½ Sunset Blvd. (bet. Argyle Ave. & Vine St.) | 323-467-0660 ●
www.magnoliala.com

"Dark" and "sleek", this "relaxed Hollywood" haunt gives its "hipstery" patrons the chance to nibble "fantastical" New American vittles late into the night in loungey environs with "movie deals being brokered at the next table"; the Downtown offshoot is equally "warm" and "well priced."

Magnolia Lounge *Eclectic*
▽ 15 | 19 | 18 | $24

Pasadena | 492 S. Lake Ave. (California Blvd.) | 626-584-1126 | www.magnoliaonlake.com

"Who can resist" a "cool" location that "used to be a speakeasy" asks the local singles and "Cal-Tech students" at this "laid-back" Pasadena lounge, notable for a central patio shaded by a magnolia tree; the Eclectic bayou fare's "not bad" "for a bar", but it's the "bargain" happy hour that gets all the attention.

❷ Maison Akira ⓜ *French/Japanese*

26 | 22 | 25 | $59

Pasadena | 713 E. Green St. (bet. El Molino & Oak Knoll Aves.) | 626-796-9501 | www.maisonakira.com

"Innovative" "master chef" Akira Hirose's "charming" French-Japanese namesake qualifies as "one of Pasadena's finest" with its "brilliant" Asian fusion "creations", "graceful service" and "unbeatable Sunday buffet brunch"; the pricing's "high-end" (as "it should be") and the "old-fashioned decor" may seem "stuffy", but overall its tranquil "inspiration" is "truly a delight."

NEW Maison Maurice ⓜ *French*

- | - | - | M

Beverly Hills | 8620 Wilshire Blvd. (Carson Rd.) | 310-967-0021 | www.maisonmauricebeverlyhills.com

Like a "trip to old Paris", this Beverly Hills arrival (in the former Bistro Baguette Cafe space) flaunts velveteen drapes, chandeliers and an ivy-lined patio as a "totally retro" backdrop for "wonderful" French bistro cooking from an eponymous chef-owner "who knows what he's doing"; its grown-up clientele welcomes a refuge that's quiet and "not expensive."

Maison Richard *Bakery/French*
(fka Michel Richard)

21 | - | 20 | $33

Hollywood | 707 N. Stanley Ave. (Melrose Ave.) | 310-275-5707 | www.maisonrichard.com

"Indulge in great pastries" at this recently relocated bistro/bakery founded by long-departed star chef Michel Richard, where the "amazing" breads and sweets complement "consistently good" French cooking; longtime followers can expect to find the same "neighborhood vibes" along with pleasant patio seating at its new Hollywood location.

❷ Mako ⓢⓜ *Asian*

26 | 18 | 25 | $54

Beverly Hills | 225 S. Beverly Dr. (bet. Charleville Blvd. & Gregory Way) | 310-288-8338 | www.makorestaurant.com

"Perfection is sought" by "dedicated chef" Makoto Tanaka at this "intimate" Asian fusion phenom "tucked away" in Beverly Hills, where the "sensational" small plates are "served beautifully" by a "first-rate" staff; it's "somewhat pricey" and the austere "decor doesn't do justice to the food", but the "consistent quality" and "charm" ensure most "leave happy."

Malibu Seafood *Seafood*

23 | 13 | 14 | $22

Malibu | 25653 PCH (bet. Corral Canyon & Malibu Canyon Rds.) | 310-456-6298 | www.malibuseafood.com

"Views across the Pacific Coast Highway of the ocean" complement "the freshest" fin fare at this Malibu "roadside hut", a longtime "low-cost" "pit stop" for "terrific" seafood basics "before or after a trip to the beach"; "long waits" and "open-air" "dining at picnic tables" are part of the package, and while no alcohol is served, you can always bring your own "wine and a tablecloth" "just like the locals do."

	FOOD	DECOR	SERVICE	COST

Malo *Mexican*

19 | 17 | 14 | $25

Silver Lake | 4326 W. Sunset Blvd. (Fountain Ave.) | 323-664-1011 | www.malorestaurant.com

Homemade tortilla chips and a "range of salsas" that'll "make you sweat" kick off the "cool" Mexican meals at this "dark" "haunt" in Silver Lake, where an attached bar boasts 150 tequilas; it's "kind of noisy" and service can be "inattentive", but that doesn't seem to hurt its popularity.

Mama D's *Italian*

19 | 12 | 20 | $24

Hermosa Beach | 1031 Hermosa Ave. (bet. Pier Ave. & 10th St.) | 310-379-6262

Manhattan Beach | 1125 Manhattan Ave. (Manhattan Beach Blvd.) | 310-546-1492

"You can smell the garlic a mile away" at these "dependable" "local" Italians in Hermosa and Manhattan Beaches, which "aim to please" with "solid" "homestyle" fare (accompanied by "yummy" "fresh bread"), "wonderful" service and "casual", "kid-friendly" vibes; they're "unassuming" "joints" with "tight" seating, but budget-conscious D-votees keep them "packed."

Manchego *Spanish*

∇ 23 | 19 | 21 | $29

Santa Monica | 2510 Main St. (Ocean Park Blvd.) | 310-450-3900 | www.manchegoonmain.com

"Don't blink" or you may miss this Santa Monica Spanish nook and its "wonderful", "inventive" tapas and cheese plates, served in "intimate", rather *rustico* digs by an "easy-on-the-eyes" staff; with a no-corkage BYO policy to boost the "value", it's a "cute" "date spot", but "expect to wait on weekends."

Mandarette *Chinese*

19 | 15 | 19 | $34

Beverly Boulevard | 8386 Beverly Blvd. (bet. Kings Rd. & Orlando Ave.) | West Hollywood | 323-655-6115 | www.mandarettecafe.com

"Sophisticated" Sichuan cooking makes this Beverly Boulevard Chinese "a rare find" in the nabe, offering an unusually "innovative menu" served by an "accommodating" crew; although the "low-key" room falls flat for a few, prices are "reasonable" for the "high quality" and it's "terrific for takeout"; N.B. now under new ownership.

Mandarin Deli *Chinese*

23 | 10 | 17 | $16

Northridge | 9305 Reseda Blvd. (Prairie St.) | 818-993-0122

Mandarin Noodle House ⬆ *Chinese*

Monterey Park | 701 W. Garvey Ave. (Chandler Ave.) | 626-570-9795

"Oh, the dumplings!" sigh surveyors smitten with the "pan-fried" signature dish at this long-standing Chinese twosome, also known for their "authentic" "handmade noodles" and "addictive, crispy" scallion pancakes; less fortunately, the downscale surroundings "could be updated" and Monterey Park is "cash only" (though "you won't need much").

Mäni's on Fairfax *Bakery/Vegan*

∇ 17 | 9 | 16 | $15

Fairfax | 519 S. Fairfax Ave. (bet. 5th St. & Maryland Dr.) | 323-938-8800 | www.manisbakery.com

Using "only natural sweeteners", this Fairfax vegan bakery concocts sugarless "goodies" served alongside a lineup of omelets, salads and

	FOOD	DECOR	SERVICE	COST

sandwiches that unsurprisingly includes "lots of veggie options" (as well as some meat); "reasonable prices" ice the cake, though some gluttons wonder "what's the point?"

NEW Manja Ⓜ *Malaysian*

	-	-	-	I

West Hollywood | 8165 Santa Monica Blvd. (Laurel Cyn. Blvd.) | 323-656-9000

Breaking stride with its neighbors in WeHo's Little Russia, this budget-friendly arrival offers Malaysian home cooking, elegantly arranged on exotically shaped plates and served in a room that could have been lifted from Kuala Lumpur, with fresh flowers, and brightly colored, ornately stitched pillows; P.S. don't spoil your appetite on the complimentary banana fritters, for there's much to sample here.

Manna *Korean*

	▽ 18	12	16	$28

Koreatown | 3377 W. Olympic Blvd. (bet. Gramercy Dr. & St. Andrews Pl.) | 323-733-8516
NEW Culver City | Westfield Culver City | 6600 Sepulveda Blvd. (Slauson Ave.) | 310-397-9901
www.mannakoreanrestaurant.com

Like manna from heaven, the "tender meat" "keeps on coming" at this K-town Korean, where "college-age" revelers assemble in a tented outdoor area for an unlimited "parade" of BBQ at a low "fixed price"; service is "spotty" and you'll "smell smoky for several days", but it's "worth it"; P.S. the new indoor site in Culver City offers a full menu.

Mantee Ⓜ *Mediterranean*

	▽ 23	20	23	$26

Studio City | 10962 Ventura Blvd. (Vineland Ave.) | 818-761-6565 | www.manteecafe.com

Matching "flavorful" Lebanese-Armenian specialties (the ravioli-like namesake dish "hits new highs") with a "comfortably homey" ambiance and "super-friendly staff", this Studio City Med is a well-priced "winner" "for the neighborhood"; an "especially charming" patio adds to the allure, so "now all they need is their liquor license."

Maria's Italian Kitchen *Italian*

	17	13	18	$24

Brentwood | 11723 Barrington Ct. (Barrington Ave.) | 310-476-6112
West LA | 10761 Pico Blvd. (Malcolm Ave.) | 310-441-3663
Pasadena | Hastings Ranch Shopping Ctr. | 3537 E. Foothill Blvd. (Rosemead Blvd.) | 626-351-2080
Encino | 16608 Ventura Blvd. (Rubio Ave.) | 818-783-2920
Northridge | 9161 Reseda Blvd. (bet. Dearborn & Nordhoff Sts.) | 818-341-5114
Sherman Oaks | 13353 Ventura Blvd. (bet. Dixie Canyon & Fulton Aves.) | 818-906-0783
Woodland Hills | El Camino Shopping Ctr. | 23331 Mulholland Dr. (Calabasas Rd.) | 818-225-0586
Agoura Hills | Ralph's Shopping Ctr. | 29035 Thousand Oaks Blvd. (Kanan Rd.) | 818-865-8999
www.mariasitaliankitchen.com

"When you don't want to cook", this "busy" "red-sauce" chain is a "family favorite" for "belt-busting" "homestyle Italian" served up with "no surprises"; the staff varies from "cordial" to "preoccupied" and you'll have to do "without a lot of fancy decor", but they're "a reliable midweek go-to" "for the price."

	FOOD	DECOR	SERVICE	COST

Marino ☒ *Italian* — 24 | 16 | 24 | $47

Hollywood | 6001 Melrose Ave. (Wilcox Ave.) | 323-466-8812 | www.marinorestaurant.net

"Old-school Italian" still rules at this "Hollywood institution", where a "second generation" of Marinos (local legend Ciro passed away in 2009) keeps "the tradition going" with "wonderful" "red-sauce" fare and "warm" servers treat regulars like "royalty"; the "quaint" space is "certainly not splashy", but it's "comfortable" if you can handle the cost.

Mario's Peruvian & Seafood *Peruvian* — 22 | 6 | 17 | $18

Hollywood | 5786 Melrose Ave. (Vine St.) | 323-466-4181

Peruvian enthusiasts pack this Hollywood hole-in-the-wall to savor "plain delicious" seafood specialties and lomo saltado that's likened to "heaven on a plate"; the setup's "very basic" and "waits can be long", but "you won't care" since the food "makes up for it" and "you definitely get your money's worth."

Marix Tex Mex Café *Tex-Mex* — 17 | 16 | 18 | $26

West Hollywood | 1108 N. Flores St. (Santa Monica Blvd.) | 323-656-8800
Marix Tex Mex Playa *Tex-Mex*
Santa Monica | 118 Entrada Dr. (PCH) | 310-459-8596
www.marixtexmex.com

"Potent" margaritas promote the "festive atmosphere" at these "affordable" Tex-Mex sibs, "standby" cantinas serving "decent gringofied" fare; even if the eating's "only average", they're "always hopping" whether with the "Boystown" crowd in WeHo or families "grabbing a bite" "right near the beach" in Santa Monica.

NEW Market Café ☒ *Eclectic* — - | - | - | I

Downtown | AT&T Center | 1150 S. Olive St. (11th St.) | 213-536-4090

New from the Patina team, this cafeteria-style quick stop draws in Downtown's lunch bunch with Eclectic eats centered around soups, sandwiches and an organic salad bar; a bright white space with primary-color accents has modern flair, but affordable pricing (nothing over $10) is the attention-getter; N.B. open weekdays till 3:30 PM.

Market City Caffe *Californian/Italian* — 18 | 18 | 18 | $27

Burbank | 164 E. Palm Ave. (bet. 1st St. & San Fernando Blvd.) | 818-840-7036

A "great antipasto bar" proffers "a variety of healthy" choices at this midrange "standby" in Burbank, and the Cal-Italian menu's pretty "dependable" too; the "friendly" service, "comfortable" interior and "quiet" patio help make it "a good bet" if you're in the market for unpretentious eats post-Ikea or the movies.

Marmalade Café *American/Californian* — 18 | 16 | 18 | $26

Fairfax | The Grove | 6333 W. Third St. (Fairfax Ave.) | 323-954-0088
Rolling Hills Estates | Avenue of the Peninsula Mall | 550 Deep Valley Dr. (Crossfield Dr.) | Rolling Hills | 310-544-6700
Malibu | 3894 Cross Creek Rd. (PCH) | 310-317-4242
Santa Monica | 710 Montana Ave. (7th St.) | 310-395-9196
El Segundo | Plaza El Segundo | 2014 E. Park Pl. (Sepulveda Blvd.) | 310-648-7200
Calabasas | The Commons | 4783 Commons Way (Calabasas Rd.) | 818-225-9092

continued)

Marmalade Café

herman Oaks | 14910 Ventura Blvd. (Kester Ave.) | 818-905-8872
Westlake Village | Promenade at Westlake | 140 Promenade Way
Thousand Oaks Blvd.) | 805-370-1331
www.marmaladecafe.com

he "huge menu" means there's "something for everyone" at this "casual", "kid-friendly" "local chain", slinging "ample portions" of California Americana that's "consistently tasty" ("especially for breakast") if "not particularly original"; "service is spotty" and the "quaint ecor evokes "your grandmother's living room", but they're "convenient" if you "bring your own excitement."

Marouch Ⓜ *Lebanese* ▽ 21 | 12 | 20 | $27

ast Hollywood | 4905 Santa Monica Blvd. (Edgemont St.) | 323-662-9325 |
www.marouchrestaurant.com

given its "moist and flavorful" shawarma, "wonderful" meze and other dependable" Lebanese eats, supporters are sure this midpriced East Hollywood vet "must be authentic"; some say the modest space "hidden in a strip mall" is looking "a little old" lately, but service is "kind nd efficient" and the eating's "always a treat."

Marrakesh *Moroccan* 21 | 23 | 23 | $40

tudio City | 13003 Ventura Blvd. (Coldwater Canyon Ave.) | 818-788-6354 |
www.marrakeshdining.com

A casbah experience" awaits at this longtime Studio City Moroccan, where nightly belly dancers and "the staff's showmanship" conjure up "party" atmosphere to enhance a "fab" selection of prix fixe spreads; nsurprisingly, "sitting on pillows and eating with your fingers" makes "fun for a group or out-of-towners."

⅃ mar'sel ⓏⓂ *Californian* 24 | 27 | 23 | $85

ancho Palos Verdes | Terranea Resort | 6610 Palos Verdes Dr. S.
Hawthorne Blvd.) | 310-265-2780 | www.terraneamarsel.com

Gorgeous" "180-degree ocean views" are just one highlight at this memorable" yearling in Ranchos Palos Verdes' tony Terranea Resort, ow "in full swing" with "exquisitely prepared" Cal cuisine and "topotch service" in a "sumptuous" setting with a "fabulous patio"; "quality n't cheap" of course, but if you're looking to "woo someone or celerate a special occasion", "this is the place."

Marston's *American* 22 | 16 | 19 | $23

asadena | 151 E. Walnut St. (bet. Marengo & Raymond Aves.) |
26-796-2459 | www.marstonsrestaurant.com

asadenans prize this "cute little" "cottage" on the outskirts of Old own for "the deliciousness" of its breakfasts and brunches, built on dreamy" pancakes, "cornflake-crusted French toast" and other traditional American fare; the overall feel is "friendly", but brace yourself or "jammed" seating and "a line on the weekends."

Martha's 22nd St. Grill *American* 24 | 12 | 20 | $16

ermosa Beach | 25 22nd St. (bet. Beach Dr. & Hermosa Ave.) |
10-376-7786

Watch the waves come in" over a "hearty breakfast" at this ramhackle Hermosa Beach "hangout", "a local landmark" with outdoor

seating "steps away from" The Strand; the "can't-miss" menu o
American "variations" draws "quite a crowd", so "be prepared" fo
"outrageous" waits on weekend mornings.

⊠ Mastro's Steakhouse *Steak* | 26 | 23 | 25 | $73

Beverly Hills | 246 N. Cañon Dr. (bet. Clifton & Dayton Ways) |
310-888-8782
Thousand Oaks | 2087 E. Thousand Oaks Blvd. (bet. Conejo School Rd. &
Los Feliz Dr.) | 805-418-1811
www.mastrosrestaurants.com

"Still the king" of carnivorous consumption, this "über-steakhouse"
chain hosts "wheeler dealer" types "paying a fortune" for "generous"
cuts of "mouthwatering" "prime meat", "extravagant" seafood tower
and "sinful" sides, all matched with "world-class" service; the Beverl
Hills branch comprises a "vibrant", "Vegas"-like piano bar and
toned-down dining room while Thousand Oaks flaunts a "classic"
"dark" look and Costa Mesa is more "showy."

⊠ Matsuhisa *Japanese* | 28 | 17 | 24 | $83

Beverly Hills | 129 N. La Cienega Blvd. (bet. Clifton Way & Wilshire Blvd.) |
310-659-9639 | www.nobumatsuhisa.com

"Oh my!" cry "enchanted" "sushi lovers" as "consummate" chef Nob
Matsuhisa continues to "wow", crafting "spectacular" Japanese far
"with Peruvian flair" at this much-"imitated" Beverly Hills fusion "tem
ple" ("where it all started"); don't be fooled by the "non-stuffy" ser
vice and "dated" decor, you'll still need to "drop off your wallet at th
door", especially for "exquisite" omakases that connoisseurs conside
"the only way to go."

Matteo's ⊠ *Italian* | 20 | 21 | 23 | $49

West LA | 2321 Westwood Blvd. (bet. Pico Blvd. & Tennessee Ave.)
310-475-4521 | www.matteosla.com

Newly refurbished, this "clubby" West LA "staple" preserves its "groov
Rat Pack feel" with a larger bar and spiffed-up leather booths ("O
Blue Eyes and friends used to hang" at table No. 8); the "Italian stand
bys" and "attentive" service remain "up to par", and consensus say
the "old-fashioned" allure is enough to distract from up-to-date pricing

Maxwell's Cafe *American* | ∇ 18 | 10 | 19 | $17

Venice | 13329 W. Washington Blvd. (Walgrove Ave.) | 310-306-7829
www.novelcafe.com

Venice natives flock to this circa-1972 "neighborhood dive" for all
American breakfasts on a budget ("garbage omelets, the best"), bu
"fast-moving lines" keep the "wait" manageable; longtimers still la
ment the departure of the "eponymous owner" a few years back, bu
come sunup it's a "very popular" spot.

M Café de Chaya *Vegetarian* | 22 | 15 | 18 | $20

Melrose | 7119 Melrose Ave. (La Brea Ave.) | 323-525-0588
Beverly Hills | 9433 Brighton Way (Beverly Dr.) | 310-858-8459
Culver City | 9343 Culver Blvd. (Ince Blvd.) | 310-838-4300
www.mcafedechaya.com

Convincing "even the most die-hard carnivores" that "tasty and vege
tarian can coexist", this "health-conscious" trio vends a slightl
"pricey" plethora of "creative" macrobiotic and vegan fare (along wit

ome fish) in "glorified cafeteria" settings; the "counter service" is helpful", but they're "popular" with throngs in "yoga gear", so there nay be a "crunch."

McCormick & Schmick's *Seafood*   20 | 20 | 20 | $41

Downtown | US Bank Tower | 633 W. 5th St., 4th fl. (Grand Ave.) | 13-629-1929
Beverly Hills | Two Rodeo | 206 N. Rodeo Dr. (Wilshire Blvd.) | 10-859-0434
El Segundo | 2101 Rosecrans Ave. (Parkway Dr.) | 310-416-1123
Pasadena | 111 N. Los Robles Ave. (Union St.) | 626-405-0064
Burbank | 3500 W. Olive Ave. (Riverside Dr.) | 818-260-0505
www.mccormickandschmicks.com

An "enjoyable" choice for "business and pleasure", this "upscale" seafood chain offers a "daily changing" menu of "freshly caught" fare in n "upbeat" atmosphere; though it feels too "stamped-out-of-a-mold" or some, its "professional" service is a plus and the "happy-hour bar nenu" wins over the after-work crowd.

McKenna's on the Bay *Seafood/Steak*   19 | 22 | 19 | $43

Long Beach | 190 Marina Dr. (PCH) | 562-342-9411 | www.mckennasonthebay.com

"Million-dollar views" over Alamitos Bay help this slightly "spendy" seafooder/steakhouse in Long Beach reel 'em in for "fresh" fish and rib-eyes in a shipshape setting with a "beautiful" patio; a pianist livens up the bar Wednesday–Sunday, though the "kitchen clatter and people chatter" can be a "drawback" on "busy weekends."

Mediterraneo *Mediterranean*   20 | 20 | 19 | $28

Hermosa Beach | 73 Pier Ave. (Hermosa Ave.) | 310-318-2666 | www.mediterraneohb.com

"People-watching" and "chilling" are de rigueur at this oceanside Med with "outdoor seating" "right at the pier" in Hermosa Beach, where youngish fans munch on "decent tapas" chased with a "wonderful selection" of beers and wines; wallet-watchers tout the weekday happy hour's "two-for-one" deals, and it's open till midnight on weekends.

Mediterraneo *Mediterranean*   ▽ 24 | 24 | 21 | $42

Westlake Village | 32037 Agoura Rd. (Lakeview Canyon Rd.) | 18-889-9105 | www.med-rest.com

A "wonderful" patio with private lake views and an "elegant" dining room provide plenty of "scenery" to bolster this Westlake Village Med's "flavorful", "often innovative" seasonal fare and 200-label wine list; "attentive service" renders the "understated" atmosphere even nore "charming", but don't be surprised if it's "expensive."

⛔ Mélisse 🅂🅼 *American/French*   28 | 26 | 27 | $105

Santa Monica | 1104 Wilshire Blvd. (11th St.) | 310-395-0881 | www.melisse.com

"Josiah Citrin is still at the top of his game" gush fans of his Santa Monica fine-dining room that continues to "hit on all cylinders" with "flawlessly composed" French–New American cuisine backed by an "incredible" 800-bottle wine list; it follows through with "almost worshipful service" (rated tops in our Survey) in a "beautiful" platinum room that's "quiet and a bit formal", adding up to an experience so exquisite", even "the bill will take your breath away."

Mel's Drive-In ● *American*

16	16	16	$18

Hollywood | 1650 N. Highland Ave. (Hollywood Blvd.) | 323-465-2111
West Hollywood | 8585 Sunset Blvd. (Sunset Plaza Dr.) | 310-854-7200
Sherman Oaks | 14846 Ventura Blvd. (Kester Ave.) | 818-990-6357
www.melsdrive-in.com

"Bring your hot rod" for a "kitschy flashback to the '50s" at these themers dishing up "filling" "American diner" eats, mostly "burgers and shakes"; spoilsports say the "retro fun" "has worn off", but they're "passable" when "it's late" and "nothing handy is open"; N.B. WeHo is 24/7.

Melting Pot *Fondue*

18	18	19	$45

Torrance | 21525 Hawthorne Blvd. (Carson St.) | 310-316-7500
Pasadena | 88 W. Colorado Blvd. (De Lacey Ave.) | 626-792-1941
Westlake Village | 3685 E. Thousand Oaks Blvd. (bet. Auburn & Marmon Aves.) | 805-370-8802
www.meltingpot.com

"It's all about sharing" and "cooking your own food" at this chain serving "every kind of fondue", including "delicious" chocolate pots; while it's a "romantic" "treat" for "younger couples" and "fun to do with a group", critics contend it's "overpriced" and "pretentious", and would prefer "more casual" setup; P.S. go with a large party if you want "two burners."

🆕 Mercantile, The *French*

▽ 21	19	22	$27

Hollywood | 6600 Sunset Blvd. (Seward St.) | 323-962-8202 |
www.themercantilela.com

"A welcome addition" to Hollywood, this French bistro and gourmet "larder" is a "cute" "haven" for "tasty" salads, sandwiches and house-made desserts at a sensible cost; the "market-type" surroundings with exposed brick and a wine bar are rustically "cool" whether you prefer to "relax" over a light bite or shop for goods "to go."

Mexicali ● *Californian/Mexican*

16	15	15	$23

Studio City | 12161 Ventura Blvd. (bet. Laurel Canyon Blvd. & Vantage Ave.) | 818-985-1744

"Amazing" margaritas and "lively" times explain why this late-night Studio City hangout "remains popular" even though the Cal-Mex chow's "hit-or-miss"; to avoid the "loud and crazy groups" that descend during happy hour (4–7 PM and 11 PM–1 AM), regulars retreat to the "quieter" patio.

Mexico City *Mexican*

20	15	18	$23

Los Feliz | 2121 Hillhurst Ave. (bet. Ambrose Ave. & Avocado St.) | 323-661-7227 | www.mexicocityla.com

The "stiff" margaritas alone cement this "neighborhood cantina" as a Los Feliz "mainstay", but it's also "flyin' high" with a "satisfying" "blend of traditional" and "innovative" Mexican eats priced for a "starving-artist clientele"; it "can be crowded" after dark when locals stop in for cervezas before "heading up the hill to the Greek."

Mexico Restaurante y Barra *Mexican*

▽ 19	19	19	$32

West Hollywood | 8512 Santa Monica Blvd. (La Cienega Blvd.) | 310-289-0088 | www.gogomexico.com

This "color-drenched" WeHo Mexican "does nothing halfway", as shown by "memorable" cooking that "avoids combo-plate sameness", a "screaming pink" paint job and a "welcoming staff" that makes it "a nonstop party" fueled by *"muy auténtico"* margaritas; it's also a "happy-hour winner", so "to escape traffic" try the patio or balcony.

Mia Sushi *Japanese*

| | - | - | - | M |

Eagle Rock | 4741 Eagle Rock Blvd. (bet. Las Colinas & Ridgeview Aves.) | 323-256-2562 | www.mia-sushi.com

Rolls with "sauces and cutesy names" rule the menu at this Eagle Rock Japanese, a "neighborhood sushi" joint where the chef may slice "something more authentic" "if you sit at the bar"; a patio offers relief from the "tight quarters", but the servers are still "overwhelmed on busy nights."

Miceli's *Italian*

| | 16 | 18 | 19 | $27 |

Hollywood | 1646 N. Las Palmas Ave. (bet. Hollywood Blvd. & Selma Ave.) | 323-466-3438

Universal City | 3655 Cahuenga Blvd. W. (Regal Pl.) | 323-851-3344 www.micelisrestaurant.com

The "singing waiters" are "an experience" at these "lively" Italians in Hollywood (since 1949) and Universal City, where "serenades" and checkered tablecloths create a hokey "old-time" milieu for pizza and pasta and "lots of it"; contras pan the "just average" eating, but they're "loud and crowded" with "visitors" looking "for a good time."

☑ Michael's ☒ *Californian*

| | 25 | 26 | 25 | $67 |

Santa Monica | 1147 Third St. (bet. California Ave. & Wilshire Blvd.) | 310-451-0843 | www.michaelssantamonica.com

When "you want to impress", this Santa Monica "landmark" from Michael McCarty (who "practically invented Californian cuisine") is a "class act all the way" serving "excellent" seasonal menus in a "romantic", art-filled space with a "gorgeous patio"; "first-rate" service rounds out the "magic", but be forewarned, "they charge accordingly."

Michael's on Naples Ristorante *Italian*

| | 26 | 23 | 23 | $52 |

Long Beach | 5620 E. Second St. (bet. Ravenna & Tivoli Drs.) | 562-439-7080 | www.michaelsonnaples.com

"Head and shoulders above" its local rivals, this Long Beacher is a "hidden treasure" where the "inspired" Italian fare is paired with "creative" wines and served with "grace"; the "semi-upscale" vibe is a "best bet" for a "romantic" meal, especially since it's "not ridiculously expensive."

Michelangelo *Italian*

| | ▽ 18 | 15 | 19 | $33 |

Silver Lake | 2742 Rowena Ave. (Glendale Blvd.) | 323-660-4843 | www.michelangelo-silverlake.com

"Plain", "old-fashioned Italian" à la "homemade" pastas and thin-crust pizza constitutes the "reliable" repertoire of this "true neighborhood joint" run by a "lovely family" in Silver Lake; if the "simple" setting's no masterpiece, supporters say it's "worth it" for the palatable prices.

Mijares *Mexican*

| | 17 | 14 | 18 | $22 |

Pasadena | 145 Palmetto Dr. (Pasadena Ave.) | 626-792-2763
Pasadena | 1806 E. Washington Blvd. (Allen Ave.) | 626-794-6674
www.mijaresrestaurant.com

"They treat everyone like a regular" at this "very casual" "Pasadena staple" (since 1910), a "fun oasis" for "margaritas on the patio" and "hearty portions" of "standard Mexican fare" "at decent prices"; the "small" East Washington sidekick works for takeout or "when you just gotta have the food and don't need atmosphere."

| | FOOD | DECOR | SERVICE | COST |

Mike & Anne's Ⓜ American
21 | 21 | 20 | $32

South Pasadena | 1040 Mission St. (Fairview Ave.) | 626-799-7199 |
www.mikeandannes.com
Out on the "lovely patio" is "the place to be" at this "comfortable"
South Pas New American where locals "linger" over "deftly prepared"
fare and "interesting cocktails"; with moderate tabs and a "semi-hip"
vibe, this "neighborhood haunt" is also a brunchtime "favorite."

Milky Way Californian
▽ 19 | 17 | 23 | $26

Pico-Robertson | 9108 W. Pico Blvd. (Doheny Dr.) | 310-859-0004
The "hospitality is terrific" at this Pico-Robertson Californian thanks
to the "warmth" of owner Leah Adler, who's also "Steven Spielberg's
mom" ("what could be cooler?"); the kosher dairy menu's "homemade blintzes" and the like are a "treat" for "observants", and the atmosphere's brimming with "haimish" charm; P.S. closed Saturdays.

Millions of Milkshakes ● American
▽ 21 | 10 | 15 | $9

West Hollywood | 8910 Santa Monica Blvd. (San Vicente Blvd.) |
213-387-4253 | www.millionsofmilkshakes.com
A "plethora of amazing goodness" awaits in WeHo at this American
shake stand where the "incredible selection" of "blended concoctions"
("even for the vegan") go by "TMZ"-esque celebrity monikers; ignore
the flashy fast-food setup and it's worth "skipping cheeseburgers to
consume your daily calories right here."

Mimi's Cafe Diner
17 | 17 | 18 | $21

Atwater Village | 2925 Los Feliz Blvd. (bet. Revere & Seneca Aves.) |
323-668-1715
Cerritos | Cerritos Towne Ctr. | 12727 Towne Center Dr. (Bloomfield Ave.) |
562-809-0510
Downey | 8455 Firestone Blvd. (bet. Brookshire & Dolan Aves.) |
562-862-2828
Long Beach | 6670 E. PCH (Studebaker Rd.) | 562-596-0831
Torrance | 25343 S. Crenshaw Blvd. (PCH) | 310-326-4477
Monrovia | 500 W. Huntington Dr. (Mayflower Ave.) |
626-359-9191
Chatsworth | 19710 Nordhoff Pl. (Corbin Ave.) | 818-717-8334
City of Industry | 17919 Gale Ave. (Azusa Ave.) | 626-912-3350
Whittier | Whittwood Town Ctr. | 15436 E. Whittier Blvd.
(Santa Gertrudes Ave.) | 562-947-0339
Santa Clarita | 24201 W. Magic Mountain Pkwy. (Auto Center Dr.) |
661-255-5520
www.mimiscafe.com
Additional locations throughout Southern California
"A few notches above Denny's", this "dressed-up coffee-shop" chain
is a "fallback" for "all-day breakfasts" boosted by "ginormous" "fresh"-
baked muffins; foes find dinner "unremarkable" and perhaps the
"cutesy" "faux French decor" is getting a little "long in the tooth", but
at least you "can count on it" for an "inexpensive" meal "with the kids."

Minestraio Trattoria Italian
23 | 19 | 21 | $39
(fka La Terza)

West Hollywood | Orlando Hotel | 8384 W. Third St. (Orlando Ave.) |
323-782-8384 | www.minestraio.com
Experience "fine Italian dining" "tapas-style" at Gino Angelini's "comfortable, low-key" trattoria in WeHo's Orlando Hotel, where the "awe-

some, freshly made pastas" are now "reformatted" as small plates; skeptics shrug "nothing special", but given "reasonable prices", "satisfactory wines" and "easier access than Angelini Osteria", most maintain it "should be busier."

Mini Bites ●⊅ Burgers
- | - | - | I

Hollywood | 4481 Santa Monica Blvd. (Virgil Ave.) | 323-666-4242 | www.minibitesinla.com

Mini is indeed the shtick at this cash-only Hollywood shack (once Jay's Jayburgers), where lettuce-and-tomato topped sliders lead a lineup of bite-size burger-joint fare; the late hours and minute prices are the perfect match for the young and munchies-minded; N.B. open till 3 AM on weekends.

Minx Ⓜ Eclectic
- | - | - | M

Glendale | 300 Harvey Dr. (bet. Hwys. 2 & 134) | 818-242-9191 | www.minx-la.com

With its breezy patio, dance floor and pumping soundtrack, this big, glammy Glendale eatery/lounge appeals to partyers who may not notice if the Eclectic menu veers from "just outstanding" to "just ok"; weekends are "extremely crowded with locals", though "lacking" service can jinx the good times.

Mio Babbo's Italian
▽ 20 | 16 | 21 | $27

Westwood | 1076 Gayley Ave. (bet. Kinross Ave. & Weyburn Dr.) | 310-208-5117 | www.miobabbos.com

"Traditional" all the way, this Westwood "neighborhood Italian" turns out "tasty" versions of "familiar" fare in a low-lit, "secluded" setting enhanced by "warm service"; it's "convenient" for UCLA sorts or "a pre-Geffen dinner", but "reasonable" prices mean it "can be crowded."

Mi Piace Californian/Italian
20 | 19 | 18 | $35

Pasadena | 25 E. Colorado Blvd. (bet. Fair Oaks & Raymond Aves.) | 626-795-3131 ●

Calabasas | The Commons | 4799 Commons Way (Calabasas Rd.) | 818-591-8822
www.mipiace.com

Ever "popular", this "trendy" "local" Pasadenan and its Calabasas off-shoot are "convenient" for "enjoyable" Cal-Italian pastas and seafood (along with "stellar desserts") at "reasonable prices"; just know the "contemporary" interiors and "delightful" outdoor tables are "crowd-gatherers", leading to "so-so service" and "noise."

Mirabelle ● Californian/Eclectic
20 | 20 | 23 | $36

West Hollywood | 8768 W. Sunset Blvd. (bet. Horn Ave. & Sherbourne Dr.) | 310-659-6022 | www.mirabelleonsunset.com

A "Sunset institution", this WeHo Cal-Eclectic pairs its "consistent", "flavorful menu" and extensive wine list with "charming service" in "upscale" surroundings with a "lively" patio; "prices are reasonable", and the "busy bar" is a "prime locale" for both "happy hour" and after hours.

Mi Ranchito Family Mexican Mexican
▽ 19 | 16 | 17 | $19

Culver City | 12223 W. Washington Blvd. (bet. Centinela Ave. & Grand View Blvd.) | 310-398-8611

Expect "nothing fancy" at this low-cost Culver City Mexican, just "solidly prepared", seafood-centric Veracruz specialties that "leave a smile on your face" whether you're out with the "family" or seeking the "perfect hangover" cure; warm "hospitality" and "crazy" "travel souvenirs on the walls" add to the "kitschy" "fun."

Mirü8691 *Asian*
∇ 24 | 15 | 21 | $30

Beverly Hills | Beverly Palm Plaza | 9162 W. Olympic Blvd. (Palm Dr.) | 310-777-8378 | www.miru8691.com

"Some of the most unusual" and "outstanding" sushi and fusion dishes grace the menu of this "reasonably priced" Beverly Hills Pan-Asian, whose "inventive rolls", Wagyu burgers and occasionally "plain weird offerings" amaze maki mavens; add an electronica soundtrack and neon lights sweeping the walls at night, and it's no wonder "it never gets old."

Mishima *Japanese*
∇ 19 | 12 | 18 | $23

Third Street | 8474 W. Third St. (La Cienega Blvd.) | 323-782-0181 | www.mishima.com

"Fast" and "reliable", this "go-to" Third Street "noodle house" lures udon and soba slurpers in for "consistently" "tasty" Japanese cheap eats; maybe the decor's "seen better days", but "you know what you're gonna get" "at a great price", so how can you mish?

Mission 261 *Chinese*
- | - | - | M

San Gabriel | 261 S. Mission Dr. (W. B'way) | 626-588-1666 | www.mission261.com

After closing for a year of renovations, this Hong Kong–style seafooder in a onetime City Hall building is back as one of San Gabriel's most elegant Cantonese, with high beamed ceilings and an outdoor patio (a rarity among Chinese restaurants); the moderately priced dim sum selection that fans call the best in town is served to order from a menu, rather than cadged from carts as they roll on by.

Misto Caffé & Bakery *Californian/Eclectic*
20 | 13 | 19 | $26

Torrance | Hillside Vill. | 24558 Hawthorne Blvd. (bet. Newton St. & Via Valmonte) | 310-375-3608 | www.mistocaffe.com

"Save room for the delicious desserts" at this "family-friendly" bakery/eatery in an "out-of-the-way" Torrance shopping center, a lunchtime "standby" for "tasty" Cal-Eclectic bites and "efficient" service at a square price; the simple space "can get crowded and squishy", but there's always "the patio on a nice day."

⊠ Mistral *French*
26 | 22 | 25 | $54

Sherman Oaks | 13422 Ventura Blvd. (bet. Dixie Canyon & Greenbush Aves.) | 818-981-6650 | www.mistralrestaurant.net

"You're in a whole new world" at this "lovely" Sherman Oaks bistro where the many "regulars" just say *oui* to "high-quality", "beautifully prepared" French fare and "excellent wines" in a setting that's "elegant without being pompous"; "the warmest" staff makes "everyone feel at home", so it gets "crowded" despite tabs that "tend to add up."

Mo-Chica ⊠ *Peruvian*
∇ 27 | 5 | 17 | $18

Downtown | Mercado La Paloma | 3655 S. Grand Ave. (bet. 35th & 37th Sts.) | 213-747-2141 | www.mo-chica.com

"If you're all about food", this Downtown Peruvian "counter" amid a "hodgepodge" of vendors in the USC-area Mercado La Paloma is an "incredible find", dishing up "exceptional" contemporary cooking from chef Ricardo Zarate (ex Wabi-Sabi) "worthy of a fancy restau-

	FOOD	DECOR	SERVICE	COST

rant" at "bargain-basement prices"; as for the locale, just "close your eyes and enjoy."

Modo Mio Cucina Rustica *Italian*   22 | 18 | 21 | $39

Pacific Palisades | 15200 W. Sunset Blvd. (La Cruz Dr.) | 310-459-0979 | www.modomiocucinarustica.com

'My way' it is at this "inviting" Palisades "neighborhood haunt", which aims to leave everyone "happy" with "satisfying" homemade pastas and other "authentic", "well-prepared" Italian cuisine smilingly served at "fair prices"; the "comfy" surroundings are suitably *rustica* with a hand-painted mural and candlelight – so "what more could you ask?"

Moishe's ⊄ *Mideastern*   ▽ 19 | 5 | 8 | $14

Fairfax | Farmers Mkt. | 6333 W. Third St. (Fairfax Ave.) | 323-936-4998

"Tasty, fresh and fast", this long-running Mideastern stall in the Farmers Market dispenses "high-quality" shawarma, falafels and the like, plus some of "the best hummus in LA"; the staff's as "surly" "as the food is delicious", but at these prices it's "one of the most popular stands" there.

NEW Momed *Mediterranean*   - | - | - | M

Beverly Hills | 233 S. Beverly Dr. (bet. Charleville Blvd. & Gregory Way) | 310-270-4444

At this Beverly Hills Med, peripatetic chef Matt Carpenter (formerly Citronelle, Bastide, BIN 8945) helms a moderately priced menu that stretches from Greece and Cyprus to Lebanon and Israel, with intriguing stops in Turkey – a cuisine little known on the Left Coast; the handsome setting, done up in soft earth tones and Middle Eastern motifs, also boasts an outdoor patio.

Monsieur Marcel *French*   20 | 16 | 20 | $26

Fairfax | Farmers Mkt. | 6333 W. Third St. (Fairfax Ave.) | 323-939-7792
Santa Monica | 1260 Third St. Promenade (Arizona Ave.) | 310-587-1166
www.mrmarcel.com

Francophiles fawn over this "relaxing" cafe fronting a French grocer at the Farmers Market, where the "reliably swell" bistro "treats", "exquisite" cheeses and charcuterie, and "fair-priced wines" will "make you want to watch *Gigi*"; the mostly "open-air" spin-off on Santa Monica's Promenade provides a "Parisian" breather "while you shop", minus "the attitude."

Monsoon Cafe *Asian*   20 | 22 | 18 | $31

Santa Monica | 1212 Third St. Promenade (bet. Arizona Ave. & Wilshire Blvd.) | 310-576-9996 | www.globaldiningca.com

Something "exotic" on Santa Monica's Promenade, this double-decker Pan-Asian extravaganza assumes a "grand colonial" look with wall-to-wall bamboo, carved masks and a huge Balinese chandelier; "a wide selection" of "distinctive" dishes "at reasonable prices" draws "tourists and locals alike", while "younger" folks focus on the "happening" "happy hour" and "bar scene."

Monte Alban ● *Mexican*   20 | 11 | 18 | $21

West LA | 11927 Santa Monica Blvd. (bet. Armacost & Brockton Aves.) | 310-444-7736

"If you want some real Mexican", this "simple" spot in a West LA "minimall" obliges with "amazingly inexpensive" Oaxacan specialties (the "terrific" mole is mandatory) from a "friendly" crew; maybe the "atmosphere is lacking", but it's hard to argue when the cooking "is totally on."

Monty's Steakhouse *Steak*
| 22 | 17 | 21 | $52 |

Woodland Hills | 5371 Topanga Canyon Blvd. (Ventura Blvd.) | 818-716-9736

"Dedicated carnivores" declare this "friendly", "family-owned" Woodland Hills meatery is a "retro" "delight" serving "humongous" steaks and sides in an "old-school" setting with "red booths" and a barful of "locals"; but in view of the "pricey" tabs, modernists insist "all that Naugahyde" is "in dire need of revamping."

NEW Mooi ⬛Ⓜ *Vegan*
| – | – | – | I |

Echo Park | Jensen Recreation Ctr. | 1700 Sunset Blvd. (Logan St.) | 213-413-1100 | www.mooifood.com

This easy-on-the-wallet Echo Parker offers creative vegan cuisine, including 20 flavors of ice cream, in a shabby-chic space with overstuffed chairs, mismatched exotic lamps and an upstairs mezzanine with a fine view of the arty crowd below; N.B. though the name sounds like a cow with a speech impediment, it's actually the Dutch word for 'nice.'

Moonshadows *American*
| 16 | 22 | 18 | $44 |

Malibu | 20356 PCH (bet. Big Rock Dr. & Las Flores Canyon Rd.) | 310-456-3010 | www.moonshadowsmalibu.com

Sit at terrace tables "right on the water" and watch the "dolphins leap" at this Malibu New American, a "popular" spot to nosh on "average" eats, knock back drinks and take in "fabulous" oceanside "scenery" that renders all else "secondary"; just be prepared to "pay for the view" and deal with DJ-driven "club vibes" on weekends.

Morels First Floor Bistro *French*
| 20 | 18 | 18 | $31 |

Fairfax | The Grove | 189 The Grove Dr. (bet. Beverly Blvd. & 3rd St.) | 323-965-9595 | www.mcchgroup.com

Take a "break from shopping madness" "the French way" at this Fairfax bistro in The Grove, where the "solid", "moderately priced" menu's a good bet "if you're in the mood" for *vin et fromage* given the 50 by-the-glass wines and on-site cheese cave; the patio's preferred as an "easy" place "to people-watch, or to have people watch you."

Morels French Steakhouse *French/Steak*
▽ | 20 | 20 | 17 | $49 |

Fairfax | The Grove | 189 The Grove Dr. (bet. Beverly Blvd. & 3rd St.) | 323-965-9595 | www.mcchgroup.com

"Location" is a virtue at this French-inflected steakhouse at The Grove where a seat on the balcony overlooking the fountains provides prime "people-watching"; dry-aged beef and "excellent" wines and cheeses make it "pretty good for a restaurant in a mall" although service is "indifferent" and skeptics aren't sure it lives up to the "top-shelf pricing."

❷ Mori Sushi ⬛ *Japanese*
| 27 | 17 | 22 | $76 |

West LA | 11500 W. Pico Blvd. (Gateway Blvd.) | 310-479-3939 | www.morisushi.org

"Sublime" sums up this "exquisite, little" Japanese in West LA where "master" chef Morihiro Onodera crafts "divine" slabs of fish and serves them up with "real wasabi" and homegrown rice on his "original" handmade ceramics; acolytes gladly "pay a lot" for the experience, even if it's all a little too "precious" for some.

	FOOD	DECOR	SERVICE	COST

Morton's The Steakhouse *Steak*

	24	22	24	$65

Downtown | 7+FIG at Ernst & Young Plaza | 735 S. Figueroa St. (bet. 7th & 8th Sts.) | 213-553-4566
Beverly Hills | 435 S. La Cienega Blvd. (bet. San Vicente & Wilshire Blvds.) | 310-246-1501
Burbank | The Pinnacle | 3400 W. Olive Ave. (Lima St.) | 818-238-0424
Woodland Hills | Warner Ctr. | 6250 Canoga Ave. (Erwin St.) | 818-703-7272
www.mortons.com

A steakhouse "standard-bearer", this "big-ticket" chain offers "excellently prepared" cuts of beef and "grand sides" "served professionally" amid an "ambiance of wealth and class"; some find it a bit "staid" and wish they'd "lose the raw-meat presentation" and "high" wine pricing, but the many who love its "traditional" ways consider it "one of the best."

Mo's *American*

	18	14	19	$21

Burbank | 4301 W. Riverside Dr. (bet. Rose & Valley Sts.) | 818-845-3009 | www.eatatmos.com

"Burbank's version of *Cheers*", this "casual" bar-and-grill – and Warner Brothers' unofficial "commissary" – is a "solid standby" for "inexpensive" American eats like "juicy" burgers customized with "do-it-yourself fixin's"; "would-be actors" provide "friendly" service, although the "tired" "1977"-style wood-paneled decor could use a face-lift.

Mosto Enoteca *Italian*

	▽ 25	18	25	$55

Marina del Rey | Marina Connection | 517 Washington Blvd. (Via Marina) | 310-821-3035 | www.mostoenoteca.com

Despite its second-floor perch in a Marina del Rey strip mall, Italophiles say this rustic enoteca is "as authentic as can be" with "homemade pastas", "great" regional wines and "knowledgeable" staffers who "make you feel right at home"; it's fit for both a nibble or a full meal, and either way, it's "easy to spend a lot of money" here.

MOZ Buddha Lounge *Asian*

	18	23	18	$42

Agoura Hills | 30105 Agoura Rd. (Reyes Adobe Rd.) | 818-735-0091 | www.mozbar.com

A bit of "Hollywood" in the "valley", this Agoura Hills nightspot tricked out in red and gold with a large Buddha hovering above dispenses "imaginative" Asian fusion plates at moderate rates; the fare garners mixed reviews, and consensus says the main attraction is the "happening bar scene" replete with live music.

NEW Mr. Beef *American*

	-	-	-	I

Venice | 1809 Ocean Front Walk (18th Pl.) | 424-228-2141 | www.mrbeefla.com

This Venice boardwalk branch of a Windy City favorite offers specialties like the eponymous "Mr. Beef" sandwich on fresh baked Turano bread, along with Scala's Italian sausage, pizza puffs, Vienna Beef hot dogs and Polish sausages; all come served in an open-to-the-air stand just down the Strand from Muscle Beach – making this the place where the beef stop for their beef.

Mr. Cecil's California Ribs *BBQ*

	19	10	15	$28

West LA | 12244 W. Pico Blvd. (bet. Amherst & Wellesley Aves.) | 310-442-1550

(continued)

(continued)

Mr. Cecil's California Ribs

NEW **Manhattan Beach** | 1209 Highland Ave. (Manhattan Beach Blvd.) | 310-546-5400

Sherman Oaks | 13625 Ventura Blvd. (bet. Ventura Canyon & Woodman Aves.) | 818-905-8400
www.mrcecilscaribs.com

These BBQ purveyors in Manhattan Beach, Sherman Oaks and West LA "hit the spot" with "fall-off-the-bone" ribs among other "habit-forming" 'cue; tabs are "not cheap", service is "unapologetically" "slow" and the digs rather plain, but hungry locals insist "when you have a hankering", "all is forgiven."

Mr. Chow ◑ *Chinese*   23 | 21 | 21 | $75

Beverly Hills | 344 N. Camden Dr. (bet. Brighton Way & Wilshire Blvd.) | 310-278-9911 | www.mrchow.com

Truly "over-the-top", this Beverly Hills "scene" since 1974 is chock-full of "celebs" and "stargazing peasants" chowing down on "excellent", "traditional" and "Americanized" Chinese dishes in a "cool", art-decked dining room that "couldn't be louder"; "pushy" service is a problem for some and whatever you do, "just don't look at the check."

Mucho Ultima Mexicana *Mexican*   ∇ 20 | 22 | 17 | $37

Manhattan Beach | 903 Manhattan Ave. (9th St.) | 310-374-4422 | www.muchomb.com

"Tanned and botoxed" tipplers tout this "sceney" Manhattan Beach Mex where "pricey margaritas" shaken with an "endless" array of te-quilas add oomph to the *comida*; despite some grumbles about "spotty" food and service, the fact that it's "always packed" speaks for itself.

Mulberry Street Pizzeria *Pizza*   23 | 9 | 17 | $16

Beverly Hills | 240 S. Beverly Dr. (bet. Charleville Blvd. & Gregory Way) | 310-247-8100

Beverly Hills | 347 N. Cañon Dr. (bet. Brighton & Dayton Ways) | 310-247-8998

Encino | 17040 Ventura Blvd. (Oak Park Ave.) | 818-906-8881
www.mulberrypizza.com

"Real thin-crust pizzas" "just like they make in NYC" are the thing at this trio also channeling the "Big Apple" with inexpensive "Little Italy"-style pastas, "fast", "indifferent" service and copies of the *NY Post* on hand; there's "not much decor to speak of", so "close your eyes" or "get it to go."

Muma *Mediterranean*   - | - | - | I

Melrose | 7275 Melrose Ave. (bet. Alta Vista Ave. & Poinsettia Pl.) | 323-936-7697 | www.mumarestaurant.com

The Pinkberry of falafel stands, this new Melrose Mediterranean wel-comes diners with mod lighting and a lime-and-white color scheme, but it's the vast topping bar that makes the scene; enhancing the cool vibe is a decidedly relaxed price point and late hours.

Murakami ✉ *Japanese*   - | - | - | I

Hollywood | 1714 N. Wilcox Ave. (Hollywood Blvd.) | 323-467-8181 | www.murakamihollywood.com

Tadashi Murakami resurrects his Japanese of the same name (closed in 2005) with this scaled back version in Hollywood offering a "limited menu" of "top-grade" rolls and rice bowls at "decent" prices; bright, casual environs and an affable vibe make it a natural for a quick "light" bite, though it closes at 7:30 PM.

Musha *Japanese*
| 25 | 15 | 19 | $30 |

Santa Monica | 424 Wilshire Blvd. (bet. 4th & 5th Sts.) | 310-576-6330 ◑
Torrance | 1725 W. Carson St. (Western Ave.) | 310-787-7344
www.musha.us

An "amazing variety" of "authentic" "Tokyo-style" pub grub turns up at these Santa Monica and Torrance izakayas that packs 'em in at communal tables creating a "noisy", "social" atmosphere; "affordable" price tags, "friendly, eccentric" staffers and free-flowing beer and sake keep the "good times" rolling "late" into the night.

Musso & Frank Grill 🅂🅼 *American*
| 20 | 21 | 21 | $41 |

Hollywood | 6667 Hollywood Blvd. (bet. Cherokee & Las Palmas Aves.) | 323-467-7788 | www.mussoandfrankgrill.com

"Like a time machine back to old Hollywood", this "Golden Age" "classic" from 1919 is a mainstay for "good" steaks and "ice-cold" drinks ("best pours in LA") served in a "dark", "well-worn" setting by a "staff that looks like it came with the place"; perhaps "the food could be better" (and the prices lower), but it's "worth it" for the "history"; P.S. the bar is now open till 2 AM on weekends.

Naga Naga Ramen *Japanese*
| - | - | - | I |

Pasadena | 49 E. Colorado Blvd. (Raymond Ave.) | 626-585-8822
NEW **Alhambra** | 46 W. Valley Blvd. (2nd St.) | 626-300-0010
www.naganagaramen.com

Noodlers "get their slurpin' on" at this Alhambra and Pasadena duo known for its traditional and not-so-traditional ramen selection featuring a variety of broths and add-ons plus accompanying rice dishes and apps; statues of Buddha and "giant aquariums" make up the decor, but it's really the affordable pricing that supplies the wow factor.

Nakkara *Thai*
| ▽ 24 | 16 | 23 | $29 |

Beverly Boulevard | 7669 Beverly Blvd. (Spaulding Ave.) | 323-937-3100 | www.nakkaraonbeverly.com

"A cut above" your everyday Thai, this Beverly Boulevard "gem" flaunts chef/co-owner Kevin Sukcharoen's "culinary ambitions" with "exciting" dishes like crispy catfish curry conveyed by a "warm staff" in a simple setting; it's "bit pricier" than its rivals, "but still extremely reasonable", especially at lunch.

Nanbankan *Japanese*
| 25 | 16 | 22 | $33 |

West LA | 11330 Santa Monica Blvd. (Corinth Ave.) | 310-478-1591
There's "grilled everything" on the menu at this "under-the-radar" Japanese yakitori "joint" in West LA where those in-the-know grab a seat at the counter and wash down "delicious" skewered meats with plenty of beer; decor offers "nothing to look at", but tabs are modest and it's a "fun place" to "go with a group."

Napa Valley Grille *Californian*
| 19 | 21 | 21 | $45 |

Westwood | 1100 Glendon Ave. (Lindbrook Dr.) | 310-824-3322 | www.napavalleygrille.com

Wine country meets Westwood at this "pleasant, spacious" chain eatery matching "pricey", "nicely presented" Cal cuisine with an "astute"

"Napa-inspired" wine list; critics chide it's a tad "generic", but service is "accommodating" and it remains a "steady" performer for "corporate" types, "happy-hour" revelers and the "brunch" crowd.

Natalee Thai *Thai* | 19 | 15 | 17 | $24 |

Beverly Hills | 998 S. Robertson Blvd. (Olympic Blvd.) | 310-855-9380

Palms | 10101 Venice Blvd. (Clarington Ave.) | 310-202-7003
www.nataleethai.com

These "popular" Thai twins in Beverly Hills and Palms turn out "silky", smooth" curries and other "spicy" standards and sushi at prices that aren't too hard "on your pocketbook"; "decent" service aside, the "waits are long" and the ambiance "noisy", so "take your earplugs" or opt for "delivery."

Nate 'n Al *Deli* | 20 | 11 | 18 | $24 |

Beverly Hills | 414 N. Beverly Dr. (bet. Brighton Way & Santa Monica Blvd.) | 310-274-0101

NEW **Thousand Oaks** | The Lakes at Thousand Oaks | 2200 E. Thousand Oaks Blvd. (Conejo School Rd.) | 805-494-3354
www.natenal.com

"Sixty-five years old and still rockin'", this "classic" Beverly Hills deli and its Thousand Oaks offshoot put "a smile on your face" with "big" pastrami sandwiches on "crusty rye" and other examples of "real-deal" "Jewish homestyle cooking" rustled up by "wisecracking waitresses" "imported from another era"; "waits at peak hours" and "dumpy" digs hardly deter its "very loyal" following from packing in each day; P.S. "keep your eye out for Larry King."

☑ Native Foods *Californian/Eclectic* | 23 | 12 | 19 | $18 |

Westwood | 1110½ Gayley Ave. (Wilshire Blvd.) | 310-209-1055 | www.nativefoods.com

"Who woulda thunk fake meat could taste this good?" ask admirers of this vegan chainlet famed for "flavorful" Cal-Eclectic eats like tempeh burgers and veggie bowls capped with "eye-opening" dairy-free desserts; the "hippie-ish" vibe is abetted by a "friendly", "bearded" staff and prices that are as "guilt"-free as the cooking.

☑ Nawab of India *Indian* | 23 | 17 | 19 | $31 |

Santa Monica | 1621 Wilshire Blvd. (bet. 16th & 17th Sts.) | 310-829-1106 | www.nawabindia.com

Spice cadets sing the praises of this "refined" Santa Monica Indian cooking up "complex and flavorful" takes on the classics; add in "capable" service and a "quiet", "comfortable" setting, and most don't mind if it's a tad more "pricey" than competitors.

☑ NBC Seafood *Chinese/Seafood* | 21 | 14 | 15 | $26 |

Monterey Park | 404 S. Atlantic Blvd. (bet. Harding & Newmark Aves.) | 626-282-2323

An enormous glass tank brimming with crabs, prawns and other "fabulous" fresh seafood helps explain the everlasting popularity of this 25-year-old Cantonese in Monterey Park, also delivering "delicate dim sum" ("some of the best in the area") for moderate sums; in spite of so-so service and a somewhat "impersonal" feel, the 700-capacity dining room is a "go-to" for banquets and other "family celebrations."

	FOOD	DECOR	SERVICE	COST

Neptune's Net *Seafood*
19 | 13 | 15 | $19

Malibu | 42505 PCH (Yerba Buena Rd.) | 310-457-3095 |
www.neptunesnet.com

Bikers, CEOs" and "surfers galore" fill up this Malibu seafood shack
serving a "nothing-fancy" lineup of "fresh" fish and chowder that
nonetheless "can't be beat"; for a place with "plastic utensils", it's not
as cheap" as you'd expect, but fans insist the "gorgeous" view of the
Pacific alone is "worth the price."

New Moon *Chinese*
21 | 17 | 18 | $24

Downtown | 102 W. Ninth St. (Main St.) | 213-624-0186 🖾
Montrose | 2138 Verdugo Blvd. (Clifton Pl.) | 818-249-4868
Valencia | Gateway Vill. | 28281 Newhall Ranch Rd. (Rye Canyon Rd.) |
661-257-4321
www.newmoonrestaurants.com

"Better than your average neighborhood Chinese", this "fairly priced"
chainlet churns out "updated" dishes with a handful of "healthy" items
like salads in "sleek, modern" digs; a minority moans that it's less-
than-authentic, but it "hits the spot" for most.

Newsroom Café *Vegetarian*
18 | 14 | 15 | $22

West Hollywood | 120 N. Robertson Blvd. (bet. Beverly Blvd. & 3rd St.) |
310-652-4444

A "great spot to read the papers and have your morning Joe", this
"hip", "well-priced" cafe chock-full of WeHo types on laptops also features "healthy" vegetarian fare, fresh-pressed juices and a full bar; despite occasional "attitude" from the staff, it's "packed on weekends"
and frequent "star sightings" are a perk.

Nick & Stef's Steakhouse *Steak*
23 | 22 | 23 | $60

Downtown | Wells Fargo Ctr. | 330 S. Hope St. (bet. 3rd & 4th Sts.) |
213-680-0330 | www.patinagroup.com

"Dangerously good" dry-aged beef leads the lineup at this Downtown
steakhouse from the Patina Group, a "popular" stop for a "business"
lunch or "quick, pre-theater" dinner; the dark wood–trimmed space
has a "pleasant" feel with a patio "overlooking the city", while "attentive" service and a no-corkage fee policy make the "expensive" bills
easier to swallow.

Nickel Diner 🅼 *Diner*
22 | 16 | 19 | $19

Downtown | 524 S. Main St. (bet. 5th & 6th Sts.) | 213-623-8301 |
www.nickeldiner.com

A "classic diner" is the inspiration for this "nostalgic" Downtowner
feeding the "hip" masses with "updated" "comfort food" elevated by
"delicious", "kitschy" desserts ("gotta love the maple-bacon dough-
nuts" and homemade Pop-Tarts); "good-value" pricing and no-attitude
service overcome the somewhat "sketchy" locale right off Skid Row,
making it a new "favorite" in the area.

Nic's ●🅼 *American*
19 | 21 | 21 | $46

Beverly Hills | 453 N. Cañon Dr. (Little Santa Monica Blvd.) | 310-550-5707 |
www.nicsbeverlyhills.com

An "old Vegas"–style "booze joint", this "swank" Beverly Hills martini
bar/lounge is centered around a "refrigerated tasting room" (aka the
VodBox) where thirsty "young executive types" don "fur coats and

hats to sip ice-cold vodka from over 100 brands"; though the moderately priced New American fare – think filet mignon and raw oysters –
"holds its own", it still "pales compared to the scene" here.

NEW 9021Pho *Vietnamese*   19 | 12 | 17 | $18

Beverly Hills | 490 N. Beverly Dr. (Santa Monica Blvd.) | 310-275-5277
www.9021pho.com

"What a treat to have pho in Beverly Hills" cheer fans of the "big bowls
of steaming noodles" at this "reasonably priced" Vietnamese "lunch
spot" (but open till 9 PM) from "inspired" chef-owner Kimmy Tang,
though "service is iffy" and the "nondescript" setting "doesn't match
its 90210 address", it's "perfect for people who want a safe introduc-
tion to the cuisine" – plus it has a "clever name."

Nine Thirty *American*   ∇ 22 | 23 | 21 | $56

Westwood | W Los Angeles Westwood | 930 Hilgard Ave. (bet. Le Conte &
Weyburn Aves.) | 310-443-8211 | www.ninethirtyw.com

"Dark" and "sophisticated", this dining room in Westwood's W hotel
hosts "power" players for "delicious", global-inflected New American
fare in glossy, modern digs; it gets its "buzz" in part from a "raucous
bar scene", so "deafening" decibels often come with the territory, as
does an "expensive" bill.

Nishimura ⊠ *Japanese*   ∇ 26 | 21 | 22 | $82

West Hollywood | 8684 Melrose Ave. (San Vicente Blvd.) | 310-659-4770

"True sushi aficionados" tout this West Hollywood edifice where chef
Hiro Nishimura delivers culinary "thrills" in the form of "exceptionally
fresh" fish that's never "disguised" by "froufrou sauces" (i.e. "do not
look for spicy tuna here"); "no signage" ensures a "cool, low-key" atmosphere and a "movie star" clientele that can foot the hefty tabs.

Nizam *Indian*   19 | 13 | 21 | $26

West LA | 10871 W. Pico Blvd. (bet. Midvale Ave. & Westwood Blvd.) |
310-470-1441 | www.nizamindianfood.com

"Good, basic Indian" is the order of the day at this "pleasant" spot
across from the Landmark movie theater on Pico, where "attractively"
priced curries and tandooris (as well as a "bargain lunch buffet") pull
in "a nice crowd"; the "run-down" digs are "not much to look at", but
"accommodating" service keeps it "tried-and-true."

☑ Nobu Los Angeles ◑ *Japanese*   26 | 24 | 23 | $86

West Hollywood | 903 N. La Cienega Blvd. (Willoughby Ave.) |
310-657-5711 | www.noburestaurants.com

A "perennial favorite", this "always packed" West Hollywood "shrine"
to Japanese cuisine from Nobu Matsuhisa pumps out "magnificent"
Peruvian-inflected plates and "melt-in-your-mouth" sushi in a "glitzy",
"star"-studded setting staffed by equally "good-looking servers";
"small portions" are a sore spot ("you need to eat a bowl of rice to get
full"), and be prepared to part with "a good portion of your paycheck."

☑ Nobu Malibu *Japanese*   26 | 19 | 23 | $76

Malibu | 3835 Cross Creek Rd. (PCH) | 310-317-9140 |
www.noburestaurants.com

"Where else can you wear jeans" while nibbling "dream"-worthy, "exceptionally fresh" sushi but at this "neighborhood-y" Malibu outpost

	FOOD	DECOR	SERVICE	COST

of Nobu Matsuhisa's empire, attracting "more celebrities than you can shake a stick at" for its "excellent", "well-presented" Japanese-Peruvian cuisine; the consensus is it "never disappoints", just don't be fooled by its "laid-back" strip-mall locale since service can be "snobby" and you'll still "pay a fortune."

Noé *American*
24 | 24 | 23 | $61

Downtown | Omni Los Angeles Hotel | 251 S. Olive St. (2nd St.) | 213-356-4100 | www.noerestaurant.com

This "elegant" "fine"-dining room inside the Omni Downtown presents an "inventive" New American menu featuring "wonderful" small plates well-suited for pre- or post–Disney Hall dining; a "lovely" patio and live piano are additional reasons it deserves to be "better known", even if prices can feel "awfully expensive" "for what you get."

NEW Noir Food & Wine *Eclectic*
25 | 20 | 25 | $46

Pasadena | 40 N. Mentor Ave. (Colorado Blvd.) | 626-795-7199 | www.noirfoodandwine.com

The "innovative" roster of small plates by chef Claud Beltran is bested only by the "terrific wine selection" (over 50 available by the glass) at this Pasadena Eclectic, also "impressing" with "on-the-ball" service and an "intimate", low-lit setting; in spite of "minuscule" portions and not-so-minuscule prices, the majority of locals labels it a "great addition" to the area.

Nonna ⑤ *Italian*
▽ 23 | 21 | 25 | $49

West Hollywood | 9255 Sunset Blvd. (Doheny Dr.) | 310-270-4455 | www.nonnaofitaly.com

This West Hollywood "sleeper" charms guests with "excellent" seasonal Italian cooking led by wood-fired pizzas, "VIP" service and an "understated" modern setting with exposed wine racks; it's "a bit pricey", but insiders insist it should be "busier", 'cuz the eating's "always a treat."

Nook Bistro ⑤ *American/Eclectic*
24 | 18 | 23 | $33

West LA | Plaza West | 11628 Santa Monica Blvd. (Barry Ave.) | 310-207-5160 | www.nookbistro.com

A strip-mall "surprise", this aptly named New American "packs a lot" in its "tiny" West LA space with "fresh", "sophisticated" takes on traditional dishes and loads of "creative beers and wines" all at a "sweet price"; a "lively" communal table and "involved", "heartfelt" service go a long way to warm up the otherwise "minimal" surroundings.

Nyala Ethiopian *Ethiopian*
23 | 15 | 20 | $23

Fairfax | 1076 S. Fairfax Ave. (bet. Olympic Blvd. & Whitworth Dr.) | 323-936-5918 | www.nyala-la.com

Diners "dig in and eat with [their] hands" at this colorful, inexpensive Fairfax Ethiopian offering a truly "finger-licking" experience via plentiful platters of "tasty", "filling" stews designed for sponging up with "blankets" of traditional injera bread; no, it's "not for the shy", but "if you're in the mood for something different", it's a whole lot of "fun."

NEW NY & C Pizzeria & Bar ◑ *Pizza*
▽ 17 | 14 | 18 | $18

Santa Monica | 1120 Wilshire Blvd. (bet. 11th & 12th Sts.) | 310-393-9099 | www.nyandcpizza.com

This pizzeria in Santa Monica channels both New York and Chicago with thin-crust and "deep dish"–style pies plus subs, salads and "good beers on tap" in a "casual", "kid"-friendly space with Gotham memorabilia on one wall and the Windy City on another; despite the novel "concept", expats insist it's "not quite" there, though the prices get no complaints and it sure beats "a trip back east."

Oak Room, The 🛂 *Californian* ▽ 16 | 16 | 18 | $37
Pacific Palisades | 1035 Swarthmore Ave. (Sunset Blvd.) | 310-454-3337 | www.oakroombistrobar.com

Nightlife options in Pacific Palisades are scarce, so this bistro co-owned by former Mayor Richard Riordan fills a niche with Cal fare led by a "standout" burger; perhaps the rest of the menu's "less than exciting" and "pricey", but a "warm" staff and cozy, oak-accented setting – not to mention a full bar – create an "enjoyable" atmosphere nonetheless.

Ocean & Vine *American* ▽ 22 | 24 | 25 | $48
Santa Monica | Loews Santa Monica Beach Hotel | 1700 Ocean Ave. (Pico Blvd.) | 310-576-3180 | www.oceanandvine.com

"The view is to die for" at this Loews Santa Monica restaurant where the windows peep out onto the ocean, and a patio with fire pits keeps things "cozy" at night; as for the food, diners deem the farm-to-table New American menu "surprisingly good" for a hotel, even if they're not sure it lives up to the prices.

Ocean Ave. Seafood *Seafood* 22 | 19 | 21 | $47
Santa Monica | 1401 Ocean Ave. (Santa Monica Blvd.) | 310-394-5669 | www.oceanave.com

This Santa Monica seafooder from the folks behind Water Grill "catches the tourist trade" off Ocean Avenue with "really fresh" fish and "a fine sampling of oysters from all over"; though "crowds", "noise" and "prices that are up there" have some "throwing this one back", most are won over by the "warm" service and the "lovely" Pacific views from the enclosed patio.

Ocean Seafood *Chinese/Seafood* 21 | 14 | 16 | $25
Chinatown | 750 N. Hill St. (bet. Alpine & Ord Sts.) | 213-687-3088 | www.oceansf.com

"The goodies keep coming and coming" at this "reliably busy" Chinatown "mecca" for "real Cantonese seafood" and "fresh, tasty" dim sum delivered straight off the carts in a "spacious", well-"worn" setting; prices are "cheap" and servers are relatively "accessible", so even if diehards declare it not up to San Gabriel standards, it still works "in a pinch."

Ocean Star *Chinese* 21 | 14 | 15 | $21
Monterey Park | 145 N. Atlantic Blvd. (bet. Emerson & Garvey Aves.) | 626-308-2128

Foodies "flock" to this dim sum "powerhouse" in Monterey Park cranking out an "endless, amazing array" of "authentic" morsels and "fresh seafood" in a space the "size of a football field"; despite some murmurs that it's "gone downhill" in recent years, weekend "crowds" are still the norm, and so are "incredibly low prices."

Off Vine *American/Californian* - | - | - | M
Hollywood | 6263 Leland Way (Vine St.) | 323-962-1900 | www.offvine.com

After two years of reconstruction following a devastating fire, this Hollywood American – built in a historic 1908 Craftsman cottage – is

	FOOD	DECOR	SERVICE	COST

open again, offering a well-priced option for those heading for performances at the nearby Pantages, along with lunch and brunch on the patio and intimate dinners in the upstairs dining room; it's a rare instance where the style of the California of a century ago meets the cooking of the California of today.

Oinkster, The *BBQ*

| | 20 | 10 | 15 | $14 |

Eagle Rock | 2005 Colorado Blvd. (Shearin Ave.) | 323-255-6465 | www.oinkster.com

A "must-visit for meat-eating Angelenos", this "popular" Eagle Rock "cue stop showcases chef André Guerrero's "rockin'" "gourmet fast food" featuring "knock-your-socks-off" pastrami and pulled pork among other "gut-busting", "habit-forming" items; a "nice selection of local beers", retro digs and "good bang for the buck" keep its "hipster" clientele "coming back"; "more locations please!"

Old Venice *Greek/Italian*

| | ∇ 18 | 16 | 18 | $26 |

Manhattan Beach | 1001 Manhattan Ave. (Manhattan Beach Blvd.) | 310-376-0242 | www.oldveniceonline.com

"Like a phoenix from the ashes", this family-run taverna in Manhattan Beach is "back in full force", reviving its "extensive" Greek-Italian menu after a fire closed its doors in 2006; with "authentic", "flavorful" fare and reasonable bills, "neighborhood" types report it's already "attracting lines at dinner."

NEW Olive Kitchen + Bar *Californian/Italian*

| | - | - | - | M |

Hollywood | Grafton on Sunset | 8462 W. Sunset Blvd. (La Cienega Blvd.) | 323-654-4600 | www.theoliveonsunset.com

The latest venture of restaurateur Greg Morris (The Belmont), this Sunset Strip Cal-Italian offers midpriced breakfasts, lunches and dinners in The Grafton's former BOA steakhouse space; the walls seem to be made of twigs, multicolored lamps warm up the space and guests are encouraged to leave their mark on a chalkboard that runs through the various rooms.

NEW Oliverio *Italian*
(fka Blue on Blue)

| | - | - | - | M |

Beverly Hills | Avalon Hotel | 9400 W. Olympic Blvd. (Cañon Dr.) | 310-277-5221 | www.avalonbeverlyhills.com

In the poolside space in the Avalon Hotel that for many years was Blue on Blue, this Beverly Hills arrival is the "in place to be" with a "cool", California-chic setting designed by Kelly Wearstler and a midpriced modern Italian menu from Mirko Paderno (ex Cecconi's); even if the food's on the "basic" side, it's still an "appealing" place for drinks, helped along by a multitude of wines and cocktails, happy-hour specials plus DJs on Tuesdays.

Omelette Parlor *American*

| | 19 | 14 | 18 | $18 |

Santa Monica | 2732 Main St. (bet. Ashland Ave. & Hill St.) | 310-399-7892

"Loosen your belt" before a visit to this Santa Monica early bird famed for "fluffy, flavorful" "oversized" omelets among other "affordable" American daytime grub; "there's "always a wait", but service is "quick" once you're seated and the "garden" patio is "lovely" for lingering anyhow.

	FOOD	DECOR	SERVICE	COST

Omino Sushi *Japanese* ▽ 26 | 13 | 21 | $32

Chatsworth | 20957 Devonshire St. (De Soto Ave.) | 818-709-8822 |
www.ominosushi.com

An "oasis in the North Valley desert", this Chatsworth Japanese is an
area "favorite" for an "excellent" array of "fresh" sushi and sashimi for
moderate sums; though the setting's simple, "fast and cheerful" service keeps the "locals" satisfied.

O-Nami *Japanese* ▽ 23 | 13 | 17 | $28

Torrance | 1925 W. Carson St. (Cabrillo Ave.) | 310-787-1632 |
www.o-nami.com

"Sushi lovers on a budget" hit up this "block-long" buffet in Torrance
and Laguna for a "vast" array of Japanese fare; what it lacks in decor
and service is made up for in "volume", though the unimpressed find
that "good value" can't compensate for only "decent" eats.

101 Coffee Shop ● *Diner* 18 | 15 | 16 | $17

Hollywood | 6145 Franklin Ave. (bet. Argyle Ave. & Gower St.) |
323-467-1175 | www.the101coffeeshop.com

"Late-night hipsters" and Hollywood Hills "locals" go to savor affordable
plates of "classic American diner food" with "modern flair" (breakfast
is a standout) at this "groovy" '70s-inspired coffee shop sporting "rock
walls, bubble lights" and a "rockin' jukebox"; music that's "crazy loud"
and service that's "hit-or-miss" doesn't deter fans who swear their
"milkshakes and fries are the best way to end any night."

NEW 101 Noodle Express ⊄ *Chinese* 22 | 12 | 17 | $15

Arcadia | 1025 S. Baldwin Ave. (Arcadia Ave.) | 626-446-8855
Alhambra | 1408 E. Valley Blvd. (bet. New Ave. & Vega St.) | 626-300-8654
"The beef roll alone is worth the trip" (and "the calories") say die-hard
fans of this Chinese located "near a bowling alley" both in Alhambra
and in an Arcadia strip mall, where "cravings" are satisfied for "authentic, tasty" noodles and more; sure, maybe "you have to jump in
front of your waiter to get noticed" and decor is "cold" and "simple", but fans shrug when it's this "cheap" and good, "what else can
you ask for?"

Z One Pico *Californian/Mediterranean* 20 | 26 | 21 | $57

Santa Monica | Shutters on the Beach | 1 Pico Blvd. (Ocean Ave.) |
310-587-1717 | www.shuttersonthebeach.com

It feels like "vacation" at this restaurant inside Santa Monica's Shutters
on the Beach that "epitomizes California living" with an "airy", "elegant" layout and "killer views" of the sand; most diners deem the Cal-
Med cuisine "good", "but not exceptional", so with "spotty" service
and "expensive" prices, perhaps "it's better for lunch."

Open Sesame *Lebanese* 22 | 16 | 20 | $24

Long Beach | 5201 E. Second St. (Nieto Ave.) | 562-621-1698
Long Beach | 5215 E. Second St. (bet. Corona & Nieto Aves.) | 562-621-1698
Manhattan Beach | 2640 N. Sepulveda Blvd. (bet. Marine Ave. & 27th St.) |
310-545-1600
www.opensesamegrill.com

"Simple, well-prepared" Middle Eastern grub "satisfies" "vegetarians and meat lovers alike" at this Lebanese chainlet cherished for
"relatively healthy" preps at "cheap" prices; despite occasionally

| | FOOD | DECOR | SERVICE | COST |

"cramped and noisy" conditions, all three thrive in "casual" digs with pleasant outdoor seating.

Original Pancake House American   22 | 12 | 18 | $15

Redondo Beach | 1756 S. PCH (bet. Palos Verdes Blvd. & Paseo De Las Delicias) | 310-543-9875 | www.originalpancakehouse.com

Some of the "best pancakes on the planet" (including the "decadent" Dutch Baby) can be found at this "popular", "competitively priced" Redondo Beach chain link that also pleases with "puffed-up" omelets and other "delicious" morning items; it's "a bit worn around the edges", but "inviting" and "quick" once you sit down – just "get there early on the weekends, or your breakfast will end up being lunch."

Original Pantry Cafe ●⌷ Diner   17 | 11 | 18 | $18

Downtown | 877 S. Figueroa St. (9th St.) | 213-972-9279 | www.pantrycafe.com

"Characters galore" fill up this Downtown "greasy spoon" owned by former Mayor Richard Riordan where "no-nonsense waiters" serve up "gigantic breakfasts fit for a Midwesterner" and other "cheap" chow 24 hours a day; true, the food's "nothing special", but "you come here for the experience."

Orris ⓜ French/Japanese   27 | 15 | 23 | $42

West LA | 2006 Sawtelle Blvd. (La Grange Ave.) | 310-268-2212 | www.orrisrestaurant.com

Each dish is "more exquisite than the next" at "master" chef Hideo Yamashiro's West LA "wonder" (and sib of Shiro) where the "delectable, little" French-Japanese plates are made "for sharing" and "served beautifully" in "tiny", "crowded" quarters with an open kitchen; a "super" staff and "semi-reasonable" prices seal the deal – now "if only they would take reservations."

Ortega 120 Mexican   20 | 18 | 18 | $31

Redondo Beach | 1814 S. PCH (bet. Palos Verdes Blvd. & Prospect Ave.) | 310-792-4120 | www.ortega120.com

This Redondo Beach Mexican goes "beyond burritos and tacos" with "inventive" south-of-the-border comida served in a "dark", "eclectic" Dia de los Muertos"–styled room; critics call the service "indifferent" and the food just "so-so", but with 120 tequilas on the menu, defenders declare it's a whole lot of "fun", as long as you "don't mind yelling."

Ortolan ⌷ⓜ French   25 | 24 | 23 | $90

Third Street | 8338 W. Third St. (bet. Orlando & Sweetzer Aves.) | West Hollywood | 323-653-3300 | www.ortolanrestaurant.com

"A rare bird indeed!", this Third Street "destination" flaunts "master" chef Christophe Émé's "exquisite", "out-there" New French creations presented in "clever", "artistic" platings in a "seductive" setting decked out with "crystal chandeliers and lots of candles"; though the usually "impeccable" servers strike some as "snooty", most agree it's a worthy "splurge."

Osteria La Buca ⓜ Italian   23 | 19 | 18 | $38

Hollywood | 5210 Melrose Ave. (Wilton Pl.) | 323-462-1900 | www.osterialabuca.com

Former chef "Mama" Cecchinato "may be gone", but this midpriced "charmer" in Hollywood "is still humming along" with "mouthwatering pastas" and other "divine" Northern "Italiano"; it's "noisy", "crowded" and the staff can be "brusque", but slip upstairs for a table by the "roaring fireplace" and you'll feel "like you're eating in someone's home."

Osteria Latini *Italian*

| 24 | 18 | 23 | $45 |

Brentwood | 11712 San Vicente Blvd. (bet. Barrington & Gorham Aves.) 310-826-9222 | www.osterialatini.com

"Charming" chef-owner Paolo Pasio makes everyone "feel like a regular" at this "low-key" Brentwood "keeper", the kind of "joint" "you wish was in your neighborhood"; sure, the seating is "cramped" and there's "always a wait", but the Italian "home cooking" is "fantastic" and prices "won't break the bank" either.

NEW Osteria Mamma 🗷 *Italian*

| - | - | - | M |

Hollywood | 5732 Melrose Ave. (Vine St.) | 323-284-7060

There are plain wood tables to eat on, and black-and-white family photos on the walls at this Italian opened by Filippo Cortivo (ex Osteria La Buca), who's taken both his mamma and her following with him a few blocks down Melrose to this space across from Paramount Studios; it serves a moderately priced menu of soul-satisfying dishes like garganelli pasta with capers and calamata olives and Florentine-style chicken breast, and there's very thin-crust pizza as well.

Z Osteria Mozza *Italian*

| 27 | 23 | 24 | $65 |

Hollywood | 6602 Melrose Ave. (Highland Ave.) | 323-297-0100 | www.mozza-la.com

"Heaven" for "foodies", this big-ticket Batali-Silverton collaboration in Hollywood is the site of "truly memorable" "Roman feasts" starring "sublime" secondi, "sensuous cheeses" from the in-house mozzarella bar and a "gorgeous" egg-filled raviolo that could make you "tear up" just thinking about it; cap it off with a "killer" vino list and a "dark" "celeb"-heavy room "abuzz" with "New York energy" and most are willing to overlook the "deadly sound level", "difficult-to-get reservations" and staff that could sometimes "use a little less 'tude."

Outback Steakhouse *Steak*

| 18 | 16 | 19 | $29 |

Lakewood | 5305 Clark Ave. (Candlewood St.) | 562-634-0353
Torrance | Del Amo Fashion Ctr. | 21880 Hawthorne Blvd. (bet. Carson St. & Sepulveda Blvd.) | 310-793-5555
Arcadia | 166 E. Huntington Dr. (bet. 1st & 2nd Aves.) | 626-447-6435
Burbank | Empire Ctr. | 1761 N. Victory Pl. (Empire Ave.) | 818-567-2717
Northridge | 18711 Devonshire St. (Reseda Blvd.) | 818-366-2341
City of Industry | Puente Hills Mall | 1418 S. Azusa Ave. (Colima Rd.) | 626-810-6765
Covina | 1476 N. Azusa Ave. (Arrow Hwy.) | 626-812-0488
Oxnard | 2341 Lockwood St. (Outlet Center Dr.) | 805-988-4329
Thousand Oaks | 137 E. Thousand Oaks Blvd. (Moorpark Rd.) | 805-381-1590
Valencia | 25261 The Old Rd. (Chiquella Ln.) | 661-287-9630
www.outback.com
Additional locations throughout Southern California

"Reliable" (if "not prime") seasoned steaks provide "real value for the dollar" at this "Aussie-themed" "middle-of-the-road" chain where folks love to "overindulge in the bloomin' onion"; it's too "kitschy" and "packaged" for pickier patrons and the "cute" service is "hit-or-miss", but "you can take all of your kids and your neighbors too" since you'll blend right into the "noisy" surroundings.

	FOOD	DECOR	SERVICE	COST

Outlaws Bar & Grill *American* ▽ 19 | 12 | 18 | $21

Playa del Rey | 230 Culver Blvd. (bet. Pershing Dr. & Vista Del Mar) | 310-822-4040 | www.outlawsrestaurant.com

"The burgers rock" at this "laid-back" Playa del Rey saloon also purveying a "fantastic" lineup of suds and "good" American eats just a block from the beach; service can be spotty, but tabs are cheap and all agree "eating on the deck on a nice day" is tough to top.

NEW Ozumo *Japanese* - | - | - | M

Santa Monica | Dining Deck, Santa Monica Pl. | 395 Santa Monica Pl. (3rd. St. Promenade) | 424-214-4560

With a clean, minimalist look straight out of Shibuya, this moderately priced Japanese newcomer in Santa Monica Place offers modern spins on the classics in dishes like black cod in miso and salt-grilled hamachi collar; there's an extensive bar up front with an encyclopedic selection of sakes and a dining room of spare wooden tables plus a sushi bar and three sedate tatami rooms with private entrances for those who want to eat their kurobuta pork unbothered by paparazzi.

Pace *Italian* 22 | 19 | 18 | $45

Laurel Canyon | 2100 Laurel Canyon Blvd. (Kirkwood Dr.) | 323-654-8583 | www.peaceinthecanyon.com

Channeling "classic Laurel Canyon bohemia", this "rustic" "hideaway" is a go-to for "delish" Italian dishes set down in a "dark", "intimate" setting that's "hip without trying too hard"; "warm service" and "fair prices" cement its status as an ideal "date spot."

Pacific Dining Car ● *Steak* 23 | 21 | 23 | $59

Downtown | 1310 W. Sixth St. (bet. Valencia & Witmer Sts.) | 213-483-6000

Santa Monica | 2700 Wilshire Blvd. (Princeton St.) | 310-453-4000 www.pacificdiningcar.com

"When you need a steak at 1 AM", look no further than these Downtown and Santa Monica "power spots" "recalling old LA at its best" with "melt-in-your-mouth" beef and "elegant" breakfasts served 24 hours a day; "fine", "traditional" "train-car" decor and "classic" waiters increase the allure, but be forewarned that all this "luxury" "comes at a price."

Paco's Tacos *Mexican* 21 | 14 | 18 | $21

Mar Vista | 4141 S. Centinela Ave. (bet. Culver & Washington Blvds.) | 310-391-9616

Westchester | 6212 Manchester Blvd. (bet. La Tijera & Sepulveda Blvds.) | 310-645-8692

www.pacoscantina.com

The "fresh, homemade tortillas" are the "main attraction" at these Mar Vista and Westchester cantinas where the staff "treats you like family" and the "good-value" Mexican "comfort food" tastes "like home"; the "festive setting strewn with lights ("tacky, but it works) is a hit with "the kids", so no surprise, there's "always a wait."

NEW Paddy Rice ⊠ *Vietnamese* - | - | - | I

Melrose | 6909 Melrose Ave. (Orange Dr.) | 323-634-7423 | www.thepaddyrice.com

This Melrose Vietnamese is dedicated to the wide and wonderful world of noodle dishes and pho, all served in a long, narrow modernist

room with dark gray walls, light wood paneling and a shiny floor; thin
of it as a nice (and inexpensive) alternative when the line for nearb
Pizzeria Mozza stretches down the block.

Padri *Italian* — 22 | 21 | 21 | $37

Agoura Hills | 29008 Agoura Rd. (Cornell Rd.) | 818-865-3700 |
www.padrirestaurant.net

"In an area underserved by fine restaurants", this "class" act in Agour
Hills stands out with "solid" seasonal Italiana served up in a contem
porary Tuscan farmhouse–styled setting at moderate rates; it boasts
"cozy, cabana-lined" patio and an adjacent martini lounge that's
"hit" with "over-35" singles on weekends.

NEW Palace Seafood & — - | - | - | M
Dim Sum *Chinese*

West LA | 11701 Wilshire Blvd. (Barrington Ave.) | 310-979-3377
Though the look hasn't changed much from the space's former incar
nation as VIP Harbor Seafood, this arrival on the second-story of
West LA mini-mall has already drawn quite a local following for it
midpriced Chinese fare; offerings include a thorough selection of din
sum served on rolling carts at lunchtime, and what's being called th
best Peking duck on the Westside – though admittedly, the compet
tion isn't all that stiff.

Palate Food + Wine *American* — 24 | 19 | 19 | $48

Glendale | 933 S. Brand Blvd. (bet. Acacia & Garfield Aves.) |
818-662-9463 | www.palatefoodwine.com

"Not too shabby for Glendale!" gush fans of this wine bar/restaurar
tucked in among the auto dealerships on Brand Boulevard, wher
chef-owner Octavio Becerra's "cutting-edge" New American far
comes in mason jars and "playful" small plates, perfect for "noshin'
true, a few find it "overpriced" and "overrated", but an "endless
array of vintages, a "passionate" staff and "modern" digs make it a
"worthwhile" for most.

Palermo *Italian* — 18 | 15 | 21 | $21

Los Feliz | 1858 N. Vermont Ave. (bet. Franklin & Russell Aves.) |
323-663-1178 | www.palermorestaurant.net

The "quintessential spaghetti joint", this "old-fashioned" Italian i
where Los Feliz locals "carb out" on "garlicky" "red-sauce" fare an
pizzas proclaimed "predictable, but totally satisfying"; add a staff tha
"makes you feel welcome" plus a "fun", "NYC" vibe and it's "undeni
ably a good time."

Z Palm, The *Steak* — 24 | 20 | 23 | $66

Downtown | 1100 S. Flower St. (11th St.) | 213-763-4600
West Hollywood | 9001 Santa Monica Blvd. (bet. Doheny Dr. &
Robertson Blvd.) | 310-550-8811
www.thepalm.com

"Perfect" lobster, "superb" steaks and "hefty" cocktails are the signa
tures of these "bustling", "special-occasion" chophouse chain link
Downtown and in WeHo with a "dark men's-club" look and "wonderfu
atmosphere" enhanced by "caricatures of celebs" (and "locals") cov
ering the walls; "impeccable", "old-school" service seals the deal, so
while it's "not cheap", most conclude it's "worth it."

	FOOD	DECOR	SERVICE	COST

almeri *Italian* 24 | 20 | 24 | $47

rentwood | 11650 San Vicente Blvd. (Darlington Ave.) |
10-442-8446

hough still something of a "secret", Ottavio Palmeri's "welcoming" rentwood Italian distinguishes itself with "fantastic cuisine "from his ative Sicily" and "excellent" service, especially "for the price"; it's usuly not crowded", but those in-the-know deem it "a definite keeper."

alms Thai ● *Thai* 21 | 13 | 19 | $22

ast Hollywood | 5900 Hollywood Blvd. (Bronson Ave.) | 323-462-5073 |
ww.palmsthai.com

ure, the "Thai Elvis impersonator" draws attention, but this East ollywood Siamese "stands on its own" foodwise with "a wide variy" of "consistent" dishes (including the "adventurous" 'wild things' enu) served with "maximum efficiency" to a "youngish", "bustling" owd; it's open till midnight or later, and "good value" redeems the inctional space; P.S. the "floor show" runs Wednesday–Sunday.

alomino *American/European* 18 | 19 | 20 | $38

Westwood | 10877 Wilshire Blvd. (Glendon Ave.) | 310-208-1960 |
ww.palomino.com

Happy hour really rocks" at this "large", "lively" Westwood outost of a national chain, a "favorite" for horsing around in the opping bar"; meanwhile the dining room is "dependable" for tandard" New American–European fare, and "moderate" tabs and a convenient" location near "UCLA and the Geffen" keep it "busy" deite the "corporate" feel.

🆕 Pan Am Room *Pan-Latin* – | – | – | M

anta Monica | Santa Monica Airport | 3221 Donald Douglas Loop S. airport Rd.) | 310-390-6565 | www.typhoon.biz

t this airport-based newcomer, located above Santa Monica's Typhoon n the space last home to The Hump), owner Brian Vidor attempts to o for Pan-Latin cuisine what he does with Asian downstairs, offering midpriced mix of dishes from Mexico and points south amid memobilia conjuring Pan Am's glory flying days; the views of Gulfstreams nd Lears negotiating the adjacent runway are a bonus.

anda Inn *Chinese* 21 | 18 | 19 | $27

ntario | 3223 E. Centrelake Dr. (Guasti Rd.) | 909-390-2888
asadena | 3488 E. Foothill Blvd. (bet. Rosemead Blvd. &
erra Madre Villa Ave.) | 626-793-7300
lendale | 111 E. Wilson Ave. (Brand Blvd.) | 818-502-1234
ww.pandainn.com

ount on sizable servings of "consistently good" (if "Americanized") hinese at these more upmarket relatives of Panda Express in Pasadena, lendale and Ontario; "fast" service and "reasonable prices" make the othing-exciting" style easy to bear, and those "chocolate-covered rtune cookies are special" too.

ane e Vino *Italian* 21 | 20 | 21 | $39

everly Boulevard | 8265 Beverly Blvd. (bet. Harper & Sweetzer Aves.) |
23-651-4600 | www.panevinola.com

he "beguiling", "romantic patios" "make all the difference" at this eparately owned Beverly Boulevard and Santa Barbara duo, long-

standing and "reliable" sources of "solid" homestyle Italian "at a fa
price"; the "warm" "hospitality" is especially "enjoyable" if you need
"hideaway" for "guests" or "date night."

Panini Cafe *Italian/Mediterranean* | 20 | 16 | 19 | $24 |

Downtown | 600 W. Ninth St. (Hope St.) | 213-489-4200
Beverly Hills | 9601 Santa Monica Blvd. (Camden Dr.) |
310-247-8300
NEW Sherman Oaks | 14622 Ventura Blvd. (Cedros Ave.) | 818-783-110
NEW Woodland Hills | 21000 Victory Blvd. (Independence Ave.) |
818-992-3330
www.mypaninicafe.com

"If you're super hungry", this ever-burgeoning chainlet offers a "sul
stantial" "chow-down" with its "better-than-average" selection
Italian panini, salads and Med-style kebabs; the digs are "very c
sual", but with "cheerful service" and high "value for the buck", it's "r
wonder" they're neighborhood "favorites."

Panzanella *Italian* | 23 | 22 | 23 | $49 |

Sherman Oaks | 14928 Ventura Blvd. (bet. Sepulveda & Van Nuys Blvds.)
818-784-4400 | www.giacominodrago.com

A "sophisticated clientele" confirms this "upscale and pricey" Sherma
Oaks entry from the Drago Group "knows how to please" with "exce
lent" Italian cuisine and "wonderful service"; though the setting
"plush" (especially "for the Valley"), it can get so "noisy" you'll b
"texting your tablemates to communicate."

⚡ Papa Cristo's 🅼 *Greek* | 24 | 10 | 18 | $19 |

Mid-City | 2771 W. Pico Blvd. (Normandie Ave.) | 323-737-2970 |
www.papacristos.com

Diners are "delighted" by the "bounteous" "feasts" at this "no-pretens
Mid-City Greek, a "treasure trove" of "authentic" eats for few "drac
mas"; the spare, spacious digs are certainly "not fancy", although t
"joyous" atmosphere's so much "fun" – especially during Thursd
night's "family-style dinners" with belly dancers – you probably wor
mind; P.S. don't miss the on-site market stocked with dry goods ar
cheeses plus "fresh-baked" breads and desserts.

Paradise Cove *American/Seafood* | 15 | 19 | 18 | $35 |

Malibu | 28128 PCH (Paradise Cove Rd.) | 310-457-2503 |
www.paradisecovemalibu.com

"It feels like a vacation" at this beachfront Malibu "getaway" from Bo
Morris where "digging your toes into the sand while you eat" mak
the only "adequate" American chow taste better; "long waits", som
what "expensive" tabs and an "overwhelmed staff" aside, you ju
can't beat the "views."

Park, The 🅼 *American* | ▽ 24 | 15 | 24 | $31 |

Echo Park | 1400 W. Sunset Blvd. (Douglas St.) | 213-482-9209 |
www.thepark1400sunset.com

Echo Park patrons hit up this "charming" "neighborhood" spot for "i
ventive" New American cuisine plus beer and wine served in mode
ately "hip" environs; though it flies a bit under the radar, the bills a
relatively "low", and the $15 three-course meal on Tuesdays is "one
the best values on the east side."

	FOOD	DECOR	SERVICE	COST

Parker's Lighthouse *Seafood*

19 | 22 | 19 | $38

Long Beach | 435 Shoreline Village Dr. (Shoreline Dr.) | 562-432-6500 | www.parkerslighthouse.com

"Stunning views" of Long Beach Harbor and the Queen Mary take center stage at this "touristy" seafooder set in a three-story lighthouse overlooking the water; "plentiful" portions and moderate pricing make it "entirely dependable", even if fare and service can feel "forgettable" at times.

Park's Barbeque *Korean*

24 | 13 | 18 | $33

Koreatown | 955 S. Vermont Ave. (bet. Olympic Blvd. & San Marino St.) | 213-380-1717 | www.parksbbq.com

Some of the "best Korean BBQ" in LA turns up at this K-town "find" distinguishing itself from the masses with "prime", "high-quality" beef, charcoal-stoked grills and "delicious" *banchan*; a "shiny", modern space, "reasonable" pricing and late hours (open till 2 AM on weekends) hit it out of the park for fans.

Parkway Grill *Californian*

26 | 25 | 25 | $54

Pasadena | 510 S. Arroyo Pkwy. (bet. California & Del Mar Blvds.) | 626-795-1001 | www.theparkwaygrill.com

"Still the gold standard" for Pasadena dining, this 25-year-old "jewel in the Smith Brothers' empire" remains a "grown-up" "delight" with "wonderful" Californian cuisine served in a "beautiful" brick-lined room that exudes "understated sophistication"; it may be "pricey", but factor in "experienced" service and "no-cover-charge" piano nightly, and you really "can't go wrong" here.

Parq at Montage Beverly Hills *American*

▽ 25 | 27 | 27 | $64

Beverly Hills | 225 N. Cañon Dr. (Wilshire Blvd.) | 310-860-7800 | www.montagebeverlyhills.com

"You get what you pay for" at this "expensive but wondrous" New American in the Montage Beverly Hills hotel, where the "innovative" cuisine is "flawlessly prepared" and delivered by "pampering" "professional" servers; most find the luxe, mosaic-bedizened setting "calm and beautiful", though a minority wonders "where's the buzz?"

Pastina Ⓢ *Italian*

21 | 18 | 22 | $38

West LA | 2260 Westwood Blvd. (bet. Olympic Blvd. & Tennessee Ave.) | 310-441-4655

It's just like "home" – if "home had better food" – at this "popular" West LA Italian pulling in a "loyal" cadre of families for "honest" Southern-style cooking at prices that "won't break the bank"; "patient" service and a "pleasant", white-tablecloth setting with candles on the tables add to the warm glow.

Patina Ⓜ *American/Californian*

26 | 26 | 25 | $79

Downtown | Walt Disney Concert Hall | 141 S. Grand Ave. (2nd St.) | 213-972-3331 | www.patinagroup.com

This Downtown "shining star" from eatery impresario Joachim Splichal "excels at the high end" with "sublime" Californian–New American dishes and "*magnifique*" wines brought on by a "polished" staff; the contemporary space adjoining Walt Disney Hall is "the epitome of elegance", so "for those special occasions" the money is "well spent."

	FOOD	DECOR	SERVICE	COST

Patrick's Roadhouse *Diner*
18 | **16** | **15** | **$22**

Santa Monica | 106 Entrada Dr. (PCH) | 310-459-4544 |
www.patricksroadhouse.info

"The food isn't great, the service isn't great and the decor isn't great,
but this "been-there-forever" hangout across from the sand in Santa
Monica "doesn't aspire to be" more than a pit stop for "solid" breakfast "grub" and burgers; the pace is "the slowest", but the "neo-hippie"
milieu can be "a real hoot"; P.S. closes at 3 PM.

Pat's *Californian/Italian*
▽ **20** | **18** | **21** | **$45**

Pico-Robertson | 9233 W. Pico Blvd. (Glenville Dr.) | 310-205-8705
"Oy gevalt is it tasty!" exclaim enthusiasts at this Pico-Robertson kosher Cal-Italian, where the "creative", "upscale" fare includes "fantastic meat dishes" and "clever desserts"; the "attentive and informed"
staff and roomy, open-kitchen setting help justify tabs that can be "a
little pricey"; P.S. closed Saturdays.

Paul Martin's American Bistro *American*
22 | **22** | **21** | **$40**

El Segundo | 2361 Rosecrans Ave. (bet. Aviation Blvd. & Redondo Ave.) |
310-643-9300 | www.paulmartinsamericanbistro.com
"Fresh, fresh, fresh" "organic and locally grown ingredients" elevate
this "inviting" El Segundo eatery's "rock-solid" American bistro fare "a
cut above the competition"; co-owned by Paul Fleming of Fleming's
Steakhouse, its "civilized" setting and "wonderful" staff are "just what
the area needs" even if "you pay a premium" for the pleasure.

Pearl Dragon *Asian*
16 | **15** | **15** | **$37**

Pacific Palisades | 15229 Sunset Blvd. (bet. Antioch St. & La Cruz Dr.) |
310-459-9790 | www.thepearldragon.com
"Locals" fall back on this Pacific Palisades "hangout" for "decent sushi"
and Pan-Asian plates even if it's "a little too family-friendly at times"
with "noisy" "children all around"; "later on" the "swinging singles" take
over since it's one of the few places "to get a stiff drink" in the area.

Pecorino *Italian*
23 | **20** | **23** | **$47**

Brentwood | 11604 San Vicente Blvd. (bet. Darlington & Mayfield Aves.) |
310-571-3800 | www.pecorinorestaurant.com
"Gracious", "old-world service" led by host-owner Mario Sabatini and
a "beautiful" "exposed-brick" interior create a "lovely, comfortable"
ambiance" at this "compact" Brentwood trattoria; the "out-of-this-
world Italian cuisine" seals the deal for the "thirty- and fortysome-
things" who keep it "busy" even though it's "on the expensive side."

Pei Wei Asian Diner *Asian*
17 | **15** | **16** | **$15**

Torrance | 2777 PCH (Crenshaw Blvd.) | 310-517-9366
Pasadena | 3455 E. Foothill Blvd. (bet. Rosemead Blvd. &
Sierra Madre Villa Ave.) | 626-325-9020
Santa Clarita | Valencia Crossroads | 24250 Valencia Blvd. (McBean Pkwy.) |
661-600-0132
www.peiwei.com
"Filling the gap between budget Chinese takeout" and higher-priced
parent P.F. Chang's, this "affordable", "order-at-the-counter" chain delivers "enjoyable", "modernized" Asian chow at a "fast pace"; maybe
the dishes could use more "pizzazz" and the "rushed" service irks
some, but families keep it "crowded" since the "kids love it."

	FOOD	DECOR	SERVICE	COST

Penthouse, The *American*   20 | 26 | 21 | $51

anta Monica | Huntley Santa Monica Beach Hotel | 1111 Second St.
Wilshire Blvd.) | 310-394-5454 | www.thehuntleyhotel.com
Epic" 360-degree vistas of the city and coastline draw an "attractive
rowd" at this "trendy" resto-lounge atop Santa Monica's Huntley
Hotel, where the "inventive" New American dishes and "classy ser-
ice" are trumped by "plush", white-gold decor replete with "gauzy
urtains", cabanas, a circular bar and a fireplace; most agree the "ex-
ensive" tabs are "justified" given the "priceless" view, but the "too-
ip scene" can be "deafening."

Peppone *Italian*   21 | 18 | 21 | $58

rentwood | 11628 Barrington Ct. (Barrington Ave.) | 310-476-7379 |
www.peppone.com
Unchanged since grandpa ate there", this "clubby" Brentwood "clas-
ic" "never goes out of fashion" for fans of hearty" Italian served by
experienced" "waiters in formal attire" who "fawn over the regulars";
"time-warp" interior with "cozy booths" and Tiffany lamps properly
ops off the "old-school" feel.

Pete's Cafe & Bar ● *American*   21 | 19 | 20 | $31

Downtown | 400 S. Main St. (4th St.) | 213-617-1000 |
www.petescafe.com
With so many "old-timey touches", this "hip" "Downtown haunt"
could be in NYC" according to the "eclectic crowd" digging into
imaginatively prepared" New American "comfort food" ("blue
heese fries are a must") at "reasonable prices"; favored for its "lively
ar" and "comfortable" environs, it's a "standby" "for pre- or post-
heater" – "plus it's open late" (till 2 AM).

Petrelli's Steakhouse *Italian/Steak*   19 | 14 | 20 | $40

ulver City | 5615 Sepulveda Blvd. (Jefferson Blvd.) | 310-397-1438 |
www.georgepetrellisteaks.com
's "not for the calorie- or cholesterol-conscious", but this "family-
wned institution in Culver City" (since 1931) still serves "fine" steak
nd "red-gravy" Italian fare at "beyond reasonable" prices; the
friendly" "old-time" staff and "retro" interior with deep black-leather
ooths are guaranteed to really "take you back."

Petros *Greek*   23 | 20 | 19 | $49

Manhattan Beach | 451 Manhattan Beach Blvd. (bet. Morningside &
alley Drs.) | 310-545-4100 | www.petrosrestaurant.com
Terrific" "upscale" cuisine "takes you to the Greek isles" at this
Manhattan Beach Hellene, where the "tempting" menu's served with
professionalism" in "crowded and lively" quarters with a white-
vashed interior and "people-watching" patio; as long as you're ready
o "rub shoulders with your neighbors" and spring for "slightly pricey"
abs, "everyone is happy."

Petrossian Paris *French*   ▽ 23 | 17 | 24 | $61

West Hollywood | 321 N. Robertson Blvd. (Rosewood Ave.) | 310-271-0576 |
www.petrossian.com
efinitely a "splurgey kind of place", this WeHo eatery/gourmet bou-
que proffers a limited lineup of "simply amazing" French "luxuries"
notably "sublime" caviar and champagne) courtesy of a former Joël

| | FOOD | DECOR | SERVICE | COST |

Robuchon chef; the cost is petrifying, but with skillful service and a recent "redesign" that's doubled the space, "the memories will be good."

P.F. Chang's China Bistro *Chinese* | 19 | 19 | 18 | $29

Beverly Hills | Beverly Ctr. | 121 N. La Cienega Blvd. (bet. Beverly Blvd. & 3rd St.) | 310-854-6467
Santa Monica | 326 Wilshire Blvd. (4th St.) | 310-395-1912
El Segundo | 2041 E. Rosecrans Ave. (Nash St.) | 310-607-9062
Pasadena | Paseo Colorado | 260 E. Colorado Blvd. (bet. Garfield & Marengo Aves.) | 626-356-9760
Sherman Oaks | Sherman Oaks Galleria | 15301 Ventura Blvd. (Sepulveda Blvd.) | 818-784-1694
Woodland Hills | The Promenade at Woodland Hills | 21821 Oxnard St. (Topanga Canyon Blvd.) | 818-340-0491
www.pfchangs.com

"Light, delicious", "Americanized" Chinese food keeps fans "coming back" – especially for the "standout" lettuce wraps – to this "trendy" "stylish" chain; though not everyone is convinced ("overpriced", "ordinary", "loud"), the "consistent" service is a plus, as is the "smart" menu "catering to people with allergies" and other needs.

NEW Phamish 🗷🍴 *Vietnamese* | - | - | - | I

Location varies; see website | 310-220-0528 | www.eatphamish.com
The legion of food trucks continues to grow with this Vietnamese arrival turning out pho, *goi cuon* (spring rolls) and a handful of banh mi options; all are washed down with industrial-strength iced coffee, and as the drill goes, check the website, Twitter or Facebook for location details.

NEW Philippe ● *Chinese* | 17 | 21 | 18 | $70

West Hollywood | 8284 Melrose Ave. (Sweetzer Ave.) | 323-951-1100
www.philippechow.com

The "splashy" "black-and-white" backdrop is tailor-made for WeHo' "trendy" types at this fledgling NYC transplant "in the old Dolc space", which features "refined Chinese" fare like the house specialty Peking duck; so far the "vibrant" "scene" is raising "high hopes" though antis advise it's "ridiculously priced" for just "ok" eating.

Philippe the Original 🍴 *Sandwiches* | 22 | 12 | 15 | $13

Chinatown | 1001 N. Alameda St. (Ord St.) | 213-628-3781 |
www.philippes.com

A "wonderful", "weird slice of LA history" in Chinatown, this circa 1908 shop – and self-proclaimed "inventor of the French dip" – pull all walks of Angelenos for "fabulous" sandwiches slathered with "potent house mustard" and chased down with coffee that's "still 9 cents a cup"; sure, the "sawdust"-sprinkled space has all "the charm of a bus station", but the "people-watching" alone makes it a "must-go" after a "Dodger game"; "may they dip for another 100 years."

☒ Phillips Bar-B-Que *BBQ* | 25 | 6 | 14 | $17

Leimert Park | 4307 Leimert Blvd. (43rd St.) | 323-292-7613 🗷
Mid-City | 2619 Crenshaw Blvd. (Adams Blvd.) | 323-731-4772 Ⓜ
Inglewood | 1517 Centinela Ave. (bet. Beach Ave. & Cedar St.) | 310-412-7135 🗷

"This ain't no Tony Roma's" crow fans of this no-frills BBQ chainlet doling out "damn good 'cue" like "melt-in-your-mouth brisket" and "finger-licking" ribs deemed a "great value" for the money; "lines are

ong, and it's "takeout only" (although Mid-City has a handful of ta-
les), but the "rewards are great", so "prepare to get down and dirty."

‍hlight *Mediterranean/Spanish*
▽ 23 | 22 | 25 | $35

Vhittier | 6724 Bright Ave. (bet. Bailey & Philadelphia Sts.) | 562-789-0578 | www.phlightrestaurant.com

his "stylish" Whittier "find" features a "creative" roster of "soulful"
panish-Med tapas and "fine wines" in a "lively" space fronting an
pen kitchen; with "so much to choose from", you'll want to "go with
group and try everything", but be advised, the "small" servings "can
uddenly add up to a whole lotta dough."

‍ho Café ●⊘ *Vietnamese*
▽ 19 | 11 | 18 | $17

ilver Lake | 2841 W. Sunset Blvd. (Silver Lake Blvd.) | 213-413-0888

his "trendy", cash-only Silver Laker ladles out "tasty" bowls of
ietnamese noodle soup for "cheap"; the minimalist storefront space
ften boasts a "line", but "fast, impersonal" service "keeps the tables
urning" quickly once you're in.

‍ Pho 79 *Vietnamese*
24 | 7 | 11 | $13

lhambra | 29 S. Garfield Ave. (Main St.) | 626-289-0239

he "pho-nomenal" noodle soups "can't be beat" at this ultra-
affordable" Alhambra outpost also featuring "crispy spring rolls"
mong its "huge" roster of Vietnamese offerings; the vibe is strictly
no frills", but its "loyal" fan base insists "you don't go there for the
ervice or decor" anyway.

‍icanha Churrascaria *Brazilian*
21 | 15 | 20 | $38

urbank | 269 E. Palm Ave. (bet. San Fernando Blvd. & 3rd St.) | 18-972-2100 | www.picanharestaurant.com

Wear your eating pants" to these Brazilian BBQ twins in Burbank and
athedral City – aka "heaven" for "carnivores" and "Atkins" dieters –
here servers unload skewered cuts of "tender, flavorful" meats till
you've had your fill"; the prix fixe meals with trips to the salad bar of-
r "good value", so those with "big appetites" are hardly put off by
e sparse settings.

‍ Piccolo *Italian*
26 | 20 | 24 | $62

enice | 5 Dudley Ave. (Spdwy.) | 310-314-3222 | www.piccolovenice.com

Like a mini-trip to the old country", this Venice "hideaway" "just off
e beach" conjures up a "wonderfully authentic" experience with
antastico" Venetian cuisine and "spectacular" wines served by an
ngaging" Italian-speaking staff; the fireplace lends it a "homey" feel,
nd now that a recent expansion has doubled the "charming", gold-
ned dining room, "the only setback is the price."

‍iccolo Paradiso *Italian*
24 | 19 | 24 | $47

everly Hills | 150 S. Beverly Dr. (bet. Charleville & Wilshire Blvds.) | 10-271-0030 | www.giacominodrago.com

ess of a scene than sister restaurant Il Pastaio", this "warm" Beverly
ills Italian from Giacomino Drago is "aces" for "first-rate" takes on
e classics (including "freshly made pasta that's a revelation")
rved up by a staff that "couldn't be friendlier"; "noisy" acoustics and
ricey" tabs hardly detract from its status as a "neighborhood favorite."

	FOOD	DECOR	SERVICE	COST

Pie 'N Burger ♥ *Diner* 22 | 10 | 18 | $15

Pasadena | 913 E. California Blvd. (bet. Lake & Mentor Aves.) |
626-795-1123 | www.pienburger.com

"Don't blow it and order a salad" at this "venerable" "Pasadena insti
tution", a "classic diner" known for its "lip-smacking" burgers, "hand
blended" shakes and "wonderful", "old-fashioned" pies; the "retro
digs include the original "long, curved counter" from 1963 and
"sweet" waitresses, so the up-to-date pricing can be jarring for many.

Pig 'n Whistle *Continental* 17 | 17 | 18 | $25

Hollywood | 6714 Hollywood Blvd. (bet. Highland & Las Palmas Aves.)
323-463-0000 | www.pignwhistle.com

A "Hollywood landmark", this restored 1927 pub in a "historic build
ing with cathedral ceilings and carved stone moldings attracts "hip
sters" and "tourists" looking to grab a drink after strolling th
boulevard; the midpriced menu of Continental "classics" is "decent
enough, but it's really about the "old-school" "vibe" here.

Pink's Famous Chili Dogs ●♥ *Hot Dogs* 20 | 7 | 14 | $11

La Brea | 709 N. La Brea Ave. (Melrose Ave.) | 323-931-4223 |
www.pinkshollywood.com

"Doing dogs proud for decades", this "iconic" stand on La Brea draw
"lines longer than Disneyland" "all day and night" for "swell" "classic
franks loaded up with "greasy", "messy" chili among a multitude c
other "fixin's"; though skeptics say it's "overhyped", at least prices ar
"cheap", and most find it "so worth" visiting if only "to say you wer
there"; P.S. look for fast-food offshoots at Universal CityWalk and LAX.

Pink Taco *Mexican* 16 | 19 | 17 | $27

Century City | Westfield Century City Shopping Ctr. |
10250 Santa Monica Blvd. (bet. Ave. of the Stars & Century Park W.)
310-789-1000 | www.pinktaco.com

"It's always a party" at this "damn noisy" stop in the Westfield Centur
City Shopping Center where "hotties in tank tops" down "big" marga
ritas and "mall-style" Mexican eats amid "blaring", "bling bling" "Day
of-the-Dead" decor; critics can't abide the "uninspiring" eats and "ai
head" service, though "happy hour" is a hit with many.

Pinot Bistro *French* 24 | 23 | 25 | $49

Studio City | 12969 Ventura Blvd. (bet. Coldwater Canyon Ave. &
Valley Vista Blvd.) | 818-990-0500 | www.patinagroup.com

A bit of "France" in Studio City, this Patina Group "winner" serve
"sensational", "real-deal" Gallic cuisine that "rivals any Paris brasse
rie"; "affable" service suits the "dark, elegant" interior while a "n
corkage fee" policy helps make it a "bargain for high-end" dining.

Pitfire Artisan Pizza *Italian* - | - | - | I

Downtown | 108 W. 2nd St. (S. Main St.) | 213-808-1200
NEW Marina del Rey | 12924 W. Washington Blvd. (Beethoven St.)
424-835-4088

West LA | 2018 Westwood Blvd. (La Grange Ave.) | 310-481-9860
North Hollywood | 5211 Lankershim Blvd. (Magnolia Blvd.) | 818-980-294
www.pitfirepizza.com

This fast-growing chain of pizzerias specializes in handmade pies, in
cluding ones topped with burrata and hazelnuts, plus a Greens, Eg

nd Ham variety with rapini, egg and prosciutto; all are served in cozy
quarters filled with the smell of good things cooking in the oven, with
the sounds of the sports of the moment on the overhead big screens.

NEW Pizza Antica *Pizza*

| – | – | – | M |

Santa Monica | Dining Deck, Santa Monica Pl. | 395 Santa Monica Pl.
3rd. St. Promenade) | 310-394-4080 | www.pizzaantica.com
With three branches in Northern California, chef Gordon Drysdale
ventures south with this new Santa Monica Place pizzeria set in a long
room dominated by an open kitchen lined with wood-burning ovens,
which cast a heavenly glow over diners seated at the counter; it churns
out a wide variety of oval-shaped pies plus midpriced pastas and mains.

🛛 Pizzeria Mozza ● *Pizza*

| 27 | 19 | 21 | $38 |

Hollywood | 641 N. Highland Ave. (Melrose Ave.) | 323-297-0101 |
www.mozza-la.com
Still one of "the hottest places in town", this "beloved" Hollywood pizzeria from Mario Batali and Nancy Silverton – LA's Most Popular
restaurant – turns a mere slice into a true "gastronomic experience"
with "delectable", "better-than-sex" pies supported by "deliciously
charred" crusts cooked to a "bubbly, chewy perfection"; no surprise,
"getting in is a challenge", service is "iffy" and the "jammed", "noisy"
quarters have the feel of "a high-end bus station", but even so, "no one
should miss it"; P.S. for takeout, try Mozza2Go around the corner.

Pizzicotto *Italian*

| 23 | 16 | 21 | $34 |

Brentwood | 11758 San Vicente Blvd. (bet. Gorham & Montana Aves.) |
310-442-7188
"Wonderful tastes" come in a "tiny package" at this diminutive
Brentwood Italian where a "charming", "old-world" crew delivers "savory" fare that "never disappoints"; "affordable" pricing trumps the
"noisy" acoustics, although upstairs and the patio offer quieter dining.

NEW Plancha ● *Mexican*

| – | – | – | I |

Mid-City | 8250 W. Third St. (Harper Ave.) | 323-951-9911 |
www.planchatacos.com
This Mid-City Mexican is notable first and foremost for being open till
midnight weekdays, and till 1 AM on weekends (no small thing in
early-night LA); the design is functional, but friendly, with an inexpensive street-food menu of tacos, quesadillas and such.

Planet Raw *Vegan*

| ▽ 20 | 13 | 14 | $31 |

Santa Monica | 609 Broadway (6th St.) | 310-587-1552 | www.planetraw.com
"It's amazing what they do with raw food" coo fans of this somewhat "pricey" Santa Monica vegan from chef-owner Juliano Brotman
spotlighting "incredibly creative" meat- and heat-free dishes like
zucchini-based pastas paired with smoothies and organic wines; a
"hippie-dippy" staff and sunny patio give it the feel of an "only-in-LA" experience, although jaded critics claim they'd "rather have a raw steak."

🛛 Polo Lounge *Californian/Continental*

| 23 | 27 | 26 | $65 |

Beverly Hills | Beverly Hills Hotel | 9641 Sunset Blvd. (Crescent Dr.) |
310-887-2777 | www.beverlyhillshotel.com
"If you have deep pockets you can see shallow celebrities" at this
"glamorous" Beverly Hills "icon" where "deals" are still brokered in the

"comfortably elegant" dining room, and even "if you're not a star", the "gracious" staff will still "treat you as one"; no surprise, it's not about the Cal-Continental cuisine, although devotees declare it's actually "quite good" too; P.S. a drink at the piano bar is a less-"expensive" option.

Pomodoro *Italian*   16 | 14 | 17 | $22

Manhattan Beach | 401 Manhattan Beach Blvd. (Morningside Dr.) | 310-545-5401

Burbank | Burbank Town Ctr. | 201 E. Magnolia Blvd. (bet. 1st & 3rd Sts.) | 818-559-1300

Pomodoro Cucina Italiana *Italian*

West Hollywood | West Hollywood Gateway Ctr. | 7100 Santa Monica Blvd. (bet. Formosa & La Brea Aves.) | 323-969-8000

www.pastapomodoro.com

For a "cheap" "pasta fix", look no further than this casual chain offering "very good value" for "ok" Italian eats, now made with more organic and locally sourced ingredients; service is "quick", however, the overabundance of "loud children" makes "takeout" awfully attractive; N.B. the Food rating may not fully reflect the recent menu updates.

Pop Champagne & Dessert Bar Ⓜ *Eclectic*   ▽ 17 | 21 | 24 | $32

Pasadena | 33 E. Union St. (bet. Fair Oaks & Raymond Aves.) | 626-795-1295 | www.popchampagnebar.com

True to its name, this "hip, young" Pasadenan plies patrons with bubbly "from all over the world" matched with midpriced Eclectic "bites" like sliders and suitably "fun" desserts in a "charming" chandelier-clad setting; perhaps it works best for a "social gathering" rather than a full meal, and it's a no-brainer for a "ladies' night" out.

Poquito Más *Mexican*   21 | 11 | 17 | $12

West Hollywood | 8555 Sunset Blvd. (Londonderry Pl.) | 310-652-7008

Westwood | 2215 Westwood Blvd. (Olympic Blvd.) | 310-474-1998

Torrance | Rolling Hills Plaza | 2625 PCH (Crenshaw Blvd.) | 310-325-1001

Burbank | 2635 W. Olive Ave. (Naomi St.) | 818-563-2252

Chatsworth | 9229 Winnetka Ave. (Prairie St.) | 818-775-1555

North Hollywood | 10651 Magnolia Blvd. (Cartwright Ave.) | 818-994-8226

Sherman Oaks | 13924 Ventura Blvd. (Colbath Ave.) | 818-981-7500

Studio City | 3701 Cahuenga Blvd. (bet. Barham & Lankershim Blvds.) | 818-760-8226 ●

Woodland Hills | 21049 Ventura Blvd. (Alhama Dr.) | 818-887-2007

www.poquitomas.com

A "fresh alternative to fast food", this "quick Mex" chain is known for its "tasty" "handmade tortillas" and "California-ized" south-of-the-border selections that you "order at the counter"; most go easy on the "hole-in-the-wall" settings (they're basically "glorified taco stands") because the prices are so easy on your "budget"; P.S. don't miss the "free tortilla soup" on rainy days.

Porta Via *Californian*   21 | 19 | 22 | $38

Beverly Hills | 424 N. Cañon Dr. (bet. Brighton Way & Santa Monica Blvd.) | 310-274-6541 | www.portaviabh.com

Beverly Hills patrons "keep coming back again and again" to this "fairly priced" "local" "favorite" known for its "nice salads", "excellent brunch" and other "fresh" Californian fare; service is "pleasant", while the ever-expanding space boasts an "inviting" brick-lined interior and "wonderful sidewalk seating" well-suited for "people-watching on Cañon Drive."

Porta Via Italian Foods *Italian* | 24 | 15 | 19 | $21 |

Pasadena | 1 W. California Blvd. (Fair Oaks Ave.) | 626-793-9000 | www.portaviafoods.com

Chowhounds hail this well-priced, "gourmet" Italian deli in Pasadena purveying "freshly made sandwiches", salads, "wonderful pastas" and a "variety of cheese, olives and antipasti" plus beer and wine available for "eat in" or "takeout"; the "bare-bones" setting's often "packed", though there's a "nice little patio" with a handful of tables out back.

Porterhouse Bistro *Steak* | 21 | 19 | 21 | $49 |

Beverly Hills | 8635 Wilshire Blvd. (Carson Rd.) | 310-659-1099 | www.porterhousebistro.com

It's all about the "exceptional prix fixe deal" at this Beverly Hills chop-house where four-course meals come at relatively modest prices in a "quiet", modern setting; "top"-tier service adds to the appeal, so even if some judge the fare a "notch below" the competition, you still "can't beat it for the price."

Portillo's Hot Dogs *Hot Dogs* | 22 | 17 | 17 | $13 |

Moreno Valley | 12840 Day St. (Gateway Dr.) | 951-653-1000 | www.portillos.com

Frankophiles "feed the urge" for "real-deal" "Chicago-style" dogs at this chain link in Moreno Valley also delivering Italian beef sandwiches and other "Windy City" eats in a Prohibition-themed setting; service is "quick" and you'll get "a lot" "for little money" here.

Porto Alegre *Brazilian/Steak* | ▽ 20 | 20 | 20 | $45 |

Pasadena | Paseo Colorado | 260 E. Colorado Blvd. (bet. Garfield & Marengo Aves.) | 626-744-0555 | www.portoalegre-churrascaria.com

Thrifty patrons "pig out on grilled meats" at this "best-for-the-buck" Brazilian steakhouse in Pasadena following through on the riodizio format with a "salad bar with lots of good choices"; solid service and a spacious earth-toned setting overlooking the Paseo complete the picture.

⚡ Porto's Bakery *Bakery/Cuban* | 24 | 14 | 17 | $14 |

Burbank | 3614 W. Magnolia Blvd. (Cordova St.) | 818-846-9100
Glendale | 315 N. Brand Blvd. (California Ave.) | 818-956-5996 | www.portosbakery.com

It's as if "you've died and gone to sweet-tooth heaven" at these Cuban bakeries in Burbank and Glendale featuring an "opulent" assortment of pastries plus savory items like "amazing" Cubano sandwiches and "must-try" potato balls ("so wrong, and yet so right"); everything comes at "bargain-basement" prices, although despite a "slew of cashiers" at the ready, "crushingly long" lines are often part of the experience.

Pourtal Wine Bar ● *Mediterranean* | ▽ 22 | 18 | 21 | $22 |

Santa Monica | 104 Santa Monica Blvd. (Ocean Ave.) | 310-393-7693 | www.pourtal.com

Let the "knowledgeable staff" guide you at this Santa Monica vino bar a block from the ocean where an ever-changing bevy of "international wines" are complemented by "great" Med "noshes"; prices are relatively "inexpensive", so grab a seat and "taste away."

Prado *Caribbean* ▽ 22 | 16 | 23 | $33

Hancock Park | 244 N. Larchmont Blvd. (bet. Beverly Blvd. & 1st St.) | 323-467-3871 | www.pradola.com

A "neighborhood" "favorite" for over 20 years, this Hancock Park Caribbean is a "solid performer" for jerk chicken and crab cakes served by a staff that "treats you like family"; a colorful setting, moderate pricing and sidewalk seating along "charming Larchmont Boulevard" mean it's hard to beat "on a beautiful LA night."

Primitivo Wine Bistro *Mediterranean* 23 | 18 | 19 | $39

Venice | 1025 Abbot Kinney Blvd. (bet. Brooks & Westminster Aves.) | 310-396-5353 | www.primitivowinebistro.com

"Delicious sangria" and "wonderful wines" fuel the "social scene" at this "dark, arty" Venice bar/restaurant rolling out "creative" midpriced Med tapas for its thirsty young crowd; the lively" atmosphere is "too noisy" and "crowded" for some, although the lush "garden" patio offers some relief.

Prizzi's Piazza *Italian* ▽ 21 | 16 | 21 | $26

Hollywood | 5923 Franklin Ave. (bet. Bronson Ave. & Gower St.) | 323-467-0168 | www.prizzispiazza.com

Regulars rely on this casual Hollywood "hang" for "garlicky" breadsticks and other "belly-filling" Italiana like lasagna and deep-dish pizza for modest sums; its usually low-key setting is kicked up a notch on weekends when a "cool" crowd takes over the patio.

Prosecco Ⓩ *Italian* ▽ 22 | 21 | 24 | $38

Toluca Lake | 10144 Riverside Dr. (bet. Forman & Talofa Aves.) | 818-505-0930

"Still going strong" after 15 years, this "dependable" "neighborhood" trattoria in Toluca Lake earns its loyal following with "very good" Northern Italian fare that's well priced too; service "with a smile" and a snug space that "feels like Greenwich Village" are part of the experience.

Z Providence *American/Seafood* 28 | 25 | 27 | $98

Hollywood | 5955 Melrose Ave. (Cole Ave.) | 323-460-4170 | www.providencela.com

"Simply sublime" sigh fans of this Hollywood New American "paragon of fine dining" showcasing "genius" chef/co-owner Michael Cimarusti's "matchless" hand with seafood, best experienced via the "utterly blissful" tasting menu featuring 16 "meticulously considered" courses; whether the ambiance is "civilized" or just "somber" is up for debate, but all agree the service is "pitch-perfect" and the overall experience "expensive", but "worth every penny."

NEW Quadrupel Brasserie Ⓜ *French* - | - | - | M

Pasadena | 43 E. Union St. (Raymond Ave.) | 626-844-2922 | www.quadrupelbrasserie.com

With its leaded stained glass, ornate polished wood and fin de siècle lamps, this combination French bistro and Belgian beer pub is an oddity in the midst of party-hearty Old Pasadena – a destination for more than 50 exotic brews from Brussels (dubbels, tripels, quadrupels, lamics and more) in a civilized setting; the moderately priced menu includes sausages and cheese, duck confit and roasted bone marrow.

R+D Kitchen *American*

20 | 19 | 20 | $34

Santa Monica | 1323 Montana Ave. (14th St.) | 310-395-3314 | www.hillstone.com

An "affluent crowd" cheers this "great little concept from the Houston's folks" serving a "tiny but tasty" lineup of "solid American comfort food" in an "airy, modern" setup on Montana's shopping row in Santa Monica; the no-reservations policy ensures constant crowds", so no one is surprised if service is of the "please get out of here as quickly as possible" variety.

Rae's ⊅ *Diner*

▽ 15 | 10 | 18 | $15

Santa Monica | 2901 Pico Blvd. (29th St.) | 310-828-7937

"When you need carbs", this "classic" Santa Monica "diner" is there with "greasy", "old-fashioned" grub like pancakes and gravy with biscuits; the service and 1950s-style setting are basic at best, but prices re low, and "the line out the door speaks for itself."

Ragin' Cajun Cafe Ⓜ *Cajun*

19 | 16 | 20 | $22

Hermosa Beach | 422 Pier Ave. (bet. Hermosa Ave. & Valley Dr.) | 310-376-7878 | www.ragincajun.com

"When you can't make it to Jazz Fest", let *les bontemps* roll at this affordable Hermosa Beach Cajun serving up "large" helpings of "fairly authentic" NOLA-inspired cooking; no, it's "not exactly health food", but it is a lot of "fun."

Rainbow Bar & Grill ● *American*

▽ 17 | 21 | 20 | $31

West Hollywood | 9015 W. Sunset Blvd. (bet. Doheny Dr. & San Vicente Blvd.) | 310-278-4232 | www.rainbowbarandgrill.com

"You'd never know it wasn't 1986" at this famed WeHo "rock 'n' roll joint", whose "funky" environs hold "all the memories" of "youth" for the aging headbangers parked in its big red booths; serving affordable American fare that's "better than expected", it's a "guilty pleasure" to start or finish a night on the Strip."

Rainforest Cafe *American*

13 | 21 | 15 | $25

Ontario | Ontario Mills | 4810 Mills Circle (Franklin Ave.) | 909-941-7979 | www.rainforestcafe.com

If the idea of "eating next to a robotic elephant that sprays water every 10 minutes" appeals, head for this jungle-themed chain filled with "spellbinding" animatronic creatures plus "families, families, families"; the American eats are "bland" and "expensive for what you get", but the "concept works" (despite being "slightly overwhelming"), so it's a "fun place to take the kids once."

Rambutan Thai *Thai*

▽ 19 | 17 | 17 | $25

Silver Lake | 2835 W. Sunset Blvd. (Silver Lake Blvd.) | 213-273-8424 | www.rambutanthai.com

"Classier" than your typical neighborhood Thai, this Silver Laker serves up a "variety" of "fresh" and "generally tasty" (if "not very authentic") Siamese eats at nice prices; the vibe is usually "quiet", though the dimly lit tropical surroundings are loungey enough to "cater to the nightlife crowd."

	FOOD	DECOR	SERVICE	COST

Ranch House ⓜ Californian
▽ 22 | 24 | 24 | $66

Ojai | 500 S. Lomita Ave. (Besant Rd.) | 805-646-2360 |
www.theranchhouse.com

The "gorgeous gardens" are "tough to beat" for "romantic outdoo[r]
dining" at this "unique" Ojai Californian, a "very rustic", "tucked-awa[y]
find" for "wonderful" seasonal fare paired with an "impressive" 1,200[-]
label wine list and "pleasant service"; yes, it's pretty "pricey", but th[e]
experience is "worth it for that special occasion."

RA Sushi Japanese
16 | 17 | 14 | $33

Torrance | Del Amo Fashion Ctr. | 3525 W. Carson St. (bet. Hawthorne Blvd. &
Madrona Ave.) | 310-370-6700 | www.rasushi.com

"Young" "singles" and "loud music" keep the "energy" up at thi[s]
Torrance link in a Japanese chain from the Benihana folks, a "busy"
nexus for "fusion sushi" in a handy mall-crawl location; the service an[d]
"average quality" rolls "may not be the best", but all agree the "bar[-]
gain" happy hour is "when it's most worth your money."

Raymond, The ⓜ Californian
25 | 24 | 24 | $52

Pasadena | 1250 S. Fair Oaks Ave. (Columbia St.) | 626-441-3136 |
www.theraymond.com

"Old-fashioned charms" are on display inside and out at thi[s]
Pasadena "hidden treasure" in a beautifully converted "Craftsma[n]
bungalow", a "longtime favorite" for its "peaceful surroundings", "fab[-]
ulous" Californian "classics" and "gracious staff"; boasting some o[f]
"the loveliest" patio seating around, it's "a special treat" that's "laste[d]
for a reason."

Real Food Daily Vegan
22 | 16 | 19 | $25

West Hollywood | 414 N. La Cienega Blvd. (Oakwood Ave.) |
310-289-9910
Santa Monica | 514-516 Santa Monica Blvd. (5th St.) |
310-451-7544
www.realfood.com

"The holy land for herbivores", this "hip", "wholesome" duo in Sant[a]
Monica and West Hollywood doles out "fresh and healthy" vegan eat[s]
headlined by "homey" dishes like tempeh Reubens and Salisbur[y]
seitan; "no-attitude" service takes the sting off tabs that feel a ta[d]
"overpriced" to some; P.S. "they can juice just about anything" too.

Red Corner Asia ◑ Thai
▽ 22 | 9 | 20 | $23

East Hollywood | Hollywood Plaza | 5267 Hollywood Blvd. (Hobart Blvd.) |
323-466-6722 | www.redcornerasia.com

"Excellent" Siamese offerings are available until 1:30 AM nightly a[t]
this East Hollywood Thai tucked into a "busy mini-mall"; the setting [is]
spare and service can be "inattentive", "but the food makes up for it["]
and the price is always right.

Reddi Chick BBQ 🖾🖘 BBQ
▽ 21 | 8 | 16 | $15

Santa Monica | Brentwood Country Mart | 225 26th St. (San Vicente Blvd.) |
310-393-5238

You "can't beat the bird" chirp champions of this Brentwood Countr[y]
Mart "tradition" for "great" rotisserie chicken and BBQ ribs served u[p]
"fast food"-style on picnic tables outside; it's "cheap", "quick an[d]
easy", so even "stars in sweats" turn out for a "fix."

Red Lion Tavern ❷ German
▽ 17 | 18 | 17 | $24

Silver Lake | 2366 Glendale Blvd. (Silver Lake Blvd.) | 323-662-5337 |
www.redliontavern.net

It's always "Oktoberfest" at this Silver Lake "hangout" where "friendly barmaids" in "dirndl skirts" ferry "hearty" German fare and "boot"-shaped steins of suds; with a beer garden and "reasonable" tabs, it's "packed" with a hipster crowd, and the only downside is the parking.

NEW Red O Mexican
- | - | - | M

Melrose | 8155 Melrose Ave. (La Jolla Ave.) | 323-655-5009 |
www.redorestaurant.com

Rick Bayless (Chicago's Frontera Grill, Topolobampo, Xoco) created the menu at this Melrose Nouvelle Mexican offering a seasonally based selection of 'savory snacks' in an ultrastylish space – including a tequila lounge entered through a glass tunnel – designed by the ubiquitous Dodd Mitchell; in a city where south-of-the-border fare is the lingua franca, it should still manage to make its mark.

Red Seven 🅰 Asian
- | - | - | M

West Hollywood | Pacific Design Ctr. | 700 N. San Vicente Blvd. (Melrose Ave.) | 310-289-1587 | www.wolfgangpuck.com

This daytime cafe in West Hollywood's Pacific Design Center proffers Pan-Asian plates courtesy of Wolfgang Puck; although the modern interior with outdoor seating on the plaza is "quiet" and comfy, service can be "short on skill" and the experience doesn't come "cheap" either.

redwhite+bluezz American
23 | 20 | 18 | $36

Pasadena | 70 S. Raymond Ave. (Green St.) | 626-792-4441 |
www.redwhitebluezz.com

If you like to talk wine", hit up this "no-pretensions" Pasadena lounge where a "friendly" crew pours "interesting flights" and glasses to the tunes of "live jazz" nightly; the "diverse" American menu's "good", but a touch "overpriced" to some, although the happy-hour lunch is a deal.

Reel Inn Seafood
20 | 15 | 14 | $23

Malibu | 18661 PCH (Topanga Canyon Blvd.) | 310-456-8221

"Funky" sums up this "no-frills" Malibu "shack", a source for "fresh, simply prepared" seafood in a "killer location" across the street from the surf; orders at the pickup window can be "slow", but the beyond-rustic" setting with surfboards and picnic tables "truly captures the SoCal beach vibe" – it's a "blast."

Reservoir 🅼 Eclectic
▽ 23 | 14 | 21 | $47

Silver Lake | 1700 Silver Lake Blvd. (Effie St.) | 323-662-8655 |
www.silverlakereservoir.com

Diners "mix-and-match" from an array of "impressive, seasonal" Eclectic dishes at this Silver Laker from chef Gloria Felix; though admirers applaud the "spot-on" fare, its "crowded", "dimly lit" dining room doesn't earn any fans, nor do prices that feel "high" for the neighborhood.

RH ❷ French
25 | 23 | 24 | $53

West Hollywood | Andaz Hotel | 8401 Sunset Blvd. (Kings Rd.) |
323-785-6090 | www.myandaz.com

"Edgy French cuisine" – in a hotel no less – turns up at this WeHo "sleeper" where "talented" chef Sebastien Archambault whips up "in-

credible" food and "even simple things like bread and butter are done
with panache"; "attentive" service and a "sleek" setting with an open
kitchen also please, as do prices that are a "bargain for the quality."

Ribs USA *BBQ*

19 | 10 | 18 | $23

Burbank | 2711 W. Olive Ave. (bet. Buena Vista & Florence Sts.) |
818-841-8872 | www.ribsusa.com

Burbankers "craving" BBQ find fixes at this area fallback for "messy"
ribs" and "hotter-than-hell wings" at budget-friendly prices; service is
efficient, but finger-lickers not into the "divey", sawdust-sprinkled
setting say it's "better for takeout."

Ristorante Villa Portofino *Italian*

- | - | - | M

Catalina Island | Hotel Villa Portofino | 101 Crescent Ave. (Marilla Ave.) |
Avalon | 310-510-2009 | www.ristorantevillaportofino.com

This old-school Italian in the elegant Villa Portofino Hotel is just a
short stroll from the vintage Avalon Casino, with its view of the sail-
boats in the harbor, presenting a moderately upscale menu of classic
pasta, chicken, veal and seafood preparations; the nice thing about
dining at a hotel on Catalina is that after too much Prosecco, you can
sleep it off in your room – and not on the deck of the last boat home.

Rive Gauche Cafe Ⓜ *French*

22 | 22 | 20 | $35

Sherman Oaks | 14106 Ventura Blvd. (Hazeltine Ave.) | 818-990-3573
"Charmingly French", this longtime Sherman Oaks bistro cooks up
"consistently good" Gallic grub in a "quaint" cottage setting; prices are a
"deal", and if you can block out busy Ventura Boulevard, it's so "relaxing" on the patio "you may be tempted to extend lunch into dinner."

Rivera *Pan-Latin*

25 | 25 | 23 | $58

Downtown | Met Lofts | 1050 S. Flower St. (11th St.) | 213-749-1460 |
www.riverarestaurant.com

"Highly creative" chef John Sedlar "transforms even the most basic
dishes into something spectacular" at this Downtown showcase for
his "revolutionary" Pan-Latin cuisine with "signature playful touches"
like "pressed flowers in the tortillas" that are "almost too pretty to
eat"; "attentive", "exuberant" service helps justify the prices, even if
the "stunning", "Vegas"-style setting is "noisy beyond belief".
P.S. don't miss the "terrific", "innovative cocktails."

Riviera Restaurant & Lounge *Italian*

24 | 22 | 23 | $49

Calabasas | 23683 Calabasas Rd. (Park Granada) | 818-224-2163 |
www.tuscany-restaurant.com

Though it "doesn't look like much from the outside", this Calabasas
Italian is a "hit with the locals" – including the occasional "celeb" –
thanks to "delicate" Northern-style dishes "lovingly prepared and
served" in a "sophisticated" earth-toned room; though prices are
geared toward "special occasions", regulars report the everyday
happy-hour discounts are a "deal."

Robata Bar ❶ *Japanese*

▽ 26 | 22 | 23 | $42

Santa Monica | 1401 Ocean Ave. (Santa Monica Blvd.) | 310-458-4771 |
www.robatabar.com

A variety of "tasty" meats and veggies are "grilled up perfectly" right
in front of you at this Japanese den and sib to Sushi Roku in Santa

Monica; service is "quick" and the "prices are right", while the dark, snug setting with an open kitchen is like "being in Tokyo."

Robata-Ya M *Japanese* ∇ 20 | 15 | 19 | $34

West LA | 2004 Sawtelle Blvd. (La Grange Ave.) | 310-481-1418

A "young, energetic crowd" gathers at this "publike" West LA Japanese for "great" grilled tidbits and small plates pumped out of an exhibition kitchen; whether you stick to the "reasonably priced" à la carte dishes or go for the omakase, either way, it's a lot of "fun."

Robin's Woodfire BBQ & Grill M *BBQ* ∇ 20 | 16 | 16 | $22

Pasadena | 395 N. Rosemead Blvd. (bet. Foothill Blvd. & Sierra Madre Villa Ave.) | 626-351-8885 | www.robinsbbq.com

"When you can't get to Kansas City", this Pasadenan doles out "decent" renditions of "wood-smoked" BBQ – and "lots" of it – at giveaway prices; it's a "nifty" place decked out with old neon soda and beer sign that works well "if you're bringing the kids."

Röckenwagner Bakery Cafe *Bakery/Californian* 21 | 14 | 15 | $18

Santa Monica | 311 Arizona Ave. (Third St. Promenade) | 310-394-4267 | www.rockenwagner.com

"Everything rocks" – especially the pretzel rolls – at this "cute" little bakery/cafe from Hans Röckenwagner also purveying "fresh" Californian salads and sandwiches alongside "OMG"-inducing pastries; "spendy" price tags and "overwhelmed" service aside, it's a solid bet for lunch or brunch "if you happen to be near the Third Street Promenade."

Rock'n Fish *Seafood/Steak* 20 | 17 | 18 | $37

Downtown | LA Live | 800 W. Olympic Blvd. (Figueroa St.) | 213-748-4020 | www.rocknfishlalive.com
Manhattan Beach | 120 Manhattan Beach Blvd. (bet. Manhattan Ave. & Ocean Dr.) | 310-379-9900 | www.rocknfishmb.com

These "hip", "high-volume" seafooders turn out "tasty", "well-fixed" "fresh fish" and steak in beyond-"lively" settings; the Manhattan Beach original is an area "favorite" just a "block from the beautiful Pacific", while Downtown's LA Live branch is especially "packed on game days" when the "potent specialty cocktails" "make the waits more bearable."

Z RockSugar Pan Asian Kitchen *Asian* 21 | 26 | 21 | $39

Century City | Westfield Century City Shopping Ctr. | 10250 Santa Monica Blvd. (bet. Ave. of the Stars & Century Park W.) | 310-552-9988 | www.rocksugarpanasiankitchen.com

A "sumptuous" "far-Eastern" setting reminiscent of "Rangoon" or "the Indiana Jones Ride at Disneyland" forms the "dramatic" backdrop at this Cheesecake Factory spin-off in the Westfield Century City Shopping Center; "fun cocktails", "flavorful" Pan-Asian small plates and "modest prices" all earn raves, but on the downside are occasionally "cloying" preps and a setting so "loud" "you can hardly hear your dinner partner talk."

NEW Rockwell ● *Eclectic* - | - | - | I

Los Feliz | 1714 N. Vermont Ave. (Prospect Ave.) | 323-669-1550 | www.rockwellvt.com

Situated down an alleyway in Los Feliz (adjacent to vermont), this largely alfresco Eclectic is a hidden destination where patrons can relax under a spreading coral tree and savor exotic cocktails complemented by an inexpensive menu featuring flatbreads, tacos and the like; it's a tad "too cool for school" for some, though for the most part tipplers tout it as a "great addition to the neighborhood."

Roll 'n Rye Deli *Deli*
| 19 | 11 | 20 | $22 |

Culver City | Studio Village Shopping Ctr. | 10990 W. Jefferson Blvd. (Machado Rd.) | 310-390-3497

"The Westside's equivalent of Canter's", this "NYC"-style deli in Culver City delivers all the "classics" like "real pastrami" sandwiches, stuffed cabbage and "matzo ball soup that's cured many a cold"; "friendly" counter guys overcome the long-in-the-tooth looks and bills that "seem a bit pricey" for some.

Romano's Macaroni Grill *Italian*
| 17 | 17 | 18 | $24 |

Cerritos | Cerritos Towne Ctr. | 12875 Towne Center Dr. (bet. Bloomfield Ave. & 183rd St.) | 562-916-7722
El Segundo | 2321 Rosecrans Ave. (bet. Aviation Blvd. & Douglas St.) | 310-643-0812
Torrance | Rolling Hills Plaza | 25352 Crenshaw Blvd. (Airport Dr.) | 310-534-1001
Northridge | Northridge Fashion Ctr. | 19400 Plummer St. (Tampa Ave.) | 818-725-2620
Thousand Oaks | Promenade Shopping Ctr. | 4000 E. Thousand Oaks Blvd. (Westlake Blvd.) | 805-370-1133
Ventura | 4880 Telephone Rd. (Portola Rd.) | 805-477-9925
Santa Clarita | 25720 The Old Rd. (bet. McBean Pkwy. & Pico Canyon Rd.) | 661-284-1850
www.macaronigrill.com

There's "much more than macaroni" at this "family-friendly" Italian franchise whose "steady" dishes offer "value for your dining dollar" even if they're "a bit ho-hum"; despite its "big-chain character", it's an easy "place to bring the gang", with "nice service" and "crayons for the kids" – though it's definitely "not cool" for a date.

NEW Rosa Mexicano *Mexican*
| 22 | 20 | 20 | $40 |

Downtown | LA Live | 800 W. Olympic Blvd. (Figueroa St.) | 213-746-0001 | www.rosamexicano.com

The "chunky" guacamole "made fresh at your table" is an "absolute must" at this NYC import in Downtown's LA Live known for its "nouveau Mexican" *comida*; though it's convenient for margaritas and a munch "before a game or concert", the acoustics are "loud", service sometimes "spotty" and anti-amigos aver it's "overpriced for rice and beans."

Roscoe's House of Chicken 'n Waffles *Soul Food*
| 21 | 10 | 16 | $18 |

Hollywood | 1514 N. Gower St. (bet. Hollywood & Sunset Blvds.) | 323-466-7453 ◐
Mid-City | 106 W. Manchester Ave. (Main St.) | 323-752-6211
Mid-City | 5006 W. Pico Blvd. (Mansfield Ave.) | 323-934-4405 ◐
Long Beach | 730 E. Broadway (bet. Alamitos & Atlantic Aves.) | 562-437-8355
Pasadena | 830 N. Lake Ave. (bet. Mountain St. & Orange Grove Blvd.) | 626-791-4890
www.roscoeschickenandwaffles.com

For a good, old-fashioned "LA chowdown", surveyors head to this "legendary" "soul-food" chain and "guilty pleasure" for the "oddly

	FOOD	DECOR	SERVICE	COST

amazing", "sweet-savory" combination of "buttery" waffles and "tender, juicy" fried chicken "with just the right amount of crunch"; "service can be slow" and the decor surely "won't make any design magazines", but when "you're blowing your diet", "there's no better place to splurge."

| | 21 | 17 | 18 | $25 |

Rose Cafe *Californian*
Venice | 220 Rose Ave. (Main St.) | 310-399-0711 |
www.rosecafe.com
An "arty" crowd digs the "healthy" "fresh" brunch dishes, baked goods and other "rock-steady" Californian bites at this "cool" Venice daytime cafe; service is "friendly", the mood "relaxed" and despite prices that are "inching" up there, "you can't beat the garden for a casual lunch on a sunny day."

| | 17 | 13 | 17 | $24 |

Rosti *Italian*
Santa Monica | 931 Montana Ave. (9th Ct.) | 310-393-3236
Encino | 16350 Ventura Blvd. (bet. Hayvenhurst & Libbit Aves.) |
818-995-7179
www.rostituscankitchen.com
Regulars rely on this affordable Encino and Santa Monica duo for "basic", "rustic" Tuscan eats headlined by a herb-coasted, brick-pressed chicken that's especially "tasty"; "average service" and "bare-bones, noisy" settings aside, it's a "dependable" bet for some "quick" "takeout."

| | – | – | – | I |

Rowdy Red Wine & Burger Bar 🅱 *Burgers*
Downtown | City Nat'l Plaza | 505 S. Flower St. (bet. 5th & 6th Sts.) |
213-627-5511 | www.mcchgroup.com
Set in a lower level of a retro Downtown mall, this burger and vino joint offers patties plain and fancy in high-tech metal-and-glass digs; serving breakfast, lunch and dinner, it could end up a favorite of the area's cubicle-bound Dilberts.

| | 17 | 22 | 20 | $22 |

Royal/T *French/Japanese*
Culver City | 8910 Washington Blvd. (Robertson Blvd.) | 310-559-6300 |
www.royal-t.org
"Definitely a novelty restaurant" nod fans of this "unique Japanese concept", a tearoom, art gallery and gift shop in Culver City, where pretty young waitresses don "kitschy" "French maid–style uniforms" and serve a "nice selection of teas" as well as bites like gyoza and Kobe sliders; though the vibe is "cool", given so much "eye candy", perhaps it's no surprise that "the food's not much to write home about."

| | 24 | 22 | 23 | $49 |

🅱 Roy's *Hawaiian*
Downtown | 800 S. Figueroa St. (8th St.) | 213-488-4994
Pasadena | 641 E. Colorado Blvd. (El Molino Ave.) | 626-356-4066
Woodland Hills | 6363 Topanga Canyon Blvd. (Victory Blvd.) |
818-888-4801
www.roysrestaurant.com
"Every meal is a delight" effuse fans of this "high-end chain" showcasing celeb chef Roy Yamaguchi's "modern mastery" of Hawaiian fusion cuisine, focusing on "beautifully prepared" fish (and "unique" local specialties) among other "innovative creations" with "bold flavors"; the "upbeat" atmosphere and "excellent" service help support the "steep" price, plus the seasonal prix fixe menu is a real "deal."

R23 *Japanese*   24 | 21 | 20 | $52

Downtown | 923 E. Second St. (bet. Alameda St. & Santa Fe Ave.) | 213-687-7178 | www.r23.com

Loyal followers makes the "trek" to this "cool" Downtown Japanese where the "sublime sushi" is the "essence of freshness" and the cooked specialties are "seldom seen elsewhere"; it's all set in a "stark", "gallerylike" space with suitably "unobtrusive service", yet while most are happy to foot the "pricey" bills, an unimpressed minority doesn't get "what all the fuss is about."

Ruby's *Diner*   17 | 17 | 18 | $17

Rolling Hills Estates | Avenue of the Peninsula Mall | 550 Deep Valley Dr. (Crossfield Dr.) | Rolling Hills | 310-544-7829
LAX | LA Int'l Airport, Terminal 6 | 209 World Way (Sepulveda Blvd.) | 310-646-2480
Long Beach | 6405 E. PCH (2nd St.) | 562-596-1914
Redondo Beach | 245 N. Harbor Dr. (Beryl St.) | 310-376-7829
Woodland Hills | Westfield Promenade | 6100 Topanga Canyon Blvd. (bet. Erwin & Oxnard Sts.) | 818-340-7829
Whittier | Whittwood Mall | 10109 Whittwood Dr. (bet. Cullen St. & Whittier Blvd.) | 562-947-7829
www.rubys.com

"Classic burgers" and "thick shakes" lead the lineup at this "bright and shiny" chain of "'50s-style" diners; sure, the food's pretty "standard", but "kids love it", and "upbeat" service and "easy-on-the-budget" tabs mean it works for a "quick bite."

Ruen Pair ●⧷ *Thai*   ▽ 23 | 8 | 15 | $20

East Hollywood | 5257 Hollywood Blvd. (Hobart Blvd.) | 323-466-0153

Surveyors seeking "authentic" "Bangkok"-style bites head to this East Hollywood Thai for "cheap, spicy" curries, noodles and a soybean-studded morning glory dish that's rightly "famous"; the strictly utilitarian setting and service are nothing to write home about, but with its late hours, fans find it "better than anything else open at 3 AM."

Rush Street *American*   17 | 18 | 16 | $29

Culver City | 9546 Washington Blvd. (Irving Pl.) | 310-837-9546 | www.rushstreetculvercity.com

It's all about the "scene" at this midpriced Culver City lounge attracting twentysomething "singles" for cocktails plus a pubby New American menu anchored by a "solid burger"; with an "energetic" rooftop patio and TVs throughout, it's basically a "glorified bar", albeit an "enjoyable" one, just "don't plan on having a conversation."

Russell's Burgers *Diner*   ▽ 24 | 17 | 19 | $20

Pasadena | 30 N. Fair Oaks Ave. (bet. Colorado Blvd. & Union St.) | 626-578-1404

"Fab" burgers and breakfasts star at this "retro" Pasadena diner also slinging shakes and pies "just like the old days"; with affordable tabs and swift service, it's no wonder it's often "packed."

Rustic Canyon *Californian/Mediterranean*   23 | 19 | 22 | $51

Santa Monica | 1119 Wilshire Blvd. (bet. 11th & 12th Sts.) | 310-393-7050 | www.rusticcanyonwinebar.com

A hip, well-heeled crowd "never tires" of this "exciting" Santa Monica eatery thanks to its ever-changing menu of "pitch-perfect"

Californian-Med small plates based on "farm-fresh" ingredients plus "fabulous" wines; seating in the "loud," modern space may be "too close for comfort", but "unpretentious" staffers and overall "great vibes" compensate.

	FOOD	DECOR	SERVICE	COST
	24	18	23	$42

Rustico *Italian*

Westlake Village | 1125 Lindero Canyon Rd. (Lakeview Canyon Rd.) | 818-889-0191 | www.rustico-restaurant.com

"A neighborhood gem" "tucked into a shopping center" in Westlake Village, this upmarket Italian (and sib of Riviera and Tuscany) proffers a "crowd-pleasing" lineup of "homestyle" dishes; regulars don't mind the "somewhat vanilla decor" and "noisy" acoustics, since the "accommodating" staff treats you like "family."

	FOOD	DECOR	SERVICE	COST
	25	22	24	$62

Z Ruth's Chris Steak House *Steak*

Beverly Hills | 224 S. Beverly Dr. (bet. Charleville Blvd. & Gregory Way) | 310-859-8744

Pasadena | 369 E. Colorado Blvd. (Euclid Ave.) | 626-583-8122

Woodland Hills | Promenade at Woodland Hills | 6100 Topanga Canyon Blvd. (bet. Erwin & Oxnard Sts.) | 818-227-9505

www.ruthschris.com

Loyalists "love the sizzling platters" of "oh-so-good buttery steaks" at this "top-quality" chophouse chain that comes through with "winning" sides too; delivering "old-style service" in a "traditional" setting, it's "expensive" (and "not for the dieter"), but "utterly reliable", especially when you're "entertaining friends and clients."

	FOOD	DECOR	SERVICE	COST
	27	26	25	$156

Z Saam at The Bazaar by José Andrés ⊠ Ⓜ *Eclectic*

Beverly Hills | SLS at Beverly Hills | 465 S. La Cienega Blvd. (Clifton Way) | 310-247-0400 | www.thebazaar.com

Devotees "delight in the brilliance of José Andrés" at this "stunning" chef's table restaurant at The Bazaar in Beverly Hills delivering 22 "bite-sized" Eclectic courses of pure "deliciousness" showcasing "fanciful" molecular techniques; add in "expert" service and a "secluded" setting in the "trippy" Philippe Starck–designed space, and it all adds up to an experience that's "expensive", but truly "unique."

	FOOD	DECOR	SERVICE	COST
	27	27	26	$71

Z Saddle Peak Lodge Ⓜ *American*

Calabasas | 419 Cold Canyon Rd. (Piuma Rd.) | 818-222-3888 | www.saddlepeaklodge.com

"Spectacular in every way" swoon admirers of this "rustic log cabin" "set on a wooded hillside" between Malibu and Calabasas where the "incredibly romantic" surroundings and "delicious" "exotic game dishes" make it the "ultimate" place to "pop the "question" – "unless she's a vegetarian"; the "staff goes above and beyond, and so do the prices", although the "excellent" brunch is much more reasonable.

	FOOD	DECOR	SERVICE	COST
	15	19	16	$29

Saddle Ranch ● *Steak*

West Hollywood | 8371 Sunset Blvd. (bet. Crescent Hts. & La Cienega Blvds.) | 323-656-2007

Universal City | Universal CityWalk | 1000 Universal Studios Blvd. (off Rte. 101) | 818-760-9680

www.srrestaurants.com

"Not a gourmet destination by any means", these "sprawling ranch-houses" on the Sunset Strip and in Universal City teem with "tourists and reality stars" lured by a "crazy" booze-soaked bar scene whose centerpiece is a mechanical bull (word to the wise: "ride before" you eat); they're "loud" and crowded and the moderately priced steak-centric fare's "nothing fancy", but if you come in "ready for a good time", it can be a lot of "fun."

Safire *American*

▽ 23	23	21	$42

Camarillo | 4850 Santa Rosa Rd. (Verdugo Way) | 805-389-1227 | www.safirebistro.com

A "foodie oasis" in Camarillo, this midpriced New American bistro "exceeds" area "expectations" with a "creative" "seasonal" menu and "beautiful" mahogany-trimmed setting with a cabana-lined patio with a fire pit; it's "pretty busy most nights", so "noisy" acoustics come with the territory.

Sagebrush Cantina *Southwestern*

13	15	16	$25

Calabasas | 23527 Calabasas Rd. (El Cañon Ave.) | 818-222-6062 | www.sagebrushcantina.com

"Rockers, bikers and surfers" fill up this "party-hearty Valley institution" in Calabasas, where "it's all about" the "beer and live music" on the patio on "warm weekend nights"; service is scattered and the Southwestern eats "passable" at best, but the "people-watching" alone makes it "well worth" a visit.

Saito's Sushi 🗷 *Japanese*

-	-	-	M

Silver Lake | 4339 W. Sunset Blvd. (Fountain Ave.) | 323-663-8890

Definitely not a see-and-be-seen kind of place, this low-key Silver Lake sushi joint slices up "amazing" raw fish for a local crowd; it's an area fixture, but not surprisingly, several surveyors find the "pricey" tabs somewhat at odds with the beyond-"minimalist" strip-mall setting.

Saketini *Asian*

▽ 20	15	23	$29

Brentwood | 150 S. Barrington Ave. (Sunset Blvd.) | 310-440-5553 | www.saketini.com

Serving "sushiphobes and sushi fanatics alike", this "neighborhood find" in Brentwood is a fallback for rolls and Asian fusion fare at "bargain" prices; the setting may be plain, but customers can count on a "helpful" staff that's "anxious to please."

Saladang *Thai*

23	18	19	$27

Pasadena | 363 S. Fair Oaks Ave. (bet. California & Del Mar Blvds.) | 626-793-8123

Saladang Song *Thai*

Pasadena | 383 S. Fair Oaks Ave. (bet. California & Del Mar Blvds.) | 626-793-5200

"Bold-flavored" Thai cooking is the forte of these "popular" side-by-side sisters in Pasadena where "delicious", if "Americanized", cuisine is brought out by the "the world's thinnest servers"; Saladang is the "more conventional" of the two, while Song specializes in "unusual" dishes served up in modern quarters with "flattering lighting" or out on a "delightful" patio.

Salt Creek Grille *Steak*

17	19	19	$37

El Segundo | Plaza El Segundo | 2015 E. Park Pl. (Sepulveda Blvd.) | 310-335-9288

(continued)

Salt Creek Grille

Valencia | Valencia Town Ctr. | 24415 Town Center Dr. (McBean Pkwy.) |
661-222-9999
www.saltcreekgrille.com

It's all about "hanging around the fire pits" "with a glass of wine" at these "comfy", Craftsman-style chain links in El Segundo and Valencia also known for a "hopping" bar scene kicked up by music on weekends; however, given the somewhat "expensive" pricing, some surveyors feel let down by the "ho-hum" steakhouse menu.

Saluté Wine Bar ●☒ *Italian/Mediterranean*

| - | - | - | I |

Santa Monica | Edgemar Complex | 2435 Main St. (bet. Hollister Ave. & Ocean Park Blvd.) | 310-450-3434 | www.salutewinebar.com

"Young" tipplers cram into this barrel-shaped Santa Monica wine bar for "self-serve" sips of wine and inexpensive Italian-Med small plates, courtesy of NYC's Joey Campanaro (Little Owl); though the jury's still out on the food, the fact that it's "crazy busy" most nights speaks for itself.

Sampa Grill ☒ *Brazilian*

| - | - | - | M |

Encino | 16240 Ventura Blvd. (bet. Libbit & Woodley Aves.) | 818-981-8818 |
www.sampagrill.net

Valley "carnivores" are keen on this spare, moderately priced Brazilian steakhouse in Encino where "attentive gauchos bring skewer after skewer" of "flavorful" cuts "until you beg them to stop"; there's also an amply stocked salad bar, although vets attest that "going here for salad is like getting *Playboy* for the articles", so "stick to the meats."

☒ Sam's by the Beach ☒ *Californian/Mediterranean*

| 26 | 22 | 27 | $50 |

Santa Monica | 108 W. Channel Rd. (PCH) | 310-230-9100

An "all-time favorite" just a block from the sand, this "intimate" Santa Monica "gem" lures a "mostly local" crowd for "delicious", "innovative" Cal-Med cuisine in a "romantic" bistro-style setting; it's not inexpensive, but "warm", "personal" service overseen by "consummate host" and owner Sam Elias makes for an eminently "pleasant" experience.

Sam Woo *Chinese*

| 22 | 8 | 13 | $19 |

Chinatown | 727 N. Broadway (bet. Alpine & Ord Sts.) | 213-680-7836
Chinatown | 803 N. Broadway (Alpine St.) | 213-687-7238 ●✑
Cerritos | 19008 Pioneer Blvd. (South St.) | 562-865-7278 ●
Van Nuys | Signature Plaza | 6450 Sepulveda Blvd. (Victory Blvd.) |
818-988-6813 ✑
Alhambra | 514 W. Valley Blvd. (bet. 5th & 6th Sts.) |
626-281-0038 ●✑
San Gabriel | 140 W. Valley Blvd. (Manley Dr.) |
626-572-8418 ●✑
San Gabriel | 425 S. California St. (Agostino Rd.) | 626-287-6528 ●✑
San Gabriel | 937 E. Las Tunas Dr. (Angelus Ave.) |
626-286-3118 ●✑

Champions cheer this "lovable" chain of "Chinese greasy spoons" specializing in "wonderful" BBQ pork and other "genuine" "Asian comfort foods" for "cheap"; just forget about the scrappy settings, "show off your Cantonese" with the counter staff and get it "to go."

	FOOD	DECOR	SERVICE	COST

Santa Monica Seafood Café *Seafood*   22 | 13 | 17 | $29

Santa Monica | 1000 Wilshire Blvd. (10th St.) | 310-393-5244 |
www.santamonicaseafood.com

For some of the "freshest" fare in Santa Monica, surveyors head to this seafood market and cafe vending "first-class oysters", chowder and other "simply prepared" items; "there's no frills, just the fish", hence "rushed, crowded" conditions are part of the package, so perhaps it's best for lunch.

Sapori *Italian*   ▽ 24 | 20 | 24 | $38

Marina del Rey | Fishermans Vill. | 13723 Fiji Way (Lincoln Blvd.) |
310-821-1740 | www.sapori-mdr.com

A "great little find" in "touristy" Fisherman's Village, this Marina del Rey Italian is a "mainstay" for "excellent", "well-priced" dishes and "lovely" "sunset views" from a "waterside" perch; "quaint", quiet environs and "accommodating" service are other ways "they always get it right."

Sashi *Japanese*   21 | 22 | 18 | $51

Manhattan Beach | Metlox Plaza | 451 Manhattan Beach Blvd.
(bet. Morningside & Valley Drs.) | 310-545-0400 | www.sashimb.com

It's a total "scene" at this "sexy" Manhattan Beach lounge/sushi bar where "surprisingly good" fish and "interesting" robata items are served in a "noisy", "modern" setting with a prime "people-watching" patio; however, those "over 30" detect a little "too much attitude" from the staff, and say the small plates come at "big prices."

Sea Empress *Chinese*   18 | 12 | 15 | $26

Gardena | Pacific Sq. | 1636 W. Redondo Beach Blvd. (bet. Normandie & Western Aves.) | 310-538-6868

A "bright spot" for "tasty" "Hong Kong–style dim sum" in the South Bay, this inexpensive Gardena Chinese is "packed" on weekends; most overlook the "tired" banquet-hall decor and "un-stellar" service because it sure "beats the long drive inland" to Chinatown.

☑ Sea Harbour *Chinese/Seafood*   25 | 14 | 15 | $29

Rosemead | 3939 N. Rosemead Blvd. (Valley Blvd.) | 626-288-3939

Regulars go early and "beat the mid-morning rush" at this Rosemead Chinese specializing in "terrific" cart-free dim sum at lunch and "great Cantonese seafood" at dinner; the setting's on the "upscale" side for the genre, ditto the relatively "pricey" tabs.

Second City Bistro 🆕 *American*   24 | 20 | 21 | $37

El Segundo | 223 Richmond St. (bet. Franklin & Grand Aves.) |
310-322-6085 | www.secondcitybistro.com

A "best-kept secret" in El Segundo, this "cute" bistro is "worth the drive" for its "delicious" New American menu and "fantastic wines" served in a rehabbed 1922 building with exposed beams and brick; prices are modest and the service "sweet", so the overall experience is "nothing short of charming."

Sedthee Thai Eatery *Thai*   - | - | - | I

Glendale | 239 N. Brand Blvd. (California Ave.) | 818-247-9789 |
www.sedtheethaieatery.com

Set on the northern edge of the Brand Boulevard shopping district in Glendale, this hyper-modernist Siamese serves a well-priced menu of

Californian interpretations of classic Thai dishes; its minimalist industrial setting is often bustling, especially during the bargain lunch.

Señor Fred *Mexican* 17 | 15 | 16 | $28

Sherman Oaks | 13730 Ventura Blvd. (bet. Woodman Ave. & Van Nuys Blvd.) | 818-789-3200 | www.senorfred.com

"Dark" and "lively", this inexpensive Sherman Oaks cantina doles out "gringo-style Mexican" eats that play second fiddle to the multitude of margaritas; middling service and "deafening" decibels suggest it's best for a "twentysomething" crowd.

Seoul Jung *Korean* ▽ 24 | 18 | 20 | $43

Downtown | Wilshire Grand | 930 Wilshire Blvd. (Figueroa St.) | 213-688-7880 | www.wilshiregrand.com

"Fine Korean cuisine" and tabletop BBQ turns up at this under-the-radar enclave ensconced in contemporary digs in Downtown's Wilshire Grand; "despite its hotel location", insiders insist it's "authentic", "tasty" and priced well too.

Seta *American/Steak* ▽ 27 | 24 | 26 | $45

Whittier | 13033 Philadelphia St. (bet. Bright & Greenleaf Aves.) | 562-698-3355 | www.dineseta.com

A "welcome addition" to Whittier, this "sophisticated" sophomore showcases "terrific" New American steakhouse fare from chef Hugo Molina (ex Pasadena's Parkway Grill) in a "slick" earth-toned space that's "hip" for the area; add a "courteous" staff that's "ready to please" plus moderate prices and it's no wonder locals are already whispering it's a "winner."

17th Street Cafe *Californian* 19 | 16 | 20 | $27

Santa Monica | 1610 Montana Ave. (bet. 16th & 17th Sts.) | 310-453-2771 | www.seventeenthstreetcafe.com

"Convenient" for Montana Avenue shopping trips, this "cheerful" Santa Monica "staple" lures "ladies who lunch" with "fresh" salads and other "well-prepared" Cal fare delivered by "happy" servers at "prices that won't kill you"; a bakery with "tempting desserts" adds "extra pizzazz" – though the "country-diner" setting is the opposite of "posh."

71 Palm Ⓩ *American/French* 22 | 21 | 20 | $41

Ventura | 71 N. Palm St. (bet. Main & Poli Sts.) | 805-653-7222 | www.71palm.com

It's like a "journey to the French countryside without the airfare" at this "cute" Ventura brasserie situated in a "historic home on a hillside" and overseen by "skilled" chef-owner Didier Poirier, who uses "high-quality ingredients" in his well-priced French-American offerings; "fine service" rounds out the experience, and though a few critics cite "uneven" execution, it mostly "exceeds expectations."

Shabu Shabu House Ⓜ *Japanese* 23 | 12 | 16 | $26

Little Tokyo | 127 Japanese Village Plaza Mall (bet. 1st & 2nd Sts.) | 213-680-3890

Cook-it-yourself types tout the "authentic" eponymous dish at this low-budget Little Tokyo Japanese where the "quality" cuts gain a lift from "flavorful" sauces and condiments; decor and service aren't their strong suit, but even still, "there's always a wait."

Shack, The *American*

17 | 12 | 14 | $17

Playa del Rey | 185 Culver Blvd. (Vista del Mar) | 310-823-6222 | www.the-shacks.com
Santa Monica | 2518 Wilshire Blvd. (26th St.) | 310-449-1171
The "quintessential beach burger shacks", these Playa del Rey and Santa Monica "dives" dole out "calorie-killing" burgers and other "bar"-style Americana washed down with "cold beer"; "unadorned" digs aside, both are favorites on game days when "Philly transplants" fill the ranks.

Shaherzad *Persian*

22 | 12 | 18 | $26

Westwood | 1422 Westwood Blvd. (bet. Santa Monica & Wilshire Blvds.) | 310-470-9131
"Delicious stews", "freshly made bread" and some of "the juiciest chicken kebabs west of Tehran" are the hallmarks of this "authentic" Westwood Persian where the "generous" plates guarantee enough "for two meals"; the setting's spare, but the "bargain" tabs win over most.

Sharky's Mexican Grill *Mexican*

19 | 11 | 17 | $12

Hollywood | 1716 N. Cahuenga Blvd. (Hollywood Blvd.) | 323-461-7881
Beverly Hills | 435 N. Beverly Dr. (bet. Brighton Way & Santa Monica Blvd.) | 310-858-0202
Long Beach | Pike at Rainbow Harbor | 51 The Paseo (Pine Ave.) | 562-435-2700
Pasadena | 841 Cordova St. (bet. Hudson & Lake Aves.) | 626-568-3500
Burbank | Burbank Empire Ctr. | 1791 N. Victory Pl. (Empire Ave.) | 818-840-9080
Calabasas | Creekside Village Shopping Ctr. | 26527 Agoura Rd. (Las Virgenes Rd.) | 818-880-0885
Sherman Oaks | 13238 Burbank Blvd. (bet. Ethel & Fulton Aves.) | 818-785-2533
Tarzana | 5511 Reseda Blvd. (Clark St.) | 818-881-8760
Simi Valley | 2410 Sycamore Dr. (Cochran St.) | 805-522-2270
Ventura | Gateway Ctr. | 4960 Telephone Rd. (Portola Rd.) | 805-339-9600
Westlake Village | 111 S. Westlake Blvd. (Thousand Oaks Blvd.) | 805-370-3701
www.sharkys.com
Additional locations throughout Southern California
There's "lots of healthy options" at this "fresh" Mexican "fast-food" chainlet offering brown rice, organic veggies and tofu in its "tasty" burritos, taco platters and protein plates; "cheap" prices are another reason "you don't feel too guilty after eating here."

Shima 🗷 Ⓜ *Japanese*

– | – | – | E

Venice | 1432 Abbot Kinney Blvd. (bet. California Ave. & Palms Blvd.) | 310-314-0882
Showing an almost "militant dedication to freshness", this Venice Japanese delivers "delicate", "beautifully presented" sushi crafted with brown rice among other deceptively "simple", "healthful" items; "unobtrusive" service and a "quiet", two-tier setting add up to a "truly Zen" experience, at least until the check arrives.

Shin ◑ Ⓜ *Korean*

– | – | – | M

Hollywood | 1600 N. Wilcox Ave. (Selma Ave.) | 323-464-4100 | www.shinbbq.com
An "interesting variety" of "delicious" "cook-it-yourself" Korean BBQ is at the forefront of this glossy Hollywood haunt with a full bar, an

"awesome" soundtrack and a 100-gallon jellyfish tank for show; it's fun for groups, especially since prices can fit "any budget."

Shiro Ⓜ *French/Japanese* | 28 | 21 | 26 | $53 |

South Pasadena | 1505 Mission St. (bet. Fair Oaks & Mound Aves.) | 626-799-4774 | www.restaurantshiro.com

Putting a "unique spin" on Asian cooking is this South Pasadena "favorite", a "go-to" for a "truly amazing" signature deep-fried catfish among other "superb" French-Japanese items backed by an "extensive" wine list; perhaps the "grand" decor feels "straight out of 1992", but service is "impeccable" and longtime fans profess they've "never had a bad meal here"; P.S. closed Monday–Tuesday.

SHU *Italian/Japanese* | ▽ 24 | 18 | 22 | $52 |

Bel-Air | The Glen | 2932½ Beverly Glen Circle (Beverly Glen Blvd.) | 310-474-2740 | www.shusushi.com

Japanese and Italian come together and it "actually works" at this Bel-Air boîte backed by Giacomino Drago, where the "excellent", "artistic" fusion-style offerings include crab and mozzarella tempura and sashimi with shaved truffles; elevating the experience is solid service and an attractive stone-clad room with frequent "star sightings", so if you can hack the prices, it's "definitely worth a try."

Sidecar Restaurant Ⓜ *American* | ▽ 24 | 19 | 25 | $39 |

Ventura | 3029 E. Main St. (bet. Mills & Telegraph Rds.) | 805-653-7433 | www.thesidecarrestaurant.com

A vintage rail car is the setting for this Ventura "gem" serving up an "ever-changing menu" of "farm-fresh" American eats based on "local", seasonal ingredients; with solid service and "decent prices", most maintain this is one train you don't want to miss; P.S. Tuesday is grilled cheese and live jazz night.

Simmzy's *American* | 21 | 15 | 19 | $25 |

Manhattan Beach | 229 Manhattan Beach Blvd. (Highland Ave.) | 310-546-1201 | www.simmzys.com

Still relatively new on the scene, this "teeny-tiny" Manhattan Beach "hangout" has been "packed" from day one, thanks to its "affordable", accessible American menu, "clever selection of microbrews" and overall "good vibes"; a patio provides stellar "people-watching", although it's "loud" and there's often a "wait."

Simon LA *American* | 22 | 24 | 22 | $47 |

West Hollywood | Sofitel LA | 8555 Beverly Blvd. (La Cienega Blvd.) | 310-278-5444 | www.sofitel.com

"Chic" twists on "comfort food" come courtesy of *Iron Chef* champ Kerry Simon at this "cool" spot in West Hollywood's Sofitel catering to a "somewhat trendy" crowd with New American plates for nibbling capped by a "don't-miss" cotton candy dessert; "attentive" service and a patio with a fire pit are added appeals, although foes find it "more touristy than foodie" and "expensive" to boot.

Simpang Asia ❶ *Indonesian* | ▽ 17 | 8 | 15 | $13 |

Palms | 10433 National Blvd. (bet. Mentone & Motor Aves.) | 310-815-9075 | www.simpangasia.com

This West LA cafe "may not be fancy", but it's one of the few places to sample Indonesian cuisine with a "satisfying" lineup of "unusual"

dishes like jackfruit curry; service isn't its strong suit, but that goes un
noticed given the "bargain" prices; N.B. the Decor score may not full
reflect a move to larger digs.

NEW Sip *American* — | — | — | M

Long Beach | Renaissance Long Beach Hotel | 111 E. Ocean Blvd.
(Pacific Ave.) | 562-437-5900

Looking like *Pee-wee's Playhouse* for grown-ups, with every color in th
rainbow, this wildly decorated hotel New American in Long Beach spe
cializes in classic cocktails made with modern ingredients; moderatel
priced sup options to go with your sips include Carolina pork ribs,
spiced lamb burger and a plate of Californian cheeses.

Sir Winston's *Californian/Continental* ∇ 24 | 28 | 22 | $61

Long Beach | Queen Mary | 1126 Queen's Hwy. (Harbor Scenic Dr.) |
562-499-1657 | www.queenmary.com

"Old-fashioned elegance" is alive and well at this "art deco" dining
room aboard the *Queen Mary* in Long Beach, where the semiforma
dress code and live piano on weekends recall the kind of place "you
don't see much anymore"; "lovely views", "exquisite" Cal-Continenta
dishes like Châteaubriand and a "staff that truly takes care of you"
make it feel "first-class" all around.

Sisley Italian Kitchen *Italian* 19 | 17 | 18 | $28

Sherman Oaks | 15300 Ventura Blvd. (Sepulveda Blvd.) | 818-905-8444
Valencia | Valencia Town Ctr. | 24201 Valencia Blvd. (McBean Pkwy.) |
661-287-4444
www.sisleykitchen.com

There's "something for everyone" at this Italian chainlet where fami
lies "fill up" on "steaming, fresh-baked" breadsticks before chowing
down on "consistent", if somewhat "ordinary", red-sauce fare; "rea
sonable" prices make it a "reliable" bet, and the ample settings are
"good for groups" too.

Skaf's Lebanese Cuisine Ⓢ *Lebanese* ∇ 22 | 10 | 18 | $21

Glendale | 367 N. Chevy Chase Dr. (Verdugo Rd.) | 818-551-5540

Glendale "locals" laud the "flavorful falafel", "wonderfully spiced ke
babs" and other "home-cooked" Lebanese dishes at this "depend
able" mainstay where the "prices can't be beat"; the setting's a bit
"drab", but the staff always makes you feel "well cared for", and
there's always "takeout."

Sky Room *American* ∇ 18 | 23 | 20 | $69

Long Beach | Historic Breakers Bldg. | 40 S. Locust Ave. (Ocean Blvd.) |
562-983-2703 | www.theskyroom.com

Aptly named for its "fabulous" panoramic views, this "'20s-style" sup
per club atop the Breakers in Long Beach is a "special-occasion" main
stay, what with its "elegantly" attired servers, live music and dancing
on weekends; the New American fare earns mixed reviews ("excel
lent" vs. "ok"), and not surprisingly, it's awfully "pricey."

NEW Slaw Dogs *Hot Dogs* ∇ 18 | 10 | 23 | $11

Pasadena | 720 N. Lake Ave. (Orange Grove Blvd.) | 626-808-9777 |
www.theslawdogs.com

A seemingly "infinite" array of hot dogs turns up at this new Pasadena
storefront focusing on fast food with a gourmet bent; it boasts speedy

	FOOD	DECOR	SERVICE	COST

counter service and picnic-y digs, but with only a handful of tables, it's an eat and run kind of place; P.S. a beer and wine license is reportedly in the works.

Smitty's Grill *American*

| 22 | 20 | 21 | $40 |

Pasadena | 110 S. Lake Ave. (bet. Cordova & Green Sts.) | 626-792-9999 | www.smittysgrill.com

"Always jammed", this "convivial" Pasadena "hangout" from the Smith Brothers (Arroyo Chop House, Parkway Grill) serves "all-American" "guy food" "classics" like chicken pot pie and meatloaf in clubby, "comfortable" quarters; factor in "excellent" service and "reasonable" prices and fans only "wish it weren't so noisy", although a quieter back room and patio offer some relief.

Smoke House *Steak*

| 20 | 18 | 21 | $36 |

Burbank | 4420 W. Lakeside Dr. (Barham Blvd.) | 818-845-3731 | www.smokehouse1946.com

"Old-school" all the way, this "been-around-forever" Burbank "institution" plies an "industry" crowd with "solid" steakhouse fare, "nicely made martinis" and "neon-orange" garlic bread that's "deservedly legendary"; perhaps the "faded" red leather–decked decor has "seen better days", but prices are moderate and for a "truly retro" experience, "it's a kick."

NEW Smokin' Joint *BBQ*

| – | – | – | M |

West Hollywood | 8486 W. Third St. (La Cienega Blvd.) | 323-655-7427 | www.smokinjointbbq.com

Everything is made from scratch at this year-old West Hollywood BBQ where "tender", "smoky" meats rated some of the "best in the area" are sided with all the fixin's; a teak bar and table service – not to mention a real neighborhood feel – help compensate for tabs that are on the steep side for the genre.

Sofi *Greek*

| 20 | 21 | 19 | $36 |

Third Street | 8030¾ W. Third St. (Laurel Ave.) | 323-651-0346 | www.sofisrestaurant.com

The "enchanting" garden patio is "the place to be" at this Third Street charmer serving "excellent" meze among other "good" Greek grub; a "lovely" staff, "reasonable" tabs and "fun" "traditional" music on weekends ensure it's "pleasant all around."

NEW Soi 7 *Thai*

| ▽ 21 | 23 | 16 | $30 |

Downtown | 518 W. Seventh St. (Olive St.) | 213-537-0333 | www.soi7la.com

"Nicer than your average Thai", this relatively new Downtown "find" delivers "upscale" takes on the classics in a "tasteful", "elegant" setting with a full bar pouring 50 sakes plus a tearoom with an "extensive selection" of brews; though it flies under the radar for now, it's aiming for the lunchtime crowd with a grab-and-go Asian-style deli.

Soleil Westwood Ⓜ *Canadian/French*

| 19 | 16 | 21 | $36 |

Westwood | 1386 Westwood Blvd. (Wilkins Ave.) | 310-441-5384 | www.soleilwestwood.com

Chef-owner Luc Alarie keeps things "*très bon*" at this "charming, neighborhood" bistro in Westwood turning out "real" French-Canadian cuisine that's otherwise "hard to find in LA"; prices are "gentle" and

the "comfortable" space is "good for conversation", so even if som
suggest the food's "only ok", it's still "busy" most nights; P.S. don'
miss the poutine menu.

NEW Sonoma Wine Garden *Californian/Italian*   − | − | − | M

Santa Monica | Dining Deck, Santa Monica Pl. | 395 Santa Monica Pl.
(3rd. St. Promenade) | 424-214-4560 | www.sonomawinegarden.com
For those who thirst for an extensive option of California wines, this
Santa Monica Place newcomer offers not just a surfeit of vino, but also
an outdoor patio that faces west toward the ocean, allowing you to
bask in the rays of the setting sun while you sip on your Viognier
there's also an assortment of artisanal cheeses and salumi, plus midpriced Cal-Italian bites like a Dungeness crab BLT.

Soot Bull Jeep *Korean*   23 | 7 | 14 | $29

Koreatown | 3136 Eighth St. (Catalina St.) | 213-387-3865
Do-it-yourself types like cooking their Korean BBQ over "real char-
coal" at this "popular" K-town source for "perfectly marinated meats"
exuding "smoky, smoky goodness" and "dynamite" *banchan*; prices offer "bang for the buck", although "dumpy" decor, "grill battles" with
the staff and clothes that "smell like a campfire for the next week" are
all part of the package.

Sor Tino *Italian*   22 | 19 | 24 | $39

Brentwood | 908 S. Barrington Ave. (San Vicente Blvd.) | 310-442-8466
"Pleasant" is the word on this "low-key" entry in Brentwood from chef-
owner Agostino Sciandri (Ago) where a "warm" staff delivers "true"
Italian home cooking" at moderate prices; inside is "cozy" and "not too
loud" but on a summer night, the "twinkle-lit patio" "sheltered by
plants" is the place to be.

NEW South Beverly Grill *American*   − | − | − | M

Beverly Hills | 122 S. Beverly Dr. (bet. Charleville & Wilshire Blvds.) |
310-550-0242 | www.hillstone.com
The latest creation from the restaurant group behind Houston's,
Gulfstream, Bandera and R+D Kitchen, this Beverly Hills arrival offers
a midpriced menu of Traditional American comfort food – think fried
oysters, juicy burgers, exotic salads and meats cooked over mesquite;
the comfortable setting shares a clean, Frank Lloyd Wright–esque design sense with its siblings, and also boasts a lively bar.

Z Spago *Californian*   27 | 25 | 26 | $77

Beverly Hills | 176 N. Cañon Dr. (Wilshire Blvd.) | 310-385-0880 |
www.wolfgangpuck.com
"The place where Wolfgang Puck started it all", this Beverly Hills
"classic" "sets the bar high" with his brand of "superb" "no-holds-
barred" Californian cuisine that still "exceeds expectations" "after all
these years"; "impeccable" service (including "frequent" tableside
visits from Puck himself), a "splashy" room "full of dealmakers" and a
garden that's "pure bliss" make it "worth every penny", even if you
have to drain "your kid's college fund" to afford it.

Spark Woodfire Grill *American*   20 | 19 | 20 | $35

Pico-Robertson | 9575 W. Pico Blvd. (Beverly Dr.) | 310-277-0133 |
www.sparkwoodfiregrill.com

(continued)

Spark Woodfire Grill

Studio City | 11801 Ventura Blvd. (bet. Carpenter & Colfax Aves.) | 818-623-8883 | www.sparkwoodfiregrill.com

Simi Valley | Simi Valley Town Ctr. | 1555 Simi Town Center Way (bet. Erringer Rd. & 1st St.) | 805-823-4756 | www.sparkredfish.com

There's "plenty to choose from" at this "casual" American chainlet firing up an "economically priced" array of roast and grilled meats via wood-burning ovens; a "cozy" atmosphere and "pleasant-enough" service mean it's "handy for lunch" or an "easy" dinner.

Spitz *Turkish*   21 | 14 | 18 | $14

Eagle Rock | 2506 Colorado Blvd. (College View Ave.) | 323-257-5600

Spitz Little Tokyo *Turkish*

Little Tokyo | 371 E. Second St. (Central Ave.) | 213-613-0101 www.eatatspitz.com

"Delicious" doner kebabs ("get them zesty-style") are the specialty of the house at these Turkish twins in Eagle Rock and Little Tokyo turning out "filling and flavorful" eats for not too much money; "fast, friendly" service and a "stylish" vibe overcomes "no-frills" decor at both locales; P.S. the Little Tokyo outpost serves beer and wine.

Spumoni *Italian*   20 | 14 | 21 | $23

Santa Monica | 713 Montana Ave. (7th St.) | 310-393-2944

Calabasas | 26500 Agoura Rd. (Las Virgenes Rd.) | 818-871-9848

Sherman Oaks | 14533 Ventura Blvd. (bet. Van Nuys Blvd. & Vesper Ave.) | 818-981-7218

Stevenson Ranch | 24917 Pico Canyon Rd. (The Old Rd.) | 661-799-0360 www.spumonirestaurants.com

"Locals" rely on these "casual" neighborhood Italians for "large" helpings of "solid" red-sauce fare and pizzas at "decent" prices; the settings are beyond-"ordinary" and service sometimes spotty, but the "convenience" alone "covers a multitude of sins", and it sure "beats cooking."

Square One Dining *American*   23 | 15 | 19 | $18

East Hollywood | 4854 Fountain Ave. (bet. Berendo & Catalina Sts.) | 323-661-1109 | www.squareonedining.com

A "favorite" for brunch, this East Hollywood American lures a "hip" crowd for "fastidiously fresh" "wholesome" eats based on organic ingredients (don't miss the "killer French toast"); the staff is "personable", but the space is "tiny", so weekends bring waits; P.S. closes at 3 PM.

Stand, The *Hot Dogs*   17 | 13 | 16 | $13

Century City | 2000 Ave. of the Stars (Constellation Blvd.) | 310-785-0400 🖂

Westwood | 1116 Westwood Blvd. (Kinross Ave.) | 310-443-0400

Encino | 17000 Ventura Blvd. (Genesta Ave.) | 818-788-2700

Woodland Hills | Warner Ctr. | 5780 Canoga Ave. (Burbank Blvd.) | 818-710-0400 www.thestandlink.com

"More dogs than you can shake a bun at" and an "endless" array of toppings turn up at this counter-service chainlet also putting out "pretty good burgers" and other "affordable" American eats; it's a "cute concept", and the "patios with twinkle lights" make it a "great summertime hangout", especially with the kids.

Standard, The ● *Eclectic* ▽ 19 | 19 | 17 | $39
West Hollywood | The Standard | 8300 Sunset Blvd. (Sweetzer Ave.)
323-650-9090 | www.standardhotel.com

There's "late-night people-watching" galore at this "hip" 24/7 coffe
shop in The Standard West Hollywood where a "cute" staff ferrie
"surprisingly good" Eclectic "diner" fare to an equally cute crowc
moderate tabs, retro digs and nightly DJs add to the "cool" factor, a
well as the "prodigious noise levels."

Standard, The ● *Eclectic* 17 | 22 | 15 | $41
Downtown | The Standard | 550 S. Flower St. (6th St.) | 213-892-8080
www.standardhotel.com

Surveyors scope out the "beautiful people" at this 24/7 "rock 'n' roll
brasserie in The Standard Downtown serving Eclectic "comfort food
in a "bright"-yellow interior that "makes you happy"; never mind th
"subpar" service and "overpriced" drinks, it's a godsend when "n
other restaurants are open"; P.S. don't miss the rooftop bar wit
"stunning views" of the city.

Stanley's *Californian* 20 | 15 | 19 | $24
Sherman Oaks | 13817 Ventura Blvd. (bet. Mammoth & Matillja Aves.)
818-986-4623 | www.stanleys83.com

"You can't go wrong with the Chinese chicken salad" at this Sherma
Oaks "ol' reliable" pulling a "loyal" cadre of fans for "tasty" Californiar
cuisine at "decent" prices; service and decor are nothing to writ
home about, but the "sunny" patio is especially "inviting" and "make
you want to stay there all day chatting with your friends."

NEW Starry Kitchen ⑤ *Asian* - | - | - | I
Downtown | 350 S. Grand Ave. (bet. 3rd & 4th Sts.) | 213-617-3474
www.starrykitchen.com

What began as a San Fernando Valley pop-up with a cult following ha
left its humble roots to bring the gospel of 'Thai Cobb' salad and crisp
tofu balls (a dish fans speak of in rapturous terms) to the Dilberts o
Downtown; the decor-free space is dominated by bright fluorescent
and a blackboard listing the dishes of the day – which tend to chang
depending on what Team SK has picked up at the market.

NEW Stefan's at L.A. Farm *Eclectic* 23 | 20 | 21 | $48
Santa Monica | 3000 W. Olympic Blvd. (Stewart St.) | 310-449-4000
www.stefansatlafarm.com

Top Chef finalist Stefan Richter "works his wonders" and works the roon
at this Santa Monica showcase for his "adventurous" Eclectic small- anc
large-plates menu that's a "grazer's paradise"; however, despite th
good vibes on the "pretty" patio, service "kinks" are a sore spot, and the
budget-conscious complain that all those "tiny" bites can "really add up.

NEW Stefan's on Montana *Eclectic* ▽ 20 | 13 | 17 | $29
Santa Monica | 1518 Montana Ave. (15th St.) | 310-394-7178 |
www.stefansonmontana.com

Santa Monicans sing the praises of this "tasty" "new addition" tc
Montana featuring *Top Chef*er Stefan Richter's "creative" Eclectic
plates like chicken pot pie and fondues in a modest storefront setting
even if some are irked by "uneven food and service" and tabs that fee
pricey for what you get", most maintain it "has potential."

	FOOD	DECOR	SERVICE	COST

Steve's Steakhouse *Steak* | - | - | - | E |

Catalina Island | 417 Crescent Ave. (Sumner Ave.) | Avalon | 310-510-0333 |
www.stevessteakhouse.com

For those who crave a taste of beef by the sea, this destination steakhouse overlooking the harbor is Avalon's most popular place to eat
meat, as well as old-style SoCal surf 'n' turf dishes; though it's not
inexpensive, the mood is casual at lunch and only slightly more
dressy at dinner.

Stevie's Creole Cafe *Cajun* | ▽ 17 | 11 | 14 | $33 |

Encino | 16911 Ventura Blvd. (Balboa Blvd.) | 818-528-3500

"Down-home" Cajun-Creole cooking comes in "huge" helpings at
this Encino restaurant and club venue; modest prices plus a
"funky" brothel-meets-honky-tonk setting with live music pull in a
"fun" crowd that's willing to forgive the "run-of-the-mill" eats and
occasionally "po'" service.

Stinking Rose, The *Italian* | 19 | 20 | 20 | $36 |

Beverly Hills | 55 N. La Cienega Blvd. (Wilshire Blvd.) | 310-652-7673 |
www.thestinkingrose.com

"Not for the faint of smell", this Beverly Hills offshoot of the SF original
presents a midpriced Italian menu of "garlic-infused" everything, from
prime rib to martinis to an ice-cream dessert that's certainly "unique";
though service is "efficient" and the "kitschy", "Alice in Garlic-land"
decor has its fans, it's all a bit "gimmicky" to some.

STK ● *Steak* | 22 | 24 | 22 | $69 |

West Hollywood | 755 N. La Cienega Blvd. (Waring Ave.) | 310-659-3535 |
www.stkhouse.com

"Bringing the steakhouse into the 21st century" is this "tragically hip"
West Hollywood chop shop where "celebs" and "wannabes" tuck into
"melt-in-your-mouth" cuts and "delicious" mac 'n' cheese; just be prepared for clublike digs that are "loud as hell" and prices that just might
empty your wallet; P.S. there's a DJ Tuesday and Thursday–Saturday.

Stonefire Grill *BBQ* | 20 | 14 | 16 | $18 |

West Hills | Fallbrook Ctr. | 6405 Fallbrook Ave. (Victory Blvd.) |
818-887-4145
Valencia | Cinema Park Plaza | 23300 Cinema Dr. (Boquet Canyon Rd.) |
661-799-8282
www.stonefiregrill.com

"Families" flock to this "value"-minded American chain for "splittable"
portions of "tasty" 'cue like tri-tip and ribs that's brought out at the
speed of fast food"; however, given the "chaotic" atmosphere, insiders insist "takeout is key."

Street *Eclectic* | 20 | 18 | 20 | $41 |

Hollywood | 742 N. Highland Ave. (Melrose Ave.) | 323-203-0500 |
www.eatatstreet.com

"Travel from Scandinavia to Thailand with a wave of the fork" at this
"vibrant" "multi-ethnic" "street-food" concept in Hollywood from
Susan Feniger (Border Grill, Ciudad) presenting Eclectic small plates
in a "hip" setting with one of the "best patios in LA"; despite some
quibbles about "hit-or-miss" service and execution and "somewhat
pricey" bills, it's still a lot of "fun" with a group.

	FOOD	DECOR	SERVICE	COST

sugarFISH *Japanese* — 24 | 18 | 21 | $38

Brentwood | 11640 San Vicente Blvd. (bet. Darlington Ave. & Wilshire Blvd.) | 310-820-4477
Marina del Rey | The Waterside | 4722¼ Admiralty Way (Mindanao Way) | 310-306-6300
www.sugarfishsushi.com

"It's all about the fish" at these "value"-minded offshoots of Sushi Nozawa in Brentwood and Marina del Rey, where the "amazingly fresh", "melt-in-your-mouth" slabs come à la carte or in a "purist"-pleasing omakase; the setting's "spare and "modern" and service is "quick", but like the original, a "no-substitutions" policy reigns.

Sunnin *Lebanese* — 23 | 12 | 17 | $20

West LA | 1776 Westwood Blvd (Santa Monica Blvd.) | 310-475-3358
Long Beach | 5110 E. Second St. (bet. Granada & Nieto Aves.) | 562-433-9000
www.sunnin.com

Admirers "throng" these "dependably delicious" Lebanese twins in Long Beach and West LA delivering "authentic", "bold-flavored" Middle Eastern eats – "wonderful hummus", "tender grilled meats" – in "huge portions"; "hospitable" service and "bargain" pricing easily override the modest settings; N.B. the Decor score may not fully reflect the West LA branch's move to "upgraded" digs.

⬧ Sur *Californian/Mediterranean* — 23 | 26 | 25 | $59

West Hollywood | 606 N. Robertson Blvd. (Melrose Ave.) | 310-289-2824
www.sur-restaurant.com

"The scene is hot" and so are the servers at this West Hollywood nightspot flaunting a "cool" all-white look tricked out with votive candles and chandeliers; given so much eye candy, many find it "hard to concentrate on" the Cal-Med menu, though allies assure it's "delicious" and relatively "reasonably priced for what you get."

Sushi Dokoro Ki Ra La *Japanese* — - | - | - | E

Beverly Hills | 9777 S. Santa Monica Blvd. (Wilshire Blvd.) | 310-275-9003
www.sushikirala.com

This "tiny, hole-in-the-wall" Japanese in Beverly Hills is a find for "highly authentic" fare, from "fresh" sushi to cooked items like grilled yellowtail collar; in spite of the simple, white-tablecloth space, bills can be "expensive", so be prepared to shell out a few clams.

Sushi Gen ⬧ *Japanese* — 26 | 15 | 19 | $45

Little Tokyo | 422 E. Second St. (Central Ave.) | 213-617-0552

Amid the sea of Little Tokyo eateries, this "traditional", "no-frills" Japanese "stands out" with "fresh", "superior quality" sushi (the "salmon's like buttah") that's "not cheap" but still a solid "value"; the setting's simple and service is nothing to write home about, but expect "long-ish waits", especially at lunch.

⬧ Sushi Masu Ⓜ *Japanese* — 27 | 13 | 23 | $48

West LA | 1911 Westwood Blvd. (bet. La Grange & Missouri Aves.) | 310-446-4368

"One of the best-kept secrets in West LA", this "tiny" Japanese is a "go-to" for "high-grade" sushi served up simply, "without pretentions"; there's "no ambiance" – just "attentive service" from chef-host Hiroshi Masuko and prices that are a "deal" given the "quality."

Sushi Mon *Japanese* ▽ 21 | 14 | 17 | $40

Third Street | 8562 W. Third St. (Holt Ave.) | West Hollywood | 310-246-9230

The "affordable" tabs are the main draw of this "solid" Third Street Japanese turning out "standard" sushi and specialty rolls; service is "friendly", though the blasé deem the digs and fare "nothing special."

⊿ Sushi Nozawa Ⓢ *Japanese* 28 | 9 | 15 | $62

Studio City | 11288 Ventura Blvd. (bet. Arch & Tropical Drs.) | 818-508-7017 | www.sushinozawa.com

Whatever you do, don't ask for soy sauce" at this "expensive", "traditional" Studio City Japanese helmed by famously "grouchy" "master chef Kazunori Nozawa that "rewards" purists with "exceptional", "top-flight" fish in "clean, straightforward" preparations; acolytes insist it's worth enduring" the "fluorescent-lit" strip-mall digs and "rushed" pace because the omakase "rocks"; P.S. closed Saturdays and Sundays.

Sushi Roku *Japanese* 23 | 21 | 20 | $51

Third Street | 8445 W. Third St. (bet. Croft Ave. & La Cienega Blvd.) | 323-655-6767
Santa Monica | 1401 Ocean Ave. (Santa Monica Blvd.) | 310-458-4771 ●
Pasadena | One Colorado | 33 Miller Alley (bet. Colorado Blvd. & Union St.) | 626-683-3000
www.sushiroku.com

Sushi and "stargazing" come together at this "loud", "hip" Japanese trio netting a "beautiful" "young" crowd for "fantastic", "fresh" fish in creative" preps in a "Zen-like", "date night–caliber" setting; perhaps the scene is "tamer" than it used to be, but unfortunately you can't say the same for the "high" price tags.

⊿ Sushi Sasabune Ⓢ *Japanese* 27 | 13 | 22 | $66

West LA | 12400 Wilshire Blvd. (Centinela Ave.) | 310-268-8380
Sushi-Don Sasabune Express *Japanese*
🆕 **Pacific Palisades** | 970 Monument St. (bet. Bashford St. & Sunset Blvd.) | 310-454-6710 | www.sushidonppl.com

Sit at the bar", "splurge" on the omakase and let the chef "feed you like Flipper" instruct fans of this "traditional" West LA Japanese known for its ultra-"fresh", "melt-in-your-mouth" cuts; a "sterile", cafeterialike" setting is part of the package, but that's no matter since "you'll leave happy"; P.S. there's now an express outlet in Pacific Palisades with takeout and a handful of tables.

Sushi Sushi ⓈⓂ *Japanese* ▽ 27 | 16 | 20 | $60

Beverly Hills | 326½ S. Beverly Dr. (bet. Gregory Way & Olympic Blvd.) | 310-277-1165

For purists only", this Beverly Hills Japanese "keeps it simple" with premium, no-frills" sushi of "quality comparable to Japan"; loyal fans overlook the lack of bells and whistles in service and decor for such a perfect" (and "expensive") experience.

⊿ Sushi Zo Ⓢ *Japanese* 29 | 13 | 21 | $104

West LA | 9824 National Blvd. (bet. Castle Heights Ave. & Shelby Dr.) | 310-842-3977

Enter with a willing palate and an empty stomach" at this "omakase-only" West LA Japanese where "every bite is exquisite" thanks to "stern" chef-owner Keizo Seki's "brilliant" yet "subtle" cuisine, ranked No. 1 for Food in this year's Survey; "shockingly expensive" prices and an "austere" strip-mall setting near the freeway hardly deter those seeking sushi that's "as good as it gets in LA."

☑ Susina Bakery & Cafe *Bakery* — 26 | 21 | 20 | $18

La Brea | 7122 Beverly Blvd. (La Brea Ave.) | 323-934-7900 | www.susinabakery.com

For "heavenly pastries", cakes and other sweets "to die for", surveyors beeline to this "adorable, little" LA Brea bakery/cafe also vending sandwiches and salads; an "enthusiastic" staff works the counter while the "relaxed" vibe at the tables makes it a natural for "meeting up with friends" over a cup of Joe.

Suzanne's Cuisine *French/Italian* — 25 | 24 | 24 | $51

Ojai | 502 W. Ojai Ave. (Bristol Ave.) | 805-640-1961 | www.suzannescuisine.com

Mother-and-daughter team Suzanne Roll and Sandra Moore are behind this midpriced Ojai eatery whipping up "wonderful" French/Italian fare from "the freshest ingredients", many harvested from the back garden; in spite of "occasionally slow" service, many say it "never disappoints" thanks to an "elegantly homey" setting graced with a "peaceful" outdoor seating area that's "magical" on a sunny day.

Sweet Lady Jane ◑ *Bakery* — 24 | 13 | 15 | $20

Melrose | 8360 Melrose Ave. (bet. Kings Rd. & Orlando Ave.) | 323-653-7145 | www.sweetladyjane.com

Groupies "give into [their] sweets cravings" at this European-style Melrose bakery noted for "fabulous" cakes and "practically tantric" pastries as well as solid lunchtime fare; "packed" digs, upper-end prices and "extremely nonchalant" service are among the downsides, even still, there's no shortage of fans and "it's always a madhouse"; P.S. a Santa Monica branch is reportedly in the works.

Swingers ◑ *Diner* — 17 | 16 | 17 | $19

Beverly Boulevard | Beverly Laurel Motor Hotel | 8020 Beverly Blvd. (Laurel Ave.) | 323-653-5858
Santa Monica | 802 Broadway (Lincoln Blvd.) | 310-393-9793
www.swingersdiner.com

When they've got the "munchies at 2 AM", "hipsters" head to these "cute" "retro-modern" diners in Santa Monica and on Beverly Boulevard where the "updated" "comfort-food" menu with a multitude of "veggie options" "hits the spot every time"; never mind the "tattooed" "attitude"-laden servers, it's open 24/7 and it's a "kick."

Taiko *Japanese* — 21 | 15 | 19 | $30

Brentwood | Brentwood Gdns. | 11677 San Vicente Blvd. (Barrington Ave.) | 310-207-7782 Ⓜ
El Segundo | 2041 Rosecrans Ave. (Sepulveda Blvd.) | 310-647-3100

"Steaming" bowls of noodles are the specialty at these "dependable" Japanese joints in Brentwood and El Segundo also doling out "decent" sushi and rice bowls in spare bamboo-accented settings; "value" pricing and ultra-"kid-friendly" service make them a "go-to" in their respective neighborhoods.

	FOOD	DECOR	SERVICE	COST

aix *French* — 17 | 18 | 22 | $31

cho Park | 1911 Sunset Blvd. (Glendale Blvd.) | 213-484-1265 |
ww.taixfrench.com

omewhere between a "golden oldie" and a "wrinkle room" sits this
hird-generation Echo Park "throwback" that's been serving "pass-
ble", "traditional" French fare complemented by crudités and soup
nce 1927; perhaps it's "not as good as it used to be", but the "quiet",
atmospheric" setting and "seasoned" staff still have their fans.

akami Sushi & Robata *Japanese* — ▽ 26 | 28 | 24 | $49

owntown | 811 Bldg. | 811 Wilshire Blvd., 21st fl. (bet. Figueroa &
ower Sts.) | 213-236-9600 | www.takamisushi.com

Unbeatable" "rooftop views" complete the "hip atmosphere" (with
he option of outdoor seating") at this Japanese aerie on the 21st
oor of a Downtown office building, which also wins wows with its
urprisingly amazing" sushi and robata grill dishes washed down with
n-point" drinks; no, it's "not for the faint-of-wallet", but given that
million-dollar" vista, the few surveyors who've weighed in urge "do try."

akao *Japanese* — 26 | 13 | 23 | $61

rentwood | 11656 San Vicente Blvd. (bet. Barrington & Darlington Aves.) |
10-207-8636

's an "unpretentious" "neighborhood" place, yet this "small"
rentwood Japanese impresses with its sushi and other fare, notably
hef-owner Takao Izumida's "outstanding omakase" deemed an "ad-
enture in dining"; it's expensive, and the decor may "leave much to be
esired", but to the majority it's a "delight" all the same.

ake a Bao *Asian* — 17 | 10 | 15 | $15

entury City | Westfield Century City Shopping Ctr. |
0250 Santa Monica Blvd. (bet. Ave. of the Stars & Century Park W.) |
10-551-1100 | www.takeabao.com

sandwichlike "twist on traditional bao" headlines the Pan-Asian menu
this "unique" "favorite" in the Westfield Century City that's consid-
ed a welcome "alternative" to the usual "food-court" fare; a few grum-
e about the "inauthenticity" of its salads, noodles and such, but most
aise it as an "interesting idea" delivering pleasingly "unusual flavors."

alésai *Thai* — 22 | 18 | 21 | $39

est Hollywood | 9043 Sunset Blvd. (Doheny Dr.) | 310-275-9724 |
ww.talesai.com

everly Hills | 9198 Olympic Blvd. (Palm Dr.) | 310-271-9345 |
ww.talesai.com

udio City | 11744 Ventura Blvd. (bet. Colfax Ave. & Laurel Canyon Blvd.) |
18-753-1001 🏶

Jpscale" and "inviting", this "terrific" trio turns out "Thailicious" rendi-
ons of classic noodles and curries; detractors say that the "small porons" are "not exactly great value", but "friendly" service and "arty"
ecor help make them "all-around" "favorites" anyway.

alia's *Italian* — ▽ 23 | 24 | 22 | $44

anhattan Beach | 1148 Manhattan Ave. (12th St.) | 310-545-6884 |
ww.taliasrestaurant.com

his upscale Manhattan Beach "gem" keeps locals loyal with its
houghtfully prepared" Italian fare and "outstanding" wine list; just

expect to "get to know your neighbors" because this "tiny" place ha
only 12 tables ("claustrophobes should use caution"), but "warm ser
vice" and a "romantic" atmosphere – courtesy of hand-blown light fix
tures and lots of dark wood – take the edge off.

Tamayo ⊠ *Mexican*

▽ 21 | 26 | 26 | $30

East LA | 5300 E. Olympic Blvd. (bet. Amalia & Hillview Aves.) | 323-260-470
A "best-kept secret in East LA", this refurbished 1928 hacienda display
paintings and tapestries by artist Rufino Tamayo in its high-ceilinge
space to provide a "delightful" backdrop for "rich", reasonably price
Mexican cooking; roomy enough for "group get-togethers", it's "a sur
prising find" that's worth the trek to this "industrial area."

Tam O'Shanter Inn *Scottish*

22 | 23 | 24 | $40

Atwater Village | 2980 Los Feliz Blvd. (Boyce Ave.) | 323-664-0228
www.lawrysonline.com
"Like Brigadoon", the Lawry's chain's "wee bit o' Scotland" in Atwate
Village is a "quaint" mockup of a Tudor "inn" that "transports" you t
"the old days" of its '20s origins, when Mary Pickford and other sta
were purportedly patrons; the "traditional fare" ("love the prime rib"
served by "cheerful" sorts in "tartan getups" is "plenty good enough" t
make "weekends and holidays feel like a crowded day at Disneyland

Tanino *Italian*

21 | 21 | 21 | $47

Westwood | 1043 Westwood Blvd. (bet. Kinross & Weyburn Aves.)
310-208-0444 | www.tanino.com
"Sophisticated but comforting", this "upmarket" "oasis in Westwoo
from chef-owner Tanino Drago is a "reliable" source of "first-rate
Southern Italian served in "warm", "elegant surroundings" by an "a
tentive" staff; it can be "pricey", but most maintain it's an "enjoyable
choice "before a play at the Geffen" or "a UCLA event."

Tantra *Indian*

- | - | - | M

Silver Lake | 3705 W. Sunset Blvd. (Edgecliffe Dr.) | 323-663-8268 |
www.tantrasunset.com
The "subterranean ambiance" and exotic decor lend some trend
karma to this Silver Lake Indian, overshadowing food that caters "t
American tastes" but can come off as "precious" and "overpriced fo
what you get"; still, given the lavish layout and "thumping" "beat fro
the adjoining" lounge, night owls own it's "a fun time."

Tanzore *Indian*

▽ 21 | 26 | 19 | $47

Beverly Hills | 50 N. La Cienega Blvd. (Wilshire Blvd.) | 310-652-3838
www.tanzore.com
"It's hard to top the decor" of this "glitzy" Beverly Hills Indian, wher
the "gorgeous room" is "a sight to see" and the "upscale" cuisine
"very good" if "a little pricey"; meanwhile foes who find it "preten
tious" fret the "food doesn't match" the "trendy vibe."

⊠ NEW Tar Pit ● *Eclectic*

20 | 27 | 23 | $52

La Brea | 609 N. La Brea Ave. (Melrose Ave.) | 323-965-1300 |
tarpitbar.squarespace.com
"One tar pit worth getting stuck in", this La Brea newcomer from che
co-owner Mark Peel (Campanile) channels a "glamorous" art dec
"supper club" where "dreamy" decor sets the stage for "inventive

ixology and an "excellent" Eclectic menu featuring faves from "years one by" like steak Diane and chicken à la king; with a "solicitous staff" nd a "noisy", "tons-of-fun" "bar scene", it's "deservedly" "a hit."

art *American* ▽ 18 | 14 | 20 | $26

airfax | Farmer's Daughter Hotel | 115 S. Fairfax Ave. (bet. Beverly Blvd. & rd St.) | 323-937-3930 | www.tartrestaurant.com

A reliable choice" for Southern-inflected grub, this "friendly" New merican occupies "quaint" quarters in the Farmer's Daughter Hotel hat extend to a "cute" patio; it's all-around "decent if you're in the area", hough morning people opine it works "best" for breakfast or lunch.

asca Winebar *Spanish* ▽ 24 | 21 | 23 | $46

hird Street | 8108 W. Third St. (Crescent Heights Blvd.) | 323-951-9890 | ww.tascawinebar.com

he "extremely knowledgeable" servers have an "uncanny" knack for airing an "awesome wine" selection with "outstanding" tapas – in-luding "not-to-be-missed" braised short ribs – at this "warm, invit-g" Spanish "gem" on Third Street; local loyalists boast they "really njoy" having "a winner" in the nabe.

aste *American* 21 | 19 | 21 | $35

Vest Hollywood | 8454 Melrose Ave. (La Cienega Blvd.) | 323-852-6888

aste at the Palisades Ⓜ *American*

acific Palisades | 538 Palisades Dr. (Sunset Blvd.) | 310-459-9808 ww.ilovetaste.com

Taste-y!" purr partisans of the "comforting", "slightly upscale" cook-g at this "casual" WeHo New American and its sib, acclaimed as a neighborhood find" in Pacific Palisades; it's a "fairly simple" formula, ut with "decent prices", "no-attitude" service and "alfresco dining ith the pretty crowd" at the Melrose locale, they're plenty "popular."

aste Chicago *Italian* ▽ 19 | 8 | 15 | $16

urbank | 603 N. Hollywood Way (Verdugo Ave.) | 818-563-2800 | ww.tastechicago.biz

carf "an authentic Chicago dog", beef sandwich or deep-dish pizza at is Burbank Italian nook co-owned by actor Joe Mantegna, "a good ttempt" to bring wistful Windy City-ites "the tastes they love"; quib-ers claim it "doesn't quite get it", but overall the results "ain't bad" ven if the "simple" counter-service setup encourages carryout.

asting Kitchen, The *Mediterranean* 22 | 21 | 20 | $51

enice | 1633 Abbot Kinney Blvd. (Venice Blvd.) | 310-392-6644 | ww.thetastingkitchen.com

These guys really care" say supporters of this recent "addition to the enice scene", where a "marvelous", ever-"changing" Med menu that elies on local ingredients" is backed up with "clever" cocktails and erved with enthusiasm"; the candlelit room gets "a bit loud" and the ll can "add up", but locals sense "it's too good not to catch on" even they wish it "would stay a secret."

Tavern *American* 23 | 25 | 21 | $53

entwood | 11648 San Vicente Blvd. (Darlington Ave.) | 310-806-6464 | ww.tavernla.com

hef/co-owner and "queen of all things local" Suzanne Goin (A.O.C., cques) brings her "Midas touch" to this Brentwood New American, a former Hamburger Hamlet "revamped" into a "stunning" bistro wit a "sunny" atrium room, where a "professional" team serves a "sump tuous", "market-fresh" menu; despite gripes over "spendy" tabs an occasional "attitude", it's a "blessing" for the "bustling crowds", espe cially when factoring in The Larder, a "casual" all-day cafe up front.

Taverna Tony *Greek* 21 | 20 | 20 | $41

Malibu | Malibu Country Mart | 23410 Civic Center Way (Cross Creek Rd.) | 310-317-9667 | www.tavernatony.com

"For a celebratory night", this "lively" Malibu "favorite" supplies "ger erous" portions of "solid" Greek fare and a high-"energy" "scene known for a random "glitterati" turnout; "you'll pay for it" and "don expect to hear" "over the racket" (especially when "wild and craz belly dancers" perform on weekends), but there's a "glorious" pati and "Tony's always there" to keep everyone "happy."

Taylor's Steak House *Steak* 21 | 19 | 21 | $40

Koreatown | 3361 W. Eighth St. (Ardmore Ave.) | 213-382-8449
La Cañada Flintridge | 901 Foothill Blvd. (Beulah Dr.) | 818-790-766 www.taylorssteakhouse.com

"Old school" "all the way", this "real steakhouse" twosome plies "pe fectly prepared" cuts and "killer martinis" with "no pretense" at "tougl to-beat" prices; the Koreatown original feels like a "piece of LA his tory" with its "red Naugahyde" booths while the La Cañada Flintridg outpost is newer, but at either "you kinda expect Sinatra to drop in."

Tender Greens *American* 22 | 14 | 17 | $17

NEW **Hollywood** | 6290 Sunset Blvd. (Vine St.) | 323-382-0380
West Hollywood | 8759 Santa Monica Blvd. (Hancock Ave.) | 310-358-191
Culver City | 9523 Culver Blvd. (Cardiff Ave.) | 310-842-8300 www.tendergreensfood.com

A "salad lover's fantasy", this New American mini-chain has a "sur fire" "genius concept": "delicious" "local produce" "fresh from th farm" and "healthful" carnivorous options tossed "to order" as yc "slide" by with your cafeteria tray; they draw "mad crowds", but th line "moves fast" and prices are so "outrageously reasonable" tha vegheads "on the go" "could eat here every day."

Tengu *Japanese* 21 | 19 | 19 | $44

Westwood | 10853 Lindbrook Dr. (Tiverton Ave.) | 310-209-0071 | www.tengu.com

"Sushi and fusion" "tantalize the tongue" at this "trendy" Westwoc Japanese, a "sophisticated" spot for "creative but not crazy" food (ii cluding "interesting" specialty rolls) delivered by an "attentive" staf "mood lighting", "flavored sakes" and a "house DJ" stoke th "loungey" vibe, and while critics cry "overpriced", most are gratef for a "hip" hangout near UCLA.

Terra ☑ *Californian* 22 | 23 | 23 | $48

Malibu | 21337 PCH (Las Flores Canyon Rd.) | 310-456-1221 | www.terramalibu.net

New chef-owner David Price adds his own "savory twists" to the "e cellent" Cal cuisine at this Malibu "sleeper", a "civilized" "gem" fc "well-thought-out" seasonal fare and "wonderful" service in a "bea tiful" Spanish-style setting with a "cozy" fireplace and tiled pati

	FOOD	DECOR	SERVICE	COST

rices reflect the "upscale" atmo, but it's "a solid choice" for "special ccasions" or wooing "a significant other."

erroni *Italian*   22 19 17 $36

everly Boulevard | 7605 Beverly Blvd. (Curson Ave.) | 323-954-0300 | ww.terroni.ca

"Phenomenal" "fresh" pastas and thin-crust pizzas keep this Beverly oulevard satellite of a Toronto-based Southern Italian chainlet "buzz-g" with "loud" "young" things; you "don't go here expecting special reatment" (many protest the "heads-will-roll" "no-substitutions pol-y"), but the bona fide eats ensure it's typically "packed."

eru Sushi *Japanese*   22 18 21 $40

tudio City | 11940 Ventura Blvd. (bet. Carpenter & Radford Aves.) | 18-763-6201 | www.terusushi.com

fter 30-plus years, this pioneering Studio City Japanese remains "re-able" for "fine sushi" from "helpful" staffers who "treat their regu-rs" (including "a lot of industry types") "like family"; some say ere's "not as much wow" these days, but with a "pleasant", garden-quipped setting and "decent prices", it's "well worth" a visit.

hai Dishes *Thai*   17 12 17 $20

Malibu | 22333 PCH (bet. Carbon Canyon & Cross Creek Rds.) | 10-456-6592

anta Monica | 111 Santa Monica Blvd. (bet. Ocean Ave. & 2nd St.) | 10-394-6189

anta Monica | 1910 Wilshire Blvd. (19th St.) | 310-828-5634

glewood | 11934 Aviation Blvd. (119th Pl.) | 310-643-6199 🖂

AX | 6234 W. Manchester Ave. (bet. Sepulveda Blvd. & Truxton Ave.) | 10-342-0046

Manhattan Beach | 1015 N. Sepulveda Blvd. (bet. 10th & 11th Sts.) | 10-546-4147

asadena | 239 E. Colorado Blvd. (bet. Garfield & Marengo Aves.) | 26-304-9975 | www.mythaidishes.com

alencia | 23328 Valencia Blvd. (bet. Bouquet Canyon Rd. & Cinema Dr.) | 61-253-3663 | www.thaidishescv.com

's "not cutting edge, but who cares?" shrug followers of this Thai hain, which dishes up "tasty" if "basic" fare at "wallet-friendly" rices; the atmosphere's "generic" at best, but they're "consistent" for "quick work lunch" and "a favorite for delivery."

hird & Olive 🖂 Ⓜ *Californian/French*   ▽ 23 22 21 $39

urbank | 250 E. Olive Ave. (3rd St.) | 818-846-3900 | ww.thirdandolive.com

urbank gets "fancy" at this "upscale venture" from "personable chef-wner" Miki Zivkovic (of "sister restaurant Bistro Provence"), where comfortably dressy decor" sets the scene for "wonderful" Cal-French boking and "attentive service"; hagglers debate the cost ("rather af-ordable" vs. "pricey"), but for the majority it's "enjoyable" enough to become a habit."

Square Cafe + Bakery *Bakery/Sandwiches*   23 17 19 $24

enice | 1121 Abbot Kinney Blvd. (bet. San Juan & Westminster Aves.) | 10-399-6504 | www.rockenwagner.com

While it's "fabulous" for all "three meals", breakfast "really rocks" at his inexpensive "German-inspired" sandwich shop in Venice, where

celebrity-chef Hans Röckenwagner "works his magic" with "outstand
ing" pastries and his "unique" pretzel bread used in "dreamy" burger
at lunchtime; those who "wait in line" to get in find "prompt service
and a "simple" "sunlight-filled" space, but if you're really in a hurry
stop at his bakery next door.

Tiara Cafe *American*   ∇ 23 | 19 | 19 | $30

Downtown | 127 E. Ninth St. (Main St.) | 213-623-3663 |
www.tiara-cafe-la.com

As expected from chef-owner Fred Eric (Fred 62), the menu's as "cre
ative" as the decor at this "unpretentious" Downtowner, an expansive
pastel-hued cafe where the "fresh and flavorful" New American lineu
highlights vegetarian/vegan options; with "accommodating" servic
from an "offbeat" staff, it's "a rare treat in this part of town", just kno
that it closes at 3 PM daily.

NEW Tiato Market Garden Café *Asian*   - | - | - | I

Santa Monica | MTV/Lionsgate | 2700 Colorado Blvd. (Princeton St.)
310-866-5228 | www.tiato.com

The An family (Crustacean) departs from its usual upscale take o
Vietnamese cooking for this casual indoor-outdoor cafe and market i
Santa Monica, where the budget-friendly Pan-Asian menu include
fare like curried kabocha bisque and snapper ceviche salad; there ar
private dining rooms in which honchos can meet and eat, and a mas
sive patio that also sports an herb garden.

Tibet Nepal House M *Nepalese/Tibetan*   ∇ 17 | 15 | 17 | $21

Pasadena | 36 E. Holly St. (Fair Oaks Ave.) | 626-585-0955 |
www.tibetnepalhouse.com

About "the only show in town" for a Nepalese-Tibetan nosh, thi
Pasadena storefront supplies "interesting", "flavorful" fare featur
ing the occasional "oddity" à la "yak meat" or butter tea; it's "no
too fancy" and service is only "adequate", but with "serene" atmo
spherics and a lunch buffet deal, devotees declare they'd "clim
Everest to eat here."

Tierra Sur at
Herzog Wine Cellars *Mediterranean*   ∇ 27 | 20 | 25 | $55

Oxnard | Herzog Wine Cellars | 3201 Camino Del Sol (Del Norte) |
805-983-1560 | www.herzogwinecellars.com

Yes, "fine dining can be kosher", as shown by chef Todd Aaron
(Zuni Cafe in SF) and his "amazing", dairy-free Med cuisine at thi
"upscale" outpost within the Herzog winery; it may seem "out of plac
in industrial Oxnard", but the sunny setting, "delightful" vinos an
"helpful" staff come as a "very pleasant surprise"; N.B. closed Frida
night and Saturday.

NEW Tiger Sushi *Japanese*   - | - | - | M

Beverly Hills | 340 N. Cañon Dr. (Brighton Way) | 310-274-3200 |
www.tigerbh.com

Sushiphiles are "impressed" as this Beverly Hills newcomer earns it
stripes with a "fantastic" array of "delicious" fish and other moder
Japanese fare, matched with a "beautiful", beige-toned space; "ser
vice is perfection", and sidewalk tables make for relaxed lunchin
among Golden Triangle shoppers.

	FOOD	DECOR	SERVICE	COST

in Roof Bistro *American* — 21 | 19 | 20 | $33

anhattan Beach | Manhattan Vill. | 3500 N. Sepulveda Blvd.
Rosecrans Ave.) | 310-939-0900 | www.tinroofbistro.com

"terrific addition" to Manhattan Beach from the family behind
mmzy's and The Lazy Dog Cafe, this "new favorite" "hits every note"
ith chef Anne Conness' "unique" "wood-fired pizzas" and "creative
vists" on New American classics, paired with "meticulously" chosen
ines; the "comfortable" interior with a porchside bocce court and
opping" bar is "always crowded" and "needs some sound dampers",
it a "wonderful" patio awaits out back.

into ⧉ *Spanish* — - | - | - | I

West Hollywood | 7511 Santa Monica Blvd. (Gardner St.) | 323-512-3095 |
ww.tintotapas.com

ke a virtual "trip to España" at this "busy" West Hollywood tapas
en, where "wonderful" expat owners oversee a "hip" milieu for
utstanding" Spanish small plates, paella and sangria; the rustic,
andelier-lit digs are "a diamond in the rough", and "specials at the
ar" add to the "real-deal" appeal.

lapazola Grill *Mexican* — 22 | 15 | 22 | $30

enice | 636 Venice Blvd. (Abbot Kinney Blvd.) | 310-822-7561 |
ww.tlapazolagrill.com
West LA | 11676 Gateway Blvd. (Barrington Ave.) | 310-477-1577 |
ww.tlapazola.com

Renowned as a cut above", this separately owned duo "dependably"
npresses with "refined" takes on "regional Oaxacan" specialties
velvety moles" included) at both the "unassuming" West LA original
nd its newly relocated, more "upscale" Venice adjunct; with
riendly" atmospherics aided by a "superb tequila selection", they're
n "unexpected" "must."

oast *American* — 20 | 14 | 18 | $22

hird Street | 8221 W. Third St. (bet. Harper & La Jolla Aves.) |
23-655-5018 | www.toastbakerycafe.net

ggs + tons of aspiring actresses" equals a total "scene" at this Third
reet "favorite", where "script"-toting types endure daytime "lines"
 long "you'd think they sprinkled crack on" the "huge selection" of
merican "griddle fare"; fans still find it "worth the chaos" to watch
amous people being famous", though it's "much more laid back and
ccessible for dinner."

Tofu-Ya *Korean* — 23 | 9 | 16 | $17

West LA | 2021 Sawtelle Blvd. (La Grange Ave.) | 310-473-2627

Volcanic tofu soups" ("heaven in a bowl"), "terrific" BBQ and "good
alue" mean "there's always a line" at this West LA "hole-in-the-wall",
hich "warms your belly" with "generous portions" of "authentic
orean" eats; admittedly, amenities are limited to "a bare table and
aper napkin", so expect to "eat and go."

okyo Table *Japanese* — ▽ 18 | 21 | 20 | $32

rcadia | Westfield Mall | 400 S. Baldwin Ave. (Huntington Dr.) |
26-445-4000 | www.tokyotable.com

's "not traditional Japanese", but fusion fanciers tout the "inventive"
ariety of Sino- and Western-influenced offerings at this mall-based

	FOOD	DECOR	SERVICE	COST

Arcadia entry; foes find it a "bit overpriced", but the "hip-looking" surroundings are suitable "for a date" or "gatherings" built around sampling "small bites" and a primo sake selection.

Tom Bergin's *Pub Food*

	13	22	20	$23

Fairfax | 840 S. Fairfax Ave. (bet. Olympic & Wilshire Blvds.) | 323-936-7151 | www.tombergins.com

"It's St. Paddy's Day all year long" at this "super-old-school" Fairfax pub (circa 1936), which is frequently "filled with locals" downing pints and "typical" Irish-American saloon grub; the "small space" can get "insanely loud and crowded", but the bartenders keep it "real" and they sure "pour a good Guinness."

🅉 Tommy's ●🍴 *Burgers/Hot Dogs*

	23	7	16	$9

Downtown | 2575 W. Beverly Blvd. (bet. Coronado St. & Rampart Blvd.) | 213-389-9060 | www.originaltommys.com

"Greasy, messy" burgers and hot dogs "dripping with chili" make the 1946-vintage Downtown "shack" "an LA institution" for "chowing down" at "stand-up" counters with "lots of napkins" at hand; you'll have "orange fingers for a week" and it's not great "for your midriff", but "heartburn be damned", this is fast food as it is "meant to be" – and "it's always open."

Tony P's Dockside Grill *American*

	17	19	19	$31

Marina del Rey | 4445 Admiralty Way (Bali Way) | 310-823-4534 | www.tonyps.com

"Sit on the patio deck" looking out over the yachts at this "on-the-water" "standby" in Marina del Rey, where an "extensive menu" of "solid" if "ordinary" Americana is served "with a smile"; for local sports junkies, "numerous giant screens" make the inside bar a popular spot to "meet for apps and drinks" "and watch the Lakers."

Tony's Bella Vista *Italian*

	▽ 15	13	15	$24

Burbank | 3116 W. Magnolia Blvd. (Fairview St.) | 818-843-0164 | www.tonysbellavista.com

"Be prepared for a serious garlic hangover" at this "cheap, old-fashioned" "neighborhood Italian" in Burbank, which is "like going back" to the "'60s" for pasta and "particularly good" pizza; those with a taste for "red leatherette booths and a healthy dose of kitsch" have "found their perfect match."

Torafuku *Japanese*

	23	19	21	$42

West LA | 10914 W. Pico Blvd. (Westwood Blvd.) | 310-470-0014 | www.torafuku-usa.com

In the eyes of "the knowledgeable aficionado", this West LA branch of a Tokyo-based franchise sets itself apart with "excellent cooked" dishes, "fresh tofu" and sushi accompanied by "exceptional" rice prepared in genuine kamado pots; the "mellow", minimalist room and "very good service" are "alluring", as are the "great lunch deals."

Toscana *Italian*

	24	18	22	$59

Brentwood | 11633 San Vicente Blvd. (Darlington Ave.) | 310-820-2448 | www.toscanabrentwood.com

"Movie directors, actors, the Governator" and bevies of Brentwoodites flock to this "tiny" Tuscan trattoria for "scrumptious" pastas and other "right-on" renditions of Northern Italian specialties; seating is "tight" the prices are "outrageous" and service ranges from "over the top" to "aloof" "unless you're Tom Cruise", but face it, "this place would be busy in the middle of an earthquake."

Toscanova *Italian*

| 20 | 19 | 20 | $39 |

Century City | Westfield Century City Shopping Ctr. | 10250 Santa Monica Blvd. (bet. Ave. of the Stars & Century Park W.) | 310-551-0499 | www.toscanova.com

When "you're hungry from shopping", wood-fired pizza and other "well-prepared Italian dishes" are served in "style" at this "newish" venture in the Westfield Century City mall from Agostino Sciandri (Ago); it's "noisy" when "crowded" and the tabs can get "pricey", but the "pretty space" lit by Murano lamps is proving "popular" so far.

Tower Bar *Californian*

| ∇ 21 | 27 | 25 | $69 |

West Hollywood | Sunset Tower Hotel | 8358 W. Sunset Blvd. (bet. La Cienega Blvd. & Sweetzer Ave.) | 323-848-6677 | www.sunsettowerhotel.com

"If California had kings", they'd hold court in WeHo at the Sunset Tower Hotel's "beautifully designed" restaurant, where a "hot-looking", "celeb"-heavy crowd enjoys "classy service" and a "dynamite" Cal menu in "old-school glamorous" digs with "amazing" city views; overseen by "excellent host" Dimitri Dimitrov, it's worth the premium price even if the eating's "not quite up to the decor."

NEW Townhouse ● *Californian*

| ∇ 12 | 15 | 14 | $29 |

Sherman Oaks | Sherman Oaks Galleria | 15301 Ventura Blvd. (Sepulveda Blvd.) | 818-453-9900 | www.restaurants-america.com

Ok, it's "not destination dining", but this newcomer to the Sherman Oaks Galleria (via a Chicago original) sates mall-walkers with "fair" Californian chow in a "chain" setting; critics dis the "bland" eats and "distracted" service, but as it "lacks the lines" of its neighbors, movie-goers in need of a "hangout" "hope for improvement."

NEW Trader Vic's *Polynesian*

| 17 | 20 | 18 | $46 |

Downtown | LA Live | 800 W. Olympic Blvd. (Figueroa St.) | 213-785-3330 | www.tradervicsla.com

Trader Vic's Lounge *Polynesian*

Beverly Hills | Beverly Hilton | 9876 Wilshire Blvd. (Santa Monica Blvd.) | 310-285-1300 | www.tradervics.com

Mixing "killer" "exotic cocktails" to wash down its Polynesian platters, LA Live's Downtown reincarnation of this legendary "staple of tiki culture" trades on the rep of its predecessor in Beverly Hills; for some the "Disneyland" ambiance and "so-so food" are "disappointing" ("especially for the cost"), but it's still a "totally tacky" "tropical paradise" and "that's the fun."

Tra Di Noi *Italian*

| 22 | 19 | 20 | $46 |

Malibu | Malibu Country Mart | 3835 Cross Creek Rd. (bet. Civic Ctr. Way & PCH) | 310-456-0169 | www.tradinoimalibu.com

The "wonderful" patio "is a must" at this "welcoming" Italian in the Malibu Country Mart, where an "affluent" "local" contingent with a high "celeb" quotient "flocks year-round" for "delicious" pastas, fish and meat "served with élan"; although "a bit pricey", for a "low-key" bite with a side of "stargazing" it's a "best bet" in the 'Bu.

	FOOD	DECOR	SERVICE	COST

Trails, The ☑ ✈ *American/Vegan*
| - | - | - | I |

Los Feliz | Griffith Park | 2333 Fern Dell Dr. (Los Feliz Blvd.) | 323-871-2102
"Reward yourself" "after a hike" at this American food stand in Griffith Park, where the sandwiches and snacks – including "healthy" vegan options – "seriously surpass the normal park" provisions; with open-air "picnic" tables and surroundings "straight out of Oregon", Los Feliz's outdoorsy sorts consider it their "little secret."

Trastevere *Italian*
| 19 | 16 | 17 | $34 |

Hollywood | Hollywood & Highland Ctr. | 6801 Hollywood Blvd. (Highland Ave.) | 323-962-3261
Santa Monica | 1360 Third St. Promenade (Santa Monica Blvd.) | 310-319-1985
www.trastevereristorante.com
Given their "shopping-center" locales in Hollywood and Santa Monica, these midpriced sibs deliver "unexpectedly good" ("if unspectacular") renditions of Italian basics "for a quick bite"; inside they can feel "cavernous", but "pleasant" outdoor seating makes for "plenty of people-watching" "on a sunny day."

Traxx ☒ *American*
| 19 | 21 | 20 | $43 |

Downtown | Union Station | 800 N. Alameda St. (bet. Cesar Chavez Ave. & Rte. 101) | 213-625-1999 | www.traxxrestaurant.com
Nostalgists are "on the right track" at this "lovely" art deco eatery that hearkens to Downtown's "glory days" with a "fabulous" indoor/outdoor location within Union Station; the New American cuisine is "satisfying" and the staff "treats you well", and while a few rail the "limited menu" "doesn't live up to its potential", it's always a "wonderful place for meeting."

Tre Venezie ☒ ☑ *Italian*
| 22 | 19 | 19 | $63 |

Pasadena | 119 W. Green St. (De Lacey Ave.) | 626-795-4455
"Don't expect your ordinary" Italian at this "cozy" Pasadena "gem" which "captures the true flavors" of Northern regional cooking with "outstanding" cuisine that's both "dependable" and "adventurous"; skeptics cite "standoffish" service and "expensive" tabs, but it remains an "unusual" "treat" with a "quiet", "date"-worthy vibe.

Trio Mediterranean Grill *Mediterranean*
| ▽ 17 | 13 | 19 | $29 |

Rolling Hills Estates | Peninsula Ctr. | 46B Peninsula Ctr. (Silver Spur Blvd.) | Rolling Hills | 310-265-5577 | www.triogrill.com
"Dependable" fare "for a mall" "draws locals in" at this "small" Med outfit in Rolling Hills Estates, a convenient option during shopping jaunts or "before the movies"; granted, it's "ordinary in all respects", but given the varied menu and "friendly service", regulars in the nabe "keep going back."

Tropicalia Brazilian Grill ● *Brazilian*
| ▽ 22 | 15 | 21 | $22 |

Los Feliz | 1966 Hillhurst Ave. (Franklin Ave.) | 323-644-1798 | www.tropicaliabraziliangrill.com
"Your taste buds will be dancing a samba" over the "ginormous" platters of "hearty Brazilian fare" at this "wonderful neighborhood" "sleeper" in Los Feliz; a "simple" setup with an "attached wine bar", it offers "charming" service, "modest prices" and a house sangria that'll "knock you out" – and "who doesn't love that?"

	FOOD	DECOR	SERVICE	COST

ruxton's American
21 | 16 | 20 | $25

Jestchester | 8611 Truxton Ave. (Manchester Ave.) | 310-417-8789 | ww.truxtonsamericanbistro.com

Westchester "favorite", this "busy" "neighborhood grill" caters to "amilies" and the "LAX" bound with a seemingly "endless" variety of well-prepared", "nothing-fancy" Americana calculated to "please all alates"; with "casually" "upbeat" environs and an "accommodating" :aff, it's a "popular" fallback for those "let's-not-cook-at-home" nights.

suji No Hana Japanese
▽ 24 | 15 | 23 | $36

Iarina del Rey | 4714 Lincoln Blvd. (Mindanao Way) | 310-827-1433

Tucked into a strip mall" in Marina del Rey, this "sweet little" Japanese akes pride" in "quality sushi" of the "traditional" variety delivered by "super" staff; "very reasonable prices" compensate for a plain set-ng, so supporters just "say yes" when they're "in the area."

uk Tuk Thai Thai
21 | 18 | 19 | $24

ico-Robertson | 8875 W. Pico Blvd. (bet. Doheny Dr. & Robertson Blvd.) | 10-860-1872 | www.tuktukla.com

Neighborhood" loyalists gather at this Pico-Robertson Thai to tuk into a winning" lineup of "well-priced" faves that includes "healthy options" olenty; the setup's snug but "attractive", a "helpful" staff fosters a riendly" vibe and soju cocktails and sake "complete the meal."

ulipano Ⓜ Italian
- | - | - | M

zusa | 530 S. Citrus Ave. (Gladstone St.) | 626-967-6670 | ww.tulipanos.com

f you want real Italian", this Azusa eatery dishes up "hearty" fare (ask bout the specials) in simple digs enlivened by a nightly guitarist; the co-wner brothers and their crew make "wonderful hosts", and those ho go "more than once" are treated "as though they're family."

urquoise Ⓜ Mediterranean/Persian
- | - | - | I

edondo Beach | 1735 S. Catalina Ave. (Vista Del Mar) | 310-373-3234 | ww.turquoise-restaurant.com

Mediterranean with a decidedly Persian touch" and "mostly organic gredients" yields an "interesting", kebab-centered menu at this edondo Beacher, run by a chef-owner who "takes a personal interest" "customer satisfaction"; the smart setup comprises a serene, blue-ued room and sidewalk tables under twinkling lights.

I Tuscany Il Ristorante Italian
26 | 22 | 25 | $50

Jestlake Village | Westlake Plaza | 968 S. Westlake Blvd. (bet. Agoura & ownsgate Rds.) | 805-495-2768 | www.tuscany-restaurant.com

Always a treat", this fixture for "fine dining in Westlake Village" is omething "special" with "wonderful" "traditional" Italian cuisine roffered by "servers who know their stuff" in "warm" environs with ne "romantic" feel "of a Tuscan villa"; even though the bills run "high", 's a "solid" "favorite in the area": *buon appetito!*

utti Mangia Italian Grill Italian
▽ 23 | 20 | 22 | $47

laremont | 102 Harvard Ave. (1st St.) | 909-625-4669 | ww.tuttimangia.com

As good as it gets" for "upscale Italian" in Claremont, this "ambitious" winner" pleases with "delicious" regional dishes, an impressive wine list

and "top-notch" service in a "refined" bi-level space; to trim back th
tab, bargain-hunters "recommend" the weekday "lunch specials."

25 Degrees ● *Burgers* | 22 | 18 | 16 | $25

Hollywood | Roosevelt Hotel | 7000 Hollywood Blvd. (Orange Dr.) |
323-785-7244 | www.25degreesrestaurant.com

Its "Guinness milkshake is proof-positive there is a God" for some, b
for most it's all about the "decadent" "design-your-own" burgers an
seemingly "endless" "gourmet" toppings at this late-night eater
(open till 1:30 AM) tricked out with "fiery bordello wallpaper" an
black leather in Hollywood's "historic" Roosevelt Hotel; downsides i
clude a "hipper-than-thou" staff and relatively "expensive tabs."

2117 Ⓜ *Asian/European* | 24 | 15 | 22 | $38

West LA | 2117 Sawtelle Blvd. (bet. Mississippi Ave. & Olympic Blvd.)
310-477-1617 | www.restaurant2117.com

Super-"fresh", "high-quality" fusion is the forte of this Euro-Asian "favo
ite" in West LA from chef-owner Hideyo Mitsuno, who "rocks" the men
with "originality" in his small plates and entrees; given the "polite se
vice" and "low prices", fans overlook the "minimalist setting" calling
"one of LA's undiscovered gems"; P.S. 2117 Coffee Café is next door.

22nd St. Landing Ⓜ *Seafood* | 17 | 18 | 18 | $31

San Pedro | 141 W. 22nd St. (Harbor Blvd.) | 310-548-4400 |
www.22ndstlandingrestaurant.com

This San Pedro seafooder does swimmingly thanks to "showstopping
views of Cabrillo Marina's commercial fishing boats and "sea lion
playing a few feet away" plus a dining room sporting a nautical theme
though finicky types cite "bland" dishes and service that "varie
wildly", the midpriced fin fare is "consistently fresh" and Sunda
brunch is a winner, especially "on the patio when it's warm."

26 Beach *Californian* | 21 | 19 | 20 | $27

Venice | 3100 Washington Blvd. (Lincoln Blvd.) | 310-823-7526 |
www.26beach.com

"Go hungry" to this "quirky" Venice Californian known for its "enor
mous menu" of "unique burgers", "abundant" salads and "other sim
ple chow" at "fair prices"; the "lovely" patio (with a retractable roo
is "popular" for "baby showers" and "Sunday brunch", while "comfor
able, shabby-chic decor" adds to the "laid-back beach charm", as d
"friendly", if sometimes "slow-as-molasses" servers.

Two Boots ● *Pizza* | ▽ 20 | 10 | 13 | $12

Echo Park | 1818 W. Sunset Blvd. (Lemoyne St.) | 213-268-2668 |
www.twoboots.com

"Where else can you find pizza with crawfish and BBQ shrimp" but th
offbeat Echo Park outpost of a NYC chain where supporters swear th
"wacky toppings" "actually work", even if "traditionalists" find them
selves yearning for a more "simple" slice; although East Coast "snarky
service is a drawback, the patio seating redeems it for many.

208 Rodeo *American* | ▽ 23 | 24 | 24 | $48

Beverly Hills | Two Rodeo | 208 Via Rodeo Dr. (Wilshire Blvd) |
310-275-2428 | www.208rodeo.com

The "see-and-be-seen" "shopping crowd" sits on the "picture
perfect" patio to best enjoy pricey "fresh" New American cuisin

	FOOD	DECOR	SERVICE	COST

...at's set down by the "superb staff" at this "crowded", flower-filled everly Hills spot; an extensive list of wines by the glass fuels the cene at this "convenient stop that's better than expected."

Typhoon *Asian*
19 | 19 | 18 | $40

Santa Monica | Santa Monica Airport | 3221 Donald Douglas Loop S. (Airport Ave.) | 310-390-6565 | www.typhoon.biz

"Watch the planes land as you eat" at this "unique" destination parked "along the runway" of the Santa Monica airport presenting a "mish-mash" of Pan-Asian specialties starring exotica like stir-fried crickets; a steady stream of locals and "out-of-towners" plus live jazz keep it "noisy" and "chaotic" most nights, though a few can't shake the feeling that it's "slid a bit" over the years.

Ugo an Italian Cafe *Italian*
17 | 16 | 19 | $28

Culver City | 3865 Cardiff Ave. (Culver Blvd.) | 310-204-1222 | www.cafeugo.com

Culver citizens soak in the "Euro vibe" at this "thriving" "indoor-outdoor" eatery dishing up "basic Italian" cooking that's "reasonably priced", if not especially "memorable"; service can be "slow", but the plethora of wines by the glass and scoops of "gelato in a zillion flavors" help make a "warm summer night" on the patio "feel like Italy"; P.S. a new outpost is coming to Santa Monica Place.

Ulysses Voyage *Greek*
20 | 18 | 19 | $30

Fairfax | Farmers Mkt. | 6333 W. Third St. (Fairfax Ave.) | 323-939-9728 | www.ulyssesvoyage.com

A "dependable" bet in the Farmers Market, this "pleasant", midpriced taverna trades in Hellenic standards like moussaka and leg of lamb; live "bouzouki" creates a "warm" atmosphere inside, though most prefer to "score a patio table", "linger over coffee" and take in some primo "people-watching."

Umami Burger *Burgers*
22 | 13 | 16 | $19

NEW **Hollywood** | 1520 N. Cahuenga Blvd. (bet. Selma Ave. & Sunset Blvd.) | 323-469-3100
Hollywood | 4655 Hollywood Blvd. (N. Vermont Ave.) | 323-669-3922
Mid-City | 850 S. La Brea Ave. (bet. 8th & 9th Sts.) | 323-931-3000
NEW **Santa Monica** | Fred Segal | 500 Broadway (5th St.) |
310-451-1300
www.umamiburger.com

Even if you're "still not sure what the fifth taste is", the consensus is the "deeply flavorful" patties are "*u-mazing*" at this "gourmet" burger chainlet also dispensing "heavenly" tempura onion rings with craft beers, wine and cocktails in "casual, typically LA sceney" digs; downsides include "double-digit" pricing ("they should call it Umami Burgerlary"), somewhat "skimpy" portions and "lackadaisical" service, although on the whole, it ultimately "gets it right"; N.B. Mid-City doesn't serve alcohol.

Uncle Bill's Pancake House *Diner*
22 | 14 | 20 | $16

Manhattan Beach | 1305 Highland Ave. (13th St.) | 310-545-5177 | www.unclebillspancakehouse.net

They "know a thing or two about breakfast" at this "beach-chic" cafe, a South Bay "institution" for the kind of "tasty", "old-fashioned" diner

fare – like "stacks of pancakes" and bacon-cheddar waffles – yo
"shouldn't tell your cardiologist" about; "ocean views" from the patio ar
a "friendly" vibe all around help make the "ridiculous waits" "worth it

Uncle Darrow's *Cajun/Creole*
19 | 8 | 19 | $17

Marina del Rey | 2560 S. Lincoln Blvd. (Washington Blvd.) | 310-306-4862
www.uncledarrows.com

It's easy to "eat too much" at this bit of "Louisiana" in Marina del Re
slinging "semi-authentic" Cajun-Creole "roadhouse" grub like jamba
laya and po' boys (but no beef or pork); it's a "substance over style
kind of place with "plain-Jane" digs, a "warm" staff and equall
down-home pricing.

NEW Upper West ●☒ *American*
- | - | - | M

Santa Monica | 3321 W. Pico Blvd. (33rd St.) | 310-586-1111 |
www.theupperwest.com

This Santa Monica entry feeds the hungry hipoisie with midprice
New American fare such as upscale mac 'n' cheese, a down-home tur
key sloppy joe and fries flavored with blue cheese or chipotle; th
barnlike, freeway exit-adjacent space, which has housed a multitud
of restaurants over the years, sports cozy booths.

Upstairs 2 ☒Ⓜ *Mediterranean*
23 | 18 | 23 | $46

West LA | Wine House | 2311 Cotner Ave. (bet. Olympic & Pico Blvds.)
310-231-0316 | www.upstairs2.com

"Hidden" above a "tremendous wine store" in West LA, this "fantastic
little" bar/restaurant is the place to "sample" "terrific" Med-inflecte
tapas "thoughtfully" paired with "numerous" "interesting" vinos "b
the bottle, glass or taste"; whether it's "intimate" or just plai
"cramped" is up for debate, but most agree it's quite a "find", even
all that nibbling can "get expensive."

☑ Urasawa ☒Ⓜ *Japanese*
27 | 22 | 26 | $455

Beverly Hills | 218 N. Rodeo Dr. (Wilshire Blvd.) | 310-247-8939

A "bucket list restaurant" if ever there was one, this omakase-only
Beverly Hills Japanese showcases a "magnificent" "all-night culinary
adventure" of "decadent" "handcrafted" courses from "master" che
Hiro Urasawa; it follows through with "exceptional" service and a
"minimalist" flower-accented space, although the price tag – $350 pe
person excluding drinks and tip – is "not for the faint of heart."

Urth Caffé *American*
21 | 15 | 16 | $20

Downtown | 451 S. Hewitt St. (5th St.) | 213-797-4534
West Hollywood | 8565 Melrose Ave. (bet. Westbourne & Westmount Drs.)
310-659-0628
Beverly Hills | 267 S. Beverly Dr. (Gregory Way) | 310-205-9311 ●
Santa Monica | 2327 Main St. (Hollister Ave.) | 310-314-7040
www.urthcaffe.com

In a city "where even the hype is hyped", these perpetually "mobbed"
"organic"-leaning cafes fit right in with "agents", "stars" and assorted
"gorgeous twentysomethings" "squishing in" for "wholesome"
American eats, "scrumptious" desserts and a Spanish latte that "deserves the Nobel Prize for coffee"; all boast "appealing" patio seating,
although skeptics dis "minimal service", relatively "high prices" and
"food that looks prettier than it tastes."

	FOOD	DECOR	SERVICE	COST

uWink *Californian*
▽ 10 | 14 | 10 | $21

Hollywood | Hollywood & Highland Ctr. | 6801 Hollywood Blvd. (Highland Ave.) | 323-466-1800 | www.uwink.com

Tabletop "computer terminals" do double duty as an ordering system and gaming console at this "high-tech" eatery and "tourist den" in Hollywood & Highland; sure, the service is "inconsistent" and the inexpensive Californian fare "mediocre", but no surprise – the "concept" "wins major points" with the "kids."

U-Zen *Japanese*
22 | 12 | 22 | $36

West LA | 11951 Santa Monica Blvd. (Brockton Ave.) | 310-477-1390

Loyalists laud this "little-known" Japanese in West LA drawing a "neighborhood" crowd for "wonderfully fresh" fish accompanied by "authentic" cooked items from the kitchen; a "kind" staff led by "gracious" chef-owner Masaru Mizokami trumps the "plain" setting, and "the price is right" too.

Z Valentino 🗷Ⓜ *Italian*
26 | 24 | 26 | $72

Santa Monica | 3115 Pico Blvd. (bet. 31st & 32nd Sts.) | 310-829-4313 | www.welovewine.com

"Aging more gracefully than most", this circa-1972 Santa Monica "icon" is "still going strong" with "refined" Italian cuisine and a "mind-boggling" array of wines set down in a "luxurious" chandelier-clad setting that's a "lovely change of pace"; a "professional" staff led by "consummate host" Piero Selvaggio makes it the "quintessential special-occasion place", just "expect to pay top dollar for the experience."

Vegan Glory *Vegan*
▽ 23 | 9 | 20 | $17

Beverly Boulevard | 8393 Beverly Blvd. (Orlando Ave.) | 323-653-4900 | www.veganglory.com

"Faux-chicken" fans tout this Beverly Boulevard fixture for its "creative" Thai-style vegan vittles; prices are "good" and service is "fast" and "cheerful", although the "downscale" digs are best-suited to a "quick bite" or takeout.

Z Veggie Grill, The *Vegan*
23 | 15 | 19 | $15

NEW **West Hollywood** | 8000 Sunset Blvd. (Laurel Ave.) | 323-822-7575
El Segundo | Plaza El Segundo | 720 Allied Way (Hughes Way) | 310-535-0025
www.veggiegrill.com

"Even hard-core meatheads" sing the praises of this vegan chainlet churning out "not-too-guilty pleasures" like "deceptively delicious" veggie burgers with "crisp" sweet-potato fries; "modest" prices and "happy" service from the counter staff mean it works well as a "healthy" alternative to "fast food."

Velvet Margarita Cantina ● *Mexican*
▽ 18 | 22 | 17 | $35

Hollywood | 1612 N. Cahuenga Blvd. (bet. Hollywood Blvd. & Selma Ave.) | 323-469-2000 | www.velvetmargarita.com

Young Hollywood types "celebrate a successful studio pitch" at this festive midpriced Mexican set in "Disney-like" Tijuana-chic digs; it's a fallback for margaritas before hitting the Cahuenga corridor, but while the kitchen is open late, the menu generally takes a backseat to the "too-cool-for-school" scene.

	FOOD	DECOR	SERVICE	COST

vermont *American* | 22 | 20 | 20 | $44 |

Los Feliz | 1714 N. Vermont Ave. (Prospect Ave.) | 323-661-6163 |
www.vermontrestaurantonline.com

"Always a pleasure", this "understated" "gem" in Los Feliz serves "solid" if "not overly ambitious" New American cuisine in a "peaceful" space with vaulted ceilings; forget about the somewhat "pricey" tabs - the "romantic" atmosphere makes it "perfect for dates"; P.S don't miss adjacent sib Rockwell for drinks.

Versailles *Cuban* | 21 | 10 | 18 | $19 |

Mid-City | 1415 S. La Cienega Blvd. (Pico Blvd.) | 310-289-0392
Palms | 10319 Venice Blvd. (Motor Ave.) | 310-558-3168
Manhattan Beach | 1000 N. Sepulveda Blvd. (10th St.) | 310-937-6829
Encino | 17410 Ventura Blvd. (bet. Louise & White Oak Aves.) |
818-906-0756
Universal City | Universal CityWalk | 1000 Universal Studios Blvd.
(off Rte. 101) | 818-505-0093
www.versaillescuban.com

The "garlicky" roast chicken and pork "could bring Fidel to his knees" at these "bang-for-your-buck" "classic" Cubans cranking out "crave-worthy" cuisine in "coma"-inducing portions; the "efficient" staff "rushes you out" – a good thing since the "packed", "hole-in-the-wall" settings are "not much to look at."

Vertical Wine Bistro Ⓜ *Eclectic/Mediterranean* | 21 | 22 | 21 | $42 |

Pasadena | 70 N. Raymond Ave. (Union St.) | 626-795-3999 |
www.verticalwinebistro.com

A "hip" crowd "crams in, elbow to elbow" at this "urbane" Pasadena bar/restaurant where more than 400 vinos pair up with "tasty" Eclectic-Med small plates; a "helpful" staff at the ready with recommendations makes it a "pleasure", even if the bill can feel "costly" for what you get.

Via Alloro *Italian* | 21 | 22 | 20 | $45 |

Beverly Hills | 301 N. Cañon Dr. (Dayton Way) | 310-275-2900 |
www.viaalloro.com

"Another Drago family hot spot", this "loud", crowded Beverly Hills Italian turns out a moderately expensive menu of pizzas and pastas in a high-end "sports-bar" setting with flat-screen TVs and ample sidewalk seating; an "unimpressed" minority feels "burned" by food and service, but overall it's a "fun" place.

Via Veneto *Italian* | 24 | 19 | 21 | $63 |

Santa Monica | 3009 Main St. (bet. Marine St. & Pier Ave.) | 310-399-1843 |
www.viaveneto.us

A well-heeled crowd touts this "terrific" Santa Monica Italian serving "delicious", "authentic" meals in "dark", "candlelit" Tuscan-styled quarters; it's "too loud and too crowded" for some, and occasional "attitude" from the staff can make the "pricey" bills hard to swallow.

ⓩ Vibrato Grill & Jazz Ⓜ *American/Steak* | 21 | 25 | 23 | $59 |

Bel-Air | 2930 N. Beverly Glen Circle (Beverly Glen Blvd.) | 310-474-9400 |
www.vibratogrilljazz.com

This "classy" "little dinner club" in Bel-Air co-owned by trumpeter Herb Alpert delivers "high-caliber" jazz, "excellent" steakhouse fare and "spot-on" cocktails in a "plush" room that "looks like a Hollywood

	FOOD	DECOR	SERVICE	COST

usical from the 1940s"; such a "transporting" experience doesn't
ome cheap, but "sophisticated" sorts say it's "worth" it.

Viet Noodle Bar ⊅ Vietnamese
▽ 21 | 18 | 18 | $17

twater Village | 3133½ Glendale Blvd. (Glenhurst Ave.) | 323-906-1575
"Noodles rule" at this diminutive Vietnamese catering to Atwater
illage's "writers and artists" with pho and other "authentic" dishes
lus freshly made juices and soy milk for cheap; it's a "neighborhood"
allback, and the bright digs furnished with "communal tables" and
lenty of books to read furthers its "welcoming" rep.

Villa Blanca Mediterranean
18 | 23 | 19 | $47

everly Hills | 9601 Brighton Way (Camden Dr.) | 310-859-7600 |
ww.villablancarestaurant.com
All the "beautiful people" come to dine at this Beverly Hills Med where
he "glam" "all-white" space is as "gorgeous" as the clientele "and the
aiters aren't bad either"; most maintain the food's "good", but "noth-
g special", and high prices and a somewhat "snobby" "Euro" vibe are
 sticking point for some.

Village Idiot, The ● American
19 | 21 | 19 | $30

Melrose | 7383 Melrose Ave. (Martel Ave.) | 323-655-3331 |
ww.villageidiotla.com
very neighborhood could use a "watering hole" like this well-priced
Melrose gastropub purveying "rustic" American grub that "sticks to your
ut" and a "great" suds selection in an "open, airy" wood-trimmed
pace; just know that weekends draw a "meat-market" "crowd", al-
hough the mood's convivial no matter how "noisy" and "packed" it gets.

Village Pantry Deli
▽ 15 | 11 | 15 | $27

acific Palisades | 1035 Swarthmore Ave. (Sunset Blvd.) | 310-454-3337 |
www.the-village-pantry.com
ormer mayor Richard Riordan is behind this "local" deli and sidewalk
afe in Pacific Palisades serving up pretty "standard" salad and sandwich fare that's "on the pricey side"; complaints of "mediocre" grub
and a "too-cold" feel mean it's "no substitute" for "longtime favorite"
Mort's (which it succeeded), even still, it draws a steady stream of
ustomers, including the occasional "star."

Village Pizzeria Pizza
25 | 11 | 16 | $15

Hancock Park | 131 N. Larchmont Blvd. (bet. Beverly Blvd. & 1st St.) |
323-465-5566
Hollywood | 6363 Yucca St. (bet. Cahuenga Blvd. & Ivar St.) | 323-790-0763
www.villagepizzeria.net
Even "ex-New Yorkers" sing the praises of these Hollywood and Hancock
Park pizza joints proffering "crisp", "thin-crust" pies loaded with
"fresh cheese" that transport you straight "back to Brooklyn"; they're
"always packed" and service is "harried", but "quick" takeout and delivery make up for it.

NEW Villains Tavern ⌧Ⓜ American
- | - | - | I

Downtown | 1356 Palmetto St. (Santa Fe Ave.) | 213-613-0766
Situated in the heart of the Arts District adjacent to Little Tokyo, this
New American offers a budget-friendly menu of New American fare
like a half-pound 'Kobe-style' burger and a grilled-cheese sandwich
flavored with sambal, accompanied by cocktails with names like the

	FOOD	DECOR	SERVICE	COST

Bella Dona and the Cerberus; the setting looks like a re-creation of 19th-century saloon, with the walls covered in every manner of bri a-brac, including vintage bottles filled with a rainbow of liquids.

Villa Piacere Ⓜ *Eclectic* | 18 | 21 | 19 | $42 |

Woodland Hills | 22160 Ventura Blvd. (bet. Shoup Ave. & Topanga Canyon Blvd.) | 818-704-1185 | www.villapiacere.com

A "lovely place for outdoor dining", this Woodland Hills Eclecti sports a "romantic" garden patio that's especially "pleasant fo Sunday brunch"; "willing" service is an added appeal, although local lament that the wide-ranging menu is "inconsistent", and price aren't inexpensive either.

Villa Sorriso *Italian* ▽ | 20 | 20 | 21 | $37 |

Pasadena | 168 W. Colorado Blvd. (Pasadena Ave.) | 626-793-8008 www.sorrisopasadena.com

Regulars report this Pasadena Italian "has a lot going for it" with "de pendable" dishes that "suit all tastes" served in a multifaceted spac with a stylish martini bar and lounge that's "fun for dancing and socializ ing" when a DJ steps in on weekends; perhaps "there's no wow factor with the fare, but tabs are modest so "you won't be disappointed" eithe

☒ Vincenti ☒ *Italian* | 26 | 23 | 25 | $66 |

Brentwood | 11930 San Vicente Blvd. (bet. Bundy Dr. & Montana Ave.) 310-207-0127 | www.vincentiristorante.com

"They take great care of you" at this Brentwood *bella* presenting "meticulously prepared" "modern" cuisine that's "always a pleasure" its "older" clientele appreciates the "warm welcome" from the staf and "civilized" atmosphere and doesn't flinch at the "very expensive prices"; P.S. Monday's pizza nights are a relative bargain.

NEW Vintage Enoteca *Italian* | - | - | - | I |

Hollywood | 7554 W. Sunset Blvd. (Gardner St.) | 323-512-5278 | www.vintageenoteca.com

This Hollywood wine bar dispenses several dozen artisanal wines from small-batch producers using grapes both familiar and unfamilia (Melon de Bourgogne, Hondarribi and Monastrell, among others), al of which go well with Italian small plates of salumi and cheese, bruschetta, panini and flatbreads; the retro setting features exposed ligh bulbs hanging from above and, yes, vintage photographs on the wall.

V.I.P. Harbor Seafood *Chinese/Seafood* | 19 | 12 | 17 | $24 |

West LA | 11701 Wilshire Blvd. (Barrington Ave.) | 310-979-3377

For "nearly Chinatown-quality dim sum" "without the drive", this strip-mall Chinese in West LA fits the bill with both "easy" and "exotic" nibbles rolled out on carts; "you have to be quick to get what you want", and be prepared to shell out more than you might in Monterey Park.

Vitello's *Italian* | 16 | 15 | 18 | $29 |

Studio City | 4349 Tujunga Ave. (Moorpark St.) | 818-769-0905 | www.vitellosrestaurant.com

An infamous "piece of Valley history" thanks to its role in the Robert Blake trial, this "been-around-forever" Studio City "spaghetti joint" still soldiers on with "ordinary", red-sauce fare served in a "kitschy", "old-school" setting; although prices are low and live jazz and opera is draw for some, those not on the "*Barreta* murder tour" may be inlined to take a "pass."

Vito *Italian*

22 | 19 | 23 | $42

Santa Monica | 2807 Ocean Park Blvd. (28th St.) | 310-450-4999 | www.vitorestaurant.com

You'll "feel like a made man" at this fairly priced "throwback" in Santa Monica, where "tuxedo-clad waiters" accommodate a "loyal" cadre of "goodfellas" and "neighborhood folks" in the mood for "traditional" italiana like red "gravy" and tableside Caesar salads; white-linen tablecloths and red-leather booths add to the "NYC" ambiance; "Frank would have loved" it.

Vittorio's Ⓜ *Italian*

18 | 11 | 21 | $27

Pacific Palisades | 16646 Marquez Ave. (Sunset Blvd.) | 310-459-9316 | www.vittoriosla.com

Pacific Palisades locals feel "lucky to have" this "handy" "little trattoria" in their neck of the woods with "reliable" Southern Italian eats and pizzas in "casual" quarters; modest prices "make it a perfect fit for families" and it's a "regular stop" for takeout too.

Ⓩ Wa Ⓜ *Japanese*

27 | 12 | 22 | $52

West Hollywood | La Cienega Plaza | 1106 N. La Cienega Blvd. (Holloway Dr.) | 310-854-7285

There's "no glitz, no glam" just "high-quality" sushi that's "as authentic as it gets" at this West Hollywood "gem", "hidden" away on the second floor of a strip mall; acolytes insist it's like "Nobu" "without the crowds or attitude", although the "high" prices can sometimes feel at odds with the "nonexistent" atmosphere.

Wabi-Sabi *Asian*

22 | 16 | 18 | $40

Venice | 1635 Abbot Kinney Blvd. (Venice Blvd.) | 310-314-2229 | www.wabisabisushi.com

A "Venice crowd" favors this "hip" stop on Abbot Kinney for "delicious" "Californiafied" sushi and "innovative" fusion items set down in an urban-industrial setting; "cute servers" and a popular happy hour with deals on cocktails and apps overcome the somewhat "expensive" price tags and keep the "good vibes" going till late.

Waffle, The ◐ *American*

17 | 12 | 15 | $20

Hollywood | 6255 W. Sunset Blvd. (bet. Argyle Ave. & Vine St.) | 323-465-6901 | www.thewaffle.us

Like "an upscale IHOP", this "hip" Hollywood "diner" lures all walks of "breakfast lovers" for "crispy waffles" (natch) and other "solid comfort-food" items served late into the night; despite grumbles of "hit-or-miss" grub, a "model-wannabe" staff and out-of-line tabs, it still works for a "pre-ArcLight bite" and predictably draws a "wait on weekends."

Walter's *Eclectic*

▽ 21 | 19 | 19 | $30

Claremont | 310 Yale Ave. (Bonita Ave.) | 909-624-4914 | www.waltersrestaurant.biz

Long a Claremont "institution", this "charming", "small-town" restaurant remains a "steady" supplier of a "wide" sampling of Eclectic cuisine, including "unusual Afghan specialties"; good-"value" pricing, a "casual" mazelike dining room and a "wonderful" leafy patio keep this "old-reliable" "popular" among the "locals."

	FOOD	DECOR	SERVICE	COST

Warehouse, The *American* | 17 | 19 | 19 | $38 |

Marina del Rey | 4499 Admiralty Way (bet. Lincoln & Washington Blvds.) | 310-823-5451 | www.mdrwarehouse.com

The patio "overlooking the marina" is about the best thing going for this "long-established" American where the "ordinary" fare comes served in a "'70s"-style, nautically themed setting evoking "*Gilligan's Island*"; several suggest it's "seen better days", though it continues to pack in the "tourists", and the "views" alone keep it "tried-and-true."

Warszawa ⓜ *Polish* | 23 | 18 | 21 | $38 |

Santa Monica | 1414 Lincoln Blvd. (Santa Monica Blvd.) | 310-393-8831 | www.warszawarestaurant.com

"Utterly charming", this Santa Monica Polish tucked into a "vintage cottage" cooks up the kind of "gutsy", "deliciously old-fashioned" dishes "your grandmother would make", like borscht, "wonderful roast duck" and pierogi; "easy-on-the-wallet" prices and "polite" service are added appeals, and there's also a "cool garden out back" for warm nights.

ⓩ Water Grill *Seafood* | 27 | 25 | 26 | $68 |

Downtown | 544 S. Grand Ave. (bet. 5th & 6th Sts.) | 213-891-0900 | www.watergrill.com

"Still top-notch after all these years" sigh fans of this 20-year-old Downtown respite that remains "in a class of its own" with chef David LeFevre's "exceptional", "artfully prepared" seafood backed by a "wonderful selection of fine wines"; impeccable" service and a "quiet", "clubby" setting make it perfect for a "power lunch" or "pre-theater" dinner, and "worth every penny" of the whale of a tab.

🆕 Waterloo & City *British* | - | - | - | M |

Culver City | 12517 W. Washington Blvd. (Venice Blvd.) | 310-391-4222 | www.waterlooandcity.com

This Culver City gastropub gets its name from the London Underground stop near the childhood home of chef-owner Brendan Collins (ex Mélisse and Anisette), and his midpriced Modern British menu includes the likes of Manchester quail with chopped liver on toast and pig's trotter with sweetbreads and salsa; the whimsical space features church pews painted pink and orange in the lounge, overstuffed suede banquettes, antique mirrors, a communal table and an outdoor patio.

West *Californian/Italian* | ▽ 20 | 24 | 20 | $48 |

Brentwood | Hotel Angeleno | 170 N. Church Ln., 17th fl. (bet. I-405 & Sunset Blvd.) | 310-481-7878 | www.westatangeleno.com

"On a clear day" "the views are spectacular" at this Cal-Italian steakhouse perched in the penthouse of Brentwood's Hotel Angeleno flaunting floor-to-ceiling windows and a sleek, wood-lined look; those "disappointed" in the food and the "splurge-worthy" tabs say it's still "good for first dates", what with a cushy bar and those "killer" vistas.

Westside Cellar Cafe & Wine Store 🈂ⓜ *Eclectic* | - | - | - | I |

Ventura | 222 E. Main St. (bet. Palm St. & Ventura Ave.) | 805-641-3500 | www.westsidecellar.com

Inhabiting a "comfortable" brick-walled space done up with the work of local artists, this Ventura bistro turns out "lovely" Eclectic creations

rom duck confit spring rolls to filet mignon, supported by a global list
of wines also available for sale at the neighboring retail shop; occasional live entertainment is an added perk.

Westside Tavern *Californian*   21 | 21 | 21 | $36
West LA | Westside Pavilion | 10850 W. Pico Blvd. (Westwood Blvd.) |
310-470-1539 | www.westsidetavernla.com
An "unexpected treat" in the Westside Pavilion in West LA, this year-
old tavern is a bona fide "hit" thanks to its "something-for-everyone"
menu featuring "fresh" Californian spins on pub fare plus "interesting
cocktails" and "artisan beers" at prices that "aren't too expensive"; a
"no-reservations" policy means "it's a zoo on weekends", although the
food arrives at an "efficient" pace, and supporters stick it out since
"post-movie dining has never been so good."

Whale & Ale, The *Pub Food*   20 | 18 | 20 | $27
San Pedro | 327 W. Seventh St. (bet. Centre & Mesa Sts.) | 310-832-0363 |
www.whaleandale.com
Channeling a "classic olde-English pub", this atmospheric Brit in San
Pedro coddles the "regulars" with "traditional" grub and a "great selection of ales" served in a "charming" Victorian interior; despite
grumbles about only "average" eats, the brass bar is "busy" and frequent live music means it's a lot of "fun."

Wharo Korean BBQ *Korean*   ▽ 21 | 16 | 20 | $32
Marina del Rey | 4029 Lincoln Blvd. (Washington Blvd.) | 310-578-7114 |
www.wharo.com
The Westside's "alternative" to K-town is this Marina del Ray standby
where diners cook up "quality meats" on tabletop grills; a few find the
prices "high" for fare that's "not quite the real deal", though it works
for a "fix" "without the drive" and you'll certainly save money on gas.

Whist *Californian*   20 | 22 | 18 | $55
Santa Monica | Viceroy Santa Monica | 1819 Ocean Ave. (Pico Blvd.) |
310-260-7500 | www.viceroysantamonica.com
For "romantic patio dining" "sit by the pool" at this "elegant" little
number in the Viceroy Santa Monica boasting an "over-the-top" British
look by Kelly Wearstler with luxe cabanas and "pretty" gardens; "ho-
hum" Cal fare, "slow" service and "premium" pricing get some surveyors
down, although the lavish Sunday brunch buffet redeems it for many.

Wilshire 🅢 *American*   23 | 24 | 22 | $54
Santa Monica | 2454 Wilshire Blvd. (bet. Chelsea Ave. & 25th St.) |
310-586-1707 | www.wilshirerestaurant.com
An "impress-your-date kind of place", this "trendy", "pricey" Santa
Monican serves its "highly imaginative" "seasonal" American menu
out on a "lovely" garden patio that "makes you forget you're in the
middle of a concrete jungle"; inside is comparatively "dreary", except
when the bar livens up on weekends luring a "hipster" crowd for "excellent" handcrafted cocktails and DJs.

Wine Bistro 🅜 *French*   23 | 19 | 23 | $43
Studio City | 11915 Ventura Blvd. (Laurel Canyon Blvd.) | 818-766-6233 |
www.winebistro.net
Ever-so-"genial" host J.B. Torchon sets a "warm" tone at this "venerable" Studio City bistro catering to a "studio"-heavy crowd with consis-

tently "tasty" French fare and, naturally, "intriguing wines"; "fair
prices", an "inviting" brass-accented setting and "tolerable" noise levels
top off the experience.

Wokcano Restaurant ✷ *Chinese/Japanese* 16 | 17 | 16 | $28

Downtown | 800 W. Seventh St. (bet. Figueroa & Flower Sts.) |
213-623-2288
West Hollywood | 8408 W. Third St. (Orlando Ave.) |
323-951-1122
Santa Monica | 1413 Fifth St. (Santa Monica Blvd.) | 310-458-3080
Long Beach | 199 The Promenade N. (B'way) | 562-951-9652
Pasadena | 33 S. Fair Oaks Ave. (bet. Colorado Blvd. & Green St.) |
626-578-1818
Burbank | 150 S. San Fernando Blvd. (Angeleno Ave.) |
818-524-2288
www.wokcanorestaurant.com

Though this affordable Chinese-Japanese chainlet may "lack authen-
ticity", a "young crowd" still digs the "tasty enough" takes on Pan-
Asian "standards" and sushi served in "lively", "modern" settings;
occasionally "neglectful" service aside, "late" hours, a full bar and frequent DJs keep it "crawling with partygoers" well into the night.

Wolfgang Puck B&G 🅢 *Californian* ▽ 22 | 21 | 22 | $44

Downtown | LA Live | 800 W. Olympic Blvd. (Figueroa St.) | 213-748-9700 |
www.wolfgangpuck.com

"Convenience" is key at this "convivial" Californian in Downtown's LA
Live, where a "not-too-expensive" menu of "reliably Puckish" signa-
tures makes it a "good call" before a game at Staples or a "show at
Nokia Theatre"; service is "prompt", and the "big and airy" indoor-
outdoor space ensures there's usually a table.

Wolfgang Puck Express *Californian* 19 | 14 | 17 | $24
(fka Wolfgang Puck Cafe)

Santa Monica | Criterion Plaza | 1315 Third St. Promenade
(bet. Arizona Ave. & Santa Monica Blvd.) | 310-576-4770
LAX | LA Int'l Airport, Terminals 2 & 7 | 209 World Way (Sepulveda Blvd.) |
310-215-5166

Wolfgang Puck LA Bistro *Californian*
(fka Wolfgang Puck Cafe)

Downtown | Library Court Bldg. | 630 W. Sixth St. (Hope St.) |
213-614-1900 🅢
Universal City | Universal CityWalk | 1000 Universal Studios Blvd.
(off Rte. 101) | 818-985-9653
www.wolfgangpuck.com

This "grab-and-go" Californian chainlet from Wolfgang Puck is a "port
in the storm" for airport travelers, nine-to-fivers and "families" seeking a "decent" enough "quick bite"; the "quasi–fast food" settings
don't offer much in the way of service or atmosphere, but tabs are
"cheap" and it "beats" more generic chains any day.

Wolfgang's Steakhouse *Steak* 23 | 23 | 23 | $73

Beverly Hills | 445 N. Cañon Dr. (Santa Monica Blvd.) | 310-385-0640 |
www.wolfgangssteakhouse.net

"Perfectly aged" porterhouses and other "high-quality" cuts are the
hallmarks of this "glammed up" "NYC"-style chophouse in Beverly
Hills from Peter Luger alum Wolfgang Zwiener; a "convivial" atmo-

sphere and a "professional staff" make it a "great place for a business dinner", ditto the "expense-account" prices.

Wood Ranch BBQ & Grill *BBQ* | 21 | 18 | 20 | $28 |

Fairfax | The Grove | 189 The Grove Dr. (bet. Beverly Blvd. & 3rd St.) | 323-937-6800
Cerritos | Cerritos Towne Ctr. | 12801 Towne Center Dr. (bet. Bloomfield & Shoemaker Aves.) | 562-865-0202
Arcadia | 400 S. Baldwin Ave. (Huntington Dr.) | 626-447-4745
Northridge | Northridge Fashion Ctr. | 9301 Tampa Ave. (bet. Nordhoff & Plummer Sts.) | 818-886-6464
Agoura Hills | Whizins Plaza | 5050 Cornell Rd. (Agoura Rd.) | 818-597-8900
Camarillo | 1101 E. Daily Dr. (Lantana St.) | 805-482-1202
Moorpark | 540 New Los Angeles Ave. (Spring Rd.) | 805-523-7253
Ventura | Pacific View Mall | 3449 E. Main St. (Mills Rd.) | 805-620-4500
Newhall | Valencia Mktpl. | 25580 The Old Rd. (bet. Constitution Ave. & McBean Pkwy.) | 661-222-9494
www.woodranch.com

There's "meat and lots of it" at these "well-priced" Traditional American-BBQ stops satisfying "hungry families" with "coma"-inducing portions of "flavorful" ribs and tri-tip all deemed "pretty good for a chain"; a "friendly, teenage" staff does its best to make the "long waits" bearable, but while the *"Ponderosa"*-themed quarters are "comfy" enough, many patrons prefer the "curbside pickup."

Woody's Bar-B-Que *BBQ* | ▽ 24 | 7 | 15 | $15 |

Mid-City | 3446 W. Slauson Ave. (Crenshaw Blvd.) | 323-294-9443
Inglewood | 475 S. Market St. (bet. Hillcrest Blvd. & La Brea Ave.) | 310-672-4200 🗷

"Tender" "smoky" 'cue capped by homemade peach cobbler is the lure at these longtime cousins churning out inexpensive, family-style feasts; prices are reasonable, but while Inglewood has a few seats, the Mid-City original is takeout only.

Woo Lae Oak *Korean* | 22 | 21 | 19 | $44 |

Beverly Hills | 170 N. La Cienega Blvd. (Clifton Way) | 310-652-4187 | www.woolaeoakbh.com

This stylish Beverly Hills Korean is a find for "cook-it-yourself" 'cue alongside other "tasty" fare; it boasts a "well-trained staff" and "sexy", "modern" setting, although "since you're doing all the work" cynics quip "it should cost less."

World Cafe ● *Eclectic* | ▽ 18 | 18 | 17 | $29 |

Santa Monica | 2820 Main St. (Ashland Ave.) | 310-392-1661 | www.worldcafela.com

Like the name suggests, this Santa Monica cafe packs in a "young" crowd for Eclectic nibbles and libations from all over the globe; most of the action is centered around the "lively" patio, even more so on weekends when a DJ kicks up the "people-watching" quotient.

NEW **WP24** *Chinese* | - | - | - | E |

Downtown | Ritz-Carlton | 900 W. Olympic Blvd., 24th fl. (Figueroa St.) | 213-743-8824 | www.wolfgangpuck.com

Situated on the 24th floor of Downtown's newly opened Ritz-Carlton Los Angeles, Wolfgang Puck's latest harks back to early Puckian concepts like Chinois on Main, though in this case, the dim sum is offset by sushi and other Asian fare, plus dishes finished tableside; a view of Nokia Theatre and the Staples Center dominates the setting, while its shiny, floor-to-ceiling metal tubes are like a bit of Las Vegas come to LA.

W's China Bistro *Chinese*

| 22 | 18 | 19 | $31 |

Redondo Beach | 1410 S. PCH (Ave. F) | 310-792-1600 | www.wschinabistro.com

Beachgoers flock to this Redondo Chinese for "updated" takes on the classics – including a handful of "healthy" salad options – served in a contemporary space that feels "upscale" for the genre; some shrug it's only "ok", but the staff "gets you in and out fast" and you won't "spend a fortune" either.

Wurstküche ● *European*

| 22 | 17 | 16 | $18 |

Downtown | 800 E. Third St. (Traction Ave.) | 213-687-4444 | www.wurstkucherestaurant.com

"Hipsters" throng this "affordable" beer hall in Downtown's Art District doling out "unique, delicious" sausages "from the mundane to the exotic" (like rattlesnake) with "unbelievable" Belgian and German brews on tap to wash it all down; the "funky", "industrial" space boasts "communal tables" and a pleasantly "raucous" vibe, so the "wurst part" is the "frequent long line" to order; P.S. it's pronounced *vurst-cook-huh*.

Xi'an *Chinese*

| 21 | 17 | 20 | $33 |

Beverly Hills | 362 N. Cañon Dr. (bet. Brighton & Dayton Ways) | 310-275-3345 | www.xian90210.com

Putting a "nouvelle" spin on familiar dishes, this "popular" Chinese keeps its "fussy Beverly Hills" clientele contented with "fresh-tasting" "Americanized" cooking at prices that are "surprisingly inexpensive" for the neighborhood; given that the "modern" space can be "noisy", luckily it also makes for some "excellent carryout."

NEW Xino *Chinese*

| - | - | - | E |

Santa Monica | Dining Deck, Santa Monica Pl. | 395 Santa Monica Pl. (3rd. St. Promenade) | 310-755-6220

The latest creation of colorful restaurateur Chris Yeo (Straits Café in SF and Sino in San Jose) is this upscale Chinese in Santa Monica Place decorated with a massive super-graphic of his wife, who seems to be wearing nothing but tattoos; it follows in the footsteps of his others, dominated by a long bar as you enter where exotic libations are mixed, while the kitchen comes through with a menu of dishes like Kobe tartar and Kung Pao chicken lollipops; P.S. don't miss the breathtaking patio, with its grand view of the city.

Xiomara ⊠ *Nuevo Latino*

| 21 | 20 | 23 | $45 |

Hollywood | 6101 Melrose Ave. (Seward St.) | 323-461-0601 | www.xiomararestaurant.com

Customers are charmed by Xiomara Ardolina's "little local gem" in Hollywood offering "unusual" Nuevo Latino dishes and "fantastic" mojitos crafted with real sugarcane juice in a "simple, elegant" space evoking 1950s Havana; service is generally "exceptional", although it's reflected in the "expensive" bills.

	FOOD	DECOR	SERVICE	COST

XIV ⊠ American
23 | 24 | 22 | $77

West Hollywood | 8117 Sunset Blvd. (bet. Crescent Heights Blvd. & Selma Dr.) | 323-656-1414 | www.xivla.com

"Eye candy" abounds at Michael Mina's "seductive" New American in WeHo, where "adventurous", "palate-pleasing" plates arrive via a "gorgeous" staff in a stunningly "ornate" Philippe Starck-designed setting recalling Louis XIV or "Liberace"; its "glitterazzi" clientele claims it's "well worth" the "pricey" bills, although cynics call it "all show and no go."

NEW Xoia Vietnamese Eats Ⓜ Vietnamese
– | – | – | I

Echo Park | 1801 W. Sunset Blvd. (Glendale Blvd.) | 213-413-3232 | www.xoiaeats.com

This storefront arrival in Echo Park brings the gospel of pho to those who hunger for the cooking of Vietnam – along with beef soup, there are spring rolls, banh mi sandwiches and a reasonable selection of vegetarian dishes; the mega-modern setting features spiderlike chandeliers, large canvases on the walls and bright-red chairs.

Yabu Japanese
23 | 18 | 22 | $33

West Hollywood | 521 N. La Cienega Blvd. (bet. Melrose & Rosewood Aves.) | 310-854-0400

West LA | 11820 W. Pico Blvd. (bet. Barrington Ave. & Bundy Dr.) | 310-473-9757
www.yaburestaurant.com

Famed for their "fabulously big bowls" of "slurp"-worthy "handmade soba", these "authentic" Japanese twins are also "reasonably priced" bets for "taste bud-tickling" small plates and a smattering of "fresh" sushi; both inhabit "spare", "unpretentious" digs, although WeHo sports a "delightful garden" that enhances the overall "charming" experience.

⊠ Yamashiro Asian/Californian
18 | 26 | 20 | $49

Hollywood | 1999 N. Sycamore Ave. (Franklin Ave.) | 323-466-5125 | www.yamashirorestaurant.com

"Magnificent views of Los Angeles" and a "breathtaking" Japanese "palace"-inspired setting like something out of a "Cecil B. DeMille" picture make this decades-old Hollywood fixture the place to "take out-of-town guests"; foodies find the midpriced Cal-Asian cuisine could be "better", but it's "good" enough, and the adjacent Pagoda Bar is a "date"-worthy drink spot.

Yamato Westwood Japanese
18 | 19 | 19 | $30

Brentwood | 1099 Westwood Blvd. (Kinross Ave.) | 310-208-0100 | www.yamatorestaurants.com

"UCLA students" and other "budget"-minded types tout this inexpensive Japanese chain link turning out "quality" sushi and "creative" small plates in a "stunning" all-white former bank building in Brentwood; the space is "noisy" and service could "be better", but oh, "what a bargain."

Yang Chow Chinese
22 | 11 | 18 | $25

Chinatown | 819 N. Broadway (bet. Alpine & College Sts.) | 213-625-0811
Pasadena | 3777 E. Colorado Blvd. (Rosemead Blvd.) | 626-432-6868
Canoga Park | 6443 Topanga Canyon Blvd. (Victory Blvd.) | 818-347-2610
www.yangchow.com

The "world-famous" slippery shrimp "are everything they're cracked up to be" swear those "hooked" on these longtime "LA staples" that set the "standard" for "classic, old-style" Chinese fare; they're "short on atmosphere" and don't look for any "warm and fuzzy service" either, but they're "always crowded" because prices are low and the food alone keeps them "tried-and-true."

Yard House ● *American* | 18 | 17 | 17 | $27 |

Downtown | LA Live | 800 W. Olympic Blvd. (Figueroa St.) | 213-745-9273
Long Beach | Shoreline Vill. | 401 Shoreline Village Dr. (Shoreline Dr.) | 562-628-0455
Pasadena | Paseo Colorado | 330 E. Colorado Blvd. (bet. Los Robles & Marengo Aves.) | 626-577-9273
www.yardhouse.com

"Brewskis galore" are the main attraction at this American chain of "glorified taverns" where over 100 draughts accompany an equally "huge" roster of reasonably priced, "better-than-expected" "bar food"; "rowdy fans" relish the "cacophony" of flat-screen TVs and "upscale frat party" atmosphere, though "peace"-seekers may be happier elsewhere.

Yatai Asian Tapas Bar ⑤ *Asian* | - | - | - | I |

West Hollywood | 8535 W. Sunset Blvd. (La Cienega Blvd.) | 310-289-0030 | www.yatai-bar.com

"Hip" West Hollywoodites hail this "affordable" Asian on the Sunset Strip that "stands out" with an "appealing variety" of "tasty" small plates set down by a "friendly" staff; "it's been discovered", hence a loud, "lively" vibe and occasional parking issues.

Yen Sushi & Sake Bar *Japanese* | 23 | 16 | 19 | $35 |

Little Tokyo | California Market Ctr. | 110 E. Ninth St. (bet. Los Angeles & Main Sts.) | 213-627-9709 ⑤
Pico-Robertson | 9618 W. Pico Blvd. (bet. Beverwil & Edris Drs.) | 310-278-0691 | www.yensushila.com
West LA | 11819 Wilshire Blvd. (Granville Ave.) | 310-996-1313
Long Beach | 4905 E. Second St. (bet. Argonne & St. Joseph Aves.) | 562-434-5757
Studio City | 12930 Ventura Blvd. (bet. Coldwater Canyon Ave. & Valley Vista Blvd.) | 818-907-6400

Regulars rely on this cheerful Japanese chainlet for "fresh", "beautifully presented" sushi and "inventive" maki sliced up by a "friendly" crew; perhaps it's "not that authentic" (Las Vegas rolls, anyone?), but the fare's certainly "consistent" and prices offer "amazing value."

Ye Olde King's Head *Pub Food* | 18 | 17 | 18 | $25 |

Santa Monica | 116 Santa Monica Blvd. (bet. Ocean Ave. & 2nd St.) | 310-451-1402 | www.yeoldekingshead.com

"English transplants" and "yanks" alike appreciate this "delightfully authentic" U.K.-style pub serving Santa Monica since 1974 with "crispy" fish 'n' chips, Guinness on tap and "footie" on the telly; a "down-to-earth" staff and "comfy" memorabilia-laden setting keep the mood congenial; "cheers."

York, The *Eclectic* | ▽ 18 | 17 | 15 | $25 |

Highland Park | 5018 York Blvd. (Ave. 50) | 323-255-9675 | www.theyorkonyork.com

Highland Park habitués fill up this "easygoing" Eclectic gastropub serving "quality bar food" and "craft beers" in a neo-industrial setting;

though the "oddball" order-at-the-bar process rubs some the wrong way, reasonable prices and a "friendly", neighborhood vibe compensate.

☑ Yuca's ☒ *Mexican*
23 | 7 | 17 | $10

Los Feliz | 4666 Hollywood Blvd. (bet. Rodney Dr. & Vermont Ave.) | 323-661-0523

Los Feliz | 2056 Hillhurst Ave. (bet. Ambrose Ave. & Price St.) | 323-662-1214 | www.yucasla.com ⊄

Surveyors seeking "burrito heaven" find it at this "funky little" "hut" and "local landmark" in Los Feliz, known for its "succulent" cochinita pibil among other "kick-ass", "real-deal" Mexican eats; the colorful Hollywood Boulevard spin-off features "a larger menu, a few tables" and a patio, although "cheap" prices are a constant at both branches.

☑ Yujean Kang's *Chinese*
26 | 17 | 22 | $37

Pasadena | 67 N. Raymond Ave. (bet. Holly & Union Sts.) | 626-585-0855 | www.yujeankangs.com

Long a Pasadena "favorite", this top-rated "upscale" Chinese presents "fabulous", "gourmet" takes on "regional" dishes that "elevate" it "way above" your ordinary take-out joint; perhaps the white-tablecloth setting could use a "spruce-up", but the staff "remembers you", and "after all these years", it's still a "pleasure"; P.S. "lunch is a bargain."

Yuzu ☒ *Japanese*
▽ 23 | 18 | 17 | $43

Torrance | 1231 Cabrillo Ave. (Torrance Blvd.) | 310-533-9898

"Teleport to Tokyo" via this "authentic", "high-end" izakaya in Torrance crafting "delicate", "inventive" small plates and sushi in "simple" earth-toned surroundings; a few find service could use "improving", although overall, the consensus is it's well "worth" seeking out.

Yxta Cocina Mexicana ☒ *Mexican*
▽ 24 | 19 | 21 | $21

Downtown | 601 S. Central Ave. (6th St.) | 213-596-5579 | www.yxta.net

Downtowners cheer this "exciting", well-priced Mexican addition serving "innovative, seasonal" takes on south-of-the-border classics coupled with "fantastic" margaritas; "intelligent" service and a pleasant white-washed setting overcome its somewhat off-the-beaten-path locale.

Zane's *Italian/Steak*
▽ 26 | 23 | 25 | $30

Hermosa Beach | 1150 Hermosa Ave. (Pier Ave.) | 310-374-7488 | www.zanesrestaurant.com

Loyalists laud this "hip" Hermosa Beacher turning out "excellent" steakhouse fare with an Italian bent and "fancy" cocktails in a "trendy" (read: "noisy") setting; with "friendly" service and "reasonable prices, it works equally well for "happy hour" or "post-party" fare.

Zankou Chicken *Mediterranean*
22 | 6 | 13 | $13

East Hollywood | 5065 W. Sunset Blvd. (Normandie Ave.) | 323-665-7845 ☾

West LA | 1716 S. Sepulveda Blvd. (Santa Monica Blvd.) | 310-444-0550

Pasadena | 1296 E. Colorado Blvd. (bet. Chester & Holliston Aves.) | 626-405-1502

Burbank | 1001 N. San Fernando Blvd. (Walnut Ave.) | 818-238-0414

Glendale | 1415 E. Colorado Blvd. (Verdugo Rd.) | 818-244-1937

Glendale | 901 W. Glenoaks Blvd. (Highland Ave.) | 818-244-0492

(continued)

(continued)

Zankou Chicken

North Hollywood | 10760 Riverside Dr. (Lankershim Blvd.) |
818-655-0469
Van Nuys | 5658 Sepulveda Blvd. (bet. Burbank Blvd. & Hatteras St.) |
818-781-0615
NEW Montebello | Newmark Mall | 125 N. Montebello Blvd.
(Whittier Blvd.) | 323-722-7200
www.zankouchicken.com

An LA "original", this "budget" Mediterranean chicken chain earns its
rabid following with "succulent, lip-smacking" birds accompanied by
"legendary" "pharmaceutical-grade" garlic sauce that makes for
"good dippin'"; given the "drab" "cafeterialike" settings and "down
right surly" counter staff ("would it kill them to smile?"), regulars offer
two words of advice: "get takeout."

Zazou *Mediterranean*

22 | 17 | 20 | $46

Redondo Beach | 1810 S. Catalina Ave. (Vista Del Mar) | 310-540-4884 |
www.zazourestaurant.com

"Locals" love this "wonderful, little" "date-night" standby in Redondo
Beach proffering a "unique" array of "excellent" Mediterranean
dishes in "casually elegant" quarters; prices are "somewhat expen
sive", but service is "attentive" and most maintain they've "never
had a bad meal" here.

Zeidler's Café Ⓜ *Californian*

15 | 15 | 16 | $24

Brentwood | Skirball Cultural Ctr. | 2701 N. Sepulveda Blvd.
(Skirball Center Dr.) | 310-440-4515 | www.skirball.org

An "oasis in a rich, cultural setting", this "reasonably priced" kosher
Californian in the Skirball Center delivers a "small but varied" lineup
of "light" lunchtime bites deemed "a step up" from typical museum
fare; service is "attentive", and the "relaxed, modern" glass-enclosed
space makes for a "pleasant" meeting place.

Zeke's Smokehouse *BBQ* ·

21 | 15 | 18 | $23

West Hollywood | West Hollywood Gateway Ctr. | 7100 Santa Monica Blvd.
(bet. Formosa & La Brea Aves.) | 323-850-9353
Montrose | 2209 Honolulu Ave. (Montrose Ave.) | 818-957-7045
www.zekessmokehouse.com

These "smoky" sibs in WeHo and Montrose satisfy 'cue "cravings"
with "saucy", "tender" meats "that fall right off the bone" and
"classic" sides like hushpuppies; factor in pleasantly "divey" quarters, a "family-friendly" vibe and "reasonable" tabs, and fans are
in "hog heaven."

NEW Zengo *Asian*

- | - | - | E

Santa Monica | Dining Deck, Santa Monica Pl. | 395 Santa Monica Pl.
(3rd. St. Promenade) | 310-899-1000

You have to walk past Richard Sandoval's La Sandia in Santa Monica
Place to get to his Zengo, a pricey Latino-Asian fusioner decked out
like a palace with high ceilings and red tile plus a patio affording an
ocean view; there's a long communal table in the middle of the restaurant, where groups can assemble for dishes including a variety of
ceviche, dim sum and such or order pre-assembled choices served in
a multitude of Zengo Boxes.

	FOOD	DECOR	SERVICE	COST

Zin Bistro Americana *American*

20 | 24 | 20 | $41

Westlake Village | 32131 Lindero Canyon Rd. (Summershore Ln.) |
818-865-0095 | www.zinbistroamericana.com

"It's all about the view" at this waterfront bistro in Westlake Village
where a "seat on the patio" can make any night feel like a "vacation";
on the downside are somewhat "pricey" tabs, so-so service and just
above "average" spins on New American "comfort food" that don't
quite live up to the "beautiful" setting.

Zip Fusion *Japanese*

19 | 15 | 18 | $25

Downtown | 744 E. Third St. (Rose St.) | 213-680-3770 | www.zipfusion.com

This "dependable, midrange" sushi chain earns a faithful "college-
aged" following with "tasty" takes on Japanese standards plus "creative" rolls and a smattering of "fusion" dishes; "fast, friendly service"
and "simple" settings complete the package, while patio seating at all
locales is an added perk.

Zucca Ristorante *Italian*

22 | 23 | 23 | $47

Downtown | 801 Tower | 801 S. Figueroa St. (8th St.) | 213-614-7800 |
www.patinagroup.com

"Business"-lunchers and "theater"-going types tout this "more affordable" member of the Patina family "set among the Downtown office
buildings" and "convenient" to the Staples Center and LA Live; it
boasts a "solid, but not spectacular" Italian menu, which gains a lift from
"accommodating" service, a "pleasant" room decorated with Tuscan
touches and a "lovely" patio.

Menus, photos, voting and more - free at ZAGAT.com

LOS ANGELES
INDEXES

Cuisines 250
Locations 269
Special Features 295

LOCATION MAPS

Hollywood | Melrose 291
Downtown 292
Marina del Rey | Santa Monica | Venice 293
Pasadena 294

Cuisines

Includes names, locations and Food ratings.

AFGHAN

Azeen's	**Pasadena**	23
Walter's	**Claremont**	21

AMERICAN

Abbey	**W Hollywood**	16
Akasha	**Culver City**	20
Alcove	**Los Feliz**	20
American Girl	**Fairfax**	11
Animal	**Fairfax**	26
☑ Apple Pan	**West LA**	23
Arsenal	**West LA**	16
Auntie Em's	**Eagle Rock**	21
Baleen	**Redondo Bch**	19
Bandera	**West LA**	22
☑ Bashan	**Montrose**	27
Beckham Grill	**Pasadena**	19
Beechwood	**Marina del Rey**	19
Belmont	**W Hollywood**	16
Belmont Brewing	**Long Bch**	18
☑ Belvedere	**Beverly Hills**	25
BJ's	**multi.**	17
Blair's	**Silver Lake**	24
bld	**Beverly Blvd**	22
Bloom	**Mid-City**	21
NEW Blue Dog	**Sherman Oaks**	21
Blue Velvet	**Downtown**	20
Blu LA Café	**Downtown**	-
Blvd 16	**Westwood**	21
Bouzy	**Redondo Bch**	22
Bowery	**Hollywood**	20
Breadbar	**multi.**	18
Brentwood	**Brentwood**	22
Brighton Coffee	**Beverly Hills**	18
Brooks	**Ventura**	25
Buffalo Club	**Santa Monica**	19
Buffalo Fire Dept.	**Torrance**	19
NEW Burger Kitchen	**Mid-City**	-
Cafe 50's	**multi.**	16
Cafe Surfas	**Culver City**	20
Cal. Chicken	**multi.**	21
Carney's	**multi.**	20
Catalina	**Redondo Bch**	22
Catalina Country Club	**Catalina Is.**	-

Cat & Fiddle	**Hollywood**	15
Central Park	**Pasadena**	19
☑ Cheesecake Factory	**multi.**	19
Chili John's	**Burbank**	18
Circa 55	**Beverly Hills**	19
Citizen Smith	**Hollywood**	17
Claim Jumper	**multi.**	18
Clearman's	**San Gabriel**	19
☑ Clementine	**Century City**	24
Clifton's	**Downtown**	13
Cole's	**Downtown**	17
Colony Café	**West LA**	18
Copa d'Oro	**Santa Monica**	17
☑ Craft	**Century City**	24
Daily Grill	**multi.**	19
NEW Daniels	**LAX**	-
Darren's	**Manhattan Bch**	24
NEW Dillon's	**Hollywood**	-
Dining Rm./Shangri-La	**Santa Monica**	22
Dish	**La Cañada Flintridge**	18
Doughboys	**Third St**	22
Du-par's	**multi.**	16
Dusty's	**Silver Lake**	22
Eat Well	**multi.**	17
Edendale Grill	**Silver Lake**	18
☑ Edison	**Downtown**	19
NEW Elements Kitchen	**Pasadena**	23
Engine Co. 28	**Downtown**	21
Farm/Bev. Hills	**multi.**	18
☑ Father's Office	**multi.**	22
FIG	**Santa Monica**	22
Firefly	**Studio City**	20
Firefly Bistro	**S Pasadena**	20
NEW First & Hope	**Downtown**	-
FOOD	**Rancho Pk**	21
Ford's	**Culver City**	20
Foundry/Melrose	**Melrose**	22
Fountain Coffee	**Beverly Hills**	25
Frysmith	**Location Varies**	-
☑ Gjelina	**Venice**	26
NEW Goal	**Fairfax**	-
Gordon Biersch	**Burbank**	16
Gram & Papas	**Downtown**	-

Green St. | **Pasadena**	22
Griddle | **Hollywood**	23
Grilled Cheese | **Location Varies**	-
Grill on Hollywood/Alley | **multi.**	22
Z Grill on Alley | **Beverly Hills**	25
Grub | **Hollywood**	22
Gulfstream | **Century City**	21
Hal's | **Venice**	21
Hamburger Hamlet | **multi.**	18
Hamburger Mary's | **W Hollywood**	14
Hard Rock | **Universal City**	13
Hash & High | **Venice**	-
Z Hatfield's | **Melrose**	27
Henry's Hat | **Universal City**	18
Heroes/Legends | **Claremont**	17
Hideout | **Hollywood**	-
Z Houston's | **multi.**	22
Huckleberry | **Santa Monica**	22
NEW Hudson | **W Hollywood**	-
Hugo's | **W Hollywood**	20
Islands | **multi.**	17
Jack n' Jill's | **multi.**	18
James' | **Venice**	19
Z Jar | **Beverly Blvd.**	25
Jer-ne | **Marina del Rey**	23
Jinky's | **multi.**	19
Z JiRaffe | **Santa Monica**	26
Joan's on 3rd | **Third St.**	23
Johnny Rockets | **multi.**	16
John O'Groats | **multi.**	20
Jones | **W Hollywood**	18
Z Josie | **Santa Monica**	26
Kate Mantilini | **multi.**	18
Ketchup | **W Hollywood**	15
Kings Rd. | **Beverly Blvd.**	16
Kitchen | **Silver Lake**	20
Kitchen 24 | **Hollywood**	20
Lab | **Downtown**	17
LA Food Show | **multi.**	17
NEW L.A. Market | **Downtown**	19
NEW Larchmont Bungalow | **Mid-Wilshire**	19
Larchmont Grill | **Hollywood**	22
Z Lasher's | **Long Bch**	24
Laurel | **Studio City**	23
Lawry's Carvery | **multi.**	20
Library Bar | **Downtown**	17
Local | **Silver Lake**	22
Lucky Devils | **Hollywood**	21
Luna Park | **La Brea**	19
NEW Lunch | **Culver City**	-
NEW Mac & Cheeza | **Downtown**	-
Madame Matisse | **Silver Lake**	-
Magnolia | **multi.**	18
Marmalade | **multi.**	18
Marston's | **Pasadena**	22
Martha's 22nd St. | **Hermosa Bch**	24
Maxwell's | **Venice**	18
Z Mélisse | **Santa Monica**	28
Mel's Drive-In | **multi.**	16
Mike & Anne's | **S Pasadena**	21
Millions/Milkshakes | **W Hollywood**	21
Mimi's | **multi.**	17
Moonshadows | **Malibu**	16
Mo's | **Burbank**	18
NEW Mr. Beef | **Venice**	-
Musso & Frank | **Hollywood**	20
Neptune's Net | **Malibu**	19
Nickel Diner | **Downtown**	22
Nic's | **Beverly Hills**	19
Nine Thirty | **Westwood**	22
Noé | **Downtown**	24
Nook Bistro | **West LA**	24
Ocean & Vine | **Santa Monica**	22
Off Vine | **Hollywood**	-
Oinkster | **Eagle Rock**	20
Omelette Parlor | **Santa Monica**	19
101 Coffee | **Hollywood**	18
Z Original Pancake | **Redondo Bch**	22
Original Pantry | **Downtown**	17
Outlaws | **Playa del Rey**	19
Palate | **Glendale**	24
Palomino | **Westwood**	18
Paradise Cove | **Malibu**	15
Park | **Echo Pk**	24
Parq/Montage | **Beverly Hills**	25
Z Patina | **Downtown**	26
Paul Martin's | **El Segundo**	22
Z Penthouse | **Santa Monica**	20
Pete's | **Downtown**	21
Z Providence | **Hollywood**	28
R+D Kitchen | **Santa Monica**	20
Rainbow B&G | **W Hollywood**	17
Rainforest Cafe | **Ontario**	13

redwhite+bluezz | **Pasadena**	23
Ruby's | **multi.**	17
Rush St. | **Culver City**	17
Russell's | **Pasadena**	24
☑ Saddle Peak | **Calabasas**	27
Safire | **Camarillo**	23
Second City | **El Segundo**	24
Seta | **Whittier**	27
71 Palm | **Ventura**	22
Shack | **multi.**	17
Sidecar | **Ventura**	24
Simmzy's | **Manhattan Bch**	21
Simon LA | **W Hollywood**	22
NEW Sip | **Long Bch**	–
Sky Room | **Long Bch**	18
Smitty's | **Pasadena**	22
NEW South Beverly Grill | **Beverly Hills**	–
Spark | **multi.**	20
Square One | **E Hollywood**	23
Stand | **multi.**	17
Swingers | **multi.**	17
Tart | **Fairfax**	18
Taste | **multi.**	21
☑ Tavern | **Brentwood**	23
Tender Greens | **multi.**	22
Tiara | **Downtown**	23
Tin Roof | **Manhattan Bch**	21
Toast | **Third St**	20
Tom Bergin's | **Fairfax**	13
Tony P's | **Marina del Rey**	17
Trails | **Los Feliz**	–
Traxx | **Downtown**	19
Truxton's | **Westchester**	21
208 Rodeo | **Beverly Hills**	23
Uncle Bill's | **Manhattan Bch**	22
NEW Upper West | **Santa Monica**	–
Urth | **multi.**	21
vermont | **Los Feliz**	22
☑ Vibrato | **Bel-Air**	21
Village Idiot | **Melrose**	19
NEW Villains | **Downtown**	–
Waffle | **Hollywood**	17
Warehouse | **Marina del Rey**	17
Wilshire | **Santa Monica**	23
Wood Ranch | **multi.**	21
XIV | **W Hollywood**	23

Yard House | **multi.**	18
Zin Bistro | **Westlake Vill**	20

ARGENTINEAN

☑ Carlitos Gardel | **Melrose**	24
1810 Rest. | **Pasadena**	23
Gaucho | **multi.**	18

ASIAN

☑ Asia de Cuba | **W Hollywood**	24
Beacon | **Culver City**	22
Buddha's Belly | **multi.**	19
Chaya Brasserie | **W Hollywood**	24
Chaya Downtown | **Downtown**	24
☑ Chinois | **Santa Monica**	26
Feast from East | **West LA**	21
NEW Flying Pig | **Location Varies**	–
Formosa | **W Hollywood**	13
Gina Lee's | **Redondo Bch**	24
☑ Mako | **Beverly Hills**	26
Mirü8691 | **Beverly Hills**	24
Monsoon | **Santa Monica**	20
MOZ | **Agoura Hills**	18
Pei Wei | **multi.**	17
Red 7 | **W Hollywood**	–
☑ RockSugar | **Century City**	21
☑ Roy's | **multi.**	24
Saketini | **Brentwood**	20
NEW Starry Kitchen | **Downtown**	–
Take a Bao | **Century City**	17
NEW Tiato | **Santa Monica**	–
2117 | **West LA**	24
Typhoon | **Santa Monica**	19
Vegan Glory | **Beverly Blvd**	23
☑ Yamashiro | **Hollywood**	18
Yatai | **W Hollywood**	–
NEW Zengo | **Santa Monica**	–

AUSTRIAN

Food + Lab | **W Hollywood**	20

BAKERIES

Breadbar | **multi.**	18
☑ Clementine | **Century City**	24
Dolce Isola | **Pico-Robertson**	–
Doña Rosa | **Pasadena**	17
Doughboys | **Third St**	22
Huckleberry | **Santa Monica**	22
Jack n' Jill's | **Santa Monica**	18
Jin Patisserie | **Venice**	23

Joan's on 3rd | **Third St.** 23

King's Hawaiian | **Torrance** 20

Le Pain Quotidien | **multi.** 20

Maison Richard | **Hollywood** 21

Mäni's | **Fairfax** 17

Misto Caffé | **Torrance** 20

Porto's | **multi.** 24

Röckenwagner | **Santa Monica** 21

Susina | **La Brea** 26

Sweet Lady Jane | **Melrose** 24

Square | **Venice** 23

ARBECUE

Baby Blues | **multi.** 21

Big Mama's | **Pasadena** 21

Boneyard | **Sherman Oaks** 21

NEW Bonnie B's | **Pasadena** -

Dr. Hogly Wogly's | **Van Nuys** 22

Gus's | **S Pasadena** 20

Johnny Rebs' | **multi.** 23

JR's | **Culver City** 22

Lucille's | **multi.** 22

Mr. Cecil's | **multi.** 19

Oinkster | **Eagle Rock** 20

Phillips BBQ | **multi.** 25

Reddi Chick | **Santa Monica** 21

Ribs USA | **Burbank** 19

Robin's | **Pasadena** 20

NEW Smokin' Joint | **W Hollywood** -

Stonefire | **multi.** 20

Wood Ranch | **multi.** 21

Woody's BBQ | **multi.** 24

Zeke's | **multi.** 21

BELGIAN

Le Pain Quotidien | **multi.** 20

Wurstküche | **Downtown** 22

BRAZILIAN

Bossa Nova | **multi.** 20

Café Brasil | **multi.** 19

Fogo de Chão | **Beverly Hills** 23

Galletto | **Westlake Vill** 23

Green Field | **multi.** 19

NEW Libra | **Culver City** -

Picanha | **Burbank** 21

Porto Alegre | **Pasadena** 20

Sampa | **Encino** -

Tropicalia | **Los Feliz** 22

BRITISH

Cat & Fiddle | **Hollywood** 15

NEW Waterloo & City | **Culver City** -

Whale & Ale | **San Pedro** 20

Ye Olde King's | **Santa Monica** 18

BURGERS

Apple Pan | **West LA** 23

Astro Burger | **multi.** 20

Barney's | **multi.** 20

Beacon | **Culver City** 22

NEW Blue Dog | **Sherman Oaks** 21

BoHo | **Hollywood** 17

Burger Continental | **Pasadena** 18

NEW Burger Kitchen | **Mid-City** -

Cassell's | **Koreatown** 21

Clearman's | **San Gabriel** 19

Comme Ça | **W Hollywood** 22

Counter | **multi.** 20

8 oz. | **Melrose** 22

Father's Office | **multi.** 22

Five Guys | **multi.** 20

Ford's | **Culver City** 20

Golden State | **Fairfax** 22

Hamburger Mary's | **W Hollywood** 14

Hole in Wall | **West LA** 21

Hungry Cat | **Hollywood** 24

In-N-Out | **multi.** 24

Islands | **multi.** 17

Johnny Rockets | **multi.** 16

Laurel | **Studio City** 23

Library Bar | **Downtown** 17

Mini Bites | **Hollywood** -

Mo's | **Burbank** 18

Oak Room | **Pacific Palisades** 16

Outlaws | **Playa del Rey** 19

Pie 'N Burger | **Pasadena** 22

Rowdy | **Downtown** -

Russell's | **Pasadena** 24

Shack | **multi.** 17

Tommy's | **Downtown** 23

25 Degrees | **Hollywood** 22

26 Beach | **Venice** 21

Umami | **multi.** 22

CAJUN

Boiling Crab | **Alhambra** 23

NEW Boiling Shrimp | **Hollywood** -

Cajun Kitchen | **Ventura**	20
Gumbo Pot | **Fairfax**	20
Ragin' Cajun | **Hermosa Bch**	19
Stevie's | **Encino**	17
Uncle Darrow's | **Marina del Rey**	19

CALIFORNIAN

Ado | **Venice**	25
Ammo | **Hollywood**	23
Angel's | **Santa Monica**	-
∠ A.O.C. | **Third St**	27
Austen's | **Ventura**	-
Babalu | **Santa Monica**	20
Barefoot B&G | **Third St**	17
Basix | **W Hollywood**	19
Beachcomber Café | **Malibu**	18
Bel-Air B&G | **Bel-Air**	20
∠ Bistro 45 | **Pasadena**	26
Bistro 31 | **Santa Monica**	-
Bloom | **Mid-City**	21
Blvd | **Beverly Hills**	23
Bono's | **Long Bch**	21
NEW Boxwood | **W Hollywood**	22
Breeze | **Century City**	18
Cabbage Patch | **multi.**	23
∠ Café Bizou/Bizou Grill | **multi.**	23
Cafe Del Rey | **Marina del Rey**	22
∠ Café 14 | **Agoura Hills**	27
Cafe Montana | **Santa Monica**	18
Café Nouveau | **Ventura**	21
NEW Café 140 S. | **Pasadena**	19
Cafe Pinot | **Downtown**	23
Cafe Rodeo | **Beverly Hills**	15
Caioti Pizza | **Studio City**	21
Camilo's | **Eagle Rock**	21
∠ Campanile | **La Brea**	26
Canal Club | **Venice**	18
Castaway | **Burbank**	17
∠ Catch | **Santa Monica**	22
Central Park | **Pasadena**	19
Cézanne | **Santa Monica**	22
∠ Chateau Marmont | **W Hollywood**	19
Checkers | **Downtown**	21
Chef Melba's | **Hermosa Bch**	27
China Grill | **Manhattan Bch**	19
∠ Cicada | **Downtown**	23
Circa 55 | **Beverly Hills**	19
∠ Cliff's Edge | **Silver Lake**	19

Coast | **Santa Monica**	21
NEW Colony | **Hollywood**	-
Coral Tree | **multi.**	17
NEW Cuvee | **W Hollywood**	-
Darren's | **Manhattan Bch**	24
∠ Derek's | **Pasadena**	26
Desert Rose | **Los Feliz**	19
Devon | **Monrovia**	24
NEW DISH | **Pasadena**	-
Emle's | **Northridge**	20
NEW Eva | **Beverly Blvd**	25
Five 61 | **Pasadena**	23
Food + Lab | **W Hollywood**	20
NEW Forage | **Silver Lake**	25
410 Boyd | **Downtown**	20
∠ Geoffrey's | **Malibu**	20
Getty Ctr. | **Brentwood**	22
Gina Lee's | **Redondo Bch**	24
NEW Glendon Bar | **West LA**	-
Golden State | **Fairfax**	23
Green St. Tav. | **Pasadena**	24
Hampton's | **Westlake Vill**	23
Hugo's | **multi.**	20
∠ Inn/Seventh Ray | **Topanga**	21
Ivy | **W Hollywood**	21
Ivy/Shore | **Santa Monica**	21
∠ Joe's | **Venice**	26
Jonathan's | **Ventura**	23
La Boheme | **W Hollywood**	21
La Grande Orange | **multi.**	21
NEW L.A. Market | **Downtown**	19
LAMILL | **Silver Lake**	21
NEW La Vida | **Hollywood**	-
∠ Leila's | **Oak Pk**	27
Lemonade Cafe | **multi.**	22
Lemon Moon | **West LA**	20
Literati | **West LA**	19
Louise's | **multi.**	15
∠ Lucques | **W Hollywood**	26
Market City | **Burbank**	16
Marmalade | **multi.**	18
∠ mar'sel | **Rancho Palos Verdes**	25
Mexicali | **Studio City**	16
∠ Michael's | **Santa Monica**	24
Milky Way | **Pico-Robertson**	19
Mi Piace | **multi.**	20
Mirabelle | **W Hollywood**	21
Misto Caffé | **Torrance**	21

Napa Valley | **Westwood**	19
Native Foods | **Westwood**	23
Oak Room | **Pacific Palisades**	16
Off Vine | **Hollywood**	-
NEW Olive | **Hollywood**	-
One Pico | **Santa Monica**	20
Parkway Grill | **Pasadena**	26
Patina | **Downtown**	26
Pat's | **Pico-Robertson**	20
Polo | **Beverly Hills**	23
Porta Via | **Beverly Hills**	21
Ranch Hse. | **Ojai**	22
Raymond | **Pasadena**	25
Röckenwagner | **Santa Monica**	21
Rose Cafe | **Venice**	21
Rustic Canyon | **Santa Monica**	23
Z Sam's/Beach | **Santa Monica**	26
17th St. Cafe | **Santa Monica**	19
Sir Winston's | **Long Bch**	24
NEW Sonoma | **Santa Monica**	-
Z Spago | **Beverly Hills**	27
Stanley's | **Sherman Oaks**	20
Z Sur | **W Hollywood**	23
Terra | **Malibu**	22
Third & Olive | **Burbank**	23
Tower Bar | **W Hollywood**	21
NEW Townhouse | **Sherman Oaks**	12
26 Beach | **Venice**	21
uWink | **Hollywood**	10
West | **Brentwood**	20
Westside Tav. | **West LA**	21
Whist | **Santa Monica**	20
Wolfgang Puck B&G | **Downtown**	22
Wolfgang Puck Café | **multi.**	19
Z Yamashiro | **Hollywood**	18
Zeidler's | **Brentwood**	15

CANADIAN
Soleil | **Westwood**	19

CARIBBEAN
Bamboo | **Culver City**	21
Cha Cha Cha | **Silver Lake**	19
Cha Cha Chicken | **Santa Monica**	20
Prado | **Hancock Pk**	22

CHINESE
(* dim sum specialist)
ABC Seafood* | **Chinatown**	20
Bamboo Cuisine | **Sherman Oaks**	23
Bamboodles | **San Gabriel**	20
Cal. Wok | **multi.**	16
CBS Seafood | **Chinatown**	20
Chi Dynasty | **Los Feliz**	21
China Grill | **Manhattan Bch**	19
Chin Chin* | **multi.**	17
Chung King | **Monterey Pk**	22
Z Din Tai Fung | **Arcadia**	25
Elite | **Monterey Pk**	24
Empress Harbor* | **Monterey Pk**	21
Empress Pavilion* | **Chinatown**	20
Fu-Shing | **Pasadena**	19
Genghis Cohen | **Fairfax**	21
Hop Li* | **multi.**	19
Hop Woo | **multi.**	19
Hu's | **Palms**	22
Lunasia* | **Alhambra**	22
Mandarette | **Beverly Blvd.**	19
Mandarin | **multi.**	23
Mission 261* | **San Gabriel**	-
Mr. Chow | **Beverly Hills**	23
Z NBC Seafood* | **Monterey Pk**	21
New Moon | **multi.**	21
Ocean Seafood* | **Chinatown**	21
Ocean Star* | **Monterey Pk**	21
NEW 101 Noodle | **multi.**	22
NEW Palace Seafood* | **West LA**	-
Panda Inn* | **multi.**	21
P.F. Chang's | **multi.**	19
NEW Philippe | **W Hollywood**	17
Sam Woo | **multi.**	22
Sea Empress* | **Gardena**	18
Z Sea Harbour* | **Rosemead**	25
V.I.P. Harbor* | **West LA**	19
Wokcano | **multi.**	16
NEW WP24 | **Downtown**	-
W's China | **Redondo Bch**	22
Xi'an | **Beverly Hills**	21
NEW Xino | **Santa Monica**	-
Yang Chow | **multi.**	22
Z Yujean Kang's | **Pasadena**	26

COFFEEHOUSES
Caffe Luxxe | **multi.**	20
Coupa | **Beverly Hills**	19
LAMILL | **Silver Lake**	21
Literati | **West LA**	17
Urth | **multi.**	21

LOS ANGELES

CUISINES

COFFEE SHOPS/ DINERS

Brighton Coffee	**Beverly Hills**	18
Cafe 50's	**multi.**	16
Z Cora's	**Santa Monica**	23
Dukes West Hollywood	**W Hollywood**	18
Du-par's	**multi.**	16
Eat Well	**W Hollywood**	17
Fountain Coffee	**Beverly Hills**	25
Fred 62	**Los Feliz**	17
Hamburger Mary's	**W Hollywood**	14
Jan's	**W Hollywood**	16
Johnnie's Pastrami	**Culver City**	20
Kate Mantilini	**multi.**	18
Mimi's	**multi.**	17
Nickel Diner	**Downtown**	22
101 Coffee	**Hollywood**	18
Z Original Pancake	**Redondo Bch**	22
Original Pantry	**Downtown**	17
Patrick's	**Santa Monica**	18
Pie 'N Burger	**Pasadena**	22
Rae's	**Santa Monica**	15
Ruby's	**multi.**	17
Russell's	**Pasadena**	24
Swingers	**multi.**	17
Uncle Bill's	**Manhattan Bch**	22
Waffle	**Hollywood**	17

CONTINENTAL

Z Bistro Gdn.	**Studio City**	21
Boccaccio's	**Westlake Vill**	20
NEW Boxwood	**W Hollywood**	22
Z Brandywine	**Woodland Hills**	28
Z Café 14	**Agoura Hills**	27
Dal Rae	**Pico Rivera**	25
NEW Drai's	**Hollywood**	-
Fins	**multi.**	21
Pig 'n Whistle	**Hollywood**	17
Z Polo	**Beverly Hills**	23
Sir Winston's	**Long Bch**	24

CREOLE

Harold & Belle's	**Mid-City**	24
Jack n' Jill's Too	**Third St**	21
Stevie's	**Encino**	17
Uncle Darrow's	**Marina del Rey**	19

CRÊPES

French Crêpe Co.	**multi.**	21
Jack n' Jill's Too	**Third St**	21
La Creperie	**Long Bch**	23

CUBAN

Z Asia de Cuba	**W Hollywood**	24
NEW Café Habana	**Malibu**	-
Cuban Bistro	**Alhambra**	20
Havana Mania	**Redondo Bch**	-
Z Porto's	**multi.**	24
Versailles	**multi.**	21

DELIS

Art's	**Studio City**	20
Barney Greengrass	**Beverly Hills**	22
Z Bay Cities	**Santa Monica**	25
Z Brent's	**multi.**	26
Broadway Deli	**Santa Monica**	15
Canter's	**Fairfax**	19
Factor's	**Pico-Robertson**	18
Fromin's	**multi.**	15
Greenblatt's	**Hollywood**	19
Junior's	**West LA**	16
La Bottega Marino	**multi.**	21
Z Langer's	**Downtown**	27
Little Dom's/Deli	**Los Feliz**	21
Nate 'n Al	**multi.**	20
Porta Via Italian	**Pasadena**	24
Roll 'n Rye	**Culver City**	19
Village Pantry	**Pacific Palisades**	15

DESSERT

Akasha	**Culver City**	20
Alcove	**Los Feliz**	20
Auntie Em's	**Eagle Rock**	21
Babalu	**Santa Monica**	20
Cafe Montana	**Santa Monica**	18
Z Cheesecake Factory	**multi.**	19
Z Clementine	**Century City**	24
Doughboys	**Third St**	23
Farm/Bev. Hills	**multi.**	18
French Crêpe Co.	**multi.**	21
Huckleberry	**Santa Monica**	22
Maison Richard	**Hollywood**	21
Pop	**Pasadena**	17
Z Porto's	**multi.**	24
Simon LA	**W Hollywood**	22
Z Susina	**La Brea**	26
Sweet Lady Jane	**Melrose**	24

Menus, photos, voting and more – free at ZAGAT.com

EASTERN EUROPEAN

Aroma | **West LA**	19

ECLECTIC

Bar*Food | **West LA**	15
Barbara's | **Downtown**	15
Barefoot B&G | **Third St**	17
Barney's Beanery | **W Hollywood**	15
NEW bar210 | **Beverly Hills**	-
Bellavino | **Westlake Vill**	19
Bistro LQ | **Fairfax**	24
BoHo | **Hollywood**	17
Boneyard | **Sherman Oaks**	21
Broadway Deli | **Santa Monica**	15
Canal Club | **Venice**	18
Chez Mélange | **Redondo Bch**	25
NEW Collection | **Malibu**	-
Corkbar | **Downtown**	22
Coupa | **Beverly Hills**	19
Depot | **Torrance**	24
NEW District | **Hollywood**	-
NEW East | **Hollywood**	25
NEW Elements Kitchen | **Pasadena**	23
Encounter | **LAX**	16
Farm Stand | **El Segundo**	22
Figtree's | **Venice**	-
NEW Gold Class | **Pasadena**	18
NEW Gorbals | **Downtown**	21
Grand Lux | **Beverly Hills**	19
NEW House Café | **Beverly Blvd**	21
Hudson Hse. | **Redondo Bch**	23
Lazy Dog | **Torrance**	17
NEW Lazy Ox | **Little Tokyo**	24
Library | **Santa Monica**	19
Literati | **West LA**	17
Z Lou | **Hollywood**	25
Magnolia Lounge | **Pasadena**	15
NEW Market Café | **Downtown**	-
Minx | **Glendale**	-
Mirabelle | **W Hollywood**	20
Misto Caffé | **Torrance**	20
Z Native Foods | **Westwood**	23
NEW Noir | **Pasadena**	25
Nook Bistro | **West LA**	24
Pop | **Pasadena**	17
Reservoir | **Silver Lake**	23
NEW Rockwell | **Los Feliz**	-

Z Saam/The Bazaar | **Beverly Hills**	27
Standard | **W Hollywood**	19
Standard | **Downtown**	17
NEW Stefan's/L.A. Farm | **Santa Monica**	23
NEW Stefan's/Montana | **Santa Monica**	20
Street | **Hollywood**	20
Z NEW Tar Pit | **La Brea**	20
Vertical Wine | **Pasadena**	21
Villa Piacere | **Woodland Hills**	18
Walter's | **Claremont**	21
Westside Cellar | **Ventura**	-
World Cafe | **Santa Monica**	18
York | **Highland Pk**	18

ETHIOPIAN

Nyala | **Fairfax**	23

EUROPEAN

BottleRock | **multi.**	16
Green St. Tav. | **Pasadena**	24
Palomino | **Westwood**	18
2117 | **West LA**	24

FONDUE

Melting Pot | **multi.**	18

FRENCH

Z A.O.C. | **Third St**	27
Z Bastide | **W Hollywood**	27
Bowery | **Hollywood**	20
Café Beaujolais | **Eagle Rock**	20
Café Pierre | **Manhattan Bch**	23
Cafe Pinot | **Downtown**	23
Café Provencal | **Thousand Oaks**	23
Cézanne | **Santa Monica**	22
Z Chateau Marmont | **W Hollywood**	19
Chaya Brasserie | **W Hollywood**	24
Chaya Downtown | **Downtown**	24
Chaya Venice | **Venice**	23
Z Chinois | **Santa Monica**	26
Z Church/State | **Downtown**	25
Clafoutis | **W Hollywood**	19
NEW Delphine | **Hollywood**	20
Z Derek's | **Pasadena**	26
Devon | **Monrovia**	24
Dusty's | **Silver Lake**	21
FIG | **Santa Monica**	22

Five 61 | **Pasadena**	23
🆉 Fraîche | **multi.**	23
French Crêpe Co. | **multi.**	21
Gordon Ramsay | **W Hollywood**	23
Jin Patisserie | **Venice**	23
🆉 JiRaffe | **Santa Monica**	26
🆉 Joe's | **Venice**	26
La Cachette | **Santa Monica**	21
La Frite | **multi.**	19
La Rive Gauche | **Palos Verdes**	20
Le Chêne | **Saugus**	25
Le Sanglier | **Tarzana**	25
Madeleine | **Tarzana**	28
🆉 Maison Akira | **Pasadena**	26
🆉 Mélisse | **Santa Monica**	28
Morels Steak | **Fairfax**	20
🆉 Orris | **West LA**	27
Ortolan | **Third St.**	25
Petrossian | **W Hollywood**	23
RH | **W Hollywood**	25
Royal/T | **Culver City**	17
71 Palm | **Ventura**	22
🆉 Shiro | **S Pasadena**	28
Soleil | **Westwood**	19
Suzanne's | **Ojai**	25
Taix | **Echo Pk**	17
Third & Olive | **Burbank**	23

FRENCH (BISTRO)

Angelique | **Downtown**	21
🆖 Bar Bouchon | **Beverly Hills**	23
Bistro/Gare | **S Pasadena**	19
Bistro LQ | **Fairfax**	24
Bistro Provence | **Burbank**	23
🆉🆖 Bouchon | **Beverly Hills**	24
🆉 Café Bizou/Bizou Grill | **multi.**	23
Cafe/Artistes | **Hollywood**	20
Cafe Stella | **Silver Lake**	21
Café Was | **Hollywood**	17
🆖 Cheval Blanc | **Pasadena**	22
Figaro | **Los Feliz**	20
Frenchy's | **Long Bch**	25
🆉 Julienne | **San Marino**	26
La Creperie | **Long Bch**	23
La Dijonaise | **Culver City**	17
Le Petit Bistro | **W Hollywood**	20
Le Petit Cafe | **Santa Monica**	21
Le Petit Four | **W Hollywood**	20

Le Petit Rest. | **Sherman Oaks**	23
Lilly's | **Venice**	19
🆖 Maison Maurice | **Beverly Hills**	–
Maison Richard | **Hollywood**	21
🆖 Mercantile | **Hollywood**	21
🆉 Mistral | **Sherman Oaks**	26
Monsieur Marcel | **multi.**	20
Morels Bistro | **Fairfax**	20
Pinot Bistro | **Studio City**	24
🆖 Quadrupel | **Pasadena**	–
Rive Gauche | **Sherman Oaks**	22
Wine Bistro | **Studio City**	23

FRENCH (BRASSERIE)

🆉 Anisette | **Santa Monica**	21
Café Chez Marie | **Century City**	–
Comme Ça | **W Hollywood**	22
Hall | **W Hollywood**	21
Kendall's | **Downtown**	19
Le St. Amour | **Culver City**	20

GASTROPUB

Bouzy | Amer. | **Redondo Bch**	22
🆖 8½ Taverna | Italian | **Studio City**	–
🆉 Father's Office | Amer./Burgers | **multi.**	22
Ford's | Amer. | **Culver City**	20
Laurel | Amer. | **Studio City**	23
Library Bar | Amer. | **Downtown**	17
R+D Kitchen | Amer. | **Santa Monica**	20
Village Idiot | Amer. | **Melrose**	19
🆖 Waterloo & City | British | **Culver City**	–
York | Eclectic | **Highland Pk**	18

GERMAN

Chalet Edelweiss | **Westchester**	17
Red Lion | **Silver Lake**	17
Wurstküche | **Downtown**	22

GREEK

Delphi | **Westwood**	16
George's Greek | **multi.**	22
Great Greek | **Sherman Oaks**	20
Le Petit Greek | **Hancock Pk**	21
Old Venice | **Manhattan Bch**	18
🆉 Papa Cristo's | **Mid-City**	24

Petros | **Manhattan Bch** 23

ofi | **Third St** 20

averna Tony | **Malibu** 21

Ulysses Voyage | **Fairfax** 20

AWAIIAN

ack Home | **multi.** 17

King's Hawaiian | **Torrance** 20

ocal Pl. | **Torrance** 17

oft | **multi.** 19

Roy's | **multi.** 24

HOT DOGS

Carney's | **multi.** 20

ab Hot Dogs | **Reseda** -

Golden State | **Fairfax** 22

ody Maroni's | **multi.** 19

Let's Be Frank | **Culver City** 21

Pink's Dogs | **La Brea** 20

Portillo's | **Moreno Valley** 22

NEW Slaw Dogs | **Pasadena** 18

Stand | **multi.** 17

Tommy's | **Downtown** 23

INDIAN

Addi's | **Redondo Bch** 24

Agra | **Silver Lake** 22

Akbar | **multi.** 22

All India | **multi.** 21

Bollywood | **Studio City** 17

Bombay Bite | **Westwood** 19

Bombay Cafe | **West LA** 22

Bombay Palace | **Beverly Hills** 21

Clay Pit | **Brentwood** 21

Cowboys/Turbans | **multi.** -

Electric Lotus | **Los Feliz** 22

Flavor of India | **multi.** 21

Holy Cow | **Third St** 22

India's Clay Oven | **Beverly Blvd** 21

India's Oven/Wilshire | **West LA** 21

India's Tandoori | **multi.** 21

Lal Mirch | **Studio City** 17

NEW Lawrence/India | **Culver City** -

Nawab | **Santa Monica** 23

Nizam | **West LA** 19

Tantra | **Silver Lake** -

Tanzore | **Beverly Hills** 21

INDONESIAN

Indo | **Palms** 20

Simpang Asia | **Palms** 17

IRISH

Auld Dubliner | **Long Bch** 16

NEW Dillon's | **Hollywood** -

Tom Bergin's | **Fairfax** 13

ISRAELI

NEW Itzik Hagadol | **Encino** 21

ITALIAN

(N=Northern; S=Southern)

Adagio | N | **Woodland Hills** 22

Ado | **Venice** 25

Ago | N | **W Hollywood** 21

Alejo's | **multi.** 21

Alessio | **multi.** 21

Allora | **Third St** -

Amalfi | **La Brea** 19

Amarone | **W Hollywood** 26

Amici | **multi.** 21

Angeli | **Melrose** 25

Angelini | **Beverly Blvd** 28

Antica | **Marina del Rey** 21

Aroma | **Silver Lake** 23

Barbrix | **Silver Lake** 23

Basix | **W Hollywood** 19

Bay Cities | **Santa Monica** 25

Bella Roma | S | **Pico-Robertson** 24

NEW Bellini Osteria | **Westlake Vill** -

Berri's | **multi.** 15

Boccali's | **Ojai** 19

Bottega Louie | **Downtown** 22

Bottle Inn | **Hermosa Bch** -

Bravo | **Santa Monica** 19

Briganti | **S Pasadena** 21

Brunello | **Culver City** 23

Buca di Beppo | S | **multi.** 15

Buona Sera | **Redondo Bch** 18

Ca'Brea | N | **La Brea** 22

Ca' del Sole | N | **N Hollywood** 21

Cafe FIORE | S | **Ventura** 22

Cafe Firenze | N | **Moorpark** 19

Cafe Med | **W Hollywood** 19

Café Piccolo | N | **Long Bch** 22

Caffé Delfini | **Santa Monica** 23

Caffe Pinguini | **Playa del Rey** 22

Caffe Primo | **W Hollywood**	18
Caffe Roma | **Beverly Hills**	18
C & O | **Marina del Rey**	19
Capo | **Santa Monica**	25
NEW Capriotti's | **Beverly Hills**	23
Casa Bianca | **Eagle Rock**	23
Cecconi's | N | **W Hollywood**	20
Celestino | **Pasadena**	25
NEW Centanni | **Venice**	19
Cheebo | **Hollywood**	20
Z Cicada | N | **Downtown**	23
Clafoutis | **W Hollywood**	19
Z Cliff's Edge | **Silver Lake**	19
Coral Tree | **multi.**	17
Cube | **La Brea**	25
NEW Cucina Rustica | **Downtown**	–
NEW Culina | **Beverly Hills**	–
D'Amore's | **Camarillo**	20
Dan Tana's | **W Hollywood**	23
Da Pasquale | S | **Beverly Hills**	23
Delancey | **Hollywood**	20
Divino | **Brentwood**	24
Dominick's | **Beverly Blvd.**	21
Drago | **Santa Monica**	23
Z Drago Centro | **Downtown**	26
NEW Eatalian | **Gardena**	–
E. Baldi | N | **Beverly Hills**	23
Enoteca Drago | **Beverly Hills**	22
Enoteca Toscana | **Camarillo**	25
Enzo/Angela | **West LA**	21
Fabiolus | N | **Hollywood**	18
Farfalla | **Los Feliz**	24
Far Niente | N | **Glendale**	23
NEW Firenze | **N Hollywood**	20
Z Fraîche | **multi.**	23
Frascati | N | **Rolling Hills Estates**	23
Fritto Misto | **multi.**	21
Gale's | N | **Pasadena**	24
Galletto | **Westlake Vill**	23
Gennaro's | N | **Glendale**	22
Giorgio Baldi | **Santa Monica**	26
Girasole | N | **Hancock Pk**	24
Guido's | N | **multi.**	20
i Cugini | **Santa Monica**	21
Il Buco | **Beverly Hills**	22
Il Capriccio | **Los Feliz**	23
Il Chianti | **Lomita**	21
Z Il Cielo | N | **Beverly Hills**	22

Il Fornaio | **multi.**	21
Il Forno | N | **Santa Monica**	21
Il Forno Caldo | **Beverly Hills**	21
Il Grano | **West LA**	26
Il Moro | **West LA**	22
Il Pastaio | **Beverly Hills**	26
Il Piccolino | **W Hollywood**	22
Il Sole | **W Hollywood**	23
Z Il Tiramisù | N | **Sherman Oaks**	24
Il Tramezzino | **multi.**	19
Ivy/Shore | **Santa Monica**	22
Johnnie's NY | **multi.**	17
Jones | **W Hollywood**	18
La Bistecca | **Downtown**	–
La Botte | **Santa Monica**	24
La Bottega Marino | **multi.**	21
La Bruschetta | **Westwood**	23
NEW La Campagna | **Hermosa Bch**	–
La Dolce Vita | **Beverly Hills**	22
La Loggia | **Studio City**	21
La Parolaccia | **multi.**	21
La Pergola | **Sherman Oaks**	23
La Piazza | **Fairfax**	18
La Scala | **multi.**	21
La Sosta | N | **Hermosa Bch**	–
La Strada | **Long Bch**	21
Z La Vecchia | **Santa Monica**	25
Lido/Manhattan | **Manhattan Bch**	18
Little Dom's/Deli | **Los Feliz**	21
Locanda/Lago | N | **Santa Monica**	22
NEW Locanda Positano | **Marina del Rey**	–
Locanda Veneta | N | **Third St**	25
L'Opera | N | **Long Bch**	23
Louise's | **multi.**	17
Madeo | N | **W Hollywood**	25
Maggiano's | **multi.**	19
Mama D's | **multi.**	19
Maria's | **multi.**	17
Marino | **Hollywood**	24
Market City | **Burbank**	18
Matteo's | **West LA**	20
Miceli's | S | **multi.**	16
Michael's/Naples | **Long Bch**	26
Michelangelo | **Silver Lake**	18
Minestraio | **W Hollywood**	23
Mio Babbo's | **Westwood**	20

Menus, photos, voting and more – free at ZAGAT.com

i Piace | multi.	20
odo Mio | Pacific Palisades	22
osto | Marina del Rey	25
ulberry St. Pizzeria | multi.	23
onna | W Hollywood	23
NY & C Pizzeria | Santa Monica	17
ld Venice | Manhattan Bch	18
Olive | Hollywood	-
Oliverio | Beverly Hills	-
steria La Buca | N | Hollywood	23
steria Latini | Brentwood	24
Osteria Mamma | Hollywood	-
Osteria Mozza | Hollywood	27
ace | Laurel Canyon	22
adri | Agoura Hills	22
alermo | Los Feliz	18
almeri | S | Brentwood	24
ane e Vino | Beverly Blvd	21
anini Cafe | multi.	20
anzanella | S | Sherman Oaks	23
astina | S | West LA	21
at's | Pico-Robertson	20
ecorino | Brentwood	23
eppone | Brentwood	21
Piccolo | N | Venice	26
ccolo Paradiso | Beverly Hills	24
tfire Artisan Pizza | multi.	-
Pizza Antica | Santa Monica	-
Pizzeria Mozza | Hollywood	27
izzicotto | Brentwood	23
omodoro | multi.	16
orta Via Italian | Pasadena	24
rizzi's | Hollywood	21
rosecco | N | Toluca Lake	22
st. Villa Portofino | Catalina Is.	-
iviera | Calabasas	24
omano's | multi.	17
osti | N | multi.	17
ustico | Westlake Vill	24
aluté | Santa Monica	-
apori | Marina del Rey	24
sley | multi.	19
Sonoma | Santa Monica	-
or Tino | Brentwood	22
pumoni | multi.	20
tinking Rose | Beverly Hills	19

Suzanne's | Ojai	25
Talia's | Manhattan Bch	23
Tanino | S | Westwood	21
Taste Chicago | Burbank	19
Terroni | S | Beverly Blvd	22
Tony's Bella Vista | Burbank	15
Toscana | N | Brentwood	24
Toscanova | Century City	20
Tra Di Noi | Malibu	22
Trastevere | multi.	19
Tre Venezie | N | Pasadena	22
Tulipano | Azusa	-
Tuscany | Westlake Vill	26
Tutti Mangia | Claremont	23
Ugo/Cafe | Culver City	17
Valentino | Santa Monica	26
Via Alloro | Beverly Hills	21
Via Veneto | Santa Monica	24
Villa Sorriso | Pasadena	20
Vincenti | Brentwood	26
NEW Vintage Enoteca | Hollywood	-
Vitello's | Studio City	16
Vito | Santa Monica	22
Vittorio's | S | Pacific Palisades	18
West | Brentwood	20
Zane's | Hermosa Bch	26
Zucca | Downtown	22

JAPANESE

(* sushi specialist)

Ahi* | Studio City	21
Asahi | West LA	20
Asaka* | Rancho Palos Verdes	16
Asakuma* | multi.	21
Asanebo* | Studio City	27
Asuka* | Westwood	19
Banzai* | Calabasas	20
Bar Hayama | West LA	22
Benihana | multi.	19
BiMi | West LA	23
Bond St. | Beverly Hills	20
Boss Sushi* | Beverly Hills	25
Cafe Sushi* | Beverly Blvd	21
Catch* | Santa Monica	22
Chabuya | West LA	21
Chaya Venice | Venice	23
Crazy Fish* | Beverly Hills	18
Echigo* | West LA	26

Name	Location	Rating
Fat Fish*	multi.	19
Geisha Hse.*	Hollywood	18
Z Gonpachi	Beverly Hills	21
Gyu-Kaku	multi.	20
Hamakaze	Marina del Rey	-
Z Hamasaku*	West LA	27
Hama*	Venice	22
Hayakawa*	Covina	28
Hide*	West LA	24
Hirosuke*	Encino	19
Hirozen*	Beverly Blvd.	26
Honda-Ya	Little Tokyo	22
Hurry Curry	West LA	18
Iroha*	Studio City	25
Itacho	Beverly Blvd	21
Izaka-Ya	multi.	26
NEW Izakaya Fu-Ga	Little Tokyo	-
Izayoi*	Little Tokyo	25
Z Japon Bistro*	Pasadena	25
Kabuki*	multi.	18
Katana*	W Hollywood	23
Z Katsu-ya	multi.	26
Z Katsuya*	multi.	23
Kiwami	Studio City	26
Koi*	W Hollywood	24
K-Zo*	Culver City	24
Lomo Arigato	Location Varies	-
Z Maison Akira	Pasadena	26
Z Matsuhisa*	Beverly Hills	28
Mia Sushi*	Eagle Rock	-
Mishima	Third St	19
Z Mori Sushi*	West LA	27
Murakami	Hollywood	-
Musha	multi.	25
Naga Naga	multi.	-
Nanbankan	West LA	25
Natalee*	Palms	19
Nishimura*	W Hollywood	26
Z Nobu LA	W Hollywood	26
Z Nobu Malibu	Malibu	26
Omino*	Chatsworth	26
O-Nami*	Torrance	23
Z Orris	West LA	27
NEW Ozumo	Santa Monica	-
Pearl Dragon*	Pacific Palisades	16
RA Sushi*	Torrance	16
Robata Bar	Santa Monica	26
Robata-Ya	West LA	20
Royal/T	Culver City	1
R23*	Downtown	2
Saito's*	Silver Lake	-
Sashi*	Manhattan Bch	2
Shabu Shabu	Little Tokyo	2
Shima	Venice	-
Z Shiro	S Pasadena	2
SHU*	Bel-Air	2
sugarFISH*	multi.	2
Sushi Dokoro*	Beverly Hills	2
Sushi Gen*	Little Tokyo	2
Z Sushi Masu*	West LA	2
Sushi Mon*	Third St.	2
Z Sushi Nozawa*	Studio City	2
Sushi Roku*	multi.	2
Z Sushi Sasabune/Sushi-Don*	multi.	2
Sushi Sushi*	Beverly Hills	2
Z Sushi Zo*	West LA	2
Taiko*	multi.	2
Takami*	Downtown	2
Takao*	Brentwood	2
Tengu*	Westwood	2
Teru Sushi*	Studio City	2
NEW Tiger Sushi*	Beverly Hills	-
Tokyo Table	Arcadia	1
Torafuku*	West LA	2
Tsuji No Hana*	Marina del Rey	2
Z Urasawa*	Beverly Hills	2
U-Zen*	West LA	2
Z Wa*	W Hollywood	2
Wabi-Sabi*	Venice	2
Wokcano*	multi.	1
Yabu*	multi.	2
Yamato	Brentwood	18
Yen*	multi.	2
Yuzu*	Torrance	2
Zip Fusion*	Downtown	19

KOREAN

(* barbecue specialist)

Name	Location	Rating
BCD Tofu	multi.	20
BonChon	Koreatown	19
NEW Chego!	Palms	-
ChoSun Galbee*	Koreatown	23
Gyenari*	Culver City	20
Jian*	Beverly Blvd	23
Kogi	Location Varies	23
NEW K-Town*	Downtown	-

Manna* | multi.	18
Park's BBQ* | Koreatown	24
Seoul Jung* | Downtown	24
Shin* | Hollywood	-
Soot Bull Jeep* | Koreatown	23
Tofu-Ya* | West LA	23
Vharo* | Marina del Rey	21
Woo Lae Oak | Beverly Hills	22

KOSHER/ KOSHER-STYLE

Fish Grill | multi.	19
Milky Way | Pico-Robertson	19
Pat's | Pico-Robertson	20
Real Food Daily | W Hollywood	22
Tierra Sur/Herzog | Oxnard	27
Zeidler's | Brentwood	15

LEBANESE

Carnival | Sherman Oaks	24
Gaby's | multi.	20
Marouch | E Hollywood	21
Open Sesame | multi.	22
Skaf's | Glendale	22
Sunnin | multi.	23

MALAYSIAN

NEW Manja | W Hollywood	-

MEDITERRANEAN

Aroma | West LA	19
Barbrix | Silver Lake	23
Beau Rivage | Malibu	19
Cabbage Patch | multi.	23
Cafe Del Rey | Marina del Rey	22
Café Pacific | Rancho Palos Verdes	22
Café Santorini | Pasadena	22
Campanile | La Brea	26
Canelé | Atwater Vill	23
Casablanca Med. | Claremont	23
Christine | Torrance	25
NEW Da Vinci | Beverly Hills	-
NEW Delphine | Hollywood	20
Desert Rose | Los Feliz	19
NEW DISH | Pasadena	-
Elf Café | Echo Pk	27
Emle's | Northridge	20
Gaby's | multi.	20
Jonathan's | Ventura	23
Lemon Moon | West LA	20

Lido/Manhattan | Manhattan Bch	18
Little Door | Third St	23
NEW Living Room/Station | Hollywood	-
Lou | Hollywood	25
Lucques | W Hollywood	27
Mantee | Studio City	23
Mediterraneo | Hermosa Bch	20
Mediterraneo | Westlake Vill	24
NEW Momed | Beverly Hills	-
Muma | Melrose	-
One Pico | Santa Monica	20
Panini Cafe | multi.	20
Phlight | Whittier	23
Pourtal | Santa Monica	22
Primitivo | Venice	23
Rustic Canyon | Santa Monica	23
Saluté | Santa Monica	-
Sam's/Beach | Santa Monica	26
Sur | W Hollywood	23
Tasting Kitchen | Venice	22
Tierra Sur/Herzog | Oxnard	27
Trio | Rolling Hills Estates	17
Turquoise | Redondo Bch	-
Upstairs 2 | West LA	23
Vertical Wine | Pasadena	21
Villa Blanca | Beverly Hills	18
Zankou | multi.	22
Zazou | Redondo Bch	22

MEXICAN

Adobe Cantina | Agoura Hills	17
Alegria/Sunset | Silver Lake	25
Antonio's | Melrose	22
Babita | San Gabriel	27
Baja Fresh | multi.	17
Best Fish Taco | Los Feliz	21
Border Grill | Santa Monica	21
Border Grill Truck | Location Varies	20
NEW Borracho | W Hollywood	-
NEW CaCao | Eagle Rock	25
Candela | Mid-City	-
Casa | Downtown	19
Casablanca | Venice	20
Casa Vega | Sherman Oaks	17
NEW Charcoal Grill | Downtown	-
NEW Chego! | Palms	-
Chichen Itza | Downtown	24

Chipotle | **multi.**	19
Cook's Tortas | **Monterey Pk**	25
Doña Rosa | **Pasadena**	17
El Carmen | **Third St**	15
El Cholo | **multi.**	18
NEW El Cholo Downtown | **Downtown**	-
El Coyote | **Beverly Blvd**	15
El Tepeyac | **East LA**	25
El Torito | **multi.**	15
El Torito Grill | **multi.**	19
Frida | **multi.**	20
NEW Fuego/Maya | **Long Bch**	19
Guelaguetza | **multi.**	21
NEW Ixtapa | **Pasadena**	-
Kay 'n Dave's | **multi.**	16
Kogi | **Location Varies**	23
La Cabanita | **Montrose**	25
La Huasteca | **Lynwood**	-
Lares | **Santa Monica**	20
NEW La Sandia | **Santa Monica**	-
La Serenata | **multi.**	22
NEW Los Arroyos | **Camarillo**	23
Lotería! | **multi.**	24
Lula | **Santa Monica**	21
Malo | **Silver Lake**	19
Mexicali | **Studio City**	16
Mexico City | **Los Feliz**	20
Mexico Rest. | **W Hollywood**	19
Mijares | **Pasadena**	17
Mi Ranchito | **Culver City**	19
Monte Alban | **West LA**	20
Mucho Ultima | **Manhattan Bch**	20
Ortega 120 | **Redondo Bch**	20
Paco's Tacos | **multi.**	21
Pink Taco | **Century City**	16
NEW Plancha | **Mid-City**	-
Poquito Más | **multi.**	21
NEW Red O | **Melrose**	-
NEW Rosa Mexicano | **Downtown**	22
Señor Fred | **Sherman Oaks**	17
Sharky's | **multi.**	19
Tamayo | **East LA**	21
Tlapazola | **multi.**	22
Velvet | **Hollywood**	18
Z Yuca's | **Los Feliz**	23
Yxta Cocina | **Downtown**	24

MIDDLE EASTERN

Burger Continental | **Pasadena**	18
Z Carousel | **multi.**	24
Falafel King | **multi.**	19
Moishe's | **Fairfax**	19

MOROCCAN

Z Dar Maghreb | **Hollywood**	23
Koutoubia | **West LA**	25
Marrakesh | **Studio City**	21

NEPALESE

Tibet Nepal | **Pasadena**	17

NEW ENGLAND

Z Lasher's | **Long Bch**	24

NOODLE SHOPS

Asahi | **West LA**	20
Bamboodles | **San Gabriel**	20
Blossom | **Downtown**	23
Chabuya | **West LA**	21
Mandarin | **multi.**	23
NEW 9021Pho | **Beverly Hills**	19
NEW 101 Noodle | **multi.**	22
Pho Café | **Silver Lake**	19
Z Pho 79 | **Alhambra**	24
Viet Noodle Bar | **Atwater Vill**	21

NUEVO LATINO

Alegria | **Long Bch**	21
Ciudad | **Downtown**	22
Xiomara | **Hollywood**	21
NEW Zengo | **Santa Monica**	-

PACIFIC RIM

Christine | **Torrance**	25
Duke's | **Malibu**	17
NEW Flying Pig | **Location Varies**	-

PAN-LATIN

Beso | **Hollywood**	21
D'Caché | **Toluca Lake**	23
NEW Fuego/Maya | **Long Bch**	19
NEW Pan Am Room | **Santa Monica**	-
Rivera | **Downtown**	25

PERSIAN

Javan | **West LA**	20
Shaherzad | **Westwood**	22
Turquoise | **Redondo Bch**	-

PERUVIAN

Choza Mama | **multi.**	19
El Pollo Inka | **multi.**	20
Domo Arigato | **Location Varies**	-
Los Balcones/Peru | **Hollywood**	-
Mario's Peruvian | **Hollywood**	22
Mo-Chica | **Downtown**	27

PIZZA

Abbot's | **multi.**	22
Antica | **Marina del Rey**	21
Berri's | **multi.**	15
BJ's | **multi.**	17
Z Bottega Louie | **Downtown**	22
Bravo | **Santa Monica**	19
Caioti Pizza | **Studio City**	21
Cal. Pizza Kitchen | **multi.**	18
Casa Bianca | **Eagle Rock**	23
Cheebo | **Hollywood**	20
D'Amore's | **multi.**	20
Farfalla | **Los Feliz**	24
Z Gjelina | **Venice**	26
Il Capriccio | **Los Feliz**	23
Joe's Pizza | **multi.**	22
Johnnie's NY | **multi.**	17
La Bottega Marino | **multi.**	21
Lamonica's | **Westwood**	22
Mulberry St. Pizzeria | **multi.**	23
NEW NY & C Pizzeria | **Santa Monica**	17
Pace | **Laurel Canyon**	22
Pitfire Artisan Pizza | **multi.**	-
NEW Pizza Antica | **Santa Monica**	-
Z Pizzeria Mozza | **Hollywood**	27
Prizzi's | **Hollywood**	21
Two Boots | **Echo Pk**	20
Village Pizzeria | **multi.**	25

POLISH

Warszawa | **Santa Monica**	23

POLYNESIAN

NEW Trader Vic's | **multi.**	17

PUB FOOD

Auld Dubliner | **Long Bch**	16
BJ's | **multi.**	17
Cat & Fiddle | **Hollywood**	15
NEW Dillon's | **Hollywood**	-
Gordon Biersch | **Burbank**	16
Heroes/Legends | **Claremont**	17
Hudson Hse. | **Redondo Bch**	23
NEW Locals Sports B&G | **Mid-City**	-
Tom Bergin's | **Fairfax**	13
Westside Tav. | **West LA**	21
Whale & Ale | **San Pedro**	20
Ye Olde King's | **Santa Monica**	18

SANDWICHES

Artisan | **Studio City**	24
Art's | **Studio City**	20
Barney Greengrass | **Beverly Hills**	22
Z Bay Cities | **Santa Monica**	25
Breadbar | **multi.**	18
Cafe Surfas | **Culver City**	20
Canter's | **Fairfax**	19
NEW Capriotti's | **multi.**	23
Cook's Tortas | **Monterey Pk**	25
Dolce Isola | **Pico-Robertson**	-
Factor's | **Pico-Robertson**	18
Greenblatt's | **Hollywood**	19
Grilled Cheese | **Location Varies**	-
Il Forno Caldo | **Beverly Hills**	21
Il Tramezzino | **multi.**	19
Johnnie's Pastrami | **Culver City**	20
Junior's | **West LA**	16
Z Langer's | **Downtown**	27
Lawry's Carvery | **multi.**	20
Lemon Moon | **West LA**	20
Little Dom's/Deli | **Los Feliz**	21
NEW Lunch | **Culver City**	-
NEW Mr. Beef | **Venice**	-
Nate 'n Al | **multi.**	20
Philippe/Original | **Chinatown**	22
Porta Via | **Beverly Hills**	21
Z Porto's | **multi.**	24
Roll 'n Rye | **Culver City**	19
3 Square | **Venice**	23
Trails | **Los Feliz**	-
Village Pantry | **Pacific Palisades**	15

SCOTTISH

NEW Gorbals | **Downtown**	21
Tam O'Shanter | **Atwater Vill**	22

SEAFOOD

ABC Seafood | **Chinatown**	20
Admiral Risty | **Rancho Palos Verdes**	20

Armstrong's	**Catalina Is.**	–
Baleen	**Redondo Bch**	19
Bluewater	**Redondo Bch**	20
Boiling Crab	**Alhambra**	23
NEW BP Oysterette	**Santa Monica**	22
Breeze	**Century City**	18
Ⓩ Brophy Bros.	**Ventura**	21
Buggy Whip	**Westchester**	18
Bull Pen	**Redondo Bch**	15
Ⓩ Catch	**Santa Monica**	22
CBS Seafood	**Chinatown**	20
Chart House	**multi.**	19
Coast	**Santa Monica**	21
Delmonico's	**Encino**	22
Duke's	**Malibu**	17
Enterprise Fish	**Santa Monica**	19
Fins	**multi.**	21
Fish Grill	**multi.**	19
Fonz's	**Manhattan Bch**	21
Galley	**Santa Monica**	17
Gladstone's	**multi.**	13
Gulfstream	**Century City**	21
Hop Woo	**Alhambra**	19
Hungry Cat	**Hollywood**	24
i Cugini	**Santa Monica**	21
Kincaid's	**Redondo Bch**	20
King's Fish	**multi.**	20
La Serenata	**multi.**	22
Lobster	**Santa Monica**	23
Lobster Trap	**Catalina Is.**	–
Lunada Bayhouse	**Palos Verdes**	–
Madison	**Long Bch**	22
Malibu Seafood	**Malibu**	23
McCormick/Schmick	**multi.**	20
McKenna's	**Long Bch**	19
Ⓩ NBC Seafood	**Monterey Pk**	21
Neptune's Net	**Malibu**	19
Ocean Ave.	**Santa Monica**	22
Ocean Seafood	**Chinatown**	21
Ⓩ Palm	**multi.**	24
Paradise Cove	**Malibu**	15
Parker's	**Long Bch**	19
Ⓩ Providence	**Hollywood**	28
Reel Inn	**Malibu**	20
Rock'n Fish	**multi.**	20
Santa Monica Seafood	**Santa Monica**	22
Ⓩ Sea Harbour	**Rosemead**	25
Spark	**Simi Valley**	20
22nd St. Landing	**San Pedro**	17
V.I.P. Harbor	**West LA**	19
Ⓩ Water Grill	**Downtown**	27

SMALL PLATES

(See also Spanish tapas specialist)

Ⓩ A.O.C.	Cal./French	**Third St**	27
NEW Bar Bouchon	French	**Beverly Hills**	23
Bar Hayama	Japanese	**West LA**	22
Beacon	Asian	**Culver City**	22
BottleRock	Euro.	**multi.**	16
Buddha's Belly	Eclectic	**Beverly Blvd**	19
Enoteca Drago	Italian	**Beverly Hills**	22
Ⓩ Gjelina	Amer.	**Venice**	26
Itacho	Japanese	**Beverly Blvd**	21
Izaka-Ya	Japanese	**multi.**	26
NEW Izakaya Fu-Ga	Japanese	**Little Tokyo**	–
Izayoi	Japanese	**Little Tokyo**	25
K-Zo	Japanese	**Culver City**	24
La Sosta	Italian	**Hermosa Bch**	–
NEW Living Room/Station	Med.	**Hollywood**	–
Ⓩ Lou	Med.	**Hollywood**	25
Ⓩ Mako	Asian	**Beverly Hills**	26
Manchego	Spanish	**Santa Monica**	23
Musha	Japanese	**multi.**	25
NEW Noir	Eclectic	**Pasadena**	25
Ⓩ Orris	French/Japanese	**West LA**	27
Pourtal	Med.	**Santa Monica**	22
Primitivo	Med.	**Venice**	23
NEW Rockwell	Eclectic	**Los Feliz**	–
Rustic Canyon	Med.	**Santa Monica**	23
Saluté	Italian	**Santa Monica**	–
Tinto	Spanish	**W Hollywood**	–
Upstairs 2	Med.	**West LA**	23
Vertical Wine	Eclectic/Med.	**Pasadena**	21
Yatai	Asian	**W Hollywood**	–
Yuzu	Japanese	**Torrance**	23

Menus, photos, voting and more – free at ZAGAT.com

SOUL FOOD

Big Mama's	Pasadena	21
Larkin's	Eagle Rock	18
Roscoe's	multi.	21

SOUTH AMERICAN

Bariloche	Ventura	22

SOUTHERN

Aunt Kizzy's	Marina del Rey	19
House of Blues	W Hollywood	16
Johnny Rebs'	multi.	23
Kokomo	Beverly Blvd	19
Larkin's	Eagle Rock	18
Lasher's	Long Bch	24
Les Sisters	Chatsworth	25
Lucille's	multi.	22

SOUTHWESTERN

Bandera	West LA	22
Coyote Cantina	Redondo Bch	21
Jinky's	multi.	19
Sagebrush	Calabasas	13

SPANISH

(* tapas specialist)

Bar Celona*	Pasadena	17
Bar Pintxo*	Santa Monica	21
Bazaar/José Andrés	Beverly Hills	26
Bokado	Studio City	19
Cafe Sevilla*	Long Bch	21
Cobras/Matadors*	Beverly Blvd	21
Enoteca Toscana	Camarillo	25
La Paella*	Beverly Hills	21
NEW La Vida	Hollywood	-
Manchego	Santa Monica	23
Phlight	Whittier	23
Tasca Winebar*	Third St	24
Tinto	W Hollywood	-

STEAKHOUSES

Arroyo	Pasadena	25
Beckham Grill	Pasadena	19
Benihana	multi.	19
Billingsley's	West LA	15
BLT Steak	W Hollywood	24
Boa	multi.	22
Buggy Whip	Westchester	18
Bull Pen	Redondo Bch	15
NEW Capital Grille	W Hollywood	-

Carlitos Gardel	Melrose	24
Chart House	multi.	19
Chez Jay	Santa Monica	16
CUT	Beverly Hills	27
Damon's	Glendale	19
Derby	Arcadia	20
555 East	Long Bch	25
Fleming's	multi.	24
Fogo de Chão	Beverly Hills	23
Fonz's	Manhattan Bch	21
Galley	Santa Monica	17
Gaucho	multi.	18
Grill on Alley	Beverly Hills	25
Holdren's	Thousand Oaks	20
Jar	Beverly Blvd.	25
Jer-ne	Marina del Rey	23
Kincaid's	Redondo Bch	20
La Bistecca	Downtown	-
Larsen's	Encino	23
Lawry's Prime Rib	Beverly Hills	26
Lunada Bayhouse	Palos Verdes	-
Madison	Long Bch	22
Mastro's Steak	multi.	26
McKenna's	Long Bch	19
Monty's	Woodland Hills	22
Morels Steak	Fairfax	20
Morton's	multi.	24
Nick & Stef's	Downtown	23
Outback	multi.	18
Pacific Dining Car	multi.	23
Palm	multi.	24
Petrelli's	Culver City	19
Porterhouse	Beverly Hills	21
Porto Alegre	Pasadena	20
Rock'n Fish	multi.	20
Ruth's Chris	multi.	25
Saddle Ranch	multi.	15
Salt Creek	multi.	17
Seta	Whittier	27
Smoke House	Burbank	20
Steve's Steak	Catalina Is.	-
STK	W Hollywood	22
Taylor's	multi.	21
Vibrato	Bel-Air	21
West	Brentwood	20
Wolfgang's Steak	Beverly Hills	23
Zane's	Hermosa Bch	26

TEX-MEX

Marix | **multi.** 17

THAI

Chaba | **Redondo Bch** 22
Z Chadaka | **Burbank** 23
Chan/Hse. of Chan | **multi.** 21
Cholada | **multi.** 23
Z Jitlada | **E Hollywood** 26
Nakkara | **Beverly Blvd** 24
Natalee | **multi.** 19
Palms Thai | **E Hollywood** 21
Rambutan | **Silver Lake** 19
Red Corner | **E Hollywood** 22
Ruen Pair | **E Hollywood** 23
Saladang | **Pasadena** 23
Sedthee | **Glendale** -
NEW Soi 7 | **Downtown** 21
Talésai | **multi.** 22
Thai Dishes | **multi.** 17
Tuk Tuk | **Pico-Robertson** 21

TIBETAN

Tibet Nepal | **Pasadena** 17

TURKISH

Spitz | **multi.** 21

VEGETARIAN

(* vegan)

A Votre Sante* | **Brentwood** 20
Elf Café | **Echo Pk** 27
Fatty's & Co. | **Eagle Rock** 25
Flore/Meet Mkt.* | **multi.** 21
Madeleine* | **Tarzana** 28
Mäni's* | **Fairfax** 17

M Café* | **multi.** 22
NEW Mooi* | **Echo Pk** -
Muma | **Melrose** -
Z Native Foods* | **Westwood** 23
Newsroom Café | **W Hollywood** 18
Planet Raw* | **Santa Monica** 20
Real Food Daily* | **multi.** 22
Tiara* | **Downtown** 23
Trails* | **Los Feliz** -
Urth* | **multi.** 21
Vegan Glory* | **Beverly Blvd** 23
Z Veggie Grill* | **multi.** 23

VENEZUELAN

Coupa | **Beverly Hills** 19

VIETNAMESE

Absolutely Pho | **multi.** 18
Benley | **Long Bch** 24
Blossom | **Downtown** 23
Blue Hen | **Eagle Rock** 17
NEW Boiling Shrimp | **Hollywood** -
Z Crustacean | **Beverly Hills** 24
Gingergrass | **Silver Lake** 22
Golden Deli | **San Gabriel** 23
Indochine Vien | **Atwater Vill** 16
Le Saigon | **West LA** 20
NEW 9021Pho | **Beverly Hills** 19
NEW Paddy Rice | **Melrose** -
NEW Phamish | **Location Varies** -
Pho Café | **Silver Lake** 19
Z Pho 79 | **Alhambra** 24
Viet Noodle Bar | **Atwater Vill** 21
NEW Xoia | **Echo Pk** -

ocations

includes names, cuisines, Food ratings and, for locations that are mapped,
op list with map coordinates.

LA Central

ATWATER VILLAGE

Canelé	*Med.*	23
Indochine Vien	*Viet.*	16
Mimi's	*Diner*	17
Tam O'Shanter	*Scottish*	22
Viet Noodle Bar	*Viet.*	21

BEVERLY BLVD.

(bet. La Brea & La Cienega;
see map on back of gatefold)

TOP FOOD

Angelini	*Italian*	**D8**	28
Hirozen	*Japanese*	**D5**	26
Jar	*Amer./Steak*	**D6**	25
Eva	*Cal.*	**E7**	25
Terroni	*Italian*	**D7**	22

LISTING

Z Angelini	*Italian*	28
bld	*Amer.*	22
Buddha's Belly	*Asian*	19
Cafe Sushi	*Japanese*	21
Cobras/Matadors	*Spanish*	21
Dominick's	*Italian*	21
El Coyote	*Mex.*	15
NEW Eva	*Cal.*	25
Fish Grill	*Seafood*	19
Hirozen	*Japanese*	26
NEW House Café	*Eclectic*	21
India's Clay Oven	*Indian*	21
Itacho	*Japanese*	21
Z Jar	*Amer./Steak*	25
Jian	*Korean*	23
Kings Rd.	*Amer.*	16
Kokomo	*Southern*	19
Mandarette	*Chinese*	19
Nakkara	*Thai*	24
Pane e Vino	*Italian*	21
Swingers	*Diner*	17
Terroni	*Italian*	22
Vegan Glory	*Vegan*	23

CHINATOWN

ABC Seafood	*Chinese/Seafood*	20
CBS Seafood	*Seafood*	20

Empress Pavilion	*Chinese*	20
Hop Li	*Chinese*	19
Hop Woo	*Chinese*	19
Ocean Seafood	*Chinese/Seafood*	21
Philippe/Original	*Sandwiches*	22
Sam Woo	*Chinese*	22
Yang Chow	*Chinese*	22

DOWNTOWN

(See map on page 292)

TOP FOOD

Water Grill	*Seafood*	**F2**	27
Langer's	*Deli*	**F1**	27
Patina	*Amer./Cal.*	**E3**	26
Drago Centro	*Italian*	**F2**	26
Rivera	*Pan-Latin*	**G1**	25
Church/State	*French*	**I5**	25
Morton's	*Steak*	**F1**	24
Noé	*Amer.*	**F3**	24
Chaya Downtown	*Asian/French*	**F2**	24
R23	*Japanese*	**G5**	24
Palm	*Steak*	**H1**	24
Fleming's	*Steak*	**G1**	24
Roy's	*Hawaiian*	**G1**	24
Cicada	*Cal./Italian*	**G2**	23
Nick & Stef's	*Steak*	**E3**	23

LISTING

Angelique	*French*	21
Barbara's	*Eclectic*	15
Blossom	*Viet.*	23
Blue Velvet	*Amer.*	20
Blu LA Café	*Amer.*	-
Z Bottega Louie	*Italian*	22
BottleRock	*Euro.*	16
Cafe Pinot	*Cal./French*	23
Cal. Pizza Kitchen	*Pizza*	18
Casa	*Mex.*	19
NEW Charcoal Grill	*Mex.*	-
Chaya Downtown	*Asian/French*	24
Checkers	*Cal.*	21
Chichen Itza	*Mex.*	24
Z Church/State	*French*	25
Z Cicada	*Cal./Italian*	23

LOS ANGELES

LOCATIONS

Restaurant	Cuisine	Rating
Ciudad	Nuevo Latino	22
Clifton's	Amer.	13
Cole's	Amer.	17
Corkbar	Eclectic	22
NEW Cucina Rustica	Italian	–
Daily Grill	Amer.	19
Z Drago Centro	Italian	26
Z Edison	Amer.	15
NEW El Cholo Downtown	Mex.	–
Engine Co. 28	Amer.	21
Farm/Bev. Hills	Amer.	18
NEW First & Hope	Amer.	–
Z Fleming's	Steak	24
410 Boyd	Cal.	20
George's Greek	Greek	22
NEW Gorbals	Eclectic	21
Gram & Papas	Amer.	–
Johnnie's NY	Pizza	17
Z Katsuya	Japanese	23
Kendall's	French	19
NEW K-Town	Korean	–
Lab	Amer.	17
La Bistecca	Italian/Steak	–
NEW L.A. Market	Amer./Cal.	19
Z Langer's	Deli	27
Lawry's Carvery	Amer.	20
Lemonade Cafe	Cal.	23
Library Bar	Amer.	17
NEW Mac & Cheeza	Amer.	–
Magnolia	Amer.	18
NEW Market Café	Eclectic	–
McCormick/Schmick	Seafood	20
Mo-Chica	Peruvian	27
Morton's	Steak	24
New Moon	Chinese	21
Nick & Stef's	Steak	23
Nickel Diner	Diner	22
Noé	Amer.	24
Original Pantry	Diner	17
Pacific Dining Car	Steak	23
Z Palm	Steak	24
Panini Cafe	Italian/Med.	20
Z Patina	Amer./Cal.	26
Pete's	Amer.	21
Pitfire Artisan Pizza	Italian	–
Rivera	Pan-Latin	25
Rock'n Fish	Seafood/Steak	20
NEW Rosa Mexicano	Mex.	22
Rowdy	Burgers	–
Z Roy's	Hawaiian	24
R23	Japanese	24
Seoul Jung	Korean	24
NEW Soi 7	Thai	21
Standard	Eclectic	17
NEW Starry Kitchen	Asian	–
Takami	Japanese	26
Tiara	Amer.	23
Z Tommy's	Burgers/Hot Dogs	23
NEW Trader Vic's	Polynesian	17
Traxx	Amer.	19
Urth	Amer.	21
NEW Villains	Amer.	–
Z Water Grill	Seafood	27
Wokcano	Chinese/Japanese	16
Wolfgang Puck B&G	Cal.	22
Wolfgang Puck Café	Cal.	19
NEW WP24	Chinese	–
Wurstküche	Euro.	22
Yard House	Amer.	18
Yxta Cocina	Mex.	24
Zip Fusion	Japanese	19
Zucca	Italian	22

EAST HOLLYWOOD

Restaurant	Cuisine	Rating
Z Carousel	Mideast.	24
Z Jitlada	Thai	26
Marouch	Lebanese	21
Palms Thai	Thai	21
Red Corner	Thai	22
Ruen Pair	Thai	23
Square One	Amer.	23
Zankou	Med.	22

ECHO PARK

Restaurant	Cuisine	Rating
Cowboys/Turbans	Indian	–
Elf Café	Med./Veg.	27
Flore/Meet Mkt.	Veg.	21
NEW Mooi	Vegan	–
Park	Amer.	24
Taix	French	17
Two Boots	Pizza	20
NEW Xoia	Viet.	–

FAIRFAX

Restaurant	Cuisine	Rating
American Girl	Amer.	11
Animal	Amer.	26
Bistro LQ	French	24
Canter's	Deli	19

Cheesecake Factory | *Amer.*	19
Chipotle | *Mex.*	19
Du-par's | *Diner*	16
Farm/Bev. Hills | *Amer.*	18
French Crêpe Co. | *French*	21
Genghis Cohen | *Chinese*	21
NEW Goal | *Amer.*	-
Golden State | *Cal.*	22
Gumbo Pot | *Cajun*	20
Johnny Rockets | *Burgers*	16
La Piazza | *Italian*	18
Lotería! | *Mex.*	24
Maggiano's | *Italian*	19
Mäni's | *Bakery/Vegan*	17
Marmalade | *Amer./Cal.*	18
Moishe's | *Mideast.*	19
Monsieur Marcel | *French*	20
Morels Bistro | *French*	20
Morels Steak | *French/Steak*	20
Nyala | *Ethiopian*	23
Tart | *Amer.*	18
Tom Bergin's | *Pub Food*	13
Ulysses Voyage | *Greek*	20
Wood Ranch | *BBQ*	21

HANCOCK PARK/ LARCHMONT VILLAGE

Chan/Hse. of Chan | *Thai*	21
Girasole | *Italian*	24
La Bottega Marino | *Italian*	21
Le Petit Greek | *Greek*	21
Louise's | *Cal./Italian*	17
Prado | *Carib.*	22
Village Pizzeria | *Pizza*	25

HIGHLAND PARK

York | *Eclectic*	18

HOLLYWOOD

(See map on page 291)

TOP FOOD

Providence | *Amer./Seafood* | **E8**	28
Pizzeria Mozza | *Pizza* | **E7**	27
Osteria Mozza | *Italian* | **E7**	27
Lou | *Eclectic/Med.* | **E8**	25
Village Pizzeria | *Pizza* | **A8**	25
Hungry Cat | *Seafood* | **B8**	24
Marino | *Italian* | **E8**	24
Lotería! | *Mex.* | **B7**	24
In-N-Out | *Burgers* | **B6**	24
Osteria La Buca | *Italian* | **E10**	23
Katsuya | *Japanese* | **B8**	23
Griddle | *Amer.* | **B4**	23
Dar Maghreb | *Moroccan* | **B4**	23
Ammo | *Cal.* | **C7**	23
Mario's Peruvian | *Peruvian* | **E8**	22

LISTING

Ammo | *Cal.*	23
Astro Burger | *Burgers*	20
Beso | *Pan-Latin*	21
BoHo | *Eclectic*	17
NEW Boiling Shrimp | *Cajun/Viet.*	-
Bossa Nova | *Brazilian*	20
Bowery | *Amer./French*	20
Cafe/Artistes | *French*	20
Café Was | *French*	17
Cal. Chicken | *Amer.*	21
Cal. Pizza Kitchen | *Pizza*	18
Cat & Fiddle | *Pub*	15
Chan/Hse. of Chan | *Thai*	21
Cheebo | *Italian*	20
Citizen Smith | *Amer.*	17
NEW Colony | *Cal.*	-
Z Dar Maghreb | *Moroccan*	23
Delancey | *Italian*	20
NEW Delphine | *French/Med.*	20
NEW Dillon's | *Pub*	-
NEW District | *Eclectic*	-
NEW Drai's | *Continental*	-
NEW East | *Eclectic*	25
Fabiolus | *Italian*	18
French Crêpe Co. | *French*	21
Geisha Hse. | *Japanese*	18
Greenblatt's | *Deli*	19
Griddle | *Amer.*	23
Grill on Hollywood/Alley | *Amer.*	22
Grub | *Amer.*	22
Hideout | *Amer.*	-
Hungry Cat | *Seafood*	24
Z In-N-Out | *Burgers*	24
Johnny Rockets | *Burgers*	16
Kabuki | *Japanese*	18
Z Katsuya | *Japanese*	23
Kitchen 24 | *Amer.*	20
Larchmont Grill | *Amer.*	22
NEW La Vida | *Cal./Spanish*	-
NEW Living Room/Station | *Med.*	-

Los Balcones/Peru | *Peruvian*	–
Lotería! | *Mex.*	24
Z Lou | *Eclectic/Med.*	25
Lucky Devils | *Amer.*	21
Magnolia | *Amer.*	18
Maison Richard | *Bakery/French*	21
Marino | *Italian*	24
Mario's Peruvian | *Peruvian*	22
Mel's Drive-In | *Amer.*	16
NEW Mercantile | *French*	21
Miceli's | *Italian*	16
Mini Bites | *Burgers*	–
Murakami | *Japanese*	–
Musso & Frank | *Amer.*	20
Off Vine | *Amer./Calif.*	–
NEW Olive | *Cal./Italian*	–
101 Coffee | *Diner*	18
Osteria La Buca | *Italian*	23
NEW Osteria Mamma | *Italian*	–
Z Osteria Mozza | *Italian*	27
Pig 'n Whistle | *Continental*	17
Z Pizzeria Mozza | *Pizza*	27
Prizzi's | *Italian*	21
Z Providence | *Amer./Seafood*	28
Roscoe's | *Soul Food*	21
Sharky's | *Mex.*	19
Shin | *Korean*	–
Street | *Eclectic*	20
Tender Greens | *Amer.*	22
Trastevere | *Italian*	19
25 Degrees | *Burgers*	22
Umami | *Burgers*	22
uWink | *Cal.*	10
Velvet | *Mex.*	18
Village Pizzeria | *Pizza*	25
NEW Vintage Enoteca | *Italian*	–
Waffle | *Diner*	17
Xiomara | *Nuevo Latino*	21
Z Yamashiro | *Asian/Cal.*	18

HUNTINGTON PARK

Guelaguetza | *Mex.*	21

KOREATOWN

BCD Tofu | *Korean*	20
BonChon | *Korean*	19
Cassell's | *Burgers*	21
ChoSun Galbee | *Korean*	23
Fat Fish | *Asian/Japanese*	19
Guelaguetza | *Mex.*	21
Manna | *Korean*	18
Z Park's BBQ | *Korean*	24
Soot Bull Jeep | *Korean*	23
Taylor's | *Steak*	21

LA BREA

Amalfi | *Italian*	19
Ca'Brea | *Italian*	22
Z Campanile | *Cal./Med.*	26
Cube | *Italian*	25
Luna Park | *Amer.*	19
Pink's Dogs | *Hot Dogs*	20
Z Susina | *Bakery*	26
Z **NEW** Tar Pit | *Eclectic*	20

LAUREL CANYON

Pace | *Italian*	22

LEIMERT PARK

Z Phillips BBQ | *BBQ*	25

LITTLE TOKYO

Honda-Ya | *Japanese*	22
NEW Izakaya Fu-Ga | *Japanese*	–
Izayoi | *Japanese*	25
NEW Lazy Ox | *Eclectic*	24
Shabu Shabu | *Japanese*	23
Spitz | *Turkish*	21
Sushi Gen | *Japanese*	26
Yen | *Japanese*	23

LOS FELIZ

Alcove | *Amer.*	20
Z Best Fish Taco | *Mex.*	21
Chi Dynasty | *Chinese*	21
Desert Rose | *Cal./Med.*	19
Electric Lotus | *Indian*	22
Farfalla | *Italian*	24
Figaro | *French*	20
Fred 62 | *Diner*	17
Il Capriccio | *Italian*	23
Little Dom's/Deli | *Italian*	21
Louise's | *Cal./Italian*	17
Mexico City | *Mex.*	20
Palermo | *Italian*	18
NEW Rockwell | *Eclectic*	–
Trails | *Amer.*	–
Tropicalia | *Brazilian*	22
vermont | *Amer.*	22
Z Yuca's | *Mex.*	23

MELROSE
(See map on page 293)

TOP FOOD

Hatfield's | *Amer.* | **E6**	27
Angeli | *Italian* | **E5**	25
Sweet Lady Jane | *Bakery* | **E2**	24

LISTING

Angeli | *Italian*	25
Antonio's | *Mex.*	22
Z Carlitos Gardel | *Argent./Steak*	24
8 oz. | *Burgers*	22
Foundry/Melrose | *Amer.*	22
Z Hatfield's | *Amer.*	27
Johnny Rockets | *Burgers*	16
M Café | *Veg.*	22
Muma | *Med.*	-
NEW Paddy Rice | *Viet.*	-
NEW Red O | *Mex.*	-
Sweet Lady Jane | *Bakery*	24
Village Idiot | *Amer.*	19

MID-CITY

Bloom | *Amer./Cal.*	21
NEW Burger Kitchen | *Burgers*	-
Candela | *Mex.*	-
El Cholo | *Mex.*	18
Harold & Belle's | *Creole*	24
NEW Locals Sports B&G | *Pub*	-
Z Papa Cristo's | *Greek*	24
Z Phillips BBQ | *BBQ*	25
NEW Plancha | *Mex.*	-
Roscoe's | *Soul Food*	21
Umami | *Burgers*	22
Versailles | *Cuban*	21
Woody's BBQ | *BBQ*	24

MID-WILSHIRE

Cowboys/Turbans | *Indian*	-
India's Tandoori | *Indian*	21
Johnnie's NY | *Pizza*	17
NEW Larchmont Bungalow | *Amer.*	19

PICO-ROBERTSON

Bella Roma | *Italian*	24
Bossa Nova | *Brazilian*	20
Dolce Isola | *Bakery/Sandwiches*	-
Factor's | *Deli*	18
Fish Grill | *Seafood*	19

Hop Li | *Chinese*	19
Milky Way | *Cal.*	19
Pat's | *Cal./Italian*	20
Spark | *Amer.*	20
Tuk Tuk | *Thai*	21
Yen | *Japanese*	23

SILVER LAKE

Agra | *Indian*	22
Z Alegria/Sunset | *Mex.*	25
Aroma | *Italian*	23
Barbrix | *Italian/Med.*	23
Blair's | *Amer.*	24
Cafe Stella | *French*	21
Cha Cha Cha | *Carib.*	19
Z Cliff's Edge | *Cal./Italian*	19
Dusty's | *Amer./French*	21
Edendale Grill | *Amer.*	18
Flore/Meet Mkt. | *Vegan*	21
NEW Forage | *Cal.*	25
Gingergrass | *Viet.*	22
Kitchen | *Amer.*	20
LAMILL | *Cal.*	21
Local | *Amer.*	22
Madame Matisse | *Amer.*	-
Malo | *Mex.*	19
Michelangelo | *Italian*	18
Pho Café | *Viet.*	19
Rambutan | *Thai*	19
Red Lion | *German*	17
Reservoir | *Eclectic*	23
Saito's | *Japanese*	-
Tantra | *Indian*	-

THIRD STREET
(bet. La Brea & Robertson; see map on back of gatefold)

TOP FOOD

A.O.C. | *Cal./French* | **E6**	27
Izaka-Ya | *Japanese* | **E5**	26
Locanda Veneta | *Italian* | **E4**	25
Ortolan | *French* | **E5**	25
Joan's on 3rd | *Amer./Bakery* | **E5**	23

LISTING

Allora | *Italian*	-
Z A.O.C. | *Cal./French*	27
Baja Fresh | *Mex.*	17
Barefoot B&G | *Cal./Eclectic*	17
Berri's | *Pizza*	15

Cal. Wok	*Chinese*	16
Doughboys	*Bakery*	22
El Carmen	*Mex.*	15
Holy Cow	*Indian*	22
Izaka-Ya	*Japanese*	26
Jack n' Jill's Too	*Creole*	21
Joan's on 3rd	*Amer./Bakery*	23
Little Door	*Med.*	23
Locanda Veneta	*Italian*	25
Mishima	*Japanese*	19
Ortolan	*French*	25
Sofi	*Greek*	20
Sushi Mon	*Japanese*	21
Sushi Roku	*Japanese*	23
Tasca Winebar	*Spanish*	24
Toast	*Amer.*	20

WEST HOLLYWOOD
(See map on back of gatefold)

TOP FOOD

Wa	*Japanese*	**B5**	27
Lucques	*Cal./Med.*	**D5**	27
Bastide	*French*	**C5**	27
Nobu LA	*Japanese*	**C5**	26
Amarone	*Italian*	**C4**	26
RH	*French*	**B5**	25
Madeo	*Italian*	**D4**	25
Koi	*Japanese*	**C5**	24
Asia de Cuba	*Asian/Cuban*	**B5**	24
BLT Steak	*Steak*	**B4**	24
Chaya Brasserie	*Asian/French*	**E4**	24
Palm	*Steak*	**D4**	24
Veggie Grill	*Vegan*	**A6**	23
Yabu	*Japanese*	**D5**	23
Sur	*Cal./Med.*	**D4**	23

LISTING

Abbey	*Amer.*	16
Absolutely Pho	*Viet.*	18
Ago	*Italian*	21
Amarone	*Italian*	26
Z Asia de Cuba	*Asian/Cuban*	24
Astro Burger	*Burgers*	20
Baby Blues	*BBQ*	21
Barney's Beanery	*Eclectic*	15
Basix	*Cal./Italian*	19
Z Bastide	*French*	27
Belmont	*Amer.*	16

BLT Steak	*Steak*	24
Z Boa	*Steak*	22
NEW Borracho	*Mex.*	–
Bossa Nova	*Brazilian*	20
NEW Boxwood	*Cal./Continental*	22
Breadbar	*Bakery*	18
Cafe Med	*Italian*	19
Caffe Primo	*Italian*	18
NEW Capital Grille	*Steak*	–
Carney's	*Hot Dogs*	20
Cecconi's	*Italian*	20
Z Chateau Marmont	*Cal./French*	19
Chaya Brasserie	*Asian/French*	24
Chin Chin	*Chinese*	17
Clafoutis	*French/Italian*	19
Comme Ça	*French*	22
Counter	*Burgers*	20
NEW Cuvee	*Cal.*	–
Dan Tana's	*Italian*	23
Dukes West Hollywood	*Diner*	18
Eat Well	*Amer.*	17
Fat Fish	*Asian/Japanese*	19
Flavor of India	*Indian*	21
Food + Lab	*Austrian/Cal.*	20
Formosa	*Asian*	13
Gordon Ramsay	*French*	23
Hall	*French*	21
Hamburger Hamlet	*Amer.*	18
Hamburger Mary's	*Diner*	14
House of Blues	*Southern*	16
NEW Hudson	*Amer.*	–
Hugo's	*Cal.*	20
Il Piccolino	*Italian*	22
Il Sole	*Italian*	23
Ivy	*Cal.*	21
Jan's	*Diner*	16
Jinky's	*SW*	19
Joe's Pizza	*Pizza*	22
Jones	*Amer./Italian*	18
Katana	*Japanese*	23
Ketchup	*Amer.*	15
Koi	*Japanese*	24
La Boheme	*Cal.*	21
Lemonade Cafe	*Cal.*	23
Le Pain Quotidien	*Bakery/Belgian*	20
Le Petit Bistro	*French*	20
Le Petit Four	*French*	20
Z Lucques	*Cal./Med.*	27

Menus, photos, voting and more – free at ZAGAT.com

Madeo	*Italian*	25
NEW Manja	*Malaysian*	-
Marix	*Tex-Mex*	17
Mel's Drive-In	*Amer.*	16
Mexico Rest.	*Mex.*	19
Millions/Milkshakes	*Amer.*	21
Minestraio	*Italian*	23
Mirabelle	*Cal./Eclectic*	20
Newsroom Café	*Veg.*	18
Nishimura	*Japanese*	26
Z Nobu LA	*Japanese*	26
Nonna	*Italian*	23
Z Palm	*Steak*	24
Petrossian	*French*	23
NEW Philippe	*Chinese*	17
Pomodoro	*Italian*	16
Poquito Más	*Mex.*	21
Rainbow B&G	*Amer.*	17
Real Food Daily	*Vegan*	22
Red 7	*Asian*	-
RH	*French*	25
Saddle Ranch	*Steak*	15
Simon LA	*Amer.*	22
NEW Smokin' Joint	*BBQ*	-
Standard	*Eclectic*	19
STK	*Steak*	22
Z Sur	*Cal./Med.*	23
Talésai	*Thai*	22
Taste	*Amer.*	21
Tender Greens	*Amer.*	22
Tinto	*Spanish*	-
Tower Bar	*Cal.*	21
Urth	*Amer.*	21
Z Veggie Grill	*Vegan*	23
Z Wa	*Japanese*	27
Wokcano	*Chinese/Japanese*	16
XIV	*Amer.*	23
Yabu	*Japanese*	23
Yatai	*Asian*	-
Zeke's	*BBQ*	21

LA East

BOYLE HEIGHTS

La Serenata	*Mex./Seafood*	22

EAST LA

El Tepeyac	*Mex.*	25
Tamayo	*Mex.*	21

LA South

BELLFLOWER

Z Johnny Rebs'	*BBQ*	23

CARSON

Back Home	*Hawaiian*	17
Five Guys	*Burgers*	20

CERRITOS

BCD Tofu	*Korean*	20
BJ's	*Pub*	17
Five Guys	*Burgers*	20
Loft	*Hawaiian*	19
Lucille's	*BBQ*	22
Mimi's	*Diner*	17
Romano's	*Italian*	17
Sam Woo	*Chinese*	22
Wood Ranch	*BBQ*	21

HAWTHORNE

Chipotle	*Mex.*	19
El Torito	*Mex.*	15
India's Tandoori	*Indian*	21

LAKEWOOD

Chipotle	*Mex.*	19
George's Greek	*Greek*	22
Outback	*Steak*	18

LAWNDALE

El Pollo Inka	*Peruvian*	20

LOMITA

Il Chianti	*Italian*	21

LYNWOOD

Guelaguetza	*Mex.*	21
La Huasteca	*Mex.*	-

PALOS VERDES PENINSULA/ ROLLING HILLS

Admiral Risty	*Seafood*	20
Asaka	*Japanese*	16
Café Pacific	*Med.*	22
Frascati	*Italian*	23
La Rive Gauche	*French*	20
Lunada Bayhouse	*Seafood/Steak*	-
Marmalade	*Amer./Cal.*	18
Z mar'sel	*Cal.*	24
Ruby's	*Diner*	17
Trio	*Med.*	17

LA West

BEL-AIR

Bel-Air B&G | *Cal.* — 20
SHU | *Italian/Japanese* — 24
Ⓩ Vibrato | *Amer./Steak* — 21

BEVERLY HILLS
(See map on back of gatefold)

TOP FOOD

Matsuhisa | *Japanese* | **F5** — 28
Saam/The Bazaar | *Eclectic* | **E5** — 27
Spago | *Cal.* | **F2** — 27
Urasawa | *Japanese* | **F2** — 27
CUT | *Steak* | **F2** — 27
Mako | *Asian* | **F2** — 26
Bazaar/José Andrés | *Spanish* | **E5** — 26
Mastro's Steak | *Steak* | **F2** — 26
Lawry's Prime Rib | *Steak* | **F5** — 26
Il Pastaio | *Italian* | **E2** — 26
Belvedere | *Amer.* | **F1** — 25
Ruth's Chris | *Steak* | **F2** — 25
Grill on Alley | *Amer.* | **F2** — 25
Boss Sushi | *Japanese* | **F5** — 25
Morton's | *Steak* | **E5** — 24

LISTING

Amici | *Italian* — 21
Asakuma | *Japanese* — 21
Baja Fresh | *Mex.* — 17
🆕 Bar Bouchon | *French* — 23
Barney Greengrass | *Deli* — 22
🆕 bar210 | *Eclectic* — -
Ⓩ Bazaar/José Andrés | *Spanish* — 26
Ⓩ Belvedere | *Amer.* — 25
Benihana | *Japanese* — 19
Blvd | *Cal.* — 23
Bombay Palace | *Indian* — 21
Bond St. | *Japanese* — 20
Bossa Nova | *Brazilian* — 20
Boss Sushi | *Japanese* — 25
Ⓩ🆕 Bouchon | *French* — 24
Brighton Coffee | *Diner* — 18
Cabbage Patch | *Cal./Med.* — 23
Cafe Rodeo | *Cal.* — 15
Caffe Roma | *Italian* — 18
Cal. Pizza Kitchen | *Pizza* — 18
🆕 Capriotti's | *Sandwiches* — 23
Ⓩ Cheesecake Factory | *Amer.* — 19

Chin Chin | *Chinese* — 17
Chipotle | *Mex.* — 19
Circa 55 | *Amer./Cal.* — 19
Coupa | *Eclectic* — 19
Crazy Fish | *Japanese* — 18
Ⓩ Crustacean | *Asian/Viet.* — 24
🆕 Culina | *Italian* — -
Ⓩ CUT | *Steak* — 27
Da Pasquale | *Italian* — 23
🆕 Da Vinci | *Med.* — -
E. Baldi | *Italian* — 23
El Torito Grill | *Mex.* — 19
Enoteca Drago | *Italian* — 22
Farm/Bev. Hills | *Amer.* — 18
Ⓩ Fogo de Chão | *Brazilian/Steak* — 23
Fountain Coffee | *Diner* — 25
Frida | *Mex.* — 20
Ⓩ Gonpachi | *Japanese* — 21
Grand Lux | *Eclectic* — 19
Ⓩ Grill on Alley | *Amer.* — 25
Gyu-Kaku | *Japanese* — 20
Il Buco | *Italian* — 22
Ⓩ Il Cielo | *Italian* — 22
Il Fornaio | *Italian* — 21
Il Forno Caldo | *Italian* — 21
Il Pastaio | *Italian* — 26
Il Tramezzino | *Italian* — 19
Islands | *Amer.* — 17
Jack n' Jill's | *Amer.* — 18
Kate Mantilini | *Amer.* — 18
La Bottega Marino | *Italian* — 21
La Dolce Vita | *Italian* — 22
LA Food Show | *Amer.* — 17
La Paella | *Spanish* — 21
La Scala | *Italian* — 21
Ⓩ Lawry's Prime Rib | *Steak* — 26
Le Pain Quotidien | *Bakery/Belgian* — 20
🆕 Maison Maurice | *French* — -
Ⓩ Mako | *Asian* — 26
Ⓩ Mastro's Steak | *Steak* — 26
Ⓩ Matsuhisa | *Japanese* — 28
M Café | *Veg.* — 22
McCormick/Schmick | *Seafood* — 20
Mirü8691 | *Asian* — 24
🆕 Momed | *Med.* — -
Morton's | *Steak* — 24
Mr. Chow | *Chinese* — 23
Mulberry St. Pizzeria | *Pizza* — 23

Natalee	*Thai*	19
Nate 'n Al	*Deli*	20
Nic's	*Amer.*	19
NEW 9021Pho	*Viet.*	19
NEW Oliverio	*Italian*	-
Panini Cafe	*Italian/Med.*	20
Parq/Montage	*Amer.*	25
P.F. Chang's	*Chinese*	19
Piccolo Paradiso	*Italian*	24
Z Polo	*Cal./Continental*	23
Porta Via	*Cal.*	21
Porterhouse	*Steak*	21
Z Ruth's Chris	*Steak*	25
Z Saam/The Bazaar	*Eclectic*	27
Sharky's	*Mex.*	19
NEW South Beverly Grill	*Amer.*	-
Z Spago	*Cal.*	27
Stinking Rose	*Italian*	19
Sushi Dokoro	*Japanese*	-
Sushi Sushi	*Japanese*	27
Talésai	*Thai*	22
Tanzore	*Indian*	21
NEW Tiger Sushi	*Japanese*	-
Trader Vic	*Polynesian*	17
208 Rodeo	*Amer.*	23
Z Urasawa	*Japanese*	27
Urth	*Amer.*	21
Via Alloro	*Italian*	21
Villa Blanca	*Med.*	18
Wolfgang's Steak	*Steak*	23
Woo Lae Oak	*Korean*	22
Xi'an	*Chinese*	21

BRENTWOOD

Amici	*Italian*	21
A Votre Sante	*Veg.*	20
Baja Fresh	*Mex.*	17
Barney's	*Burgers*	20
Brentwood	*Amer.*	22
Caffe Luxxe	*Coffee*	20
Cal. Wok	*Chinese*	16
Z Cheesecake Factory	*Amer.*	19
Chin Chin	*Chinese*	17
Clay Pit	*Indian*	21
Coral Tree	*Cal./Italian*	17
Daily Grill	*Amer.*	19
Divino	*Italian*	24
Fish Grill	*Seafood*	19

Gaucho	*Argent./Steak*	18
Getty Ctr.	*Cal.*	22
Z Katsuya	*Japanese*	23
La Scala	*Italian*	21
Le Pain Quotidien	*Bakery/Belgian*	20
Maria's	*Italian*	17
Osteria Latini	*Italian*	24
Palmeri	*Italian*	24
Pecorino	*Italian*	23
Peppone	*Italian*	21
Pizzicotto	*Italian*	23
Saketini	*Asian*	20
Sor Tino	*Italian*	22
sugarFISH	*Japanese*	24
Taiko	*Japanese*	21
Takao	*Japanese*	26
Z Tavern	*Amer.*	23
Toscana	*Italian*	24
Z Vincenti	*Italian*	26
West	*Cal./Italian*	20
Yamato	*Japanese*	18
Zeidler's	*Cal.*	15

CENTURY CITY

Breadbar	*Bakery*	18
Breeze	*Cal./Seafood*	18
Café Chez Marie	*French*	-
Z Clementine	*Amer.*	24
Coral Tree	*Cal./Italian*	17
Z Craft	*Amer.*	24
Gulfstream	*Amer./Seafood*	21
Z Houston's	*Amer.*	22
Johnnie's NY	*Pizza*	17
Lawry's Carvery	*Amer.*	20
Pink Taco	*Mex.*	16
Z RockSugar	*Asian*	21
Stand	*Hot Dogs*	17
Take a Bao	*Asian*	17
Toscanova	*Italian*	20

CULVER CITY

Akasha	*Amer.*	20
Bamboo	*Carib.*	21
Beacon	*Asian*	22
BottleRock	*Euro.*	16
Z Brunello	*Italian*	23
Cafe Surfas	*Amer.*	20
Z Father's Office	*Amer./Burgers*	22
Ford's	*Amer.*	20

Z Fraîche | *French/Italian*	23
Gyenari | *Korean*	20
Z In-N-Out | *Burgers*	24
Johnnie's Pastrami | *Diner*	20
JR's | *BBQ*	22
Kay 'n Dave's | *Mex.*	16
K-Zo | *Japanese*	24
La Dijonaise | *French*	17
NEW Lawrence/India | *Indian*	–
Le St. Amour | *French*	20
Z Let's Be Frank | *Hot Dogs*	21
NEW Libra | *Brazilian*	–
NEW Lunch | *Amer.*	–
Manna | *Korean*	18
M Café | *Veg.*	22
Mi Ranchito | *Mex.*	19
Petrelli's | *Italian/Steak*	19
Roll 'n Rye | *Deli*	19
Royal/T | *French/Japanese*	17
Rush St. | *Amer.*	17
Tender Greens | *Amer.*	22
Ugo/Cafe | *Italian*	17
NEW Waterloo & City | *British*	–

MALIBU

Beachcomber Café | *Cal.*	18
Beau Rivage | *Med.*	19
NEW Café Habana | *Cuban*	–
Chart House | *Seafood/Steak*	19
Cholada | *Thai*	23
NEW Collection | *Eclectic*	–
D'Amore's | *Pizza*	20
Duke's | *Pac. Rim*	17
Fish Grill | *Seafood*	19
Z Geoffrey's | *Cal.*	20
Guido's | *Italian*	20
Malibu Seafood | *Seafood*	23
Marmalade | *Amer./Cal.*	18
Moonshadows | *Amer.*	16
Neptune's Net | *Seafood*	19
Z Nobu Malibu | *Japanese*	26
Paradise Cove | *Amer./Seafood*	15
Reel Inn | *Seafood*	20
Taverna Tony | *Greek*	21
Terra | *Cal.*	22
Thai Dishes | *Thai*	17
Tra Di Noi | *Italian*	22

MARINA DEL REY

(See map on page 293)

TOP FOOD

sugarFISH | *Japanese* | **K3**	24
Cafe Del Rey | *Cal./Med.* | **J3**	22
Akbar | *Indian* | **J3**	22
Antica | *Pizza* | **J3**	21
Alejo's | *Italian* | **J3**	21

LISTING

Akbar | *Indian*	22
Alejo's | *Italian*	21
Antica | *Pizza*	21
Aunt Kizzy's | *Southern*	19
Baja Fresh | *Mex.*	17
Beechwood | *Amer.*	19
Cafe Del Rey | *Cal./Med.*	22
Cal. Wok | *Chinese*	16
C & O | *Italian*	19
Chart House | *Seafood/Steak*	19
Z Cheesecake Factory | *Amer.*	19
Chipotle | *Mex.*	19
Counter | *Burgers*	20
El Torito | *Mex.*	15
Gaby's | *Med.*	20
Hamakaze | *Japanese*	–
Islands | *Amer.*	17
Jer-ne | *Amer./Steak*	23
NEW Locanda Positano | *Italian*	–
Mosto | *Italian*	25
Pitfire Artisan Pizza | *Italian*	–
Sapori | *Italian*	24
sugarFISH | *Japanese*	24
Tony P's | *Amer.*	17
Tsuji No Hana | *Japanese*	24
Uncle Darrow's | *Cajun/Creole*	19
Warehouse | *Amer.*	17
Wharo | *Korean*	21

MAR VISTA

Paco's Tacos | *Mex.*	21

PACIFIC PALISADES

Gladstone's | *Seafood*	13
Kay 'n Dave's | *Mex.*	16
Modo Mio | *Italian*	22
Oak Room | *Cal.*	16
Pearl Dragon | *Asian*	16
Z Sushi Sasabune/Sushi-Don | *Japanese*	27

Taste | *Amer.* 21

Village Pantry | *Deli* 15

Vittorio's | *Italian* 18

PALMS

Café Brasil | *Brazilian* 19

NEW Chego! | *Korean/Mex.* -

Hu's | *Chinese* 22

Indo | *Indonesian* 20

Johnnie's NY | *Pizza* 17

Natalee | *Thai* 19

Simpang Asia | *Indonesian* 17

Versailles | *Cuban* 21

PLAYA DEL REY

Berri's | *Pizza* 15

Caffe Pinguini | *Italian* 22

Outlaws | *Amer.* 19

Shack | *Amer.* 17

RANCHO PARK

FOOD | *Amer.* 21

John O'Groats | *Amer.* 20

SANTA MONICA

(See map on page 293)

TOP FOOD

Mélisse | *Amer./French* | **D2** 28

Valentino | *Italian* | **F5** 26

JiRaffe | *Amer./French* | **D2** 26

Chinois | *Asian/French* | **G1** 26

Sam's/Beach | *Cal./Med.* | **B1** 26

Josie | *Amer.* | **F4** 26

Giorgio Baldi | *Italian* | **B1** 26

Capo | *Italian* | **E1** 25

Bay Cities | *Italian* | **E2** 25

Michael's | *Cal.* | **D1** 25

La Vecchia | *Italian* | **G1** 25

Musha | *Japanese* | **D2** 25

La Botte | *Italian* | **D2** 24

Via Veneto | *Italian* | **G1** 24

Warszawa | *Polish* | **D2** 23

LISTING

Abbot's | *Pizza* 22

Akbar | *Indian* 22

Angel's | *Cal.* -

☑ Anisette | *French* 21

Babalu | *Cal.* 20

Baja Fresh | *Mex.* 17

Barney's | *Burgers* 20

Bar Pintxo | *Spanish* 21

☑ Bay Cities | *Italian* 25

Benihana | *Japanese* 19

Bistro 31 | *Cal.* -

☑ Boa | *Steak* 22

Border Grill | *Mex.* 21

NEW BP Oysterette | *Seafood* 22

Bravo | *Italian/Pizza* 19

Broadway Deli | *Deli* 15

Buca di Beppo | *Italian* 15

Buddha's Belly | *Asian* 19

Buffalo Club | *Amer.* 19

☑ Café Bizou/Bizou Grill | Cal./French 23

Cafe Montana | *Cal.* 18

Caffé Delfini | *Italian* 23

Caffe Luxxe | *Coffee* 20

Cal. Chicken | *Amer.* 21

Cal. Pizza Kitchen | *Pizza* 18

Capo | *Italian* 25

☑ Catch | *Cal./Seafood* 22

Cézanne | *Cal./French* 22

Cha Cha Chicken | *Carib.* 20

Chez Jay | *Steak* 16

☑ Chinois | *Asian/French* 26

Coast | *Cal./Seafood* 21

Copa d'Oro | *Amer.* 17

☑ Cora's | *Diner* 23

Counter | *Burgers* 20

Daily Grill | *Amer.* 19

Dining Rm./Shangri-La | *Amer.* 22

Drago | *Italian* 23

El Cholo | *Mex.* 18

Enterprise Fish | *Seafood* 19

Falafel King | *Mideast.* 19

☑ Father's Office | *Amer./Burgers* 22

FIG | *Amer./French* 22

☑ Fraîche | *French/Italian* 23

Frida | *Mex.* 20

Fritto Misto | *Italian* 21

Fromin's | *Deli* 15

Galley | *Seafood/Steak* 17

Giorgio Baldi | *Italian* 26

☑ Houston's | *Amer.* 22

Huckleberry | *Amer.* 22

i Cugini | *Italian/Seafood* 21

Il Fornaio | *Italian* 21

Il Forno | *Italian* 21

Ivy/Shore | *Cal./Italian* 22

Jack n' Jill's | *Amer.* 18

Jinky's | *SW* 19

🅉 JiRaffe | *Amer./French* 26

Joe's Pizza | *Pizza* 22

Johnnie's NY | *Pizza* 17

🅉 Josie | *Amer.* 26

Kay 'n Dave's | *Mex.* 16

La Botte | *Italian* 24

La Cachette | *French* 21

La Grande Orange | *Amer.* 20

Lares | *Mex.* 20

NEW La Sandia | *Mex.* -

La Serenata | *Mex./Seafood* 22

🅉 La Vecchia | *Italian* 25

Le Pain Quotidien | *Bakery/Belgian* 20

Le Petit Cafe | *French* 21

Library | *Eclectic* 19

Lobster | *Seafood* 23

Locanda/Lago | *Italian* 22

Louise's | *Cal./Italian* 17

Lula | *Mex.* 21

Manchego | *Spanish* 23

Marix | *Tex-Mex* 17

Marmalade | *Amer./Cal.* 18

🅉 Mélisse | *Amer./French* 28

🅉 Michael's | *Cal.* 25

Monsieur Marcel | *French* 20

Monsoon | *Asian* 20

Musha | *Japanese* 25

🅉 Nawab | *Indian* 23

NEW NY & C Pizzeria | *Pizza* 17

Ocean & Vine | *Amer.* 22

Ocean Ave. | *Seafood* 22

Omelette Parlor | *Amer.* 19

🅉 One Pico | *Cal./Med.* 20

NEW Ozumo | *Japanese* -

Pacific Dining Car | *Steak* 23

NEW Pan Am Room | *Pan-Latin* -

Patrick's | *Diner* 18

🅉 Penthouse | *Amer.* 20

P.F. Chang's | *Chinese* 19

NEW Pizza Antica | *Pizza* -

Planet Raw | *Vegan* 20

Pourtal | *Med.* 22

R+D Kitchen | *Amer.* 20

Rae's | *Diner* 15

Real Food Daily | *Vegan* 22

Reddi Chick | *BBQ* 21

Robata Bar | *Japanese* 26

Röckenwagner | *Bakery/Cal.* 21

Rosti | *Italian* 17

Rustic Canyon | *Cal./Med.* 23

Saluté | *Italian/Med.* -

🅉 Sam's/Beach | *Cal./Med.* 26

Santa Monica Seafood | *Seafood* 22

17th St. Cafe | *Cal.* 19

Shack | *Amer.* 17

NEW Sonoma | *Cal./Italian* -

Spumoni | *Italian* 20

NEW Stefan's/L.A. Farm | *Eclectic* 23

NEW Stefan's/Montana | *Eclectic* 20

Sushi Roku | *Japanese* 23

Swingers | *Diner* 17

Thai Dishes | *Thai* 17

NEW Tiato | *Asian* -

Trastevere | *Italian* 19

Typhoon | *Asian* 19

Umami | *Burgers* 22

NEW Upper West | *Amer.* -

Urth | *Amer.* 21

🅉 Valentino | *Italian* 26

Via Veneto | *Italian* 24

Vito | *Italian* 22

Warszawa | *Polish* 23

Whist | *Cal.* 20

Wilshire | *Amer.* 23

Wokcano | *Chinese/Japanese* 16

Wolfgang Puck Café | *Cal.* 19

World Cafe | *Eclectic* 18

NEW Xino | *Chinese* -

Ye Olde King's | *Pub* 18

NEW Zengo | *Asian* -

TOPANGA

🅉 Inn/Seventh Ray | *Cal.* 21

VENICE

(See map on page 293)

TOP FOOD

Piccolo | *Italian* | **G1** 26

Joe's | *Cal./French* | **H1** 26

Gjelina | *Amer.* | **I2** 26

Ado | *Cal./Italian* | **H1** 25

Jin Patisserie | *Bakery/French* | **H2** 23

LISTING

Abbot's | *Pizza* 22
Ado | *Cal./Italian* 25
Asakuma | *Japanese* 21
Baby Blues | *BBQ* 21
Cafe 50's | *Diner* 16
Cal. Chicken | *Amer.* 21
Canal Club | *Cal./Eclectic* 18
Casablanca | *Mex.* 20
NEW Centanni | *Italian* 19
Chaya Venice | *Japanese/French* 23
Figtree's | *Eclectic* -
Z Gjelina | *Amer.* 26
Hal's | *Amer.* 21
Hama | *Japanese* 22
Hash & High | *Amer.* -
James' | *Amer.* 19
Jin Patisserie | *Bakery/French* 23
Jody Maroni's | *Hot Dogs* 19
Z Joe's | *Cal./French* 26
Johnnie's NY | *Pizza* 17
Lemonade Cafe | *Cal.* 23
Lilly's | *French* 19
Maxwell's | *Amer.* 18
NEW Mr. Beef | *Amer.* -
Z Piccolo | *Italian* 26
Primitivo | *Med.* 23
Rose Cafe | *Cal.* 21
Shima | *Japanese* -
Tasting Kitchen | *Med.* 22
3 Square | *Sandwiches* 23
Tlapazola | *Mex.* 22
26 Beach | *Cal.* 21
Wabi-Sabi | *Asian* 22

WEST LA

All India | *Indian* 21
Z Apple Pan | *Amer.* 23
Aroma | *E Euro./Med.* 19
Arsenal | *Amer.* 16
Asahi | *Japanese* 20
Asakuma | *Japanese* 21
Bandera | *Amer./SW* 22
Bar*Food | *Eclectic* 15
Bar Hayama | *Japanese* 22
Billingsley's | *Steak* 15
BiMi | *Japanese* 23
Bombay Cafe | *Indian* 22
Cabbage Patch | *Cal./Med.* 23

Café Brasil | *Brazilian* 19
Cafe 50's | *Diner* 16
Cal. Chicken | *Amer.* 21
Chabuya | *Japanese* 21
Chan/Hse. of Chan | *Thai* 21
Colony Café | *Amer.* 18
Echigo | *Japanese* 26
Enzo/Angela | *Italian* 21
Feast from East | *Asian* 21
Gaby's | *Med.* 20
NEW Glendon Bar | *Cal.* -
Guido's | *Italian* 20
Gyu-Kaku | *Japanese* 20
Z Hamasaku | *Japanese* 27
Hide | *Japanese* 24
Hole in Wall | *Burgers* 21
Hop Li | *Chinese* 19
Hop Woo | *Chinese* 19
Hurry Curry | *Japanese* 18
Il Grano | *Italian* 26
Il Moro | *Italian* 22
India's Oven/Wilshire | *Indian* 21
India's Tandoori | *Indian* 21
Z In-N-Out | *Burgers* 24
Islands | *Amer.* 17
Javan | *Persian* 20
Johnnie's NY | *Pizza* 17
Junior's | *Deli* 16
Koutoubia | *Moroccan* 25
La Bottega Marino | *Italian* 21
La Serenata | *Mex./Seafood* 22
Lemon Moon | *Cal./Med.* 20
Le Saigon | *Viet.* 20
Literati | *Cal./Eclectic* 17
Louise's | *Cal./Italian* 17
Maria's | *Italian* 17
Matteo's | *Italian* 20
Monte Alban | *Mex.* 20
Z Mori Sushi | *Japanese* 27
Mr. Cecil's | *BBQ* 19
Nanbankan | *Japanese* 25
Nizam | *Indian* 19
Nook Bistro | *Amer./Eclectic* 24
Z Orris | *French/Japanese* 27
NEW Palace Seafood | *Chinese* -
Pastina | *Italian* 21
Pitfire Artisan Pizza | *Italian* -
Robata-Ya | *Japanese* 20

LOS ANGELES

LOCATIONS

Restaurant		Score
Sunnin	*Lebanese*	23
🛚 Sushi Masu	*Japanese*	27
🛚 Sushi Sasabune/Sushi-Don	*Japanese*	27
🛚 Sushi Zo	*Japanese*	29
Tlapazola	*Mex.*	22
🛚 Tofu-Ya	*Korean*	23
Torafuku	*Japanese*	23
2117	*Asian/Euro.*	24
Upstairs 2	*Med.*	23
U-Zen	*Japanese*	22
V.I.P. Harbor	*Chinese/Seafood*	19
Westside Tav.	*Cal.*	21
Yabu	*Japanese*	23
Yen	*Japanese*	23
Zankou	*Med.*	22

WESTWOOD

Restaurant		Score
Asuka	*Japanese*	19
Baja Fresh	*Mex.*	17
BJ's	*Pub*	17
Blvd 16	*Amer.*	21
Bombay Bite	*Indian*	19
Cal. Pizza Kitchen	*Pizza*	18
D'Amore's	*Pizza*	20
Delphi	*Greek*	16
Falafel King	*Mideast.*	19
🛚 In-N-Out	*Burgers*	24
La Bruschetta	*Italian*	23
Lamonica's	*Pizza*	22
Le Pain Quotidien	*Bakery/Belgian*	20
Mio Babbo's	*Italian*	20
Napa Valley	*Cal.*	19
🛚 Native Foods	*Cal./Eclectic*	23
Nine Thirty	*Amer.*	22
Palomino	*Amer./Euro.*	18
Poquito Más	*Mex.*	21
Shaherzad	*Persian*	22
Soleil	*Canadian/French*	19
Stand	*Hot Dogs*	17
Tanino	*Italian*	21
Tengu	*Japanese*	21

South Bay

CATALINA ISLAND

Restaurant		Score
Armstrong's	*Seafood*	–
Catalina Country Club	*Amer.*	–
Lobster Trap	*Seafood*	–
Rist. Villa Portofino	*Italian*	–
Steve's Steak	*Steak*	–

DOWNEY

Restaurant		Score
Mimi's	*Diner*	17

EL SEGUNDO

Restaurant		Score
Chipotle	*Mex.*	19
Counter	*Burgers*	20
Farm Stand	*Eclectic*	22
🛚 Fleming's	*Steak*	24
Marmalade	*Amer./Cal.*	18
McCormick/Schmick	*Seafood*	20
Paul Martin's	*Amer.*	22
P.F. Chang's	*Chinese*	19
Romano's	*Italian*	17
Salt Creek	*Steak*	17
Second City	*Amer.*	24
Taiko	*Japanese*	21
🛚 Veggie Grill	*Vegan*	23

GARDENA

Restaurant		Score
NEW Eatalian	*Italian*	–
El Pollo Inka	*Peruvian*	20
Sea Empress	*Chinese*	18

HERMOSA BEACH

Restaurant		Score
Akbar	*Indian*	22
Bottle Inn	*Italian*	–
Chef Melba's	*Cal.*	27
El Pollo Inka	*Peruvian*	20
Fritto Misto	*Italian*	21
NEW La Campagna	*Italian*	–
La Sosta	*Italian*	–
Mama D's	*Italian*	19
Martha's 22nd St.	*Amer.*	24
Mediterraneo	*Med.*	20
Ragin' Cajun	*Cajun*	19
Zane's	*Italian/Steak*	26

INGLEWOOD

Restaurant		Score
🛚 Phillips BBQ	*BBQ*	25
Thai Dishes	*Thai*	17
Woody's BBQ	*BBQ*	24

LAX

Restaurant		Score
Daily Grill	*Amer.*	19
NEW Daniels	*Amer.*	–
El Cholo	*Mex.*	18
Encounter	*Eclectic*	16
Gladstone's	*Seafood*	13

uby's | *Diner* 17

hai Dishes | *Thai* 17

Volfgang Puck Café | *Cal.* 19

ONG BEACH

legria | *Nuevo Latino* 21

uld Dubliner | *Pub* 16

aja Fresh | *Mex.* 17

elmont Brewing | *Amer.* 18

enley | *Viet.* 24

J's | *Pub* 17

ono's | *Cal.* 21

afé Piccolo | *Italian* 22

afe Sevilla | *Spanish* 21

laim Jumper | *Amer.* 18

l Torito | *Mex.* 15

55 East | *Steak* 25

renchy's | *French* 25

NEW Fuego/Maya | 19
   Mex./Pan-Latin

eorge's Greek | *Greek* 22

reen Field | *Brazilian* 19

ohnnie's NY | *Pizza* 17

Z Johnny Rebs' | *BBQ* 23

ohnny Rockets | *Burgers* 16

ing's Fish | *Seafood* 20

a Creperie | *French* 23

a Parolaccia | *Italian* 21

Z Lasher's | *Amer.* 24

a Strada | *Italian* 21

'Opera | *Italian* 23

ucille's | *BBQ* 22

adison | *Seafood/Steak* 22

cKenna's | *Seafood/Steak* 19

ichael's/Naples | *Italian* 26

imi's | *Diner* 17

pen Sesame | *Lebanese* 22

arker's | *Seafood* 19

oscoe's | *Soul Food* 21

uby's | *Diner* 17

harky's | *Mex.* 19

NEW Sip | *Amer.* —

ir Winston's | *Cal./Continental* 24

ky Room | *Amer.* 18

unnin | *Lebanese* 23

okcano | *Chinese/Japanese* 16

ard House | *Amer.* 18

en | *Japanese* 23

MANHATTAN BEACH

Back Home | *Hawaiian* 17

Café Pierre | *French* 23

Cal. Pizza Kitchen | *Pizza* 18

China Grill | *Cal./Chinese* 19

Darren's | *Amer./Cal.* 24

Fonz's | *Seafood/Steak* 21

Z Houston's | *Amer.* 22

Il Fornaio | *Italian* 21

Islands | *Amer.* 17

Izaka-Ya | *Japanese* 26

Johnny Rockets | *Burgers* 16

LA Food Show | *Amer.* 17

Le Pain Quotidien | *Bakery/Belgian* 20

Lido/Manhattan | *Italian/Med.* 18

Mama D's | *Italian* 19

Mr. Cecil's | *BBQ* 19

Mucho Ultima | *Mex.* 20

Old Venice | *Greek/Italian* 18

Open Sesame | *Lebanese* 22

Z Petros | *Greek* 23

Pomodoro | *Italian* 16

Rock'n Fish | *Seafood/Steak* 20

Sashi | *Japanese* 21

Simmzy's | *Amer.* 21

Talia's | *Italian* 23

Thai Dishes | *Thai* 17

Tin Roof | *Amer.* 21

Uncle Bill's | *Diner* 22

Versailles | *Cuban* 21

REDONDO BEACH

Z Addi's | *Indian* 24

Baleen | *Amer.* 19

Bluewater | *Seafood* 20

Bouzy | *Amer.* 22

Buca di Beppo | *Italian* 15

Bull Pen | *Seafood/Steak* 15

Buona Sera | *Italian* 18

Catalina | *Amer.* 22

Chaba | *Thai* 22

Chart House | *Seafood/Steak* 19

Z Cheesecake Factory | *Amer.* 19

Chez Mélange | *Eclectic* 25

Coyote Cantina | *SW* 21

El Torito | *Mex.* 15

Gina Lee's | *Asian/Cal.* 24

Havana Mania | *Cuban* —

Hudson Hse. | *Pub* 23
Kincaid's | *Seafood/Steak* 20
☑ Original Pancake | *Amer.* 22
Ortega 120 | *Mex.* 20
Ruby's | *Diner* 17
Turquoise | *Med./Persian* –
W's China | *Chinese* 22
Zazou | *Med.* 22

SAN PEDRO

22nd St. Landing | *Seafood* 17
Whale & Ale | *Pub* 20

TORRANCE

BCD Tofu | *Korean* 20
Benihana | *Japanese* 19
Buffalo Fire Dept. | *Amer.* 19
Chipotle | *Mex.* 19
Christine | *Med./Pac. Rim* 25
Claim Jumper | *Amer.* 18
Counter 20
Depot | *Eclectic* 24
El Pollo Inka | *Peruvian* 20
El Torito Grill | *Mex.* 19
Gyu-Kaku | *Japanese* 20
Islands | *Amer.* 17
King's Hawaiian | *Hawaiian* 20
Lazy Dog | *Eclectic* 17
Local Pl. | *Hawaiian* 17
Loft | *Hawaiian* 19
Lucille's | *BBQ* 22
Melting Pot | *Fondue* 18
Mimi's | *Diner* 17
Misto Caffé | *Cal./Eclectic* 20
Musha | *Japanese* 25
O-Nami | *Japanese* 23
Outback | *Steak* 18
Pei Wei | *Asian* 17
Poquito Más | *Mex.* 21
RA Sushi | *Japanese* 16
Romano's | *Italian* 17
Yuzu | *Japanese* 23

WESTCHESTER

Alejo's | *Italian* 21
Buggy Whip | *Seafood/Steak* 18
Chalet Edelweiss | *German* 17
☑ In-N-Out | *Burgers* 24
Johnny Rockets | *Burgers* 16

Kabuki | *Japanese* 18
Paco's Tacos | *Mex.* 21
Truxton's | *Amer.* 21

Inland Empire

MORENO VALLEY

BJ's | *Pub* 17
Portillo's | *Hot Dogs* 22

ONTARIO

Benihana | *Japanese* 19
Panda Inn | *Chinese* 21
Rainforest Cafe | *Amer.* 13

Pasadena & Environs

ARCADIA

BJ's | *Pub* 17
☑ Cheesecake Factory | *Amer.* 19
Derby | *Steak* 20
☑ Din Tai Fung | *Chinese* 25
Hop Li | *Chinese* 1
Johnny Rockets | *Burgers* 16
NEW 101 Noodle | *Chinese* 2
Outback | *Steak* 18
Tokyo Table | *Japanese* 18
Wood Ranch | *BBQ* 2

EAGLE ROCK

Auntie Em's | *Amer.* 2
Blue Hen | *Viet.* 1
NEW CaCao | *Mex.* 2
Café Beaujolais | *French* 20
Camilo's | *Cal.* 2
Casa Bianca | *Pizza* 2
Fatty's & Co. | *Veg.* 2
Larkin's | *Southern* 1
Mia Sushi | *Japanese* –
Oinkster | *BBQ* 2
Spitz | *Turkish* 2

LA CAÑADA FLINTRIDGE

Dish | *Amer.* 1
Taylor's | *Steak* 2

MONROVIA

Claim Jumper | *Amer.* 1
Devon | *Cal./French* 2
Mimi's | *Diner* 1

TOP FOOD

Bistro 45	*Cal.*	**D5**	26
Derek's	*Cal./French*	**H3**	26
Parkway Grill	*Cal.*	**F2**	26
Maison Akira	*French/Japanese*	**E4**	26
Yujean Kang's	*Chinese*	**D2**	26
Arroyo	*Steak*	**F2**	25
Japon Bistro	*Japanese*	**D5**	25
Ruth's Chris	*Steak*	**D3**	25
Noir	*Eclectic*	**D5**	25
Raymond	*Cal.*	**H2**	25
Celestino	*Italian*	**E5**	25
Gale's	*Italian*	**F2**	24
Porta Via Italian	*Italian*	**F2**	24
Green St. Tav.	*Cal./Euro.*	**D2**	24
Roy's	*Hawaiian*	**D4**	24

LISTING

Akbar	*Indian*	22
All India	*Indian*	21
☑ Arroyo	*Steak*	25
Azeen's	*Afghan*	23
Bar Celona	*Spanish*	17
Beckham Grill	*Amer.*	19
Big Mama's	*BBQ/Soul Food*	21
☑ Bistro 45	*Cal.*	26
NEW Bonnie B's	*BBQ*	–
Buca di Beppo	*Italian*	15
Burger Continental	*Mideast.*	18
☑ Café Bizou/Bizou Grill	*Cal./French*	23
NEW Café 140 S.	*Cal.*	19
Café Santorini	*Med.*	22
Cal. Pizza Kitchen	*Pizza*	18
Celestino	*Italian*	25
Central Park	*Amer./Cal.*	19
☑ Cheesecake Factory	*Amer.*	19
NEW Cheval Blanc	*French*	22
Chipotle	*Mex.*	19
Choza Mama	*Peruvian*	19
Counter	*Burgers*	20
☑ Derek's	*Cal./French*	26
NEW DISH	*Cal./Med.*	–
Doña Rosa	*Bakery/Mex.*	17
1810 Rest.	*Argent./Steak*	23
El Cholo	*Mex.*	18

NEW Elements Kitchen	*Amer./Eclectic*	23
El Torito	*Mex.*	15
Five 61	*Cal./French*	23
Fu-Shing	*Chinese*	19
Gale's	*Italian*	24
NEW Gold Class	*Eclectic*	18
Green St.	*Amer.*	22
Green St. Tav.	*Cal./Euro.*	24
Gyu-Kaku	*Japanese*	20
Hamburger Hamlet	*Amer.*	18
☑ Houston's	*Amer.*	22
Il Fornaio	*Italian*	21
Islands	*Amer.*	17
NEW Ixtapa	*Mex.*	–
☑ Japon Bistro	*Japanese*	25
Kabuki	*Japanese*	18
La Grande Orange	*Amer.*	20
Le Pain Quotidien	*Bakery/Belgian*	20
Louise's	*Cal./Italian*	17
Magnolia Lounge	*Eclectic*	15
☑ Maison Akira	*French/Japanese*	26
Maria's	*Italian*	17
Marston's	*Amer.*	22
McCormick/Schmick	*Seafood*	20
Melting Pot	*Fondue*	18
Mijares	*Mex.*	17
Mi Piace	*Cal./Italian*	20
Naga Naga	*Japanese*	–
NEW Noir	*Eclectic*	25
Panda Inn	*Chinese*	21
☑ Parkway Grill	*Cal.*	26
Pei Wei	*Asian*	17
P.F. Chang's	*Chinese*	19
Pie 'N Burger	*Diner*	22
Pop	*Eclectic*	17
Porta Via Italian	*Italian*	24
Porto Alegre	*Brazilian/Steak*	20
NEW Quadrupel	*French*	–
Raymond	*Cal.*	25
redwhite+bluezz	*Amer.*	23
Robin's	*BBQ*	20
Roscoe's	*Soul Food*	21
☑ Roy's	*Hawaiian*	24
Russell's	*Diner*	24
☑ Ruth's Chris	*Steak*	25
Saladang	*Thai*	23

LOS ANGELES

LOCATIONS

Sharky's | *Mex.* 19

NEW Slaw Dogs | *Hot Dogs* 18

Smitty's | *Amer.* 22

Sushi Roku | *Japanese* 23

Thai Dishes | *Thai* 17

Tibet Nepal | *Nepalese/Tibetan* 17

Tre Venezie | *Italian* 22

Vertical Wine | *Eclectic/Med.* 21

Villa Sorriso | *Italian* 20

Wokcano | *Chinese/Japanese* 16

Yang Chow | *Chinese* 22

Yard House | *Amer.* 18

Z Yujean Kang's | *Chinese* 26

Zankou | *Med.* 22

SAN MARINO

Z Julienne | *French* 26

SOUTH PASADENA

Bistro/Gare | *French* 19

Briganti | *Italian* 21

Firefly Bistro | *Amer.* 20

Gus's | *BBQ* 20

Mike & Anne's | *Amer.* 21

Z Shiro | *French/Japanese* 28

San Fernando Valley & Burbank

BURBANK

Baja Fresh | *Mex.* 17

Bistro Provence | *French* 23

BJ's | *Pub* 17

Cal. Pizza Kitchen | *Pizza* 18

Castaway | *Cal.* 17

Z Chadaka | *Thai* 23

Chili John's | *Amer.* 18

Chipotle | *Mex.* 19

Choza Mama | *Peruvian* 19

Daily Grill | *Amer.* 19

El Torito | *Mex.* 15

Flavor of India | *Indian* 21

Gordon Biersch | *Pub* 16

Islands | *Amer.* 17

Johnny Rockets | *Burgers* 16

Kabuki | *Japanese* 18

Market City | *Cal./Italian* 18

McCormick/Schmick | *Seafood* 20

Morton's | *Steak* 24

Mo's | *Amer.* 18

Outback | *Steak* 18

Picanha | *Brazilian* 21

Pomodoro | *Italian* 16

Poquito Más | *Mex.* 21

Z Porto's | *Bakery/Cuban* 24

Ribs USA | *BBQ* 19

Sharky's | *Mex.* 19

Smoke House | *Steak* 20

Taste Chicago | *Italian* 19

Third & Olive | *Cal./French* 21

Tony's Bella Vista | *Italian* 19

Wokcano | *Chinese/Japanese* 16

Zankou | *Med.* 22

CALABASAS

Banzai | *Japanese* 20

Fins | *Continental/Seafood* 21

King's Fish | *Seafood* 20

Marmalade | *Amer./Cal.* 18

Mi Piace | *Cal./Italian* 20

Riviera | *Italian* 2

Z Saddle Peak | *Amer.* 2

Sagebrush | *SW* 1

Sharky's | *Mex.* 1

Spumoni | *Italian* 2

CANOGA PARK

D'Amore's | *Pizza* 2

Gyu-Kaku | *Japanese* 2

Yang Chow | *Chinese* 2

CHATSWORTH

Z Les Sisters | *Southern* 2

Mimi's | *Diner* 1

Omino | *Japanese* 2

Poquito Más | *Mex.* 2

ENCINO

Absolutely Pho | *Viet.* 1

Benihana | *Japanese* 1

Buca di Beppo | *Italian* 1

Cal. Chicken | *Amer.* 2

Cal. Wok | *Chinese* 1

NEW Capriotti's | *Sandwiches* 2

Coral Tree | *Cal./Italian* 1

Delmonico's | *Seafood* 1

Fromin's | *Deli* 1

Hirosuke | *Japanese* 1

Islands | *Amer.* 1

NEW Itzik Hagadol | *Israeli* 1

ohnny Rockets	*Burgers*	16
ohn O'Groats	*Amer.*	20
⊋ Katsu-ya	*Japanese*	26
⊋ Larsen's	*Steak*	23
Maria's	*Italian*	17
Mulberry St. Pizzeria	*Pizza*	23
Rosti	*Italian*	17
Sampa	*Brazilian*	-
Stand	*Hot Dogs*	17
Stevie's	*Cajun/Creole*	17
Versailles	*Cuban*	21

GLENDALE

⊠ Carousel	*Mideast.*	24
Damon's	*Steak*	19
Eat Well	*Amer.*	17
Far Niente	*Italian*	23
Frida	*Mex.*	20
Gennaro's	*Italian*	22
Islands	*Amer.*	17
Jody Maroni's	*Hot Dogs*	19
⊠ Katsuya	*Japanese*	23
Minx	*Eclectic*	-
Palate	*Amer.*	24
Panda Inn	*Chinese*	21
⊠ Porto's	*Bakery/Cuban*	24
Sedthee	*Thai*	-
Skaf's	*Lebanese*	22
Zankou	*Med.*	22

MONTROSE

⊠ Bashan	*Amer.*	27
La Cabanita	*Mex.*	25
New Moon	*Chinese*	21
Zeke's	*BBQ*	21

NORTH HOLLYWOOD

Ca' del Sole	*Italian*	21
NEW Firenze	*Italian*	20
⊠ In-N-Out	*Burgers*	24
Pitfire Artisan Pizza	*Italian*	-
Poquito Más	*Mex.*	21
Zankou	*Med.*	22

NORTHRIDGE

Alessio	*Italian*	21
⊠ Brent's	*Deli*	26
Cal. Chicken	*Amer.*	21
Claim Jumper	*Amer.*	18
El Torito	*Mex.*	15

Emle's	*Cal./Med.*	20
Mandarin	*Chinese*	23
Maria's	*Italian*	17
Outback	*Steak*	18
Romano's	*Italian*	17
Wood Ranch	*BBQ*	21

RESEDA

BCD Tofu	*Korean*	20
Fab Hot Dogs	*Hot Dogs*	-

SHERMAN OAKS

Bamboo Cuisine	*Chinese*	23
Barney's	*Burgers*	20
NEW Blue Dog	*Amer.*	21
Boneyard	*BBQ/Eclectic*	21
⊠ Café Bizou/Bizou Grill	*Cal./French*	23
Cafe 50's	*Diner*	16
⊠ Carnival	*Lebanese*	24
Casa Vega	*Mex.*	17
⊠ Cheesecake Factory	*Amer.*	19
El Torito	*Mex.*	15
El Torito Grill	*Mex.*	19
Great Greek	*Greek*	20
Gyu-Kaku	*Japanese*	20
Hamburger Hamlet	*Amer.*	18
⊠ Il Tiramisù	*Italian*	24
⊠ In-N-Out	*Burgers*	24
Jinky's	*SW*	19
La Frite	*French*	19
La Pergola	*Italian*	23
Le Petit Rest.	*French*	23
Maria's	*Italian*	17
Marmalade	*Amer./Cal.*	18
Mel's Drive-In	*Amer.*	16
⊠ Mistral	*French*	26
Mr. Cecil's	*BBQ*	19
Panini Cafe	*Italian/Med.*	20
Panzanella	*Italian*	23
P.F. Chang's	*Chinese*	19
Poquito Más	*Mex.*	21
Rive Gauche	*French*	22
Señor Fred	*Mex.*	17
Sharky's	*Mex.*	19
Sisley	*Italian*	19
Spumoni	*Italian*	20
Stanley's	*Cal.*	20
NEW Townhouse	*Cal.*	12

STUDIO CITY

Ahi	*Japanese*	21
Artisan	*Cheese/Sandwiches*	24
Art's	*Deli*	20
🄩 Asanebo	*Japanese*	27
Baja Fresh	*Mex.*	17
🄩 Bistro Gdn.	*Continental*	21
Bokado	*Spanish*	19
Bollywood	*Indian*	17
Caioti Pizza	*Pizza*	21
Cal. Pizza Kitchen	*Pizza*	18
Carney's	*Hot Dogs*	20
Chin Chin	*Chinese*	17
Counter	*Burgers*	20
Daily Grill	*Amer.*	19
Du-par's	*Diner*	16
NEW 8½ Taverna	*Gastropub*	–
Firefly	*Amer.*	20
Hugo's	*Cal.*	20
Il Tramezzino	*Italian*	19
🄩 In-N-Out	*Burgers*	24
Iroha	*Japanese*	25
🄩 Katsu-ya	*Japanese*	26
Kiwami	*Japanese*	26
Lal Mirch	*Indian*	17
La Loggia	*Italian*	21
Laurel	*Amer.*	23
Le Pain Quotidien	*Bakery/Belgian*	20
Lotería!	*Mex.*	24
Louise's	*Cal./Italian*	17
Mantee	*Med.*	23
Marrakesh	*Moroccan*	21
Mexicali	*Cal./Mex.*	16
Pinot Bistro	*French*	24
Poquito Más	*Mex.*	21
Spark	*Amer.*	20
🄩 Sushi Nozawa	*Japanese*	28
Talésai	*Thai*	22
Teru Sushi	*Japanese*	22
Vitello's	*Italian*	16
Wine Bistro	*French*	23
Yen	*Japanese*	23

TARZANA

D'Amore's	*Pizza*	20
Il Tramezzino	*Italian*	19
India's Tandoori	*Indian*	21
Le Sanglier	*French*	25

Madeleine	*French/Vegan*	28
Sharky's	*Mex.*	19

TOLUCA LAKE

D'Caché	*Pan-Latin*	23
Prosecco	*Italian*	22

UNIVERSAL CITY

Buca di Beppo	*Italian*	15
Hard Rock	*Amer.*	13
Henry's Hat	*Amer.*	18
Jody Maroni's	*Hot Dogs*	19
Miceli's	*Italian*	16
Saddle Ranch	*Steak*	15
Versailles	*Cuban*	21
Wolfgang Puck Café	*Cal.*	19

VAN NUYS

Dr. Hogly Wogly's	*BBQ*	22
🄩 In-N-Out	*Burgers*	24
Sam Woo	*Chinese*	22
Zankou	*Med.*	22

WEST HILLS

Alessio	*Italian*	21
Stonefire	*BBQ*	20

WOODLAND HILLS

Adagio	*Italian*	22
Baja Fresh	*Mex.*	17
BJ's	*Pub*	17
🄩 Brandywine	*Continental*	28
Cal. Chicken	*Amer.*	21
🄩 Cheesecake Factory	*Amer.*	19
El Torito	*Mex.*	15
🄩 Fleming's	*Steak*	24
Gaucho	*Argent./Steak*	18
🄩 In-N-Out	*Burgers*	24
Islands	*Amer.*	17
Kabuki	*Japanese*	18
Kate Mantilini	*Amer.*	18
La Frite	*French*	19
Maggiano's	*Italian*	19
Maria's	*Italian*	17
Monty's	*Steak*	22
Morton's	*Steak*	24
Panini Cafe	*Italian/Med.*	20
P.F. Chang's	*Chinese*	19
Poquito Más	*Mex.*	21
🄩 Roy's	*Hawaiian*	24
Ruby's	*Diner*	17

☑ Ruth's Chris | *Steak* — 25

Stand | *Hot Dogs* — 17

Villa Piacere | *Eclectic* — 18

San Gabriel Valley

ALHAMBRA

Boiling Crab | *Cajun* — 23

Cuban Bistro | *Cuban* — 20

Hop Woo | *Chinese* — 19

Lunasia | *Chinese* — 22

Naga Naga | *Japanese* — -

NEW 101 Noodle — 22

☑ Pho 79 | *Viet.* — 24

Sam Woo | *Chinese* — 22

AZUSA

Tulipano | *Italian* — -

CITY OF INDUSTRY

Benihana | *Japanese* — 19

Claim Jumper | *Amer.* — 18

Mimi's | *Diner* — 17

Outback | *Steak* — 18

CLAREMONT

Buca di Beppo | *Italian* — 15

Casablanca Med. | *Med.* — 23

Heroes/Legends | *Pub* — 17

La Parolaccia | *Italian* — 21

Tutti Mangia | *Italian* — 23

Walter's | *Eclectic* — 21

COVINA/
WEST COVINA

BJ's | *Pub* — 17

Green Field | *Brazilian* — 19

Hayakawa | *Japanese* — 28

Outback | *Steak* — 18

MONTEBELLO

Astro Burger | *Burgers* — 20

Zankou | *Med.* — 22

MONTEREY PARK

Chung King | *Chinese* — 22

Cook's Tortas | *Mex.* — 25

Elite | *Chinese* — 24

Empress Harbor | *Chinese* — 21

Mandarin | *Chinese* — 23

☑ NBC Seafood | *Chinese/Seafood* — 21

Ocean Star | *Chinese* — 21

PICO RIVERA

Dal Rae | *Continental* — 25

ROSEMEAD

☑ Sea Harbour | *Chinese/Seafood* — 25

ROWLAND HEIGHTS

BCD Tofu | *Korean* — 20

SAN GABRIEL

☑ Babita | *Mex.* — 27

Bamboodles | *Chinese* — 20

Clearman's | *Amer.* — 19

Golden Deli | *Viet.* — 23

Mission 261 | *Chinese* — -

Sam Woo | *Chinese* — 22

WHITTIER

Mimi's | *Diner* — 17

Phlight | *Med./Spanish* — 23

Ruby's | *Diner* — 17

Seta | *American/Steak* — 27

Conejo/
Simi Valley/
Oxnard/
Ventura & Environs

AGOURA HILLS/
OAK PARK

Adobe Cantina | *Mex.* — 17

☑ Café 14 | *Cal./Continental* — 27

☑ Leila's | *Cal.* — 27

Maria's | *Italian* — 17

MOZ | *Asian* — 18

Padri | *Italian* — 22

Wood Ranch | *BBQ* — 21

CAMARILLO

D'Amore's | *Pizza* — 20

Enoteca Toscana | *Italian/Spanish* — 25

NEW Los Arroyos | *Mex.* — 23

Safire | *Amer.* — 23

Wood Ranch | *BBQ* — 21

MOORPARK

Cafe Firenze | *Italian* — 19

Wood Ranch | *BBQ* — 21

OJAI

Boccali's | *Italian* — 19

Ranch Hse. | *Cal.* — 22

Suzanne's | *French/Italian* — 25

OXNARD

Baja Fresh | *Mex.* — 17
BJ's | *Pub* — 17
Du-par's | *Diner* — 16
Outback | *Steak* — 18
Tierra Sur/Herzog | *Med.* — 27

SIMI VALLEY

Sharky's | *Mex.* — 19
Spark | *Amer.* — 20

THOUSAND OAKS

Buca di Beppo | *Italian* — 15
Café Provencal | *French* — 23
Ⓩ Cheesecake Factory | *Amer.* — 19
Cholada | *Thai* — 23
Claim Jumper | *Amer.* — 18
D'Amore's | *Pizza* — 20
El Torito | *Mex.* — 15
Grill on Hollywood/Alley | *Amer.* — 22
Holdren's | *Steak* — 20
Ⓩ Mastro's Steak | *Steak* — 26
Nate 'n Al | *Deli* — 20
Outback | *Steak* — 18
Romano's | *Italian* — 17

VENTURA

Austen's | *Cal.* — –
Baja Fresh | *Mex.* — 17
Bariloche | *S Amer.* — 22
Brooks | *Amer.* — 25
Ⓩ Brophy Bros. | *Seafood* — 21
Cafe FIORE | *Italian* — 22
Café Nouveau | *Cal.* — 21
Cajun Kitchen | *Cajun* — 20
Jonathan's | *Cal./Med.* — 23
Romano's | *Italian* — 17
71 Palm | *Amer./French* — 22
Sharky's | *Mex.* — 19
Sidecar | *Amer.* — 24
Westside Cellar | *Eclectic* — –
Wood Ranch | *BBQ* — 21

WESTLAKE VILLAGE

Bellavino | *Eclectic* — 19
🆕 Bellini Osteria | *Italian* — –
BJ's | *Pub* — 17
Boccaccio's | *Continental* — 20
Ⓩ Brent's | *Deli* — 26
Counter | *Burgers* — 20
Fins | *Continental/Seafood* — 21
Galletto | *Brazilian/Italian* — 23
Hampton's | *Cal.* — 21
Marmalade | *Amer./Cal.* — 18
Mediterraneo | *Med.* — 24
Melting Pot | *Fondue* — 18
Rustico | *Italian* — 24
Sharky's | *Mex.* — 19
Ⓩ Tuscany | *Italian* — 26
Zin Bistro | *Amer.* — 20

Santa Clarita Valley & Environs

SANTA CLARITA

Mimi's | *Diner* — 17
Pei Wei | *Asian* — 17
Romano's | *Italian* — 17

SAUGUS/NEWHALL

Le Chêne | *French* — 25
Wood Ranch | *BBQ* — 21

STEVENSON RANCH

Spumoni | *Italian* — 20

VALENCIA

BJ's | *Pub* — 17
Buca di Beppo | *Italian* — 15
Claim Jumper | *Amer.* — 18
New Moon | *Chinese* — 21
Outback | *Steak* — 18
Salt Creek | *Steak* — 17
Sisley | *Italian* — 19
Stonefire | *BBQ* — 20
Thai Dishes | *Thai* — 17

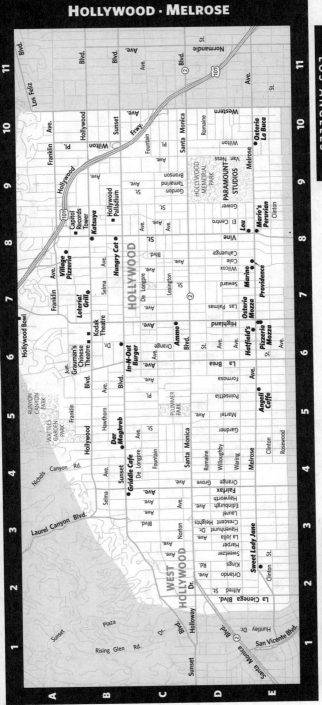

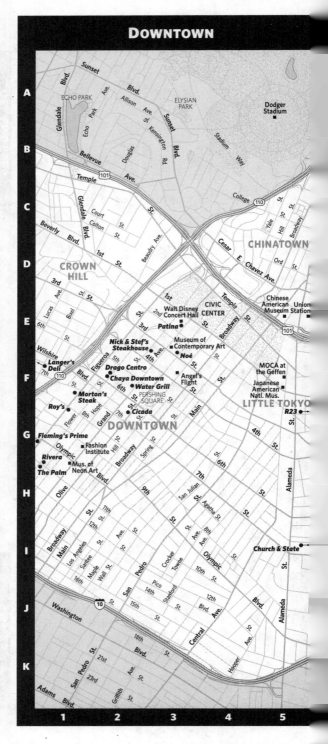

DOWNTOWN

A

Sunset Blvd.

Glendale Blvd.

ECHO PARK

Echo Park Ave.

ELYSIAN PARK

Dodger Stadium

Allison Ave.

B

Bellevue

Douglas

Kensington Rd.

Stadium Way

Temple 101

College 110

C

Glendale Blvd.

Court St.

Colton St.

Beaudry Ave.

Cesar E. Chavez Ave.

CHINATOWN

Yale St.

Hill St.

Broadway

Beverly Blvd.

1st St.

Ord St.

D

CROWN HILL

3rd St.

Lucas Ave.

Bixel St.

6th St.

Temple St.

Broadway

CIVIC CENTER

Chinese American Museum

Union Station

101

E

Wilshire Blvd.

Langer's Deli

7th 110

Figueroa St.

1st 2nd 3rd St.

Walt Disney Concert Hall

Patina

Nick & Stef's Steakhouse

4th Ave.

Museum of Contemporary Art

Noé

MOCA at the Geffen

Japanese American Natl. Mus.

F

Drago Centro

Chaya Downtown

Water Grill

5th 6th St.

PERSHING SQUARE

Angel's Flight

Main St.

LITTLE TOKYO

R23

Morton's Steak

Roy's

Flower St.

Grand St.

8th St.

Cicada

DOWNTOWN

Spring St.

4th St.

G

Fleming's Prime

Olympic

Fashion Institute

Hill St.

Broadway

6th St.

Rivera

The Palm

Mus. of Neon Art

Blvd.

7th St.

Alameda St.

H

Olive

9th St.

San Julian St.

Agatha St.

Church & State

I

Broadway

Main

Los Angeles St.

Santee St.

Maple Ave.

Wall St.

San Pedro St.

Crocker St.

Towne

Olympic

10th St.

Pico

Stanford

12th Blvd.

Alameda St.

J

Washington

10

14th St.

15th St.

Central Ave.

Hooper Ave.

K

San Pedro St.

21st St.

23rd St.

Griffith Ave.

18th St.

Blvd.

Adams Blvd.

1 2 3 4 5

292   Menus, photos, voting and more – free at ZAGAT

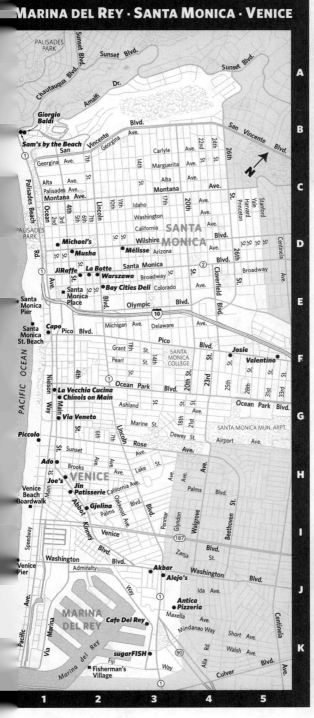

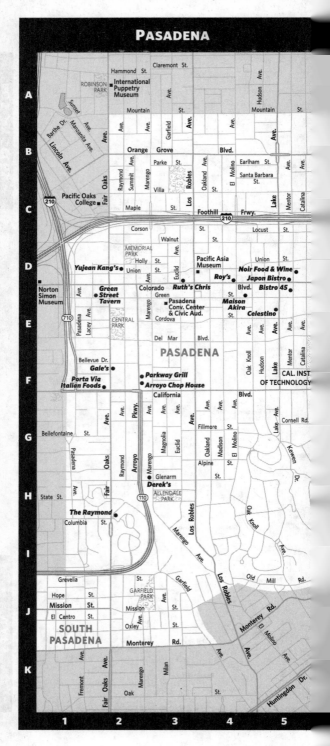

PASADENA

Special Features

Listings cover the best in each category and include names, locations and food ratings. Multi-location restaurants' features may vary by branch.

BEACHSIDE/WATERSIDE

Baleen | **Redondo Bch**	19
Belmont Brewing | **Long Bch**	18
Bluewater | **Redondo Bch**	20
🔢 Boa | **Santa Monica**	22
Boccaccio's | **Westlake Vill**	20
Cafe Del Rey | **Marina del Rey**	22
🔢 Catch | **Santa Monica**	22
Chart House | **multi.**	19
🔢 Cheesecake Factory | **Redondo Bch**	19
NEW Drai's | **Hollywood**	–
Duke's | **Malibu**	17
Figtree's | **Venice**	–
NEW Fuego/Maya | **Long Bch**	19
Gaby's | **Marina del Rey**	20
🔢 Geoffrey's | **Malibu**	20
Gladstone's | **Pacific Palisades**	13
Guido's | **Malibu**	20
🔢 Inn/Seventh Ray | **Topanga**	21
Ivy/Shore | **Santa Monica**	22
Jer-ne | **Marina del Rey**	23
Jody Maroni's | **Venice**	19
Kincaid's | **Redondo Bch**	20
Lobster | **Santa Monica**	23
🔢 mar'sel | **Rancho Palos Verdes**	24
Martha's 22nd St. | **Hermosa Bch**	24
McKenna's | **Long Bch**	19
Mediterraneo | **Westlake Vill**	24
Moonshadows | **Malibu**	16
Neptune's Net | **Malibu**	19
NEW Oliverio | **Beverly Hills**	–
🔢 One Pico | **Santa Monica**	20
Paradise Cove | **Malibu**	15
Parker's | **Long Bch**	19
Ruby's | **Redondo Bch**	17
Sapori | **Marina del Rey**	24
Sir Winston's | **Long Bch**	24
Tony P's | **Marina del Rey**	17
22nd St. Landing | **San Pedro**	17
Warehouse | **Marina del Rey**	17
Yard House | **Long Bch**	18
Zin Bistro | **Westlake Vill**	20

BREAKFAST
(See also Hotel Dining)

Alcove | **Los Feliz**	20
🔢 Anisette | **Santa Monica**	21
Art's | **Studio City**	20
Astro Burger | **multi.**	20
Auntie Em's | **Eagle Rock**	21
Barney Greengrass | **Beverly Hills**	22
bld | **Beverly Blvd**	22
Brighton Coffee | **Beverly Hills**	18
Cajun Kitchen | **Ventura**	20
🔢 Clementine | **Century City**	24
🔢 Cora's | **Santa Monica**	23
Doughboys | **Third St**	22
Dukes West Hollywood | **W Hollywood**	18
Du-par's | **multi.**	16
Farm/Bev. Hills | **multi.**	18
Fred 62 | **Los Feliz**	17
Griddle | **Hollywood**	23
Huckleberry | **Santa Monica**	22
Hugo's | **multi.**	20
John O'Groats | **Rancho Pk**	20
Lemon Moon | **West LA**	20
Le Pain Quotidien | **multi.**	20
Literati | **West LA**	17
Lotería! | **Fairfax**	24
Mäni's | **Fairfax**	17
Marmalade | **multi.**	18
Marston's | **Pasadena**	22
Martha's 22nd St. | **Hermosa Bch**	24
Maxwell's | **Venice**	18
Mel's Drive-In | **Hollywood**	16
Mimi's | **Atwater Vill**	17
Newsroom Café | **W Hollywood**	18
Nickel Diner | **Downtown**	22
🔢 Original Pancake | **Redondo Bch**	22
Pacific Dining Car | **multi.**	23
Patrick's | **Santa Monica**	18
Roscoe's | **Mid-City**	21
Ruby's | **multi.**	17
Square One | **E Hollywood**	23
🔢 Susina | **La Brea**	26

Sweet Lady Jane	**Melrose**	24
Swingers	**Santa Monica**	17
Toast	**Third St**	20
Uncle Bill's	**Manhattan Bch**	22
Urth	**multi.**	21

BRUNCH

☑ Anisette	**Santa Monica**	21
☑ Belvedere	**Beverly Hills**	25
☑ NEW Bouchon	**Beverly Hills**	24
☑ Campanile	**La Brea**	26
☑ Cliff's Edge	**Silver Lake**	19
Comme Ça	**W Hollywood**	22
Dusty's	**Silver Lake**	21
Firefly Bistro	**S Pasadena**	20
☑ Gjelina	**Venice**	26
Hugo's	**multi.**	20
Jer-ne	**Marina del Rey**	23
☑ Joe's	**Venice**	26
La Huasteca	**Lynwood**	-
Lilly's	**Venice**	19
McCormick/Schmick	**El Segundo**	20
Morels Bistro	**Fairfax**	20
Napa Valley	**Westwood**	19
Nine Thirty	**Westwood**	22
Ocean Seafood	**Chinatown**	21
☑ One Pico	**Santa Monica**	20
☑ Polo	**Beverly Hills**	23
Porta Via	**Beverly Hills**	21
Raymond	**Pasadena**	25
☑ Saddle Peak	**Calabasas**	27
☑ Tavern	**Brentwood**	23
3 Square	**Venice**	23
Whist	**Santa Monica**	20

BUFFET

(Check availability)

Akbar	**Hermosa Bch**	22
All India	**West LA**	21
Austen's	**Ventura**	-
Bollywood	**Studio City**	17
Bombay Palace	**Beverly Hills**	21
Burger Continental	**Pasadena**	18
Café Pacific	**Rancho Palos Verdes**	22
Castaway	**Burbank**	17
Circa 55	**Beverly Hills**	19
Clay Pit	**Brentwood**	21
Delmonico's	**Encino**	22
El Torito	**multi.**	15
El Torito Grill	**Torrance**	19

Flavor of India	**multi.**	21
Frida	**Glendale**	20
Hampton's	**Westlake Vill**	21
House of Blues	**W Hollywood**	16
India's Oven/Wilshire	**West LA**	21
India's Tandoori	**multi.**	21
NEW Ixtapa	**Pasadena**	-
NEW K-Town	**Downtown**	-
La Huasteca	**Lynwood**	-
Lal Mirch	**Studio City**	17
☑ Maison Akira	**Pasadena**	26
Flore/Meet Mkt.	**Echo Pk**	21
Mijares	**Pasadena**	17
☑ Nawab	**Santa Monica**	23
Nizam	**West LA**	19
O-Nami	**Torrance**	23
Panda Inn	**multi.**	21
Sagebrush	**Calabasas**	13
Salt Creek	**Valencia**	17
Smoke House	**Burbank**	20
Tanzore	**Beverly Hills**	21
Tibet Nepal	**Pasadena**	17
Walter's	**Claremont**	21
Whist	**Santa Monica**	20

BUSINESS DINING

☑ Arroyo	**Pasadena**	25
Barney Greengrass	**Beverly Hills**	22
NEW Bellini Osteria | **Westlake Vill**	-
☑ Belvedere	**Beverly Hills**	25
☑ Bistro 45	**Pasadena**	26
Bistro LQ	**Fairfax**	24
BLT Steak	**W Hollywood**	24
Blvd	**Beverly Hills**	23
Blvd 16	**Westwood**	21
☑ NEW Bouchon	**Beverly Hills**	24
NEW Boxwood	**W Hollywood**	22
Breeze	**Century City**	18
Brooks	**Ventura**	25
☑ Campanile	**La Brea**	26
☑ Catch	**Santa Monica**	22
Celestino	**Pasadena**	25
Chaya Downtown	**Downtown**	24
Checkers	**Downtown**	21
NEW Cheval Blanc	**Pasadena**	22
☑ Cicada	**Downtown**	23
Coast	**Santa Monica**	21
☑ Craft	**Century City**	24

NEW Culina | **Beverly Hills**	–
Z CUT | **Beverly Hills**	27
Dan Tana's | **W Hollywood**	23
Drago | **Santa Monica**	23
Z Drago Centro | **Downtown**	26
555 East | **Long Bch**	25
Z Fleming's | **multi.**	24
Z Fraîche | **Culver City**	23
NEW Fuego/Maya | **Long Bch**	19
Gordon Ramsay | **W Hollywood**	23
Grill on Hollywood/Alley | **Hollywood**	22
Z Grill on Alley | **Beverly Hills**	25
Hampton's | **Westlake Vill**	21
Z Hatfield's | **Melrose**	27
Il Grano | **West LA**	26
Il Moro | **West LA**	22
Z Jar | **Beverly Blvd.**	25
Z Josie | **Santa Monica**	26
Kincaid's | **Redondo Bch**	20
La Bistecca | **Downtown**	–
La Botte | **Santa Monica**	24
NEW L.A. Market | **Downtown**	19
Z Larsen's | **Encino**	23
Madeo | **W Hollywood**	25
Z mar'sel | **Rancho Palos Verdes**	24
Z Mélisse | **Santa Monica**	28
Z Michael's | **Santa Monica**	25
Z Mistral | **Sherman Oaks**	26
Morton's | **multi.**	24
Nick & Stef's | **Downtown**	23
Nic's | **Beverly Hills**	19
Z Nobu LA | **W Hollywood**	26
Ocean & Vine | **Santa Monica**	22
NEW Olive | **Hollywood**	–
Z One Pico | **Santa Monica**	20
Parq/Montage | **Beverly Hills**	25
Z Patina | **Downtown**	26
Paul Martin's | **El Segundo**	22
Peppone | **Brentwood**	21
Z Petros | **Manhattan Bch**	23
NEW Philippe | **W Hollywood**	17
Pinot Bistro | **Studio City**	24
Z Polo | **Beverly Hills**	23
Z Providence | **Hollywood**	28
Rivera | **Downtown**	25
Z Roy's | **Downtown**	24
Rustic Canyon | **Santa Monica**	23

Z Ruth's Chris | **multi.**	25
Safire | **Camarillo**	23
Salt Creek | **El Segundo**	17
Z Spago | **Beverly Hills**	27
STK | **W Hollywood**	22
Sushi Dokoro | **Beverly Hills**	–
Taylor's | **multi.**	21
Tierra Sur/Herzog | **Oxnard**	27
Z Valentino | **Santa Monica**	26
Z Vincenti | **Brentwood**	26
Z Water Grill | **Downtown**	27
Westside Tav. | **West LA**	21
Wilshire | **Santa Monica**	23
Wolfgang Puck B&G | **Downtown**	22
Wolfgang's Steak | **Beverly Hills**	23
Z Yujean Kang's | **Pasadena**	26
Zucca | **Downtown**	22

CELEBRITY CHEFS

José Andrés
Z Bazaar/José Andrés | **Beverly Hills**	26
Z Saam/The Bazaar | **Beverly Hills**	27

Gino Angelini
Z Angelini | **Beverly Blvd**	28
Minestraio | **W Hollywood**	23

Govind Armstrong
8 oz. | **Melrose**	22

Mario Batali, Nancy Silverton
Z Osteria Mozza | **Hollywood**	27
Z Pizzeria Mozza | **Hollywood**	27

Rick Bayless
NEW Red O | **Melrose**	–

Octavio Becerra
Palate | **Glendale**	24

Michael Cimarusti
Z Providence | **Hollywood**	28

Josiah Citrin
Lemon Moon | **West LA**	20
Z Mélisse | **Santa Monica**	28

Tom Colicchio
Z Craft | **Century City**	24

Celestino Drago
Z Drago Centro | **Downtown**	26

Gordon Drysdale
NEW Pizza Antica | **Santa Monica**	–

Todd English
  Beso | **Hollywood** 21

Susan Feniger
  Border Grill | **Santa Monica** 21
  Ciudad | **Downtown** 22
  Street | **Hollywood** 20

Ben Ford
  Ford's | **Culver City** 20

Neal Fraser
  bld | **Beverly Blvd** 22
  Cole's | **Downtown** 17

Alain Giraud
  🅩 Anisette | **Santa Monica** 21

Suzanne Goin
  🅩 A.O.C. | **Third St** 27
  🅩 Lucques | **W Hollywood** 27
  🅩 Tavern | **Brentwood** 23

Ilan Hall
  NEW Gorbals | **Downtown** 21

Thomas Keller
  NEW Bar Bouchon | **Beverly Hills** 23
  🅩**NEW** Bouchon | **Beverly Hills** 24

Bruce Marder
  Capo | **Santa Monica** 25
  NEW House Café | **Beverly Blvd** 21

Nobu Matsuhisa
  🅩 Matsuhisa | **Beverly Hills** 28
  🅩 Nobu LA | **W Hollywood** 26
  🅩 Nobu Malibu | **Malibu** 26

Joe Miller
  Bar Pintxo | **Santa Monica** 21
  🅩 Joe's | **Venice** 26

Michael Mina
  XIV | **W Hollywood** 23

David Myers
  Comme Ça | **W Hollywood** 22

Mark Peel
  🅩 Campanile | **La Brea** 26
  🅩**NEW** Tar Pit | **La Brea** 20

Wolfgang Puck
  🅩 Chinois | **Santa Monica** 26
  🅩 CUT | **Beverly Hills** 27
  Red 7 | **W Hollywood** –
  🅩 Spago | **Beverly Hills** 27
  Wolfgang Puck B&G | **Downtown** 22

Wolfgang Puck Café | **multi.** 19
  NEW WP24 | **Downtown** –

Laurent Quenioux
  Bistro LQ | **Fairfax** 24

Gordon Ramsay
  NEW Boxwood | **W Hollywood** 22
  Gordon Ramsay | **W Hollywood** 23

Akasha Richmond
  Akasha | **Culver City** 20

Stefan Richter
  NEW Stefan's/L.A. Farm | **Santa Monica** 23
  NEW Stefan's/Montana | **Santa Monica** 20

Hans Röckenwagner
  Röckenwagner | **Santa Monica** 21
  3 Square | **Venice** 23

Richard Sandoval
  NEW La Sandia | **Santa Monica** –
  NEW Zengo | **Santa Monica** –

John Sedlar
  Rivera | **Downtown** 25

Claude Segal
  NEW Drai's | **Hollywood** –

Jimmy Shaw
  Lotería! | **multi.** 24

Kerry Simon
  NEW L.A. Market | **Downtown** 19
  Simon LA | **W Hollywood** 22

Laurent Tourondel
  BLT Steak | **W Hollywood** 24

Roy Yamaguchi
  🅩 Roy's | **multi.** 24

Sang Yoon
  🅩 Father's Office | **multi.** 22

CHEESE TRAYS

Ago	**W Hollywood**	21
🅩 Angelini	**Beverly Blvd**	28
🅩 A.O.C.	**Third St**	27
Artisan	**Studio City**	24
Barbrix	**Silver Lake**	23
🅩 Bastide	**W Hollywood**	27
Bellavino	**Westlake Vill**	19
🅩 Belvedere	**Beverly Hills**	25
Bistro LQ	**Fairfax**	24
Cafe FIORE	**Ventura**	22
Cafe Pinot	**Downtown**	23
Cafe Stella	**Silver Lake**	21

Café Was | **Hollywood**	17
Chez Mélange | **Redondo Bch**	25
☑ Church/State | **Downtown**	25
☑ Cicada | **Downtown**	23
Comme Ça | **W Hollywood**	22
Copa d'Oro | **Santa Monica**	17
Corkbar | **Downtown**	22
☑ Craft | **Century City**	24
Cube | **La Brea**	25
FIG | **Santa Monica**	22
☑ Fraîche | **Culver City**	23
Joan's on 3rd | **Third St.**	23
La Bottega Marino | **multi.**	21
☑ Leila's | **Oak Pk**	27
Little Door | **Third St**	23
☑ Lou | **Hollywood**	25
☑ mar'sel | **Rancho Palos Verdes**	24
☑ Mélisse | **Santa Monica**	28
Monsieur Marcel | **Fairfax**	20
Morels Bistro | **Fairfax**	20
Morels Steak | **Fairfax**	20
Palate | **Glendale**	24
☑ Patina | **Downtown**	26
Pourtal | **Santa Monica**	22
Primitivo | **Venice**	23
☑ Providence | **Hollywood**	28
Rustic Canyon | **Santa Monica**	23
☑ Saddle Peak | **Calabasas**	27
17th St. Cafe | **Santa Monica**	19
71 Palm | **Ventura**	22
☑ Spago | **Beverly Hills**	27
Taste | **multi.**	21
Tasting Kitchen | **Venice**	22
Terra | **Malibu**	22
Tiara | **Downtown**	23
Tinto | **W Hollywood**	-
☑ Tuscany | **Westlake Vill**	26
208 Rodeo | **Beverly Hills**	23
Ugo/Cafe | **Culver City**	17
Upstairs 2 | **West LA**	23
Vertical Wine | **Pasadena**	21
Via Alloro | **Beverly Hills**	21
Via Veneto | **Santa Monica**	24
☑ Vincenti | **Brentwood**	26
Westside Cellar | **Ventura**	-
Wilshire | **Santa Monica**	23
Wine Bistro | **Studio City**	23
Zazou | **Redondo Bch**	22

CHEF'S TABLE

☑ Bastide | **W Hollywood**	27
Casa | **Downtown**	19
Catalina | **Redondo Bch**	22
NEW Culina | **Beverly Hills**	-
Depot | **Torrance**	24
NEW East | **Hollywood**	25
NEW Firenze | **N Hollywood**	20
Foundry/Melrose | **Melrose**	22
Hampton's | **Westlake Vill**	21
Hungry Cat | **Hollywood**	24
Il Pastaio | **Beverly Hills**	26
LAMILL | **Silver Lake**	21
Michael's/Naples | **Long Bch**	26
Parq/Montage | **Beverly Hills**	25
☑ Patina | **Downtown**	26
☑ Providence | **Hollywood**	28
☑ Saam/The Bazaar | **Beverly Hills**	27
Safire | **Camarillo**	23
Spark | **Simi Valley**	20
Terroni | **Beverly Blvd**	22

CHILD-FRIENDLY

(Alternatives to the usual fast-food places; * children's menu available)

Abbot's | **multi.**	22
Amici | **multi.**	21
Angeli | **Melrose**	25
Asaka* | **Rancho Palos Verdes**	16
Astro Burger | **multi.**	20
Asuka | **Westwood**	19
Babalu | **Santa Monica**	20
Back Home* | **Manhattan Bch**	17
Barbara's | **Downtown**	15
Barney's* | **Santa Monica**	20
Benihana* | **multi.**	19
Big Mama's* | **Pasadena**	21
BJ's* | **multi.**	17
Bluewater* | **Redondo Bch**	20
Bravo* | **Santa Monica**	19
Brighton Coffee | **Beverly Hills**	18
Buca di Beppo* | **multi.**	15
Burger Continental* | **Pasadena**	18
Cafe 50's* | **multi.**	16
Cafe Med | **W Hollywood**	19
Cafe Pinot | **Downtown**	23
Caffé Delfini | **Santa Monica**	23
Caffe Pinguini | **Playa del Rey**	22

Cal. Chicken*	multi.	21
Cal. Pizza Kitchen*	multi.	18
Cal. Wok	multi.	16
C & O*	Marina del Rey	19
☑ Carnival*	Sherman Oaks	24
Casa Bianca	Eagle Rock	23
Casablanca	Venice	20
Chaba	Redondo Bch	22
Cha Cha Cha	Silver Lake	19
Cha Cha Chicken	Santa Monica	20
Chart House*	multi.	19
☑ Cheesecake Factory*	multi.	19
Chi Dynasty	Los Feliz	21
Chili John's*	Burbank	18
Claim Jumper*	multi.	18
Clay Pit	Brentwood	21
☑ Clementine*	Century City	24
Coral Tree*	Brentwood	17
Counter*	Santa Monica	20
Daily Grill*	multi.	19
D'Amore's	multi.	20
Da Pasquale	Beverly Hills	23
Delphi	Westwood	16
Dish*	La Cañada Flintridge	18
Doña Rosa*	Pasadena	17
Duke's*	Malibu	17
El Coyote*	Beverly Blvd	15
El Tepeyac	East LA	25
El Torito*	multi.	15
El Torito Grill*	multi.	19
Enterprise Fish*	Santa Monica	19
Fabiolus	Hollywood	18
Farfalla	Los Feliz	24
Feast from East	West LA	21
Fritto Misto*	multi.	21
Fromin's*	multi.	15
Gaucho*	multi.	18
Gladstone's*	Pacific Palisades	13
Green Field	multi.	19
Gulfstream	Century City	21
Hamburger Hamlet*	multi.	18
Hop Li	multi.	19
Hop Woo	West LA	19
Il Forno Caldo	Beverly Hills	21
Indo	Palms	20
Islands*	multi.	17
Jinky's*	multi.	19
Jody Maroni's*	multi.	19

Johnnie's NY*	multi.	17
Johnnie's Pastrami*	Culver City	20
Johnny Rockets*	multi.	16
John O'Groats*	Rancho Pk	20
Kay 'n Dave's*	multi.	16
La Dijonaise	Culver City	17
☑ Langer's	Downtown	27
Le Petit Cafe	Santa Monica	21
Le Petit Greek	Hancock Pk	21
☑ Les Sisters*	Chatsworth	25
Louise's*	multi.	17
Lucille's*	multi.	22
Mama D's*	Manhattan Bch	19
Mandarin	multi.	23
Maria's*	multi.	17
Marston's*	Pasadena	22
Martha's 22nd St.*	Hermosa Bch	24
Maxwell's*	Venice	18
Miceli's*	Hollywood	16
Mi Piace*	multi.	20
Mi Ranchito*	Culver City	19
Mishima*	Third St	19
Misto Caffé*	Torrance	20
Moishe's	Fairfax	19
Mo's*	Burbank	18
Mulberry St. Pizzeria	multi.	23
☑ NBC Seafood	Monterey Pk	21
Outback*	multi.	18
Outlaws*	Playa del Rey	19
Paco's Tacos*	Westchester	21
Palms Thai	E Hollywood	21
Panda Inn	multi.	21
Paradise Cove*	Malibu	15
Pastina	West LA	21
P.F. Chang's*	multi.	19
Pie 'N Burger	Pasadena	22
Pizzicotto	Brentwood	23
Poquito Más*	multi.	21
Rae's*	Santa Monica	15
Ribs USA	Burbank	19
Robin's*	Pasadena	20
Romano's*	multi.	17
Rosti*	multi.	17
Ruby's*	multi.	17
17th St. Cafe*	Santa Monica	19
Sisley*	multi.	19
Smoke House*	Burbank	20
Stanley's	Sherman Oaks	20

Menus, photos, voting and more – free at ZAGAT.com

Stinking Rose | **Beverly Hills** 19
Swingers* | **Beverly Blvd** 17
Taste Chicago | **Burbank** 19
Thai Dishes | **multi.** 17
Tibet Nepal* | **Pasadena** 17
Tony P's* | **Marina del Rey** 17
22nd St. Landing* | **San Pedro** 17
Ulysses Voyage* | **Fairfax** 20
Uncle Bill's* | **Manhattan Bch** 22
Versailles* | **multi.** 21
Vittorio's | **Pacific Palisades** 18
Wokcano | **Pasadena** 16
Wood Ranch* | **multi.** 21
Zankou | **multi.** 22
Zeke's* | **multi.** 21

COOL LOOS

Blue Velvet | **Downtown** 20
Firefly | **Studio City** 20
Z Katsuya | **Brentwood** 23
LA Food Show | **Manhattan Bch** 17
Ortolan | **Third St.** 25
Z Patina | **Downtown** 26
Z Penthouse | **Santa Monica** 20
Z Roy's | **Downtown** 24
Smitty's | **Pasadena** 22
Z Spago | **Beverly Hills** 27

DANCING

Buffalo Club | **Santa Monica** 19
Cafe FIORE | **Ventura** 22
Cuban Bistro | **Alhambra** 20
El Pollo Inka | **Gardena** 20
NEW Fuego/Maya | **Long Bch** 19
NEW La Vida | **Hollywood** –
Madison | **Long Bch** 22
Monsoon | **Santa Monica** 20
Padri | **Agoura Hills** 22
Rainbow B&G | **W Hollywood** 17
Rush St. | **Culver City** 17
Saddle Ranch | **Universal City** 15
Smoke House | **Burbank** 20
Villa Sorriso | **Pasadena** 20
Warehouse | **Marina del Rey** 17

DESSERT SPECIALISTS

Akasha | **Culver City** 20
Alcove | **Los Feliz** 20
Auntie Em's | **Eagle Rock** 21

Babalu | **Santa Monica** 20
Z NEW Bouchon | **Beverly Hills** 24
Cafe Montana | **Santa Monica** 18
Z Campanile | **La Brea** 26
Z Cheesecake Factory | **multi.** 19
Z Clementine | **Century City** 24
Doughboys | **Third St** 22
Farm/Bev. Hills | **multi.** 18
French Crêpe Co. | **multi.** 21
Huckleberry | **Santa Monica** 22
Jack n' Jill's | **Santa Monica** 18
Jack n' Jill's Too | **Third St** 21
Jin Patisserie | **Venice** 23
Joan's on 3rd | **Third St.** 23
La Creperie | **Long Bch** 23
Maison Richard | **Hollywood** 21
Mäni's | **Fairfax** 17
Melting Pot | **multi.** 18
NEW Mercantile | **Hollywood** 21
Mi Piace | **multi.** 20
Misto Caffé | **Torrance** 20
Nickel Diner | **Downtown** 22
Pop | **Pasadena** 17
Z Porto's | **multi.** 24
17th St. Cafe | **Santa Monica** 19
Simon LA | **W Hollywood** 22
Z Spago | **Beverly Hills** 27
Z Susina | **La Brea** 26
Sweet Lady Jane | **Melrose** 24

DINING ALONE

(Other than hotels and places with counter service)

Z Addi's | **Redondo Bch** 24
Akbar | **Pasadena** 22
All India | **West LA** 21
Antica | **Marina del Rey** 21
Art's | **Studio City** 20
Z Asanebo | **Studio City** 27
Back Home | **Manhattan Bch** 17
Banzai | **Calabasas** 20
BCD Tofu | **Cerritos** 20
Belmont Brewing | **Long Bch** 18
Bistro/Gare | **S Pasadena** 19
BJ's | **multi.** 17
Buddha's Belly | **Beverly Blvd** 19
Ca' del Sole | **N Hollywood** 21
China Grill | **Manhattan Bch** 19
Chin Chin | **W Hollywood** 17

Clafoutis | **W Hollywood** 19

☑ Cora's | **Santa Monica** 23

Dish | **La Cañada Flintridge** 18

El Pollo Inka | **Lawndale** 20

Engine Co. 28 | **Downtown** 21

Factor's | **Pico-Robertson** 18

☑ Father's Office | **Santa Monica** 22

555 East | **Long Bch** 25

☑ Fleming's | **multi.** 24

Fred 62 | **Los Feliz** 17

Fromin's | **Santa Monica** 15

Galletto | **Westlake Vill** 23

Gaucho | **multi.** 18

George's Greek | **Downtown** 22

Grand Lux | **Beverly Hills** 19

Grub | **Hollywood** 22

Il Capriccio | **Los Feliz** 23

Iroha | **Studio City** 25

Jinky's | **Sherman Oaks** 19

Johnny Rockets | **Encino** 16

JR's | **Culver City** 22

☑ Katsu-ya | **Encino** 26

Kincaid's | **Redondo Bch** 20

La Dijonaise | **Culver City** 17

La Scala | **Beverly Hills** 21

Lotería! | **Fairfax** 24

Lucille's | **Long Bch** 22

Maria's | **Encino** 17

Mio Babbo's | **Westwood** 20

Mr. Cecil's | **West LA** 19

Musso & Frank | **Hollywood** 20

O-Nami | **Torrance** 23

Padri | **Agoura Hills** 22

☑ Palm | **multi.** 24

Pei Wei | **multi.** 17

Prizzi's | **Hollywood** 21

Rambutan | **Silver Lake** 19

Ribs USA | **Burbank** 19

Roll 'n Rye | **Culver City** 19

Spark | **Studio City** 20

Stand | **Encino** 17

Sushi Dokoro | **Beverly Hills** -

Takao | **Brentwood** 26

Talésai | **W Hollywood** 22

Tiara | **Downtown** 23

Trails | **Los Feliz** -

Trio | **Rolling Hills Estates** 17

2117 | **West LA** 24

Typhoon | **Santa Monica** 19

Versailles | **Manhattan Bch** 21

Wood Ranch | **Northridge** 21

ENTERTAINMENT

(Call for days and times
of performances)

Alegria | live music | **Long Bch** 21

Amalfi | varies | **La Brea** 19

Antonio's |
classical guitar/mariachis |
Melrose 22

☑ Arroyo | piano | **Pasadena** 25

Auld Dubliner | Irish | **Long Bch** 16

Bandera | jazz | **West LA** 22

☑ Brandywine | guitar |
Woodland Hills 28

Buffalo Club | DJ | **Santa Monica** 19

Buggy Whip | piano | **Westchester** 18

Cafe Del Rey | live music |
Marina del Rey 22

Canter's | varies | **Fairfax** 19

☑ Carlitos Gardel | piano | **Melrose** 24

☑ Carousel | belly dancing/
vocals | **Glendale** 24

Casablanca | guitar/Latin | **Venice** 20

☑ Catch | jazz | **Santa Monica** 22

☑ Crustacean | live music |
Beverly Hills 24

☑ Dar Maghreb | belly dancing |
Hollywood 23

El Cholo | varies | **Pasadena** 18

Electric Lotus | DJ | **Los Feliz** 22

El Pollo Inka | live music | **multi.** 20

Fins | live music | **multi.** 21

Frenchy's | jazz | **Long Bch** 25

Galletto | varies | **Westlake Vill** 23

Geisha Hse. | karaoke | **Hollywood** 18

Genghis Cohen | varies | **Fairfax** 21

Great Greek | Greek |
Sherman Oaks 20

Hal's | jazz | **Venice** 21

House of Blues | live music |
W Hollywood 16

Koutoubia | belly dancing |
West LA 25

Lucille's | blues | **Long Bch** 22

Madison | piano | **Long Bch** 22

Market City | varies | **Burbank** 18

Marrakesh | belly dancing |
Studio City 21

Menus, photos, voting and more – free at ZAGAT.com

Z Mastro's Steak | piano/vocals | **Beverly Hills** — 26

Moonshadows | DJ | **Malibu** — 16

Nic's | varies | **Beverly Hills** — 19

Z One Pico | bass/piano | **Santa Monica** — 20

Padri | DJ/'80s cover band | **Agoura Hills** — 22

Z Papa Cristo's | belly dancing | **Mid-City** — 24

Parker's | jazz | **Long Bch** — 19

Z Parkway Grill | piano | **Pasadena** — 26

Pig 'n Whistle | varies | **Hollywood** — 17

Z Polo | guitar/piano | **Beverly Hills** — 23

Saddle Ranch | varies | **multi.** — 15

Sir Winston's | piano | **Long Bch** — 24

Sky Room | live music | **Long Bch** — 18

Velvet | DJ | **Hollywood** — 18

Z Vibrato | jazz | **Bel-Air** — 21

Villa Sorriso | DJ | **Pasadena** — 20

FAMILY-STYLE

Buca di Beppo | **multi.** — 15

Buddha's Belly | **Beverly Blvd** — 19

C & O | **Marina del Rey** — 19

Z Carnival | **Sherman Oaks** — 24

Z Carousel | **multi.** — 24

Casa Bianca | **Eagle Rock** — 23

Cha Cha Cha | **Silver Lake** — 19

Chan/Hse. of Chan | **Hollywood** — 21

Chi Dynasty | **Los Feliz** — 21

China Grill | **Manhattan Bch** — 19

Chin Chin | **multi.** — 17

Z Chinois | **Santa Monica** — 26

Cholada | **multi.** — 23

Z Crustacean | **Beverly Hills** — 24

Dominick's | **Beverly Blvd.** — 21

Enoteca Drago | **Beverly Hills** — 22

Farm Stand | **El Segundo** — 21

Itacho | **Beverly Blvd** — 26

Izaka-Ya | **multi.** — 22

Lamonica's | **Westwood** — 24

NEW Lazy Ox | **Little Tokyo** — 21

Le Petit Greek | **Hancock Pk** — 19

Maggiano's | **multi.** — 19

Mandarette | **Beverly Blvd.** — 17

Maria's | **multi.** — 16

Miceli's | **multi.**

Mission 261 | **San Gabriel** — -

Natalee | **Beverly Hills** — 19

Ocean Seafood | **Chinatown** — 21

Ocean Star | **Monterey Pk** — 21

Riviera | **Calabasas** — 24

Robin's | **Pasadena** — 20

Romano's | **Cerritos** — 17

Sapori | **Marina del Rey** — 24

Sea Empress | **Gardena** — 18

Shin | **Hollywood** — -

Sisley | **multi.** — 19

Stonefire | **multi.** — 20

V.I.P. Harbor | **West LA** — 19

Woody's BBQ | **Mid-City** — 24

Zeke's | **multi.** — 21

FIREPLACES

Abbey | **W Hollywood** — 16

Admiral Risty | **Rancho Palos Verdes** — 20

Amalfi | **La Brea** — 19

Austen's | **Ventura** — -

Baleen | **Redondo Bch** — 19

Barefoot B&G | **Third St** — 17

Beau Rivage | **Malibu** — 19

Beckham Grill | **Pasadena** — 19

Bel-Air B&G | **Bel-Air** — 20

Z Bistro Gdn. | **Studio City** — 21

Blue Velvet | **Downtown** — 20

Bluewater | **Redondo Bch** — 20

BoHo | **Hollywood** — 17

Bond St. | **Beverly Hills** — 20

Buggy Whip | **Westchester** — 18

Bull Pen | **Redondo Bch** — 15

Ca' del Sole | **N Hollywood** — 21

Cafe Del Rey | **Marina del Rey** — 22

Cafe/Artistes | **Hollywood** — 20

Cafe FIORE | **Ventura** — 22

Cafe Firenze | **Moorpark** — 19

Café Pacific | **Rancho Palos Verdes** — 22

Capo | **Santa Monica** — 25

Z Catch | **Santa Monica** — 22

Chart House | **multi.** — 19

Claim Jumper | **multi.** — 18

Clearman's | **San Gabriel** — 19

Coupa | **Beverly Hills** — 19

Dal Rae | **Pico Rivera** — 25

Dan Tana's | **W Hollywood** — 23

D'Caché | **Toluca Lake** — 23

Derby | **Arcadia**	20
Z Derek's | **Pasadena**	26
Dish | **La Cañada Flintridge**	18
Dominick's | **Beverly Blvd.**	21
NEW East | **Hollywood**	25
El Cholo | **multi.**	18
El Coyote | **Beverly Blvd**	15
El Torito | **Long Bch**	15
Fins | **Calabasas**	21
Geisha Hse. | **Hollywood**	18
Gennaro's | **Glendale**	22
Guido's | **West LA**	20
Hamburger Hamlet | **Pasadena**	18
Z Houston's | **multi.**	22
Z Il Cielo | **Beverly Hills**	22
Il Fornaio | **multi.**	21
Z Inn/Seventh Ray | **Topanga**	21
Ivy | **W Hollywood**	21
James' | **Venice**	19
Javan | **West LA**	20
Jer-ne | **Marina del Rey**	23
Z Josie | **Santa Monica**	26
Koi | **W Hollywood**	24
La Boheme | **W Hollywood**	21
NEW Larchmont Bungalow | **Mid-Wilshire**	19
Larchmont Grill | **Hollywood**	22
La Rive Gauche | **Palos Verdes**	20
Z Lasher's | **Long Bch**	24
NEW La Vida | **Hollywood**	-
Z Lawry's Prime Rib | **Beverly Hills**	26
Literati | **West LA**	17
Little Door | **Third St**	23
Z Lucques | **W Hollywood**	27
Marrakesh | **Studio City**	21
Z mar'sel | **Rancho Palos Verdes**	24
Z Mastro's Steak | **Thousand Oaks**	26
McCormick/Schmick | **Pasadena**	20
Mediterraneo | **Westlake Vill**	24
Z Mélisse | **Santa Monica**	28
Minx | **Glendale**	-
Mission 261 | **San Gabriel**	-
Monty's | **Woodland Hills**	22
Napa Valley | **Westwood**	19
Ocean & Vine | **Santa Monica**	22
Off Vine | **Hollywood**	-
Z One Pico | **Santa Monica**	20

Ortolan | **Third St.**	25
Osteria La Buca | **Hollywood**	23
Padri | **Agoura Hills**	22
Panda Inn | **Ontario**	21
Paradise Cove | **Malibu**	15
Z Parkway Grill | **Pasadena**	26
Z Penthouse | **Santa Monica**	20
Petrelli's | **Culver City**	19
R+D Kitchen | **Santa Monica**	20
Raymond | **Pasadena**	25
Reel Inn | **Malibu**	20
Rive Gauche | **Sherman Oaks**	22
Romano's | **Ventura**	17
Z Saddle Peak | **Calabasas**	27
Safire | **Camarillo**	23
Salt Creek | **El Segundo**	17
71 Palm | **Ventura**	22
Simon LA | **W Hollywood**	22
Smoke House | **Burbank**	20
Stinking Rose | **Beverly Hills**	19
Suzanne's | **Ojai**	25
Taix | **Echo Pk**	17
Tam O'Shanter | **Atwater Vill**	22
Tanino | **Westwood**	21
Taverna Tony | **Malibu**	21
Terra | **Malibu**	22
Tom Bergin's | **Fairfax**	13
Tower Bar | **W Hollywood**	21
Vertical Wine | **Pasadena**	21
Z Vibrato | **Bel-Air**	21
Villa Piacere | **Woodland Hills**	18
Walter's | **Claremont**	21
Westside Cellar | **Ventura**	-
Whale & Ale | **San Pedro**	20
XIV | **W Hollywood**	23
Ye Olde King's | **Santa Monica**	18
Zin Bistro | **Westlake Vill**	20

FOOD TRUCKS

Border Grill Truck | **Location Varies**	20
NEW Flying Pig | **Location Varies**	-
Frysmith | **Location Varies**	-
Grilled Cheese | **Location Varies**	-
Kogi | **Location Varies**	23
Z Let's Be Frank | **Culver City**	21
Lomo Arigato | **Location Varies**	-
NEW Phamish | **Location Varies**	-

Menus, photos, voting and more – free at ZAGAT.com

GREEN/LOCAL/ ORGANIC

Akasha | **Culver City**	20
Ammo | **Hollywood**	23
Animal | **Fairfax**	26
Austen's | **Ventura**	-
A Votre Sante | **Brentwood**	20
Bloom | **Mid-City**	21
Blue Hen | **Eagle Rock**	17
Blvd 16 | **Westwood**	21
Border Grill Truck | **Location Varies**	20
Brooks | **Ventura**	25
Cabbage Patch | **Beverly Hills**	23
Copa d'Oro | **Santa Monica**	17
Coral Tree | **multi.**	17
Cube | **La Brea**	25
Dining Rm./Shangri-La | **Santa Monica**	22
NEW DISH | **Pasadena**	-
Eat Well | **W Hollywood**	17
Elf Café | **Echo Pk**	27
NEW Eva | **Beverly Blvd**	25
Farm Stand | **El Segundo**	22
Fatty's & Co. | **Eagle Rock**	25
NEW Forage | **Silver Lake**	25
Golden State | **Fairfax**	22
NEW House Café | **Beverly Blvd**	21
Huckleberry | **Santa Monica**	22
Hugo's | **multi.**	20
Hungry Cat | **Hollywood**	24
Inn/Seventh Ray | **Topanga**	21
Jar | **Beverly Blvd.**	25
Jinky's | **Sherman Oaks**	19
Joe's | **Venice**	26
Jonathan's | **Ventura**	23
Kitchen | **Silver Lake**	20
Kitchen 24 | **Hollywood**	20
Kokomo | **Beverly Blvd**	19
La Bistecca | **Downtown**	-
La Grande Orange | **Pasadena**	20
La Pergola | **Sherman Oaks**	23
NEW Larchmont Bungalow | **Mid-Wilshire**	19
Larchmont Grill | **Hollywood**	22
Larkin's | **Eagle Rock**	18
La Serenata | **multi.**	22
La Sosta | **Hermosa Bch**	-
NEW Lazy Ox | **Little Tokyo**	24

Le Pain Quotidien | **multi.**	20
Literati | **West LA**	17
Local | **Silver Lake**	22
Lucques | **W Hollywood**	27
Madeleine | **Tarzana**	28
Mäni's | **Fairfax**	17
M Café | **multi.**	22
NEW Mooi | **Echo Pk**	-
Native Foods | **Westwood**	23
Newsroom Café | **W Hollywood**	18
Planet Raw | **Santa Monica**	20
Real Food Daily | **multi.**	22
Shima | **Venice**	-
Square One | **E Hollywood**	23
Standard | **W Hollywood**	19
NEW Stefan's/L.A. Farm | **Santa Monica**	23
Suzanne's | **Ojai**	25
Tender Greens | **multi.**	22
Urth | **multi.**	21
Vegan Glory | **Beverly Blvd**	23

HISTORIC PLACES

(Year opened; * building)

1874 | Arsenal* | **West LA**	16
1877 | Jonathan's* | **Ventura**	23
1900 | Porta Via Italian* | **Pasadena**	24
1900 | Raymond* | **Pasadena**	25
1900 | Saddle Peak* | **Calabasas**	27
1902 | Blu LA Café* | **Downtown**	-
1906 | Pete's* | **Downtown**	21
1908 | Cole's* | **Downtown**	17
1908 | Off Vine* | **Hollywood**	-
1908 | Philippe/Original | **Chinatown**	22
1910 | Austen's* | **Ventura**	-
1910 | 71 Palm* | **Ventura**	22
1910 | Sidecar* | **Ventura**	24
1910 | Via Veneto* | **Santa Monica**	24
1910 | Warszawa* | **Santa Monica**	23
1911 | Larkin's* | **Eagle Rock**	18
1912 | Engine Co. 28* | **Downtown**	21
1912 | Polo* | **Beverly Hills**	23
1916 | Alcove* | **Los Feliz**	20
1916 | Madison* | **Long Bch**	22
1917 | Enterprise Fish* | **Santa Monica**	19
1919 | Musso & Frank* | **Hollywood**	20

Year	Restaurant	Location	Rating
1920	Barney's Beanery	W Hollywood	15
1920	Clafoutis*	W Hollywood	19
1920	Farm/Bev. Hills*	Beverly Hills	18
1920	La Paella*	Beverly Hills	21
1920	Lasher's*	Long Bch	24
1920	Mijares	Pasadena	17
1921	Pacific Dining Car	Downtown	23
1922	Casablanca Med.*	Claremont	23
1922	Derby*	Arcadia	20
1922	Second City*	El Segundo	24
1922	Tam O'Shanter	Atwater Vill	22
1923	El Cholo	Mid-City	18
1923	Farfalla*	Los Feliz	24
1923	Lobster	Santa Monica	23
1924	Canter's	Fairfax	19
1924	Edendale Grill*	Silver Lake	18
1924	Grub*	Hollywood	22
1924	Original Pantry	Downtown	17
1925	Bay Cities	Santa Monica	25
1925	Church/State*	Downtown	25
1925	Palm*	Downtown	24
1925	Taste*	W Hollywood	21
1926	Greenblatt's	Hollywood	19
1926	Sky Room*	Long Bch	18
1927	Benihana*	Santa Monica	19
1927	Far Niente*	Glendale	23
1927	Pig 'n Whistle*	Hollywood	17
1927	Taix	Echo Pk	17
1928	Cafe Stella*	Silver Lake	21
1928	Tamayo*	East LA	21
1929	Campanile*	La Brea	26
1929	Chateau Marmont*	W Hollywood	19
1929	Tanino*	Westwood	21
1929	Tower Bar*	W Hollywood	21
1930	Brighton Coffee	Beverly Hills	18
1931	El Coyote	Beverly Blvd	15
1931	Lucques*	W Hollywood	27
1931	Petrelli's	Culver City	19
1932	Fatty's & Co.*	Eagle Rock	25
1934	Galley*	Santa Monica	17
1935	Café Chez Marie*	Century City	-
1935	Clifton's	Downtown	1
1935	Stand*	Westwood	1
1936	Sir Winston's*	Long Bch	2
1936	Tom Bergin's	Fairfax	1
1937	Damon's	Glendale	1
1937	Traxx*	Downtown	1
1938	Du-par's	multi.	16
1938	Lawry's Prime Rib	Beverly Hills	20
1939	Bistro 45*	Pasadena	26
1939	Formosa	W Hollywood	13
1939	Luna Park*	La Brea	19
1939	Pink's Dogs	La Brea	20
1940	Il Cielo*	Beverly Hills	22
1940	Yamashiro	Hollywood	18
1942	Mr. Cecil's*	West LA	19
1945	Nate 'n Al	Beverly Hills	20
1946	Billingsley's	West LA	15
1946	Chili John's	Burbank	18
1946	Fountain Coffee	Beverly Hills	25
1946	Paradise Cove*	Malibu	15
1946	Smoke House	Burbank	20
1946	Tommy's*	Downtown	23
1946	Uncle Bill's	Manhattan Bch	22
1947	Apple Pan	West LA	23
1947	Langer's	Downtown	27
1948	Bull Pen	Redondo Bch	15
1948	Cassell's	Koreatown	21
1948	Dominick's	Beverly Blvd.	21
1948	Factor's	Pico-Robertson	18
1948	Papa Cristo's	Mid-City	24
1948	Reddi Chick	Santa Monica	21
1949	Miceli's	Hollywood	16
1950	Hamburger Hamlet	W Hollywood	18
1952	Buggy Whip	Westchester	18
1952	Cafe 50's*	West LA	16
1952	Johnnie's Pastrami	Culver City	20
1953	Father's Office	Santa Monica	22
1953	Ranch Hse.*	Ojai	22
1953	Taylor's	Koreatown	21
1954	El Torito	multi.	15
1955	Casa Bianca	Eagle Rock	23
1955	El Tepeyac	East LA	25
1955	Trader Vic	Beverly Hills	17
1956	Antonio's	Melrose	22

1956 | Casa Vega | **Sherman Oaks**	17
1956 | La Scala | **Beverly Hills**	21
1957 | Art's | **Studio City**	20
1957 | Jan's | **W Hollywood**	16
1957 | Walter's | **Claremont**	21
1958 | Dal Rae | **Pico Rivera**	25
1958 | Neptune's Net | **Malibu**	19
1958 | Rae's | **Santa Monica**	15
1959 | Chez Jay | **Santa Monica**	16
1959 | Junior's | **West LA**	16
1959 | Red Lion | **Silver Lake**	17
1960 | Porto's | **Glendale**	24

HOLIDAY MEALS

(Special prix fixe meals offered at major holidays)

Amalfi | **La Brea**	19
Ƶ A.O.C. | **Third St**	27
Austen's | **Ventura**	-
Bariloche | **Ventura**	22
Barney Greengrass | **Beverly Hills**	22
Bel-Air B&G | **Bel-Air**	20
Ƶ Bistro 45 | **Pasadena**	26
Ƶ NEW Bouchon | **Beverly Hills**	24
Cafe FIORE | **Ventura**	22
Ƶ Campanile | **La Brea**	26
Ƶ Chinois | **Santa Monica**	26
Ƶ Craft | **Century City**	24
Ƶ Derek's | **Pasadena**	26
NEW Firenze | **N Hollywood**	20
Great Greek | **Sherman Oaks**	20
Hampton's | **Westlake Vill**	21
Ƶ Jar | **Beverly Blvd.**	25
Ƶ Joe's | **Venice**	26
Ƶ Josie | **Santa Monica**	26
Kate Mantilini | **Beverly Hills**	18
La Cachette | **Santa Monica**	21
Locanda/Lago | **Santa Monica**	22
Madison | **Long Bch**	22
Ƶ Mastro's Steak | **Beverly Hills**	26
Mediterraneo | **Westlake Vill**	24
Ƶ Mélisse | **Santa Monica**	28
Michael's/Naples | **Long Bch**	26
Moonshadows | **Malibu**	16
Napa Valley | **Westwood**	19
Paul Martin's | **El Segundo**	22
Ƶ Saddle Peak | **Calabasas**	27
71 Palm | **Ventura**	22
Ƶ Spago | **Beverly Hills**	27

Suzanne's | **Ojai**	25
Ƶ Tavern | **Brentwood**	23
Ƶ Vincenti | **Brentwood**	26
Westside Cellar | **Ventura**	-
Whist | **Santa Monica**	20

HOTEL DINING

Alexandria Hotel	
NEW Gorbals | **Downtown**	21
Andaz Hotel	
RH | **W Hollywood**	25
Angeleno, Hotel	
West | **Brentwood**	20
Avalon Hotel	
NEW Oliverio | **Beverly Hills**	-
Beverly Hills Hotel	
Fountain Coffee | **Beverly Hills**	25
Ƶ Polo | **Beverly Hills**	23
Beverly Hilton	
NEW bar210 | **Beverly Hills**	-
Circa 55 | **Beverly Hills**	19
Trader Vic | **Beverly Hills**	17
Beverly Laurel Motor Hotel	
Swingers | **Beverly Blvd**	17
Beverly Terrace Hotel	
Amici | **Beverly Hills**	21
Beverly Wilshire	
Blvd | **Beverly Hills**	23
Ƶ CUT | **Beverly Hills**	27
Burbank Marriott	
Daily Grill | **Burbank**	19
Casa Del Mar, Hotel	
Ƶ Catch | **Santa Monica**	22
Chateau Marmont	
Ƶ Chateau Marmont | **W Hollywood**	19
Erwin, Hotel	
Hash & High | **Venice**	-
Fairmont Miramar Hotel	
FIG | **Santa Monica**	22
Farmer's Daughter Hotel	
Tart | **Fairfax**	18
Four Seasons Beverly Hills	
NEW Culina | **Beverly Hills**	-
Four Seasons Westlake Vill.	
Hampton's | **Westlake Vill**	21
Hilton Checkers	
Checkers | **Downtown**	21

Hollywood Heights Hotel
Hideout | **Hollywood** ⁻|

Huntley Santa Monica Bch.
Z Penthouse | **Santa Monica** 20|

Hyatt Regency Century Plaza
Breeze | **Century City** 18|

J.W. Marriott at LA Live
NEW L.A. Market | **Downtown** 19|

Le Merigot Hotel
Cézanne | **Santa Monica** 22|

Loews Santa Monica Beach
Ocean & Vine | **Santa Monica** 22|

London West Hollywood
Gordon Ramsay |
W Hollywood 23|

Luxe Hotel Rodeo Dr.
Cafe Rodeo | **Beverly Hills** 15|

Malibu Country Inn
NEW Collection | **Malibu** ⁻|

Maya, Hotel
NEW Fuego/Maya |
Long Bch 19|

Millennium Biltmore Hotel
La Bistecca | **Downtown** ⁻|

Mondrian Hotel
Z Asia de Cuba | **W Hollywood** 24|

Omni Los Angeles Hotel
Noé | **Downtown** 24|

Orlando Hotel
Minestraio | **W Hollywood** 23|

Palihouse
Hall | **W Hollywood** 21|

Palomar, Hotel
Blvd 16 | **Westwood** 21|

Peninsula Hotel of Beverly Hills
Z Belvedere | **Beverly Hills** 25|

Pierpont Inn
Austen's | **Ventura** ⁻|

Portofino Hotel & Yacht Club
Baleen | **Redondo Bch** 19|

Renaissance Long Beach Hotel
NEW Sip | **Long Bch** ⁻|

Ritz-Carlton
NEW WP24 | **Downtown** ⁻|

Ritz-Carlton, Marina Del Rey
Jer-ne | **Marina del Rey** 23|

Roosevelt Hotel
25 Degrees | **Hollywood** 22|

Shangri-La Hotel
Dining Rm./Shangri-La | 22|
Santa Monica

Shutters on the Beach
Coast | **Santa Monica** 21|
Z One Pico | **Santa Monica** 20|

SLS at Beverly Hills
Z Bazaar/José Andrés | 26|
Beverly Hills
Z Saam/The Bazaar | 27|
Beverly Hills

Sofitel LA
Simon LA | **W Hollywood** 22|

Standard Hotel Downtown
Standard | **Downtown** 17|

Standard Hotel Hollywood
Standard | **W Hollywood** 19|

Sunset Tower Hotel
Tower Bar | **W Hollywood** 21|

Terranea Resort
Z mar'sel | 24|
Rancho Palos Verdes

Thompson Beverly Hills Hotel
Bond St. | **Beverly Hills** 20|

Viceroy Santa Monica
Whist | **Santa Monica** 20|

Villa Portofino, Hotel
Rist. Villa Portofino | **Catalina Is.** ⁻|

W Hollywood Hotel
NEW Delphine | **Hollywood** 20|
NEW Drai's | **Hollywood** ⁻|
NEW Living Room/Station | ⁻|
Hollywood

Wilshire Grand
Seoul Jung | **Downtown** 24|

W Los Angeles Westwood
Nine Thirty | **Westwood** 22|

LATE DINING

(Weekday closing hour)

Abbey | 2 AM | **W Hollywood** 16|
Z Apple Pan | 12 AM | **West LA** 23|
Arsenal | 2 AM | **West LA** 16|
Astro Burger | varies | **multi.** 20|
Bar*Food | 12 AM | **West LA** 15|
NEW Bar Bouchon | 12 AM | 23|
Beverly Hills
Barney's Beanery | 1 AM | 15|
W Hollywood
BCD Tofu | varies | **multi.** 20|

Berri's | varies | **Third St** — 15
SJ's | varies | **multi.** — 17
NEW Borracho | 1 AM | — -
W Hollywood
Bossa Nova | varies | **multi.** — 20
Bowery | 2 AM | **Hollywood** — 20
Brentwood | 12 AM | **Brentwood** — 22
Cafe/Artistes | 12 AM | — 20
Hollywood
Cafe 50's | varies | **West LA** — 16
Cafe Sushi | 12 AM | **Beverly Blvd** — 21
Café Was | 2 AM | **Hollywood** — 17
Caffe Primo | varies | **W Hollywood** — 18
Caffe Roma | 2 AM | **Beverly Hills** — 18
Canter's | 24 hrs. | **Fairfax** — 19
Carney's | varies | **W Hollywood** — 20
Casa Bianca | 12 AM | **Eagle Rock** — 23
Casa Vega | 1 AM | **Sherman Oaks** — 17
Cecconi's | varies | **W Hollywood** — 20
Z Chateau Marmont | 24 hrs. | — 19
W Hollywood
Citizen Smith | 4 AM | **Hollywood** — 17
Dan Tana's | 1 AM | **W Hollywood** — 23
NEW Dillon's | 1 AM | **Hollywood** — -
Dominick's | 12:45 AM | — 21
Beverly Blvd.
Doña Rosa | varies | **Pasadena** — 17
Doughboys | 12 AM | **Third St** — 22
Dukes West Hollywood | 2 AM | — 18
W Hollywood
Du-par's | 24 hrs. | **multi.** — 16
NEW 8½ Taverna | 12 AM | — -
Studio City
8 oz. | 12 AM | **Melrose** — 22
El Carmen | 1:30 AM | **Third St** — 15
Electric Lotus | 12 AM | **Los Feliz** — 22
Factor's | 12 AM | **Pico-Robertson** — 18
Firefly | 12 AM | **Studio City** — 20
Fred 62 | 24 hrs. | **Los Feliz** — 17
Gaby's | varies | **Marina del Rey** — 20
Galletto | 12:30 AM | — 23
Westlake Vill
Geisha Hse. | 12 AM | **Hollywood** — 18
Z Gjelina | varies | **Venice** — 26
NEW Glendon Bar | 2 AM | — -
West LA
NEW Goal | 12 AM | **Fairfax** — -
NEW Gorbals | 12 AM | — 21
Downtown

Greenblatt's | 1:30 AM | — 19
Hollywood
Hamburger Mary's | 12 AM | — 14
W Hollywood
Honda-Ya | 1 AM | **Little Tokyo** — 22
Hop Woo | varies | **multi.** — 19
Hudson Hse. | varies | — 23
Redondo Bch
Z In-N-Out | varies | **multi.** — 24
Iroha | 12 AM | **Studio City** — 25
Jan's | 2 AM | **W Hollywood** — 16
Joe's Pizza | varies | **multi.** — 22
Johnnie's Pastrami | varies | — 20
Culver City
Jones | 1:30 AM | **W Hollywood** — 18
Z Katsuya | varies | **Hollywood** — 23
Ketchup | 12:30 AM | — 15
W Hollywood
Kitchen | 12 AM | **Silver Lake** — 20
Kitchen 24 | 24 hrs. | **Hollywood** — 20
Lamonica's | varies | **Westwood** — 22
Lares | 1 AM | **Santa Monica** — 20
NEW Lazy Ox | 12 AM | — 24
Little Tokyo
NEW Living Room/Station | — -
12 AM | **Hollywood**
Lotería! | varies | **Hollywood** — 24
Z Lou | 12 AM | **Hollywood** — 25
Madison | 12 AM | **Long Bch** — 22
Mel's Drive-In | varies | **multi.** — 16
Mexicali | 1 AM | **Studio City** — 16
Millions/Milkshakes | 2 AM | — 21
W Hollywood
Mini Bites | 12 AM | **Hollywood** — -
Mirabelle | 12:30 AM | — 20
W Hollywood
Monte Alban | 12 AM | **West LA** — 20
NEW NY & C Pizzeria | varies | — 17
Santa Monica
NEW Olive | 12 AM | **Hollywood** — -
101 Coffee | 3 AM | **Hollywood** — 18
NEW 101 Noodle | 1 AM | — 22
Alhambra
Original Pantry | 24 hrs. | — 17
Downtown
Pacific Dining Car | 24 hrs. | **multi.** — 23
Palms Thai | 12 AM | **E Hollywood** — 21
Pete's | 2 AM | **Downtown** — 21
NEW Philippe | 12 AM | — 17
W Hollywood

Pho Café | 12 AM | **Silver Lake**	19
Pink's Dogs | 2 AM | **La Brea**	20
Z Pizzeria Mozza | 12 AM | **Hollywood**	27
Poquito Más | varies | **Studio City**	21
Pourtal | 12 AM | **Santa Monica**	22
Rainbow B&G | 1:45 AM | **W Hollywood**	17
Red Corner | 1:30 AM | **E Hollywood**	22
Red Lion | 12 AM | **Silver Lake**	17
NEW Rockwell | 12 AM | **Los Feliz**	-
Roscoe's | varies | **multi.**	21
Ruen Pair | 4 AM | **E Hollywood**	23
Saddle Ranch | varies | **multi.**	15
Saluté | varies | **Santa Monica**	-
Sam Woo | 12 AM | **multi.**	22
Shin | 1 AM | **Hollywood**	-
Simpang Asia | 12 AM | **Palms**	17
Standard | 24 hrs. | **W Hollywood**	19
Standard | 24 hrs. | **Downtown**	17
Swingers | varies | **multi.**	17
Z NEW Tar Pit | 12 AM | **La Brea**	20
Z Tommy's | 24 hrs. | **Downtown**	23
NEW Townhouse | 1:30 AM | **Sherman Oaks**	12
25 Degrees | 1:30 AM | **Hollywood**	22
Two Boots | varies | **Echo Pk**	20
NEW Upper West | 12 AM | **Santa Monica**	-
Velvet | 2 AM | **Hollywood**	18
Village Idiot | 12 AM | **Melrose**	19
Waffle | 2:30 AM | **Hollywood**	17
Wokcano | varies | **multi.**	16
World Cafe | varies | **Santa Monica**	18
Wurstküche | 12 AM | **Downtown**	22
Zankou | 11:45 PM | **E Hollywood**	22

MICROBREWERIES

Belmont Brewing | **Long Bch**	18
BJ's | **multi.**	17
Gordon Biersch | **Burbank**	16

NEWCOMERS

Bar Bouchon | **Beverly Hills**	23
bar210 | **Beverly Hills**	-
Bellini Osteria | **Westlake Vill**	-
Blue Dog | **Sherman Oaks**	21
Boiling Shrimp | **Hollywood**	-
Bonnie B's | **Pasadena**	-
Borracho | **W Hollywood**	-
Z Bouchon | **Beverly Hills**	24
Boxwood | **W Hollywood**	22
BP Oysterette | **Santa Monica**	22
Burger Kitchen | **Mid-City**	-
CaCao | **Eagle Rock**	25
Café Habana | **Malibu**	-
Café 140 S. | **Pasadena**	19
Capital Grille | **W Hollywood**	-
Capriotti's | **Beverly Hills**	23
Centanni | **Venice**	19
Charcoal Grill | **Downtown**	-
Chego! | **Palms**	-
Cheval Blanc | **Pasadena**	22
Collection | **Malibu**	-
Colony | **Hollywood**	-
Cucina Rustica | **Downtown**	-
Culina | **Beverly Hills**	-
Cuvee | **W Hollywood**	-
Daniels | **LAX**	-
Da Vinci | **Beverly Hills**	-
Delphine | **Hollywood**	20
Dillon's | **Hollywood**	-
DISH | **Pasadena**	-
District | **Hollywood**	-
Drai's | **Hollywood**	-
East | **Hollywood**	25
Eatalian | **Gardena**	-
8½ Taverna | **Studio City**	-
El Cholo Downtown | **Downtown**	-
Elements Kitchen | **Pasadena**	23
Eva | **Beverly Blvd**	25
Firenze | **N Hollywood**	20
First & Hope | **Downtown**	-
Flying Pig | **Location Varies**	-
Forage | **Silver Lake**	25
Fuego/Maya | **Long Bch**	19
Glendon Bar | **West LA**	-
Goal | **Fairfax**	-
Gold Class | **Pasadena**	18
Gorbals | **Downtown**	21
House Café | **Beverly Blvd**	21
Hudson | **W Hollywood**	-
Itzik Hagadol | **Encino**	21
Ixtapa | **Pasadena**	-
Izakaya Fu-Ga | **Little Tokyo**	-
K-Town | **Downtown**	-
La Campagna | **Hermosa Bch**	-

Menus, photos, voting and more – free at ZAGAT.com

..A. Market | **Downtown**	19
archmont Bungalow | **Mid-Wilshire**	19
.a Sandia | **Santa Monica**	-
.a Vida | **Hollywood**	-
.awrence/India | **Culver City**	-
.azy Ox | **Little Tokyo**	24
.ibra | **Culver City**	-
.iving Room/Station | **Hollywood**	-
.ocals Sports B&G | **Mid-City**	-
.ocanda Positano | **Marina del Rey**	-
.os Arroyos | **Camarillo**	23
.unch | **Culver City**	-
Mac & Cheeza | **Downtown**	-
Maison Maurice | **Beverly Hills**	-
Manja | **W Hollywood**	-
Market Café | **Downtown**	-
Mercantile | **Hollywood**	21
Momed | **Beverly Hills**	-
Mooi | **Echo Pk**	-
Mr. Beef | **Venice**	-
9021Pho | **Beverly Hills**	19
Noir | **Pasadena**	25
NY & C Pizzeria | **Santa Monica**	17
Olive | **Hollywood**	-
Oliverio | **Beverly Hills**	-
101 Noodle | **Arcadia**	22
Osteria Mamma | **Hollywood**	-
Ozumo | **Santa Monica**	-
Paddy Rice | **Melrose**	-
Palace Seafood | **West LA**	-
Pan Am Room | **Santa Monica**	-
Phamish | **Location Varies**	-
Philippe | **W Hollywood**	17
Pizza Antica | **Santa Monica**	-
Plancha | **Mid-City**	-
Quadrupel | **Pasadena**	-
Red O | **Melrose**	-
Rockwell | **Los Feliz**	-
Rosa Mexicano | **Downtown**	22
Sip | **Long Bch**	-
Slaw Dogs | **Pasadena**	18
Smokin' Joint | **W Hollywood**	-
Soi 7 | **Downtown**	21
Sonoma | **Santa Monica**	-
South Beverly Grill | **Beverly Hills**	-
Starry Kitchen | **Downtown**	-
Stefan's/L.A. Farm | **Santa Monica**	23

Stefan's/Montana | **Santa Monica**	20
⚡ Tar Pit | **La Brea**	20
Tiato | **Santa Monica**	-
Tiger Sushi | **Beverly Hills**	-
Townhouse | **Sherman Oaks**	12
Trader Vic's | **Downtown**	17
Upper West | **Santa Monica**	-
Villains | **Downtown**	-
Vintage Enoteca | **Hollywood**	-
Waterloo & City | **Culver City**	-
WP24 | **Downtown**	-
Xino | **Santa Monica**	-
Xoia | **Echo Pk**	-
Zengo | **Santa Monica**	-

OUTDOOR DINING
(G=garden; P=patio; S=sidewalk; T=terrace)

Alcove | P | **Los Feliz**	20
Antonio's | S | **Melrose**	22
⚡ Asia de Cuba | P | **W Hollywood**	24
Babalu | S | **Santa Monica**	20
Barefoot B&G | P | **Third St**	17
Barney Greengrass | T | **Beverly Hills**	22
Barney's | P | **multi.**	20
⚡ Bastide | G, P | **W Hollywood**	27
Beacon | P | **Culver City**	22
Beau Rivage | P | **Malibu**	19
Beechwood | P | **Marina del Rey**	19
Bel-Air B&G | P | **Bel-Air**	20
⚡ Belvedere | G, P | **Beverly Hills**	25
bld | P | **Beverly Blvd**	22
BottleRock | P | **Culver City**	16
Bravo | P | **Santa Monica**	19
Breadbar | P | **multi.**	18
Brooks | P | **Ventura**	25
Burger Continental | P | **Pasadena**	18
Ca' del Sole | P | **N Hollywood**	21
Cafe/Artistes | G | **Hollywood**	20
Cafe Med | P | **W Hollywood**	19
Cafe Pinot | P | **Downtown**	23
Café Santorini | P | **Pasadena**	22
C & O | P | **Marina del Rey**	19
Cha Cha Chicken | P | **Santa Monica**	20
⚡ Chateau Marmont | G | **W Hollywood**	19
China Grill | P | **Manhattan Bch**	19
⚡ Clementine | P, S | **Century City**	24

☑ Cliff's Edge | G, P | **Silver Lake**	19
Coral Tree | P | **multi.**	17
☑ Cora's | P | **Santa Monica**	23
Dominick's | G, P | **Beverly Blvd.**	21
Edendale Grill | G, P | **Silver Lake**	18
Farm/Bev. Hills | P, S | **multi.**	18
Fat Fish | P | **W Hollywood**	19
Fins | P | **multi.**	21
Firefly | P | **Studio City**	20
Firefly Bistro | P | **S Pasadena**	20
Ford's | P, S | **Culver City**	20
☑ Fraîche | P | **Culver City**	23
Foundry/Melrose | G | **Melrose**	22
☑ Geoffrey's | P | **Malibu**	20
Gladstone's | P | **Pacific Palisades**	13
Gumbo Pot | P | **Fairfax**	20
Hungry Cat | P | **Hollywood**	24
i Cugini | P | **Santa Monica**	21
☑ Il Cielo | G, P | **Beverly Hills**	22
Il Moro | P | **West LA**	22
☑ Inn/Seventh Ray | G | **Topanga**	21
Ivy | G, P | **W Hollywood**	21
Ivy/Shore | P, T | **Santa Monica**	22
James' | P | **Venice**	19
Jin Patisserie | G | **Venice**	23
☑ Joe's | P | **Venice**	26
Katana | P | **W Hollywood**	23
Koi | G, P | **W Hollywood**	24
Library | P | **Santa Monica**	19
Lilly's | P | **Venice**	19
Little Door | G, P | **Third St**	23
Locanda/Lago | P | **Santa Monica**	22
Lotería! | P | **Fairfax**	24
☑ Lucques | P | **W Hollywood**	27
Marix | P | **W Hollywood**	17
Martha's 22nd St. | S | **Hermosa Bch**	24
Mediterraneo | P | **Hermosa Bch**	20
Mediterraneo | P | **Westlake Vill**	24
☑ Michael's | G, P | **Santa Monica**	25
Minx | P, T | **Glendale**	-
Mi Piace | P | **multi.**	20
Moonshadows | T | **Malibu**	16
Morels Bistro | P | **Fairfax**	20
Neptune's Net | P | **Malibu**	19
☑ Nobu Malibu | P | **Malibu**	26
Noé | T | **Downtown**	24
Off Vine | G | **Hollywood**	-

Padri | P | **Agoura Hills**	22
Pane e Vino | G, P | **Beverly Blvd**	21
Pink's Dogs | P | **La Brea**	20
☑ Polo | P | **Beverly Hills**	23
Pomodoro | P | **multi.**	16
☑ Porto's | S | **multi.**	24
Ranch Hse. | G, P | **Ojai**	22
Raymond | G, P | **Pasadena**	25
Reel Inn | P | **Malibu**	20
Rose Cafe | P | **Venice**	21
☑ Saddle Peak | P, T | **Calabasas**	27
Safire | P | **Camarillo**	23
Salt Creek | P | **multi.**	17
Shack | P | **multi.**	17
Simon LA | P | **W Hollywood**	22
Sor Tino | P | **Brentwood**	22
☑ Spago | P | **Beverly Hills**	27
Stand | G, P | **multi.**	17
Standard | P, T | **W Hollywood**	19
Standard | P | **Downtown**	17
Taverna Tony | P | **Malibu**	21
Tony P's | P | **Marina del Rey**	17
Tra Di Noi | P | **Malibu**	22
Traxx | P | **Downtown**	19
Urth | P, S | **multi.**	21
Villa Piacere | P | **Woodland Hills**	18
Whist | T | **Santa Monica**	20
Wood Ranch | P | **multi.**	21
☑ Yamashiro | G | **Hollywood**	18
Zin Bistro | P | **Westlake Vill**	20

PARTIES/ PRIVATE ROOMS

(Restaurants charge less at off times; call for capacity)

Antonio's | **Melrose**	22
☑ A.O.C. | **Third St**	27
☑ Arroyo | **Pasadena**	25
Banzai | **Calabasas**	20
Barefoot B&G | **Third St**	17
Beau Rivage | **Malibu**	19
Beckham Grill | **Pasadena**	19
☑ Belvedere | **Beverly Hills**	25
☑ Bistro Gdn. | **Studio City**	21
Bravo | **Santa Monica**	19
Buca di Beppo | **Universal City**	15
Buffalo Club | **Santa Monica**	19
Buggy Whip | **Westchester**	18
Buona Sera | **Redondo Bch**	18

Ca'Brea | **La Brea** 22

Ca' del Sole | **N Hollywood** 21

☑ Café Bizou/Bizou Grill | **multi.** 23

Cafe Del Rey | **Marina del Rey** 22

Cafe Pinot | **Downtown** 23

Café Santorini | **Pasadena** 22

☑ Campanile | **La Brea** 26

Canal Club | **Venice** 18

Castaway | **Burbank** 17

Cézanne | **Santa Monica** 22

Chart House | **Redondo Bch** 19

Checkers | **Downtown** 21

Chez Jay | **Santa Monica** 16

Christine | **Torrance** 25

☑ Cicada | **Downtown** 23

Dal Rae | **Pico Rivera** 25

☑ Dar Maghreb | **Hollywood** 23

Depot | **Torrance** 24

Derby | **Arcadia** 20

☑ Derek's | **Pasadena** 26

Devon | **Monrovia** 24

Drago | **Santa Monica** 23

Duke's | **Malibu** 17

El Cholo | **multi.** 18

El Torito | **multi.** 15

Enoteca Drago | **Beverly Hills** 22

☑ Fleming's | **El Segundo** 24

Geisha Hse. | **Hollywood** 18

Giorgio Baldi | **Santa Monica** 26

Gladstone's | **Pacific Palisades** 13

Gordon Biersch | **Burbank** 16

Hal's | **Venice** 21

☑ Il Cielo | **Beverly Hills** 22

Il Fornaio | **multi.** 21

Il Moro | **West LA** 22

Il Sole | **W Hollywood** 23

☑ Inn/Seventh Ray | **Topanga** 21

James' | **Venice** 19

Jonathan's | **Ventura** 23

Jones | **W Hollywood** 18

Katana | **W Hollywood** 23

Kate Mantilini | **Beverly Hills** 18

Kendall's | **Downtown** 19

King's Fish | **Long Bch** 20

La Cachette | **Santa Monica** 21

☑ Lawry's Prime Rib | **Beverly Hills** 26

Little Door | **Third St** 23

L'Opera | **Long Bch** 23

Madison | **Long Bch** 22

Maggiano's | **multi.** 19

Marino | **Hollywood** 24

☑ Mastro's Steak | **Beverly Hills** 26

☑ Matsuhisa | **Beverly Hills** 28

McCormick/Schmick | **multi.** 20

McKenna's | **Long Bch** 19

☑ Michael's | **Santa Monica** 25

Monsoon | **Santa Monica** 20

Morels Steak | **Fairfax** 20

Morton's | **multi.** 24

Napa Valley | **Westwood** 19

Nick & Stef's | **Downtown** 23

Off Vine | **Hollywood** –

☑ One Pico | **Santa Monica** 20

Ortolan | **Third St.** 25

Pacific Dining Car | **multi.** 23

☑ Palm | **multi.** 24

☑ Parkway Grill | **Pasadena** 26

☑ Patina | **Downtown** 26

Pinot Bistro | **Studio City** 24

☑ Polo | **Beverly Hills** 23

R23 | **Downtown** 24

☑ Ruth's Chris | **Beverly Hills** 25

Simon LA | **W Hollywood** 22

Smitty's | **Pasadena** 22

☑ Spago | **Beverly Hills** 27

Tanino | **Westwood** 21

Tantra | **Silver Lake** –

☑ Urasawa | **Beverly Hills** 27

☑ Valentino | **Santa Monica** 26

☑ Vibrato | **Bel-Air** 21

Villa Sorriso | **Pasadena** 20

Woo Lae Oak | **Beverly Hills** 22

☑ Yamashiro | **Hollywood** 18

Zucca | **Downtown** 22

PEOPLE-WATCHING

Abbey | **W Hollywood** 16

Akasha | **Culver City** 20

Animal | **Fairfax** 26

☑ Anisette | **Santa Monica** 21

☑ A.O.C. | **Third St** 27

☑ Asia de Cuba | **W Hollywood** 24

NEW Bar Bouchon | **Beverly Hills** 23

Barney Greengrass | **Beverly Hills** 22

☑ Bazaar/José Andrés | **Beverly Hills** 26

Beso | **Hollywood**	21
bld | **Beverly Blvd**	22
BoHo | **Hollywood**	17
Z NEW Bouchon | **Beverly Hills**	24
Bowery | **Hollywood**	20
Brentwood | **Brentwood**	22
Z Brophy Bros. | **Ventura**	21
Café Was | **Hollywood**	17
Cecconi's | **W Hollywood**	20
Z Chateau Marmont | **W Hollywood**	19
Chaya Brasserie | **W Hollywood**	24
Chaya Venice | **Venice**	23
Z Church/State | **Downtown**	25
Citizen Smith | **Hollywood**	17
Cole's | **Downtown**	17
NEW Colony | **Hollywood**	–
Comme Ça | **W Hollywood**	22
Copa d'Oro | **Santa Monica**	17
Z Craft | **Century City**	24
Z CUT | **Beverly Hills**	27
Delancey | **Hollywood**	20
Z Drago Centro | **Downtown**	26
NEW Drai's | **Hollywood**	–
Z Edison | **Downtown**	15
Z Father's Office | **Culver City**	22
Figtree's | **Venice**	–
Ford's | **Culver City**	20
Geisha Hse. | **Hollywood**	18
NEW Gorbals | **Downtown**	21
Gordon Ramsay | **W Hollywood**	23
Z Grill on Alley | **Beverly Hills**	25
Z Hatfield's | **Melrose**	27
NEW House Café | **Beverly Blvd**	21
NEW Hudson | **W Hollywood**	–
Hudson Hse. | **Redondo Bch**	23
Hungry Cat | **Hollywood**	24
Il Sole | **W Hollywood**	23
Ivy | **W Hollywood**	21
Jones | **W Hollywood**	18
Katana | **W Hollywood**	23
Z Katsuya | **multi.**	23
Kogi | **Location Varies**	23
Koi | **W Hollywood**	24
Larkin's | **Eagle Rock**	18
Laurel | **Studio City**	23
NEW La Vida | **Hollywood**	–
Little Door | **Third St**	23

NEW Living Room/Station | **Hollywood**	–
Locanda/Lago | **Santa Monica**	22
Z Lou | **Hollywood**	25
Magnolia | **Hollywood**	18
Magnolia Lounge | **Pasadena**	15
Z Mastro's Steak | **Beverly Hills**	26
Mr. Chow | **Beverly Hills**	23
Mucho Ultima | **Manhattan Bch**	20
Nate 'n Al | **multi.**	20
Z Nobu Malibu | **Malibu**	26
NEW Olive | **Hollywood**	–
Z Osteria Mozza | **Hollywood**	27
Z Palm | **W Hollywood**	24
Parq/Montage | **Beverly Hills**	25
Z Penthouse | **Santa Monica**	20
Z Petros | **Manhattan Bch**	23
NEW Philippe | **W Hollywood**	17
Pink Taco | **Century City**	16
Z Pizzeria Mozza | **Hollywood**	27
NEW Red O | **Melrose**	–
Red 7 | **W Hollywood**	–
Reservoir | **Silver Lake**	23
Rivera | **Downtown**	25
Z RockSugar | **Century City**	21
Royal/T | **Culver City**	17
Rustic Canyon | **Santa Monica**	23
Saluté | **Santa Monica**	–
Santa Monica Seafood | **Santa Monica**	22
Sashi | **Manhattan Bch**	21
Z Spago | **Beverly Hills**	27
Standard | **W Hollywood**	19
STK | **W Hollywood**	22
Street | **Hollywood**	20
Sushi Roku | **multi.**	23
Z NEW Tar Pit | **La Brea**	20
Z Tavern | **Brentwood**	23
Tin Roof | **Manhattan Bch**	21
Tom Bergin's | **Fairfax**	13
Tower Bar | **W Hollywood**	21
NEW Villains | **Downtown**	–
XIV | **W Hollywood**	23

POWER SCENES

Ago | **W Hollywood**	21
Akasha | **Culver City**	20
Z Angelini | **Beverly Blvd**	28
Z Anisette | **Santa Monica**	21

Menus, photos, voting and more – free at ZAGAT.com

A.O.C. | **Third St**	27
NEW Bar Bouchon | **Beverly Hills**	23
...rney Greengrass | **Beverly Hills**	22
Bazaar/José Andrés | **Beverly Hills**	26
Belvedere | **Beverly Hills**	25
...T Steak | **W Hollywood**	24
NEW Bouchon | **Beverly Hills**	24
NEW Boxwood | **W Hollywood**	22
...rooks | **Ventura**	25
...ecconi's | **W Hollywood**	20
...haya Downtown | **Downtown**	24
...omme Ça | **W Hollywood**	22
Craft | **Century City**	24
NEW Culina | **Beverly Hills**	-
CUT | **Beverly Hills**	27
...an Tana's | **W Hollywood**	23
Drago Centro | **Downtown**	26
...ordon Ramsay | **W Hollywood**	23
...rill on Hollywood/Alley | **Hollywood**	22
Hamasaku | **West LA**	27
Katsuya | **multi.**	23
Mastro's Steak | **Beverly Hills**	26
Matsuhisa | **Beverly Hills**	28
Morton's | **multi.**	24
Nick & Stef's | **Downtown**	23
Nobu LA | **W Hollywood**	26
Osteria Mozza | **Hollywood**	27
Palm | **W Hollywood**	24
Patina | **Downtown**	26
NEW Philippe | **W Hollywood**	17
Pizzeria Mozza | **Hollywood**	27
Polo | **Beverly Hills**	23
Providence | **Hollywood**	28
RH | **W Hollywood**	25
Rivera | **Downtown**	25
Saam/The Bazaar | **Beverly Hills**	27
Spago | **Beverly Hills**	27
STK | **W Hollywood**	22
Tavern | **Brentwood**	23
Toscana | **Brentwood**	24
Valentino | **Santa Monica**	26
Vincenti | **Brentwood**	26
Water Grill | **Downtown**	27
Wilshire | **Santa Monica**	23
Wolfgang's Steak | **Beverly Hills**	23

QUIET CONVERSATION

NEW Bar Bouchon | **Beverly Hills**	23
NEW bar210 | **Beverly Hills**	-
Bastide | **W Hollywood**	27
Belvedere | **Beverly Hills**	25
Bistro LQ | **Fairfax**	24
Blossom | **Downtown**	23
Blvd | **Beverly Hills**	23
Bottle Inn | **Hermosa Bch**	-
NEW Bouchon | **Beverly Hills**	24
NEW Boxwood | **W Hollywood**	22
Breeze | **Century City**	18
Brooks | **Ventura**	25
Cafe FIORE | **Ventura**	22
Café 14 | **Agoura Hills**	27
Caffe Primo | **W Hollywood**	18
Cézanne | **Santa Monica**	22
Checkers | **Downtown**	21
NEW Cheval Blanc | **Pasadena**	22
Circa 55 | **Beverly Hills**	19
Coast | **Santa Monica**	21
NEW Collection | **Malibu**	-
Coupa | **Beverly Hills**	19
Cube | **La Brea**	25
NEW Culina | **Beverly Hills**	-
Derek's | **Pasadena**	26
Dining Rm./Shangri-La | **Santa Monica**	22
Drago | **Santa Monica**	23
Dusty's | **Silver Lake**	21
NEW Elements Kitchen | **Pasadena**	23
Encounter | **LAX**	16
Enzo/Angela | **West LA**	21
Five 61 | **Pasadena**	23
Fraîche | **Culver City**	23
NEW Fuego/Maya | **Long Bch**	19
Gordon Ramsay | **W Hollywood**	23
Hampton's | **Westlake Vill**	21
Hatfield's | **Melrose**	27
Il Grano | **West LA**	26
NEW Izakaya Fu-Ga | **Little Tokyo**	-
La Botte | **Santa Monica**	24
La Cachette | **Santa Monica**	21
NEW L.A. Market | **Downtown**	19
Le St. Amour | **Culver City**	20
Madeo | **W Hollywood**	25
Magnolia Lounge | **Pasadena**	15

NEW Maison Maurice	Beverly Hills	-
Marino	Hollywood	24
Z mar'sel	Rancho Palos Verdes	24
Z Mélisse	Santa Monica	28
Z Michael's	Santa Monica	25
Mirü8691	Beverly Hills	24
NEW Momed	Beverly Hills	-
NEW Noir	Pasadena	25
Oak Room	Pacific Palisades	16
Ocean & Vine	Santa Monica	22
Z Polo	Beverly Hills	23
Porto Alegre	Pasadena	20
Z Providence	Hollywood	28
Raymond	Pasadena	25
RH	W Hollywood	25
Z Saam/The Bazaar	Beverly Hills	27
71 Palm	Ventura	22
Sidecar	Ventura	24
Tasca Winebar	Third St	24
Third & Olive	Burbank	23
NEW Tiato	Santa Monica	-
Tierra Sur/Herzog	Oxnard	27
Tre Venezie	Pasadena	22
Ugo/Cafe	Culver City	17
Upstairs 2	West LA	23
Z Valentino	Santa Monica	26
Vito	Santa Monica	22
Wilshire	Santa Monica	23
Wolfgang's Steak	Beverly Hills	23

RAW BARS

Z Anisette	Santa Monica	21
Armstrong's	Catalina Is.	-
BLT Steak	W Hollywood	24
Bluewater	Redondo Bch	20
NEW BP Oysterette	Santa Monica	22
Z Brophy Bros.	Ventura	21
Canal Club	Venice	18
Coast	Santa Monica	21
Comme Ça	W Hollywood	22
Delmonico's	Encino	22
NEW East	Hollywood	25
Gulfstream	Century City	21
Gumbo Pot	Fairfax	20
Hall	W Hollywood	21
Hungry Cat	Hollywood	24

Z Joe's	Venice	2
Kendall's	Downtown	1
King's Fish	multi.	2
McKenna's	Long Bch	1
Neptune's Net	Malibu	1
Ocean Ave.	Santa Monica	2
Santa Monica Seafood	Santa Monica	2
Z Water Grill	Downtown	2

ROMANTIC PLACES

Z Anisette	Santa Monica	2
Baleen	Redondo Bch	1
NEW bar210	Beverly Hills	-
Z Bastide	W Hollywood	2
Z Bazaar/José Andrés	Beverly Hills	2
Beau Rivage	Malibu	1
Bella Roma	Pico-Robertson	2
Z Belvedere	Beverly Hills	2
Bistro/Gare	S Pasadena	1
Z Bistro 45	Pasadena	2
Bistro LQ	Fairfax	2
Blvd	Beverly Hills	2
Z NEW Bouchon	Beverly Hills	2
Z Brandywine	Woodland Hills	2
Brentwood	Brentwood	2
Brooks	Ventura	2
Cafe Del Rey	Marina del Rey	2
Cafe/Artistes	Hollywood	2
Cafe FIORE	Ventura	2
Caffe Roma	Beverly Hills	1
Capo	Santa Monica	2
Z Catch	Santa Monica	2
Cézanne	Santa Monica	2
Checkers	Downtown	2
NEW Collection	Malibu	-
Comme Ça	W Hollywood	2
Z Craft	Century City	2
NEW Culina	Beverly Hills	-
Z Derek's	Pasadena	2
Dominick's	Beverly Blvd.	2
Z Drago Centro	Downtown	2
Z Fraîche	Culver City	2
NEW Fuego/Maya	Long Bch	1
Z Geoffrey's	Malibu	2
Getty Ctr.	Brentwood	2
Gordon Ramsay	W Hollywood	2
Hampton's	Westlake Vill	2

Hatfield's | **Melrose**	27		**NEW** Xino | **Santa Monica**	-
Il Cielo | **Beverly Hills**	22		**Z** Yamashiro | **Hollywood**	18
Sole | **W Hollywood**	23			

SINGLES SCENES

Inn/Seventh Ray | **Topanga**	21		Abbey | **W Hollywood**	16
er-ne | **Marina del Rey**	23		Beechwood | **Marina del Rey**	19
Josie | **Santa Monica**	26		**NEW** Blue Dog | **Sherman Oaks**	21
a Bistecca | **Downtown**	-		Blue Velvet | **Downtown**	20
a Boheme | **W Hollywood**	21		Blvd 16 | **Westwood**	21
a Botte | **Santa Monica**	24		**Z** Boa | **W Hollywood**	22
a Cachette | **Santa Monica**	21		Border Grill | **Santa Monica**	21
a Sosta | **Hermosa Bch**	-		BottleRock | **Culver City**	16
e Chêne | **Saugus**	25		Bouzy | **Redondo Bch**	22
e St. Amour | **Culver City**	20		Bowery | **Hollywood**	20
ittle Door | **Third St**	23		Brooks | **Ventura**	25
Lou | **Hollywood**	25		**Z** Brophy Bros. | **Ventura**	21
Lucques | **W Hollywood**	27		Café Santorini | **Pasadena**	22
mar'sel | **Rancho Palos Verdes**	24		Caffe Roma | **Beverly Hills**	18
Mélisse | **Santa Monica**	28		Canal Club | **Venice**	18
Michael's | **Santa Monica**	25		Cecconi's | **W Hollywood**	20
Michael's/Naples | **Long Bch**	26		Chaya Brasserie | **W Hollywood**	24
Noé | **Downtown**	24		Chaya Venice | **Venice**	23
NEW Noir | **Pasadena**	25		Cheebo | **Hollywood**	20
Ortolan | **Third St.**	25		**NEW** Cheval Blanc | **Pasadena**	22
NEW Ozumo | **Santa Monica**	-		Citizen Smith | **Hollywood**	17
Parq/Montage | **Beverly Hills**	25		Ciudad | **Downtown**	22
Patina | **Downtown**	26		**NEW** Colony | **Hollywood**	-
Penthouse | **Santa Monica**	20		Comme Ça | **W Hollywood**	22
Z Piccolo | **Venice**	26		Copa d'Oro | **Santa Monica**	17
Pinot Bistro | **Studio City**	24		Corkbar | **Downtown**	22
Porto Alegre | **Pasadena**	20		Dominick's | **Beverly Blvd.**	21
Z Providence | **Hollywood**	28		**NEW** Drai's | **Hollywood**	-
Raymond | **Pasadena**	25		**NEW** East | **Hollywood**	25
RH | **W Hollywood**	25		**Z** Edison | **Downtown**	15
Rivera | **Downtown**	25		El Coyote | **Beverly Blvd**	15
Rustic Canyon | **Santa Monica**	23		**Z** Father's Office | **multi.**	22
Z Saddle Peak | **Calabasas**	27		Ford's | **Culver City**	20
71 Palm | **Ventura**	22		Foundry/Melrose | **Melrose**	22
Sir Winston's | **Long Bch**	24		Geisha Hse. | **Hollywood**	18
Sky Room | **Long Bch**	18		**NEW** Glendon Bar | **West LA**	-
NEW Sonoma | **Santa Monica**	-		Hal's | **Venice**	21
Z Spago | **Beverly Hills**	27		Hama | **Venice**	22
Z Sur | **W Hollywood**	23		Henry's Hat | **Universal City**	18
Tierra Sur/Herzog | **Oxnard**	27		Hideout | **Hollywood**	-
Z Valentino | **Santa Monica**	26		Hudson Hse. | **Redondo Bch**	23
Vertical Wine | **Pasadena**	21		James' | **Venice**	19
Via Alloro | **Beverly Hills**	21		Jones | **W Hollywood**	18
Villa Blanca | **Beverly Hills**	18		**Z** Katsuya | **multi.**	23
Vito | **Santa Monica**	22		Ketchup | **W Hollywood**	15

Kitchen 24	**Hollywood**	20
Koi	**W Hollywood**	24
Laurel	**Studio City**	23
NEW La Vida	**Hollywood**	-
NEW Living Room/Station	**Hollywood**	-
Magnolia	**Hollywood**	18
Magnolia Lounge	**Pasadena**	15
NEW Mercantile	**Hollywood**	21
Minx	**Glendale**	-
Moonshadows	**Malibu**	16
Mucho Ultima	**Manhattan Bch**	20
Ocean Ave.	**Santa Monica**	22
Z Palm	**W Hollywood**	24
Z Parkway Grill	**Pasadena**	26
Z Penthouse	**Santa Monica**	20
Z Pizzeria Mozza	**Hollywood**	27
Pourtal	**Santa Monica**	22
Primitivo	**Venice**	23
RA Sushi	**Torrance**	16
Rock'n Fish	**Manhattan Bch**	20
Rush St.	**Culver City**	17
Rustic Canyon	**Santa Monica**	23
Safire	**Camarillo**	23
Salt Creek	**El Segundo**	17
Simon LA	**W Hollywood**	22
Standard	**W Hollywood**	19
Stanley's	**Sherman Oaks**	20
Sushi Roku	**multi.**	23
Swingers	**Beverly Blvd**	17
Tanzore	**Beverly Hills**	21
Z NEW Tar Pit	**La Brea**	20
Tasca Winebar	**Third St**	24
Tengu	**Westwood**	21
Tinto	**W Hollywood**	-
25 Degrees	**Hollywood**	22
Village Idiot	**Melrose**	19
Wabi-Sabi	**Venice**	22
Wolfgang Puck B&G	**Downtown**	22
Yatai	**W Hollywood**	-
York	**Highland Pk**	18

SLEEPERS

(Good food, but little known)

Bella Roma	**Pico-Robertson**	24
Benley	**Long Bch**	24
Cabbage Patch	**multi.**	23
Casablanca Med.	**Claremont**	23
Chef Melba's	**Hermosa Bch**	27

Chichen Itza	**Downtown**	2
Cook's Tortas	**Monterey Pk**	2
D'Caché	**Toluca Lake**	2
Devon	**Monrovia**	2
Elf Café	**Echo Pk**	2
Enoteca Toscana	**Camarillo**	2
Fatty's & Co.	**Eagle Rock**	2
Five 61	**Pasadena**	2
Fountain Coffee	**Beverly Hills**	2
Hayakawa	**Covina**	2
Hudson Hse.	**Redondo Bch**	2
Izayoi	**Little Tokyo**	2
Jer-ne	**Marina del Rey**	2
Jian	**Beverly Blvd**	2
Jonathan's	**Ventura**	2
Koutoubia	**West LA**	2
Le Chêne	**Saugus**	2
Madeleine	**Tarzana**	2
Manchego	**Santa Monica**	2
Mantee	**Studio City**	2
Mediterraneo	**Westlake Vill**	2
Mirü8691	**Beverly Hills**	2
Mo-Chica	**Downtown**	2
Mosto	**Marina del Rey**	2
Nakkara	**Beverly Blvd**	2
Nishimura	**W Hollywood**	2
Nonna	**W Hollywood**	2
Omino	**Chatsworth**	2
O-Nami	**Torrance**	2
Park	**Echo Pk**	2
Parq/Montage	**Beverly Hills**	2
Petrossian	**W Hollywood**	2
Phlight	**Whittier**	2
Reservoir	**Silver Lake**	2
Robata Bar	**Santa Monica**	2
Ruen Pair	**E Hollywood**	2
Russell's	**Pasadena**	2
Safire	**Camarillo**	2
Sapori	**Marina del Rey**	2
Seoul Jung	**Downtown**	2
Seta	**Whittier**	2
SHU	**Bel-Air**	2
Sidecar	**Ventura**	2
Sir Winston's	**Long Bch**	2
Sushi Sushi	**Beverly Hills**	2
Takami	**Downtown**	2
Talia's	**Manhattan Bch**	2
Tasca Winebar	**Third St**	2

Third & Olive | **Burbank**	23	🅉 Patina | **Downtown**	26
Tiara | **Downtown**	23	Paul Martin's | **El Segundo**	22
Tierra Sur/Herzog | **Oxnard**	27	🅉 Petros | **Manhattan Bch**	23
Tsuji No Hana | **Marina del Rey**	24	🅉 Providence | **Hollywood**	28
Tutti Mangia | **Claremont**	23	Ranch Hse. | **Ojai**	22
208 Rodeo | **Beverly Hills**	23	RH | **W Hollywood**	25
Vegan Glory | **Beverly Blvd**	23	🅉 Roy's | **multi.**	24
Woody's BBQ | **multi.**	24	🅉 Ruth's Chris | **Pasadena**	25
Yuzu | **Torrance**	23	🅉 Saam/The Bazaar | **Beverly Hills**	27
Xixta Cocina | **Downtown**	24	🅉 Saddle Peak | **Calabasas**	27
Zane's | **Hermosa Bch**	26	71 Palm | **Ventura**	22

SPECIAL OCCASIONS

🅉 Anisette | **Santa Monica**	21	**NEW** Sonoma | **Santa Monica**	–
NEW Bar Bouchon | **Beverly Hills**	23	🅉 Spago | **Beverly Hills**	27
🅉 Bazaar/José Andrés | **Beverly Hills**	26	Tierra Sur/Herzog | **Oxnard**	27
🅉 Belvedere | **Beverly Hills**	25	🅉 Tuscany | **Westlake Vill**	26
🅉 Bistro 45 | **Pasadena**	26	🅉 Urasawa | **Beverly Hills**	27
Bistro LQ | **Fairfax**	24	🅉 Valentino | **Santa Monica**	26
🅉**NEW** Bouchon | **Beverly Hills**	24	🅉 Water Grill | **Downtown**	27
Brooks | **Ventura**	25	Westside Tav. | **West LA**	21
Cecconi's | **W Hollywood**	20	Wolfgang's Steak | **Beverly Hills**	23
🅉 Chinois | **Santa Monica**	26		

STARGAZING

🅉 Cicada | **Downtown**	23	Ammo | **Hollywood**	23
Comme Ça | **W Hollywood**	22	BLT Steak | **W Hollywood**	24
🅉 Craft | **Century City**	24	🅉 Boa | **multi.**	22
NEW Culina | **Beverly Hills**	–	Brentwood | **Brentwood**	22
🅉 CUT | **Beverly Hills**	27	**NEW** Café Habana | **Malibu**	–
Drago | **Santa Monica**	23	Cafe Med | **W Hollywood**	19
🅉 Drago Centro | **Downtown**	26	Cecconi's | **W Hollywood**	20
🅉 Fleming's | **multi.**	24	🅉 Chateau Marmont | **W Hollywood**	19
🅉 Fraîche | **Culver City**	23	🅉 Craft | **Century City**	24
Gordon Ramsay | **W Hollywood**	23	**NEW** Culina | **Beverly Hills**	–
🅉 Hatfield's | **Melrose**	27	🅉 CUT | **Beverly Hills**	27
🅉 Jar | **Beverly Blvd.**	25	Dan Tana's | **W Hollywood**	23
🅉 Josie | **Santa Monica**	26	Fountain Coffee | **Beverly Hills**	25
Marino | **Hollywood**	24	Giorgio Baldi | **Santa Monica**	26
🅉 mar'sel | **Rancho Palos Verdes**	24	Griddle | **Hollywood**	23
🅉 Mastro's Steak | **Beverly Hills**	26	🅉 Grill on Alley | **Beverly Hills**	25
🅉 Matsuhisa | **Beverly Hills**	28	🅉 Hamasaku | **West LA**	27
🅉 Nobu LA | **W Hollywood**	26	Il Sole | **W Hollywood**	23
Noé | **Downtown**	24	Ivy | **W Hollywood**	21
Ocean & Vine | **Santa Monica**	22	Ivy/Shore | **Santa Monica**	22
🅉 One Pico | **Santa Monica**	20	Koi | **W Hollywood**	24
Ortolan | **Third St.**	25	Madeo | **W Hollywood**	25
🅉 Osteria Mozza | **Hollywood**	27	🅉 Matsuhisa | **Beverly Hills**	28
🅉 Palm | **W Hollywood**	24	M Café | **multi.**	22
Parq/Montage | **Beverly Hills**	25	Mr. Chow | **Beverly Hills**	23

LOS ANGELES

SPECIAL FEATURES

Nishimura | **W Hollywood**	26
☑ Nobu LA | **W Hollywood**	26
☑ Nobu Malibu | **Malibu**	26
☑ Osteria Mozza | **Hollywood**	27
☑ Pizzeria Mozza | **Hollywood**	27
☑ Polo | **Beverly Hills**	23
SHU | **Bel-Air**	24
☑ Spago | **Beverly Hills**	27
Sushi Roku | **multi.**	23
☑ Tavern | **Brentwood**	23
Taverna Tony | **Malibu**	21
Toast | **Third St**	20
Tower Bar | **W Hollywood**	21
Tra Di Noi | **Malibu**	22
☑ Urasawa | **Beverly Hills**	27
Urth | **multi.**	21

TASTING MENUS

Ado | **Venice**	25
Amarone | **W Hollywood**	26
Aroma | **Silver Lake**	23
☑ Asia de Cuba | **W Hollywood**	24
Bar Hayama | **West LA**	22
Bar Pintxo | **Santa Monica**	21
☑ Bashan | **Montrose**	27
☑ Bazaar/José Andrés | **Beverly Hills**	26
Bella Roma | **Pico-Robertson**	24
Bistro LQ | **Fairfax**	24
Bond St. | **Beverly Hills**	20
Boss Sushi | **Beverly Hills**	25
Briganti | **S Pasadena**	21
Brooks | **Ventura**	25
Cafe Firenze | **Moorpark**	19
Capo | **Santa Monica**	25
Catalina | **Redondo Bch**	22
Christine | **Torrance**	25
☑ Cicada | **Downtown**	23
☑ Dar Maghreb | **Hollywood**	23
☑ Derek's | **Pasadena**	26
Devon | **Monrovia**	24
☑ Drago Centro | **Downtown**	26
Echigo | **West LA**	26
NEW Firenze | **N Hollywood**	20
Five 61 | **Pasadena**	23
Foundry/Melrose | **Melrose**	22
Gordon Ramsay | **W Hollywood**	23
☑ Hatfield's | **Melrose**	27
Hayakawa | **Covina**	28

Hirozen | **Beverly Blvd.**	26
☑ Il Cielo | **Beverly Hills**	22
Il Grano | **West LA**	26
Indo | **Palms**	20
☑ Inn/Seventh Ray | **Topanga**	21
☑ Japon Bistro | **Pasadena**	25
☑ Joe's | **Venice**	26
Katana | **W Hollywood**	23
☑ Katsu-ya | **multi.**	26
☑ Katsuya | **multi.**	23
Kiwami | **Studio City**	26
Koutoubia | **West LA**	25
K-Zo | **Culver City**	24
La Botte | **Santa Monica**	24
Locanda/Lago | **Santa Monica**	22
☑ Lucques | **W Hollywood**	27
☑ Maison Akira | **Pasadena**	26
☑ Matsuhisa | **Beverly Hills**	28
☑ Mélisse | **Santa Monica**	28
☑ Michael's | **Santa Monica**	25
☑ Nobu Malibu | **Malibu**	26
Noé | **Downtown**	24
Ortolan | **Third St.**	25
☑ Osteria Mozza | **Hollywood**	27
☑ Patina | **Downtown**	26
NEW Philippe | **W Hollywood**	17
☑ Piccolo | **Venice**	26
☑ Providence | **Hollywood**	28
Raymond | **Pasadena**	25
☑ Saam/The Bazaar | **Beverly Hills**	27
☑ Saddle Peak | **Calabasas**	27
Shin | **Hollywood**	–
☑ Shiro | **S Pasadena**	28
☑ Spago | **Beverly Hills**	27
NEW Stefan's/L.A. Farm | **Santa Monica**	23
Sushi Dokoro | **Beverly Hills**	–
Sushi Roku | **multi.**	23
☑ Sushi Sasabune/Sushi-Don | **West LA**	27
Sushi Sushi | **Beverly Hills**	27
Takao | **Brentwood**	26
Third & Olive | **Burbank**	23
Tiara | **Downtown**	23
Tutti Mangia | **Claremont**	23
Upstairs 2 | **West LA**	23
☑ Valentino | **Santa Monica**	26
☑ Vincenti | **Brentwood**	26

Menus, photos, voting and more – free at ZAGAT.com

Wa | **W Hollywood**	27
Water Grill | **Downtown**	27
NEW WP24 | **Downtown**	–
XIV | **W Hollywood**	23
Yabu | **W Hollywood**	23
Yuzu | **Torrance**	23

TEEN APPEAL

Abbot's | **Venice**	22
Angeli | **Melrose**	25
Apple Pan | **West LA**	23
Babalu | **Santa Monica**	20
Back Home | **Manhattan Bch**	17
Benihana | **Ontario**	19
BJ's | **multi.**	17
Border Grill | **Santa Monica**	21
Broadway Deli | **Santa Monica**	15
Buca di Beppo | **multi.**	15
Buddha's Belly | **Beverly Blvd**	19
Burger Continental | **Pasadena**	18
Cafe 50's | **multi.**	16
Caioti Pizza | **Studio City**	21
Canter's | **Fairfax**	19
Casa Bianca | **Eagle Rock**	23
Cha Cha Chicken | **Santa Monica**	20
Cheebo | **Hollywood**	20
Chipotle | **multi.**	19
Dukes West Hollywood | **W Hollywood**	18
El Coyote | **Beverly Blvd**	15
Gale's | **Pasadena**	24
Gladstone's | **Pacific Palisades**	13
Gordon Biersch | **Burbank**	16
Grand Lux | **Beverly Hills**	19
Hama | **Venice**	22
Hard Rock | **Universal City**	13
Islands | **multi.**	17
Jack n' Jill's | **Santa Monica**	18
Johnnie's NY | **multi.**	17
Johnny Rockets | **multi.**	16
Lamonica's | **Westwood**	22
Lucille's | **Torrance**	22
Martha's 22nd St. | **Hermosa Bch**	24
Mel's Drive-In | **Sherman Oaks**	16
Mexico City | **Los Feliz**	20
Natalee | **multi.**	19
Paco's Tacos | **multi.**	21
Palms Thai | **E Hollywood**	21
Pink's Dogs | **La Brea**	20

Poquito Más | **multi.**	21
Rae's | **Santa Monica**	15
Ribs USA | **Burbank**	19
Saladang | **Pasadena**	23
Shack | **multi.**	17
Sharky's | **multi.**	19
Stand | **Encino**	17
Swingers | **Beverly Blvd**	17
Teru Sushi | **Studio City**	22
Thai Dishes | **multi.**	17
Typhoon | **Santa Monica**	19
Wabi-Sabi | **Venice**	22
Zankou | **Burbank**	22

TRANSPORTING EXPERIENCES

☑ Anisette | **Santa Monica**	21
Barney Greengrass | **Beverly Hills**	22
☑ Bazaar/José Andrés | **Beverly Hills**	26
Blue Velvet | **Downtown**	20
☑ Campanile | **La Brea**	26
☑ Cicada | **Downtown**	23
☑ Cliff's Edge | **Silver Lake**	19
Comme Ça | **W Hollywood**	22
☑ Crustacean | **Beverly Hills**	24
☑ Dar Maghreb | **Hollywood**	23
☑ Edison | **Downtown**	15
☑ Gonpachi | **Beverly Hills**	21
☑ Inn/Seventh Ray | **Topanga**	21
La Boheme | **W Hollywood**	21
Little Door | **Third St**	23
Marrakesh | **Studio City**	21
☑ Michael's | **Santa Monica**	25
Musso & Frank | **Hollywood**	20
☑ RockSugar | **Century City**	21
☑ Urasawa | **Beverly Hills**	27
☑ Vibrato | **Bel-Air**	21
Whist | **Santa Monica**	20
XIV | **W Hollywood**	23
☑ Yamashiro | **Hollywood**	18

TRENDY

Ago | **W Hollywood**	21
Akasha | **Culver City**	20
Ammo | **Hollywood**	23
Animal | **Fairfax**	26
☑ Asia de Cuba | **W Hollywood**	24
NEW Bar Bouchon | **Beverly Hills**	23
NEW bar210 | **Beverly Hills**	–

Bazaar/José Andrés | **Beverly Hills** — ▯ — 26

Beechwood | **Marina del Rey** — 19

bld | **Beverly Blvd** — 22

BoHo | **Hollywood** — 17

▯ NEW Bouchon | **Beverly Hills** — 24

Cecconi's | **W Hollywood** — 20

▯ Chateau Marmont | **W Hollywood** — 19

Chaya Venice | **Venice** — 23

▯ Church/State | **Downtown** — 25

Citizen Smith | **Hollywood** — 17

Cobras/Matadors | **Beverly Blvd** — 21

Cole's | **Downtown** — 17

NEW Colony | **Hollywood** — –

Comme Ça | **W Hollywood** — 22

Copa d'Oro | **Santa Monica** — 17

▯ Craft | **Century City** — 24

▯ CUT | **Beverly Hills** — 27

Delancey | **Hollywood** — 20

NEW Drai's | **Hollywood** — –

▯ Edison | **Downtown** — 15

NEW El Cholo Downtown | **Downtown** — –

▯ Father's Office | **Culver City** — 22

NEW First & Hope | **Downtown** — –

Ford's | **Culver City** — 20

Foundry/Melrose | **Melrose** — 22

▯ Fraîche | **Culver City** — 23

Frysmith | **Location Varies** — –

NEW Glendon Bar | **West LA** — –

NEW Gorbals | **Downtown** — 21

Gordon Ramsay | **W Hollywood** ▯ — 23

Grilled Cheese | **Location Varies** — –

Hama | **Venice** — 22

Hash & High | **Venice** — –

NEW House Café | **Beverly Blvd** — 21

Hudson Hse. | **Redondo Bch** — 23

Hungry Cat | **Hollywood** — 24

Izaka-Ya | **Third St** — 26

▯ Jar | **Beverly Blvd.** — 25

Jones | **W Hollywood** — 18

Katana | **W Hollywood** — 23

▯ Katsu-ya | **multi.** — 26

▯ Katsuya | **multi.** — 23

Ketchup | **W Hollywood** — 15

Kitchen 24 | **Hollywood** — 20

Kogi | **Location Varies** — 23

Koi | **W Hollywood** — 24

LAMILL | **Silver Lake** — 21

NEW La Vida | **Hollywood** — –

Library Bar | **Downtown** — 17

Little Door | **Third St** — 23

NEW Living Room/Station | **Hollywood** — –

Local | **Silver Lake** — 22

Lomo Arigato | **Location Varies** — –

▯ Lou | **Hollywood** — 25

Magnolia | **Hollywood** — 18

▯ Mastro's Steak | **Beverly Hills** — 26

NEW Mercantile | **Hollywood** — 21

Mexico Rest. | **W Hollywood** — 19

Mucho Ultima | **Manhattan Bch** — 20

▯ Nobu LA | **W Hollywood** — 26

▯ Nobu Malibu | **Malibu** — 26

NEW Olive | **Hollywood** — –

NEW Oliverio | **Beverly Hills** — –

▯ Osteria Mozza | **Hollywood** — 27

NEW Ozumo | **Santa Monica** — –

Palate | **Glendale** — 24

▯ Penthouse | **Santa Monica** — 20

NEW Pizza Antica | **Santa Monica** — –

▯ Pizzeria Mozza | **Hollywood** — 27

NEW Red O | **Melrose** — –

Rock'n Fish | **Manhattan Bch** — 20

Saluté | **Santa Monica** — –

Street | **Hollywood** — 20

Sushi Roku | **multi.** — 23

▯ NEW Tar Pit | **La Brea** — 20

▯ Tavern | **Brentwood** — 23

Tin Roof | **Manhattan Bch** — 21

Urth | **W Hollywood** — 21

Vertical Wine | **Pasadena** — 21

Village Idiot | **Melrose** — 19

Wabi-Sabi | **Venice** — 22

Whist | **Santa Monica** — 20

NEW Xino | **Santa Monica** — –

XIV | **W Hollywood** — 23

York | **Highland Pk** — 18

NEW Zengo | **Santa Monica** — –

VIEWS

Admiral Risty | **Rancho Palos Verdes** — 20

▯ Asia de Cuba | **W Hollywood** — 24

Austen's | **Ventura** — –

Baleen | **Redondo Bch** — 19

arney Greengrass | **Beverly Hills** 22

eachcomber Café | **Malibu** 18

eau Rivage | **Malibu** 19

elmont Brewing | **Long Bch** 18

ue Velvet | **Downtown** 20

Boa | **Santa Monica** 22

occaccio's | **Westlake Vill** 20

afe Del Rey | **Marina del Rey** 22

Catch | **Santa Monica** 22

hart House | **multi.** 19

EW Collection | **Malibu** -

EW Drai's | **Hollywood** -

uke's | **Malibu** 17

Torito | **Marina del Rey** 15

ncounter | **LAX** 16

gtree's | **Venice** -

ns | **Calabasas** 21

EW Fuego/Maya | **Long Bch** 19

Geoffrey's | **Malibu** 20

etty Ctr. | **Brentwood** 22

ladstone's | **Pacific Palisades** 13

ampton's | **Westlake Vill** 21

ash & High | **Venice** -

y/Shore | **Santa Monica** 22

nathan's | **Ventura** 23

incaid's | **Redondo Bch** 20

obster | **Santa Monica** 23

Malibu Seafood | **Malibu** 23

mar'sel | **Rancho Palos Verdes** 24

artha's 22nd St. | **Hermosa Bch** 24

cKenna's | **Long Bch** 19

oonshadows | **Malibu** 16

oé | **Downtown** 24

One Pico | **Santa Monica** 20

EW Pan Am Room |
Santa Monica -

aradise Cove | **Malibu** 15

arker's | **Long Bch** 19

atrick's | **Santa Monica** 18

Penthouse | **Santa Monica** 20

anch Hse. | **Ojai** 22

eel Inn | **Malibu** 20

Saam/The Bazaar | **Beverly Hills** 27

Saddle Peak | **Calabasas** 27

apori | **Marina del Rey** 24

ir Winston's | **Long Bch** 24

ky Room | **Long Bch** 18

teve's Steak | **Catalina Is.** -

Taverna Tony | **Malibu** 21

Tony P's | **Marina del Rey** 17

Tower Bar | **W Hollywood** 21

Trader Vic | **Beverly Hills** 17

22nd St. Landing | **San Pedro** 17

208 Rodeo | **Beverly Hills** 23

Typhoon | **Santa Monica** 19

Warehouse | **Marina del Rey** 17

West | **Brentwood** 20

NEW WP24 | **Downtown** -

Z Yamashiro | **Hollywood** 18

Yard House | **Long Bch** 18

VISITORS ON EXPENSE ACCOUNT

Ago | **W Hollywood** 21

Z Anisette | **Santa Monica** 21

Z A.O.C. | **Third St** 27

Z Arroyo | **Pasadena** 25

NEW Bar Bouchon | **Beverly Hills** 23

Barbrix | **Silver Lake** 23

Z Bastide | **W Hollywood** 27

Z Bazaar/José Andrés |
Beverly Hills 26

Z Belvedere | **Beverly Hills** 25

Beso | **Hollywood** 21

Bistro LQ | **Fairfax** 24

BLT Steak | **W Hollywood** 24

Blue Velvet | **Downtown** 20

Blvd | **Beverly Hills** 23

Blvd 16 | **Westwood** 21

Z Boa | **W Hollywood** 22

Z NEW Bouchon | **Beverly Hills** 24

NEW Boxwood | **W Hollywood** 22

Brooks | **Ventura** 25

Buffalo Club | **Santa Monica** 19

Z Campanile | **La Brea** 26

Capo | **Santa Monica** 25

Z Catch | **Santa Monica** 22

Cecconi's | **W Hollywood** 20

Celestino | **Pasadena** 25

Chaya Brasserie | **W Hollywood** 24

Chaya Downtown | **Downtown** 24

Checkers | **Downtown** 21

NEW Cheval Blanc | **Pasadena** 22

Z Chinois | **Santa Monica** 26

Z Cicada | **Downtown** 23

Comme Ça | **W Hollywood** 22

Z Craft | **Century City** 24

Z Crustacean | **Beverly Hills** — 24

NEW Culina | **Beverly Hills** — -

Z CUT | **Beverly Hills** — 27

NEW Delphine | **Hollywood** — 20

Devon | **Monrovia** — 24

Dining Rm./Shangri-La | **Santa Monica** — 22

Dominick's | **Beverly Blvd.** — 21

Drago | **Santa Monica** — 23

Z Drago Centro | **Downtown** — 26

E. Baldi | **Beverly Hills** — 23

NEW Elements Kitchen | **Pasadena** — 23

Z Fleming's | **Downtown** — 24

Z Fogo de Chão | **Beverly Hills** — 23

NEW Fuego/Maya | **Long Bch** — 19

Geisha Hse. | **Hollywood** — 18

Z Geoffrey's | **Malibu** — 20

NEW Gorbals | **Downtown** — 21

Gordon Ramsay | **W Hollywood** — 23

Grill on Hollywood/Alley | **Hollywood** — 22

Hampton's | **Westlake Vill** — 21

Z Hatfield's | **Melrose** — 27

Hideout | **Hollywood** — -

Holdren's | **Thousand Oaks** — 20

Ivy | **W Hollywood** — 21

Ivy/Shore | **Santa Monica** — 22

Z Jar | **Beverly Blvd.** — 25

Jer-ne | **Marina del Rey** — 23

JiRaffe | **Santa Monica** — 26

Z Joe's | **Venice** — 26

Z Josie | **Santa Monica** — 26

Lobster | **Santa Monica** — 23

L'Opera | **Long Bch** — 23

Z Lucques | **W Hollywood** — 27

Z Mako | **Beverly Hills** — 26

Z mar'sel | **Rancho Palos Verdes** — 24

Z Mastro's Steak | **Beverly Hills** — 26

Z Matsuhisa | **Beverly Hills** — 28

Z Mélisse | **Santa Monica** — 28

Z Michael's | **Santa Monica** — 25

Minestraio | **W Hollywood** — 23

Morton's | **multi.** — 24

Mr. Chow | **Beverly Hills** — 23

Nick & Stef's | **Downtown** — 23

Nic's | **Beverly Hills** — 19

Z Nobu LA | **W Hollywood** — 26

Z Nobu Malibu | **Malibu** — 26

Z One Pico | **Santa Monica** — 20

Ortolan | **Third St.** — 25

Z Osteria Mozza | **Hollywood** — 27

NEW Ozumo | **Santa Monica** — -

Pacific Dining Car | **multi.** — 23

Z Palm | **W Hollywood** — 24

Z Parkway Grill | **Pasadena** — 26

Parq/Montage | **Beverly Hills** — 25

Z Patina | **Downtown** — 26

Paul Martin's | **El Segundo** — 22

Petros | **Manhattan Bch** — 23

NEW Philippe | **W Hollywood** — 17

Z Polo | **Beverly Hills** — 23

Z Providence | **Hollywood** — 28

Ranch Hse. | **Ojai** — 22

Raymond | **Pasadena** — 25

NEW Red O | **Melrose** — -

RH | **W Hollywood** — 25

Rivera | **Downtown** — 25

Z Roy's | **multi.** — 24

Z Ruth's Chris | **Pasadena** — 25

Z Saam/The Bazaar | **Beverly Hills** — 27

Z Saddle Peak | **Calabasas** — 27

Z Shiro | **S Pasadena** — 28

SHU | **Bel-Air** — 24

STK | **W Hollywood** — 22

Z Sur | **W Hollywood** — 23

Z Sushi Nozawa | **Studio City** — 28

Sushi Roku | **multi.** — 23

Takao | **Brentwood** — 26

Z Tavern | **Brentwood** — 23

Tierra Sur/Herzog | **Oxnard** — 27

Tin Roof | **Manhattan Bch** — 21

Z Valentino | **Santa Monica** — 26

Z Vincenti | **Brentwood** — 26

Z Water Grill | **Downtown** — 27

Westside Tav. | **West LA** — 21

Wilshire | **Santa Monica** — 23

Wolfgang's Steak | **Beverly Hills** — 23

NEW Xino | **Santa Monica** — -

XIV | **W Hollywood** — 23

Z Yujean Kang's | **Pasadena** — 26

NEW Zengo | **Santa Monica** — -

WINE BARS

Z A.O.C. | **Third St** — 27

Bar Pintxo | **Santa Monica** — 21

Bellavino | **Westlake Vill** — 19

stro/Gare | **S Pasadena**	19
ttleRock | **Culver City**	16
oadway Deli | **Santa Monica**	15
afe Stella | **Silver Lake**	21
& O | **Marina del Rey**	19
orkbar | **Downtown**	22
ube | **La Brea**	25
noteca Drago | **Beverly Hills**	22
noteca Toscana | **Camarillo**	25
Fleming's | **multi.**	24
enchy's | **Long Bch**	25
ungry Cat | **Hollywood**	24
nathan's | **Ventura**	23
Sosta | **Hermosa Bch**	-
Leila's | **Oak Pk**	27
lly's | **Venice**	19
Lou | **Hollywood**	25
onsieur Marcel | **Fairfax**	20
NEW Noir | **Pasadena**	25
alate | **Glendale**	24
etrossian | **W Hollywood**	23
op | **Pasadena**	17
urtal | **Santa Monica**	22
rimitivo | **Venice**	23
ustic Canyon | **Santa Monica**	23
aluté | **Santa Monica**	-
asca Winebar | **Third St**	24
nto | **W Hollywood**	-
5 Degrees | **Hollywood**	22
pstairs 2 | **West LA**	23
Valentino | **Santa Monica**	26
ertical Wine | **Pasadena**	21
Vestside Cellar | **Ventura**	-
Vine Bistro | **Studio City**	23

WINNING
WINE LISTS

go | **W Hollywood**	21
kasha | **Culver City**	20
Anisette | **Santa Monica**	21
A.O.C. | **Third St**	27
Arroyo | **Pasadena**	25
aleen | **Redondo Bch**	19
NEW Bar Bouchon | **Beverly Hills**	23
Bastide | **W Hollywood**	27
Bazaar/José Andrés | **Beverly Hills**	26
eacon | **Culver City**	22
eechwood | **Marina del Rey**	19

Bella Roma | **Pico-Robertson**	24
Z Bistro 45 | **Pasadena**	26
Bistro LQ | **Fairfax**	24
Bistro Provence | **Burbank**	23
BLT Steak | **W Hollywood**	24
Blue Velvet | **Downtown**	20
Blvd | **Beverly Hills**	23
Blvd 16 | **Westwood**	21
Z Boa | **Santa Monica**	22
BottleRock | **Culver City**	16
Z NEW Bouchon | **Beverly Hills**	24
Bouzy | **Redondo Bch**	22
Brooks | **Ventura**	25
Cafe Del Rey | **Marina del Rey**	22
Cafe Pinot | **Downtown**	23
Z Campanile | **La Brea**	26
Cecconi's | **W Hollywood**	20
Chaya Downtown | **Downtown**	24
Chez Mélange | **Redondo Bch**	25
Z Chinois | **Santa Monica**	26
Circa 55 | **Beverly Hills**	19
Comme Ça | **W Hollywood**	22
Corkbar | **Downtown**	22
Z Craft | **Century City**	24
NEW Culina | **Beverly Hills**	-
Z CUT | **Beverly Hills**	27
NEW Da Vinci | **Beverly Hills**	-
NEW Delphine | **Hollywood**	20
Drago | **Santa Monica**	23
Z Drago Centro | **Downtown**	26
E. Baldi | **Beverly Hills**	23
NEW Elements Kitchen | **Pasadena**	23
555 East | **Long Bch**	25
Z Fleming's | **multi.**	24
Foundry/Melrose | **Melrose**	22
Z Fraîche | **multi.**	23
Z Gonpachi | **Beverly Hills**	21
NEW Gorbals | **Downtown**	21
Gordon Ramsay | **W Hollywood**	23
Z Grill on Alley | **Beverly Hills**	25
Hampton's | **Westlake Vill**	21
Il Moro | **West LA**	22
Jer-ne | **Marina del Rey**	23
Z JiRaffe | **Santa Monica**	26
Kendall's | **Downtown**	19
King's Fish | **Calabasas**	20
La Bistecca | **Downtown**	-

La Botte	**Santa Monica**	24	Tropicalia	**Los Feliz**	22
La Cachette	**Santa Monica**	21	Ugo/Cafe	**Culver City**	17
⊠ Larsen's	**Encino**	23	Upstairs 2	**West LA**	23
⊠ Lucques	**W Hollywood**	27	⊠ Valentino	**Santa Monica**	26
⊠ mar'sel	**Rancho Palos Verdes**	24	Vertical Wine	**Pasadena**	21
⊠ Mélisse	**Santa Monica**	28	Via Alloro	**Beverly Hills**	21
⊠ Michael's	**Santa Monica**	25	⊠ Water Grill	**Downtown**	27
Minestraio	**W Hollywood**	23	Westside Tav.	**West LA**	21
Minx	**Glendale**	⌐	Wilshire	**Santa Monica**	23
Mosto	**Marina del Rey**	25	Wolfgang's Steak	**Beverly Hills**	23
Napa Valley	**Westwood**	19	XIV	**W Hollywood**	23
Nick & Stef's	**Downtown**	23	⊠ Yujean Kang's	**Pasadena**	26

WORTH A TRIP

⊠ Nobu LA	**W Hollywood**	26
NEW Noir	**Pasadena**	25

Arcadia

⊠ Din Tai Fung   25

Calabasas

Ocean Ave.	**Santa Monica**	22
Ortolan	**Third St.**	25

Mi Piace   20

⊠ Saddle Peak   27

Conejo Valley/Simi Valley

Pacific Dining Car	**multi.**	23
Palate	**Glendale**	24
⊠ Parkway Grill	**Pasadena**	26
Parq/Montage	**Beverly Hills**	25

⊠ Leila's   27

Padri   22

Safire   23

⊠ Tuscany   26

Malibu

⊠ Patina	**Downtown**	26
Paul Martin's	**El Segundo**	22
Peppone	**Brentwood**	21

⊠ Geoffrey's   20

⊠ Nobu Malibu   26

Monrovia

Pinot Bistro	**Studio City**	24
Pop	**Pasadena**	17
Pourtal	**Santa Monica**	22

Devon   24

San Gabriel Valley

Primitivo	**Venice**	23
Raymond	**Pasadena**	25
NEW Red O	**Melrose**	⌐
redwhite+bluezz	**Pasadena**	23
Rivera	**Downtown**	25
Rowdy	**Downtown**	⌐
⊠ Roy's	**Downtown**	24

⊠ Babita   27

Empress Harbor   21

Golden Deli   23

Hayakawa   28

⊠ NBC Seafood   21

Ocean Star   21

Saugus

⊠ Saam/The Bazaar	**Beverly Hills**	27

Le Chêne   25

South Bay

Safire	**Camarillo**	23
Saluté	**Santa Monica**	⌐
Simon LA	**W Hollywood**	22
NEW Sonoma	**Santa Monica**	⌐

Café Pierre   23

Chez Mélange   25

Christine   25

⊠ Spago	**Beverly Hills**	27
STK	**W Hollywood**	22
Street	**Hollywood**	20
⊠ Sur	**W Hollywood**	23

555 East   25

Frenchy's   25

L'Opera   23

Paul Martin's   22

Taste	**W Hollywood**	21
⊠ Tavern	**Brentwood**	23
Tierra Sur/Herzog	**Oxnard**	27
Tin Roof	**Manhattan Bch**	21
Tinto	**W Hollywood**	⌐

⊠ Petros   23

Sea Empress   18

Sky Room   18

ORANGE COUNTY

Top Food

28 Marché Moderne | *French*
Basilic | *French/Swiss*
Tradition by Pascal | *French*
Hobbit | *Continental/French*

27 Studio | *Californian/French*

Napa Rose | *Californian*
Bluefin | *Japanese*

26 Tabu Grill | *Seafood/Steak*
Mastro's | *Steak*
Park Ave | *American*

Top Decor

29 Studio

28 Pelican Grill
Andrea

26 Stonehill Tavern
Ritz

Mastro's Ocean Club
Napa Rose

25 Charlie Palmer
Leatherby's Café Rouge
Pinot Provence

Top Service

28 Hobbit

27 Studio

26 Tradition by Pascal
Mr. Stox
Marché Moderne

Ritz
Basilic
Andrea
Napa Rose

25 Stonehill Tavern

BY LOCATION

ANAHEIM

27 Napa Rose

25 Mr. Stox
Ruth's Chris

COSTA MESA

28 Marché Moderne

26 Mastro's
Golden Truffle

IRVINE

25 Ruth's Chris
Bistango

24 Wasa

LAGUNA BEACH

27 Studio

26 Tabu Grill
Cafe Zoolu

NEWPORT BEACH

28 Basilic
Tradition by Pascal

24 Cucina Alessá

NEWPORT COAST

27 Bluefin

25 Mastro's Ocean Club
Andrea

	FOOD	DECOR	SERVICE	COST

◪ Andrea *Italian* 25 | 28 | 26 | $69

Newport Coast | Pelican Hill Resort | 22800 Pelican Hill Rd.
Newport Coast Dr.) | 949-467-6800 | www.pelicanhill.com
A "breathtaking" view of the Pacific Ocean meets "excellent", "gracious"
service in a "refined, elegant" space at this Newport Coaster proffering "delicious" Italian cuisine including "amazing" pasta housemade in
a temperature-controlled room; grumblers note the menu's "inflated
prices", but those in-the-know shrug that's "not a surprise" given the
"über-posh" location in the multimillion-dollar Pelican Hill resort.

Antonello ◪ *Italian* 25 | 23 | 25 | $54

Santa Ana | South Coast Plaza | 3800 S. Plaza Dr. (Sunflower Ave.) |
714-751-7153 | www.antonello.com
Regulars "love every bite" at this "reliable" South Coast Plaza "time-
tested treasure", where the "waiters are delightful", and "terrific",
"high-end Italian" fare comes in "ample portions"; while some call the
decor "dated", nostalgists say the rustic frescoes evoke a street scene
that will "transport you back" to the old country, and an "extensive
wine list" further warms the mood.

◪ Basilic ◪◪ *French/Swiss* 28 | 20 | 26 | $59

Newport Beach | 217 Marine Ave. (Park Ave.) | 949-673-0570 |
www.basilicrestaurant.com
Chef Bernard Althaus "continues to amaze" at this enduring, "enchanting" "hideaway" on Balboa Island, where the "delicious" French-Swiss
specialties, "spot-on service" and "old-world charm" evoke "the best bistros in Europe"; prices are on the high side, but the experience is "always
a treat"; P.S. "reserve well ahead", since this "quaint" nook only seats 24.

Bistango ◪ *American* 25 | 24 | 24 | $47

Irvine | Atrium Bldg. | 19100 Von Karman Ave. (bet. Campus Dr. &
DuPont Ave.) | 949-752-5222 | www.bistango.com
This "well-disguised" "oasis" of "upscale" New American cuisine
tucked inside a "sterile" Irvine office building summons "high-
powered lunch" types by day and "special-occasion" jazz-lovers by
night; walls hung with "classy, approachable" exhibits that "change often" frame an "art gallery"-esque setting that's manned by a "quality
crew", with "prix fixe menus" that are actually "quite affordable"
boosting the allure.

Black Sheep Bistro ◪◪ *French/Spanish* 26 | 16 | 25 | $41

Tustin | 303 El Camino Real (3rd St.) | 714-544-6060 |
www.blacksheepbistro.com
"Husband-and-wife team" Rick and Diana Boufford's "romantic" "little"
Tustin bistro is a "neighborhood favorite" for "creative" French-
Spanish cuisine including "outstanding paella" and lamb dishes
"better than Mary ever had"; there's a nominal stemware-rental fee
standing in for standard corkage, while "professional, personal service" helps keep things "cozy" and "comfortable."

Bluefin *Japanese* 27 | 21 | 22 | $60

Newport Coast | Crystal Cove Promenade | 7952 E. PCH (Crystal Heights Dr.) |
949-715-7373 | www.bluefinbyabe.com
"Blue-finatics" urge you to just "open your wallet" for the "delectable
experience" of chef-owner Takashi Abe's "art gallery"-worthy sushi

and "adventurous" "fusions" at this sparsely decorated Newport Coast Japanese eatery hidden inside the Crystal Cove Promenade; sure, the staff can be "a bit cool" and the dining room is so "small" that "eavesdropping is part of the experience", but "lunch is a deal."

Brasserie Pascal *French*

24 | 22 | 20 | $42

Newport Beach | Fashion Island | 327 Newport Center Dr. (San Miguel Dr.) | 949-640-2700 | www.pascalnpb.com

More "Parisian brasserie" than Fashion Island mall restaurant, Pascal Olhats' French venue is "authentic" right down to the "decor and waiters" insist fans of "favorites" including boeuf bourguignon and coq au vin; "frequent promotions" and "specials" "keep the prices down", adding to the "excellent value" and "pleasant surprise."

Break of Dawn Ⓜ *Eclectic/Vietnamese*

25 | 17 | 21 | $20

Laguna Hills | 24351 Avenida De La Carlota (Los Alisos Blvd.) | 949-587-9418 | www.breakofdawnrestaurant.com

"Faithful morning foodies are a testament" to chef Dee Nguyen's "casual" "hidden gem" – tucked in an "unassuming" Laguna Hills strip mall – where eclectic Vietnamese and French-inspired breakfast and lunch items such as sausage and rice and crème brûlée French toast challenge any "health-conscious" resolve; although "it can be crowded", "sincere" service assures that the "innovative" fare arrives in a speedy fashion, leading fans to only "wish they were open for dinner."

Cafe Zoolu Ⓜ *Californian*

26 | 14 | 21 | $48

Laguna Beach | 860 Glenneyre St. (bet. St. Anns Dr. & Thalia St.) | 949-494-6825 | www.cafezoolu.com

"Locals" assure "you'll become a regular" after one taste of the "fantastic" fare including "excellent" charbroiled mesquite swordfish at this "quirky" Californian where the surrounding Laguna Beach scene blends with tropical Polynesian decor; while entree portions are "large", the dining room is "tiny", so to be among the "lucky few", reservations are recommended.

Cellar, The Ⓜ *French*

24 | 23 | 24 | $50

Fullerton | Villa del Sol | 305 N. Harbor Blvd. (Wilshire Ave.) | 714-525-5682 | www.cellardining.com

"Classic", "romantic" and "nostalgic", this longtime "OC institution" is where you'll find all of the "heavy sauces and heavy staffing" associated with pricey yet "superb" "old-world" French cuisine – plus an "outstanding" wine list; adding to the "elegant" experience is the "unique" Downtown Fullerton locale – "underground" in the "secluded", "cavelike" cellar of an old hotel and ideal for a "special-occasion" "rendezvous."

Ⓩ Charlie Palmer at Bloomingdale's South Coast Plaza *American*

22 | 25 | 23 | $62

Costa Mesa | South Coast Plaza | 3333 S. Bristol St. (Anton Blvd.) | 714-352-2525 | www.charliepalmer.com

"Quiet and sophisticated without being stuffy", chef Charlie Palmer's "contemporary" New American eatery in South Coast Plaza offers "shopping-mall" dining that "can't be beat" with its "spacious" room, "sleek" leather seating and "faultless" service; expect "high-style

| | FOOD | DECOR | SERVICE | COST |

temptation" (with prices to match) in the form of "small portions" and the "freshest ingredients"; P.S. wine lovers can find the restaurant's selections next door at the Next Vintage shop.

Cucina Alessá *Italian*　　　　24 | 19 | 23 | $34
NEW Huntington Beach | 520 Main St. (6th St.) | 714-969-2148
Newport Beach | 6700 W. PCH (Orange St.) | 949-645-2148
www.cucinaalessa.com

Fans of this Italian kitchen duo brave the "noisy" dining room and "parking hassles" in quest of chef-owner Alessandro Pirozzi's "high-quality" thin-crust pizzas and housemade pastas at prices that are "so reasonable" – ergo it's "always busy" at both Huntington Beach and the "very small" Newport Beach venue; though there are "long waits" on weekends, the "personal", "efficient" staff will "make you feel welcome."

⚡ Five Crowns *Continental*　　　24 | 23 | 25 | $50
Corona del Mar | 3801 E. PCH (Poppy Ave.) | 949-760-0331 |
www.lawrysonline.com

Offering a "trip across the pond without a passport", this Corona del Mar "standby" caters to the "old-school Newport crowd" with Continental plates – including the "best dang" Lawry's prime rib and Yorkshire pudding around; though the "tired" English-inn decor draws some yawns, fans appreciate this "step back in time" (especially "at Christmas when they have carolers") aided by a "been-here-for-years" staff, and the Sunday brunch on the patio is "fabulous."

Five Feet *Chinese/French*　　　25 | 18 | 23 | $49
Laguna Beach | 328 Glenneyre St. (bet. Forest Ave. & Mermaid St.) |
949-497-4955 | www.fivefeetrestaurants.com

"A treat for sure", this pricey Chinese-French spot in Laguna Beach is "unusual from every angle", swathed in "over-the-top" "'80s-vibe" decor and featuring chef-owner Michael Kang's "inventive" "fusion" prix fixes and à la carte menu items ("oh, the catfish!") showing "great care in preparation"; the only quibbles are with quarters so "crowded and noisy" that "you might as well eat in a train station" – but fans are "not complaining."

Fukada Ⓜ *Japanese*　　　　24 | 15 | 18 | $20
Irvine | 8683 Irvine Center Dr. (Research Dr.) | 949-341-0111

Surveyors say "you don't know how good udon can be" until you've slurped the "satisfying" housemade noodles of this Irvine establishment – slithery elixirs for the often "unbearable" waits, "curt" service and modest decor; inexpensive price tags for these "steaming bowls" and other Japanese fare seal the deal.

Gabbi's Mexican Kitchen *Mexican*　　26 | 21 | 22 | $32
Orange | 141 S. Glassell St. (Chapman Ave.) | 714-633-3038 |
www.gabbipatrick.com

"It's not your typical tacos-and-beans place" aver admirers of this "up-scale" Mexican eatery in "funky" Old Town Orange, where "creative twists" and "better ingredients" equal "spectacular gastronomic experiences"; agreeable service amid hacienda-style decor and a dimly lit dining room make for a "worthwhile date" spot, but when driving by, "don't look for signage" because there is none.

	FOOD	DECOR	SERVICE	COST

Gemmell's *Continental/French* · 25 · 20 · 23 · $45

Dana Point | 34471 Golden Lantern St. (Dana Point Harbor Dr.) |
949-234-0064 | www.gemmellsrestaurant.com

Chef-owner Byron Gemmell's "intimate" French-Continental venue
"hidden" in Dana Point Harbor is a "bastion" of "fabulous fine dining",
where "rich" fare is ferried by a staff that "accommodates your every
need"; "time is taken to make each dish special", so it's not cheap –
but bargain-hunters take pleasure in lunch and dinner prix fixe deals.

Golden Truffle, The 🅢🅜 *Caribbean/French* · 26 · 13 · 20 · $45

Costa Mesa | 1767 Newport Blvd. (bet. 17th & 18th Sts.) | 949-645-9858 |
www.goldentruffle.com

"Don't be fooled" by its "casual", strip-mall feel and "makeover"-
ready decor say the "open-minded" "admirers" of Costa Mesa's
"golden treasure" offering an "inspired" ever-changing menu of
French-Caribbean fare; service might range from "haphazard" to
"overly friendly", but when chef-owner Alan Greeley is in the kitchen,
regulars assure "you will not be disappointed."

Ẓ Hobbit, The 🅜 *Continental/French* · 28 · 23 · 28 · $84

Orange | 2932 E. Chapman Ave. (Malena St.) | 714-997-1972 |
www.hobbitrestaurant.com

"Epicures and oenophiles alike" "treat their palates" at chef-owner
Michael Philippi's Orange standout offering a seven-course French-
Continental "adventure" served by an "elegant" staff that earns OC's
No. 1 spot for Service; though prices are equally "extravagant", the
"charming" converted Spanish-style dwelling adds to a "unique experience" that unfolds "like a play", beginning with champagne and
hors d'oeuvres "in the wine cellar" and spanning "several hours of
heaven"; P.S. "reservations are necessary", as there's only one seating
a night (Wednesday–Sunday).

NEW House of Big Fish & · - · - · - · M
Ice Cold Beer 🅢🅜 *Seafood*

Laguna Beach | 450 S. Pacific Coast Hwy. (Legion) | 949-715-4500 |
www.houesofbigfish.com

Laguna tourists wriggle past locals to get their fill of fresh, affordable
seafood (think oysters, crab, sashimi) and beachy grub (gumbo and
lobster rolls) at this already packed Pacific Coast Highway newcomer with a no-worries aura and ocean views from the primo seats;
scores of frosty beers by the tap, bottle or bucket reinforce the
chillin' vibe, and happy hour is truly one hour, but is filled with bargain sips and bites.

NEW Il Barone Ristorante 🅢 *Italian* · - · - · - · M

Newport Beach | 4251 Martingale Way (bet. Birch St. & MacArthur Blvd.) |
949-955-2755 | www.ilbaroneristorante.com

Franco and Donatella Barone, he the longtime chef at Antonello, she
the veteran GM at Nello Cucina, break loose to reinvent the old
Pleasant Peasant digs near John Wayne airport and create the stylish ristorante of their dreams; Sicily-born Franco's menu is packed
with classics for his loyal followers plus fresh pastas, seafood and
new game dishes with Northern twists, and housemade desserts are
a special treat.

	FOOD	DECOR	SERVICE	COST

☑ In-N-Out Burger ● *Burgers* | 24 | 11 | 20 | $9 |

Costa Mesa | 594 W. 19th St. (bet. Anaheim & Maple Aves.)
Huntington Beach | 18062 Beach Blvd. (Talbert Ave.)
Irvine | 4115 Campus Dr. (Bridge Rd.)
Laguna Niguel | 27380 La Paz Rd. (Avila Rd.)
Tustin | Tustin Mktpl. | 3020 El Camino Real (Jamboree Rd.)
800-786-1000 | www.in-n-out.com
Additional locations throughout Southern California
See review in Los Angeles Directory.

Leatherby's Café Rouge Ⓜ *Californian* | 26 | 25 | 24 | $54 |

Costa Mesa | Orange County Performing Arts Ctr. | 615 Town Center Dr.
(Bristol St.) | 714-429-7640 | www.patinagroup.com
"Terrific before the theater", this Patina Group venue inhabits a
"gorgeous, modern" setting within the Segerstrom Concert Hall,
where new chef Ross Pangilinan is "working magic in the kitchen" with
his Californian creations; some patrons find the pricing a little "over
the top", although pre-show prix fixe meals and happy-hour apps
are also options; P.S. it's only open during performance season, so call
ahead for hours.

☑ Marché Moderne *French* | 28 | 24 | 26 | $58 |

Costa Mesa | South Coast Plaza | 3333 Bristol St. (Anton Blvd.) |
714-434-7900 | www.marchemoderne.net
"Yes, it's in a mall", but "get over it" say the many fans of this "joyous
discovery", a "sophisticated" South Coast Plaza bistro where chef-
owners Florent and Amelia Marneau turn out "unforgettable" French
fare – from "comforting" classics to "adventurous" small plates –
ranked No. 1 for Food and Most Popular in Orange County; it's not
cheap, but it pays off with an "elegant" setting complete with "romantic" cabanas on the patio and service that makes you feel "well taken
care of"; P.S. the "prix fixe lunch" is one of the "best deals" around.

Mastro's Ocean Club *Seafood/Steak* | 25 | 26 | 25 | $76 |

Newport Coast | Crystal Cove Promenade | 8112 E. PCH (Reef Point Dr.) |
949-376-6990 | www.mastrosrestaurants.com
A glittery crowd tucks into "fantastic" *Flintstones*-size" steaks,
seafood towers and "decadent" sides at this "outrageously expensive" Crystal Cove chophouse set in luxe ocean liner–inspired digs
with "stunning views" of the Pacific; it's a tad "pretentious" to some,
but "first-class" service makes it "the place to go celebrate something special", and you just can't beat the "people-watching" either
("yow, the cleavage!").

☑ Mastro's Steakhouse *Steak* | 26 | 23 | 25 | $73 |

Costa Mesa | 633 Anton Blvd. (Park Center Dr.) | 714-546-7405 |
www.mastrosrestaurants.com
See review in Los Angeles Directory.

Morton's The Steakhouse *Steak* | 24 | 22 | 24 | $65 |

Anaheim | 1895 S. Harbor Blvd. (Convention Way) | 714-621-0101
Santa Ana | South Coast Plaza | 1641 W. Sunflower Ave. (bet. Bear &
Bristol Sts.) | 714-444-4834
www.mortons.com
See review in Los Angeles Directory.

Mr. Stox *American*   25 | 24 | 26 | $52

Anaheim | 1105 E. Katella Ave. (bet. Lewis St. & State College Blvd.) | 714-634-2994 | www.mrstox.com

"It's class all the way" at this Anaheim "icon" presenting the "best of everything", from the "wonderful", meat-heavy American menu and "extensive" array of wines to the cushy setting that exudes "old-school elegance"; prices are high, but service is "warm" and "knowledgeable", and you really "can't go wrong here", especially for a special occasion.

⛿ Napa Rose *Californian*   27 | 26 | 26 | $65

Anaheim | Disney's Grand Californian Hotel & Spa | 1600 S. Disneyland Dr. (Katella Ave.) | 714-300-7170 | www.disneyland.com

"There's not a mouse in sight" at this "first-class", "grown-up" "oasis of calm" within the Disneyland theme park showcasing "brilliant" seasonal Californian fare by chef Andrew Sutton and an "epic" wine list; the Craftsman-style setting boasts "engaging, knowledgeable" servers and a "surprisingly kid-friendly" vibe, though a few find the experience marred by "high" prices and an abundance of diners "dragging in from the park" in "sweatshirts and tennis sneakers" ("wish they had a dress-up only room!").

Nirvana Grille Ⓜ *Californian*   24 | 18 | 24 | $47

Laguna Beach | 303 Broadway St. (Beach St.) | 949-497-0027
Mission Viejo | Marguerite Shopping Ctr. | 24031 Marguerite Pkwy. (Trabuco Rd.) | 949-380-0027
www.nirvanagrille.com

An "oasis" in a "fuddy-duddy" strip mall", this Mission Viejo Californian and its Laguna offshoot draw a dedicated following for chef-owner Lindsey Smith-Rosales' "innovative", seasonal cooking; since they're some of the "best bets" foodwise in their respective areas, most have "no complaints" about the upper-end pricing and "plain-Jane" white-tablecloth settings.

Old Vine Café *Eclectic*   25 | 17 | 22 | $32

Costa Mesa | The Camp | 2937 Bristol St. (Baker St.) | 714-545-1411 | www.oldvinecafe.com

For wine tasting without the "snob" factor, a "young" crowd favors this rustic little cafe in Costa Mesa's retail venue The Camp, where "refined" Eclectic small plates meet up with an "excellent" array of bottles; prices are modest, and the "fresh" fare's also a "favorite" for breakfast and brunch.

Onotria Wine Country Cuisine ⛿ *Eclectic/Italian*   25 | 20 | 25 | $51

Costa Mesa | 2831 Bristol St. (Bear St.) | 714-641-5952 | www.onotria.com

Though it houses an "amazing", "extensive" collection of premium vinos, admirers insist the "real attraction" at this Costa Mesa "gem" is chef-owner Massimo Navarretta's "delicious" Italian-Eclectic menu that changes with the seasons; prices are high, but it has a "personal touch", from the "knowledgeable" service down to the farmhouse-styled setting that "feels like someone's home in Napa."

	FOOD	DECOR	SERVICE	COST

Original Fish Co. *Seafood*

25 | 18 | 22 | $35

Los Alamitos | 11061 Los Alamitos Blvd. (Katella Ave.) | 562-594-4553 | www.originalfishcompany.com

"Fanatically fresh" fish and some of the "best chowder in Orange County" are the hallmarks of this "big barn of a seafood restaurant" in Los Alamitos; tabs are "affordable" and service is "friendly", although it's "always bustling", so "long waits" are a regular occurrence; P.S. an on-site market vends the daily catch.

Park Ave Ⓜ *American*

26 | 23 | 24 | $40

Stanton | 11200 Beach Blvd. (bet. Katella & Ruthann Aves.) | 714-901-4400 | www.parkavedining.com

"Yes Virginia, there is a reason to drive to Stanton" brag boosters of this "unlikely" "find" where "hands-on" chef-partner David Slay presents "exceptional" American "comfort food" crafted with "fresh" "veggies picked from their own garden"; refreshingly "reasonable" prices, "personable" service and a delightfully "retro" setting in a "beautifully maintained midcentury Googie masterpiece" make it "worth a visit"; P.S. "don't miss the special brined fried chicken" on Sunday nights.

Ⓩ Pelican Grill *Californian*

24 | 28 | 25 | $61

Newport Coast | Pelican Hill Resort | 22800 Pelican Hill Rd. (Newport Coast Dr.) | 949-467-6800 | www.pelicanhill.com

A "fabulous" location with "panoramic views" of the Pacific forms the backdrop for this "luxurious" resort restaurant in Pelican Hill featuring an "inventive" Californian menu; indeed it's "expensive", but service is "attentive" and the vibe so "peaceful", that you just can't beat it for a "lazy lunch" on the veranda.

Pinot Provence *French*

24 | 25 | 24 | $56

Costa Mesa | Westin South Coast Plaza Hotel | 686 Anton Blvd. (Bristol St.) | 714-444-5900 | www.patinagroup.com

Loyalists insist this "timeless" enclave in the Westin South Coast Plaza "always comes through" for "business lunches" and "romantic" dinners alike with "solid if not spectacular" French cuisine and "attentive" service in a "quiet", "lovely" Provençal setting; indeed, it's "pricey", but "no corkage" on bottles makes it quite the "deal" for fine dining.

Pizzeria Ortica Ⓩ *Pizza*

24 | 17 | 20 | $38

Costa Mesa | 650 Anton Blvd. (bet. Bristol St. & Park Center Dr.) | 714-445-4900 | www.pizzeriaortica.com

"OC's answer to Pizzeria Mozza" is this Costa Mesa Italian and instant "favorite" from David Myers (Comme Ça in LA) purveying "amazing, thin-crust" Neapolitan pies and "perfectly al dente" pastas in a stripped-down space with an open kitchen; "quick" service and accessible pricing help mitigate oft-"crowded" conditions and a setting so "loud" that "sign language" is almost a necessity.

Plums Café & Catering *Pacific NW*

25 | 16 | 20 | $24

Costa Mesa | Westport Square Shopping Ctr. | 369 E. 17th St. (Tustin Ave.) | 949-722-7586 | www.plumscafe.com

"Oregon comes to California" via this well-priced "breakfast favorite" in Costa Mesa turning out "terrific" Pacific Northwestern cuisine worthy of a "four-star restaurant"; the bright, lofty space tends toward "noisy", although regulars assure dinners are more sedate.

Ramos House Café ⓜ *American*

25 | 18 | 22 | $35

San Juan Capistrano | 31752 Los Rios St. (Ramos St.) | 949-443-1342 | www.ramoshouse.com

Set in an "adorable", little cottage "right on the train tracks" in "historic Old San Juan Capistrano, this "delightful" New American showcases chef-owner John Q. Humphreys' "incredible" Southern-inflected day time fare backed by an "overstuffed Bloody Mary" that's a meal in itself; the seating outside on a "rustic", tree-shaded patio is sure to "melt your stress away" providing you can overlook the "rather pricey" bills.

NEW Raya *Pan-Latin*

- | - | - | E

Dana Point | Ritz-Carlton Laguna Niguel | 1 Ritz-Carlton Dr. (PCH) | 949-240-2000 | www.ritzcarlton.com

Richard Sandoval (La Sandia and Zengo in LA) brings his acclaimed Pan-Latin cuisine to this Dana Point newcomer, a retooling of the Ritz-Carlton's plush fine-dining room; the pricey menu takes many cues from the sea, including a rotating selection of ceviche, and decor follows suit with a silver kelp sculpture wall; P.S. the rooftop lounge is also new, offering small plates, signature cocktails and a sweeping view of the coast.

Ritz Restaurant & Garden, The ⒮ⓜ *Continental*

24 | 26 | 26 | $61

Newport Beach | 880 Newport Center Dr. (Santa Barbara Dr.) | 949-720-1800 | www.ritzrestaurant.com

Channeling old-fashioned "glamour and glitz", this longtime Newport Beach fine-dining venue pulls a well-heeled crowd for "classic" Continental plates and martinis ferried by a "professional", tuxedoed staff; it's all a tad "too stuffy" for some, although its following insists the "clubby", "elegant" ambiance enhanced by live piano Wednesday–Sunday is just the thing for a "dressed-up" night on the town.

Roy's *Asian Fusion/Hawaiian*

24 | 22 | 23 | $49

Anaheim | Anaheim GardenWalk | 321 W. Katella Ave. (Clementine St.) | 714-776-7697

Newport Beach | Fashion Island | 453 Newport Center Dr. (San Miguel Dr.) | 949-640-7697

www.roysrestaurant.com

See review in Los Angeles Directory.

☑ Ruth's Chris Steak House *Steak*

25 | 22 | 24 | $62

Anaheim | 2041 S. Harbor Blvd. (bet. Katella & Orangewood Aves.) | 714-750-5466

Irvine | Park Pl. | 2961 Michelson Dr. (Carlson Ave.) | 949-252-8848

www.ruthschris.com

See review in Los Angeles Directory.

Santouka Ramen ⌫ *Japanese*

24 | 7 | 12 | $12

Costa Mesa | Mitsuwa Mktpl. | 665 Paularino Ave. (bet. Bristol St. & Costa Mesa Frwy.) | 714-434-1101 | www.japaneserestaurantinfo.com/santoka

Parked inside the Mitsuwa market, this low-cost Costa Mesa branch of a Japanese chain supplies some of the "best ramen" around, with "fresh noodles", "fatty pork" and an "earthy broth" that's absolutely "addictive"; the "food court" setting doesn't offer much in the way of

	FOOD	DECOR	SERVICE	COST

ecor or service, but even still, it's "so busy" that it's often "impossible
o find a seat."

NEW Seasons 52 🅂🅜 *Californian*

| - | - | - | E |

Costa Mesa | South Coast Plaza | 3333 Bristol St. (Sunflower) |
714-437-5252 | www.seasons52.com

South Coast Plaza debuts another hot operator with the first California
outpost of this upscale wine bar/grill chain with a farmer's market
spin; expect brick-oven cooking, wood-fire grilling and other tricks
that coax flavors from nature's current bounty backed by 60 wines by
the glass and for the finale, a bevy of indulgent shot glass desserts.

Spaghettini Italian Grill & Jazz Club *Italian*

| 24 | 22 | 21 | $43 |

Seal Beach | 3005 Old Ranch Pkwy. (bet. I-405 & Seal Beach Blvd.) |
562-596-2199 | www.spaghettini.com

"Wonderful" Northern Italian cuisine and "terrific smooth jazz" come
together at this "wildly popular" Seal Beach supper club, a "great
date" place that's also favored for its "fabulous brunch" with "free-
flowing" champagne; the handsome space has a "classy", "comfortable" feel, just beware of "sticker shock" with the bill.

Stonehill Tavern 🅜 *American*

| 25 | 26 | 25 | $73 |

Dana Point | St. Regis Resort, Monarch Bch. | 1 Monarch Beach Resort
Niguel Rd.) | 949-234-3318 | www.michaelmina.net

Truly "refined", this "elegant" Dana Point resort restaurant from
Michael Mina "pampers" its "blond and botoxed" clientele with "spectacular" New American cuisine set down in a "gorgeous" room with
"views of the ocean"; "splurge"-worthy bills should come as no surprise, although a few tut "it should be tastier" given the chef.

☑ Studio 🅜 *Californian/French*

| 27 | 29 | 27 | $102 |

Laguna Beach | Montage Laguna Bch. | 30801 S. PCH (Montage Dr.) |
949-715-6420 | www.studiolagunabeach.com

A "picture-perfect" clifftop locale affording "sublime" sunset views
over the Pacific help earn this "fine-dining" venue in the Montage Laguna
Beach resort the No. 1 score for Decor in Orange County; equally
"wow"-worthy is chef Craig Strong's "imaginative" Cal-New French
menu and "flawless" service, so "what more can you ask for" aside
from "a loan to pay for it" all?

Tabu Grill *Seafood/Steak*

| 26 | 20 | 24 | $63 |

Laguna Beach | 2892 S. PCH (bet. Hinkle & Nyes Pls.) | 949-494-7743 |
www.tabugrill.com

Now flaunting a newly expanded dining room, this "dark", "sophisticated" Laguna Beach "gem" continues to "delight" with chef Kevin
Jerrold-Jones' "beautifully presented" surf 'n' turf fare prepared with
Pacific Rim influences and presented by an effortlessly "hip" staff;
prices are "expensive" and a few note a "dip in quality" since the re-
vamp (indeed, the Food score's down three points), though it's still
"crowded" most nights, so make a "reservation."

☑ Tradition by Pascal *French*

| 28 | 22 | 26 | $62 |

Newport Beach | 1000 N. Bristol St. (Jamboree Rd.) | 949-263-9400 |
www.pascalnewportbeach.com

"Simply terrific" declare devotees of this "little bit of France" tucked in
a ho-hum Newport Beach strip mall, where chef-owner Pascal Olhats

himself turns out "top-notch" Gallic cuisine and his crew offers table side finishes on Thursday evenings; a "quiet", "elegant" setting an "attentive" service that "isn't snooty" all make it "easy to drop a bun dle" here; P.S. Sunday's prix fixe is a "good deal."

![NEW] True Food Kitchen 🅂🅼 *Health Food*

| – | – | – | E |

Newport Beach | Fashion Island | 451 Newport Center Dr. (Avocado)
949-644-2400 | www.foxrc.com

Maximum nutrients with maxed-out flavors are the formula at thi sleek Fashion Island newcomer anchored by the healthy-living pre cepts of author/lifestyle guru Dr. Andrew Weil as translated by che Michael Stebner; it features a globally inspired, seasonal menu tha spans brunch to dinner, washed down with power juice blends, elixir and organic wines; a sprawling patio with fire pit and living succulen wall furthers the green theme.

230 Forest Avenue *Californian*

| 24 | 19 | 21 | $42 |

Laguna Beach | 230 Forest Ave. (PCH) | 949-494-2545 |
www.230forestavenue.com

"Locals and tourists" alike flock to this "trendy spot" in the "heart o Laguna Beach", where chef Marc Cohen's "innovative" Californian menu is buoyed by a "modern", "artistic vibe" and some stellar "people watching"; try nabbing tables on the patio, as "cramped" seating in the dining room makes some feel like "sardines in a can" – still, "top notch" (if "pricey") cuisine and "fine service" "make it all worthwhile."

Walt's Wharf *Seafood*

| 25 | 17 | 23 | $38 |

Seal Beach | 201 Main St. (Central Ave.) | 562-598-4433 |
www.waltswharf.com

"Some of the finest, fresh-grilled seafood" in town is the hook for both lo cals and "tourists" at this popular Seal Beach "staple" near the pier where the "wonderful" wines and pier-side setting make it a "great place to spend a summer evening"; decor is of the "salty dog", "no frills" variety, but prices are "fair" and the servers "hustle" so most don't seem to mind; P.S. no reservations at dinner, so try lunch or expect a "wait."

Wasa *Japanese*

| 24 | 18 | 19 | $40 |

Irvine | The Market Pl. | 13124 Jamboree Rd. (Irvine Blvd.) | 714-665-3338
Lake Forest | The Orchard | 23702 El Toro Rd. (Rockfield Blvd.) | 949-770-3280
Newport Beach | Bluffs Shopping Ctr. | 1346 Bison Ave. (Macarthur Blvd.) |
949-760-1511
www.wasasushi.com

Smitten customers "can't get enough" of the "tasty", "nontraditional" hand rolls and "fresh, fresh, fresh" sushi and sashimi at this "popular" Japanese mini-chain; iffy service and a somewhat "sterile" atmo sphere are overcome by "reasonable" prices and a "fun" vibe, and Newport especially is quite the "hot spot."

Watermarc *American/Eclectic*

| 24 | 21 | 23 | $47 |

Laguna Beach | 448 S. PCH (bet. Legion St. & Park Ave.) | 949-376-6272 |
www.watermarcrestaurant.com

"Hip" from day one, this Laguna Beach "locals'" spot from chef Marc Cohen (230 Forest, Opah) rolls out an "imaginative", "expertly pre pared" roster of Eclectic–New American "grazing" plates backed by

	FOOD	DECOR	SERVICE	COST

"drink options galore" like "top-notch cocktails" and well-priced wines; communal tables and an active bar encourage a "noisy", "upbeat" vibe – so those in-the-know head to the "Zen-like" patio on the second floor for a quieter atmosphere.

Wildfish Seafood Grille *American/Seafood*

	24	22	21	$54

Newport Beach | The Bluffs | 1370 Bison Ave. (Macarthur Blvd.) | 949-720-9925 | www.wildfishseafoodgrille.com

"Exceptional" seafood plus a "lively" bar with some of the best "people-watching" around keep this handsome Newport Beach American "buzzing" with a "typical OC" crowd (think *"Real Housewives"*); regulars note the bills "add up quickly" although the "fantastic" happy hour every night offers some relief.

Winery, The *Californian*

	24	23	23	$50

Tustin | The District | 2647 Park Ave. (bet. Tustin Ranch Rd. & Warner Ave.) | 714-258-7600 | www.thewineryrestaurant.net

A real "impress-your-date" kind of place, this Tustin entry in The District earns kudos for its "terrific" *vin*-focused Cal cuisine featuring prime steaks and game elevated by an eclectic 600-bottle wine list; its "beautiful, open layout" is done up in wine-country style, although "noisy" acoustics are a drawback, as are the "expensive" tabs.

PALM SPRINGS/
SANTA BARBARA
RESTAURANT
DIRECTORY

Palm Springs & Environs

<table>
<tr><td colspan="2">

TOP FOOD

26   Wally's Desert | *Continental*
     Le Vallauris | *French/Med.*
     Cuistot | *Cal./French*
     Sirocco | *Italian*
     Jillian's | *Continental*

TOP DECOR

27   Le Vallauris
     Cuistot
26   Wally's Desert
24   Copley's
     Jillian's

</td><td colspan="2">

TOP SERVICE

26   Wally's Desert
     Sirocco
     Le Vallauris
25   Copley's
     Cuistot

BEST BUYS

1. In-N-Out
2. Original Pancake
3. Johnny Rockets
4. Native Foods
5. Ruby's

</td></tr>
</table>

Adobe Grill *Mexican*

| 16 | 19 | 16 | $37 |

La Quinta | La Quinta Resort & Club | 49-499 Eisenhower Dr. (bet. Fernando & 50th Aves.) | 760-564-5725 | www.laquintaresort.com

Pretty "patio dining" is the main "attraction" at this midpriced Mexican on the grounds of the lush '20s-era La Quinta Resort & Club (once an Old Hollywood hideaway), where south-of-the-border standards are accompanied by nightly mariachis and margaritas; for "hotel" fare, it's "better-than-usual", and the hacienda decor and margaritas served in hand-blown glassware enhance the mood.

Arnold Palmer's *Steak*

| 21 | 24 | 21 | $48 |

La Quinta | 78164 Ave. 52 (Washington St.) | 760-771-4653 | www.arnoldpalmers.net

Expect an "older crowd" "with a martini in hand" at this La Quinta steakhouse owned by the namesake legend and frequented for its "reliable" chops and service as well as its nine-hole green; with so much "fabulous memorabilia" around, "it's like visiting the Hall of Fame", but the real draw is the nightly "entertainment in the bar", which extends to "much more than the music."

Bellini *Italian*

| - | - | - | E |

Palm Desert | 73111 El Paseo (bet. Ocotillo Dr. & Sage Ln.) | 760-341-2626
Named for the famed Venetian cocktail, this "chef-owned establishment" in Palm Desert delivers classic Italian cuisine and a "welcoming atmosphere" in a modern trattoria setup with tapestries and textured walls; insiders insist it's "wonderful" all around, but it still flies a bit under the radar, perhaps because of pricey tabs and limited hours; N.B. closed July–August.

Billy Reed's *American*

| 16 | 14 | 20 | $26 |

Palm Springs | 1800 N. Palm Canyon Dr. (Vista Chino) | 760-325-1946 | www.billyreedspalmsprings.com

"Palm Springs snowbirds" and "families of all ages" get their "sugar, grease and caffeine" fix at this "homey" coffee-shop "staple"; the Victorian-inspired decor may "look like grandma's house in the Midwest" and the "simple" fare doesn't rise above "mediocre", but "daily dinner specials", "generous portions" and "pleasant" service keep 'em coming back.

BJ's *Pub Food*
17 | 16 | 17 | $21

Corona | Crossings at Corona | 2520 Tuscany St. (bet. Cajalco Rd. & Grand Oaks) | 951-271-3610

Rancho Cucamonga | 11520 Fourth St. (bet. Pittsburgh Ave. & Richmond Pl.) | 909-581-6750

San Bernardino | 1045 E. Harriman Pl. (Tippecanoe Ave.) | 909-380-7100

Temecula | 26500 Ynez Rd. (Overland Dr.) | 951-252-8370

www.bjsbrewhouse.com

Additional locations throughout Southern California

See review in Los Angeles Directory.

Cafe des Beaux-Arts *French*
21 | 18 | 21 | $38

Palm Desert | 73640 El Paseo (Larkspur Ln.) | 760-346-0669 | www.cafedesbeauxarts.com

"*Très bon*" declare devotees of this Palm Desert "standard", a longtime lunch favorite on El Paseo whose "efficient" staff delivers "well-prepared, traditional" Gallic bistro classics "without pretense"; the "quaint, old-style French cafe" decor is "nothing fancy", but "reasonable prices for the location" and "streetside seating" guaranteeing primo "people-watching" boost the appeal; it's closed July–August.

California Pizza Kitchen *Pizza*
18 | 14 | 17 | $22

Rancho Cucamonga | Victoria Gdns. | 12517 N. Main St. (bet. Kew & Monet Aves.) | 909-899-8611

Riverside | Riverside Plaza | 3540 Riverside Plaza Dr. (Riverside Ave.) | 951-680-9362

Temecula | Promenade in Temecula | 40820 Winchester Rd. (bet. Margarita & Ynez Rds.) | 951-296-0575

Palm Desert | Shops at El Paseo | 73080 El Paseo (bet. Hwy. 74 & Ocotillo Dr.) | 760-776-5036

Palm Springs | Desert Fashion Plaza | 123 N. Palm Canyon Dr. (bet. Amado Rd. & Tahquitz Canyon Way) | 760-322-6075

www.cpk.com

Additional locations throughout Southern California

See review in Los Angeles Directory.

Castaway *Californian*
17 | 22 | 19 | $37

San Bernardino | 670 Kendall Dr. (H St.) | 909-881-1502 | www.castawayrestaurant.com

See review in Los Angeles Directory.

Castelli's *Italian*
21 | 16 | 20 | $49

Palm Desert | 73098 Hwy. 111 (Monterey Ave.) | 760-773-3365 | www.castellis.cc

An "old-style" Palm Desert "favorite" that feels like a place the "Rat Pack" might've dined at, this "high-priced" Italian is appreciated for its "personable" service and "decent" classics offered in "enormous" servings; it's often "crowded" and "noisy", and could use a "freshen-up", but given the "unmatched people-watching" and nightly "piano player in the bar", most don't mind; P.S. limited hours in July and August.

Cheeky's *American*
∇ 26 | 17 | 20 | $20

Palm Springs | 622 N. Palm Canyon Dr. (bet. Grande Valmonte & Tamarisk Rd.) | 760-327-7595 | www.cheekysps.com

A breakfast and lunch "delight" in the desert, this "hip", affordable Palm Springs New American dishes up "excellent", "fresh, sometimes daring" fare ("don't miss the bacon flights") delivered by a "friendly" staff; though you can "watch the world go by from the inviting patio", seating inside its small, "modern" space is limited, so "prepare to wait in line."

☑ Cheesecake Factory *American*   19 | 18 | 19 | $27

Rancho Cucamonga | Victoria Gdns. | 12379 N. Main St. (bet. Monet & Monticello Aves.) | 909-463-3011
Rancho Mirage | The River | 71800 Hwy. 111 (Rancho Las Palmas Dr.) | 760-404-1400
www.thecheesecakefactory.com
Additional locations throughout Southern California
See review in Los Angeles Directory.

Chez Pierre *French*   ▽ 27 | 19 | 25 | $49

Palm Desert | 44250 Town Center Way (Fred Waring Dr.) | 760-346-1818 | www.chezpierrebistro.com

Those seeking frogs' legs Provençal and other "*magnifique*" Country French classics are "rewarded" at this Palm Desert "gem", where the "extraordinarily talented chef" is "hands-on" yet makes time to "chat with customers"; despite the "hidden" "strip-mall" location, its "convivial" setting manages to be both "casual" and "classy" – with "posh" prices to match (though the $30 prix fixe is a deal).

Chop House *Steak*   23 | 20 | 23 | $53

Palm Desert | 74040 Hwy. 111 (Portola Ave.) | 760-779-9888
Palm Springs | 262 S. Palm Canyon Dr. (bet. Arenas & Baristo Rds.) | 760-320-4500
www.restaurantsofpalmsprings.com

With its "melt-in-your-mouth" beef, "cozy", quiet, "clublike" environs and "impeccable" service, supporters say you "can't go wrong" at this Palm Springs–Palm Desert steakhouse twosome; a few feel it falls short of what you might "expect for the price", but to the majority it offers "excellent value", all things considered.

Citron *Californian*   ▽ 22 | 22 | 21 | $61

Palm Springs | Viceroy Palm Springs | 415 S. Belardo Rd. (Ramon Rd.) | 760-320-4117 | www.viceroypalmsprings.com

"Feel like a movie star while dining poolside under chic striped umbrellas" at this "small", "hip" Californian "hot spot" with a "big-city vibe" situated in the "boutique" Viceroy Palm Springs hotel; though some gripe that the "precious portions" are "expensive" and served up with a "side of snooty", most call the "seasonal" fare "tops" and like the "cool bar."

Citrus City Grille *Californian*   23 | 19 | 21 | $33

Corona | 2765 Lakeshore Dr. (Temescal Canyon Rd.) | 951-277-2888
Riverside | Riverside Plaza | 3555 Riverside Plaza Dr. (Riverside Ave.) | 951-274-9099
www.citruscitygrille.com

Daily specials from the "carefully designed" Californian menu are "fresh and tasty" at this affordable "neighborhood" mini-chain with Corona and Riverside offshoots; a casual, "relaxed" mood prevails with "friendly, dependable" service, and though naysayers find the "ambiance lacking", patio seating strikes the right note on a nice day.

Claim Jumper *American* | 18 | 17 | 19 | $26 |

Corona | 380 McKinley St. (Promenade Ave.) | 951-735-6567
Rancho Cucamonga | 12499 Foothill Blvd. (I-15) | 909-899-8022
San Bernardino | 1905 S. Commercenter E. (Hospitality Ln.) | 909-383-1818
www.claimjumper.com
See review in Los Angeles Directory.

Copley's on Palm Canyon *American* | 25 | 24 | 25 | $57 |

Palm Springs | 621 N. Palm Canyon Dr. (bet. Alejo & Tamarisk Rds.) |
760-327-9555 | www.copleyspalmsprings.com
"Not to be missed for a special night out", this pricey Palm Springs
"jewel in the desert" set in a "romantic" "period hacienda" (formerly
Cary Grant's residence) has "its own herb garden" and offers "fantastic, gourmet" New American cuisine courtesy of chef Andrew Copley;
a "heavenly patio" and excellent service add to the pricey "pleasure"
(except from mid-July until September, when it's closed).

Cork Tree *Californian* | 23 | 22 | 22 | $52 |

Palm Desert | Desert Springs Mktpl. | 74950 Country Club Dr. (Cook St.) |
760-779-0123 | www.thecorktree.com
"Excellent", "creative" yet "approachable" Californian cuisine draws
surveyors to this Palm Desert "gem" "tucked in a corner of a shopping plaza"; locals overlook pricey tabs while "meeting for drinks
in the cozy bar or dining on the patio" and being tended to by
"professional", "personable servers."

☑ Cuistot Ⓜ *Californian/French* | 26 | 27 | 25 | $67 |

Palm Desert | 72595 El Paseo (Hwy. 111) | 760-340-1000 |
www.cuistotrestaurant.com
"Extraordinary" Cal-French dishes and "spectacular surroundings",
including a patio with an outdoor fireplace, make this "elegant" Palm
Desert "favorite" a "destination that never disappoints"; the service is
"top-notch", as are the "sommelier's excellent recommendations",
but given the prices, it's all "best enjoyed on an expense account, except for the seasonal prix fixe."

Daily Grill *American* | 19 | 17 | 20 | $30 |

Palm Desert | 73061 El Paseo (Monterey Ave.) | 760-779-9911 |
www.dailygrill.com
See review in Los Angeles Directory.

Davey's Hideaway *Seafood/Steak* | ▽ 21 | 18 | 23 | $39 |

Palm Springs | 292 E. Palm Canyon Dr. (Via Entrada) | 760-320-4480
Recalling "supper clubs of days gone by", this Palm Springs "throwback" lures locals with a "professional" yet "friendly" staff and a menu
of prime rib, "loaded baked potatoes" and other surf 'n' turf favorites;
a "cozy, midcentury" look with circular booths and a pianist "tickling
the ivories in the corner" nightly completes the package nostalgists
dub a "tremendous value."

Europa Ⓜ *Continental* | ▽ 26 | 25 | 27 | $46 |

Palm Springs | Villa Royale Inn | 1620 S. Indian Trail (Palm Canyon Dr.) |
760-327-2314 | www.villaroyale.com
Set in Palm Springs' "gorgeous" Villa Royale Inn, this "old-world", "romantic" "hideaway" in a "vintage building" with a fireplace and a pool-

side patio offers "fabulous albeit pricey" Continental cuisine; "spot-or
service" simply ups the appeal.

Falls, The *Steak*

▽ 21 | 22 | 21 | $53

Palm Springs | Mercado Plaza | 155 S. Palm Canyon Dr., 2nd fl. (Arenas Rd.) |
760-416-8664 | www.thefallsrestaurants.com

Watch the "moon rise between the palms" and the "hustle and bustle
of Palm Canyon Drive" from the balcony seating at this steakhouse
"overlooking Palm Springs" or sit inside for a view of the waterfall over
the bar; while some call the fare "excellent" and others claim it's overpriced, the "half-off-the-bar-menu happy hour" is a real "deal."

⚡ Fleming's Prime Steakhouse & Wine Bar *Steak*

24 | 23 | 24 | $58

Rancho Cucamonga | Victoria Gdns. | 7905 Monet Ave. (bet. Foothill Blvd. &
Victoria Gardens Ln.) | 909-463-0416
Rancho Mirage | The River | 71800 Hwy. 111 (Rancho Las Palmas Dr.) |
760-776-6685
www.flemingssteakhouse.com
See review in Los Angeles Directory.

Gyu-Kaku *Japanese*

20 | 17 | 18 | $34

Rancho Cucamonga | Victoria Gdns. | 7893 Monet Ave. (Foothill Blvd.) |
909-899-4748 | www.gyu-kaku.com
See review in Los Angeles Directory.

Hog's Breath Inn *American*

18 | 18 | 16 | $43

La Quinta | Old Town La Quinta | 78-065 Main St. (Calle Tampico) |
760-564-5556 | www.hogsbreathinnlaquinta.com

"Covered with Clint posters" (and co-owned by Mr. Eastwood), this
"quaint Old Town" La Quinta offshoot of the Carmel original "appeals to fans" of the actor-director while serving "reliable" if "unexcit-
ing" American fare; supporters favor "happy hours" and "live music"
by a pianist Wednesday–Sunday, but detractors quip it just didn't
"make my day."

⚡ In-N-Out Burger ● *Burgers*

24 | 11 | 20 | $9

Corona | 2305 Compton Ave. (bet. Ontario Ave. & Taber St.)
Corona | 450 Auto Center Dr. (bet. Rte. 91 & Wardlow Rd.)
Riverside | 6634 Clay St. (Van Buren Blvd.)
Riverside | 72265 Varner Rd. (Ramon Rd.)
Riverside | 7467 Indiana Ave. (Madison St.)
800-786-1000 | www.in-n-out.com
Additional locations throughout Southern California
See review in Los Angeles Directory.

Islands *American*

17 | 16 | 18 | $18

Chino | 3962 Grand Ave. (Pipeline Ave.) | 909-591-6056
Corona | 1295 Magnolia Ave. (Montecito Dr.) | 951-279-7724
Rancho Cucamonga | 11425 Foothill Blvd. (Milliken Ave.) | 909-944-6661
Riverside | Riverside Plaza | 3645 Central Ave. (bet. Magnolia &
Riverside Aves.) | 951-782-7471
Palm Desert | Desert Crossing Shopping Ctr. | 72-353 Hwy. 111
(Desert Crossing) | 760-346-4007
www.islandsrestaurants.com
Additional locations throughout Southern California
See review in Los Angeles Directory.

Jillian's ☒ *Continental*

26 | 24 | 24 | \$63

alm Desert | 74155 El Paseo (Hwy. 111) | 760-776-8242 |
www.jilliansfinedining.com

"Classy" through and through, this formal Palm Desert venue stands
out for its "consistently wonderful" Continental cuisine and "beauti-
ul" hacienda-home setting graced by a "charming" courtyard "that
would put even Scrooge in a romantic mood"; the staff "treats every-
ne like a special guest", but given the "expensive" bills and the jacket-
suggested policy, some suggest saving this site for "special evenings."

Johannes *Eclectic*

26 | 18 | 23 | \$54

alm Springs | 196 S. Indian Canyon Dr. (Arenas Rd.) | 760-778-0017 |
www.johannesrestaurants.com

"Austrian meets Asian" at this "brilliant" Eclectic in Palm Springs
helmed by "talented" chef-owner Johannes Bacher, whose "food is at
he top of its game"; while "simple", the "contemporary" setting is
nevertheless "comfortable" and colorful, making the overall package –
which includes an "intriguing wine list" that's "half-bottle heaven" –
another of the desert's finest."

ohn Henry's ☒ *Eclectic/French*

20 | 14 | 21 | \$34

Palm Springs | 1785 E. Tahquitz Canyon Way (Sunrise Way) | 760-327-7667
"Prices that are beyond reasonable" mean "it's hard to get a reservation" at this Palm Springs "hangout" serving "large portions" of "varied" Eclectic-French fare; "quantity trumps quality" quibblers cry, but
try telling that to the "enthusiastic crowd of locals" who "pack the patio nightly"; P.S. it's closed June–October.

Johnny Rockets *Burgers*

16 | 15 | 16 | \$14

Rancho Cucamonga | Victoria Gdns. | 7800 Kew Ave. (Main St.) |
909-463-2800 | www.johnnyrockets.com
Additional locations throughout Southern California
See review in Los Angeles Directory.

Kaiser Grille *American*

14 | 16 | 17 | \$37

Palm Springs | 205 S. Palm Canyon Dr. (Arenas Rd.) | 760-323-1003 |
www.restaurantsofpalmsprings.com

The patio provides a perch for "watching the passing parade" at this
"Palm Springs standby" more valued for its "good location" than for
American fare that, while "varied", lacks the "wow factor"; mostly "catering to tourists and early-bird diners", overall it "needs a refresh",
though service is "friendly."

King's Fish House *Seafood*

20 | 18 | 19 | \$34

Corona | 2530 Tuscany Rd. (Calico Rd.) | 951-284-7900
Rancho Cucamonga | Victoria Gdns. | 12427 N. Main St. (Monet Ave.) |
909-803-1280
www.kingsfishhouse.com
See review in Los Angeles Directory.

La Quinta Cliffhouse *American*

19 | 21 | 21 | \$41

La Quinta | 78250 Hwy. 111 (Washington St.) | 760-360-5991 |
www.laquintacliffhouse.com

"Surrounded by the mountains", this New American perched atop
La Quinta's Point Happy boasts a "beautiful" backdrop (try for the

FOOD | DECOR | SERVICE | COST

patio "around sunset") along with "decent food" and a "relaxed" ranch-style setting; naturally the tabs can run up, so surveyor who seek "real value" "stick to the bar menu", especially durin the "lively" happy hour.

Las Casuelas *Mexican*

20 | 20 | 20 | $27

Rancho Mirage | 70-050 Hwy. 111 (bet. Country Club & Frank Sinatra Drs.) 760-328-8844 | www.lascasuelasnuevas.com
La Quinta | 78480 Hwy. 111 (Washington St.) | 760-777-7715 | www.lascasuelasquinta.com
Palm Springs | 222 S. Palm Canyon Dr. (Arenas Rd.) | 760-325-2794 www.lascasuelas.com
Palm Springs | 368 N. Palm Canyon Dr. (bet. Alejo & Amado Rds.) | 760-325-3213 | www.lascasuelas.com

Casuelas Café *Mexican*

Palm Desert | 73703 Hwy. 111 (San Luis Rey Ave.) | 760-568-0011 www.casuelascafe.com

These "popular", family-owned "institutions" charm compadres wit "straightforward", "inexpensive" Mexican fare and "margs" that "pac a punch"; "lively" vibes and "inviting" patios also contribute to the "long-running success", though sticklers snub "standard-issue" eatin *para las turistas."*

La Spiga Ristorante Italiano 🅢 *Italian*

▽ 24 | 26 | 24 | $69

Palm Desert | 72557 Hwy. 111 (El Paseo) | 760-340-9318 | www.laspigapalmdesert.com

Rose gardens, fruit trees and three gazebos grace the "beautifu grounds" of this "gorgeous" Palm Desert Italian, designed to replicat a Tuscan villa and presided over by "a lovely husband-and-wife" che owner team; the menu follows through with "wonderful", "hand crafted" pasta and meat dishes, but given the "astounding" price some suggest it's best saved for "special occasions."

Le St. Germain *Californian/French*

24 | 24 | 22 | $61

Indian Wells | 74985 Hwy. 111 (Cook St.) | 760-773-6511 | www.lestgermain.com

Have a "fine-dining experience in the desert" at this spacious India Wells Cal-French, which caters to "discerning palates" with "depenc able" cuisine and an "extensive wine list" served by an "attentiv staff"; the "elegant" interior and "lovely", tree-lined patio add a touc of "class", but expect prices to match.

🆉 Le Vallauris *French/Mediterranean*

26 | 27 | 26 | $65

Palm Springs | 385 W. Tahquitz Canyon Way (Museum Dr.) | 760-325-5059 | www.levallauris.com

"Delightful" alfresco dining is the raison d'être of this "elegant" "oasis voted No. 1 for Decor and the Most Popular in Palm Springs thanks part to its "sublime" patio "shaded with great old trees" that a "magically lit at night"; the "consistently wonderful" French Mediterranean food and "personal service" "set the standard" fc these parts, and though you may need to "win the lotto" to pay, th "treat" is "worth every dollar."

🆉 LG's Prime Steakhouse *Steak*

23 | 22 | 22 | $62

La Quinta | 78525 Hwy. 111 (Washington St.) | 760-771-9911
Palm Desert | 74225 Hwy. 111 (El Paseo) | 760-779-9799

ontinued)

G's Prime Steakhouse

alm Springs | 255 S. Palm Canyon Dr. (bet. Arenas & Baristo Rds.) |
60-416-1779
ww.lgsprimesteakhouse.com

oachella Valley meat mavens "roll out" of this "family-owned" chop-
ouse trio "content" after gorging on "excellent steaks" and Caesar
alad prepared "tableside" ("a must"); they're "classy" but "comfort-
ole" with "top-notch service", and though beefs arise over the "pre-
ium prices", "you get what you pay for."

ord Fletcher's 🖾Ⓜ *Continental* ∇ 21 | 17 | 20 | $40

ancho Mirage | 70385 Hwy. 111 (Country Club Dr.) | 760-328-1161 |
ww.lordfletcher.com

ancho Miragers tout the "generous" helpings of "enjoyable"
ontinental grub (e.g. "reliable prime rib") at this '60s-era British pub
throwback", a multiroom jumble of "very English" art and antiques;
ome say it "needs to update", but it remains an "old standard."

ucille's Smokehouse Bar-B-Que *BBQ* 22 | 18 | 19 | $28

ancho Cucamonga | Victoria Gdns. | 12624 N. Main St. (Foothill Blvd.) |
09-463-7427 | www.lucillesbbq.com
ee review in Los Angeles Directory.

Matchbox *American/Pizza* ∇ 23 | 20 | 19 | $30

alm Springs | Mercado Plaza | 155 S. Palm Canyon Dr., 2nd fl.
Arenas Rd.) | 760-778-6000 | www.matchboxpalmsprings.com

Highly addictive" wood-fired pizza leads the "something-for-everyone"
ineup at this Palm Springs New American, a "solid choice" for "casual"
ites in "an upstairs setting" with a "refreshing" patio "overlooking
ruisy Palm Canyon Drive"; "reasonable" prices and "upbeat" atmo-
pherics strike the fancy of "fun-loving" "tourists and locals" alike.

Mel's Drive-In *Diner* 16 | 16 | 16 | $18

Rancho Cucamonga | 11550 Fourth St. (Richmond St.) | 909-484-9100 |
www.melsdrive-in.com
See review in Los Angeles Directory.

Melvyn's Restaurant & Lounge *Continental* ∇ 18 | 21 | 21 | $49

Palm Springs | Ingleside Inn | 200 W. Ramon Rd. (Palm Canyon Dr.) |
760-325-2323 | www.inglesideinn.com

A "blast from the past", this '70s "throwback" in the "quaint", Spanish-
style Ingleside Inn recalls "old Palm Springs" and a time "when movie
stars hung out here", offering "civilized" service from "tuxedoed" waiters
and "standard" Continental fare like veal and pepper steak; the lounge's
nightly piano and "intimate dance floor" are a sentimental "bonus."

Mimi's Cafe *Diner* 17 | 17 | 18 | $21

Chino | 3890 Grand Ave. (Rosewell Ave.) | 909-465-1595
Corona | 2230 Griffin Way (McKinley St.) | 951-734-2073
Rancho Cucamonga | 10909 Foothill Blvd. (Spruce Ave.) | 909-948-1130
Rancho Mirage | 71861 Hwy. 111 (Bob Hope Dr.) | 760-836-3905
La Quinta | 79765 Hwy. 111 (Jefferson St.) | 760-775-4470
www.mimiscafe.com
Additional locations throughout Southern California
See review in Los Angeles Directory.

	FOOD	DECOR	SERVICE	COST

Mister Parker's ☑ French
— | — | — | E

Palm Springs | Parker Palm Springs | 4200 E. Palm Canyon Dr. (Cherokee Way) | 760-321-4629 | www.misterparkers.com

This "trendy" "hideout for the entertainment crowd" in the Parke Palm Springs resort boasts an "amazingly hip" Jonathan Adler desig blinged out with mirrored ceilings, kitschy art and a white baby gran the familiar French fare will set you back "a lot of bucks", but it's "fu if you're in the mood" for "starlets" and a "scene."

Morton's The Steakhouse Steak
24 | 22 | 24 | \$65

Palm Desert | Desert Springs Mktpl. | 74880 Country Club Dr. (Cook St.) | 760-340-6865 | www.mortons.com
See review in Los Angeles Directory.

☑ Native Foods Californian/Eclectic
23 | 12 | 19 | \$18

Palm Desert | 73890 El Paseo (Portola Ave.) | 760-836-9396
Palm Springs | 1775 E. Palm Canyon Dr. (Sunrise Way) | 760-416-0070
www.nativefoods.com
See review in Los Angeles Directory.

Okura Robata Grill & Sushi Bar Japanese
▽ 24 | 22 | 23 | \$46

La Quinta | Point Happy Plaza | 78370 Hwy. 111 (Washington St.) | 760-564-5820
Palm Springs | 105 S. Palm Canyon Dr. (Tahquitz Canyon Way) | 760-327-1333
www.okurasushi.com

Sushi's scarce in the desert, so these contemporary twins in La Quint and Palm Springs fill the void with "excellent" takes on Japanes cooking – from "terrific" raw items to Kobe beef – all chased dow with saketinis; true, there may be "lots of other places that offe better value", but the fact that they're "reliable" counts a lot in th neck of the woods.

☑ Original Pancake House American
22 | 12 | 18 | \$15

Temecula | 41377 Margarita Rd. (Winchester Rd.) | 951-296-9016 | www.originalpancakehouse.com
See review in Los Angeles Directory.

Outback Steakhouse Steak
18 | 16 | 19 | \$29

Corona | 151 McKinley St. (Sampson Ave.) | 951-273-1336
San Bernardino | 620 E. Hospitality Ln. (Waterman Ave.) | 909-890-0061
Temecula | 40275 Winchester Rd. (Margarita Rd.) | 951-719-3700
Upland | 530 N. Mountain Ave. (Arrow Hwy.) | 909-931-1050
Palm Desert | Waring Plaza | 72220 Hwy. 111 (Fred Waring Dr.) | 760-779-9068
www.outback.com
Additional locations throughout Southern California
See review in Los Angeles Directory.

Pacifica Seafood Restaurant Seafood
24 | 23 | 23 | \$48

Palm Desert | The Gardens | 73505 El Paseo (bet. Larkspur Ln. & San Pablo Ave.) | 760-674-8666 | www.pacificaseafoodrestaurant.com
Savvy guests "sit on the balcony" overlooking El Paseo and drink in th panoramic views of the mountains at this "lively" Palm Desert des nation; "simply delicious" "fresh" seafood, "some of the best martin

the desert" and a "convivial" staff help justify the "upmarket"
bs; P.S. check their website for details on "half-price wine" nights
nd prix fixe specials.

.F. Chang's China Bistro *Chinese*   19 | 19 | 18 | $29

ancho Cucamonga | Victoria Gdns. | 7870 Monticello Ave. (Main St.) |
09-463-4095
ancho Mirage | The River | 71800 Hwy. 111 (Rancho Las Palmas Dr.) |
60-776-4912
iverside | Galleria at Tyler | 3475 Tyler St. (bet. Hemet St. & Rte. 91) |
51-689-4020
emecula | 40762 Winchester Rd. (bet. Margarita & Ynez Rds.) |
51-296-6700
ww.pfchangs.com
ee review in Los Angeles Directory.

icanha Churrascaria *Brazilian*   21 | 15 | 20 | $38

athedral City | 68-510 Hwy. 111 (Cathedral Canyon Dr.) | 760-328-1818 |
ww.picanharestaurant.com
ee review in Los Angeles Directory.

urple Palm, The *Mediterranean*   - | - | - | E

alm Springs | Colony Palms Hotel | 572 N. Indian Canyon Dr. (Via Colusa) |
60-969-1818 | www.colonypalmshotel.com
rank and Ava would have loved" this luxuriously "retro" "find" in the
nic Colony Palms Hotel set in "elegant" Moroccan-style digs over-
oking the pool; it serves a "surprising" Med menu made up of small
nd more substantial plates, and the upper-end pricing qualifies it as
"special place for a special meal."

istorante Mamma Gina *Italian*   23 | 21 | 24 | $47

alm Desert | 73705 El Paseo (bet. Larkspur Ln. & San Luis Rey Ave.) |
60-568-9898 | www.mammagina.com
Palm Desert "classic", this "long-established" Italian with a twin in
uscany delivers "delicious" Northern-style cuisine in an "elegant"
etting that evokes "the past"; maybe it's "not always exciting" (and
ot cheap either), but the service from "old-time waiters" is "topotch" so it "shines" for a "special occasion."

istorante Tuscany *Italian*   ▽ 25 | 23 | 24 | $67

alm Desert | JW Marriott Desert Springs | 74855 Country Club Dr.
Cook St.) | 760-341-1839 | www.desertspringsresort.com
n "unexpected" "gem" tucked into the JW Marriott Desert Springs,
is Northern Italian provides "excellent" cuisine and "wonderful ser-
ice" in a muraled setting enhanced by lake views; indeed, it's pricey,
ut that's ok with supporters who swear it "never misses."

omano's Macaroni Grill *Italian*   17 | 17 | 18 | $24

orona | 3591 Grand Oaks (Cajalco Rd.) | 951-278-0999
emecula | 41221A Margarita Rd. (General Kearny Rd.) | 951-296-0700
ww.macaronigrill.com
ee review in Los Angeles Directory.

Roy's *Hawaiian*   24 | 22 | 23 | $49

ancho Mirage | 71959 Hwy. 111 (Bob Hope Dr.) | 760-340-9044 |
ww.roysrestaurant.com
ee review in Los Angeles Directory.

	FOOD	DECOR	SERVICE	COST

Ruby's *Diner*   17 | 17 | 18 | $17

Rancho Mirage | 71885 Hwy. 111 (Bob Hope Dr.) | 760-836-0788
Riverside | Galleria at Tyler | 1298 Galleria at Tyler (Magnolia Ave.) |
951-359-7829
Palm Springs | 155 S. Palm Canyon Dr. (Arenas Rd.) |
760-406-7829
www.rubys.com
See review in Los Angeles Directory.

☒ Ruth's Chris Steak House *Steak*   25 | 22 | 24 | $62

Palm Desert | 74-740 Hwy. 111 (bet. Cook St. & Portola Ave.) |
760-779-1998 | www.ruthschris.com
See review in Los Angeles Directory.

Shame on the Moon *American*   21 | 20 | 23 | $46

Rancho Mirage | 69950 Frank Sinatra Dr. (bet. Da Vall Dr. & Hwy. 111)
760-324-5515 | www.shameonthemoon.com
A "warm welcome" sets the tone at this "campy" Rancho Mirage "throw
back" delivering "classic retro" American fare like liver and onions an
"huge martinis" to an "eclectic" crowd; prices are "fair", and if it's "
little noisy" in the main dining room, those in-the-know request a sea
on the porch for quieter dining; P.S. reservations recommended.

☒ Sirocco *Italian*   26 | 24 | 26 | $62

Indian Wells | Renaissance Esmeralda Resort & Spa |
44-400 Indian Wells Ln. (Hwy. 111) | 760-773-4444 |
www.renaissanceesmeralda.com
"Still as stunning as ever", this longtime "jewel" in the Renaissanc
Esmeralda Resort in Indian Wells impresses guests with "beautiful
views of the Santa Rosa mountains and "sublime" Northern Italian cu
sine that's "not your typical hotel restaurant" fare; "excellent"
"knowledgeable" service qualifies it as "one of the best in the desert"
although "you may need a second mortgage" to foot the bill; N.B. th
Decor score does not reflect a recent spruce-up.

TAPS Fish House & Brewery *American/Seafood*   23 | 22 | 21 | $36

Corona | Promenade Shops at Dos Lagos | 2745 Lakeshore Dr.
(Temescal Canyon Rd.) | 951-277-5800 | www.tapsbrea.com
"Dependable" is the word on this midpriced Traditional American sea
food chain churning out "excellent", "fresh" food "with Cajun touches
in "bustling" quarters with an oyster bar; brew buffs come for th
"good-value" happy hours and "award-winning" lagers, while Sunday
bring the crowds for a "spectacular" brunch buffet that "will have yo
reaching for your Lipitor."

Tommy Bahama's Tropical Café *Caribbean*   22 | 23 | 20 | $40

Palm Desert | The Gardens | 73595 El Paseo (bet. Larkspur Ln. &
San Pablo Ave.) | 760-836-0188 | www.tommybahama.com
There's a real "beachy feel" to these "themed" chain links around LA
and Orange County, where the "fresh" Caribbean flavors and "fes
tive", "tropical-inspired" settings are "like a mini-vacation without th
luggage"; though detractors decry the "kitschy", "touristy" vibe, th
"beautifully planted" patios with live steel drums are certainly pleas
ant for sipping a "strong" rum drink, and many like perusing th
attached retail stores.

	FOOD	DECOR	SERVICE	COST

Tropicale Restaurant & Coral Seas Lounge *Eclectic*

-	-	-	M

Palm Springs | 330 E. Amado Rd. (bet. Cll Encilia & Indian Canyon Dr.) | 760-866-1952 | www.thetropicale.com

Palm Springs lounge lizards laud this "spectacular" "'50s" "throwback", "lovingly designed" "hot spot" where "stunning" "retro" decor and a "fantastic" patio set the "scene" for wide-ranging Eclectic eats that'll "bring you back for more"; fashionable types sporting "trendy glasses and funky shoes" raise a designer drink to "the Rat Pack experience."

Wally's Desert Turtle *Continental*

26	26	26	$80

Rancho Mirage | 71775 Hwy. 111 (Rancho Las Palmas Dr.) | 760-568-9321 | www.wallys-desert-turtle.com

For a "dress-up night on the town", devotees "drop big bucks" at this Rancho Mirage "classic" that elevates desert dining with "outstanding" old-fashioned Continental cuisine" and "impeccable" treatment – indeed, it's ranked tops for Food and Service in Palm Springs; perhaps the "formal" dining room's a tad "stuffy" ("it feels like the kind of place Dick Cheney would like"), but its following finds it "worth every penny" for a "special" evening.

Wood Ranch BBQ & Grill *BBQ*

21	18	20	$28

Corona | Promenade Shops at Dos Lagos | 2785 Lakeshore Dr. (Temescal Canyon Rd.) | 951-667-4200 | www.woodranch.com

See review in Los Angeles Directory.

Yard House *American*

18	17	17	$27

Rancho Cucamonga | Victoria Gdns. | 12473 N. Main St. (bet. Day Creek Blvd. & Victoria Gardens Ln.) | 909-646-7116 ●

Rancho Mirage | 71800 Hwy. 111 (Rancho Las Palmas Dr.) | 760-779-1415

Riverside | Galleria at Tyler | 3775 Tyler St. (bet. Magnolia Ave. & Riverside Frwy.) | 951-688-9273 ●

NEW Temecula | The Promenade | 40770 Winchester Rd. (bet. Margarita & Ynez Rds.) | 951-296-3116 ●

www.yardhouse.com

See review in Los Angeles Directory.

Zin *American/French*

22	16	20	$46

Palm Springs | 198 S. Palm Canyon Dr. (Arenas Rd.) | 760-322-6300 | www.zinamericanbistro.com

A "dependable" bet "right on the strip in Palm Springs", this "popular" bistro serves "steady" American-French cooking that gets a boost from an "outstanding" wine list; some wish it were more "exciting", but with a reputation for "good value", as well as a cosmopolitan, art-filled dining room, it remains a valley "favorite."

Zip Fusion *Japanese*

19	15	18	$25

Corona | Crossings at Corona | 2560 Tuscany St. (Grand Oaks) | 951-272-2177 | www.zipfusion.com

See review in Los Angeles Directory.

Santa Barbara & Environs

TOP FOOD

28 Downey's | Cal./French
27 Ca' Dario | Italian
    Trattoria Grappolo | Italian
    Olio e Limone | Italian
26 Arigato | Japanese

TOP DECOR

28 Stonehouse
25 Bella Vista
24 Lucky's
    Cold Spring Tavern
    Coast

TOP SERVICE

28 Downey's
    Stonehouse
25 bouchon
    Louie's
    Bella Vista

BEST BUYS

1. In-N-Out
2. La Super-Rica
3. Cajun Kitchen
4. Los Arroyos
5. China Pavilion

All India Cafe *Indian*   21 | 14 | 19 | $25

Santa Barbara | 431 State St. (bet. Gutierrez & Haley Sts.) | 805-882-1000
www.allindiacafe.com
See review in Los Angeles Directory.

Arigato Sushi *Japanese*   26 | 18 | 22 | $42

Santa Barbara | 1225 State St. (bet. Anapamu & Victoria Sts.) |
805-965-6074 | www.arigatosantabarbara.com
"Fresh", "rock-star quality" fish gets a creative touch, resulting in "out
standing sushi" at this "no-reservations" Santa Barbara Japanese wher
you'll sit "elbow-to-elbow" in a "bustling" brick-walled room and b
tended by a "friendly" staff; despite "expensive" tabs and a "so noisy yo
can't think" setting, there are long "waits" if you don't "get there early."

Ballard Inn & Restaurant, The 🅼 *French*   26 | 23 | 25 | $66

Ballard | Ballard Inn | 2436 Baseline Ave. (bet. Alamo Pintado &
Refugio Rds.) | 805-688-7770 | www.ballardinn.com
"An elegant haven in the midst of wine country" in Santa Ynez, this "re
laxed getaway" set in a "cozy inn" overlooking the "tiny town" o
Ballard offers a "mind-blowing" blend of French cuisine with "Asia
touches" and "perfect pairings" of local vintages; a "lovely" dinin,
room with a three-sided fireplace and an "expert" staff add to the "ro
mantic" if "expensive" experience.

🖪 Bella Vista *Californian*   24 | 25 | 25 | $59

Montecito | Four Seasons Resort, The Biltmore | 1260 Channel Dr.
(Hill & Olive Mill Rds.) | 805-565-8237 | www.fourseasons.com
"Gorgeous" is the word on this Californian nestled in Montecito'
Biltmore Four Seasons Resort, a "wonderful" source for seasona
wine-country cuisine, with champagne and caviar headlining wha
may be the area's "best Sunday brunch"; "killer ocean views" from th
terrace are matched by near-"perfect service" and a casually "elegant
dining room, which seems even better "if someone else is paying."

Blue Agave ⬤ *Eclectic*   20 | 23 | 21 | $35

Santa Barbara | 20 E. Cota St. (State St.) | 805-899-4694 |
www.blueagavesb.com
Aptly named for the top-shelf tequilas it serves, this late-night bi-leve
Eclectic in Downtown Santa Barbara couples the elixir and other "hearty

rinks" with a globe-trotting menu highlighted by "fresh" organic in-
redients; the "chic", "lounge"-like setting includes "romantic" velvet
booths, a smoking balcony (cigars are sold on-site) and a "lively bar"
abetted by "cheerful, helpful" service.

ouchon *Californian/French*

25 | 23 | 25 | $58

anta Barbara | 9 W. Victoria St. (bet. Chapala & State Sts.) |
05-730-1160 | www.bouchonsantabarbara.com

"Quality" dining is alive and well at this "memorable" Santa Barbara
Cal-French "wine-connoisseur's choice", where the "imaginative",
"always-changing" menu skews toward organic and a "terrific" cellar
grants "access to wonderful local" labels; "informed service" and a
"picturesque" French country setting with a "romantic patio" add to its
allure, though the upscale pricing relegates it to "special occasions."

☑ Brophy Bros.
Clam Bar & Restaurant *Seafood*

21 | 17 | 18 | $29

Santa Barbara | 119 Harbor Way (Shoreline Dr.) | 805-966-4418 |
www.brophybros.com

Fans say the "clam chowda's so good, you'd swear you were in Boston"
but for the location off the Santa Barbara pier at this "elbow-to-elbow",
indoor-outdoor seafooder boasting some of the "freshest fish"
around, as well as a "noisy" bar fueled by "generous drinks"; the sibling "right on the docks" in Ventura has the same "casual" service and
"ample portions" at "reasonable prices" – just watch out for the errant
"seagull making a bid for your bread."

Brothers Restaurant at
Mattei's Tavern *American*

25 | 22 | 22 | $49

Los Olivos | 2350 Railway Ave. (Foxen Canyon Rd.) | 805-688-4820 |
www.matteistavern.com

The "cowboy meets *The Galloping Gourmet*" at this Los Olivos American
run by brothers Matt and Jeff Nichols who "pump out" "melt-in-your-
mouth" prime rib, chops and other "outstanding", "hearty" dishes ferried by a "friendly staff"; "strong drinks" make for a "rollicking good
time", but the "beautiful" setting in a "historic" "Old West" tavern
(circa 1886) is the real ace-in-the-hole.

Bucatini *Italian*

▽ 22 | 18 | 21 | $39

Santa Barbara | 436 State St. (bet. Gutierrez & Haley Sts.) |
805-957-4177 | www.bucatini.com

When it comes to "fresh", "simple" pasta and wood-fire pizza, this
Santa Barbara Italian will "knock your socks off" with its "tasty" fare
served on a "great people-watching" patio that's bigger than the restaurant itself; moderate prices and "casual" service are additional reasons locals "love" it for dining alfresco "on warm summer evenings."

☑ Ca' Dario *Italian*

27 | 19 | 22 | $46

Santa Barbara | 37 E. Victoria St. (Anacapa St.) | 805-884-9419 |
www.cadario.net

"Anything grilled is divine" and the rest of the menu is "delectable" at
this "charming" Italian in Santa Barbara known for its "excellent" execution of "simple" pastas, meats and other classics plus a "fantastic"
wine list with many available by the glass; despite an old-world-
inspired setting that's "noisy" and "usually crowded" (resulting in ser-

vice that "sometimes suffers"), it's a local "favorite, so reservation
are a must."

Cafe Buenos Aires *Argentinean*
20 | 23 | 21 | $36

Santa Barbara | 1316 State St. (bet. Arlington Ave. & Victoria St.) |
805-963-0242 | www.cafebuenosaires.com

The "romantic patio" might put your date into a "trance" predict pa
trons of this "beautiful" Argentinean with a view of the "histori
Arlington Theatre" in Santa Barbara that's a "favorite" thanks to it
"fairly priced" "quality" beef dishes and "excellent cocktails"; a "pleas
ant" staff and "live tango dancers weekly" up the appeal.

Cafe del Sol *Californian*
20 | 19 | 22 | $32

Montecito | 30 Los Patos Way (Cabrillo Blvd.) | 805-969-0448

"Smell the ocean breeze" and "watch the sunset" while sippin
"fine margaritas" on the patio at this Spanish-style Californian i
Montecito known for "huge drinks" plus food and service that ar
"sure to please"; "locals love it for good reason" – but most of all fo
the "wonderful" ambiance.

Cajun Kitchen *Cajun*
20 | 12 | 19 | $18

Goleta | 6831 Hollister Ave. (Storke Rd.) | 805-571-1517
Carpinteria | 865 Linden Ave. (bet. 8th & 9th Sts.) | 805-684-6010
Santa Barbara | 1924 De La Vina St. (bet. Mission & Pedregosa Sts.) |
805-687-2062
Santa Barbara | 901 Chapala St. (Cañon Perdido St.) | 805-965-1004
www.cajunkitchensb.com

"Breakfast is the meal to eat" at this Santa Barbara–Ventura chain of
fering "solid coffee-shop fare" and "New Orleans–style" Cajun "com
fort food" dished up in "large servings"; easy-on-the-wallet prices anc
attentive service help offset "hole-in-the-wall" decor; P.S. no dinner.

California Pizza Kitchen *Pizza*
18 | 14 | 17 | $22

Santa Barbara | Paseo Nuevo Mall | 719 Paseo Nuevo (De La Guerra St.)
805-962-4648 | www.cpk.com
Additional locations throughout Southern California
See review in Los Angeles Directory.

Carlitos Café y Cantina *Mexican*
16 | 19 | 17 | $30

Santa Barbara | 1324 State St. (bet. Sola & Victoria Sts.) | 805-962-7117 |
www.carlitos.com

"Perfect for sangria and apps on the patio", this "colorful" Santa
Barbara Mexican boasts a prime location "near the theaters" and live
music Wednesday–Saturday; there are gripes about "slow service"
and standard fare that's merely "pretty good", yet "a little expensive"
for the genre – but the fact that this place has been around for three
decades speaks for itself.

Cava *Pan-Latin*
21 | 20 | 18 | $40

Montecito | 1212 Coast Village Rd. (Olive Mill Rd.) | 805-969-8500 |
www.cavarestaurant.com

A "sunny" patio, "homey" interior and an "interesting" lineup of "well-
done" "upscale" Pan-Latin dishes set apart this midpriced Montecito
cantina, a sister to Carlito's Café; the service is on the "laid-back" side
and the scene can get a little "noisy" at prime times, but out "under the
nighttime sky" all that's easy to forgive.

	FOOD	DECOR	SERVICE	COST

China Palace *Chinese* | 20 | 19 | 21 | $26

Montecito | 1070 Coast Village Rd. (bet. Hermosillo Dr. & Hot Springs Rd.) | 05-565-9380 | www.chinapalacesb.com

China Pavilion *Chinese*

anta Barbara | 1202 Chapala St. (Anapamu St.) | 805-560-6028
www.china-pavilion.com

Light", "well-prepared" dim sum and other Chinese standards
rought to table by a "fast" staff keep 'em coming back to this Santa
arbara–Montecito pair; "pleasantly decorated" digs and affordable
rices are two more reasons they're local "favorites."

Coast *Californian/Seafood* | 21 | 24 | 21 | $45

anta Barbara | Canary Hotel | 31 W. Carrillo St. (Chapala St.) |
05-879-9100 | www.canarysantabarbara.com
ee review in Los Angeles Directory.

Cold Spring Tavern *American* | 21 | 24 | 20 | $33

anta Barbara | 5995 Stagecoach Rd. (Rte. 154) | 805-967-0066 |
www.coldspringtavern.com

Drawing a crowd" arriving by "Harleys" and "limos", this Santa Barbara
original stagecoach depot" dating from 1886 features a "roaring fire-
lace", "antiques" and a "breathtaking" mountain setting as well as "rea-
onably priced" "classic American cuisine" including game; a "friendly
taff" and "local wine list" add to the appeal; P.S. regulars recommend
he "afternoon tri-tip sandwich with entertainment" on Sundays.

⋣ Downey's Ⓜ *Californian/French* | 28 | 23 | 28 | $65

Santa Barbara | 1305 State St. (Victoria St.) | 805-966-5006 |
www.downeyssb.com

t's "foodie heaven" at this "glittering jewel" claiming the No. 1 spot for
ood and Service in Santa Barbara thanks to chef-owner John Downey's
masterfully prepared" Cal-French fare and a "cordial", "thoughtful"
taff led by his wife, Liz; her paintings also adorn a "lovely, understated
oom" that simply adds to the "superb", if costly, "dining experience."

Elements *Californian* | ▽ 21 | 22 | 21 | $43

Santa Barbara | 129 E. Anapamu St. (bet. Anacapa & Santa Barbara Sts.) |
805-884-9218 | www.elementsrestaurantandbar.com

Earth, air, water and fire are the theme behind this Santa Barbara
Californian, where a "wonderful terrace view of the courthouse and
sunken gardens" creates an "attractive" backdrop for the "excellent"
"eclectic" eats and "interesting bar scene"; capable service and "reasonable pricing" further elevate the experience.

El Torito *Mexican* | 15 | 15 | 17 | $21

Santa Barbara | 29 E. Cabrillo Blvd. (State St.) | 805-963-1968 |
www.eltorito.com
Additional locations throughout Southern California
See review in Los Angeles Directory.

Emilio's *Eclectic* | 20 | 17 | 22 | $37

Santa Barbara | 324 W. Cabrillo Blvd. (bet. Bath & Castillo Sts.) |
805-966-4426 | www.emiliosrestaurant.com

'Attentive" servers deliver an "inventive" Eclectic "menu and wine
ist to please all palates", drawing a "loyal crowd of customers" to

this moderately priced Santa Barbara "neighborhood joint"; a "top notch location" across from the ocean contributes to the "inviting ambiance", all prompting fans to say it's "nice to know some places never change."

Enterprise Fish Co. *Seafood*

19 | 17 | 18 | $35

Santa Barbara | 225 State St. (Montecido St.) | 805-962-3313
See review in Los Angeles Directory.

☒ Hitching Post *BBQ*

23 | 16 | 22 | $44

Buellton | 406 E. Rte. 246 (½ mi. east of Rte. 101) | 805-688-0676 | www.hitchingpost2.com
Casmalia | 3325 Point Sal Rd. (Santo Rd.) | 805-937-6151 | www.hitchingpost1.com

"*Sideways*" brought "crowds" and "pop-star fame" to the Buellton out post of these fraternal BBQs, but they keep "oak-grilling" "juicy steaks" just as they "always did", serving them up in a "blue-jeans and-boots" setting alongside their "famous" "house-label Pinot Noir" and other Santa Barbara County wines; the older Casmalia locale, op erating since 1952, is "not on the tourist route" like its sibling, but places like these make allies "proud to be Californian."

Holdren's Steaks & Seafood *Seafood/Steak*

20 | 19 | 20 | $52

Santa Barbara | 512 State St. (Haley St.) | 805-965-3363 | www.holdrens.com
See review in Los Angeles Directory.

Hungry Cat, The *Seafood*

24 | 17 | 20 | $47

Santa Barbara | 1134 Chapala St. (bet. Anapamu & Figueroa Sts.) | 805-884-4701 | www.thehungrycat.com
See review in Los Angeles Directory.

☒ In-N-Out Burger ● *Burgers*

24 | 11 | 20 | $9

Goleta | 4865 Calle Real (Turnpike Rd.) | 800-786-1000 | www.in-n-out.com
Additional locations throughout Southern California
See review in Los Angeles Directory.

Jade ☒Ⓜ *Pacific Rim*

▽ 23 | 15 | 23 | $32

Santa Barbara | 3132 State St. (bet. Calle Palo Colorado & Las Positas Rd.) | 805-563-2007 | www.jadesb.com

"Mostly frequented by the natives" of SB, this "fusion kitchen" run by "fantastic", "caring" chef-owners Dustin and Jeannine Green turns out a "unique" menu of "fairly priced" Pacific Rim cuisine; it's "not in the Downtown area", so it remains a bit of a "sleeper", but that suits locals who "don't want tourists to find it."

☒ La Super-Rica Taqueria ⊅ *Mexican*

25 | 5 | 13 | $15

Santa Barbara | 622 N. Milpas St. (Alphonse St.) | 805-963-4940

"Legendary" as a "Julia Child favorite", this longtime taco stand – and Santa Barbara's Most Popular restaurant – "lives up to" the "hype" according to those who "brave" "lines around the building" to "rel ish" "magnificent tortillas" ("homemade" before your eyes) and "dee lish" fillings that rank with "the best" "for the peso"; just be prepared for service "through a take-out window" and patio seating that "looks like nothing."

	FOOD	DECOR	SERVICE	COST

os Arroyos *Mexican* | 23 | 17 | 20 | $23 |

Montecito | 1280 Coast Village Rd. (Olive Mill Rd.) | 805-969-9059
anta Barbara | 14 W. Figueroa St. (bet. Chapala & State Sts.) |
05-962-5541
www.losarroyos.net
ee review in Los Angeles Directory.

os Olivos Cafe *Californian/Mediterranean* | 24 | 19 | 21 | $37 |

os Olivos | 2879 Grand Ave. (Alamo Pintado Ave.) | 805-688-7265 |
www.losolivoscafe.com

Famous from *Sideways*", this "charming little cottage" in "quaint" Los
Olivos lets "wine country" pilgrims "nosh in between tastings" on
wonderful", "incredibly fresh" Cal-Med fare served by a "friendly"
taff; the "superb" (natch) cellar "showcasing local" vintages makes
or "perfect" pairings, and oenophiles can snag a bottle from the "re-
ail wall" to take home.

ouie's *Californian* | 26 | 21 | 25 | $47 |

anta Barbara | Upham Hotel | 1404 De La Vina St. (Sola St.) |
805-963-7003 | www.louiessb.com

Set in a "lovely" Victorian hotel, this longtime Santa Barbaran matches
a "warm" bistro locale (extending to a wraparound veranda) with "re-
iably delicious" Californian "classics" and "fabulous Central Coast
wines", all served by an "amenable" team; the "quiet" ambiance sig-
nals it's still a "well-kept secret" of locals "in-the-know."

Lucky's *Steak* | 25 | 24 | 25 | $64 |

Montecito | 1279 Coast Village Rd. (Olive Mill Rd.) | 805-565-7540 |
www.luckys-steakhouse.com

"Well-heeled locals", vacationing "celebs" and other fortunate carnivores steer to this "deluxe" Montecito meatery (owned by the founder
of Lucky Brand jeans) to feast on "grand steaks" presented by "terrific"
servers; the "formal" interior and "jumping" "bar scene" up the "glam"
quotient, but "stop by the ATM and withdraw your max" en route.

Marmalade Café *American/Californian* | 18 | 16 | 18 | $26 |

Santa Barbara | La Cumbre Plaza | 3825 State St. (La Cumbra Rd.) |
805-682-5246 | www.marmaladecafe.com
See review in Los Angeles Directory.

Mimosa *French* | ∇ 18 | 15 | 20 | $41 |

Santa Barbara | 2700 De La Vina St. (Alamar Ave.) | 805-682-2272 |
www.mimosasantabarbara.com

Something of "a Santa Barbara secret" sited away from the main
drag, this long-standing bistro is a "laid-back" haven for "traditional
French" fare and service that recall "1960s Paris"; its mature admirers
appreciate the prix fixe dinner "deals", but critics contend it's
"faded" and "dated."

Miró ⊠ 🅜 *Spanish* | - | - | - | VE |

Santa Barbara | Bacara Resort & Spa | 8301 Hollister Ave. (Rte. 101) |
805-968-0100 | www.bacararesort.com

Santa Barbara's rich and "fabulous" dine oceanside amid the sculp-
tures of artist Joan Miró at this Spaniard in the Bacara Resort & Spa,
where the "fantastic" Basque-Catalonian cuisine utilizes "fresh" or-

ganic produce from a nearby ranch; dishes are "beautifully delivered and heightened by a 1,200-label wine cellar, but it's all priced "for very special occasions."

Montecito Cafe *Californian*

23 | 20 | 21 | $37

Montecito | Montecito Inn | 1295 Coast Village Rd. (Olive Mill Rd.) | 805-969-3392 | www.montecitocafe.com

"From teens to 90-year-olds", this "cheerful" Montecito Californian is "everybody's go-to" for a "consistently" "tasty" lineup that's "one of the better values" in the area; "capable" staffers and a "comfortable" setting" in a "quaint" 1920s inn boost the appeal – now if only they could "reduce the noise level."

Olio e Limone *Italian*

27 | 20 | 22 | $60

Santa Barbara | 11 W. Victoria St. (bet. Chapala & State Sts.) | 805-899-2699 | www.olioelimone.com

"Rich, earthy" Sicilian dishes crafted from the "freshest" ingredients are supported by a "superb" wine list at this "top-notch" Santa Barbara Italian set in exceedingly "pleasant" – if "tiny" – quarters; even though service can be a smidge "pretentious", it's a "favorite" in the area and "always packed" accordingly.

Opal *Californian/Eclectic*

21 | 20 | 21 | $42

Santa Barbara | 1325 State St. (Arlington Ave.) | 805-966-9676 | www.opalrestaurantandbar.com

A "well-priced" local mainstay, this 20-year-old "in the heart of Santa Barbara" presents a "diverse", "reliable" Cal-Eclectic menu, though vets suggest you "stick to the simple" stuff; "attentive" staffers, "specialty" drinks and "comfy chairs" keep the mood "relaxing", despite the constant "buzz."

Outback Steakhouse *Steak*

18 | 16 | 19 | $29

Goleta | 5690 Calle Real (bet. Fairview & Patterson Aves.) | 805-964-0599 | www.outback.com
Additional locations throughout Southern California
See review in Los Angeles Directory.

Palace Grill *Cajun/Creole*

20 | 17 | 22 | $38

Santa Barbara | 8 E. Cota St. (State St.) | 805-963-5000 | www.palacegrill.com

This "bustling" Santa Barbara standby earns nods for its gratis cornbread muffins ("mmm") that kick off "festive" feasts of "ersatz" Cajun-Creole eats washed down with "potent" jalapeño martinis; the constant "lines" outside are a downer, but live music and weekend sing-alongs perk things up.

Pane e Vino *Italian*

21 | 20 | 21 | $39

Montecito | Upper Montecito Vill. | 1482 E. Valley Rd. (bet. Santa Angela Ln. & San Ysidro Rd.) | 805-969-9274
See review in Los Angeles Directory.

Piatti *Italian*

20 | 20 | 18 | $36

Montecito | 516 San Ysidro Rd. (Valley Rd.) | 805-969-7520 | www.piatti.com
"Inexpensive for the neighborhood", this Montecito link in a regional chain presents "reliable" renditions of Italian cooking – like "interesting salads and pizzas" – in a "comfy", rustic setting with two "pretty"

atios and a fireplace; "indifferent" service can be a sore spot, though
he experience is usually "enjoyable" for most.

low & Angel Californian/Eclectic
▽ 24 | 26 | 23 | $58

Montecito | San Ysidro Ranch | 900 San Ysidro Ln. (bet. Las Tunas Rd. &
Mountain Dr.) | 805-565-1745 | www.sanysidroranch.com

A "wonderfully cozy" "British pub"–style interior with stone walls and
xposed beams beckons guests to this "informal" dining room at the
osh San Ysidro Ranch in Santa Barbara; it serves a wide-ranging Cal-
clectic menu enhanced by a 1,500-bottle wine list, although bills can
eel "overpriced for what you get."

❸ Ruth's Chris Steak House Steak
25 | 22 | 24 | $62

Santa Barbara | La Cumbre Plaza | 3815 State St. (bet. Hope Ave. &
La Cumbre Rd.) | 805-563-5674 | www.ruthschris.com

See review in Los Angeles Directory.

Sakana Ⓜ Japanese
▽ 27 | 15 | 22 | $43

Montecito | 1046 Coast Village Rd. (Hot Springs Rd.) | 805-565-2014

This "teeny-tiny" Japanese tucked away in a Montecito shopping center delivers well-priced fish that's "among the best" in the area; a "no-
reservations" policy makes for "waits", but acolytes insist it's "oh
so worth it."

Seagrass Ⓜ Seafood
▽ 29 | 26 | 28 | $58

Santa Barbara | 30 E. Ortega St. (bet. Anacapa & State Sts.) |
805-963-1012 | www.seagrassrestaurant.com

For some of "the best seafood in Santa Barbara", locals and visitors
alike angle for a table at this "pricey" boîte serving up "fantastic" fish
and other "wonderful", "local" specialties in a cushy, Cape Cod–
inspired dining room; "top-notch" service "complements" the meal,
and helps justify the tabs.

❼ Stonehouse American
23 | 28 | 28 | $74

Montecito | San Ysidro Ranch | 900 San Ysidro Ln. (bet. Las Tunas Rd. &
Mountain Dr.) | 805-565-1724 | www.sanysidroranch.com

"You couldn't ask for a more romantic setting" swoon those smitten with
this New American in the San Ysidro Ranch, voted No. 1 for Decor in
Santa Barbara thanks to its "enchanting" ambiance in a "beautiful" 19th-
century stone house with a wood-burning fireplace; "over-the-top"
doting service makes it well suited to a "special occasion", although a
minority notes the "food should be better" given the ultrapricey bills.

Tee-Off Seafood/Steak
- | - | - | M

Santa Barbara | Ontare Plaza | 3627 State St. (Ontare Rd.) | 805-687-1616 |
www.teeoffsb.com

"Beef galore" and "big drinks" define this "neighborhood" surf 'n' turf
"joint" in Santa Barbara, a golf-themed "fossil" from the "'50s" locally
known for its "terrific prime rib" and "good value"; it's such a "throwback", cynics smirk "they should really call this place the Time Warp."

❼ Trattoria Grappolo Italian
27 | 19 | 24 | $43

Santa Ynez | 3687 Sagunto St. (Meadowvale Rd.) | 805-688-6899 |
www.trattoriagrappolo.com

"Hidden away in Santa Ynez" wine country, this "little" Italian "treat"
wins raves with "wonderful", ultra-"authentic" cooking served in a

muraled setting with "fuss"-free atmospherics and a few counter seats overlooking the open kitchen; a haven for "memorable dining" that costs "way less" than others in its class, it's "very popular, and you can see why."

Trattoria Mollie ☒ *Italian*   25 | 18 | 21 | $58

Montecito | 1250 Coast Village Rd. (Elizabeth Ln.) | 805-565-9381 | www.tmollie.com

"Lively" chef-owner Mollie Ahlstrand's "exemplary" Northern Italian cooking ("homemade pasta", "perfect" pizzas) "is a revelation" at this upmarket Montecito "charmer", an "Oprah"-approved "haven" for the "beautiful people"; detractors detect "too much attitude", but with "attentive service" and a "nice patio", a majority deems it a "destination."

Tre Lune *Italian*   24 | 21 | 23 | $51

Montecito | 1151 Coast Village Rd. (bet. Butterfly Ln. & Middle Rd.) | 805-969-2646

A "highly favored" spot for Montecito "locals" from "celebs to families", this "smallish" trattoria is known for "excellent Italian" standards as well as "one of the better breakfast menus around"; "you pay for the privilege", but for fans of the "warm" "neighborhood feel" the verdict is unanimously *"bene."*

Tupelo Junction *Southern*   21 | 18 | 20 | $33

Santa Barbara | 1218 State St. (bet. Anapamu & Victoria Sts.) | 805-899-3100 | www.tupelojunction.com

"Leave your diet at the door and indulge" in "down-home" "comfort food" prepared with a "clever" "modern spin" at this Santa Barbara Southerner, favored equally for "unique breakfasts" and "tasty" lunches and dinners; it's "not fine dining", but the "casual", "cozy" atmo gets a lift from "pleasant" servers and live music some nights.

Via Vai *Italian*   23 | 17 | 21 | $34

Montecito | Upper Vill. | 1483 E. Valley Rd. (bet. Santa Angela Ln. & San Ysidro Rd.) | 805-565-9393

"Excellent pizza" is at the forefront of this "casual" Montecito fixture that puts out "super thin–crust" pies and Italian "home cooking" at reasonable rates; it's a real "locals' place" with a "simple" muraled interior and a "beautifully planted patio" dotted with "brightly colored umbrellas" adding to the "charm."

ORANGE COUNTY/
PALM SPRINGS/
SANTA BARBARA
INDEXES

Cuisines 364
Locations 368
Special Features 372

Cuisines

Includes names, locations and Food ratings.

AMERICAN

Arnold Palmer's | **La Quinta/PS**	21
Billy Reed's | **PS**	16
Bistango | **Irvine/OC**	25
BJ's | **multi.**	17
Brothers | **Los Olivos/SB**	25
☑ Charlie Palmer | **Costa Mesa/OC**	22
Cheeky's | **PS**	26
☑ Cheesecake Factory | **multi.**	19
Claim Jumper | **multi.**	18
Cold Spring | **SB**	21
Copley's | **PS**	25
Daily Grill | **Palm Desert/PS**	19
Hog's Breath | **La Quinta/PS**	18
Islands | **multi.**	17
Johnny Rockets | **Rancho Cuca/PS**	16
Kaiser Grille | **PS**	14
La Quinta Cliffhouse | **La Quinta/PS**	19
Matchbox | **PS**	23
Mel's Drive-In | **Rancho Cuca/PS**	16
Mimi's | **multi.**	17
Mr. Stox | **Anaheim/OC**	25
☑ Original Pancake | **Temecula/PS**	22
Park Ave | **Stanton/OC**	26
Ramos Hse. | **San Juan Cap/OC**	25
Ruby's | **multi.**	17
Shame on Moon | **Rancho Mirage/PS**	21
Stonehill | **Dana Pt/OC**	25
☑ Stonehouse | **Montecito/SB**	23
TAPS | **Corona/PS**	23
Watermarc | **Laguna Bch/OC**	24
Wildfish | **Newport Bch/OC**	24
Yard House | **multi.**	18
Zin | **PS**	22

ARGENTINEAN

Cafe Buenos Aires | **SB**	20

ASIAN

☑ Roy's | **multi.**	24

BARBECUE

☑ Hitching Post | **multi.**	23
Lucille's | **Rancho Cuca/PS**	22
Wood Ranch | **Corona/PS**	21

BRAZILIAN

Picanha | **Cathedral City/PS**	21

BURGERS

Hungry Cat | **SB**	24
☑ In-N-Out | **multi.**	24
Islands | **multi.**	17
Johnny Rockets | **Rancho Cuca/PS**	16

CAJUN

Cajun Kitchen | **multi.**	20
Palace Grill | **SB**	20

CALIFORNIAN

☑ Bella Vista | **Montecito/SB**	24
bouchon | **SB**	25
Cafe del Sol | **Montecito/SB**	20
Cafe Zoolu | **Laguna Bch/OC**	26
Castaway | **San Bern/PS**	17
Citron | **PS**	22
Citrus City | **multi.**	23
Coast | **SB**	21
Cork Tree | **Palm Desert/PS**	23
☑ Cuistot | **Palm Desert/PS**	26
☑ Downey's | **SB**	28
Elements | **SB**	21
Leatherby's Café Rouge | **Costa Mesa/OC**	26
Le St. Germain | **Indian Wells/PS**	24
Los Olivos | **Los Olivos/SB**	24
Louie's | **SB**	26
Marmalade | **SB**	18
Montecito | **Montecito/SB**	23
☑ Napa Rose | **Anaheim/OC**	27
☑ Native Foods | **multi.**	23
Nirvana | **multi.**	24
Opal | **SB**	21
☑ Pelican Grill | **Newport Coast/OC**	24
Plow & Angel | **Montecito/SB**	24
NEW Seasons 52 | **Costa Mesa/OC**	–
☑ Studio | **Laguna Bch/OC**	27
230 Forest Ave. | **Laguna Bch/OC**	24
Winery | **Tustin/OC**	24

CARIBBEAN

Golden Truffle | **Costa Mesa/OC**	26
Tommy Bahama's | **Palm Desert/PS**	22

Menus, photos, voting and more – free at ZAGAT.com

CHINESE

China Palace/Pavilion	**multi.**	20
Five Feet	**Laguna Bch/OC**	25
P.F. Chang's	**multi.**	19

COFFEE SHOPS/ DINERS

Billy Reed's	**PS**	16
Mimi's	**multi.**	17
Original Pancake	**Temecula/PS**	22
Ruby's	**multi.**	17

CONTINENTAL

Europa	**PS**	26
Five Crowns	**Corona del Mar/OC**	24
Gemmell's	**Dana Pt/OC**	25
Hobbit	**Orange/OC**	28
Jillian's	**Palm Desert/PS**	26
Lord Fletcher's	**Rancho Mirage/PS**	21
Melvyn's	**PS**	18
Ritz	**Newport Bch/OC**	24
Wally's Desert	**Rancho Mirage/PS**	26

CREOLE

Palace Grill	**SB**	20

DESSERT

Cheesecake Factory	**multi.**	19

ECLECTIC

Blue Agave	**SB**	20
Break of Dawn	**Laguna Hills/OC**	25
Emilio's	**SB**	20
Johannes	**PS**	26
John Henry's	**PS**	20
Native Foods	**multi.**	23
Old Vine	**Costa Mesa/OC**	25
Onotria	**Costa Mesa/OC**	25
Opal	**SB**	21
Plow & Angel	**Montecito/SB**	24
Tropicale	**PS**	-
Watermarc	**Laguna Bch/OC**	24

FRENCH

Ballard Inn	**Ballard/SB**	26
Basilic	**Newport Bch/OC**	28
bouchon	**SB**	25
Cellar	**Fullerton/OC**	24
Cuistot	**Palm Desert/PS**	26

Downey's	**SB**	28
Five Feet	**Laguna Bch/OC**	25
Gemmell's	**Dana Pt/OC**	25
Golden Truffle	**Costa Mesa/OC**	26
Hobbit	**Orange/OC**	28
John Henry's	**PS**	20
Le St. Germain	**Indian Wells/PS**	24
Le Vallauris	**PS**	26
Marché Moderne	**Costa Mesa/OC**	28
Mimosa	**SB**	18
Mister Parker's	**PS**	-
Pinot Provence	**Costa Mesa/OC**	24
Studio	**Laguna Bch/OC**	27
Tradition/Pascal	**Newport Bch/OC**	28

FRENCH (BISTRO)

Black Sheep	**Tustin/OC**	26
Cafe/Beaux-Arts	**Palm Desert/PS**	21
Chez Pierre	**Palm Desert/PS**	27
Zin	**PS**	22

FRENCH (BRASSERIE)

Brass. Pascal	**Newport Bch/OC**	24

HAWAIIAN

Roy's	**multi.**	24

HEALTH FOOD

(See also Vegetarian)

NEW True Food	**Newport Bch/OC**	-

INDIAN

All India	**SB**	21

ITALIAN

(N=Northern)

Andrea	**Newport Coast/OC**	25
Antonello	**Santa Ana/OC**	25
Bellini	**Palm Desert/PS**	-
Bucatini	**N**	**SB**	22
Ca' Dario	**SB**	27
Castelli's	**Palm Desert/PS**	21
Cucina Alessà	**multi.**	24
Il Barone Ristorante	**Newport Bch/OC**	-
La Spiga	**Palm Desert/PS**	24
Olio e Limone	**SB**	27
Onotria	**Costa Mesa/OC**	25

Pane e Vino | N | **Montecito/SB**	21
Piatti | **Montecito/SB**	20
Pizzeria Ortica | **Costa Mesa/OC**	24
Rist. Mamma Gina | N | **Palm Desert/PS**	23
Rist. Tuscany | N | **Palm Desert/PS**	25
Romano's | **multi.**	17
☑ Sirocco | **Indian Wells/PS**	26
Spaghettini | N | **Seal Bch/OC**	24
☑ Tratt. Grappolo | **Santa Ynez/SB**	27
Tratt. Mollie | N | **Montecito/SB**	25
Tre Lune | **Montecito/SB**	24
Via Vai | **Montecito/SB**	23

JAPANESE

(* sushi specialist)

Arigato* | **SB**	26
Bluefin* | **Newport Coast/OC**	27
Fukada | **Irvine/OC**	24
Gyu-Kaku | **Rancho Cuca/PS**	20
Okura Robata | **multi.**	24
Sakana* | **Montecito/SB**	27
Santouka | **Costa Mesa/OC**	24
Wasa* | **multi.**	24
Zip Fusion* | **Corona/PS**	19

MEDITERRANEAN

☑ Le Vallauris | **PS**	26
Los Olivos | **Los Olivos/SB**	24
Purple Palm | **PS**	-

MEXICAN

Adobe Grill | **La Quinta/PS**	16
Carlitos Café | **SB**	16
Las Casuelas | **multi.**	20
El Torito | **SB**	15
Gabbi's | **Orange/OC**	26
☑ La Super-Rica | **SB**	25
Los Arroyos | **multi.**	23

PACIFIC NORTHWEST

Plums | **Costa Mesa/OC**	25

PACIFIC RIM

Jade | **SB**	23

PAN-LATIN

Cava | **Montecito/SB**	21
NEW Raya | **Dana Pt/OC**	-

PIZZA

BJ's | **multi.**	17
Cal. Pizza Kitchen | **multi.**	18
Matchbox | **PS**	23
Pizzeria Ortica | **Costa Mesa/OC**	24

PUB FOOD

BJ's | **multi.**	17

SEAFOOD

☑ Brophy Bros. | **SB**	21
Coast | **SB**	21
Davey's | **PS**	21
Enterprise Fish | **SB**	19
Holdren's | **SB**	20
NEW House of Big Fish | **Laguna Bch/OC**	-
Hungry Cat | **SB**	24
King's Fish | **multi.**	20
Mastro's Ocean | **Newport Coast/OC**	25
Morton's | **multi.**	24
Original Fish Co. | **Los Alamitos/OC**	25
Pacifica | **Palm Desert/PS**	24
Seagrass | **SB**	29
Tabu Grill | **Laguna Bch/OC**	26
TAPS | **Corona/PS**	23
Tee-Off | **SB**	-
Walt's Wharf | **Seal Bch/OC**	25
Wildfish | **Newport Bch/OC**	24

SMALL PLATES

☑ Marché Moderne | French | **Costa Mesa/OC**	28
Old Vine | Eclectic | **Costa Mesa/OC**	25

SOUTHERN

Lucille's | **Rancho Cuca/PS**	22
Tupelo Junction | **SB**	21

SPANISH

Black Sheep | **Tustin/OC**	26
Miró | **SB**	-

STEAKHOUSES

Arnold Palmer's | **La Quinta/PS**	21
Chop Hse. | **multi.**	23
Davey's | **PS**	21
Falls | **PS**	21
☑ Fleming's | **multi.**	24
Holdren's | **SB**	20

Menus, photos, voting and more – free at ZAGAT.com

LG's | multi. 23

ucky's | Montecito/SB 25

Mastro's Ocean | 25
Newport Coast/OC

Mastro's Steak | 26
Costa Mesa/OC

Morton's | multi. 24

Outback | multi. 18

Ruth's Chris | multi. 25

Tabu Grill | Laguna Bch/OC 26

Tee-Off | SB -

SWISS

Basilic | Newport Bch/OC 28

VEGETARIAN

(* vegan)

Native Foods* | multi. 23

VIETNAMESE

Break of Dawn | Laguna Hills/OC 25

Locations

Includes names, cuisines and Food ratings.

Orange County

ANAHEIM/ ANAHEIM HILLS

Morton's | *Steak*	24
Mr. Stox | *Amer.*	25
Z Napa Rose | *Cal.*	27
Z Roy's | *Asian Fusion/Hawaiian*	24
Z Ruth's Chris | *Steak*	25

CORONA DEL MAR

Z Five Crowns | *Continental*	24

COSTA MESA

Z Charlie Palmer | *Amer.*	22
Golden Truffle | *Carib./French*	26
Z In-N-Out | *Burgers*	24
Leatherby's Café Rouge | *Amer.*	26
Z Marché Moderne | *French*	28
Z Mastro's Steak | *Steak*	26
Old Vine | *Eclectic*	25
Onotria | *Eclectic/Italian*	25
Pinot Provence | *French*	24
Pizzeria Ortica | *Pizza*	24
Plums | *Pac. NW*	25
Santouka | *Japanese*	24
NEW Seasons 52 | *Cal.*	-

DANA POINT

Gemmell's | *Continental/French*	25
NEW Raya | *Pan-Latin*	-
Stonehill | *Amer.*	25

FULLERTON

Cellar | *French*	24

HUNTINGTON BEACH

Cucina Alessá | *Italian*	24
Z In-N-Out | *Burgers*	24

IRVINE

Bistango | *Amer.*	25
Fukada | *Japanese*	24
Z In-N-Out | *Burgers*	24
Z Ruth's Chris | *Steak*	25
Wasa | *Japanese*	24

LAGUNA BEACH

Cafe Zoolu | *Cal.*	26
Five Feet | *Chinese/French*	25
NEW House of Big Fish | *Seafood*	-
Nirvana | *Cal.*	24
Z Studio | *Cal./French*	27
Tabu Grill | *Seafood/Steak*	26
230 Forest Ave. | *Cal.*	24
Watermarc | *Amer./Eclectic*	24

LAGUNA HILLS

Break of Dawn | *Eclectic/Viet.*	25

LAGUNA NIGUEL

Z In-N-Out | *Burgers*	24

LAKE FOREST

Wasa | *Japanese*	24

LOS ALAMITOS

Original Fish Co. | *Seafood*	25

MISSION VIEJO

Nirvana | *Cal.*	24

NEWPORT BEACH

Z Basilic | *French/Swiss*	28
Brass. Pascal | *French*	24
Cucina Alessá | *Italian*	24
Il Barone Ristorante | *Italian*	-
Ritz | *Continental*	24
Z Roy's | *Asian Fusion/Hawaiian*	24
Z Tradition/Pascal | *French*	28
NEW True Food | *Health*	-
Wasa | *Japanese*	24
Wildfish | *Amer./Seafood*	24

NEWPORT COAST

Z Andrea | *Italian*	25
Bluefin | *Japanese*	27
Mastro's Ocean | *Seafood/Steak*	25
Z Pelican Grill | *Cal.*	24

ORANGE

Gabbi's | *Mex.*	26
Z Hobbit | *Continental/French*	28

SAN JUAN CAPISTRANO

Ramos Hse. | *Amer.*	25

SANTA ANA

Antonello | *Italian*	25
Morton's | *Steak*	24

SEAL BEACH

Spaghettini	*Italian*	24
Walt's Wharf	*Seafood*	25

STANTON

Park Ave	*Amer.*	26

TUSTIN

Black Sheep	*French/Spanish*	26
� In-N-Out	*Burgers*	24
Winery	*Cal.*	24

Palm Springs & Environs

CATHEDRAL CITY

Picanha	*Brazilian*	21

CHINO

Islands	*Amer.*	17
Mimi's	*Diner*	17

CORONA

BJ's	*Pub*	17
Citrus City	*Cal.*	23
Claim Jumper	*Amer.*	18
🔋 In-N-Out	*Burgers*	24
Islands	*Amer.*	17
King's Fish	*Seafood*	20
Mimi's	*Diner*	17
Outback	*Steak*	18
Romano's	*Italian*	17
TAPS	*Amer./Seafood*	23
Wood Ranch	*BBQ*	21
Zip Fusion	*Japanese*	19

INDIAN WELLS

Le St. Germain	*Cal./French*	24
🔋 Sirocco	*Italian*	26

LA QUINTA

Adobe Grill	*Mex.*	16
Arnold Palmer's	*Steak*	21
Hog's Breath	*Amer.*	18
La Quinta Cliffhouse	*Amer.*	19
Las Casuelas	*Mex.*	20
🔋 LG's	*Steak*	23
Mimi's	*Diner*	17
Okura Robata	*Japanese*	24

PALM DESERT

Bellini	*Italian*	-
Cafe/Beaux-Arts	*French*	21
Cal. Pizza Kitchen	*Pizza*	18
Castelli's	*Italian*	21
Las Casuelas	*Mex.*	20
Chez Pierre	*French*	27
Chop Hse.	*Steak*	23
Cork Tree	*Cal.*	23
🔋 Cuistot	*Cal./French*	26
Daily Grill	*Amer.*	19
Islands	*Amer.*	17
🔋 Jillian's	*Continental*	26
La Spiga	*Italian*	24
🔋 LG's	*Steak*	23
Morton's	*Steak*	24
🔋 Native Foods	*Cal./Eclectic*	23
Outback	*Steak*	18
Pacifica	*Seafood*	24
Rist. Mamma Gina	*Italian*	23
Rist. Tuscany	*Italian*	25
🔋 Ruth's Chris	*Steak*	25
Tommy Bahama's	*Carib.*	22

PALM SPRINGS

Billy Reed's	*Amer./Coffee*	16
Cal. Pizza Kitchen	*Pizza*	18
Cheeky's	*Amer.*	26
Chop Hse.	*Steak*	23
Citron	*Cal.*	22
Copley's	*Amer.*	25
Davey's	*Seafood/Steak*	21
Europa	*Continental*	26
Falls	*Steak*	21
🔋 Johannes	*Eclectic*	26
John Henry's	*Eclectic/French*	20
Kaiser Grille	*Amer.*	14
Las Casuelas	*Mex.*	20
🔋 Le Vallauris	*French/Med.*	26
🔋 LG's	*Steak*	23
Matchbox	*Amer./Pizza*	23
Melvyn's	*Continental*	18
Mister Parker's	*French*	-
🔋 Native Foods	*Cal./Eclectic*	23
Okura Robata	*Japanese*	24
Purple Palm	*Med.*	-
Ruby's	*Diner*	17
Tropicale	*Eclectic*	-
Zin	*Amer./French*	22

RANCHO CUCAMONGA

BJ's	*Pub*	17
Cal. Pizza Kitchen	*Pizza*	18
🔋 Cheesecake Factory	*Amer.*	19

Claim Jumper | *Amer.*	18
🅩 Fleming's | *Steak*	24
Gyu-Kaku | *Japanese*	20
Islands | *Amer.*	17
Johnny Rockets | *Burgers*	16
King's Fish | *Seafood*	20
Lucille's | *BBQ*	22
Mel's Drive-In | *Diner*	16
Mimi's | *Diner*	17
P.F. Chang's | *Chinese*	19
Yard House | *Amer.*	18

RANCHO MIRAGE

🅩 Cheesecake Factory | *Amer.*	19
🅩 Fleming's | *Steak*	24
Las Casuelas | *Mex.*	20
Lord Fletcher's | *Continental*	21
Mimi's | *Diner*	17
P.F. Chang's | *Chinese*	19
🅩 Roy's | *Hawaiian*	24
Ruby's | *Diner*	17
Shame on Moon | *Amer.*	21
🅩 Wally's Desert | *Continental*	26
Yard House | *Amer.*	18

RIVERSIDE

Cal. Pizza Kitchen | *Pizza*	18
Citrus City | *Cal.*	23
🅩 In-N-Out | *Burgers*	24
Islands | *Amer.*	17
P.F. Chang's | *Chinese*	19
Ruby's | *Diner*	17
Yard House | *Amer.*	18

SAN BERNARDINO

BJ's | *Pub*	17
Castaway | *Cal.*	17
Claim Jumper | *Amer.*	18
Outback | *Steak*	18

TEMECULA

BJ's | *Pub*	17
Cal. Pizza Kitchen | *Pizza*	18
🅩 Original Pancake | *Amer.*	22
Outback | *Steak*	18
P.F. Chang's | *Chinese*	19
Romano's | *Italian*	17
Yard House | *Amer.*	18

UPLAND

Outback | *Steak*	18

Santa Barbara & Environs

(See page 289 for Ventura & Environs)

BALLARD

Ballard Inn | *French*	26

BUELLTON

🅩 Hitching Post | *BBQ*	23

CARPINTERIA

Cajun Kitchen | *Cajun*	20

CASMALIA

🅩 Hitching Post | *BBQ*	23

GOLETA

Cajun Kitchen | *Cajun*	20
🅩 In-N-Out | *Burgers*	24
Outback | *Steak*	18

LOS OLIVOS

Brothers | *Amer.*	25
Los Olivos | *Cal./Med.*	24

MONTECITO

🅩 Bella Vista | *Cal.*	24
Cafe del Sol | *Cal.*	20
Cava | *Pan-Latin*	21
China Palace/Pavilion | *Chinese*	20
Los Arroyos | *Mex.*	23
Lucky's | *Steak*	25
Montecito | *Cal.*	23
Pane e Vino | *Italian*	21
Piatti | *Italian*	20
Plow & Angel | *Cal./Eclectic*	24
Sakana | *Japanese*	27
🅩 Stonehouse | *Amer.*	23
Tratt. Mollie | *Italian*	25
Tre Lune | *Italian*	24
Via Vai | *Italian*	23

SANTA BARBARA

All India | *Indian*	21
Arigato | *Japanese*	26
Blue Agave | *Eclectic*	20
bouchon | *Cal./French*	25
🅩 Brophy Bros. | *Seafood*	21
Bucatini | *Italian*	22
🅩 Ca' Dario | *Italian*	27
Cafe Buenos Aires | *Argent.*	20

Cajun Kitchen | *Cajun*	20	
Cal. Pizza Kitchen | *Pizza*	18	
Carlitos Café | *Mex.*	16	
China Palace/Pavilion | *Chinese*	20	
Coast | *Cal./Seafood*	21	
Cold Spring | *Amer.*	21	
☑ Downey's | *Cal./French*	28	
Elements | *Cal.*	21	
El Torito | *Mex.*	15	
Emilio's | *Eclectic*	20	
Enterprise Fish | *Seafood*	19	
Holdren's | *Seafood/Steak*	20	
Hungry Cat | *Seafood*	24	
Jade | *Pac. Rim*	23	
☑ La Super-Rica | *Mex.*	25	

Los Arroyos | *Mex.*	23
Louie's | *Cal.*	26
Marmalade | *Amer./Cal.*	18
Mimosa | *French*	18
Miró | *Spanish*	-
Olio e Limone | *Italian*	27
Opal | *Cal./Eclectic*	21
Palace Grill | *Cajun/Creole*	20
☑ Ruth's Chris | *Steak*	25
Seagrass | *Seafood*	29
Tee-Off | *Seafood/Steak*	-
Tupelo Junction | *Southern*	21

OC/PS/SB

SANTA YNEZ

☑ Tratt. Grappolo | *Italian*	27

LOCATIONS

Visit ZAGAT.mobi from your mobile phone   371

Special Features

Listings cover the best in each category and include names, locations and
Food ratings. Multi-location restaurants' features may vary by branch.

BEACHSIDE/WATERSIDE

🔢 Bella Vista | **Montecito/SB**	24
🔢 Cheesecake Factory | **Rancho Mirage/PS**	19
Citron | **PS**	22
Emilio's | **SB**	20
Mastro's Ocean | **Newport Coast/OC**	25
Miró | **SB**	-
🔢 Studio | **Laguna Bch/OC**	27

BREAKFAST

(See also Hotel Dining)

Billy Reed's | **PS**	16
Break of Dawn | **Laguna Hills/OC**	25
Cajun Kitchen | **multi.**	20
Old Vine | **Costa Mesa/OC**	25
🔢 Original Pancake | **Temecula/PS**	22
Plums | **Costa Mesa/OC**	25
Ramos Hse. | **San Juan Cap/OC**	25
Ruby's | **Riverside/PS**	17
Tupelo Junction | **SB**	21

BRUNCH

🔢 Charlie Palmer | **Costa Mesa/OC**	22
🔢 Five Crowns | **Corona del Mar/OC**	24
Pinot Provence | **Costa Mesa/OC**	24
Plums | **Costa Mesa/OC**	25
Ramos Hse. | **San Juan Cap/OC**	25
Spaghettini | **Seal Bch/OC**	24

BUFFET

(Check availability)

All India | **SB**	21
🔢 Bella Vista | **Montecito/SB**	24
Castaway | **San Bern/PS**	17
Citrus City | **multi.**	23
El Torito | **SB**	15
Las Casuelas | **Rancho Mirage/PS**	20
Picanha | **Cathedral City/PS**	21
TAPS | **Corona/PS**	23

BUSINESS DINING

Antonello | **Santa Ana/OC**	25
Arnold Palmer's | **La Quinta/PS**	21
Bistango | **Irvine/OC**	25
Bucatini | **SB**	22
Cellar | **Fullerton/OC**	24
🔢 Charlie Palmer | **Costa Mesa/OC**	22
China Palace/Pavilion | **SB**	20
Leatherby's Café Rouge | **Costa Mesa/OC**	26
Mastro's Ocean | **Newport Coast/OC**	25
🔢 Mastro's Steak | **Costa Mesa/OC**	26
Morton's | **multi.**	24
Mr. Stox | **Anaheim/OC**	25
Park Ave | **Stanton/OC**	26
Pinot Provence | **Costa Mesa/OC**	24
NEW Raya | **Dana Pt/OC**	-
Ritz | **Newport Bch/OC**	24
🔢 Roy's | **Newport Bch/OC**	24
🔢 Ruth's Chris | **Irvine/OC**	25
NEW Seasons 52 | **Costa Mesa/OC**	-
Spaghettini | **Seal Bch/OC**	24
Stonehill | **Dana Pt/OC**	25
🔢 Stonehouse | **Montecito/SB**	23
🔢 Tradition/Pascal | **Newport Bch/OC**	28

CELEBRITY CHEFS

Takashi Abe

Bluefin | **Newport Coast/OC**	27

Marc Cohen

Watermarc | **Laguna Bch/OC**	24

Andrew Copley

Copley's | **PS**	25

Michael Kang

Five Feet | **Laguna Bch/OC**	25

Florent Marneau

🔢 Marché Moderne | **Costa Mesa/OC**	28

David Myers

Pizzeria Ortica | **Costa Mesa/OC**	24

Charlie Palmer

🔢 Charlie Palmer | **Costa Mesa/OC**	22

Pierre Pelech

Chez Pierre | **Palm Desert/PS**	27

ichard Sandoval
NEW Raya | **Dana Pt/OC** | – |

ndrew Sutton
Z Napa Rose | **Anaheim/OC** | 27 |

oy Yamaguchi
Z Roy's | **Rancho Mirage/PS** | 24 |

CHEESE TRAYS

a Basilic	**Newport Bch/OC**	28
Black Sheep	**Tustin/OC**	26
Cafe/Beaux-Arts	**Palm Desert/PS**	21
Cork Tree	**Palm Desert/PS**	23
a Cuistot	**Palm Desert/PS**	26
Z Downey's	**SB**	28
Elements	**SB**	21
Z Five Crowns	**Corona del Mar/OC**	24
Gemmell's	**Dana Pt/OC**	25
Golden Truffle	**Costa Mesa/OC**	26
Z Johannes	**PS**	26
Leatherby's Café Rouge	**Costa Mesa/OC**	26
Los Olivos	**Los Olivos/SB**	24
Z Marché Moderne	**Costa Mesa/OC**	28
Onotria	**Costa Mesa/OC**	25
Pinot Provence	**Costa Mesa/OC**	24
Stonehill	**Dana Pt/OC**	25
Z Tradition/Pascal	**Newport Bch/OC**	28
Z Wally's Desert	**Rancho Mirage/PS**	26
Watermarc	**Laguna Bch/OC**	24
Zin	**PS**	22

CHEF'S TABLE

Cork Tree	**Palm Desert/PS**	23
Z Cuistot	**Palm Desert/PS**	26
Five Feet	**Laguna Bch/OC**	25
Gemmell's	**Dana Pt/OC**	25
Z Napa Rose	**Anaheim/OC**	27
Rist. Tuscany	**Palm Desert/PS**	25
NEW Seasons 52	**Costa Mesa/OC**	–
Z Studio	**Laguna Bch/OC**	27
TAPS	**Corona/PS**	23
Winery	**Tustin/OC**	24

CHILD-FRIENDLY

(Alternatives to the usual fast-food places; * children's menu available)

Billy Reed's*	**PS**	16
Z Brophy Bros.	**SB**	21
Carlitos Café*	**SB**	16
Cold Spring*	**SB**	21
Z In-N-Out	**Laguna Niguel/OC**	24
Las Casuelas*	**PS**	20
Z La Super-Rica	**SB**	25
Louie's	**SB**	26
Mimosa	**SB**	18
Z Napa Rose	**Anaheim/OC**	27
Original Fish Co.*	**Los Alamitos/OC**	25
Ruby's*	**multi.**	17
Tratt. Mollie	**Montecito/SB**	25

DANCING

Arnold Palmer's	**La Quinta/PS**	21
Bistango	**Irvine/OC**	25
Cafe Buenos Aires	**SB**	20
Las Casuelas	**multi.**	20
Melvyn's	**PS**	18

DESSERT SPECIALISTS

Z Marché Moderne	**Costa Mesa/OC**	28
Plums	**Costa Mesa/OC**	25

DINING ALONE

(Other than hotels and places with counter service)

Arigato	**SB**	26
Bluefin	**Newport Coast/OC**	27
Cafe Zoolu	**Laguna Bch/OC**	26
Carlitos Café	**SB**	16
Z Fleming's	**multi.**	24
Z Jillian's	**Palm Desert/PS**	26
Z Marché Moderne	**Costa Mesa/OC**	28
Morton's	**Anaheim/OC**	24
Mr. Stox	**Anaheim/OC**	25
Z Roy's	**multi.**	24
NEW Seasons 52	**Costa Mesa/OC**	–
Wasa	**Irvine/OC**	24
Watermarc	**Laguna Bch/OC**	24

ENTERTAINMENT

(Call for days and times of performances)

Bistango	varies	**Irvine/OC**	25
Lucille's	blues	**Rancho Cuca/PS**	22
Spaghettini	jazz	**Seal Bch/OC**	24

FIREPLACES

Adobe Grill	**La Quinta/PS**	16
Arnold Palmer's	**La Quinta/PS**	21

Ballard Inn | **Ballard/SB**	26
🄩 Bella Vista | **Montecito/SB**	24
Blue Agave | **SB**	20
Brothers | **Los Olivos/SB**	25
Cafe del Sol | **Montecito/SB**	20
Cafe Zoolu | **Laguna Bch/OC**	26
Cava | **Montecito/SB**	21
Cellar | **Fullerton/OC**	24
Citron | **PS**	22
Claim Jumper | **multi.**	18
Cold Spring | **SB**	21
🄩 Cuistot | **Palm Desert/PS**	26
Falls | **PS**	21
🄩 Five Crowns | **Corona del Mar/OC**	24
Gemmell's | **Dana Pt/OC**	25
🄩 Hitching Post | **Buellton/SB**	23
Hog's Breath | **La Quinta/PS**	18
La Quinta Cliffhouse | **La Quinta/PS**	19
Las Casuelas | **La Quinta/PS**	20
La Spiga | **Palm Desert/PS**	24
🄩 Le Vallauris | **PS**	26
🄩 LG's | **La Quinta/PS**	23
Lord Fletcher's | **Rancho Mirage/PS**	21
Los Olivos | **Los Olivos/SB**	24
Lucky's | **Montecito/SB**	25
Matchbox | **PS**	23
Miró | **SB**	-
Mr. Stox | **Anaheim/OC**	25
🄩 Napa Rose | **Anaheim/OC**	27
Park Ave | **Stanton/OC**	26
🄩 Pelican Grill | **Newport Coast/OC**	24
Piatti | **Montecito/SB**	20
Pinot Provence | **Costa Mesa/OC**	24
Plow & Angel | **Montecito/SB**	24
Spaghettini | **Seal Bch/OC**	24
Stonehill | **Dana Pt/OC**	25
🄩 Studio | **Laguna Bch/OC**	27
Winery | **Tustin/OC**	24

GREEN/LOCAL/ ORGANIC

Ballard Inn | **Ballard/SB**	26
Bellini | **Palm Desert/PS**	-
Blue Agave | **SB**	20
Brothers | **Los Olivos/SB**	25
Bucatini | **SB**	22
Cafe del Sol | **Montecito/SB**	20
China Palace/Pavilion | **Montecito/SB**	20

Citron | **PS**	22
Copley's | **PS**	25
🄩 Downey's | **SB**	28
Elements | **SB**	21
Falls | **PS**	21
Fukada | **Irvine/OC**	24
Gemmell's | **Dana Pt/OC**	25
Hungry Cat | **SB**	24
Jade | **SB**	23
🄩 Johannes | **PS**	26
John Henry's | **PS**	20
La Spiga | **Palm Desert/PS**	24
Leatherby's Café Rouge | **Costa Mesa/OC**	26
Le St. Germain | **Indian Wells/PS**	24
🄩 Le Vallauris | **PS**	26
Louie's | **SB**	26
🄩 Marché Moderne | **Costa Mesa/OC**	28
Mimosa | **SB**	18
Miró | **SB**	-
🄩 Native Foods | **multi.**	23
Nirvana | **Mission Viejo/OC**	24
Onotria | **Costa Mesa/OC**	25
Opal | **SB**	21
Pizzeria Ortica | **Costa Mesa/OC**	24
Plow & Angel | **Montecito/SB**	24
Ramos Hse. | **San Juan Cap/OC**	25
🆕 Seasons 52 | **Costa Mesa/OC**	-
🄩 Tradition/Pascal | **Newport Bch/OC**	28
Tratt. Mollie | **Montecito/SB**	25
🆕 True Food | **Newport Bch/OC**	-
Tupelo Junction | **SB**	21
Winery | **Tustin/OC**	24
Zin | **PS**	22

HISTORIC PLACES

(Year opened; * building)

1800 | Tupelo Junction* | **SB**	21
1881 | Ramos Hse.* | **San Juan Cap/OC**	25
1886 | Brothers* | **Los Olivos/SB**	25
1886 | Cold Spring* | **SB**	21
1893 | Plow & Angel* | **Montecito/SB**	24
1893 | Stonehouse* | **Montecito/SB**	23
1909 | Hitching Post* | **Casmalia/SB**	23
1922 | Cellar* | **Fullerton/OC**	24

927 | Bella Vista* | **Montecito/SB**	24
930 | Elements* | **SB**	21
930 | Hobbit* | **Orange/OC**	28
930 | Las Casuelas* | **PS**	20
933 | Citron* | **PS**	22
934 | Five Crowns* | **Corona del Mar/OC**	24
947 | Copley's* | **PS**	25
956 | Tee-Off | **SB**	-
958 | Las Casuelas | **PS**	20
960 | Castaway | **San Bern/PS**	17

HOLIDAY MEALS

(Special prix fixe meals offered at major holidays)

Ballard Inn | **Ballard/SB**	26
☒ Bella Vista | **Montecito/SB**	24
Blue Agave | **SB**	20
Brothers | **Los Olivos/SB**	25
☒ Downey's | **SB**	28
☒ Hitching Post | **Buellton/SB**	23
Jade | **SB**	23
Los Olivos | **Los Olivos/SB**	24
Louie's | **SB**	26
Lucky's | **Montecito/SB**	25
Miró | **SB**	-
Montecito | **Montecito/SB**	23
Olio e Limone | **SB**	27
Plow & Angel | **Montecito/SB**	24
Seagrass | **SB**	29
☒ Tratt. Grappolo | **Santa Ynez/SB**	27
Tre Lune | **Montecito/SB**	24

HOTEL DINING

Bacara Resort & Spa	
Miró | **SB**	-
Ballard Inn	
Ballard Inn | **Ballard/SB**	26
Canary Hotel	
Coast | **SB**	21
Colony Palms Hotel	
Purple Palm | **PS**	-
Disney's Grand Californian	
☒ Napa Rose | **Anaheim/OC**	27
Four Seasons, The Biltmore	
☒ Bella Vista | **Montecito/SB**	24
Ingleside Inn	
Melvyn's | **PS**	18
JW Marriott Desert Springs	
Rist. Tuscany | **Palm Desert/PS**	25
La Quinta Resort & Club	
Adobe Grill | **La Quinta/PS**	16
Montage Laguna Bch.	
☒ Studio | **Laguna Bch/OC**	27
Montecito Inn	
Montecito | **Montecito/SB**	23
Parker Palm Springs	
Mister Parker's | **PS**	-
Pelican Hill Resort	
☒ Andrea | **Newport Coast/OC**	25
☒ Pelican Grill | **Newport Coast/OC**	24
Renaissance Esmeralda Resort	
☒ Sirocco | **Indian Wells/PS**	26
Ritz-Carlton Laguna Niguel	
NEW Raya | **Dana Pt/OC**	-
San Ysidro Ranch	
Plow & Angel | **Montecito/SB**	24
☒ Stonehouse | **Montecito/SB**	23
St. Regis Resort, Monarch Bch.	
Stonehill | **Dana Pt/OC**	25
Upham Hotel	
Louie's | **SB**	26
Viceroy Palm Springs	
Citron | **PS**	22
Villa Royale Inn	
Europa | **PS**	26
Westin South Coast Plaza Hotel	
Pinot Provence | **Costa Mesa/OC**	24

LATE DINING

(Weekday closing hour)

☒ In-N-Out | varies | **multi.**	24
Yard House | varies | **multi.**	18

MICROBREWERIES

TAPS | **Corona/PS**	23
Yard House | **multi.**	18

NEWCOMERS

House of Big Fish | **Laguna Bch/OC**	-
Raya | **Dana Pt/OC**	-
Seasons 52 | **Costa Mesa/OC**	-
True Food | **Newport Bch/OC**	-

OUTDOOR DINING

(G=garden; P=patio; T=terrace)

Bistango | P | **Irvine/OC**	25
Citron | P | **PS**	22
Copley's | P | **PS**	25
☒ Le Vallauris | P | **PS**	26

OC/PS/SB

SPECIAL FEATURES

Marché Moderne | P | **Costa Mesa/OC** 28

Matchbox | P | **PS** 23

Pinot Provence | P | **Costa Mesa/OC** 24

Plums | P | **Costa Mesa/OC** 25

Ramos Hse. | P | **San Juan Cap/OC** 25

Ritz | G | **Newport Bch/OC** 24

🆕 Seasons 52 | P | **Costa Mesa/OC** -

🔟 Stonehouse | T | **Montecito/SB** 23

🆕 True Food | P | **Newport Bch/OC** -

PARTIES/ PRIVATE ROOMS

(Restaurants charge less at off times; call for capacity)

Antonello | **Santa Ana/OC** 25

Bistango | **Irvine/OC** 25

🔟 Five Crowns | **Corona del Mar/OC** 24

🔟 Hobbit | **Orange/OC** 28

Mr. Stox | **Anaheim/OC** 25

Pinot Provence | **Costa Mesa/OC** 24

Ritz | **Newport Bch/OC** 24

🔟 Roy's | **Newport Bch/OC** 24

🔟 Studio | **Laguna Bch/OC** 27

PEOPLE-WATCHING

Antonello | **Santa Ana/OC** 25

Arigato | **SB** 26

Bistango | **Irvine/OC** 25

🔟 Charlie Palmer | **Costa Mesa/OC** 22

🆕 House of Big Fish | **Laguna Bch/OC** -

Mastro's Ocean | **Newport Coast/OC** 25

Plow & Angel | **Montecito/SB** 24

🆕 Raya | **Dana Pt/OC** -

Shame on Moon | **Rancho Mirage/PS** 21

Stonehill | **Dana Pt/OC** 25

🔟 Stonehouse | **Montecito/SB** 23

230 Forest Ave. | **Laguna Bch/OC** 24

Watermarc | **Laguna Bch/OC** 24

Wildfish | **Newport Bch/OC** 24

POWER SCENES

Antonello | **Santa Ana/OC** 25

Arnold Palmer's | **La Quinta/PS** 21

Bistango | **Irvine/OC** 25

Cellar | **Fullerton/OC** 2

🔟 Charlie Palmer | **Costa Mesa/OC** 2

🔟 Marché Moderne | **Costa Mesa/OC** 2

Mastro's Ocean | **Newport Coast/OC** 2

🔟 Mastro's Steak | **Costa Mesa/OC** 2

Morton's | **multi.** 2

Mr. Stox | **Anaheim/OC** 2

Ritz | **Newport Bch/OC** 2

🔟 Roy's | **Newport Bch/OC** 2

Stonehill | **Dana Pt/OC** 2

🔟 Studio | **Laguna Bch/OC** 2

QUIET CONVERSATION

Antonello | **Santa Ana/OC** 2

Arnold Palmer's | **La Quinta/PS** 2

Ballard Inn | **Ballard/SB** 2

🔟 Basilic | **Newport Bch/OC** 2

Black Sheep | **Tustin/OC** 2

Bluefin | **Newport Coast/OC** 2

Bucatini | **SB** 2

Cellar | **Fullerton/OC** 2

🔟 Charlie Palmer | **Costa Mesa/OC** 2

🔟 Five Crowns | **Corona del Mar/OC** 2

Jade | **SB** 2

🔟 Marché Moderne | **Costa Mesa/OC** 2

🔟 Mastro's Steak | **Costa Mesa/OC** 2

Morton's | **Anaheim/OC** 2

Mr. Stox | **Anaheim/OC** 2

🔟 Napa Rose | **Anaheim/OC** 2

Nirvana | **Mission Viejo/OC** 2

🆕 Raya | **Dana Pt/OC** -

Ritz | **Newport Bch/OC** 2

🆕 Seasons 52 | **Costa Mesa/OC** -

Stonehill | **Dana Pt/OC** 2

🔟 Stonehouse | **Montecito/SB** 23

🔟 Studio | **Laguna Bch/OC** 2

🔟 Tradition/Pascal | **Newport Bch/OC** 28

🆕 True Food | **Newport Bch/OC** -

Watermarc | **Laguna Bch/OC** 24

RAW BARS

Coast | **SB** 2

Enterprise Fish | **SB** 19

NEW House of Big Fish | Laguna Bch/OC | - |
Hungry Cat | **SB** | 24 |
King's Fish | **multi.** | 20 |
APS | **Corona/PS** | 23 |
Wildfish | **Newport Bch/OC** | 24 |

ROMANTIC PLACES

Antonello | **Santa Ana/OC** | 25 |
Arnold Palmer's | **La Quinta/PS** | 21 |
Ballard Inn | **Ballard/SB** | 26 |
Basilic | **Newport Bch/OC** | 28 |
Bucatini | **SB** | 22 |
Cellar | **Fullerton/OC** | 24 |
Charlie Palmer | Costa Mesa/OC | 22 |
Elements | **SB** | 21 |
Europa | **PS** | 26 |
Hobbit | **Orange/OC** | 28 |
Leatherby's Café Rouge | Costa Mesa/OC | 26 |
Le Vallauris | **PS** | 26 |
Marché Moderne | Costa Mesa/OC | 28 |
Mastro's Steak | Costa Mesa/OC | 26 |
Mr. Stox | **Anaheim/OC** | 25 |
Napa Rose | **Anaheim/OC** | 27 |
Pinot Provence | **Costa Mesa/OC** | 24 |
Plow & Angel | **Montecito/SB** | 24 |
Ritz | **Newport Bch/OC** | 24 |
Stonehill | **Dana Pt/OC** | 25 |
Stonehouse | **Montecito/SB** | 23 |
Studio | **Laguna Bch/OC** | 27 |
Tradition/Pascal | Newport Bch/OC | 28 |

SINGLES SCENES

Bistango | **Irvine/OC** | 25 |
Elements | **SB** | 21 |
Fleming's | **multi.** | 24 |
NEW House of Big Fish | Laguna Bch/OC | - |
Plow & Angel | **Montecito/SB** | 24 |
Shame on Moon | Rancho Mirage/PS | 21 |
Spaghettini | **Seal Bch/OC** | 24 |

SLEEPERS

(Good food, but little known)
Cafe Zoolu | **Laguna Bch/OC** | 26 |
Cheeky's | **PS** | 26 |
Chez Pierre | **Palm Desert/PS** | 27 |

Europa | **PS** | 26 |
Fukada | **Irvine/OC** | 24 |
Jade | **SB** | 23 |
La Spiga | **Palm Desert/PS** | 24 |
Louie's | **SB** | 26 |
Matchbox | **PS** | 23 |
Nirvana | **multi.** | 24 |
Okura Robata | **multi.** | 24 |
Plow & Angel | **Montecito/SB** | 24 |
Plums | **Costa Mesa/OC** | 25 |
Rist. Tuscany | **Palm Desert/PS** | 25 |
Sakana | **Montecito/SB** | 27 |
Seagrass | **SB** | 29 |
Tratt. Mollie | **Montecito/SB** | 25 |
Tre Lune | **Montecito/SB** | 24 |

SPECIAL OCCASIONS

Antonello | **Santa Ana/OC** | 25 |
Arnold Palmer's | **La Quinta/PS** | 21 |
Bistango | **Irvine/OC** | 25 |
Cellar | **Fullerton/OC** | 24 |
Charlie Palmer | Costa Mesa/OC | 22 |
Cuistot | **Palm Desert/PS** | 26 |
Downey's | **SB** | 28 |
Elements | **SB** | 21 |
Five Crowns | Corona del Mar/OC | 24 |
Hobbit | **Orange/OC** | 28 |
Johannes | **PS** | 26 |
Leatherby's Café Rouge | Costa Mesa/OC | 26 |
Le St. Germain | **Indian Wells/PS** | 24 |
Le Vallauris | **PS** | 26 |
Marché Moderne | Costa Mesa/OC | 28 |
Mastro's Ocean | Newport Coast/OC | 25 |
Mastro's Steak | Costa Mesa/OC | 26 |
Miró | **SB** | - |
Morton's | **multi.** | 24 |
Napa Rose | **Anaheim/OC** | 27 |
Pinot Provence | **Costa Mesa/OC** | 24 |
NEW Raya | **Dana Pt/OC** | - |
Roy's | **multi.** | 24 |
Stonehill | **Dana Pt/OC** | 25 |
Stonehouse | **Montecito/SB** | 23 |
Studio | **Laguna Bch/OC** | 27 |
Tradition/Pascal | Newport Bch/OC | 28 |
Wally's Desert | Rancho Mirage/PS | 26 |

OC/PS/SB

SPECIAL FEATURES

TASTING MENUS

Ballard Inn	**Ballard/SB**	26
Bluefin	**Newport Coast/OC**	27
Cellar	**Fullerton/OC**	24
Five Feet	**Laguna Bch/OC**	25
Miró	**SB**	-
Old Vine	**Costa Mesa/OC**	25
Rist. Tuscany	**Palm Desert/PS**	25
Stonehill	**Dana Pt/OC**	25
☑ Studio	**Laguna Bch/OC**	27

TEEN APPEAL

Cheeky's	**PS**	26
☑ In-N-Out	**multi.**	24
Los Arroyos	**multi.**	23
Matchbox	**PS**	23
Piatti	**Montecito/SB**	20
Via Vai	**Montecito/SB**	23
Zip Fusion	**Corona/PS**	19

TRANSPORTING EXPERIENCES

☑ Basilic	**Newport Bch/OC**	28
Bluefin	**Newport Coast/OC**	27
☑ Hobbit	**Orange/OC**	28
☑ Marché Moderne	**Costa Mesa/OC**	28
Mastro's Ocean	**Newport Coast/OC**	25
☑ Studio	**Laguna Bch/OC**	27

TRENDY

Bistango	**Irvine/OC**	25
Bluefin	**Newport Coast/OC**	27
Citron	**PS**	22
NEW House of Big Fish	**Laguna Bch/OC**	-
Hungry Cat	**SB**	24
☑ Marché Moderne	**Costa Mesa/OC**	28
Mastro's Ocean	**Newport Coast/OC**	25
☑ Mastro's Steak	**Costa Mesa/OC**	26
Mister Parker's	**PS**	-
NEW Seasons 52	**Costa Mesa/OC**	-
Shame on Moon	**Rancho Mirage/PS**	21
Stonehill	**Dana Pt/OC**	25
☑ Stonehouse	**Montecito/SB**	23
NEW True Food	**Newport Bch/OC**	-

VIEWS

Adobe Grill	**La Quinta/PS**	16
☑ Andrea	**Newport Coast/OC**	25
Arnold Palmer's	**La Quinta/PS**	21
Ballard Inn	**Ballard/SB**	26
☑ Bella Vista	**Montecito/SB**	24
Bellini	**Palm Desert/PS**	-
bouchon	**SB**	25
Cafe Buenos Aires	**SB**	20
Castaway	**San Bern/PS**	17
☑ Cuistot	**Palm Desert/PS**	26
Elements	**SB**	21
Emilio's	**SB**	20
Falls	**PS**	21
Hog's Breath	**La Quinta/PS**	18
NEW House of Big Fish	**Laguna Bch/OC**	-
☑ Johannes	**PS**	26
La Quinta Cliffhouse	**La Quinta/PS**	19
Mastro's Ocean	**Newport Coast/OC**	25
Miró	**SB**	-
Pacifica	**Palm Desert/PS**	24
☑ Pelican Grill	**Newport Coast/OC**	24
Rist. Mamma Gina	**Palm Desert/PS**	23
Rist. Tuscany	**Palm Desert/PS**	25
☑ Sirocco	**Indian Wells/PS**	26
Stonehill	**Dana Pt/OC**	25
☑ Studio	**Laguna Bch/OC**	27

VISITORS ON EXPENSE ACCOUNT

Antonello	**Santa Ana/OC**	25
Arnold Palmer's	**La Quinta/PS**	21
Bistango	**Irvine/OC**	25
Bluefin	**Newport Coast/OC**	27
Cellar	**Fullerton/OC**	24
☑ Charlie Palmer	**Costa Mesa/OC**	22
☑ Cuistot	**Palm Desert/PS**	26
☑ Downey's	**SB**	28
☑ Five Crowns	**Corona del Mar/OC**	24
Five Feet	**Laguna Bch/OC**	25
☑ Hobbit	**Orange/OC**	28
☑ Johannes	**PS**	26
Leatherby's Café Rouge	**Costa Mesa/OC**	26
Le St. Germain	**Indian Wells/PS**	24
☑ Le Vallauris	**PS**	26

Marché Moderne | **Costa Mesa/OC** — 28

Mastro's Ocean | **Newport Coast/OC** — 25

Mastro's Steak | **Costa Mesa/OC** — 26

Miró | **SB** — –

Morton's | **multi.** — 24

Mr. Stox | **Anaheim/OC** — 25

Z Napa Rose | **Anaheim/OC** — 27

Onotria | **Costa Mesa/OC** — 25

Pinot Provence | **Costa Mesa/OC** — 24

NEW Raya | **Dana Pt/OC** — –

Ritz | **Newport Bch/OC** — 24

Z Roy's | **multi.** — 24

Z Ruth's Chris | **Irvine/OC** — 25

Stonehill | **Dana Pt/OC** — 25

Z Stonehouse | **Montecito/SB** — 23

Z Studio | **Laguna Bch/OC** — 27

Z Tradition/Pascal | **Newport Bch/OC** — 28

Z Wally's Desert | **Rancho Mirage/PS** — 26

WINE BARS

Z Ca' Dario | **SB** — 27

Citrus City | **Riverside/PS** — 23

Hungry Cat | **SB** — 24

Los Olivos | **Los Olivos/SB** — 24

Rist. Mamma Gina | **Palm Desert/PS** — 23

Winery | **Tustin/OC** — 24

WINNING WINE LISTS

Antonello | **Santa Ana/OC** — 25

Bistango | **Irvine/OC** — 25

Black Sheep | **Tustin/OC** — 26

Cellar | **Fullerton/OC** — 24

Z Charlie Palmer | **Costa Mesa/OC** — 22

Cold Spring | **SB** — 21

Z Cuistot | **Palm Desert/PS** — 26

Elements | **SB** — 21

Z Five Crowns | **Corona del Mar/OC** — 24

Golden Truffle | **Costa Mesa/OC** — 26

Z Hobbit | **Orange/OC** — 28

Le St. Germain | **Indian Wells/PS** — 24

Z Le Vallauris | **PS** — 26

Z Marché Moderne | **Costa Mesa/OC** — 28

Z Mastro's Steak | **Costa Mesa/OC** — 26

Miró | **SB** — –

Mr. Stox | **Anaheim/OC** — 25

Z Napa Rose | **Anaheim/OC** — 27

Old Vine | **Costa Mesa/OC** — 25

Onotria | **Costa Mesa/OC** — 25

Pinot Provence | **Costa Mesa/OC** — 24

Plow & Angel | **Montecito/SB** — 24

Ritz | **Newport Bch/OC** — 24

Z Roy's | **Newport Bch/OC** — 24

NEW Seasons 52 | **Costa Mesa/OC** — –

Stonehill | **Dana Pt/OC** — 25

Z Stonehouse | **Montecito/SB** — 23

Z Studio | **Laguna Bch/OC** — 27

Z Wally's Desert | **Rancho Mirage/PS** — 26

Walt's Wharf | **Seal Bch/OC** — 25

Wildfish | **Newport Bch/OC** — 24

WORTH A TRIP

Anaheim
  Z Napa Rose — 27

Costa Mesa
  Z Marché Moderne — 28
  Pinot Provence — 24

Dana Point
  Stonehill — 25

Fullerton
  Cellar — 24

Laguna Beach
  Z Studio — 27

Newport Beach
  Ritz — 24
  Z Tradition/Pascal — 28

Orange
  Z Hobbit — 28

Santa Ana
  Antonello — 25

Wine Vintage Chart

This chart is based on our 0 to 30 scale. The ratings (by U. of South Carolina law professor **Howard Stravitz**) reflect vintage quality and the wine's readiness to drink. A dash means the wine is past its peak or too young to rate. Loire ratings are for dry whites.

Whites	95	96	97	98	99	00	01	02	03	04	05	06	07	08
France:														
Alsace	24	23	23	25	23	25	26	23	21	24	25	24	26	-
Burgundy	27	26	23	21	24	24	24	27	23	26	27	25	25	24
Loire Valley	-	-	-	-	-	23	24	26	22	24	24	23	23	24
Champagne	26	27	24	23	25	24	21	26	21	-	-	-	-	-
Sauternes	21	23	25	23	24	24	29	25	24	21	26	23	27	25
California:														
Chardonnay	-	-	-	-	23	22	25	26	22	26	29	24	27	-
Sauvignon Blanc	-	-	-	-	-	-	-	-	25	26	25	27	25	-
Austria:														
Grüner V./Riesl.	24	21	26	23	25	22	23	25	26	25	24	26	24	22
Germany:	21	26	21	22	24	20	29	25	26	27	28	25	27	25

Reds	95	96	97	98	99	00	01	02	03	04	05	06	07	08
France:														
Bordeaux	26	25	23	25	24	29	26	24	26	24	28	24	23	25
Burgundy	26	27	25	24	27	22	24	27	25	23	28	25	24	-
Rhône	26	22	24	27	26	27	26	-	26	24	27	25	26	-
Beaujolais	-	-	-	-	-	-	-	-	24	-	27	24	25	23
California:														
Cab./Merlot	27	25	28	23	25	-	27	26	25	24	26	23	26	24
Pinot Noir	-	-	-	-	24	23	25	26	25	26	24	23	27	25
Zinfandel	-	-	-	-	-	-	25	23	27	22	22	21	21	25
Oregon:														
Pinot Noir	-	-	-	-	-	-	-	26	24	25	26	26	25	27
Italy:														
Tuscany	24	-	29	24	27	24	27	-	25	27	26	25	24	-
Piedmont	21	27	26	25	26	28	27	-	25	27	26	25	26	-
Spain:														
Rioja	26	24	25	-	25	24	28	-	23	27	26	24	25	-
Ribera del Duero/ Priorat	26	27	25	24	25	24	27	20	24	27	26	24	26	-
Australia:														
Shiraz/Cab.	24	26	25	28	24	24	27	27	25	26	26	24	22	-
Chile:	-	-	24	-	25	23	26	24	25	24	27	25	24	-
Argentina:														
Malbec	-	-	-	-	-	-	-	-	-	25	26	27	24	-

ZAGATWINE™
Stay home and paint the town red.
SAVE $100
Enjoy 12 great wines for ONLY $69.99
(Plus FREE GIFT)
Order at zagatwine.com/2161018
or call 1-800-892-4427 quote code 2161018
You must be at least 21 years old to order. All wine orders will be processed and fulfilled by a licensed retailer in the industry and applicable taxes are paid. Offer may vary. Void where prohibited by law. Please visit our website for complete list of shipping states, terms and conditions.

ZAGAT

Los Angeles/Southern California Region

LA's Most Popular Restaurants

Map coordinates follow each name. For chains, only flagship or central locations are plotted. The detailed map on the reverse shows Top Food-rated properties in Beverly Hills and West Hollywood, and on nearby Beverly Blvd. and Third St.

1 Pizzeria Mozza (C-5)

2 Bazaar/José Andrés (C-5)

3 Spago (C-5)

4 Osteria Mozza (C-5)

5 Angelini Osteria (C-5)

6 Café Bizou † (B-4)

7 Mélisse (D-4)

8 A.O.C. (C-5)

9 Mastro's Steak (B-1, C-5)

10 Bouchon (C-5)

11 Providence (C-5)

12 Campanile (C-5)

13 Brent's Deli (A-3, B-1)

14 Lucques (C-5)

15 Joe's (D-4)

16 Cheesecake Factory † (C-5)

17 CUT (C-5)

18 In-N-Out † (C-5)

19 Chinois on Main (D-4)

20 Gjelina (D-4)

21 Lawry's Prime Rib (C-5)

22 Matsuhisa (C-5)

23 JiRaffe (D-4)

24 Bottega Louie (C-6)

25 Fraîche (D-4, D-5)

26 Water Grill (C-6)

27 Apple Pan (C-4)

28 Din Tai Fung (C-8)

29 Ruth's Chris † (C-5)

30 Church & State (D-6)

31 Valentino (D-4)

32 Crustacean (C-5)

33 Fleming's † (E-5)

34 Boa (C-5, D-4)

35 Katsuya † (C-4)

36 Father's Office (D-4, D-5)

37 Houston's † (C-5)

38 Katsu-ya (B-4, C-5)

39 Palm (C-5, D-6)

40 Roy's † (D-6)

41 Langer's Deli (C-6)

42 Grill on Alley (C-5)

43 Patina (C-6)

44 Anisette (D-4)

45 Hatfield's (C-5)

46 Drago Centro (C-6)

47 Josie* (D-4)

48 Parkway Grill* (B-7)

49 Tavern (C-4)

50 Jar (C-5)

51 Saddle Peak* (C-2)

52 Bay Cities Deli (D-4)

---

*Indicates tie with above   † Indicates multiple branches